An Economic Survey of Communist China

An Economic Survey

of Communist China

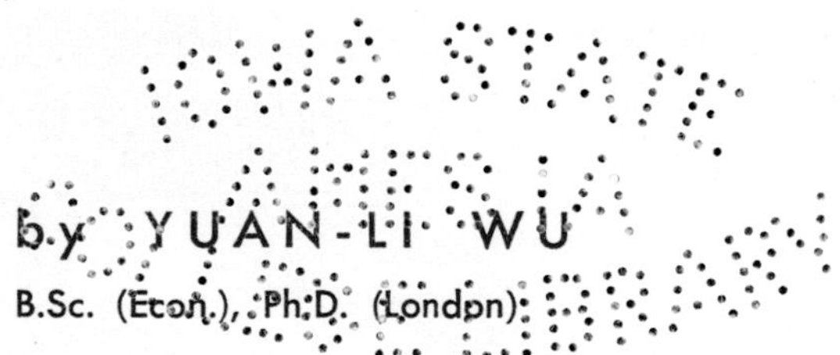

by YUAN-LI WU
B.Sc. (Econ.), Ph.D. (London)

BOOKMAN ASSOCIATES

New York

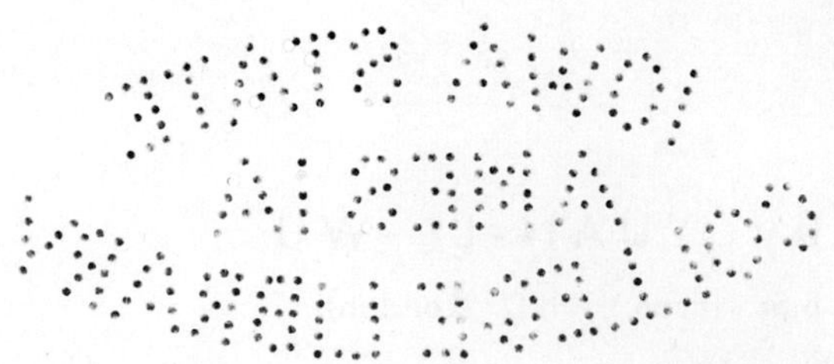

MANUFACTURED IN THE UNITED STATES OF AMERICA
PRINTED BY RECORD PRESS, NEW YORK, N. Y.

"TO MY MOTHER AND TO THE
MEMORY OF MY FATHER"

Preface

As an account of Chinese economic development this book attempts to tell only one part of the complex story about Communist China, but it is a part that has not yet been told to western readers in detail. As the title shows, this is a non-political book, and every effort has been made to avoid partisanship. Partly for this reason and partly because of the book's primary interest in the Chinese mainland, there is no discussion on the economic development of Taiwan (Formosa). Similarly, other controversial political issues have been avoided. This does not imply, of course, that the reader cannot draw certain deductions of political significance on his own, as the concluding chapter will show quite clearly. This is perhaps as it should be.

Extensive use of official Communist Chinese statistics is made in this book, but by no means uncritically. This practice cannot be avoided due to the complete absence of other independent sources of first-hand information as far as published material is concerned. For even non-Communist publications in Hongkong and Formosa are compelled to rely on Communist sources. The reader will be well advised to bear this fact in mind.

It is a pleasure to express my gratitude to the many persons and institutions without whose help, indulgence, and support this book could not have been written. Thanks are due especially to the Hoover Library and the Stanford Research Institute for the many sources of information and research opportunities they have given me; to the Tsinghua University Fund and President Y. C. Mei of the National Tsinghua University of China for the timely fellowship that has enabled me to complete my writing; to Professor Franklin L. Ho of Columbia University, Professor David N. Rowe of Yale, and Dr. Eugene Staley and Mr. William L. White of the Stanford Research Institute for their invaluable encouragement and counsel; to Dr. Mary C. Wright, Mrs. Lienche Fang, and their past and present colleagues at the Hoover Library for the tireless help in material search given me over a long period of time; to Miss Margaret Sparks for her indispensable assistance in the editing and preparation of the manuscript; to Major John K. Jouett, U. S. Army, for his painstaking and generous co-operation in preparing the transportation maps and charts; and to my many other friends and colleagues both at Stanford and elsewhere for some of the inspiring examples of scholarship they have set in research on China.

I wish also to thank my wife for her active and competent assistance in innumerable ways and all members of my family for their indulgence, patient understanding, and constant encouragement in a work which, interesting as it is to me, has deprived them of much that is rightfully theirs.

This book represents only a small and faltering step in an as yet incompletely charted field of inquiry. However, if, in spite of its many shortcomings, it should prove to be useful as a stepping stone to further and better work in its field, it will not have been undertaken in vain.

Stanford, 1955

Contents

CHAPTER ONE

Introduction

I

PURPOSE AND NATURE OF THE STUDY

The postwar success of the Communist Party in China is one of the most important international developments of our time. Not only has the new regime left an indelible mark on Chinese society, its impact on the rest of the world has been equally far-reaching. The unsettled state of affairs in Asia and the changed and changing balance of power in the world as a whole are intimately related to the recent upheaval in China. Under the circumstances, it would certainly be helpful if we could familiarize ourselves with the course of events in Communist China and interpret correctly the actions and policies of the new regime. In particular, as industrialization and the development of military power are officially described to be Communist China's major objectives,[1] it would be useful if we could appraise the country's actual and potential capacity in these two respects.

During the past few years, Communist China has become no less an enigma to most of us than the Soviet Union. Since there is no free flow of information, the rest of the world, with the possible exception of the Soviet countries, is often very poorly informed on Chinese developments. This lack of knowledge is probably most evident in the area of material and economic factors which constitute some of the primary considerations in the formulation of policy by Communist leaders. If we are not to fail in the task of explaining and predicting Communist Chinese policies, this gap in our knowledge must be bridged. This is precisely the task we have set for ourselves here.

At this point, the question will no doubt be raised whether it would be wiser to postpone the writing of a book on Communist

China's economy until some later date when the facts can be viewed in their proper perspective and with less emotion. The answer to this question is definitely in the negative. Not only will a book written several years from now be of no practical value to us at the present time, but the facts themselves, unless recorded and analyzed without further delay, may be lost to us altogether. The present partial blackout of information has been assiduously cultivated by the Communist Chinese government. Its Decree of February 1951 on the Suppression of Counter-Revolutionary Activities, reinforced by a later Decree on the Security of State Secrets, has gone so far as to make the disclosure of "vital" economic information a capital offense.[2] Since the epithet "vital" is exceedingly flexible, a strong deterrent to reporting from Communist China, objective and otherwise, has been imposed. Accordingly, whatever information that can still be gleaned from published sources is usually of a piecemeal and disjointed nature and must be systematically sifted and organized. Under the circumstances, it is necessary to make full use of the fact that the Communists' conquest of China was completed only in 1949 and that this recent date affords us still ample opportunity to survey the course of current development in the light of our knowledge about the former years. If such a review is not undertaken now, the difficulty in reconstructing basic data will increase as time passes.

However, if the present need for a searching study on Communist Chinese economy is well-established, the nature of the problems that will emerge in such an analysis may not be entirely obvious. For, apart from its practical significance to statesmen and historians, knowledge about the current economic experiment in China will also be extremely useful in studying the diverse and knotty problems of economic development in less developed countries in general. The rise of Communist China has in effect posed a challenge to the imagination of the peoples outside the Soviet sphere, especially with regard to the future of Asian and other economically less developed countries, some of which have only just started to grope their way towards a definitive future free from the former guiding, though not necessarily benevolent, hand of foreign powers. This is because Communism as a form of organization and a mode of life, while purporting to offer a solution to the pressing economic and social problems of China, also lays claim to a larger area of validity and application, and, most of us would agree that many of the problems confronting the other less developed countries are essentially similar to the Chinese ones. We only have to look towards India or Burma or Indonesia to appreciate the significance of this comparison. The Communist experiment in China is in this sense a test case. Its success or failure in attaining the goals chosen by its promoters will doubtless help to sway the attitude of non-Chinese peoples who have the same thoughts in mind. At the same time, whether or not these goals are consonant with the promotion of human welfare and dignity will concern us all.

For a number of years before World War II, industrialization—a term often used loosely and synonymously with "economic development"—was deemed to be the only effective way to raise China from economic debility and political impotence. While this over-all objective was probably advanced by most of the educated Chinese, there was, however, no clear agreement on the manner of its accomplishment. The extent of government planning and intervention, the desirable speed of development, the priority of capital goods versus consumers' goods industries, the degree of self-sufficiency, the treatment of foreign capital and the manner of promoting and coordinating social and economic changes were, for instance, among the many topics of protracted debate. Although a gradual shift towards statism could be detected before the war with Japan, the direction was by no means irrevocable or resolute. As the war drew to its close, discussion of these issues was again revived. However, it was not until the establishment of the Communist regime that a general plan was not only firmly laid out, but also carried well beyond the blueprint stage.

From the time a course of development was charted—that of forced industrialization under the centralized planning of a Communist government—the new regime has gone about its way ruthlessly and methodically in dealing with the various problems involved in managing and expanding a rather confused and lethargic economy. The errors it makes, the manner in which it attempts to deal with specific issues, the cost and necessary conditions of its limited success, and the human suffering and sacrifice its policy has exacted—in short, the entire content of its experience—present some excellent case material to the student of economic development and the planners of other countries. To say the least, it would be exceedingly difficult to find a better current illustration of how certain things might or might not be done if specific end results in the development of a poor country are in question, including the conversion of a pre-capitalistic economy to socialism and the organization of a large, overpopulated area for forced development. These are realistic issues in many parts of the world today and will remain so for a long time to come. Thus, a survey of Communist China's economic conditions is interesting not only because China is currently under Communist domination, but also because China is undergoing a stage of development which may very well have its parallel in other underdeveloped countries. The freshness of the Chinese experience, which is well worth watching in any event, makes the lesson all the more valuable if the tragedy of China is not to be re-enacted elsewhere.

A WORD ON THE METHOD OF APPROACH

To say that we should study Chinese economic development for some very good reasons does not, however, tell us how the study should be conducted. The matter at issue is one of general attitude, as well as technique, and a few words of explanation may be in order.

First of all, it should be pointed out that although discussion involving Communist China has a tendency to arouse strong emotions at the present time, we will attempt to present a strictly factual description and analysis. We will not allow our opposition to the doctrines of Chinese Communism as a political principle or a way of life to prevent us from gaining a correct view of the known facts. In other words, we will, as a rule, refrain from making value judgments. Even where comments involving subjective evaluation appear to be in order, we will clearly label them as such.

In the second place, we will adopt the working assumption that the Chinese Communists are guided by rational considerations of self-interest, but are not inhibited by the mores and ethical ideas generally accepted in the non-Communist world, and that the recent economic development of China is largely the result of the Communist Party's attempt to solve certain economic problems in its own way. These problems are defined for the Communist planners by the nature of the economic order they envisage, the external circumstances they have to take into account, and their unmistakable desire to remain in power, at, we shall assume, virtually any cost.

OUTLINE OF THE STUDY

A practical plan of inquiry emerges rather logically from our particular approach. First, since government policy plays a central role in a planned economy, it is both a logical and convenient starting point for our survey. A brief sketch of this policy in very general terms will, therefore, be attempted in the remaining pages of this chapter. It will be followed in the next chapter by a summary of the various material and intangible factors which constitute the economic heritage Communist China has inherited from the past and which, in the first instance, it must accept as given data. These preliminary steps will then lead to the main body of the book beginning with Chapter III, dealing with the various phases of economic activity, from which, it is believed, a clear view of Communist Chinese economy will crystalize.

II

FORERUNNERS OF CURRENT POLICY

The present stage of Communist China's economic development is characterized in official Communist phraseology as the period of "New Democracy," or alternatively, that of "democratic dictatorship[3] of the workers' and peasants' alliance." It is regarded as a transitional period bridging traditional China, which is usually depicted as "semi-feudalistic" or "semi-capitalistic," with a full-fledged socialistic society. This rather confusing use of terms is explained by the Communists' dogma that peasants and workers are the only democratic elements in a society and that a dictatorship must be maintained by them, under the leadership of the Communist Party, over the other social classes that are still permitted to exist before the advent of socialism.[4] This basic characteristic of such a transitional society is, of course, reflected in the organization of the economy.

Thus, according to Mao Tse-tung in his wartime volume on *The New Democracy,* the economic system he envisaged would possess the following features: First, there would be state control and operation of all monopolistic or large-scale enterprises irrespective of the nationality of their ownership so that private capital would not be allowed to control the economic life of the country. Banks, railways, and civil aviation were cited as examples of such enterprises destined for nationalization. Second, this partial nationalization would not be confiscatory and would not entail the suppression of such private business as could not exercise any decisive influence on general economic conditions. Third, in the agricultural sector, certain "necessary measures" would be taken to appropriate the land owned by large landowners and to redistribute it among the landless and poor peasants. Fourth, the redistributed land would still be privately owned so that there would not be any socialization of land, but only an abolition of "feudalistic" relationships on the farms.[5] These objectives were, according to Mao, entirely in conformity with the Kuomintang's platform as originally adopted by the latter at its First National Congress.

It should be recalled that when the above statement was made the Chinese Communist Party was still essentially an armed opposition party and was eagerly bidding for popular support, both at home and abroad. This circumstance would seem to explain the relatively restrained tone and, for a Communist party, the moderate objectives in nationalization and land redistribution.[6] For this reason, the wartime statement of policy may be profitably compared with another pronouncement by Mao Tse-tung some seven years later when conditions had altered vastly in favor of the Communist Party, although no final decision in the struggle for power had yet been reached. This somewhat revised version was contained in Mao's address to the Party's Central Committee in December, 1947, on the proper way to deal with the prevailing political situation and the Party's immediate goal.[7]

On this particular occasion Mao declared that the Party's economic objectives consisted of (1) the confiscation of land owned by "feudalistic exploiters" and its restitution to the peasantry, (2) the expropriation of the "monopolistic capital" of the Chiang, Soong, Kung, and Chen families for reversion to state ownership, and (3) the protection of national industries and trade. These three "economic principles of the new democratic revolution" followed the pattern of the earlier outline except that they seemed to suggest a clearer demarcation of the area of expropriation. Only a section of the capitalist class who represented what was termed "bureaucratic capital" was to be expropriated outright. The lesser capitalists, on the other hand, were regarded as "national capitalists" as they did not have close ties with "bureaucratic capital" and "foreign imperialistic elements" and were often oppressed by the last two. As "national capitalists" they would be permitted either to participate in the revolution or even to observe neutrality. However, it was also pointed out that the criterion in distinguishing one capitalist from another would not be the size of the enterprise, but rather the function he performed in relation to the national economy. It was, therefore, still perfectly possible for small businesses to be expropriated should their activity be regarded as detrimental to public welfare. In the light of what has since taken place, it would appear that this combination of qualified assurance and veiled threat to the country's businessman was not unrelated to the political advantage expected from such a maneuver. Consequently, the exact nature of the economy remained to be further clarified.

AN OUTLINE OF THE "COMMON PROGRAM" OF 1949

This anticipated step was taken in October, 1949, when the People's Political Consultative Conference, called to mark the official birth of the new regime, adopted a comprehensive political platform. The latter was described as the "Common Program" by virtue of the fact that it was ostensibly subscribed to by all the parties, as well as persons of no known political affiliations, taking part in the Conference.

An analysis of the economic section of the Common Program[8] shows that it contains both an outline of the basic principles in organizing the economy during the transitional period of "New Democracy" and a priority schedule of the various problems with which it had to deal. The main points are as follows:

First, the Common Program proposes the division of the economy into five sectors, viz., (1) a state sector consisting of socialistic enterprises, (2) a "semi-socialistic" sector of cooperative enterprises, (3) a sector of "state capitalism" composed of joint private and public enterprises, (4) a sector of small, individualistic enterprises including the small farms and handicraft industries, and (5) a sector of "national capitalists."

Second, economic activity in all the sectors is to be governed by a central plan, with the state sector acting as the coordinating factor. The state may take whatever measures deemed necessary in regulating markets and raw material supplies, business operations, working conditions, technical facilities, and fiscal and monetary matters.

Third, as a prerequisite of industrialization and expansion of production, land reform is to be carried out in the whole country. In all the newly acquired areas, this is to be preceded by such preparatory steps as the liquidation of persons described as "local despots" and the reduction of land rent and interest rates on loans.

Fourth, as for industrialization, rehabilitation and expansion would proceed first in such fields as mining, the iron and steel industry, the generation of electric power, and the manufacture of machinery, electrical equipment, and chemicals. Only secondary importance is to be attached to the production of consumers' goods such as textiles.

Fifth, international trade is to be controlled under the principle of protection of domestic industry.

Sixth, state trading enterprises are to be established to curb speculation, to balance supply and demand, to stabilize prices, and to promote the organization of cooperatives.

Seventh, the participation of labor in the management of state enterprises and the introduction of collective bargaining in the private sectors are also stipulated. Unions are to be organized both to fulfill their usual functions, and to assure the realization of government production plans.

Finally, the Common Program stresses the need to institute strict control over all financial establishments, together with balancing the budget and adoption of a taxation policy that would assure supplies for the continued prosecution of the civil war, the rehabilitation of production, and the fulfilment of the country's investment program.

IMPLICATIONS OF THE COMMON PROGRAM

While the economic provisions of the Common Program as just described do not offer too many details, it is nevertheless possible to deduce the nature of the economy which the Chinese Communist Party apparently wishes to create. The development of heavy industries in preference to the expansion of consumers' goods production under government planning on a more or less self-sufficient basis and the redistribution of land are the two major constituents of the economic program. These objectives are to be carried out without immediate socialization of the entire economy. Instead, two sectors of the economy will retain their individualistic character for the time being; namely, (1) peasant farming and handicraft industries and (2) certain larger private enterprises. However, the existing status of these private institutions will not remain stationary because the promotion of cooperatives in farming and in small-scale manufacturing and trade and the establishment of joint enterprises with the government offer the two intermediate stages through which they will pass into socialized production. In short, the period of "New Democracy" is to be one of gradual transition, though what gradualness means remains to be seen.

The obvious desire to avoid plunging the entire economy into total chaos through any overzealous attempt at socialization was no doubt well calculated. The new regime suffered from a severe shortage of trained technicians and managerial personnel and was forced to utilize certain qualified persons whose loyalty to the Party was not above suspicion. Its past experience in the rural areas of Northwest China and elsewhere had not provided it with much opportunity to prepare for the present challenge. The victory over its adversary had probably arrived earlier than it was altogether prepared for. Consequently, in a limited sense, the Communists' assertion that certain capitalists still had a social function to perform was perfectly genuine.[9] Production was lagging, and inflation was still rampant. Confusion would have been further confounded if the regime had sought to adhere to its ideological preconceptions in complete disregard of certain urgent issues.

It was perfectly clear what the Communists considered their urgent tasks. Above all, there were the continuing prosecution of the civil war and the achievement of a certain degree of currency stability. These pressing issues, together with land redistribution, posed a serious challenge to the Communist Party's grip on the country. It appears logical, therefore, that unless the Party's newly gained power could be consolidated—or at least a firm beginning made in that direction—its long-term program would be in jeopardy. Accordingly, the length of the period of transition depends upon the Communist Party's success in consolidating its power and the speed with which socialization can be achieved without serious disruption of production.

THE 1954 CONSTITUTION

That the above inferences are correct has been borne out by the Constitution, adopted in 1954, which replaces the Common Program as the organic law of the regime. Economically it is essentially a reaffirmation of the Party's policy as reviewed above although now in several respects provisions of the Constitution are clearer and more explicit than the corresponding articles of the Common Program, thus reflecting the progress made by the Communist Party since 1949 in striving towards its original objectives, some of which, such as land reform and industrial recovery, have already been realized.

In the first place, where the Common Program spoke of land reform, the Constitution now enunciates a policy of "voluntary co-operativization" and of the "restriction and gradual elimination" of rich peasants.[10] Secondly, while private capitalists were half-assured of their continued usefulness and protection under the new regime in 1949, national policy towards private business is now positively described as one of "utilization, restriction, and reform."[11] The socialization of all business enterprises in areas where the cooperative form does not prevail accordingly looms more imminent than before. Finally, while the Constitution pays lip service to the protection of private property in means of production[12] during the period of transition, Article 13 of the Constitution expressly reserves to the state the right to requisition, purchase, and nationalize private land and other means of production "according to law."[13] Apparently, the end of the transitional period is now somewhat closer at hand.

NOTES

1. The theme that national defense is dependent upon industrialization while industrialization must give top priority to defense industries runs through all Communist declarations of policy. It has become particularly evident since the beginning of Communist China's First Five-Year Plan in 1953 and the elaboration by party leaders of the "general party line" as of 1954.

2. For the texts of these regulations see *Compendium of Central Government Financial and Economic Policy Directives and Regulations,* 3rd issue, p. 108, edited by the Economic and Financial Commission, Peking, March, 1952 (hereafter cited as *Compendium*); and *New China Monthly,* Vol. III, No. 5, Peking, March, 1951. All references of Chinese sources in Chinese, unless otherwise noted.

3. For an explanation of the apparent contradiction in the term "democratic dictatorship" see, for instance, Mao Tse-tung, *"The People's Democratic Dictatorship,"* Peking, 1949.

4. Cf. Mao Tse-tung, *The New Democracy, Chieh-fang she* edition, 1940, p. 17.

5. By "feudalistic" relationships Mao meant the payment of land rent and the employment of hired farm laborers. See Chapter IV below.

6. It should, however, be noted that Mao did not elaborate on the nature of the "necessary measures" for the promised land reform.

7. See Mao Tse-tung, *The Current Situation and Our Task,* p. 27, report to the Central Committee of the Chinese Communist Party, December 25, 1947. *Chieh-fang she* standard edition of collected official documents, 1949.

8. The English text of the "Common Program" may be found in *The Important Documents of the First Plenary Session of the Chinese People's Political Consultative Conference,* Peking, Foreign Languages Press, 1949.

9. The Communist authorities, however, did not describe at this time the degree and nature of control private business would be subject to during the period when its existence would be tolerated.

10. Cf. Article 8 of the draft Constitution as adopted by the Government Council on June 14, 1954. *Draft Constitution of the People's Republic of China, Jeu-min ch'u-pan she* edition, Peking, June, 1954

11. Cf. Article 10. In addition, it should be noted that the sector of state capitalism is no longer regarded as a "permanent" form and is treated primarily as a transient stage in the course of socialization.

12. See Articles 8, 9, and 10.

13. It will be recognized that, even allowing for these changes in emphasis, the economic provisions of the 1954 Constitution are not drastically different from those of the Common Program. The Constitution, therefore, is not really "necessary" as a statement on economic organization. Its function is essentially political inasmuch as its adoption in 1954 marked the end of the Communists' nominal coalition with other parties and further purged the government of all non-Communist influence.

CHAPTER TWO

Background and Heritage

I

INTRODUCTION

When the Chinese Communists took over the country in 1949, the economy they inherited left a great deal to be desired. Basically, the Chinese economy cannot boast of any special abundance except in its supply of manpower. As far as underground resources are concerned, although the deposits of a few minerals are large and a few other items are probably found in greater quantities than the country is usually credited with, there was, and there still is, only incomplete knowledge about many other important raw materials. While the country is predominantly agricultural, the ratio of land to labor is exceedingly small, so that intensive, subsistence farming on small farms made up of scattered parcels of land was the rule in 1949, as it had been for many centuries before. Neither mining nor manufacturing was highly developed except in one or two instances. The small industrial output was further concentrated in a few areas, and most of it had been developed with foreign skill and under foreign management. Of the few industrial centers, heavy industry had been built up almost entirely in Manchuria where destruction, as a result of removals of stock, equipment, and installations by Soviet occupation troops at the end of World War II, was most severe. For these reasons the country's future industrial development, as seen in 1949, was handicapped not only by the critical shortage of technical and management personnel, as well as skilled labor, but also by the slight material foundation on which further construction had to be based. Furthermore, production had been brought to a standstill through a combination of military hostilities, disruption of transportation links between sources of raw materials and manufacturing and marketing centers, and the monetary chaos resulting from the prolonged inflation that, begun after the outbreak of the war with Japan in 1937, had finally reached a point of utter confusion and hopelessness. As a matter of fact, by 1947, the inflation psychosis had established such a firm hold on the population that, from the government down, the country was more concerned with the daily gyration of commodity prices and financial index numbers than the task of maintaining the economy and the government as a going concern. In the face of the worsening inflation and the impending political upheaval, the flight of capital from China had been gradually accelerated, and the country's balance of international payments was in a most precarious position. Only a small part of the gold and dollar exchange reserves formerly under the control of the Nationalist government had remained within the reach of the mainland authorities so that there was not much available in terms of foreign exchange resources. As for future economic development, although there had been many paper plans, the situation in 1949 could hold out no bright promise for the immediate future because stability and rehabilitation would have to precede the adoption of any program of a more far-reaching import.

Any attempt to review the state of the entire economy in detail would call for a thorough examination of the economic history of modern China. Since this is not our objective, we shall only try to cover some of the most salient issues, a fair conception of which is necessary for the understanding of subsequent developments under the Communist regime. In doing so, we shall also try to present some of the statistical data on China's economic resources that, while essential for our study, are not always readily available in any single volume.

THE SIZE AND GEOGRAPHICAL DISTRIBUTION OF THE POPULATION

As students of most underdeveloped countries are aware, availability of adequate statistical information can never be taken for granted. This deficiency becomes most glaring as we try to evaluate the potential of China's largest productive factor, its population. According to the Nationalist Ministry of the Interior,[1] the population of China in 1947, excluding Formosa, totaled 454.9 million. This figure, which is the sum of data for individual provinces and cities estimated at different times by various sources, is of course little more than a very approximate magnitude. It may be compared with the prewar figure of 450 million, perhaps one of the most frequently quoted numbers in publications on China,[2] or that of 475 million, which is another one of the many prewar estimates derived from incomplete information.[3]

The figure of 475 million was temporarily used by the Chinese Communists who, however, proceeded to revise it almost immediately. Between 1950 and 1952 the Communist Ministry of the Interior is said to have worked over it six times on the basis of local and regional reports and studies by government agencies.[4] The successively revised population statistics are not all available although a few may be mentioned here. First, following the Ministry of the Interior's figure of May, 1950, of 483,869,687, including Formosa, the Communist military authorities reported two months later in the same year that the Chinese population was 492,530,000. In 1951, however, the Economic and Financial Commission again put the population total at 483 million. In 1952, the figure of 486,571,231 was reported by the Shanghai *Ta-kung pao* which presumably quoted from some official source. Finally, in 1953 the figure of 545,156,042 was given by the Ya-kuang Geographical Society. All these figures include the population of Formosa.[5]

The above data represent interim estimates which were finally brought up to date through a general census carried out by the Communist authorities in 1953 in connection with the election of the National People's Congress of 1954. According to Teng Hsiao-p'ing's report to the Government Council,[6] the Chinese population at the end of June, 1953, or less than four years after the establishment of the new regime, stood at 601,912,371 on the basis of the census. Of this total, however, 7 million represented the population of Formosa, while 12,337,532 were persons of Chinese descent resident in foreign countries. Thus, the total population for the Chinese mainland was 582,584,839. Of the last figure, according to Teng, 573,876,670 were accounted for by "direct investigation" although it is not clear whether a complete census count took place with respect to the entire number.[7] The remaining 8,708,169 persons belonged to the non-Chinese minority races whose number was estimated indirectly.

Following Teng's report, the National Bureau of Statistics stated in November, 1954, that the total population of China was 601,-938,035 which was composed of (1) 582,603,417 for the mainland;

(2) 7,591,298 for Formosa, and (3) 11,743,320 for overseas Chinese. The total figures, as well as provincial and regional breakdowns, as published in the *Enlightenment Daily* on November 1, 1954, may be checked on the basis of the number of delegates returned to the 1954 Congress, which, apart from representatives from special groups, was composed of delegates from the individual provinces and cities at the ratio of one delegate to 800,000 persons for all the provinces and one delegate to every 100,000 persons for the 14 municipalities then under the direct jurisdiction of the Communist Central Government, as well as for the ten "industrial towns" in the country, together with some 150 delegates for the minority races. If we assume that the Communist census was reasonably accurate and that there was no deliberate padding, we could use the figure of 583 million as a close approximation of the present population on the Chinese mainland.[8] The provincial figures as given in the last available published source prior to the census report, as well as those of the census report and estimates based on representation in the National People's Congress, are given in the table appearing on pages 16, 17 and 18.

CHARACTERISTICS OF THE POPULATION

As one might expect, information on the other characteristics of the Chinese population is not very adequate. However, the following points may be noted:

First, all pre-Communist studies have invariably indicated both a high birth rate and a high death rate for China. According to an estimate by Ch'en Ta for the entire country, the crude birth rate in 1934 was 38 per thousand, while the crude death rate was 33 per thousand.[9] Studies by other scholars, such as Lossing Buck and Ch'iao Ch'i-ming, are in general agreement with Ch'en on the birth rate, but have tended to give lower figures for the death rate. Following the 1953 Communist Chinese census, Pai Chien-hua wrote: "According to the census check for 29 large and medium cities, the whole province of Ningsia, 10 counties of other provinces, as well as one representative *ch'ü* (administrative district), 2 representative *chen* (rural township), 58 representative *hsiang* (group of villages), and 7 representative *ts'un* (villages) of 35 counties, covering a total population of 30,180,000, the present birth rate of China averages 37 per thousand; the death rate, 17 per thousand; and the annual rate

CHINA'S POPULATION
(IN THOUSAND PERSONS)

	1953 Census Report			*Estimates Based on 1953 Census*			*Prior to 1953 Census*		
Northeast (Manchuria)									
Liaoning[1]	—			16,240			15,950		
Shen-yang (Mukden)	—			2,420			1,551		
Lü-ta (Port Arthur & Dairen)	—			1,200			1,054		
Fu-shun	—			700			233		
An-shan	—			600			380		
Pen-ch'i	—	18,545		500	21,660		95	19,263	
Kirin		11,290		6,580				6,931	
Ch'ang-ch'un				800	7,380				
Heilungkiang[2]		11,897		12,180				11,151	
Ha-erh-pin (Harbin)				1,200	13,380				
Jehol		5,161	46,893		4,860	47,280		4,899	42,244
Inner Mongolia[3]			6,100			5,220			5,817
North									
Hopeh	35,985			37,360			32,257		
Pei-ching (Peking)	2,768			2,720			2,031		
T'ien-ching (Tientsin)	2,694	41,447		2,760	42,840		2,000	36,288	
Shansi		14,314	55,761		15,700	58,540		12,316	48,604

Northwest									
Shensi	—			15,200			14,710		
Hsi-an (Sian)	—	15,881		800	16,000		560	15,270	
Kansu[4]		12,928			14,080			12,016	
Tsinghai		1,677			2,760			1,317	
Sinkiang		4,874	35,360		3,480	36,320		5,300	33,903
East									
Shantung		48,877			53,860			45,212	
Kiangsu	41,252			45,860			40,000		
Shanghai	6,204	47,456		6,260	52,120		6,000	46,000	
Chekiang		22,866			24,500			21,000	
Anhwei		30,344			30,660			30,000	
Fukien		13,143	162,686		13,660	174,800		12,000	154,212
Central-South									
Honan		44,215			42,580			40,195	
Hupeh	—			26,400			21,470		
Wu-han[5]	—	27,790		1,460	27,860		1,200	22,670	
Kiangsi		16,773			16,800			17,000	
Hunan		33,227			33,540			31,000	
Kwangtung	—			34,580			31,740		
Kuang-chou (Canton)	—	34,770		1,600	36,180		1,500	33,240	
Kwangsi		19,561	176,336		14,120	171,080		18,480	162,585

	1953 Census Report			*Estimates Based on 1953 Census*			*Prior to 1953 Census*		
Southwest									
Szechwan	—			60,920			56,000		
Ch'ung-ch'ing (Chungking)	—	62,304		1,600	62,520		1,100	57,100	
Sikang		3,381			3,060			3,307	
Yunnan		17,473			12,570			17,000	
Kweichow		15,037	98,195		11,920	90,070		13,000	90,407
Tibet			1,274			1,000			1,000
TOTAL			582,605			584,310			538,772

1. Sum of Liaotung (8,559) and Liaohsi (7,391), merged in June, 1954.

2. Including Sungkiang (5,151), incorporated into Heilungkiang in June, 1954.

3. Including Suiyuan (3,317), formerly in North China, incorporated into Inner Mongolia, approved by the Government Council in June, 1954.

4. Including Ningsia (716), incorporated into Kansu in June, 1954.

5. Including Wu-ch'ang, Han-k'ou (Hankow), and Han-yang.

The estimates prior to the 1953 census are taken from *Atlas of the People's Republic of China*, revised edition, Shanghai, August 1953.

of population growth 2 per cent."[10] Since the above sample contains an unduly large representation of urban population, the death rate, abstracting from any deliberate distortion, tends to be underestimated. Consequently, the rate of population growth may be less than 2 per cent a year although it is in all probability higher than Ch'en's estimate for 1934, and possibly somewhat above one per cent.

Second, in spite of high infant mortality, the high birth rate and the high mortality of persons more than 50 years old give rise to a relatively large proportion of persons within the age group of zero to 14 years. According to Ch'en's tabulation for the Kun-ming Lake region, the age distribution is as follows:

Age Group	*Per Cent Distribution*
0–14 years	33.7
15–49 years	52.8
50 years and over	13.5

The working population, according to Ch'en, constitutes 53.5 per cent of the total population, which is higher than in most other countries.

There may be some question as to the representativeness of the above figures. For this reason, reference may also be made to the estimates used by T. H. Shen in his recent study on *China's Agricultural Resources*.[11] The age distribution given is as follows:

Age Group	*Per Cent Distribution*
Under 6 months	2
6 months–2 years	5
2–5 years	8
5–15 years	22
15–20 years	8
20 years and over	55
TOTAL	100

Not much information has been published by the Communist authorities on age distribution. "According to statistics covering over 574.2 million persons, 15.6 per cent of the total population represents infants of 1 to 4 years old, born in the five years after the liberation. 11 per cent of the total population consists of children of 5 to 9 years of age."[12] Furthermore, it is reported that 14.5 per cent of the population falls within the age group of 10 to 17 years. Thus 58.9 per cent of the population is in the group of 18 years and above, which would constitute a very large working population.

Third, the sex ratio or the number of males per 100 females varies from 89.1 to 115 at birth and 90.7 to 129.4 for all ages according to nine local censuses taken before the Communist regime and with varying coverages. For the country as a whole, according to the 1948 *Statistical Yearbook,* the sex ratio appears to be 110 for all ages. The 1953 census speaks of a ratio of male and female infants in the age group of 1 to 4 years that is almost equal. In the age group of 5 to 9 years, however, it is said that there are far more males than females. For all age groups the sex ratio is said to be 107.5.

In this connection one should not fail to mention a very significant phenomenon regarding China's population trend. According to Carr-Saunders, the total population of China probably increased from 150 million in 1650 to 450 million in 1933. At any rate, population growth increased rapidly after 1850. If the recent census is reliable, then the present population has again increased to 583 million. It has been suggested by some students of China's demographic problems that population growth in China in the past followed certain cyclical patterns. These cyclical trends are explained by Ch'en Ta as follows: "At the beginning of a new dynasty, when peace and order were maintained, population normally increased by the excess of births over deaths, and cultural developments advanced apace through the division of labor. As time went on, the increased and increasing density, coupled with the lack of inventions and improvements in farming technology, gradually intensified the struggle for existence by the masses. Nevertheless, population continued to increase until it reached a saturation point, the apex of the cycle. Then came pestilence and famine, symptoms of overpopulation, until life became increasingly more intolerable and revolution or war broke out. This temporarily relieved the pressure of population and brought a new dynasty into being. Population continued to decrease until it reached the lowest possible level, the bottom of the cycle."[13]

To say that the establishment of the new regime after years of war and revolution coincided with a new apex of the population cycle would be an oversimplification. However, the hypothesis advanced by Ch'en and held by others as well has its merits, and the Malthusian ghost is far from being dead in China. Yet the introduction of new technology and social organization and the possibilities opened up by ruthless authoritarian control in reducing consumption and increasing investment may conceivably more than offset the effect of population growth. Population pressure is a meaningful concept only in relation to the amount of natural resources with which the country is endowed and the effectiveness of the economic system in their utilization. Consequently, we must now turn first to an examination of some of the material resources at the disposal of Communist China.

AGRICULTURAL RESOURCES

The land mass of the Chinese mainland covers an area of 9,700,327 square kilometers. If an imaginary line were drawn from Yunnan province in Southwest China to Heilungkiang in the northeast, it would divide the country into two natural regions with great contrasts. Excluding Tibet, the western part would consist of some 42 per cent of the land area with less than 4 per cent of the total population. The eastern part, on the other hand, would account for 96 per cent of the population, but less than 58 per cent of the land area. To the west of this line lie the major mountain ranges, the plateaus, deserts, and uninhabited wastes. To the east are the fertile plains and deltas.

According to the latest figures prepared by the Ministry of Agriculture and Forestry of the Nationalist Government in 1946[14] there were 63.2 million farm households in the country and a total farm population of 331.8 million or about 72.4 per cent of the entire population. The total farm population, excluding Formosa, was 62.8 million households and 328.9 million persons. According to the same source, the proportion of farm to total population exceeded 80 per cent. At the same time, the total cultivated land was reported to be 94 million hectares (1,410.7 million *shih mow*) or about 93 million hectares excluding Formosa.[15] Thus the amount of cultivated land would average 1.48 hectares for every farm household or just above 0.28 hectare per capita of the farm population. Without Formosa the figures would be about the same. Only in certain underpopulated areas, such as Manchuria, the former province of Suiyuan, and Sinkiang, did the 1946 report give an average amount of cultivated land of approximately 2/3 of a hectare per head of the farm population, whereas in most provinces in China Proper the amount was around 1/5 of a hectare.

According to Communist statistics published in 1950, the total farm population, excluding Formosa, was estimated at 392.4 million out of a total population of 477.3 million, and the total cultivated land was given as 97.4 million hectares.[16] Finally, on the basis of the percentage shares of the farm population in total population and the estimated population figures for the major regions of the Chinese mainland based on the 1953 census, both the farm population and the available cultivated land are given in the table below.

Estimates of Farm Population and
Cultivated Land in Communist China, 1953[1]

	Total Population (in million	*Farm Population persons)*	*Cultivated Land (in thousand hectares)*	*Cultivated Land per capita of Farm Population (in hectares)*
Northeast	46.9	38.1	15,041	0.39
Inner Mongolia	6.1	5.3	4,544	0.85
North	55.8	43.6	11,556	0.26
Northwest	35.4	32.1	8,841	0.27
East	162.7	141.2	21,539	0.15
Central-South	176.3	137.6	22,267	0.16
Southwest	98.2	79.4	13,656	0.17
TOTAL	581.4	477.3	97,444	0.20

1. **Excluding Tibet. Territorial divisions based on provinces after 1954 readjustments.**

UNCULTIVATED LAND

Although the above tentative estimates are only approximate, the shortage of cultivated land relative to the farm population is an indisputable fact. With 82 per cent of the total population engaged in agriculture, the amount of cultivated land per capita of the farm population now amounts to no more than 0.2 hectare, which gives an average of about one hectare per farm household. Even if the population figure from the 1953 census should be an overestimate, the severe shortage of farm land would still exist as may be seen in the data published under the Nationalists or in the revised figures first released under the new regime in 1950.

As for the size of uncultivated but arable land, there are a number of estimates which differ widely from one another.[17] Among the higher estimates we may quote Baker's figure of 213 million hectares or Wong Wen-hao's estimate of 167-227 million hectares. Next in scale is C. H. Chen's estimate of 93-107 million hectares. The 1930 *Yearbook* of the Ministry of the Interior puts the uncultivated area at 44 million hectares, later revised to only 9 million hectares. The Department of Agricultural Economics of the former Nanking University has estimated the same at 14 million hectares, which is also the figure used by Buck in his monumental study on *Land Utilization in China*. Finally, the Communist authorities have suggested that some 53 million hectares of wasteland can probably be reclaimed in Northwest China.[18]

The larger estimates mentioned all tend to fall into the common error of considering all uncultivated, arable land as available for cultivation without paying due regard to several important factors. First, some of the land that has remained uncultivated so far is required for other purposes such as animal husbandry, afforestation, and the gathering of fuels. Second, some of the land, though arable, may be of extremely poor quality. Third, the topographical conditions may be such that, if cultivated, soil erosion would set in, which would endanger farm land in the vicinity. This is true especially in areas where terraced farming is practiced. Finally, reclamation cannot be carried out on a large scale without adequate irrigation and transportation facilities, especially in Northwest China.

For these reasons, any substantial increase in cultivated land through reclamation is rather improbable in the near future. Moreover, even if much of the wasteland were brought under cultivation, the relief of population pressure would be slight because of the high ratio of farm population to land. Barring some spectacular technological revolution in agriculture, any appreciable betterment of the country's economic well-being must therefore be sought in the development of other resources.

SOME OF THE UNDERGROUND RESOURCES

The extent to which important mineral deposits are available in China is not completely known mainly because of the lack of thorough geological surveys in many remote areas. For this reason any general conclusion must be of a tentative nature. However, on the basis of available information, China does not appear to be especially favorably endowed by nature in this respect although recent discoveries in several items, in so far as they have been reported and can be relied upon, have tended to modify the extremely gloomy picture painted heretofore by some students. The known reserves of some of the principal mineral resources and the provinces in which they are found in sizable quantities are given in the following table:

Mineral Reserves in Communist China
(in thousand metric tons)

	Quantity	*Occurrence*
Iron Ore	5,432,934–6,778,000[1]	Some deposit in all provinces
Manganese Ore	29,389	Kwangtung, Kiangsi, Kwangsi, Hunan, Fukien, Kansu, and Liaoning
Tungsten	2,035– 2,469	Kiangsi, Kwangtung, Hunan, Kwangsi, Sinkiang, and Fukien
Copper	967	Yunnan, Sikang, Kweichow, Szechwan, Hupeh, Liaoning, Shansi, and Shensi
Antimony	3,803	Hunan, Kwangtung, Kweichow, Kwangsi, and Yunnan
Tin	652– 1,873	Yunnan, Kiangsi, Kwangsi, Kwangtung, and Hunan
Bauxite	142,267	Shantung, Kweichow, Liaoning, Yunnan, and Hopeh
Magnesite	5,083,000	Liaoning, Shantung, and Ningsia
Coal	454,000,000[1]	Some deposit in all provinces
Petroleum	206,000[1]	Sinkiang, Kansu, Shensi, Tsinghai, and Szechwan
Oil Shale (petroleum content)	521,000	Liaoning, Shensi, Kwangtung, Kirin, and Kansu

Sources: Geological Survey of China, *General Statement on the Mining Industry,* No. 7, Chungking, 1945; Bureau of Statistics, *Statistical Yearbook of the Republic of China,* Nanking, 1948; and U.S. Bureau of Mines, *Foreign Minerals Survey,* Washington, D.C., 1948.

1. See the following discussion in the text. Also for sources.

Since coal and iron are the traditional basic ingredients of heavy industries, the extent to which they are available is of primary importance to the future of Communist China. In this respect recent information has been quite favorable.

The abundance of China's coal reserves is well established. Moreover, as a result of extensive geological surveys, the amount of known reserves has been increasing during recent years. The total reserve in China Proper was reported at 260.7 billion metric tons in the 1945 *General Statement on China's Mining Industry.* This figure was subsequently raised to 431.7 billion tons.[19] For Manchuria, the amount of reserves, reported at only 4.6 billion tons in the *General Statement,* was estimated at 22.4 billion tons by the former South Manchuria Railway Company. Mention has been made both under the Nationalist regime and in Communist reports of sizable new discoveries at Huai-nan in Anhwei and P'ing-hsiang in Kiangsi, as well as in western Suiyuan and Shensi. Altogether the volume of new deposits found during 1950-1952 has been put at over 1.8 billion tons.[20] Thus the total coal reserves of Communist China may be conservatively estimated at 454 billion tons.

As for iron ore, a recent Communist publication has put the total reserve at 6,778 million metric tons,[21] considerably higher than previous estimates. However, the latter were revised upward several times under the Nationalist regime. In its 1932 issue of the *General Statement on the Mining Industry,* the Geological Survey of China estimated total iron ore deposits at no more than one billion tons. Based on subsequent information, the same agency revised its estimate in 1945 to 2.1 billion tons. This was later revised to 2.5 billion tons in the 1948 *Chinese Yearbook,* and was finally changed to over 5 billion tons by the National Resources Commission. Although no information is at present available on the geographical distribution of the 6.8 billion tons last reported, it is believed that sizable discoveries may have been made in the Pao-t'ou area in Suiyuan where a new iron and steel center appears to be in the making. To facilitate comparison, the distribution of both coal and iron deposits by provinces, as far as it is known, is listed in the table appearing on page 26.

Finally, it should be noted that according to a recent Communist Chinese report, the petroleum deposit of the Northwest is said to be about 1.7 billion tons.[22] If this figure represents recoverable oil, it would add considerably to the potentiality of the country's industrial development.

However, in spite of possible future discoveries, it is still true that with the exception of such minerals as antimony, tungsten, and tin, known reserves in Communist China are exceedingly small in comparison with total deposits in the rest of the world. This relative,

Geographical Distribution of Coal and Iron Ore Deposits in Communist China
(in thousand metric tons)

	Coal		*Iron Ore*	
Northeast (Manchuria)		22,395,000		3,575,070
Inner Mongolia[1]				
North				
Hopeh	4,366,000		91,467	
Shansi	295,600,000		80,000	
Chahar	526,000		526,000	
Suiyuan	476,000	300,968,000	117,000	814,467
Northwest				
Shensi	71,950,000		10,847	
Kansu	1,513,000		10,075	
Tsinghai	824,000		50,000	
Sinkiang	31,980,000	106,267,000	48,737	119,659
East				
Shantung	2,126,000		107,264	
Kiangsu	217,000		5,700	
Chekiang	100,000		3,224	
Anhwei	760,000		19,204	
Fukien	153,000	3,356,000	92,562	227,954
Central-South				
Honan	8,034,000		4,541	
Hupeh	354,000		193,174	
Kiangsi	700,000		15,466	
Hunan	1,293,000		31,753	
Kwangtung	333,000		257,155	
Kwangsi	1,157,000	11,871,000	2,067	504,156
Southwest				
Szechwan	3,833,000		22,023	
Sikang	531,000		39,849	
Yunnan	2,310,000		12,156	
Kweichow	2,518,000	9,192,000	117,600	191,628
Total		454,049,000		5,432,924

Sources: For coal, see Bureau of Information, *Coal*, Nanking, 1947; and U.S. Bureau of Mines, *Foreign Minerals Survey*, p. 178, Washington D.C., 1948. For iron ore, see Bureau of Information, *Iron and Steel*, pp. 6-10, and 22-23, Nanking, 1947; Geological Survey of China, *General Statement on the Mining Industry*, No. 7, pp. 88-89, Chungking, 1945; and *Chinese Yearbook*, Vol. II, p. 1568, Nanking, 1948.

1. Data for Inner Mongolia are included in those of Suiyuan and Chahar, and, in the case of coal, also to a very small extent, in that of Manchuria.

if not absolute, poverty in underground resources stands in sharp contrast to the large population of China and rivals the land shortage pointed out earlier. Moreover, at the time the Communist regime was established, production of most of these minerals was at their all-time low. In fact, exploitation of mineral deposits had never been highly developed partly because domestic industrial demand was virtually non-existent except in the case of coal. The retarded state of the mining industry in general can best be seen in the production data assembled on pages 28 and 29.

III

ESTIMATES OF NATIONAL INCOME

So much about the human and natural resources at the disposal of Communist China. Attention should next be directed to the effectiveness with which the resources were employed in the production of goods and services prior to the establishment of the Communist regime.

There exist a number of national income estimates for China that vary a great deal both in conceptual precision and in the extensiveness of data used. Some are little more than intelligent guesses while others are based on sample studies. Only a few are the results of extensive statistical research and investigation.[23]

Among the detailed studies the most extensive is the one conducted by the Academia Sinica under the direction of Ou Pao-san.[24]

According to Ou, the per capita income produced in 1933, if computed on the basis of a population of 429,494,138 persons, would be no more than CN$47 at 1933 prices, or an equivalent of US$12. At such a low level of national income, there was very little left after consumption. In fact, according to Ou, consumption often exceeded the volume of current production so that disinvestment had to take place during the greater part of the 1931-1936 period.[25] While Ou's estimates may not be entirely accurate, the general poverty of the country was most striking. This situation had not changed appreciably by 1949.

Mineral Production in China, 1900-1948
(in thousand metric tons)

	Iron Ore	Manganese	Tungsten	Copper	Antimony	Tin	Aluminum	Magnesium	Coal	Crude Oil (in thousand gallons)
1900				0.6		2.9				
1901				0.6		3.1				
1902				0.6	2.0	3.8				
1903				0.6	7.0	2.5				
1904				0.6	5.7	3.0				
1905				0.6	5.3	4.5				
1906				0.6	6.7	4.0				
1907				0.8	8.3	3.5				
1908				0.8	9.9	4.6				
1909				0.8	8.8	4.3				
1910				0.8	12.4	6.2				
1911				0.8	13.0	5.8				
1912				0.8	16.0	8.9				
1913				0.8	15.8	9.1				
1914				0.1	27.3	7.3				
1915				0.1	21.9	8.1				
1916				0.1	20.0	7.7				
1917				0.1	33.4	11.1				
1918			9.9	0.1	17.0	8.8				
1919			5.8	0.1	9.2	9.0				
1920			6.9	0.1	15.6	11.5				
1921			7.5	0.1	13.1	6.2				
1922			7.9	0.1	14.6	9.3				
1923			5.5	0.4	16.3	8.2				
1924			6.0	0.3	13.0	7.2				

1925	1,519	43.4	5.3	1.1	21.3	9.4			24,255	50
1926	1,562	42.8	8.1	0.2	15.5	10.2			23,040	563
1927	1,710	71.3	8.4	0.2	20.0	9.5			24,172	834
1928	2,004	63.6	8.0	0.4	—	7.6			25,092	992
1929	2,630	61.2	9.7	0.3	20.3	7.5			25,437	1,219
1930	2,252	70.7	6.7	0.3	18.0	7.2			26,037	15,294
1931	2,250	31.9	6.6	0.5	14.4	8.6			27,245	19,002
1932	2,249	21.6	2.2	0.6	14.1	7.3			26,376	21,754
1933	2,313	10.3	5.7	0.5	14.2	8.4			28,379	26,742
1934	2,544	2.6	6.3	0.5	16.3	8.0			32,724	28,454
1935	3,136	15.0	14.5	0.4	15.2	11.0			35,803	—
1936	3,360	21.0	9.8	0.3	14.3	13.0			39,646	—
1937	3,216	38.0	14.0	0.4	17.1	13.4			37,055	—
1938	3,190	1.0	14.1	0.6	10.6	15.4	1.0		33,835	—
1939	4,621	1.0	11.9	0.6	13.3	14.2	3.3		39,399	—
1940	7,172	3.4	9.4	1.4	7.6	10.7	5.0		47,581	—
1941	8,223	0.5	12.5	0.8	8.0	11.4	8.0		58,550	—
1942	9,727	0.5	12.0	0.7	5.1	7.9	7.4	0.1	64,974	—
1943	10,096	4.4	9.0	0.6	0.4	4.4	8.6	0.2	57,885	75,396
1944	5,592	6.7	3.2	0.9	0.2	1.6	7.6	0.4	56,697	62,213
1945	—	4.0	—	0.6	—	1.9	1.5	—	—	53,979
1946	—	8.2	2.6	0.9	1.0	1.2	—	—	17,158	21,600
1947	—	9.0	6.4	1.1	1.6	1.5	—	—	18,387	16,000
1948	—	—	10.3	—	3.3	2.1	—	—	—	—

Sources: Geological Survey of China, *General Statement on the Mining Industry,* Nos. 1-7; Bureau of Statistics, *Statistical Yearbook of the Republic of China,* Nanking, 1948; *Chinese Yearbook,* Nanking, 1948; *Thirty Years of Chinese Engineering,* 2nd edition, Nanking, 1948; National Resources Commission, *Summary Report of the Work of the National Resources Commission since Demobilization,* Nanking, 1948; *National Resources Commission Quarterly,* Vol. VI, Nos. 1-2; U.S. Bureau of Mines, *Foreign Minerals Survey,* Washington, D.C., 1948; United Nations, *Statistical Yearbook,* 1951; and Pauley Commission, *Report on Japanese Assets in Manchuria,* Washington, D.C., 1946.

National Income of China in 1931-1936 at Current Prices
(in CN$ million)

	1931	*1932*	*1933*	*1934*	*1935*	*1936*
Agriculture	15,315	15,094	12,593	11,325	12,906	16,641
Mining & Metallurgy	257	234	238	241	258	294
Manufacturing	1,927	1,870	1,889	1,813	2,002	2,475
Building & Construction	200	139	221	260	190	195
Transportation & Communication	980	885	922	995	1,052	1,042
Commerce	3,989	2,718	2,541	2,286	2,236	2,566
Banking & Insurance	176	176	200	235	251	294
Dwelling Service	934	934	934	934	934	934
Professional Service	164	160	171	161	173	215
Domestic Service	141	141	141	141	141	141
Government Service	725	635	642	918	835	1,001
Total	24,808	22,986	20,492	19,309	20,978	25,798
Deduction	153	153	173	203	217	254
Income Produced	24,655	22,833	20,319	19,106	20,761	25,544
International Net Inpayments						
(1) Excluding Foreign Borrowing & Contributions	172	126	68	106	65	171
(2) Including Foreign Borrowing & Contributions	216	989	98	337	341	1,214
Disposable Income	24,827	22,959	20,387	19,212	20,826	25,715
Disposable Goods & Services	24,871	23,822	20,417	19,443	21,102	26,758

Source: Ou Pao-san, *National Income of China, 1933, 1936 and 1946* (English), Nanking, 1947. Data represent revised figures from Ou's earlier work on *China's National Income, 1933,* Shanghai, 1947.

LOW RATE OF CAPITAL ACCUMULATION

One may question whether the potential capacity to accumulate capital in China is not larger than the estimates by Ou Pao-san for the 1931-1936 period would suggest. But the more optimistic estimates, such as that of Liu Ta-chung, appear definitely to be on the high side as far as actual conditions before the war with Japan were concerned. Liu's assumption was that some ten per cent of the gross national product would be saved every year. This would be equivalent to about US$1.7 billion, which, less depreciation and other forms of capital consumption, would point to an annual net investment of US$1 billion. That this was definitely too high for the prewar period may be roughly demonstrated by considering the following factors.

First, we may consider the size of the capital stock in China before the war. Although estimates of the capital stock of China are even less reliable than the national income figures, we could perhaps use the one advanced by Wang Foh-shen in 1948.[26] According to Wang, China's total capital stock in 1933, estimated on the basis of the discounted value of future income, was between US$4-16 billion. On the other hand, estimated on the basis of annual depreciation multiplied by the average life of the capital stock, it was between US$4-19 billion. The wide range results from the use of different interest rates and different estimates of average durability respectively. Even if the higher figures were correct, it would appear rather unlikely that China's capital stock could be so small if an annual net investment of US$1 billion had been maintained for any length of time.

Second, net investment was low in prewar China because of the high frequency of natural disasters which were destructive of existing capital stock and because of population growth which tended to increase current consumption. According to Ch'en Ta, from 206 B.C. to 1933, China experienced no less than 1,057 droughts and 1,030 floods of major proportions or an average of 49 droughts and 48 floods in every one hundred years.[27] These, together with the cyclical movement of the population, may very well underlie the small rate of growth of capital.

Finally, since, according to Wang, about one-half of the capital stock was, and probably still is, in the agricultural sector which is especially susceptible to the effect of natural disasters, the slow rate of capital accumulation by the farm population inevitably leads to a low net investment in the aggregate. Moreover, as we shall see in Chapter IV, certain institutional factors were also at work which tended to prevent the productive employment of rural savings.

During the sixteen years that elapsed between 1933 and the Communists' accession to power, there were both a considerable increase in population and some expansion of industrial capital. But all in all the amount of capital per capita of China's working population was probably smaller. This lack of productive equipment thus further reinforced the shortage of land and natural resources described above.

IV

CHARACTERISTICS OF INDUSTRIAL DEVELOPMENT

The Chinese Communists inherited not only the economic burden of over-population in the agricultural sector, but also the small industrial base from which further expansion might be carried out. In order to appreciate the actual situation, the following characteristics of the country's past industrial development should be noted.

First, prior to the establishment of the Communist regime, modern industry in China was concentrated in Manchuria and a few treaty ports in China Proper. Second, foreign capital predominated in all modern enterprises. Third, there was a serious shortage in modern transportation and communication facilities, power supply, and organized investment markets, all prerequisites of economic development. Fourth, light industries producing certain consumers' goods were relatively more developed than such industries as iron and steel and machinery manufacturing. Fifth, the typical Chinese industrial enterprise had very small capital, most of which was tied in fixed equipment so that there was as a rule very little working capital available. Finally, management and business organization were extremely backward, partly as a result of certain traditional social factors and the so-called cultural lags, partly as a result of government policy and the influence of foreign economic relations.

GEOGRAPHICAL DISTRIBUTION OF INDUSTRY

Outside Manchuria, the principal manufacturing centers in China before World War II were Shanghai, Tientsin in North China, Hankow in Central China, Canton in South China, and Tsingtao on the eastern seabord. This geographical concentration at a few sea and river ports became only slightly less pronounced after the war. Wartime industrial development in Southwest China and in a few areas in the North had somewhat shifted the geographical distribution of industries. However, the center of gravity in 1949 was still located in Shanghai in China Proper and in the southern section of Manchuria in the Northeast.

During 1933, a little over one-half of the country's industrial output was derived from Shanghai, with Manchuria, North China, Central China, and South China about equally responsible for the remainder.[28] As a result of Japanese investments, the industrial growth of Manchuria went forward by leaps and bounds during the late thirties and early forties. Accordingly, the relative importance of Manchuria in Chinese industrial production rose greatly in relation to Shanghai as well as the rest of the country. The annual rate of increase in industrial employment in Manchuria between 1935 and 1940 reached 32 per cent while output per capita of the employed industrial population increased from CN$2,800 per annum according to Ou Pao-san to CN$6,100 in 1939 for the Kwantung Leased Territory. On the other hand, between 1936 and 1941, industrial production in Shanghai as measured by a simple average for eight manufacturing industries experienced an annual increase of 12 per cent only. However, since this index does not give sufficient weight to the important cotton textile and flour industries which lagged behind the growth of industry in general, there is even an upward bias in the above measurement. The fall in the relative importance of Shanghai during the war was partly due to the wholesale removal of certain industrial equipment to Free China and wartime restrictions and other dislocations under the occupation. Finally, the importance of North China and Free China also increased slightly relative to Shanghai as industrial production in these areas rose at an annual rate of 19 per cent between 1939 and 1945. However, these shifts were not large enough to create other manufacturing centers in China Proper to rival Shanghai. That such was the situation on the eve of the establishment of the Communist regime may be seen in the statistics on page 34.

THE INFLUENCE OF FOREIGN CAPITAL

The concentration of modern industry in the river and sea ports was the direct result of the predominance of foreign firms in China's manufacturing industries. In 1933, for instance, one-half of the industrial workers in Shanghai were employed by foreign firms. In Manchuria, the steady growth of employment in Japanese firms from 1933 to 1940 was twice as fast as that in Chinese firms in the same area.[29] The expansion of Japanese investments in Manchurian industry was, of course, largely due to Japan's political domination

Employment, Motive Power, and Number of Manufacturing Concerns in Major Cities in China Proper, 1947

	Number of Factories	Total Employment	Motive Power H.P.	Motive Power Kilovoltampere
Shanghai	7,738	406,371	325,268.2	73,063.8
Nanking	888	12,010	18,077.5	4.0
Tientsin	1,211	65,734	110,476.9	9,624.0
Peiping (Peking)	272	9,974	13,256.9	24,509.0
Hankow	459	23,863	10,167.0	4,527.0
Ch'ang-sha & Heng-yang	216	10,289	4,040.5	39.3
Nan-ch'ang & Chiu-chiang	161	7,192	4,059.0	636.0
Chungking	661	36,940	11,709.5	3,545.0
Kun-ming	66	7,543	5,298.5	—
Kwei-yang	83	5,597	1,311.1	94.4
Canton	473	30,016	10,022.1	476.0
Swatow	121	5,942	266.0	5.0
Hsi-an	69	7,090	3,655.0	506.0
Lan-chou	39	3,212	1,974.2	28.0
Fu-chou	176	3,698	3,291.0	—
Tsingtao	185	31,518	34,403.0	14,734.0

Source: National Economic Commission, *Industrial Survey of Principal Cities in China, Preliminary Report,* Nanking, 1948.

of the area. Comparable development in the treaty ports, of which Shanghai was the most important, also led to the gravitation of foreign firms to these cities.

The establishment of trade posts by foreign merchants at the treaty ports resulted in the creation of settlements and concessions. The military weakness of the Manchu regime and its successors further permitted the perpetration of extra-territoriality. Given extra-territoriality, however objectionable it might be from a purely nationalistic point of view, it was only natural for foreign businessmen to congregate in the treaty ports and to establish their manufacturing enterprises. Given the political instability of the period, the exactions of warlords, and the fear of physical loss, the foreign concessions also provided the infant Chinese industries with a much needed sanctuary. Physical safety, however, was not the only consideration. Some of the early Chinese industrialists had originally been compradores of foreign firms. They had grown up in the economic organization in close association with their foreign counterparts, and it was no less natural for them to establish their enterprises within the original treaty ports or in their immediate vicinity.

Even aside from this personal and human factor, the growth of foreign firms helped to create external economies. Banking, communications, servicing, insurance, the stock exchange, and all the ancillary facilities of modern business were all far more developed in these new economic centers than elsewhere. This factor exerted a gravitational pull to all new business, whether Chinese or foreign-owned.

While foreign capital played a pioneering role in the development of Chinese industries, it also obstructed the expansion of Chinese firms in a different way. Perhaps the most important factor was the availability of capital. No Chinese firm could borrow at a rate of interest comparable to that at which foreign firms could obtain financing. The undeveloped state of the security exchange made public issues exceedingly difficult and rare. The small capital available to the average Chinese firm was reflected in the predominance of individual proprietors and partnerships in business organization. It was often used in procuring the necessary plant and equipment so that more frequently than not there was a shortage of working capital. The quantitative restriction of credit and the high interest rate made it necessary for the Chinese entrepreneur to earn a higher profit margin than his foreign competitors, which made him particularly vulnerable to price competition. If he was dependent upon domestic supplies of raw materials from the interior provinces, he was further confronted with the high transport cost, unreliability of supply due to lack of standardization, and an inefficient system of purchase and collection. It has been frequently pointed out, for instance, that it was usually much better for Shanghai flour and cotton mills to buy their wheat and cotton from Canada and the United States respectively than from North China. These conditions, on the one hand, affected the position of Chinese firms *vis-à-vis* their foreign competitors in the treaty ports. On the other hand, they resulted in the slow expansion of industry in the interior provinces until the war with Japan brought about the wholesale removal of industry to the West and the subsequent expansion of small-scale production in Southwest and Northwest China.

SOCIAL FACTORS RETARDING INDUSTRIAL PROGRESS

The absence of an orgainized investment market imposed certain limitations on the form of business organization. As long as potential investors looked upon the flotation of share capital as something similar to the solicitation of charity contributions, the entrepreneur was compelled to operate with his own resources, as well as those of his immediate family circle and close friends. The predominance of small proprietorships and partnerships also had its root in the social structure of the country which centered around the family institution. As long as business enterprise was an appendage of the family, its organization and management had to evolve around it. On the one hand, control was not allowed to pass out of the hands of the closest family members. On the other hand, the business organization frequently became a place for the relief of unemployed relatives. This led to inefficiency in management and technical performance, which, in turn, affected adversely the profitability of industrial pursuits, internal accumulation, and the recruitment of outside capital for expansion. The form of business organization and the availability of capital thus reacted upon each other.

Another factor inherent in the traditional Chinese society which affected economic development adversely was the lack of mechanical skill and other background technical knowledge on the part of the workers. The peasant who is accustomed to the plow must undergo a fundamental change in mentality and working habits in order to adapt himself to handling machinery in organized groups. Although this is a common obstacle faced by all underdeveloped countries, in the case of China the situation was somewhat worsened by the large traditional gap between mental and manual labor. Unfortunately, most work with machines, especially on a level below that of engineers in the drafting room, falls within the latter category and was held in low esteem. The factory workman, if he was literate, not only aspired to an office job, but considered his work with machinery on the production line as a status he should leave behind as soon as possible. This attitude accounted for the appalling lack of supervisory personnel on the factory floor in China and the consequent poor performance in maintenance and repair of machinery.

Closely connected with this general attitude was the failure to develop the practical sciences and the resultant lag in technological innovations which were not infrequently looked upon as inconsequential in comparison with philosophy and the arts. In short, the social and cultural values were not such as to permit the development of any irrepressible urge to innovate and to adopt the ways of factory production.

RELATIVE IMPORTANCE OF CONSUMER'S GOODS INDUSTRIES

Outside Manchuria, which was built up by the Japanese before and during World War II as a center of heavy industry, the little modern industry China possessed was devoted mostly to the production of consumer's goods. In this, one could perhaps say that China followed the typical pattern of economic development in most underdeveloped areas. In particular, the cotton textiles, food processing, and the manufacture of such light chemicals as matches constituted the principal activities in manufacturing. As for the metallurgical and machinery industries, the factories in China Proper were little more, by western standards, than repair and assembly shops. The few modern enterprises in basic chemicals, steel production, and the like, established in the late thirties and during the war, stood out as notable exceptions. This situation is well illustrated in the distribution of employment and other related statistics by industries according to the 1947 survey.

Employment, Motive Power, and
Number of Firms in China by Industries, 1947

		Motive Power		
	Employment	*H.P.*	*KVA*	*Number of Factories*
Textiles	337,734	329,213.5	36,408.5	3,773
Food Processing	108,297	74,661.0	14,547.3	1,379
Chemicals	78,905	80,423.3	9,841.5	1,553
Apparel	51,981	8,482.4	20.0	1,783
Paper and Printing	38,569	56,624.3	2,489.0	1,669
Machinery	36,392	20,670.5	161.5	1,505
Metallurgical	28,747	65,781.8	12,252.2	494
Metal Products	21,893	26,744.4	61,041.0	682
Electrical Equipment	16,213	7,093.6	42.8	303
Clay and Stone	15,731	117,676.3	24,965.0	152
Transportation Equipment	12,380	4,845.5	255.0	269
Wood Working	4,497	4,693.5	60.0	156
Miscellaneous	20,311	30,362.3	127.5	360
Total	771,650	827,272.4	162,211.3	14,078

Source: National Economic Commission, *Industrial Survey of Principal Cities in China, Preliminary Report,* Nanking, 1948. In addition to the cities listed in the previous table, the above data also include Formosa and the Manchurian cities of Shen-yang, Liao-yang, Sze-p'ing, Fu-shun, An-shan, Pen-ch'i, Ch'ang-ch'un, Chi-lin, and Su-chia-tun. If the Manchurian factories were excluded, the predominance of the light manufacturing industries would be even more obvious.

V

PUBLIC FINANCE AND FISCAL POLICY[30]

The industrial development of China in the pre-Communist period was greatly influenced by the government. In the first place, it was affected by the government's taxation and fiscal policy which, during the greater part of the last decade, was unfavorable to steady economic development. In the second place, an increasingly important role was played by the state through its direct participation in industrial production.

The government failed to exert a consistently beneficial influence on economic development largely because of the lack of a sound system of public finance. With the exception of 1914 and 1916, the entire history of the Republic was one of budget deficits. The existence of budget deficits as such would not be a necessary evil but for the fact that they were due to large military expenditures in all the years and the failure to develop a reliable and equitable system of taxation.

Military expenditure, together with debt services, was responsible throughout the prewar period for 60 to 70 per cent of the total outlay of the central government. This reflected the effect of the rule of warlords prior to the firm establishment of the Nationalist government in 1927 and the subsequent civil war with the Communists. The large portion of the budget taken up by debt services was the result of indiscriminate borrowing for consumption purposes. From 1932 to 1936, tax receipts were rarely above 80 per cent of government revenue throughout. The predominant part or about 90 per cent of the tax receipts was again made up by indirect taxes. In 1936, for instance, the salt tax accounted for 27.8 per cent of total tax proceeds or 19.1 per cent of the government's total revenue. In the same year, the consolidated excise tax imposed on rolled and cured tobacco, cotton yarn, wheat flour, matches, cement, and alcohol constituted 19.5 per cent of total tax preceeds and 14.6 per cent of the government's revenue. Customs receipts in the same year accounted for 40.2 per cent of total tax proceeds and 30.9 per cent of the government's revenue. The inequitable nature of taxation was particularly evident in the salt tax from which about one-third of the total tax revenue was derived. The income tax was not introduced in China until shortly before the war with Japan so that indirect taxation was the mainstay of government finance. As the particular nature of these taxes made them dependent upon the continued maintenance of free foreign trade and government control of the coastal provinces where the salt fields and the manufacturing plants were situated, war developments soon deprived the government of its major sources of revenue. This helped to spark the uncontrolled inflation of the war and postwar years.

What we have just mentioned deals with taxation by the central government. In addition, there was, of course, local taxation to face. Prior to the establishment of the Nationalist government in Nanking, the Peking government was especially notorious with respect to its financial confusion. Theoretically, the central and local governments shared in total government revenue, and surtaxes were imposed by the provincial and local authorities over and above the various categories of central government taxation. However, control over various provinces by individual warlords prevented the tax proceeds from being transmitted to the central government most of the time. Local taxes were many and varied. Such taxes were levied, for instance, on domestic animals, groceries, hotels, entertainment, restaurants and tea houses, fisheries, business turnover, and land.

Following the establishment of the Nationalist government in Nanking, the mainstay of local taxation consisted of the land or agricultural tax and the business tax. By 1937 some 7,100 different local taxes previously imposed by provincial and local governments had been abolished. The local governments were further given subsidies by the central government. Before a uniform and simplified system of central and local taxation could be established in practice, however, the war had broken out, and military operations soon rendered inoperative the previous attempt to differentiate local and central taxation. In 1941, as a wartime measure, the imposition of land tax in kind was introduced, and this was made a revenue of the central government.

Since the government failed to develop direct taxation, its continued expenditure on military activities led to dependence on borrowing. However, because, until the last few years before the war, most of the borrowing done was for unproductive purposes, government credit was extremely low. The government was unable to borrow except at an extremely high interest rate. In addition, it was obliged to pledge specific revenues against individual bond issues. From 1927 to September, 1937, there were altogether 38 public issues totalling CN$1.9 million and £1.5 million. These were in addition to the loans floated during the earlier years of the Republic which totalled 27 issues and CN$610 million. An attempt was made in 1932 to reduce the rate of interest on the outstanding issues and to extend their maturity dates. The customs revenue was pledged to the extent of CN$8.6 million a month to establish a sinking fund for domestic debt. Again in 1936 the government issued five different groups of consolidated bonds as a refunding loan to replace 33 different previous issues. The refunding operation brought about a general lowering of the rate of interest from 7-8 per cent to 6 per cent.

The difficulty in borrowing was seen not only in the high interest rate. The absence of a highly developed investment market meant that in most cases the government was not able to sell its bonds directly to the public. It relied instead upon the financial houses to absorb its bonds, and as this became increasingly difficult, especially during the war years, most of the borrowing was done in the form of overdrafts from the government banks. This, of course, led directly to credit expansion and monetary inflation.

THE BROADER ASPECT OF GOVERNMENT ECONOMIC POLICY[31]

In the broader aspect of government economic policy, prewar development in China illustrated very aptly the situation common to most underdeveloped countries. It was characterized by the desire to industrialize rapidly, together with the conviction that this could not be achieved without the extensive intervention of the state. Two ideological influences also underlay the outlook of the government. The tradition of paternalism regarded the expansion of state enterprise as a most natural development while the impact of western socialist thought had impressed upon the policy-makers and economic planners the need to avert the disadvantages of untrammelled private enterprise, and the importance of establishing economic and social equality, however nebulous these concepts might be, especially in their practical application.

The basic principles of the economic policy of the Kuomintang, as outlined by Sun Yat-sen in his proposal for the international development of China, may be summarized as follows: First, foreign capital should be invited for the industrial development of China.

Second, private enterprise should expand side by side with government undertakings organized in national trusts. Third, private capital should be controlled through progressive taxation, including income and inheritance taxes. Fourth, farmers should own their own land.

However, Sun Yat-sen did not make clear whether the abolition of private property was his ultimate goal. Nor did he distinctly delineate the private and government sectors of the economy. Thus, there is some ambiguity as to whether he envisaged a basically capitalistic system for China and, if not, how he thought the elimination of private property and enterprise might be brought about. This confusion is enhanced because, although he pointed out that his "principle of people's livelihood" was socialistic, his failure to identify it with one of the 57 varieties of socialism which he professed to have found shed little light on the issue.

Upon close examination of Sun Yat-sen's writings, however, the burden of his arguments appears to be in favor of a liberal interpretation. In the first place, the employment of progressive taxation as a means of curbing the influence of private capital and the idea of enabling farmers to own their own land are not revolutionary measures however radical they may have sounded thirty years ago. Nor are these proposals inimical to the institution of private property. Moreover, Sun Yat-sen was most outspoken in his opposition to class struggle as an integral part of the social theory of dialectic materialism. To him class struggle was a phenomenon in social pathology because the good society should be based upon the harmony of interests instead. Finally, it should be noted that at the time he identified his "principle of the people's livelihood" with socialism in general, he was the head of a political party which, having failed to win allies among the western powers, had turned to the Soviet Union for help, especially because the latter had only just relinquished of its own accord the extra-territorial rights of the Czarist regime in China, though possibly because it was then in no position to defend these rights. Socialism promised then to many people in the world an era of prosperity and justice—the imperialistic and authoritarian tendencies of the Soviet regime not having yet been apparent—and the need for an ally to help unify the country was no doubt paramount in Sun's mind.

With the break between the Nationalists and the Communists, the sharp schism within the Kuomintang between the issues of socialism and capitalism was for a time buried, but not completely, for the period between 1927 and 1937 was marked by a spate of paper plans for the economic development of the country, all of which envisaged an active and expanding role for the state. Most of these plans were completely devoid of any practical significance, but the formation of the National Economic Council in the latter part of 1931 marked the beginning of a short episode of development along rational lines. Following upon the wake of the 1931 flood, the NEC, though vested with very wide powers, did not engage in any grandiose and unpractical planning. Instead, it rendered valuable assistance to certain industries, such as cotton and silk, through financial assistance and technical help. As the economic depression passed its lowest point in 1934, this period of least irrational planning was also a period of great economic progress.

The threat of war was already mounting, and with it the development of a war economy with increasing government participation began to take shape. The National Resources Commission, established in 1933, drew up in 1936 its first concrete plan to develop certain heavy industries in China, including iron and steel, copper, zinc, tungsten, antimony, synthetic oil and alcohol, electrical equipment, and basic chemicals. After the outbreak of the war and the subsequent loss of the established industrial areas and the partial removal of certain industrial establishments to the Southwest, the predominance of state enterprise in industry and mining in Free China became unmistakable. The few large enterprises under Chinese control in wartime were for the most part operated and owned by the National Resources Commission. This development of statism was further enhanced immediately after the end of the war as the government took over all the enterprises formerly owned by Japanese interests and Chinese collaborators. These included the large Japanese textile industry in China, practically all the iron and steel mills, and many other industrial plants, as well as, theoretically at any rate, virtually all the industrial plants in Manchuria. However, the transfer of government enterprise to private hands was contemplated by the government during the last few years of its rule on the mainland as a result of the pressing need to raise revenue. This never came to pass because the Communists soon swept the country.

Because the government had played an increasingly important role in the actual allocation and use of resources both before and after the war, and because inadequate attention had been given to the development of the economy through individual initiative within a well-ordered economy and established rule of law, there was not a broad and vigorous capitalistic economy in China at the time the Communists took over. The transition to a system of greater regimentation, at the beginning at any rate, was made all the easier both physically and ideologically.

VI

SOVIET DEVASTATION OF MANCHURIA

The above review has summarized some of the material and institutional factors which helped to shape the economic development of China up to 1949. However, most of these factors represented long-term, underlying developments that were only indirectly related to the Sino-Japanese war and its aftermath. While they may have provided the setting for future development, the impetus to the fall of the Nationalists was given by two events, the immediate cause of which was the war.

Foremost on the list of external events that contributed to the downfall of the Nationalists after World War II was the destruction of the Manchurian industrial complex through planned removals of installations and stocks on the part of Soviet occupation troops. On the one hand, Nationalist China was denied the benefit of the production of the many Japanese enterprises in providing the country's reconstruction needs. On the other hand, the political necessity forced upon the Nationalists, i.e., from their particular point of view, to keep control of Manchuria in spite of initial setbacks helped to sap their military strength in successive futile campaigns which only added to the inflationary movement in the economy. We have already noted the extremely fragile industrial base China possessed inside the Great Wall and the consequent importance of Manchuria. The serious effect of Soviet removals on Manchurian industry and on the industrial production of China as a whole can be easily perceived from the following data:

Summary of Damage to Basic Manchurian Industry

	Estimated Loss Due to Removals and Damage during Soviet Occupation (US $million)	*Estimated Per Cent Reduction in Productive Capacity*
Electric Power	201.00	71
Coal	50.00	90[1]
Iron and Steel	131.26	51–100[2]
Railways	221.39	50–100[2]
Metal Working	163.00	80
Non-ferrous Metals	10.00	75
Liquid Fuels and Lubricants	11.38	75
Chemicals	14.00	50
Cement	23.00	50
Textiles	38.00	75
Paper and Pulp	7.00	30
Radio, Telegraph and Telephone	25.00	20–100[2]
Total	895.03	

Source: Pauley Commission, *Report on Japanese Assets in Manchuria,* p. 37, Washington, D.C., 1946.

1. Based on investigation of mines responsible for 50 per cent of total Manchurian coal production.
2. Percentage varies in sub-categories.

"After the removals the Soviet forces permitted and even encouraged Chinese mobs to pillage, taking official movies of the process in some instances . . . (They) also confiscated approximately three million U.S. dollars worth of gold bullion stocks and over a half billion Manchurian *yuan* from Manchukuo banks. They also circulated nearly ten billion *yuan* in occupational currency, almost doubling the total Manchurian note issue. In addition to the removals, mentioned above, occupational currency was used to purchase factories and properties and some privately-owned merchandise and materials . . .

"The value of the properties removed by the Soviets is probably one-tenth of the amount of damage and economic collapse resulting from these same removals. Many of the items removed were key installations. The removal of one essential item often stopped production in an entire plant . . . At least one-third of the original Japanese investment would be required to restore the damaged and destroyed plants to their original productive level. This does not take into account further deterioration and the loss of production before the old level is reached. These would probably double the cost. Taking all this into consideration, two billion U.S. dollars (are) considered to be a conservative estimate of the damage to Manchuria resulting from the Soviet occupation." [32]

It is difficult to say whether the removals would have been ordered had the Soviet Union foreseen the eventual triumph of the Chinese Communists on the mainland. If the removals had not taken place, it is conceivable that restoration of Manchurian industrial and agricultural production would have bolstered the economic and political position of the Nationalist government to such an extent that its fight against inflation and internal deterioration might have been won. The great economic benefit Communist China had been able to derive from Manchuria in its own attempt at economic stabilization and recovery during the last few years (once rehabilitation has taken place) offers substantial support to this view. On the other hand, since the removals did take place, the Chinese Communists, once installed in power, have been made far more dependent upon the Soviet Union as a result than they might otherwise have been.

VII

WARTIME INFLATION

The course of China's monetary inflation may be divided into three periods—the wartime inflation between the latter part of 1939 and 1945, the postwar inflation up to the collapse of *fapi*[33] in August, 1948, and the final stage ending with the Nationalists' evacuation of the mainland in 1949. Although inflation was brought about by the war and the failure of the government's financial and fiscal policy, it in turn bred inefficiency and corruption, undermined the authority of the central government in relation to dissident groups and provincial interests, transformed the average citizen into a speculator, and created a mass despondence and moral vacuum that made the country ripe for the picking by the militant Communist Party.

The fortunes of war had turned against the Chinese after the first few months of fighting in Shanghai in 1937. The retreat westward initiated a large population movement to the province of Szechwan and beyond. Specific shortages soon developed, especially in areas of concentrated population and with respect to such commodities as rice, cotton yarn, and cloth. Transportation difficulties also led to certain regional price discrepancies. However, as far as the general price level was concerned, its rise continued to be moderate until the latter part of 1939. Several factors accounted for the relative price stability of these first two years of the war with Japan.

In the first place, total government revenue in 1937 still amounted to one-half of total expenditure. The relative importance of non-borrowed revenue continued to account for at least one-quarter of total government outlay up to 1939. This relatively "small" budget deficit did not require any sudden, large increase in note issue. Nor had the fear of inflation yet taken its hold on popular imagination. Moreover, the writ of *fapi* still ran in the whole country at the beginning of the war, even in Japanese-occupied areas. The Federal Reserve Bank of the North China regime, sponsored by the Japanese, was not established until 1938 while the Hwa-hsin Bank, forerunner of the Central Reserve Bank of the Japanese-sponsored regime in Nanking, was not established until 1939. Apart from the blockade, the Japanese had not yet initiated their economic offensive by their attempt to eliminate the circulation of *fapi* in areas under their control and by their use of *fapi* acquired through compulsory conversion for purchasing supplies in Free China and for other operations designed to undermine price stability and the foreign exchange value of the official Chinese currency. For these various reasons, the rise of prices in Free China was reasonably moderate up to 1939 and generally paralleled the expansion of money supply.

From June, 1937, to June, 1939, the volume of note issue increased from CN$1.4 billion to CN$2.6 billion, i.e., about 97 per cent. In the same period, the wholesale price index in Chungking rose from 101 (July–December, 1937 = 100) to 216, the increase being closely comparable to that in note issue. However, from December, 1939, to December, 1940, while the note issue of the Central Bank of China increased from CN$3.1 billion to CN$8 billion, and the total money supply, i.e., including demand deposits, from CN$7.4 billion to CN$13.5 billion, there was a greater than threefold increase in the Chungking wholesale price index which went up from 325 to 1,121. This phenomenon of the price level rising at a faster rate than the supply of money continued throughout the war, until the scene was briefly changed with the war's end.[34]

The rise of the price level was the result of the uninterrupted expansion of spending which came from several different sources. First and foremost, there was the ever-widening budget deficit. The loss of ordinary sources of government revenue had brought about a revamping of the tax structure. Taxes on excess profit and inheritance were both introduced in 1939. The land tax in kind was inaugurated in 1941 and its proceeds were earmarked for the central government. Total government revenue was derived at the time in the following manner: (1) land tax, 45 per cent; (2) government monoplies, 25 per cent; (3) indirect taxes, 15 per cent; and (4) income, profit, and other direct taxes, 15 per cent. In spite of this attempt to open up new sources of revenue, however, government income lagged far behind government outlay. Out of a total expenditure of CN$8 billion in 1941, the above revenue sources accounted for no more than CN$1.3 billion or 15 per cent. Although the tax changes adopted during the year brought about an improvement in 1942 when 30 per cent of the total expenditure of CN$25 billion was covered by revenue, the situation deteriorated again in the subsequent years. As government expenditure increased, the budget deficit also continued to mount, even allowing for a fairly constant ratio of expenditure to revenue. Thus, while a total budget deficit of CN$183.5 billion was incurred during the entire five-year period from 1940 to 1944, by the end of 1945 this cumulative total had risen to over CN$450 billion.

To meet this mounting deficit, the government issued a number of internal loans, including the U.S. dollar bonds and savings certificates of 1942. It also initiated the public sale of government gold holdings in 1943, which, up to June, 1945, realized a total of CN$80 billion. Unfortunately, all this was to no avail. Borrowing directly from the public being impossible, the deficit could not be made up by voluntary or even forced savings, and the various measures designed to drain off the public's excessive purchasing power proved to be ineffective.[35]

While the wartime increase in prices in Free China was related to the expansion of money supply consisting chiefly of currency issued by the Central Bank of China, and, for the first few years, also notes of the Bank of China, the Bank of Communications, and the Farmers' Bank of China, the official *fapi* was not the only currency in use in the entire country. Other banks of issue under Japanese occupation were busily engaged in a similar process of monetary inflation. The Central Reserve Bank of the Nanking regime, established in 1941 as successor of the Hwa-hsin Bank, had increased its note issue from CRB$65 million in June, 1941, to CRB$75 billion at the end of 1944, and, as a final splurge, an additional issue of CRB$2,000 billion was made immediately before V.J. day. The outstanding issue of the Federal Reserve Bank of the regime in North China, totalling FRB $162 million at the end of 1938, stood at 5 billion by the middle of 1944. The Bank of Mongolia which was established in 1937 and acted as an issuing bank for the area of southern Chahar, northern Shansi, and the province of Suiyan, increased its note issue from 13 million at the end of 1937 to approximately 124 million at the end of 1942. Although these three banks were established by the Japanese, at the end of the war it was necessary to liquidate their outstanding notes, and the conversion into CN dollars, even though at very low exchange rates, was another source of the increasing money supply. In addition to these relatively well-known banks there were still other currencies in circulation. Among these were the various issues of the Communist-controlled regional banks. Between 1938 and 1943 there were, furthermore, large amounts of Japanese military Yen in circulation in Central and South China. An estimate by Tamagna put the total volume of the latter at about one billion in 1942.

Over and above all these currencies which circulated in China Proper there were the currencies of Manchuria and Formosa. Although they were not integrated with the CN dollar following the end of the war, their wartime inflation also constituted a part of the total monetary chaos that prevailed in China. The note issue of the Central Bank of Manchuria stood at Y179 million in the middle of 1937. By mid-1943 this amount had increased tenfold. By the end of 1944 it reached 5.9 billion Yen. The Bank of Taiwan, perhaps the most stable of all the issuing banks, also increased its total note issue from Y75 million in the middle of 1937 to probably Y850 million at the end of 1944.

Disregarding the Japanese military Yen and the currencies of the Communist banks, the total amount of currency in circulation, including the *fapi*, the CRB, the FRB, and the currencies of the Bank of Mongolia, the Central Bank of Manchou, and the Bank of Taiwan, amounted to an approximate value of CN$375 billion at the end of 1944. The picture we have thus painted is one of general inflation in all of China although the intensity of inflation varied in different regions as a result of differences in monetary management and regional productivity.

THE COURSE OF POSTWAR INFLATION

The sudden surrender of Japan and the replacement of the Japanese-sponsored currencies in Central and North China by *fapi*, which greatly increased its area of circulation almost overnight, gave the inflation-weary population a short respite. Thus, while the volume of note issue in September, 1945, was about 465 times that of July, 1937, the wholesale price index as compiled by the Central Bank of China for Shanghai stood at 345 times that of the average for January to June, 1937. Unfortunately, large and unbridled government expenditure in re-occupation and troop deployment, together with a buying spree on the part of those who had descended from Chungking, soon altered the picture. By November, 1945, the relative increase in note issue, compared with its mid-1937 level, had been surpassed by that of the wholesale price index in Shanghai. If we regard changes in the size of note issue as representative of changes in the total volume of money, while considering the relation between the relative increase of the price level and that of the volume of money as indicative of any change in the population's willingness to hold cash balances, we could safely conclude that hyper-inflation was resumed at the end of 1945.

As a center of commercial and speculative activities, Shanghai was not a typical city in China, and the price level in Shanghai probably tended to be more volatile than elsewhere. However, for our purpose, we can disregard this factor and use the various price indices in Shanghai to describe the general course of the inflation. On this basis it will be noted (1) that the wholesale price index rose approximately twelvefold from January, 1946, to March, 1947, another forty-five fold from March, 1947, to May, 1948, and almost another ten fold by August 19, 1948, when the "gold *yuan*" (GY) was introduced; and (2) that while during 1946 the price indices for gold bars and United States dollar notes, the two major objects of speculation on the exchange market, lagged behind the rise of the wholesale price index, the gap in the relative rates of increase was gradually closed during 1947 so that by April, 1948, the initial lag had been completely wiped out and from then on to August 19 of the same year the three indices rose at virtually the same rate. Although gold and United States dollar rates were subject to the effect of govern-

The Course of *Fapi* Depreciation

September 1945—August 19, 1948

September 1945=100		*Note Issue*[1]	*Shanghai Whole-Sale Price Index*[2]	*Shanghai Gold Bar Price Index*[2]	*Shanghai U. S. Dollar Note Price Index*[2]
1945	September	100.00	100.00	100.00	100.00
	October	119.53	109.72	121.68	157.88
	November	133.64	287.61	177.12	171.38
	December	153.06	256.58	155.78	152.37
1946	January	170.56	269.04	184.87	181.16
	February	187.07	508.86	306.35	258.94
	March	199.58	741.82	337.63	252.82
	April	226.65	748.30	330.93	262.28
	May	266.39	1,103.26	375.41	289.40
	June	313.33	1,070.07	404.21	322.26
	July	320.17	1,179.93	412.47	314.92
	August	352.43	1,241.85	423.90	363.65
	September	400.56	1,475.43	454.02	444.86
	October	442.58	1,554.09	474.88	527.84
	November	488.90	1,540.87	535.46	566.35
	December	552.67	1,655.55	670.87	732.50

1947	January	668.87	1,990.30	808.31	836.25
	February	717.56	3,090.35	1,300.00	1,582.12
	March	851.99	3,247.98	1,323.08	1,754.75
	April	1,023.60	4,130.10	1,507.37	2,036.00
	May	1,243.15	7,045.50	2,797.48	3,398.12
	June	1,453.00	8,673.39	4,081.41	4,606.00
	July	1,746.04	9,032.14	5,059.57	5,455.00
	August	2,210.68	9,556.93	5,243.40	5,285.00
	September	2,525.70	12,533.83	6,080.69	6,314.87
	October	3,106.00	17,351.70	9,468.09	10,132.25
	November	4,012.38	19,295.55	13,484.04	13,671.87
	December	4,940.86	24,282.36	18,034.04	18,640.00
1948	January	5,191.34	36,939.35	22,198.58	22,390.62
	February	—	52,900.40	30,085.11	26,656.25
	March	10,382.68	85,502.33	57,013.40	55,416.62
	April	—	99,116.75	77,454.99	82,644.25
	May	20,023.73	142,468.34	125,491.00	140,456.75
	June	—	256,396.88	239,361.70	284,850.00
	July	—	755,165.32	648,854.34	770,750.00
	August	296,647.88	1,368,048.91	1,080,784.57	1,207,421.87

1. Compiled from private estimates.

2. The Shanghai wholesale price index is that compiled by the Central Bank of China which included twenty-three commodities.

See *Central Bank Monthly*. The gold bar and United States dollar quotations are derived from private files.

ment stabilization efforts during 1946 and the first part of 1947, large-scale government sales had more or less ceased during the latter part of 1947. In the absence of such official pressure, these rates began to climb, and it may not be far-fetched to assert that sometime during the winter of 1947–48 the official currency was being progressively replaced by dollars and gold not only as a standard of account and a storage of value, which the latter had been for some time, but also as a medium of exchange. This demonetization of *fapi* was finally given official sanction when its replacement by the "gold *yuan*" was decreed on August 19, 1948. The introduction of GY marked the end of what might still be regarded as a relatively "orderly" stage of hyper-inflation. It ushered in a very short respite as a result of the currency conversion, which had the psychological effect of lowering price tags, and the most stringent administrative price control China had seen up to that time. This temporary relief was followed by an inflation that proved to be even more virulent than before and that completely discredited the new currency within six months from the time of its adoption. (See preceding table, pages 50 and 51.)

THE FINAL DEBACLE

The "currency reform" of August, 1948, was accompanied by the imposition of wholesale and retail price ceilings in a few major economic centers. These ceilings were strictly enforced by police methods—especially in Shanghai. This administrative control was reasonably successful during September, 1948, the first month after the "currency reform," but began to break down shortly thereafter. Underlying the failure were the large volume of new note issue necessitated by war requirements and the decision of the government on the forcible conversion of specie and foreign currencies hitherto hoarded by the population, and lack of general rationing and price control in rural areas. While around GY50 million only were issued in the conversion of the former *fapi,* GY672 million were issued between August 23 and October 30, 1948, in exchange for specie, silver dollars, and foreign currencies surrendered by the population. The total volume of GY issued increased from 296.83 million at the end of August to 1,595.37 million two months later.[36] In line with this development, the wholesale price index in Shanghai rose from 157.4 on August 19, 1948 (January to June 1937 = 100), to 220.4

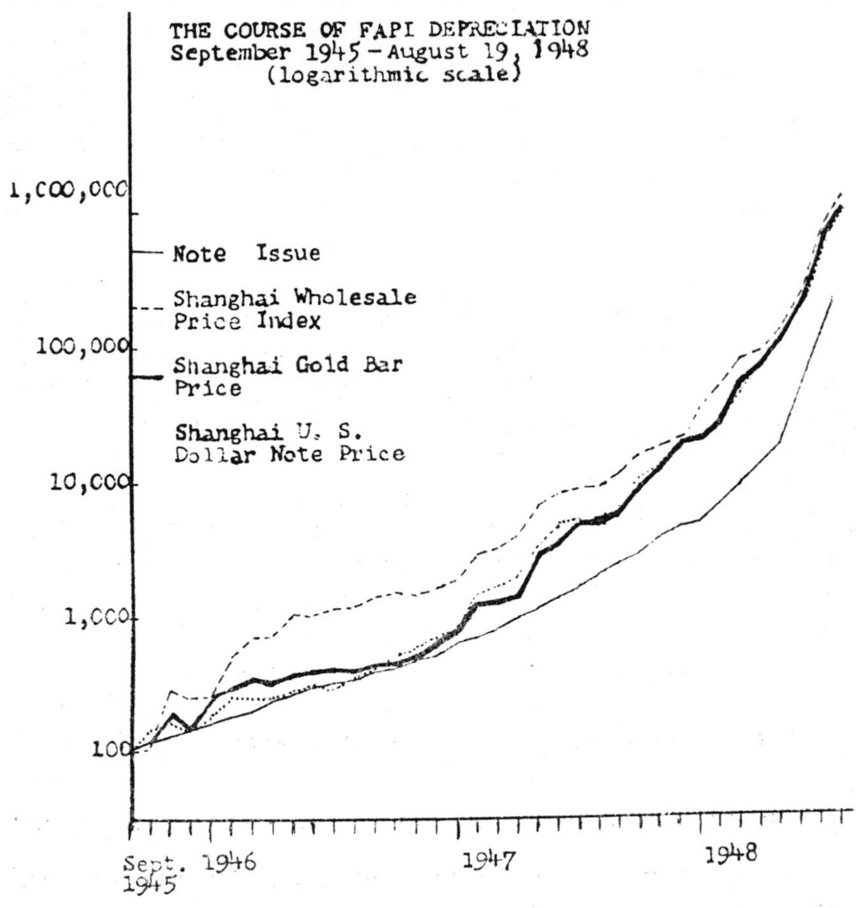

in October when the price ceiling was in force. With the lifting of the price ceiling at the beginning of November, the index shot up immediately. It stood at 3,683.8 in the second week of November, 1948, remained at an even level through December, jumped to 5,482.9 in the first week of 1949, and reached 95,552.0 in the third week of February, 1949. Thus the wholesale price index registered a six-hundred fold rise in six months during the short life of the GY. In the meantime the United States dollar, which was quoted at GY4.00 each on August 19, 1948, rose to GY150 on January 6, 1949, and GY2,893 at the end of February, 1949, or about 709 times[37] in six months.

Although the "gold *yuan*" was not officially abandoned until the beginning of July, 1949, when the Nationalist Government was in Canton and when Shanghai had already passed to Communist control for over a month, its demise was officially heralded at the end of February, 1949, when the Minister of Finance announced his program to legalize the open sale of gold and silver and the free circulation of the silver dollar, and to collect the major taxes either in kind as was the case with the salt and excise taxes or in Customs *yuan,* a fictitious accounting unit used in computing customs duties. After February, the depreciation of GY was further accelerated so that by the third week of April, 1949, the Shanghai wholesale price index stood at 5,057,889 as against 95,552 in the third week of February and 157.4 on August 19, 1948. The increase between the third week of February and that of April, a space of two months only, was fifty-two fold.

While a final attempt was made in July, 1949, to go back on silver, and silver dollar notes were issued, this was no more than a futile gesture. The silver dollar notes soon became inconvertible and fell into complete disuse in October, 1949, before the fall of Canton. Even their temporary position as legal tender was marred by the independent issue of regional currencies while the silver dollar itself actually held sway even before the official abandonment of GY.

FOREIGN EXCHANGE, INFLATION, AND THE BALANCE OF PAYMENTS[38]

When the war came to an end in 1945 and the Nationalist government returned to Nanking from Chungking, negotiations between the Kuomintang and the Communist Party were actively conducted, and for a while it looked as though peaceful political settlement was within reach. Later on, when the failure of the Marshall Mission was officially admitted and when the work of the truce teams was replaced by active hostilities, the superior strength of the government army was considered adequate enough to make the end of the civil war a relatively short-term proposition. Since the Sino-Japanese war had meant considerable privations for the civilian population now clamoring for consumers' goods, and, since industry at the same time was asking for imported raw materials, the government took the position that foreign supplies should be encouraged. In other words, the government was ready to resort to the disinvestment of its foreign

The Course of "Gold *Yuan*" Depreciation[1]
August 19, 1948–April, 1949

		Note Issue (GY Million)	Wholesale Price Index (January–June 1937 = 100)	
			Shanghai	Canton
1948	August 19	296.82	157.4	146.1
	September	956.75	197.0	297.5
	October	1,595.37	220.4	494.0
	November			
	1st week		—	—
	2nd week		3,683.8	2,405.1
	3rd week		3,576.0	1,632.1
	4th week		3,461.7	1,578.0
	December			
	1st week		3,204.2	2,152.4
	2nd week		3,049.6	3,099.8
	3rd week		3,181.4	3,376.9
	4th week		3,677.1	4,848.9
1949	January			
	1st week		5,482.9	7,492.0
	2nd week		8,158.2	10,094.7
	3rd week		13,572.5	12,296.4
	4th week		14,850.3	15,153.1
	5th week		16,012.6	17,071.9
	February			
	1st week		56,308.9	63,267.1
	2nd week		73,976.0	101,937.2
	3rd week		95,552.0	159,217.9
	4th week		117,975.7	161,025.9
	March			
	1st week		184,637.0	203,756.0
	2nd week		301,280.0	347,554.0
	3rd week		441,720.0	420,427.0
	4th week		647,136.0	887,330.0
	April			
	1st week		975,115.0	1,113,026.0
	2nd week		1,803,000.0	2,146,050.0
	3rd week		5,057,889.0	5,001,875.0

1. Data taken from the Central Bank of China series. See *Central Bank Monthly*, and *Central Bank Weekly*.

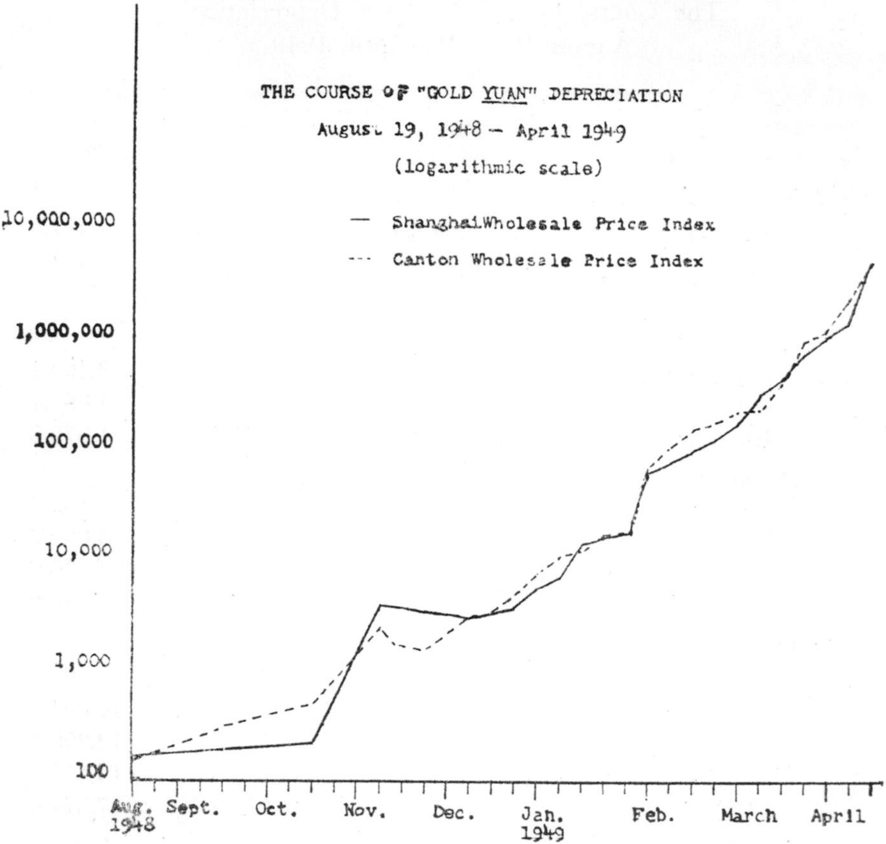

assets in order to increase the immediate supply of goods in the hope that the inflationary pressure generated by military expenditure would soon disappear. This official attitude was reflected in the liberal foreign trade regulations first promulgated in the beginning of 1946. Very few imports were restricted, and, although foreign exchange purchases had to be sanctioned by the government through the Central Bank and its appointed banks, there was no serious rationing of exchange to speak of. At the same time, the exchange rate was fixed at CN$2,020 to US$1. This policy was continued until August, 1946, when the official exchange rate was revised to CN$3,350 to US$1.

The depreciation of the official exchange rate became necessary because of the increasing gap between the official exchange rate and the black market rate that had developed in the meantime, for, even though imports were more or less free, there were certain demands for foreign exchange such as capital transfers which could not be met under the official system. Besides, as exporters were required to sell the foreign exchange proceeds of their exports at the official rate to the monetary control, the overvaluation of the Chinese currency tended to discourage exports and acted as a disguised subsidy to importers. The greater the gap between the official and the black market rates, the more serious was the drain on the official exchange reserve, which the government found progressively more difficult to bear. Simultaneously with exchange depreciation, import restrictions were tightened. A quota system was set up for a large number of raw materials while import permits for other commodities also became more scarce.

Further tightening of control was carried out in February, 1947, following another serious upsurge of the price level, and the exchange rate was now depreciated to CN$12,000 to US$1. This occasional revision of the exchange rate in order to stimulate exports and to conserve the foreign exchange resources under the control of the government, however, proved once again to be ineffective as the gap between the official and the black market rates continued to widen after every revision. Finally, by August, 1947, the policy of a fixed official exchange rate was abandoned in favor of a more flexible exchange rate.

An exchange equalization fund was established this time to prevent large fluctuations in the exchange rate, but the rate itself was left to the play of demand and supply as represented primarily by imports and exports. However, this method also failed to yield an exchange rate reflecting the conditions of the market. For instance, in the beginning of September, 1947, when the daily average of the HK dollar quotation in terms of the CN dollar stood at a little over CN$7,000 on the free market of Hongkong, the cover rate of the exchange equalization fund in Canton was about CN$6,700. In other words, the market rate of the HK dollar was then some 9 per cent above the official exchange quotation. But by the end of October in the same year the market rate in Hongkong was 50 per cent higher than the official quotation of the HK dollar in Canton. Occasionally, the premium ran as high as over 100 per cent. The fund consistently overvalued the CN dollar in the market because every official act of depreciation was looked upon as an acknowledgement of greater instability of the currency, which further stimulated the flight away from the currency to foreign exchange, gold, etc. Thus it was believed that any attempt to catch up with the market rate by revising the official rate constantly would only nullify the advantage of its flexibility. In addition to the psychological factor, every increase in the price of foreign currencies also raised the cost of imports. As essential raw materials and foodstuffs had to be imported, the effect was very obviously undesirable.

As mentioned before, towards the end of 1947, the rise of the price of gold in Shanghai, which had lagged behind the increase in the price of rice and other commodities, began to catch up with the latter, and, by April, 1948, it was almost consistently leading the rise of commodity prices. A similar story can be told about the relative increase in the price of the US dollar compared with that of the price of rice, etc. Here we have a graphic example of the dilemma facing the Nationalist government. As long as the budget could not be balanced, prices would continue to rise; people would buy foreign currencies in order to salvage their capital; the official exchange rate would lag behind the market rate; and the drain of foreign exchange reserves would continue. Since foreign exchange resources of the government were not unlimited and imports were necessary to keep some of the country's industries going and to provide ammunition for the civil war, the drain on reserves could not be allowed to continue. Quantitative restrictions apart, the government sought to encourage current exports through exchange depreciation, but, since exchange depreciation stimulated commodity prices as well as flight from the currency, the result was a further rise of prices and consequently a larger budget deficit.

Capital flight during this period took the form of black market purchases of foreign exchange and gold in the large cities, especially Shanghai and Canton, and these operations were facilitated by the free exchange market in the British Crown Colony of Hongkong. Gold merchants would import gold into Hongkong—frequently via the adjacent Portuguese settlement of Macao—smuggle it to the Chinese mainland, sell the gold there at a premium price, and then cover by disposing of the CN dollar proceeds of their gold sales on the Hongkong free market. The gold purchases from abroad took up the foreign exchange proceeds of smuggled Chinese exports, as well as Chinese overseas remittances, while the sale of the CN dollar, which helped to generate speculative sales in anticipation of further depreciation, served to lower the exchange value of the Chinese currency and thus further stimulated capital flight.

The loss of government foreign exchange reserves during the last few years of the Nationalists' rule in China may be seen in the following table although, for obvious reasons, the extent of illicit transactions cannot be discerned in these figures.

China's Balance of Payments
1946–1948
(in US$ million)

	1946		*1947*		*1948*	
	Credit	*Debit*	*Credit*	*Debit*	*Credit*	*Debit*
Current Account						
Merchandise Imports and Exports	205	1,161	291	845	248	456
Specie Import and Export	—	9	—	40	44	—
Travel	4	4	10	10	4	3
Transportation	4	—	10	—	8	—
Service of Foreign Loans	—	4	—	5	—	5
Government	35	109	52	26	22	25
Miscellaneous	—	34	—	20	—	37
Total Goods and Service	248	1,321	363	946	326	526
Donations	533	3	365	10	312	—
Capital	529[1]	—	252[1]	—	—	30
Unaccounted for	14	—	24	—	—	82

Source: International Monetary Fund, *Balance of Payments Yearbook*, Washington, D.C., 1948. For the definitions of the terms, see the same.

1. Largely disinvestment of Chinese foreign holdings.

The depleted government reserves received a sizable replenishment during the "gold *yuan*" conversion in the latter part of 1948. Although some of the reserve was later withdrawn as a result of renewed open sales of gold and silver, virtually the entire remaining government stock of specie was reported to have been shipped out from the mainland prior to the Nationalists' evacuation. Thus, apart from private holdings, only a part of the foreign exchange deposits available were seized by the Communist authorities when they took over, and they consisted essentially of sterling and Hongkong dollars.

The latter probably accounted for the bulk of the official foreign exchange assets available to the Communists in 1949.

VIII

CONCLUSION

Even to those who are neither social philosophers nor political theorists the tortuous course of monetary inflation in China since the end of World War II which we have just described at some length would appear to reflect quite plainly the undercurrents of the Chinese society which finally succumbed to Communism. The Kuomintang, though increasingly identifying itself with the interests of the urban capitalists, nevertheless failed to develop a social framework within which a healthy capitalistic system could thrive. Its inability to put the government on a "pay as you go" basis led it to rely upon the only course that was to take it to a dismal and ignominious end Yet, when the end was approaching, it even chose to hasten it by the futile currency conversion of 1948, which utterly alienated the middle class from which its supporters came without even the compensation of thereby endearing itself to any other group of the population. On the other hand, the middle class was no less responsible for the Kuomintang's failure because of its own notorious lack of self-discipline. For them the pursuit of individual interests had apparently degenerated into complete license. Thus began the period of a new experiment under the "people's dmocratic dictatorship," the working of which we shall now explore.

NOTES

1. Bureau of Statistics, *Statistical Yearbook of the Republic of China,* Nanking, 1948, pp. 46-47. Data released in July, 1947.
2. Estimate for 1933; cf. Sir Alexander M. Carr-Saunders, *World Population,* 1937.
3. Estimate of 1931 by the Ministry of Interior. (One curious point that emerges from these figures is that although they represent estimates for years separated by over a decade, they show a remarkable stability. Since population growth is rarely, if ever, slowed down by war, and since there were few large-scale military operations in the latter part of the Sino-Japanese war, the 1947 estimate does not tally with those of the prewar period.)
4. See Pai Chien-hua's article in *People's Daily,* Peking, November 1, 1954.
5. Cf. *Committee for Free Asia Bulletin,* San Francisco, June 29, 1954.
6. Cf. *Ta-kung pao,* Tientsin, June 20, 1954.

7. This figure may be compared with the population of the entire area in which "election at the basic level" was held. The latter was reported to be 571,434,511 by Teng. The November, 1954, report of the Bureau of Statistics gave the number obtained by direct census count as 574,205,940, and that by indirect methods as 27,732,095.

8. The population in 1949 would, of course, be somewhat smaller. According to Pai Chien-hua, the returns of a population of 52,950,000 were checked, and the result showed that duplication of registration amounted to 0.139 per cent only while the number of persons unregistered was only 0.255 per cent. *People's Daily,* Peking, November 1, 1954.

9. The following data on birth and death rates may be listed here:

	Birth Rate	*Death Rate*
	(per thousand persons)	
C. M. Ch'iao's survey of 12,456 farm families in 22 counties, 10 provinces	35.7	25.0
Lossing Buck's survey of 4,216 farm families in 4 provinces	42.2	27.9
Buck's survey of 38,256 farm families in 22 provinces	38.3	27.1
Ch'en Ta's 1934 study	38.0	33.0
1953 Communist Chinese census	37.0	17.0

Cf. Ch'en Ta, *Population in Modern China,* Chicago, 1946.

10. *People's Daily,* Peking, November 1, 1954.

11. Shen, *op. cit.,* p. 172, University of Chicago Press, 1951.

12. Pai Chien-Hua, *op. cit.*

13. Ch'en Ta, *op. cit.,* p. 4.

14. Bureau of Statistics, *Statistical Yearbook of the Republic of China,* pp. 70-71, Nanking, 1948.

15. Both the metric and the *shih* systems are now used in China. One *shih mow* is equal to one-fifteenth of a hectare and 0.1647 of an acre.

16. *A manual for Newspaper Readers,* pp. 562-563, Hankow, 1950.

17. For sources see Bureau of Statistics, *Statistical Yearbook of the Republic of China,* p. 70, Nanking, 1948.

18. NCNA (New China News Agency), February 5, 1954. Unless otherwise specified, all NCNA reports emanate from Peking.

19. Bureau of Information, *Coal,* Nanking, 1947.

20. NCNA, Shanghai, March 23, 1953; NCNA, January 15, February 5, and May 10, 1953, and January 17, 1954; and China News Service, Nan-ch'ang, December 28, 1952.

21. *Economic Weekly,* No. 15, p. 2, Shanghai, April, 1953.

22. *Wen-hui pao,* Hongkong, June 15, 1953.

23. Among the rough estimates we may mention (1) Wong Wen-hao's figure of CN$18 billion for China's prewar national income, (2) the estimate of CN$12,150 million by Franklin Ho for the prewar period, (3) Buck's estimate in his *China's Farm Economy* of a per capita income of CN$52.9 for the farm population for the 1921-1925 period, from which a total national income of CN$23,485 million has been calculated by others. Still others owe their origin to such persons as Sun Ch'en Ch'eng Hsiao-kang, and Ch'en Cheng-han. In the same category we may also mention an estimate by the Dresdner Bank, as well as Colin Clark's estimate of 22.7 billion international units in his *Conditions of Economic Progress.* For a fuller discussion and sources see Ting Ku, "Five Estimates of China's National Income," *Central Bank Monthly,* new series, Vol. I, No. 6, Shanghai, June, 1946.

24. The other estimates are those of Liu Ta-chün (D. K. Lieu) and Liu Ta-chung. Compared with Ou's findings, the following figures may be noted:

	1931-1936 Per Capita Income CN$
Lieu	41.2
Liu	71.0
Ou	47.0

Lieu's estimate, as quoted by Ting, employs the method of distributive shares. It tends to be too low because of certain omissions and his exclusion of the income of non-Chinese residents in China. Liu Ta-chung's estimate as published in his 1946 Brookings Institution study on *The National Income of China, 1931-1936* is the gross national product and the per capita figure is derived from a population of 410 million. Cf. Ting, *op. cit.*

25. See the discussion in Chapter VII below.

26. Cf. Wang Foh-shen, "Problems Concerning China's Capital Stock," *Economic Review*, Vol. IV, No. 2, Shanghai, October, 1948.

27. Ch'en Ta, *op. cit.*

28. See Wang Foh-shen, *China's Industrial Production, 1931-1946,* (English) Nanking, 1948, for a fuller discussion and for sources.

29. Cf. Wang Foh-shen, "The Relative Importance of Chinese and Foreign Firms in China's Prewar Industrial Production," *Central Bank Monthly,* new series, Vol. II, No. 3, Shanghai, March, 1947.

30. On public finance in modern China cf. Chu Shih-huang, *An Economic History of the Republic,* Shanghai, 1948; and Arthur N. Young, *China's Economic and Financial Reconstruction* (English), New York, 1947.

31. Cf. Wu Yuan-Li, *China's Postwar Economic Policy—Planning or Free Enterprise,* New York, 1946.

32. Pauley, *op. cit.*, pp. 10-11, and 36-37.

33. The term *fapi* means "legal tender," but has become synonymous with the Chinese national *yuan* or dollar (CN$) through usage.

34. For wartime changes in prices and money supply cf. Frank M. Tamagna, *Financial Problems in Postwar China,* New York, 1946; Liu Ta-chun (D. K. Lieu), *China's Economic Stabilization and Reconstruction,* New Brunswick, 1948; and *Economic Review,* Vol. I, No. 1, Shanghai, April, 1947, and Vol. II, No. 14, January, 1948.

35. The Chinese government's own military expenditure was not the only important source of increasing money supply. Expenditures by United States military establishments in China represented another important source of spending. Prior to January, 1944, thanks to the unrealistic exchange rate of CN$20 to US$1, all local currency expenditure by the United States was financed by converting U.S. dollars into *fapi* at this rate. While this rate was advantageous from the Chinese point of view of controlling inflation, it was obviously unrealistic and worked against the interest of the United States. Thus, in January, 1944, while maintaining the same rate as before, the Chinese government agreed to grant a 100 per cent supplement for the conversion of U.S. dollar expenditures into Chinese currency, thus making the effective rate CN$40 to US$1. This practice was continued for a few months and was again regarded as unsatisfactory. Under a subsequent arrangement, the Central Bank of China agreed to make CN dollar advances to the American authorities in order to meet the latter's local currency expenditure, pending periodic settlements between the U.S. Treasury and the Chinese Ministry of Finance. On January 22, 1945, a settlement involving US$150 million was announced which completed a total settlement of US$210 million covering all advances up to November of the preceding year.

Although the exchange rate employed was not made known it stands to reason that the effective rate was higher than 40 to 1.

36. The note issue data are taken from *Central Bank Monthly,* Shanghai, issues from August, 1948, to 1949. See also *Central Bank Monthly,* Vol. XX, Nos. 5-6, p. 1, Shanghai, February, 1949.

37. Market quotations derived from private sources.

38. The above description of the final stage of China's economic development in the postwar period would not be complete without a word on the international economic position of the country on the eve of the Communist victory. An understanding of this particular aspect is essential in order to appreciate the country's present foreign economic relations which, as we shall see, play an important role in its economic planning.

CHAPTER THREE

Economic Stabilization and Fiscal Policy

I

INTRODUCTION

If there was one single indispensable factor on which the Chinese Communists depended for the initial consolidation of their hold on China, it was undoubtedly the creation of an adequate fiscal system and the restoration of currency stability. The Communists were keenly aware of the fact that galloping inflation had contributed largely to the downfall of their opponents, not only because of its direct effect on the normal function of the economy, but, perhaps even more so, because of its corrupting and disintegrating influence on social standards and administrative efficiency. A repetition of the experience would have caused utter disillusion on the part of those who had assumed the incalculable risk of a violent political upheaval in the hope of securing economic stability and security. Even more damaging would have been the indirect effect of sustained inflation on the Communists' continued ability to govern. Little wonder, therefore, that Communist China considered currency stabilization one of its first tasks and was quick in trumpeting the success it scored.

In an article extolling the Communists' role in China's economic rehabilitation,[1] written in commemoration of the Party's thirtieth anniversary, the Chairman of the Communist government's Economic and Financial Commission singled out as a major achievement of the first eighteen months of the new regime the restoration of currency stability after a twelve-year-old inflation. Approximately one year later, in August, 1952, when the then Minister of Finance, Po I-p'o, reviewed the progress of the country's fiscal affairs, a keynote of his address[2] was again the government's success in balancing the budget. The same impression was conveyed early in 1953 when Po made his last budget speech.[3] These are some of the more notable instances in which the achievement of currency stability and of a balanced budget is pointed out as an irrefutable argument for confidence in the future of China under the Communists.

Several questions are involved in evaluating Communist China's performance in its fiscal affairs. First, to what extent and how has monetary inflation actually been brought under control? Second, what is the real significance of the so-called "balanced budgets?" Third, in what manner has the country's fiscal system been overhauled and adjusted to the exigencies of present economic policy? Finally, is the Communist government in a position to prevent the rekindling of inflation, or at least to mitigate the political consequences of inflation, if it continues to pursue its averred policy of forced industrialization and/or if it should choose to embark upon further foreign military adventures such as the intervention in Korea?

II

DEVELOPMENTS PRIOR TO MARCH, 1950

There were a number of favorable factors which the *jen-min pi* or "people's currency" enjoyed initially. In the first place, as the Communist armies advanced, there was a steady expansion of the geographical area within which it circulated as legal tender. Second, the new currency was exchanged for the Nationalist currencies through rapidly concluded conversions which entailed the repudiation of what was probably a sizable portion of the latter's outstanding issues.[4] Moreover, since the conversion was fully anticipated, the accelerated depreciation of the old issues in the final days of their life contributed to the establishment of conversion rates highly advantageous from the point of view of the new issuing authority. Third, the customary practice of rapid spending and commodity hoarding, which had been the underlying cause of the rise of commodity prices at a rate proportionately much greater than the increase in the volume of money, was at least slightly curbed through fear of political retribution and drastic Communist police measures. Finally, as a result of the military advance, important rail transportation lines had been opened so that external impediments to inter-regional goods movement became progressively less. Yet all these factors were unable to stem the tide of inflation which was being constantly fed by government spending.

If we take the fall of Shanghai, which was until recently the economic capital of China, to mark the beginning of the new economic period, we find a virtually uninterrupted rise of the price level up to the spring of 1950. This upward movement was interspersed with four periods of violent price hikes which took place in May, July, and November, 1949, and February, 1950. The wholesale price index in Shanghai as prepared by the city government rose nearly fivefold within a short space of thirteen days from May 28 to June 9, 1949. From June 9 to December 1, 1949, the increase was again tenfold.[5] Thus the average wholesale price level in February, 1950, was virtually seventy times as high as that of May 28, 1949. The situation in Shanghai was merely a sample of developments in the country as a whole.

The replacement of the Nationalist currency by the *jen-min-pi* had its latest parallel in the abolition of the Japanese-sponsored currencies in Occupied China at the end of World War II. In both cases, currencies which were severely depreciated at the time of conversion were replaced by only relatively less inflated currencies. Since the underlying cause of inflation continued to be present, the replacement of one currency by another, of course, could not in itself halt the inflationary spiral.

Large deficit spending was the immediate cause of the galloping rise of prices in 1949 and early 1950. Although the exact monetary value of the budget deficit in 1949 is not known, it has been officially reported to be three-fourths of total government outlay in that year.[6] While there was a slight improvement in early 1950, the deficit continued to run at a rate equal to 40 per cent of total outlay.[7] The disparity between revenue and expenditure was the result both of increased military and administrative outlay and of the breakdown of tax collection. In particular, one important cause of the expansion of expenditure was the Communists' policy to keep provisionally on the payroll all administrative and military personnel who had either actively defected from the Nationalist government or had simply stayed behind during the latter's withdrawal. Although the pay scale was reduced and the political effect of such a policy was undoubtedly favorable to the Communists, the number of persons on the new government's payroll was increased from seven to about nine million in the course of a few months.[8] On the other hand, in spite of the expanding territory from which revenue could be derived, the increase could not but lag behind that of expenditure, partly because of the disruption of normal economic activity. Furthermore, there was no unified tax system in all the areas under Communist rule, and the division of tax and other income between the new central and local governments stood in sharp contrast to the concentration of outlay through the central government. Obviously, short of a drastic overhaul of the entire fiscal system and the adoption of emergency measures the new regime might very well have toppled under its own weight.

PRELIMINARY STEPS TO INCREASE REVENUE

The series of measures aiming at currency stabilization which were adopted in 1950 may be divided into two categories. The first group was principally concerned with the reduction of the budget deficit of the central government and the adoption of non-inflationary measures to bridge the remaining gap. The second group was directed towards a general contraction of spending and, in a broad sense, included the entire mechanism of monetary control.[9] Chronologically speaking, it was the first group of measures that received early attention although, as we shall see, the effect of the second group was equally decisive, if not more so.

The first two important steps in raising goverment revenue through non-inflationary means consisted of the establishment of a unified taxation system and the flotation of a compulsory loan. Both measures were decided upon at the end of 1949 and thus constituted the vanguard of a more far-reaching program for the centralization of financial and economic controls proclaimed in March of the following year.

A national taxation conference had been called during November, 1949, when commodity prices went on a rampage. It was followed by the announcement of a preliminary 1950 budget a month later and again of a unified tax law at the end of January, 1950. These must now be considered in some detail.

A. *The Victory Bonds*

Speaking with a frankness that was not characteristic of his later reports, the Communist Finance Minister stated very clearly during his presentation of the new regime's first budget that because of continuing military operations the 1950 budget could not be balanced and that the deficit was anticipated to be 18.7 per cent of total government outlay.[10] Less than two-fifths of this deficit—or 7.18 per cent of total expenditure—would be met by the flotation of a five-year 5 per cent bond while the remainder, or 9.52 per cent of total expenditure, would have to be met by increasing note issue. In view of the rapid depreciation of the currency, the new bonds were to be issued in "commodity-equivalent units," each of which consisted of specified quantities of four basic staples. The monetary value of one bond unit which represented also the subscription, as well as redemption, price of the bond, was to be the sum of the weighted average wholesale values of these commodities in six different cities.[11] The total authorized amount was fixed at 200 million such units, to be issued in two equal installments during 1950. Subscription for the first half of the entire issue was to be completed by the end of March, 1950, while the second half was to be issued later in the year.[12] In addition, it was stipulated that the bonds were non-transferable and could not be discounted or used as collaterals for borrowing. These features were clearly designed to reduce credit expansion and the general liquidity of business while making the bonds more attractive to subscribers by allowing their monetary value to fluctuate with price changes.

The significance of the Victory Bonds was, however, not limited to the deflationary role intended by their authors. They also provide us with a useful tool in gauging the absolute magnitude of the budget and some of its constituent items. Although the Communist authorities did not then release monetary figures, the percentage data given may be used to translate the budget items into bond units in the table appearing on page 69.

It should be noted that the price of one bond unit when it was officially quoted for the first time on January 6, 1950, was ¥14,055.[13] At the same time, the official exchange rate for one United States dollar was approximately ¥18,500.[14] Thus the total budgeted expenditure was equivalent to ¥38,918.6 billion or US$2,084.7 million as against a total revenue of ¥31,638.6 billion or US$1,694.7 million, both figures being unprecedentedly large for China.

Although the budget still registered a deficit, it had been prepared on the assumption of a substantially increased tax revenue which was divided more or less evenly between agricultural and non-agricul-

The Preliminary Budget of 1950
(in million Victory Bond units)

Revenue	*Amount*		*Percentage Value*	
Taxes				
The Agricultural or Grain Tax	935.6		41.4	
Other Taxes	879.1	1,814.7	38.9	80.3
Profit from State Enterprises		386.5		17.1
Proceeds from Warehouse Clearance[1]		54.2		2.4
Other		4.5		0.2
Total Revenue		2,259.9		100.0
Expenditure				
Defense		1,078.6		38.8
Administration[2]		594.9		21.4
Investment in State Enterprises		664.4		23.9
Public Health, Education and Cultural Activities[3]		114.0		4.1
Debt Service[4]		2.8		0.1
Subsidy to Local Governments		63.9		2.3
General Reserve		261.3		9.4
		2,779.9		100.0
Deficit				
Victory Bonds		200.0		38.5
Note Issue		320.0		61.5
		520.0		100.0

Source: Po I-p'o, *ibid.*

1. For the significance of this item, see the next section.
2. Expenses of military governments in occupied areas and Communist Party expenditure are included under this item.
3. Propaganda expenditure included.
4. This refers to interest payments on a 1949 bond issue in Manchuria.

tural sources.[15] This division represented an elevation of the non-agricultural taxes to a position of major importance and was distinctly an innovation in the fiscal system.

B. *Codification of Non-agricultural Taxes*

The new tax program[16] was outlined in a series of statements and regulations published on January 31, 1950, and shortly thereafter.[17] In place of the numerous different imposts in force in individual areas fourteen taxes were henceforth to be levied by the central and local governments. These were (1) an excise tax on selected commodities; (2) an "industrial and commercial tax" payable by all profit-making enterprises, corporate or otherwise, including such small businessmen as stall keepers, hawkers and itinerant merchants, and further divided into (a) a tax on total net sales or commissions and (b) a business income tax; (3) a tax on salt; (4) customs duties; (5) an income tax on wages and salaries; (6) a tax on interest income; (7) a stamp tax; (8) an exchange tax on business transactions concluded on organized exchanges,[18] (9) a slaughter tax, (10) a tax on houses and buildings, (11) a tax on real estate for non-agricultural use, (12) a special consumption tax on entertainment, cold refreshments, restaurant meals and hotel rooms, (13) an inheritance tax, and (14) license fees. Although no explicit mention was made at this time about the division of the tax revenue between the central and local governments, it was stipulated that all taxes of national importance were subject to the sole jurisdiction of the central government and that local authorities were not allowed to make unilateral changes in the regulations, rates, and other related matters. Even in the case of taxes earmarked for local use, alterations in all tax regulations were contingent upon the prior approval of superior administrative levels[19] and, in many cases, that of the central government itself.

THE SPIRIT OF THE NEW TAX STRUCTURE

While the reduction of the number of taxes to fourteen was a simplification in the tax structure, the step was taken primarily in the interest of administrative efficiency. No decrease in the tax burden, was, of course, intended. On the contrary, as the Communist authorities have since commented themselves,[20] the spirit of the new tax structure was "to impose a variety of taxes to be collected a large number of times." The tax on net sales especially reflected this aspect of official policy inasmuch as taxes could be collected every time a commodity changed hands. In an economy where the merchant and the middleman predominate in the market, as was the case in China at this time, such a tax is clearly advantageous from the treasury's point of view, at least in the short run.

The tax on net sales and business income was the most important factor among the non-agricultural taxes in the 1950 budget and stood out as probably the most effective means both in broadening the tax base and in augmenting revenue. In the first place, having elevated the tax on sales from its traditional place in local finance, the authorities saw to it that all profit-making businesses in the country would fall within its domain, including both cooperatives and state enterprises. The explicit inclusion of single transactions, of itinerant merchants, and of stall vendors was designed to serve the same purpose. Second, in view of the fact that the sales tax is levied, as a rule, several times before a commodity reaches the final consumer, the rates as fixed in the January 1950 regulations—from one to three per cent—are rather high. Moreover, tax is also levied on business net income at rates ranging from five to thirty per cent, with the progressive rates applicable to the *entire* income of the taxpayer. Special reductions are granted to businesses in a few industries such as shipbuilding, mining, machinery manufacturing, and the like, while the rates are as a rule lower for manufacturers than for commercial concerns.

To safeguard the real value of the proceeds from the all-important "industrial and commercial tax" provision was made for the possible effect of violent price changes. Thus it was stipulated that the tax rates that appeared in the January, 1950, regulations were fixed at a time when the price of rice in Shanghai was ¥800 per catty, and that rate adjustments would be made by tax collectors in accordance with price changes.[21] Obviously these rates were determined sometime in November, 1949, when the price of rice was at the stated level in Shanghai. By the time the regulations were made public in January, 1950, it had already increased nearly threefold. Similarly, in the case of the excise taxes, it was provided that for tax purposes the price of a commodity should be determined once a month, except when price fluctuations should exceed fifteen per cent from one month to another.[22] In the latter case, prompt adjustments would be made.

Clearly, the Communist government's policy at this time was, first and foremost, to collect enough revenue to meet its needs. Any serious consideration of either equity or the determinateness of the tax burden, if present at all, was not conspicuously in evidence.[23]

METHODS OF TAX ASSESSMENT

While some of the features of the new tax system as described above are sufficiently revealing, the nature of the tax policy cannot be fully understood without a word on the manner of assessment in the case of the "industrial and commercial tax." Abstracting for the moment from the flexible nature of tax rates due to price fluctuations, the assessment of tax liability on sales and income would appear definitive enough but for the fact that most small businesses in China do not keep complete records while even the larger ones may not have proper accounting systems. Thus it is not always possible to determine the income or even the net sales of a business. To obviate this difficulty the Communist authorities have devised a rather ingenious method which was incorporated in the 1950 tax law and has not been materially changed since.

Under the law three different methods of tax assessment are available. In the first place, a taxpayer with an accounting system deemed adequate by the tax collector may file regular reports himself. Since most taxpayers do not belong to this category, two other alternatives are available. These are known respectively as (1) "democratic appraisal and assessment at fixed rates" and (2) "periodic payments of fixed sums." Under the first of these two methods, which was, in fact, the only one in use before mid-1950, the taxable income or value of sales of an individual business is nominally determined by the trade association or sub-group to which it belongs by comparison with certain selected sample enterprises which are divided into three grades with respect to volume of business and profitability. Self-assessments are theoretically first submitted by individual taxpayers and are then appraised, in open forum, by the sub-groups of their respective trade associations. If approved by the authorities whose agents participate in the discussion as *ex-officio* members, the tax liability of the business is determined.[24] Under the second method, which is applied in smaller urban areas, and in cases where organized appraisal is impracticable, tax is assessed directly by the government and fixed payments are then made periodically. In short, the government charges what it thinks it can get, relying in part upon denunciation by workers and competitiors for the necessary information.

The question may be raised as to how under the method of "democratic appraisal," a concerted effort to lower tax liability all-round through collusion within the group can be avoided. It seems that the authorities are protected by two different safeguards. First, the main function of the forum is to classify the members into different grades while the tax liability of representative firms in a given grade is determined by the government. Tax collection quotas are usually assigned both by geographical areas and by trades and industries within an area so that the division into grades is tantamount to a method of apportionment, the minimum total tax liability of the group being more or less determined beforehand. Moreover, the participation of government agents within the groups helps to facilitate the process of tax assessment according to the wishes of the government. Business jealousy and denunciations by disgruntled workers are utilized with full effect. Thus, while there may be some procrastination, it is not known to have reached any serious proportions.[25]

The term "democratic appraisal" is apparently invented to give this rather arbitrary method of tax assessment a semblance of popular justice. On the one hand, if applied honestly and without bias, the claim to a rough-and-ready form of equity may not be entirely without substance. On the other hand, at a time when every effort was bent to augment government revenue, the net effect of this method would appear to be unavoidably arbitrary. Of course, given the need to increase revenue and the absence of accounting records, it must be admitted that a difficult problem exists. Since the Communists are not particularly concerned with the reasonableness of assessment methods, they have adopted this direct solution.

III

CENTRALIZATION OF ECONOMIC AND FINANCIAL CONTROLS

As we have just seen, government deliberations at the end of 1949 had already resulted in the decision to issue the Victory Bonds and in the promulgation of the new tax regulations. However, these measures were clearly quite inadequate. Although bond subscription had begun in January, 1950, the first new year under Communist rule started with a larger deficit than expected.[26] Government expenditure in the first month of 1950 exceeded, while government revenue fell short of, the respective budgeted amounts. The rise of the official bond quotation from ¥14,843 in mid-January to ¥23,353 in mid-February was indicative of the situation. In spite of the time lag that was to be expected before the deflationary effects of the bond issue and of the increasing taxes could be felt, more drastic measures had to be taken if the immediate political tasks of the regime were to be accomplished at all.

These immediate objectives were expressly re-defined at a National Financial Conference held in early February, 1950, as (1) the conquest of Formosa, the Hainan Island and Tibet, (2) rehabilitation of economic activity in pivotal areas, (3) support of some nine million persons on the government's payroll, and (4) assuring of adequate food supply to the country's large urban centers and the feeding of refugees from extensive areas afflicted by natural disasters.[27] Since large expenditures could not be entirely obviated under these conditions, the control of inflation continued to be the most important issue.

The February Conference was highly successful inasmuch as it led to the adoption of a comprehensive program which has since come to be known as the directive to "unify government financial and economic work." The principal, over-all plan as expounded in this directive and other supporting decrees[28] constituted a thorough attempt to overhaul the entire structure of government finance and fiscal administration. Its major points may be analyzed as follows:

1. Curtailment of Expenditures. An austerity campaign was set in motion in all government agencies while government enterprises were told to fix standard output quotas, to lower their costs, and to increase their capital turnover.[29] At the same time, a national commission was established to eliminate fictitious personnel on the government's payroll and to centralize the allocation of surplus government employees among individual agencies. All new hiring without the commission's prior approval was stopped.

2. Opening of New Revenue Sources. Another commission was set up to take a complete inventory of the supplies in the country's warehouses which had been stockpiled by agencies of the Nationalist government and by others whose property had since been expropriated. Following this census, the commission was to decide what part of the supplies could be used directly by the government and its productive enterprises in lieu of current purchases and what part should be sold on the open market. Such public sales were calculated not only to increase revenue, but also to induce the liquidation of similar private stocks. In addition, the government's many productive enterprises were instructed to transmit to the central treasury at

regular intervals both their operating profits and payments into their depreciation reserves.

3. Centralization of Revenue. With the exception of local agricultural surtaxes, the maximum amount of which was fixed at 15 per cent[30] of the agricultural tax proper, the "public grains," collected in kind, were placed under the sole control of the central government. Local authorities were required to assist in storing and transporting the grains, but were not allowed to draw upon them without special permission. The only exceptions tolerated were withdrawals for army rations and emergency relief.

In the case of the now equally important non-agricultural taxes, by far the largest portion, as represented by the taxes on salt and other commodities, the "industrial and commercial tax" and customs duties, was earmarked for the central government. Even the proceeds of those minor taxes which were reserved for local governments could be used by the latter only in accordance with their respective budgets as approved by the central government.

4. Control of Tax Proceeds. All tax proceeds due to the central government were to be deposited with the government depository on the very day of collection in all cities and large villages, or within five days after collection in small villages which are at some distance from the nearest depository. In the case of food grains, they had to be placed in government warehouses within fifteen days from the time of collection. Daily reports to the central government's Bureau of Taxation by telephone or telegraph on all tax proceeds collected on the preceding day were required from all larger cities[31] while reports at 10-day intervals were to be made by all others.

5. Control over Government Cash Balance. Funds appropriated for individual government departments, agencies, and enterprises were to be released only by installment and according to approved schedules. The outstanding unreleased balance would be placed on deposit in terms of "commodity-equivalent" units. All funds released to individual agencies, however, would have to be deposited with the People's Bank of China,[32] instead of private banks, the same rule being applicable to the revenue of local governments. Finally, all government organs, including military contingents and productive enterprises, were allowed to have only enough currency on hand to

meet the necessary cash payments for three days. All other payments were to be made by check drawn on the People's Bank.

6. Price and Market Control. Finally, the interregional movement of selected commodities,. including food grains, cotton, cotton yarn and piece goods, salt, coal and miscellaneous consumers' goods was placed under the unified control of the Ministry of Trade. Six government trading corporations were established to exercise control over market fluctuations, both through wholesale and through government retail outlets. The government obtains its supplies either through taxation in kind as in the case of grain and, to a less extent, cotton, or through the production of its own enterprises, supplemented by purchases where necessary, such as cotton yarn and coal.[33]

The upshot of all these regulations was to give the central government the predominant part of increased tax collections, to keep it advised promptly of all changes in revenue, to reduce, regulate and slow down cash disbursements, to minimize the possibility of unauthorized expenditure, and, last but by no means the least, to deprive the private banking system of its major base of credit expansion. The net effect on currency stabilization was soon evident.

CHANGES IN THE BASIC COST OF LIVING

The month of March, 1950, during which the various measures described above began to make their appearance, marked the peak of the uncontrolled inflation since the establishment of the new regime. The price of Victory Bonds fell from ¥31,310 per unit in mid-March, 1950, to ¥21,232 in mid-October, a drop of 32 per cent. This has since been followed by a steady rise, interspersed with periods of relative stability. Since the bond price represents the aggregate monetary value of specific quantities of several commodities essential to everyday life and could therefore be regarded as a crude cost of living index for urban centers, this movement is extremely significant.

In addition to the bond index, a number of cities instituted in 1949 their own "commodity-equivalent units" quotations of which were regularly published. These indices, abolished in 1954, were widely used by government and private institutions in their financial plans and accounting procedures. Occasionally there are also separate indices known as "wage units" which are essentially similar to the other indices and are used to determine the money wage of workers whose base pay is expressed in terms of such units. Although they differ from one another slightly in composition, it is noteworthy, as a glance over the following table clearly shows, that since March, 1950, the indices of seven cities, which are widely apart geographically, showed a trend that was virtually identical. The initial break after March, 1950, was general and fairly severe.

With the exception of Canton, the end of the downward movement came towards the latter part of the third quarter of the year, i.e., shortly after the outbreak of the Korean war. Since then there has been a steady rise, with the capital city of Peking and its port city, Tientsin, exhibiting the greatest upward strength although, on the whole, stability has been maintained to a remarkable degree.

Monthly Quotations of Victory Bonds[1]

		Price[2] *(Jen-min-pi per Bond Unit)*	*Index (March 1950 = 100)*
1950	January	14,843	47.4
	February	23,353	71.7
	March	31,310	100.00
	April	—	—
	May	—	—
	June	—	—
	July	—	—
	August	—	—
	September	21,888	69.7
	October	21,232	68.0
	November	21,696	69.2
	December	21,250	67.8
1951	January	22,401	71.5
	February	22,461	71.7
	March	22,741	72.6
	April	23,706	75.6
	May	23,582	75.2
	June	23,910	76.3
	July	24,103	76.8
	August	24,367	77.7
	September	24,412	77.9
	October	24,542	78.3
	November	24,735	78.9
	December	24,667	78.7

		Price[2] (Jen-min-pi per Bond Unit)	Index (March 1950 = 100)
1952	January	24,727	78.8
	February	24,611	78.7
	March	24,794	79.1
	April	24,715	78.8
	May	24,402	77.9
	June	24,375	77.8
	July	24,350	77.7
	August	24,402	77.9
	September	24,635	78.6
	October	24,342	78.1
	November	24,536	78.4
	December	24,483	78.2
1953	January	24,781	79.1
	February	24,783	79.2
	March	24,723	79.0
	April	24,856	79.4
	May	24,774	79.1
	June	24,827	79.3
	July	24,848	79.4
	August	24,756	79.1
	September	24,926	79.6
	October	24,915	79.6
	November	24,804	79.2
	December	24,423	78.0
1954	January	24,638	78.7
	February	24,639	78.7
	March	24,639	78.7
	April	24,588	78.5
	May	24,790	79.2
	June	24,887	79.5
	July	24,888	79.5
	August	24,692	78.9
	September	24,692	78.9
	October	24,788	79.2
	November	24,788	79.2
	December	24,788	79.2
1955	January	24,849	79.3

1. 1950-52, *Ta-kung pao,* Shanghai, 1951-52.
   1953-54, *Jen-min jih-pao,* Peking.

2. Mid-month quotations.

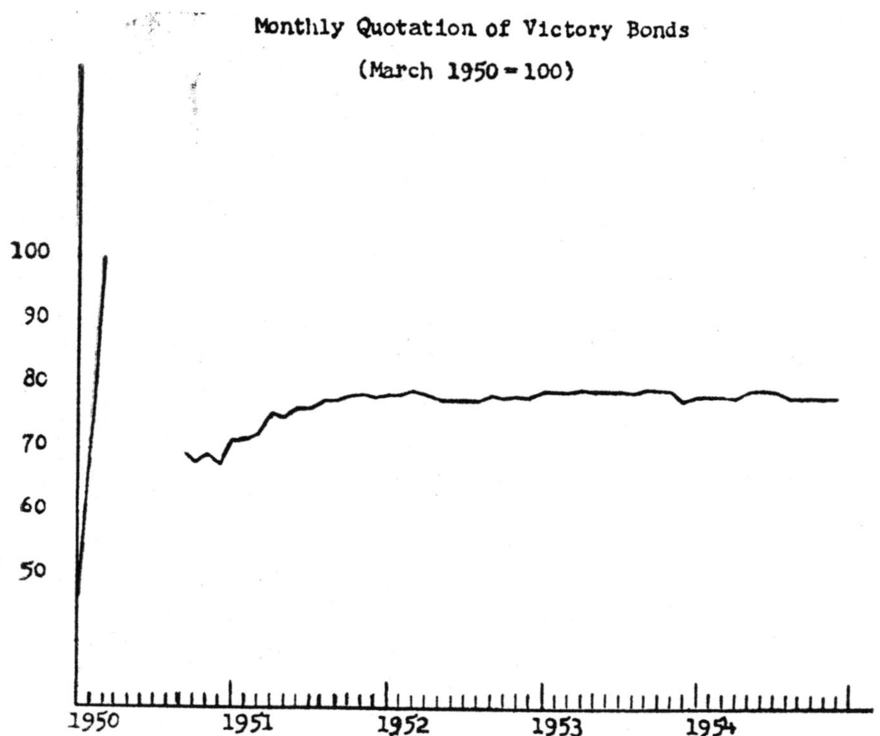
Monthly Quotation of Victory Bonds
(March 1950 = 100)
100
90
80
70
60
50
1950
1951
1952
1953
1954

“Commodity-Equivalent Unit” Indices in Seven Cities[1]
(March 1950 = 100)

	East China	North China		Central-South China		Southwest China	Northwest China
	Shanghai	*Tientsin*	*Peking*	*Wuhan*	*Canton*	*Chungking*	*Hsi-an*
1949							
March		1.48					
April		1.75	1.58				
May		3.64	3.56				
June	5.47	4.07	3.95	10.32			
July	11.77	6.71	6.09	15.26			5.76
August	13.21	12.82	11.75	14.52			9.18
September	12.73	12.28	11.94	14.12			9.74
October	13.18	13.56	13.22	17.86			11.83
November	32.00	37.35	31.89	39.29			28.80
December	45.93	49.24	48.84	61.78	41.21		42.86
1950							
January	63.78	57.17	56.42	50.83	41.79	32.31	58.59
February	93.10	85.52	79.86	80.60	74.58	67.50	92.14
March	100.00	100.00	100.00	100.00	100.00	100.00	100.00
April	91.19	91.61	87.80	80.04	72.87	80.05	77.79
May	86.47	84.62	80.12	73.69	65.85	74.13	63.69
June	84.09	82.26	78.28	70.21	62.66	75.95	58.12
July	83.18	78.72	75.88	71.12	64.88	73.90	57.38
August	83.48	77.68	73.69	69.81	59.99	74.43	57.63
September	83.48	77.57	73.57	64.27	57.38	68.06	60.54
October	79.74	80.26	76.35	66.24	55.18	69.27	64.01
November	80.32	83.47	80.06	70.34	54.40	70.67	67.76
December	79.98	84.31	80.34	72.67	54.55	69.64	70.50

1951							
January	80.70	90.03	84.13	73.73	52.16	71.12	73.83
February	80.85	90.10	84.32	73.59	52.37	71.70	74.14
March	80.17	90.05	83.94	74.97	57.39	74.38	74.14
April	83.72	93.84	86.00	75.04	54.38	78.73	76.94
May	84.94	94.36	85.99	75.30	56.29	81.97	77.14
June	85.58	93.75	85.99	75.88	56.34	83.47	77.14
July	86.74	93.67	85.89	76.52	56.51	84.95	77.25
August	87.62	96.23	88.48	74.85	56.98	83.07	79.05
September	87.57	96.67	91.14	74.15	56.08	78.81	79.79
October	87.53	99.41	91.45	74.51	55.66	78.99	80.30
November	87.53	100.18	91.64	74.75	56.38	83.33	80.45
December	87.53	100.39	91.75	75.50	55.70	83.06	81.20
1952							
January	87.53	100.4	—				
February	87.53	100.3	—				
March	88.73	100.8	91.61				
April	88.73	100.1	90.72				
May	88.62	98.6	90.00				
June	88.62	97.2	88.30				
July	88.62	97.1	88.66				
August	88.62	97.9	89.45				
September	88.09	99.2	90.64				
October	86.56	99.5	90.97				
November	—		91.92				
December	86.22		92.04				
1953							
January	86.22		93.34				
February			93.34				
March			93.34				

	East China	North China		Central-South China		Southwest China	Northwest China
	Shanghai	*Tientsin*	*Peking*	*Wuhan*	*Canton*	*Chungking*	*Hsi-an*
April			93.68				
May			93.70				
June			94.27				
July			94.48				
August			94.48				
September			94.48				
October			93.93				
November			93.01				
December			92.01				
1954							
January			93.69				

Sources: *People's Handbook*, pp. 298-299, Shanghai, 1953; *Liberation Daily*, Shanghai; *Tientsin Daily*, Tientsin; *Progress Daily*, Tientsin; *Enlightenment Daily*, Peking.

1. The above indices represent monthly averages calculated from daily quotations published by the local offices of the People's Bank the only exception being the 1952 data for Shanghai which are for the beginning of each month.

The commodities included in the above units are as follows:

	Rice (Shih Catties)	Wheat Flour (Shih Catties)	Corn Meal (Shih Catties)	Cooking Oil (Shih Liang)	Salt (Shih Liang)	Cotton Cloth (Shih Ch'ih)	Coal (Shih Catties)
Shanghai	1.56	—	—	1.00	—	1.00*	0.75
Tientsin	—	1.00	1.00	—	—	1.00	—
Peking	—	1.00	1.00	—	—	1.00	—
Wuhan	1.50	—	—	0.50	0.50	0.40*	3.00
Canton	1.00	—	—	0.75	1.00	0.50**	1.00
Chungking	3.00	—	—	1.00	1.00	1.00	3.00
Sian	—	2.00	—	—	—	1.00	5.00

* Firewood
** Coal briquettes

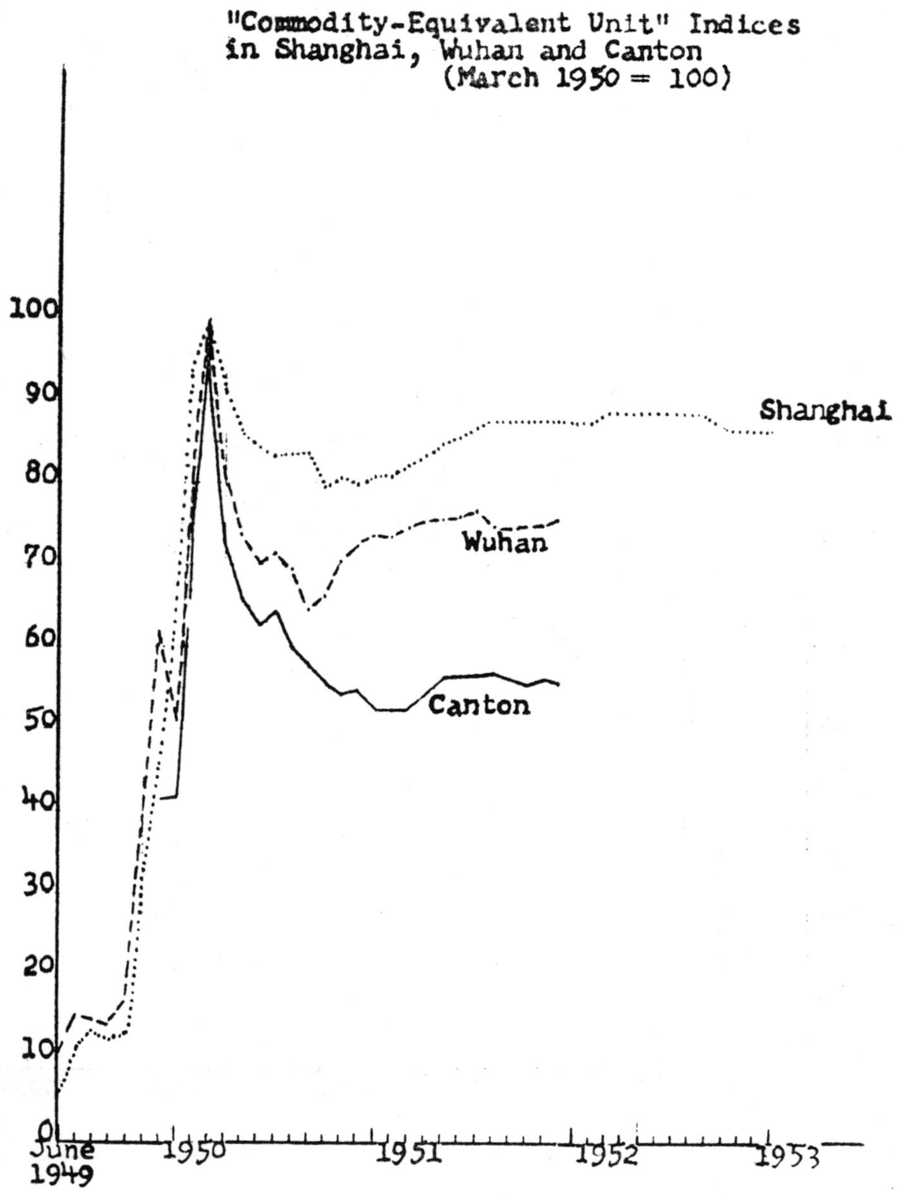
"Commodity-Equivalent Unit" Indices
in Shanghai, Wuhan and Canton
(March 1950 = 100)
100
90
80
70
60
50
40
30
20
10
0
Shanghai
Wuhan
Canton
June
1949
1950
1951
1952
1953

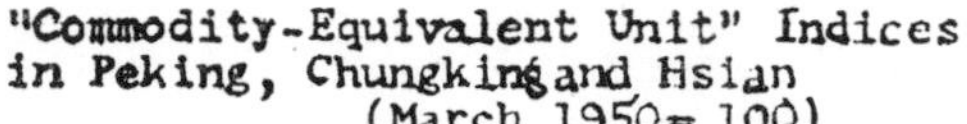

"Commodity-Equivalent Unit" Indices in Peking, Chungking and Hsian (March 1950 = 100)

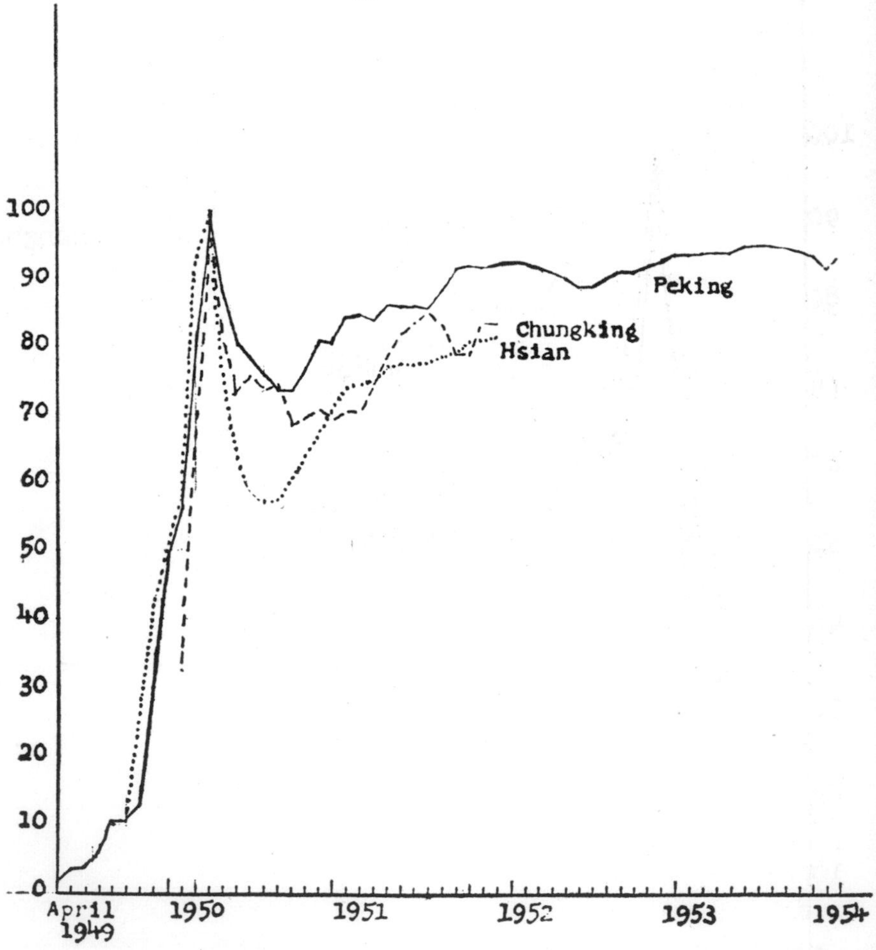

RELATIVE IMPORTANCE OF THE STABILIZING FACTORS

Granted that a high degree of price stability has ostensibly been achieved, the immediate question is to analyze its causes and to gain a better understanding of its nature. In this respect, it is significant to note that the downward movement of prices began immediately after the introduction of the control measures while the budget deficit continued to be of sizable proportions all through the second quarter of 1950. As the following data demonstrate, proceeds from non-agricultural taxes during the first half of 1950 represented only 38.1 per cent of the annual total of proceeds from this source as against 61.9 per cent in the second half. On the other hand, slightly less than one-half of total annual outlay was incurred in the first half of the year. In the case of the agricultural tax, receipts are, as a rule, greater after the autumn harvest than in the first half of the year. The discrepancy between revenue and expenditure resulted in deficits amounting to 43 per cent of total expenditure in the first quarter of the year and 40 per cent in the second quarter. Yet the price level had begun to recede even before the end of the first quarter. However important the increase in taxation may be at a later stage in reducing inflationary pressure, the immediate cause of the downward movement would appear to lie elsewhere.

The compulsory subscription of Victory Bonds, begun well before March, was doubtless useful in contracting the volume of money in circulation. However, the second 100 million units were never issued while not more than 70 per cent of the first hundred million units were actually paid for. The sum involved was, therefore, much too small to offset the inflationary pressure of the budget deficit. The real cause of the fall of prices must be sought in a sudden desire on the part of the business community and the public to spend less money less rapidly and to sell more goods they held for money. The need to pay cash for bond subscription and for the increased taxes was reinforced by the additional uncertainty as to how much more might have to be paid. For one thing, the new taxes were supplemented by collection of "back taxes" allegedly delinquent under the Nationalist regime, and it was even more difficult for the taxpayer to determine his liability in this case. Police measures, which included the employment of Communist youths to go into private homes to detect "hoarding" and "wasteful" consumption, and the possibility of keeping one's

Communist China's Central Government Revenue and Expenditure 1950

	Quarterly Figures in % of Annual Total				*Deficit in % of Cash Outlay*
	Tax Revenue[1] *from Cities*	*Receipts from Local Governments*	*Subsidies to Local Governments*	*Cash Outlay*	
First Quarter	16.5	7.9	43.0	21.4	43.0
Second Quarter	21.6	—	—	25.5	40.0
Third Quarter	23.3	—	—	24.4	9.8
Fourth Quarter	38.6	39.9	14.7	28.7	6.4
Annual Total	100.0	100.0	100.0	100.0	16.7

Source: The above data are taken from Jung Tzu-ho's report on public finance in 1950 and 1951, *New China Monthly,* Vol. III, No. 6, pp. 1354-5, Peking, April, 1951.

1. The same pattern is exhibited by income from salt tax and custom duties.

savings in "commodity-equivalent" units also served to reduce the premium on consumption and commodity hoarding. No less important from the point of view of both economic and psychological effects was the rapid liquidation of private commodity stocks induced by large-scale government dumping on the market, reinforced by the contraction of credit that followed the withdrawal of goverment funds from private banks. Once the forced liquidation of business inventory and of hoarded stocks began and prices started to fall, the desire to liquidate increased even faster so that the effect was bound to be cumulative.

Thus the overhaul of the tax structure was probably not primarily responsible for the *initial* decline of prices. Nor should the bond issue be entirely credited with it. A more plausible explanation is that the break in the inflationary spiral was brought about, in the first instance, largely by government open market commodity operations, supplemented by compulsory austerity and credit deflation. However, while these measures might be regarded as belonging to the sphere of monetary control, they came into being as an integral part of the new fiscal system. On the one hand, the concentration of government deposits in the state banks and the rationing of cash were part and parcel of the reform in fiscal administration. On the other hand, if tax and other revenue had not been increased, in the long run, stability would have been impossible under persistent and increasing budget deficits, which, in the circumstances, would most likely have been the case. Nor should one forget that success in market control was predicated upon the government's command over large commodity stocks, especially food grains, cotton yarn, and coal. Of these three items, the most important one or grain was, and continues to be, obtained from taxation in kind. The government would probably have been unable to acquire the large supplies necessary for market control if the agricultural tax had been levied entirely in money and grain had then been purchased, especially during a period of rapidly rising prices. Thus, in the ultimate analysis, it was the combined effort of all the measures adopted in the spring of 1950, reinforced by other subsequent developments, that has brought about the degree of stability observed above.

DIVERGENCE BETWEEN CONTROLLED PRICES AND THE GENERAL PRICE LEVEL

At this point, it should be further noted that the trend of controlled prices as reflected in the various "cost of living" indices has probably depicted a more favorable picture than the general price level would have done. While analysis is somewhat handicapped by the lack of long series of general price indices, available information in this respect concerning widely scattered areas and covering different periods of time reveals certain uniformity. That is, if a common base period is adopted, the wholesale price level has tended to remain much higher than the cost of living index in all geographical areas. This is well illustrated by the following data. The cause of this difference lies in the fact that all wholesale price indices include a far wider range of commodities than the corresponding "cost of living" indices. The latter do not comprise any manufactured products other than cotton yarn.[34]

Comparative Trends Between Controlled Prices and the General Price Level

	Period	*Controlled Prices*[1]	*General Wholesale Prices*
I. All China			
A. Average for 15 cities[2]			
	1950		
	January	47.4	56.5
	February	71.7	89.9
	March	100.0	100.0

Period	Controlled Prices[1]	General Wholesale Prices
April	—	75.1
May	—	69.5
June	—	69.2
July	—	75.2
August	—	76.8
September	69.7	77.6
October	68.0	81.9
November	69.2	85.8
December	67.8	85.7
B. Average for 6 cities[3]		
1950		
March	100.0	100.0
December	67.8	88.6
1951		
March	72.6	118.5
May	75.2	123.0
July	76.8	125.6
September	77.9	101.3
December	78.7	100.3
1952		
June	77.8	95.2
C. Average for 7 cities[4]		
1950		
March	100.0	100.0
1951		
December	78.7	96.6
1952		
December	78.2	90.6
1953		
December	78.0	91.7
1954		
December	79.3	92.3
II. East China—Shanghai		
1949		
End September	12.19	13.6
End October	16.8	20.5
End November	44.6	60.5
End December	49.9	62.4
1950		
End January	78.8	83.6
End February	107.0	110.6
End March	100.0	100.0
End April	90.9	88.4
End May	87.7	84.3
End June	85.4	93.6
End July	84.6	99.3
End August	84.6	100.8

	Period	Controlled Prices[1]	General Wholesale Prices
	End September	80.7	102.2
	End October	81.5	106.4
	End November	81.7	106.4
	End December	81.2	102.6
	1951		
	End January	82.4	102.6
	End February	81.0	103.0
III. Northwest China[5]			
	December	78.7	96.6
	1951		
	January	104.7	105.5
	February	105.2	108.7
	March	105.2	110.5
	April	109.1	108.5
	May	109.4	110.0
	June	109.4	117.7
	July	109.6	118.1
	August	112.1	122.2
	September	113.2	126.4
IV. South China—Canton[6]			
	1951		
	January	90.4	97.4
	February	90.7	97.1
	March	90.8	98.6
	April	94.2	99.0
	May	97.5	100.7
	June	97.6	102.7
	July	97.9	105.1
	August	98.7	113.5
	September	97.1	118.4
	October	96.4	118.9

Sources: New China Monthly, Vol. VI, No. 4, p. 1350, Peking, October, 1951; *Economic Yearbook,* p. 12, Hongkong, 1953; and *Ta-kung pao,* Tientsin, February 22, 1955.

1. For "controlled prices" the indices used are the Victory Bond index for all China and the "commodity-equivalent unit" indices for the other areas.

2. The fifteen cities are Peking, Tientsin, Kalgan, Taiyüan, Shanghai, Tsingtao, Tsinan, Fu-chou, Hankow, Canton, Changsha, Nan-ch'ang, Hsi-an, Lan-chou, and Chungking. The wholesale price index is originally compiled by the Bureau of Prices of Communist China's Ministry of Trade.

3. The six cities are Shanghai, Tientsin, Hankow, Canton, Chungking, and Hsi-an.

4. The seven cities are the same six listed in note 3 plus Shen-yang. (Official index of the Ministry of Commerce.)

5. Average for six cities: Hsi-an, Lan-chou, Ying-ch'uan, Ti-hua, Hsi-ning, and Nan-cheng. See *Economic Yearbook,* p. 80, Hongkong, 1951.

6. July-December, 1950—100. Wholesale price index compiled by the Lingnan University. *Economic Yearbook,* p. 120, Hongkong, 1952.

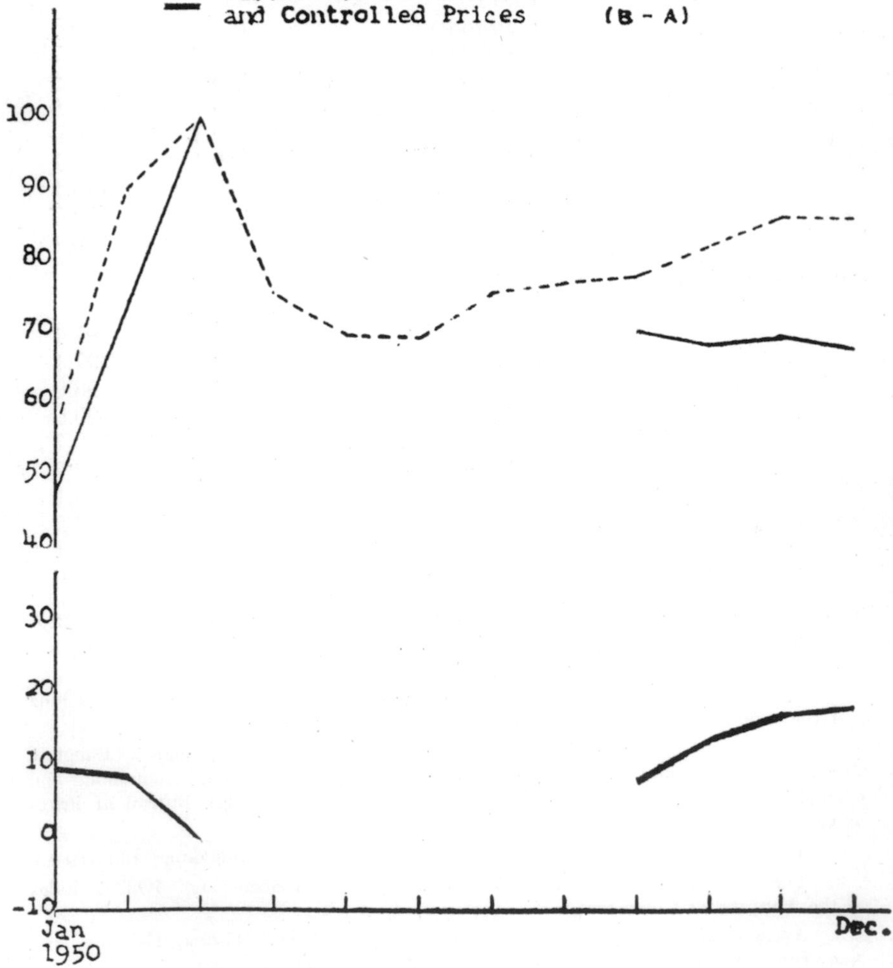
Comparative Trends between the Controlled Prices and the General Price Level
(average for 15 cities)
Controlled Prices (A)
General Price Level(B)
Difference in Trends between General and Controlled Prices (B - A)
100
90
80
70
60
50
40
30
20
10
0
-10
Jan
1950
Dec.

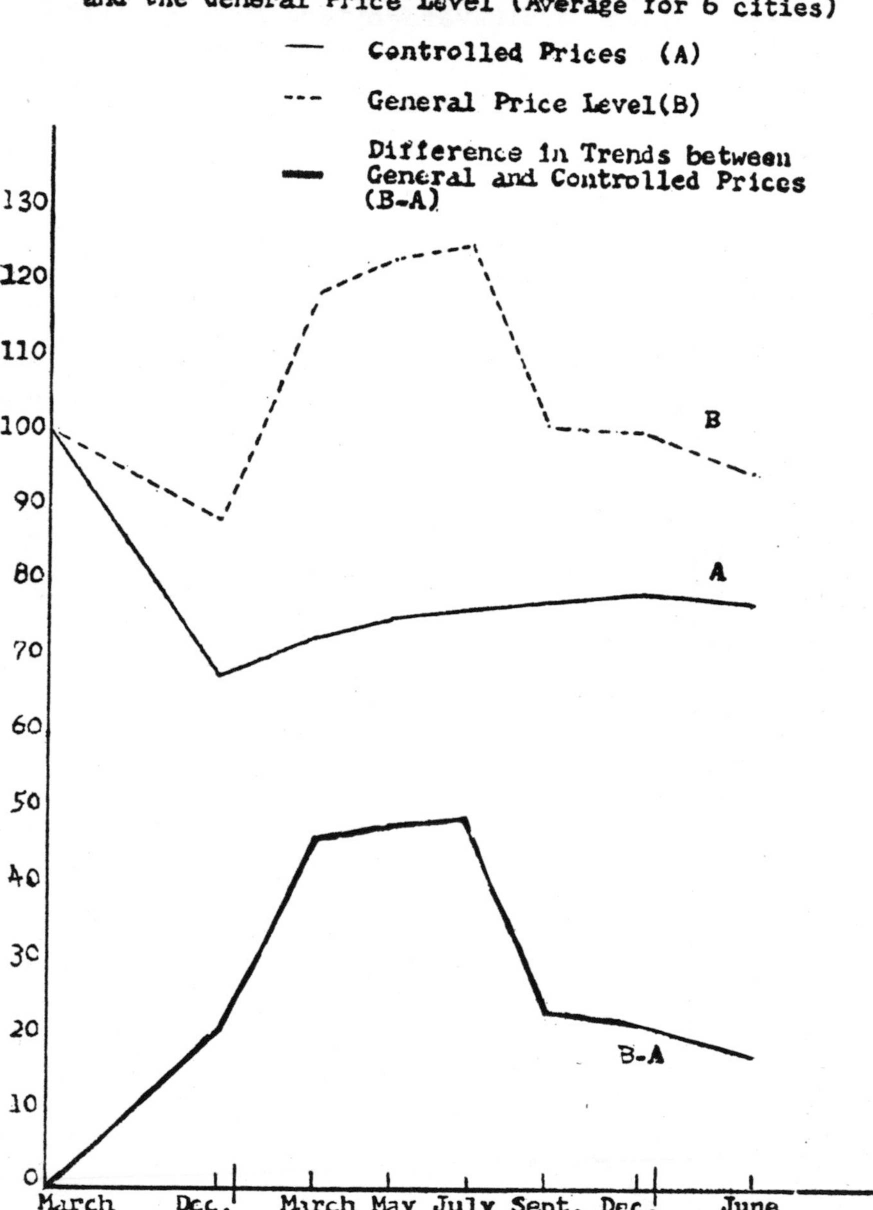
Couparative Trends between the Controlled Prices and the General Price Level (Average for 6 cities)
Controlled Prices (A)
General Price Level(B)
Difference in Trends between General and Controlled Prices (B-A)
130
120
110
100
90
80
70
60
50
40
30
20
10
0
B
A
B-A
March 1950
Dec.
1951
March
May
July
Sept.
Dec.
1952
June

Comparative Trends Between the Controlled Prices and the General Price Level(Average for 7 cities)

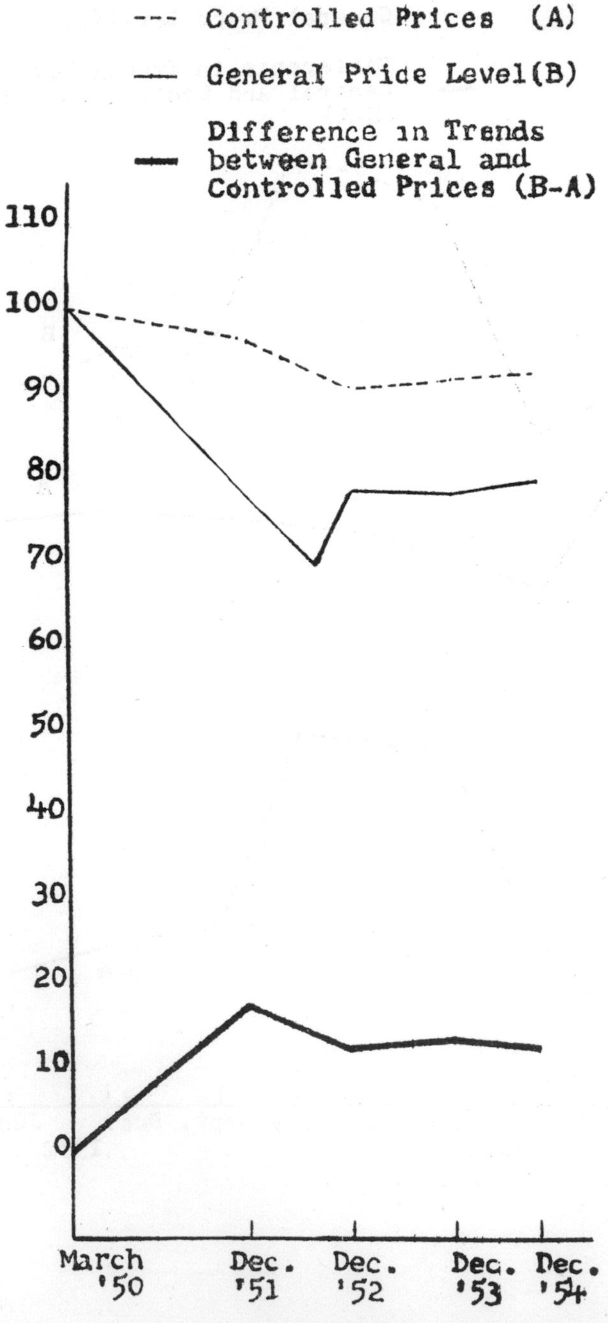

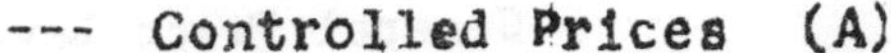

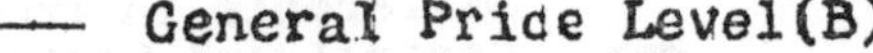

--- Controlled Prices (A)
— General Price Level(B)
Difference in Trends between General and Controlled Prices (B-A)
110
100
90
80
70
60
50
40
30
20
10
0
March '50
Dec. '51
Dec. '52
Dec. '53
Dec. '54

Comparative Trends between the Controlled Prices and the General Price Level (East China–Shanghai)

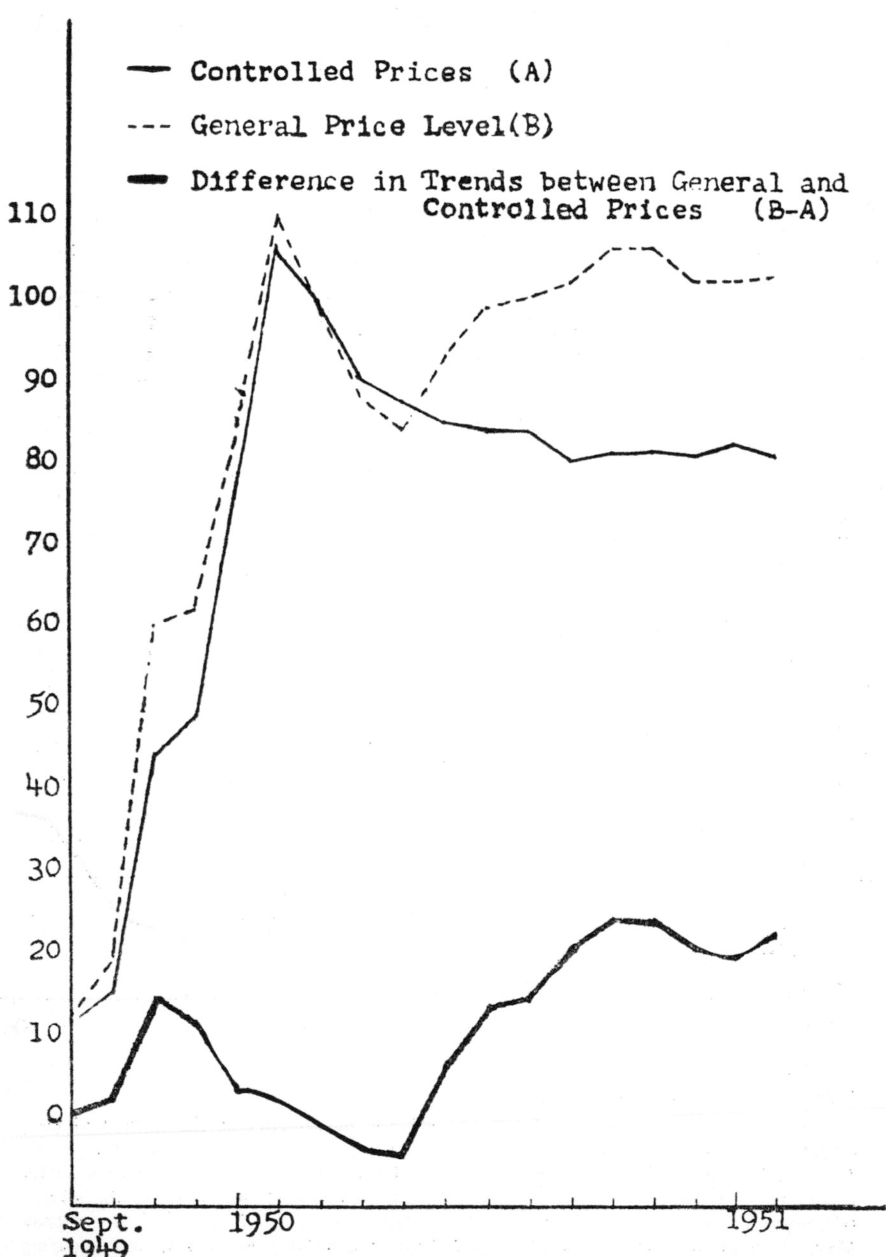

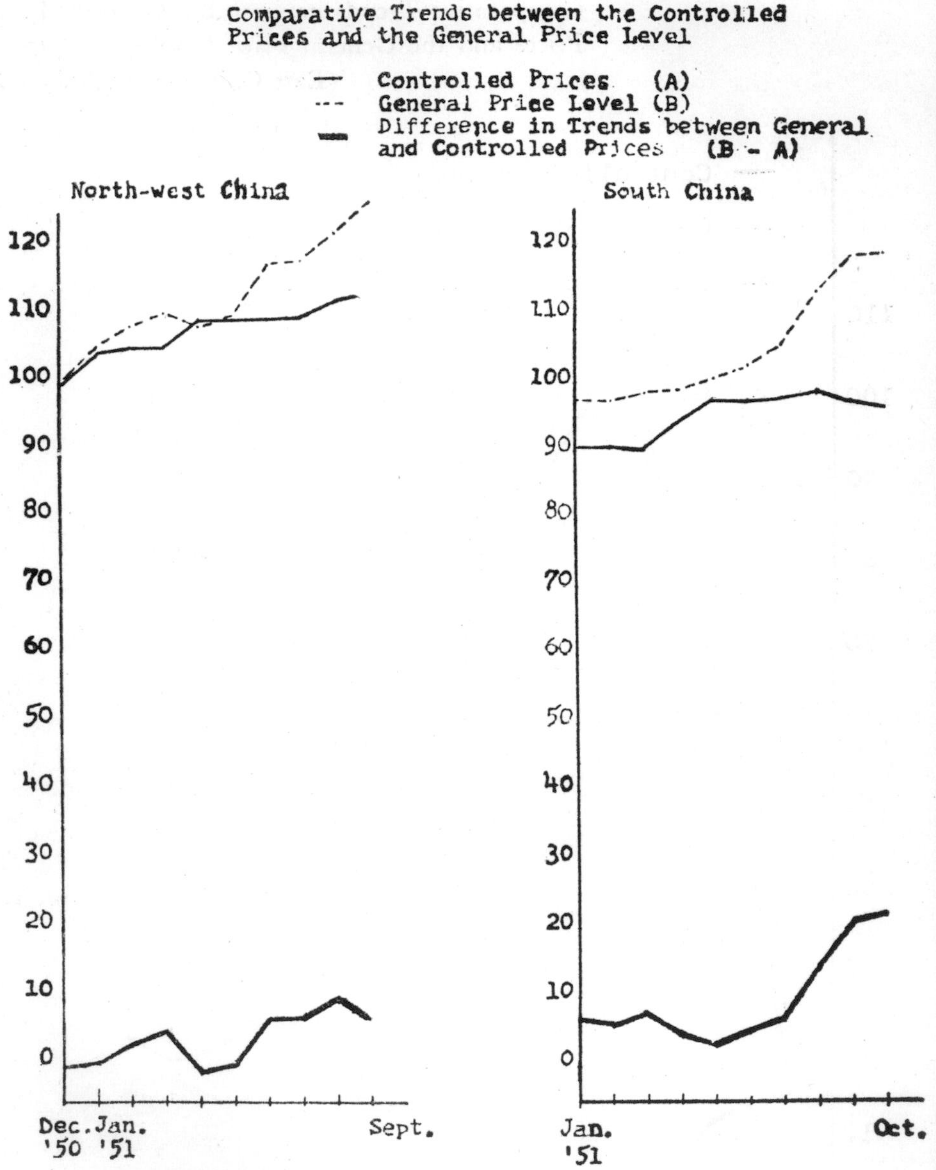

Comparative Trends between the Controlled Prices and the General Price Level

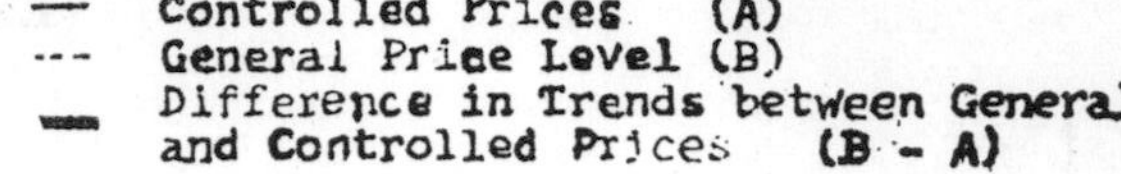

North-west China

120 110 100 90 80 70 60 50 40 30 20 10 0

Dec. '50 Jan. '51 Sept.

South China

120 110 100 90 80 70 60 50 40 30 20 10 0

Jan. '51 Oct.

Note to preceding diagrams:

The preceding diagrams each depict the *relative* movements of the indices of controlled prices and general wholesale prices for an area as from a common base period. Accordingly, even if the difference between the latter and the former becomes negative at any time, it does not necessarily mean that the controlled prices exceed the wholesale prices in any absolute sense. (For instance, in the case of Shanghai, if we took May, 1950, as base, all differences would become positive.) Moreover, in comparing

They are heavily weighted by their two major components—namely, food and cotton textile. The stability of such a crude index is therefore assured as long as grain and cotton yarn prices and the cost of manufacturing yarn into cloth are stable. To this day the Communist government still does not possess absolute and water-tight control over the distribution of the peasants' surplus crops, although it has gone a long way in this direction through the grain tax, the organization of government-sponsored marketing cooperatives, and compulsory purchases, a subject which we shall discuss in another place. Large initial stocks were acquired through both taxation and expropriation, which are not always distinguishable from each other. Withdrawals from these stocks have been compensated by proceeds from the grain tax, supplemented to a small extent by purchases. In the case of cotton yarn, price control was consolidated in January, 1951, when the state trading corporation was given monopoly for the purchase and sale of all yarns produced by the country's mills.[35] Suppression of all alternative channels of distribution, at least at the distributors' level, and possession of sizable stocks have given the government trading concerns a commanding position over the market price of the key commodities constituting the "cost of living" indices.

Since wages and other contractual payments are as a rule tied to such indices and since other cash outlay by government and private organizations is often similarly measured, price stability in the two groups of commodities has exerted an enormous influence in stabilizing manufacturers' costs and other prices in general. Moreover, as savings deposits in banks were until recently often tied to the same or similar indices, stability in the latter had a salutary effect in increasing the propensity to save, quite apart from the discouragement to consumption by police measures. Since the government apparently has not been in a position to control all industrial prices, the general price level has been higher and has exhibited less stability than the prices of the controlled commodities. For the same reason the Communist authorities have been extremely reticent concerning

---

the trends regionally, it is important to remember that not only the base periods may be different from one region to another, but the price levels in different regions during a common base period (as, for instance, in the diagrams of regional trends of commodity-equivalent units) are not the same. Thus, starting from the same base period, region A's price level may fall much more than that of region B although it may still be higher absolutely.

detailed changes in the general price level, especially since 1951. This means, also, that the *real* cost of living for the population is higher than the crude indices would have us believe. Moreover, the step-by-step introduction of rationing also suggests that some of the fixed prices may be nominal prices in the sense that only limited quantities can be purchased, if at all. However, the stabilization of the controlled prices has helped keep the general price level in rein.

However, in the long run, the effectiveness of such price control is very doubtful if the volume of money is constantly expanded. The state of the budget, therefore, remains a highly sensitive subject and deserves close scrutiny.

IV

A REVIEW OF THE 1950–1955 BUDGETS

To the often-asked question as to how Communist China's fiscal affairs stand the official reply is that the country has not had an unbalanced budget since 1949. This claim is officially substantiated by the following data made available by the Finance Minister.

Some doubt may be expressed concerning the overall picture presented by these figures, and on their meaningfulness. For the broad claim made by the Communist authorities has given rise to a very interesting discrepancy. Thus, according to the published report of the Vice Minister of Finance, Jung Tzu-ho, in April, 1951,[36] actual revenue during 1950 was 31.7 per cent higher, while actual outlay was 14 per cent higher than the respective budgeted figures. This performance, attributed to the control measures introduced during 1950, led to a somewhat smaller deficit than expected. The actual deficit was 16.7 per cent of actual expenditure, or 96.6 per cent of the budgeted deficit. The somewhat smaller deficit was covered, according to Jung, by funds from three separate sources; namely, subscriptions received from bonds issued, credit from the Soviet Union, and bank overdraft (i.e., creation of new money). Payments received for the bonds were further reported to be 70.4 per cent of the first issue, while new bank credit was put at 86.9 per cent of the budgeted amount.

If the reported percentage changes in revenue, outlay, and deficit are applied to the original data in the 1950 provisional budget, several different estimates of the realized deficit may be obtained.[37]

Revenue and Expenditure of the Communist Chinese Government 1950–1955

A. In Billions of Jen-min-pi

	1950	1951	1952	1953[1] Budget	1954 Budget	1954 Actual	1955[4] Budget
Revenue							
Taxes	48,985.5	81,133.0	96,218.2	114,695.8	135,596.8	132,180.8	137,805.7
Non-agricultural	29,878.3	58,477.8	68,983.0	87,468.8	104,455.1	89,715.4	100,000.0
Agricultural	19,104.8	21,699.2	25,602.3	25,661.6	31,141.7	32,775.1	28,000.0
Other	2.4	956.0	1,632.9	1,564.4	—	9,690.3	9,805.7
Income from State Enterprises	8,694.4	30,534.7	46,578.8	69,979.7	83,341.8	99,615.0	111,158.1
Credit and Insurance Income	3,274.2	5,678.4	2,510.0	10,273.9	—	30,572.5	31,534.0
Subtotal	60,954.1	117,346.1	145,307.0	194,948.4	218,938.6	262,368.3	280,497.8
Other Revenue	8,485.5	24,739.5	43,971.1	38,550.7	12,943.0	[2]	[2]
Balance from Previous Year	—	—	—	—	42,827.0	45,090.0	31,427.4
Total	69,439.6	142,085.6	189,278.1	233,499.1	274,708.6	307,458.3	311,925.2
Expenditure							
Economic Development	17,356.1	35,109.7	73,069.9	103,527.6	113,227.0	123,582.2	141,887.6
Social, Cultural, and Educational Activities	7,552.2	13,436.1	22,332.5	34,807.5	36,692.0	34,605.1	38,506.9
National Defense	28,274.3	50,608.2	42,777.0	52,253.7	52,670.0	58,135.3	71,931.5

Administration	13,132.0	17,456.4	19,336.9	23,779.6	46,868.8	21,620.7	22,415.6
Other Expenditure	1,767.4	2,413.4	5,702.3	3,647.0		8,381.1	12,453.3
Subtotal	68,082.0	119,023.8	163,218.6	218,015.4	249,457.8	246,324.4	287,194.9
Reserve or Carry-over	—	—	—	15,483.7	25,250.8	61,133.9[3]	24,730.3[5]
Total	68,082.0	119,023.8	163,218.6	233,499.1	274,708.6	307,458.3	311,925.2

Sources: The above data are taken from Po I-p'o's report on February 12, 1953, Teng Hsiao-p'ing's report in the *People's Daily*, Peking, June 18, 1954, and Li Hsien-nien's report on the 1955 budget, NCNA, July 9, 1955.

1. Actual revenue in 1953 was reported by Teng to be Y215,477.4 billion. In addition, Y41,232.2 billion were carried over from 1952. Against the total financial resource of Y256,709.6 billion, actual outlay during 1953 amounted to Y213,882.6 billion and Y42,827.0 billion were reported carried over to 1954. The smaller actual outlay in 1953 was attributed by Teng to reductions in all items other than defense for which expenditure was stepped up during the first half of the year. The last figure, however, differs from the actual figure given for 1954.

2. Included in "credit and insurance income."

3. The actual amount carried over was only Y31,427.4 billion. For details see Li Hsien-nien's report on July 9, 1955.

4. For the sake of comparison the 1955 data are still expressed in terms of the old *jen-min-pi*.

5. Including a General Reserve Fund of Y10,172.3 billion.

B. In Millions of US Dollars[1]

	1950	*1951*	*1952*	*1953 Budget*	*1954 Budget*	*1954 Actual*	*1955 Budget*
Revenue							
Taxes	1,518	3,570	4,330	4,685	5,501	5,373	5,602
Non-agricultural	926	2,573	3,104	3,573	4,237	3,647	4,065
Agricultural	592	955	1,152	1,048	1,264	1,332	1,138
Other	neg.	42	74	64	—	394	399
Income from State Enterprises	270	1,343	2,096	2,859	3,380	4,049	4,519
Credit and Insurance Income	102	250	113	420	—	1,243	1,281
Subtotal	1,890	5,163	6,539	7,963	8,881	10,665	11,402
Other Revenue	263	1,088	1,979	1,575	525	—	—
Balance from Previous Year	—	—	—	—	1,738	1,832	1,278
Total	2,153	6,251	8,518	9,538	11,144	12,497	12,680
Expenditure							
Economic Development	538	1,545	3,288	4,229	4,593	5,023	5,768
Social, Cultural, and Educational Activities	234	591	1,005	1,421	1,489	1,407	1,565
National Defense	876	2,227	1,925	2,134	2,137	2,363	2,924
Administration	407	768	870	971		879	911
Other Expenditure	55	106	257	149	1,901	340	506
Subtotal	2,110	5,237	7,345	8,904	10,120	10,012	11,674
Reserve or Carry-over	—	—	—	634	1,024	2,485	1,006
Total	2,110	5,237	7,345	9,538	11,144	12,497	12,680

1. The following monthly average exchange rates in thousand *jen-min-pi* per US dollar are used in conversion:

1950	Y32.6	1952	22.3	1954	24.6
1951	22.5	1953	24.6	1955	24.6

It is suggested that reasons for this discrepancy are to be found in (1) the possibility that total revenue and expenditure figures were revised in the national financial conference held in February, 1950, when changes in the relative shares of agricultural and non-agricultural taxes were later reported, and (2) the possible practice of using both monetary values and commodity indices (e.g., Victory Bond units) in comparing actual performance with the original budget and violent changes in the value of the currency during the year.

However, the report by Jung agreed with the provisional 1950 budget on one point. That is, there was distinctly a deficit. Since Jung went into some details concerning the manner in which this deficit was made up, and since his official report has never been repudiated, one can be justifiably surprised when, two years after Jung's review, Po I-p'o stated that government revenue in 1950 was greater than government expenditure. As long as one does not assume that all the official figures are phony, which is an improbable proposition, there must be a plausible explanation for this apparent contradiction. It appears to us that in fact several possibilities are present.

THE NATURE OF "OTHER REVENUE"

In the first place, according to Po I-p'o, total revenue is divided into four categories: tax income, revenue from government enterprises, credit and insurance income, and "other revenue." There have been several revisions in the classification of budgetary items between 1950 and the end of 1952.[38] According to the revised classification as adopted in September, 1952, government revenue is classified into 27 major categories. Of these some undoubtedly fall under the first two broad divisions given by Po, i.e., tax income and revenue from state enterprises. The remaining divisions are (1) administrative income, such as fines, (2) income from sale of public property, such as the liquidation of warehouse inventory, (3) income from domestic and foreign loans, (4) other income, such as donations by the public and extraordinary levies, and (5) income from note issue. The question is which of these items have been lumped together under the term, "other revenue," by the Minister of Finance and how important they are individually. If income from borrowing and/or note issue has actually been included—and it may well have been—it is perfectly clear why the 1950 budget deficit has disappeared in the 1953 report. Another factor that should be considered is that according to the official classification method, revenue from government credit institutions is a part of the income from state enterprises. Its presentation as a separate division by Po is a departure from normal practice and raises the question whether it represents income from government credit institutions as it should or whether it also includes income from government borrowing. The latter possibility appears to have been substantiated by Li Hsien-nien in his budget report in 1955. According to Li, income under the category of "credit, loan, and insurance" in 1954 greatly exceeded the planned figure not only because of greater income from government bonds than expected, but mainly because of the addition to this account of a Soviet loan.

A further point of interest is that there was no mention of the budget during the entire year of 1951 when the Korean war was at its height. Yet on the occasion of his report on the 1952 budget in August, 1952, the Minister of Finance also mentioned that although the budget for 1951 had shown a deficit at the time it was drawn up, *by June, 1952,* actual revenue had been materially increased so that the "realized" 1951 budget was more than balanced. This observation was somewhat curious in view of the fact that Communist China's fiscal year coincides with the calendar year. As Po's remark has since been corroborated by other writers,[39] a possible explanation is that for accounting purposes, revenue accrued in 1951 but not collected until 1952 was credited to 1951, and that, by the same token, the 1950 budget was given identical treatment. The fact that large revenue was obtained in early 1952 during the drive against urban business communities, the greater part of which consisted of back taxes allegedly due in 1951 or earlier and may have been credited to an earlier year, lends support to the above argument. The budget mentioned by Po was, in all probability, not the cash budget, which was definitely unbalanced in both 1950 and 1951. For 1952 and subsequent years whether the budget was actually in balance or not in the orthodox sense depends upon how important note issue, government borrowing, and credit expansion were in relation to the term "other revenue" and "credit and insurance income." As may be seen from the previous tables, if "other revenue" were excluded completely, government outlay would be in excess of income throughout 1950–1953 and again in 1955. Even in 1954, a budget deficit would appear if a part of the "credit and insurance income" were excluded from ordinary revenue and treated as government borrowing. For the other years the deficit would be even larger under the same treatment.

THE IMPORTANCE OF EXTRAORDINARY REVENUE

Although a budget deficit is inflationary in its effect, it is quite compatible with a deflationary movement and falling prices if contraction in private spending more than offsets the government's excessive outlay. This appears to represent actual developments in Communist China during 1950–1951. Nevertheless, if a persistent budget deficit should again develop, it may conceivably bring about a renewal of the inflation spiral. The likelihood of such a development is of considerable interest.

In this respect, attention should be directed to the role of "other revenue" in Po's 1953 report. Apart from the questionable points that have already been raised, many of the heterogeneous items included as "other revenue" are of a non-recurring character. The liquidation of inventory through warehouse clearance, the disposal, in one way or another, of other government property, the confiscation of private assets belonging to former members of the Nationalist government and to landowners cannot be repeated. Even in the case of such extraordinary levies, disguised as donations to the Arms Fund and the "Resist America and Aid Korea" Fund, or fines imposed on business for "illegal" practices and tax evasion, to have to continue them year after year might also prove politically impracticable. Although the exact amount added to the coffers of the state from these sources cannot be determined, that it is of material import in the composition of "other revenue" cannot be denied.[40]

A call was issued by the Communist authorities in the last quarter of 1953 to strive to fulfill the revenue target set for the year. It appears that sizable amounts of tax payments were in arrears; that more than one-third of the year's taxes still remained to be collected, including all the income taxes from private business; and that administrative inefficiency was particularly noticeable in the case of a few non-agricultural taxes.[41] Less than two months later, the issue of a 4 per cent, 8-year, new Construction Bond, totalling ¥6,000 billion, was announced. This was followed by the decision a year later to float a similar issue for 1955. If these developments are indicative of the Communist government's fiscal situation, some doubt would appear to be justified as to the state of government finance in 1953 and 1954. The problem of increasing revenue from regular sources is apparently still the central issue.

V

TAX ADJUSTMENTS SINCE 1950

Before we can evaluate the future prospect of the Communist government's ability to finance its increasing expenditure without resorting to inflationary means, some of the changes in tax structure and fiscal policy that have taken place since the introduction of the emergency stabilization measures in the first part of 1950 should be briefly reviewed. These changes may be divided into two groups, of which the greater part have grown out of adjustments to the original taxes that were either too high to be of long-term advantage to the treasury or too cumbersome to be administered efficiently.

As early as June, 1950, it was admitted by high Communist officials that there had been a number of "deviations" in the collection of public grain and of the "industrial and commercial" tax. Among others, inequitable distribution of the tax burden, tax evasions, the multiplicity of taxes, and divergence in interpretation and methods of assessment were given as examples of errors that should be corrected.[42] In addition, it appears that the concentration of revenue in the hands of the central government had gone too far and that local authorities were unable to carry on their normal functions.

It was to correct some of these errors that the first group of tax changes was introduced in the latter part of 1950. The changes were mainly technical and involved the consolidation of some of the excise tax items and of a few of the minor taxes and the revision of certain tax rates, none of which, with the exception of the salt and alcohol taxes, were, however, of any importance.[43] Then in March, 1951, the respective shares of the central and local governments in tax revenue were redefined, the latter being now given (1) in the case of the agricultural tax, a larger share of the amount, (2) a small portion of the tax on sales and business income, and (3) more clearly defined privileges in tagging surtaxes on established national taxes.[44] Finally, in the case of the all-important agricultural tax, an effort was made during 1952 in streamlining the rather confusing practice hitherto employed in different areas.[45]

THE TURNOVER TAX

Another development during this period is of a somewhat different character. This is the introduction as of 1953 of a turnover tax for 24 commodities in place of the original excise, sales, and stamp taxes. The purpose of this tax is to levy a single tax at a higher rate for those commodities in the marketing of which the numerous echelons of the traditional distribution channel have now disappeared through changes in the economic structure.[46] Hailed as a major innovation and significant development towards the establishment of a tax system more closely resembling that of the Soviet Union, the turnover tax, together with minor changes in further consolidation introduced at the same time, constituted the latest adjustment. The basic tax structure as well as fiscal administration, however, has remained unchanged. Even the special method of assessing the sales and business income taxes discussed before is still in force.

THE NATIONAL CONSTRUCTION BONDS

It is interesting to note that following the issue of the Victory Bonds in 1950 no attempt was made by the Chinese Communists to make further public bond offerings. Instead, reliance was placed upon other revenue sources, including the various extraordinary levies mentioned so far. This policy was reversed only at the end of 1953 when the government decided to float an issue of four per cent, 8-year National Construction Bonds to the tune of ¥6,000 billion during 1954. Since then another four per cent, 10-year issue has been ordered for 1955.

As may be seen from the following table, in both cases, the largest share was alloted to private business, while persons on the government's payroll, including the armed forces, subscribed for the next largest share. Farmers, on the other hand, were called upon to subscribe for the smallest portion.

Whether this distribution means that there was considerable resistance in rural areas to the bonds or rather that the government was well aware at the outset of the peasants' inability to pay is open

Bond Subscription Allotments
in Communist China
(¥ billion)

	1954 Bonds			*1955 Bonds*
	Subscription Targets	*Subscriptions up to March 24, 1954*		*Subscription Targets*[1]
Private Business	3,200.0	3,761.9		2,700.0
Government Employees, Teachers, and Industrial Workers)			(1,400.0)	
)	1,000.0	2,107.4		2,400.0
Armed Forces)			(1,000.0)	
Farmers	1,800.0	556.0		1,800.0
Total	6,000.0	6,425.3		6,900.0

Sources: NCNA, December 9, 1953; China News Service, Peking, April 1, 1954; and Chinese News Service, New York, January 11, 1955; and *People's Daily,* Peking, December 24, 1954.

1. The total target exceeds the Y6,000 billion issue considerably.

to conjecture. Probably both explanations are true to some extent. Furthermore, the bond issues and the heavy allotment to private business suggest that the Communist authorities have begun to feel the impact of the non-recurring nature of the extraordinary levies, as well as the diminishing return of increasing taxation.

The question may be raised as to whether the bond issues are adequate enough to meet the government's needs. According to Teng Hsiao-p'ing's 1954 budget report, up to April, 1954, bond subscriptions amounted to ¥8,160 billion, which may be compared to the ¥12,943 under "other revenue" in the 1954 budget. However, there is some doubt on the amount of subscriptions actually collected. Up to March 24, 1954, payments received on the total subscription of ¥6,425.3 billion amounted to no more than ¥1,668.0 billion, or about 25 per cent.[47] Even though subscription through payroll deductions may assure a part of the receipts, it is by no means certain that Communist China could succeed in balancing its budget by bond issues. In fact, the adoption of such direct controls as rationing and price fixing suggest that they have only suppressed some of the symptoms of price inflation without removing their cause.

THE CURRENCY CONVERSION OF 1955

At this point mention should be made of the conversion operation of 1955, under which new *jen-min-pi* notes were exchanged for old notes at the rate of 1 (new) to 10,000 (old) and all contractual relations and other matters expressed in terms of the old currency were likewise converted.[48] Since no limitation to the conversion of the old currency was officially imposed, barring any administrative manipulation, the operation could not in itself change anything, of course. However, all Communist writers have so far unanimously asserted that the adoption of the new currency would bring about even greater economic stability, and have warned against panic buying, refusal to accept old notes during the conversion period, and illegal speculative activities. Among other things, they have pointed to a ten-fold increase in the government's gold holdings since 1949 although the currency is in no way related to gold. Apart from the convenience of eliminating several digits in bookkeeping, the only valid explanation given for conversion at this time was that the old notes consisted of many diverse issues and could be easily defaced and counterfeited.[49] This sounds a rather sinister note, especially if we bear in mind that currency conversion is a costly operation and that the official warnings against sabotage during the conversion could not be reconciled with the rather facile explanation that the country's economic stability was such as to warrant the undertaking of conversion merely to facilitate bookkeeping and to put crisp new notes into the hands of the population who resents the inconvenience of the old notes. Moreover, abandonment of the old notes had the effect of bringing private cash balances to the open, thus facilitating the increase of compulsory savings. Furthermore, the argument advanced by some writers that the new currency would be conducive to better planning and closer supervision, which as such it could not be expected to do, suggests that there might be something seriously wrong with the old currency and its general acceptability. Perhaps, in adopting the new currency, the Communists hoped to achieve a certain psychological advantage which always accompanies the reduction of price tabs. But this is no more than a conjecture which future events alone can prove or disprove.[50]

THE FUTURE OUTLOOK

The end of the Korean war removed a major source of inflation. However, the large investment program begun in 1953, together with expansion of military expenditure, has again reversed the deflationary trend observed during the 1952 "five-anti" movement and has brought about what, to say the least, must be regarded as a creeping inflation. Given the present array of taxes it would appear in the light of the above analysis that additional revenue must be sought in other ways. In this connection, Communist Chinese writers and officials have frequently pointed to the increasing importance of government income derived from state enterprises in the form of profits and amortization payments. As more and more productive activities are nationalized, revenue from this source will continue to mount.[51] Theoretically, the government should have little difficulty in raising revenue if it controlled the entire apparatus of production and were able to price, in addition to factors of production, that part of the national output reserved for the population just high enough to absorb the latter's expenditure. In other words, the economy would then resemble a large military camp with all the production in excess of the rations reserved for the controlling authorities. The amount of the rations could, in turn, be fixed at such a level that the authorities would have all that is required. However, until such a stage is reached and until the government can wipe out most of the surplus purchasing power of the population by monetary or other means, restriction of consumption through price changes alone has its psychological drawbacks,[52] and the government has to face the possibility that its regular revenue may not give it command over all the services and goods it desires, especially if its demand for the country's resources is unduly large.

Of course, if revenue cannot be increased, the possibility of reducing expenditure must be examined. To the question whether some reduction in government expenditure might not be made by Communist China in the future there is really no unequivocal reply. The most important items of expenditure in the budgts are economic construction and defense.[53] Their reduction would have to be predicated upon a radical change in major policy—either a slowdown of industrialization or the abandonment of militarism. If such a change does not take place, continued reliance on "extraordinary revenue"[54] would ensue. However, since increasing resistance to such levies may be encountered, the danger of a resurgence of monetary inflation may be quite real, especially if the government should choose to enlarge its expenditure further by stepping up its industrialization program and/or by embarking upon foreign adventures.[55]

In the final analysis, given the minimum level of consumption, the availability of an increasing revenue to the government for its industrialization and other programs depends, of course, upon the rate of increase of the national output. From the point of view of the inflation threat, the issue, therefore, is whether productivity in all major activities can be substantially increased in Communist China without the prior investment of capital and whether new material and human resources can be found. For a consideration of this problem we shall turn first to the field of agricultural production and the closely related problem of land reform.

NOTES

1. Chen Yün, "The Chinese Communist Party's Leading Role in National Construction," *Compendium,* Vol. III, p. 5.

2. Cf. Po I-p'o's report to the 16th meeting of the Central People's Government Council, August 11, 1952.

3. Po I-p'o, *On the 1953 Budget,* report to the Central People's Government Council, February 12, 1953, Peking, 1953.

4. This was particularly true after the occupation of Shanghai in May, 1949, where more than one-half of the outstanding issue of the Nationalist currency circulated. For details see the chapter on monetary control.

5. Changes in the Shanghai wholesale price index during this period are as follows:

(End of March, 1950 = 100)

1949—May	28	1.6	Oct.	10	12.9
June	9	6.2	Oct.	31*	20.5
June	27	6.4	Nov.	26	54.0
July	30	16.1	Nov.	30*	60.5
Sept.	30*	13.6	Dec.	31*	62.4
1950—Jan.	31	83.6			
Feb.	28*	110.6			
Mar.	31*	100.0			

The above data taken from *Economic Yearbook,* Hongkong, 1951, and various issues of the *Liberation Daily,* Shanghai. Figures with an asterisk are averages of the last ten days of the month.

6. See Chen Yün's report to the seventh meeting of the Central People's Government Council, April 13, 1950, on the financial situation and food supply, *A Manual for Newspaper Readers,* p. 402, Hankow, 1950.

7. See Jung Tze-ho's report on government finance in 1950 and 1951 in *New China Monthly,* Vol. III, No. 6, pp. 1354-1355, Peking, April, 1951.

8. See *People's Daily,* editorial, Peking, December 3, 1949. The same figures had been quoted by Communist officials in reports on the preliminary 1950 budget.

9. We will confine our discussion in the present chapter to the first group and only those elements in the second group which were part and parcel of the fiscal overhaul. Discussion on monetary control proper will be postponed to a later chapter.

10. Po I-p'o, *Report on Drafting of the 1950 Preliminary National Budget,* presented to the fourth meeting of the Central People's Government Council, December 2, 1949. Text in *A Manual for Newspaper Readers,* p. 388 et seq., Hankow, 1950.

11. The commodities and their specified quantities are (1) rice or, in the case of Tientsin, millet (six *shih* catties); (2) flour (one and one-half catties); (3) white cotton cloth (four *shih ch'ih*), and (4) coal (sixteen catties). The wholesale values of the above commodities at six cities are averaged with the following weights: Shanghai (45%), Tientsin (20%), Hankow (10%), Canton (10%), Hsi-an (5%), and Chungking (10%). The value of one bond unit is equal to the sum of the above averages. One *shih* catty and one *shih-ch'ih* are equivalent respectively to 1.1023 lbs. and 1.0936 ft.

12. The second 100 million units were never issued.

13. The "Y" sign has been adopted as the official symbol for the *jen-min-pi.*

14. This was the US dollar T.T. rate in Canton, as well as the US dollar currency rate in Shanghai.

15. The proportion between the agricultural and non-agricultural taxes was slightly altered later. The revised percentage distribution of the revenue items was: non-agricultural taxes, 40.1%; agricultural tax, 37.2%; income from state enterprises, 17.9%; other, 4.8%, *People's Daily,* Peking, March 22, 1950.

16. The tax program was decided upon after a national taxation conference held in November, 1949.

17. For the texts of the various tax regulations see, for instance, *A Manual for Newspaper Readers,* pp. 435-460, Hankow, 1950.

18. The exchange tax is payable by the buyer while the sales tax on the same transaction is payable by the seller.

19. The government structure of China was divided into three major levels, viz., the central government, the governments of "large administrative areas" and provincial governments. The term, "local authorities," is used here to denote the two lower levels.

20. *People's Daily,* editorial, Peking, December 22, 1950.

21. See Article 6, Chapter 2, of the provisional regulations of the "industrial and commercial tax."

22. This was later changed to ten per cent.

23. Some Communist Party members who had been taught to regard all heavy taxation as exploitation of the masses were reported to have found it hard to reconcile this view with the revised official outlook of a party in power. See *People's Daily,* editorial, Peking, March 22, 1950.

24. In case the forum fails to reach an agreement, the tax authority will make the final decision.

25. See *People's Daily,* Peking, December 22, 1950.

26. See Fan Ch'ang-chiang, "A New Era in Financial and Economic Work," *People's Daily,* Peking, March 3, 1950.

27. The population affected by natural calamities in 1949, mostly floods, totalled 40 million, of whom 7 million were desperate cases. The area of farm land affected was 121,560,000 *mow* or about 8 per cent of the country's total cultivated area. See Chen Yün, *Report on the Financial and Food Situation* to the Central People's Gov-

ernment, April 13, 1950. On this point and subsequent developments see also *China Wins Economic Battles,* Peking, Foreign Languages Press, 1950.

28. Among the many important documentary sources see, in particular, *Directive on the Unification of National Financial and Economic Work,* March 3, 1950, and an official communication of the same date by the Central Committee of the Chinese Communist Party to its subordinate organs; *Regulations of the Central Depository,* March 3, 1950; *Directive on the Liquidation and Allocation of Warehouse Supplies,* March 14, 1950; *Directive on the Procedure of Unifying State Trading,* March 14, 1950; *Directive on the Unification of the Receipt, Disbursement, Safekeeping, and Allocation of Public Grains,* March 26, 1950; *Directive on the Unified Control of Fiscal Receipts and Expenditures in 1950,* April 1, 1950; and *Directive on the Implementation of Cash Control in Government Agencies,* April 7, 1950. For articles in English dealing with the above topic see, for instance, the *Far Eastern Economic Review,* Hongkong, of this period.

29. An increase in capital turnover implies a reduction of inventory and goods in process relative to sales and output. More finished goods would thus be made available on the market.

30. The surtax was increased to 20 per cent of the national tax in 1951. It was nominally abolished in 1952.

31. Over 55 cities were observing this practice by April, 1950.

32. I.e., the central bank of Communist China.

33. Government coal mines and cotton mills were predominant in both industries. Control over cotton yarns was further tightened as of January, 1951, when sales of yarn were channeled through the government corporation and direct sales by private mills were prohibited. See *New China Monthly,* Vol. III, No. 3, p. 622, Peking, January, 1951.

34. For this reason, they should not be regarded as genuine measurements of the cost of living.

35. Following the outbreak of the Korean war, "speculators once again began to hoard cotton yarn. The price of yarn on the black market in North and Central China was at one time over one-third higher than the official price." The effect on the prices of other basic commodities of consumption such as salt and edible oil was reported to be disturbing, and "there was a serious threat to price stability in general." *People's Daily,* Peking, January 4, 1951.

36. Jung Tzu-ho, *loc. cit.*

37. In the first place, since total expenditure and revenue in the 1950 budget are estimated at 2,779.9 and 2,259.9 million bond units, and since actual expenditure and revenue are 114 and 131.7 per cent of the budget figures, the latter should amount to 3,169.1 and 2,976.3 million bond units. This would give us a deficit of 192.8 million units. Second, if the realized deficit is calculated as 96.6 per cent of the budgeted deficit, or 520 million bond units, it would amount to 502.3 million bond units. Third, if total realized expenditure is taken as 3,169.1 million and the realized deficit as 16.7 per cent of actual outlay, the latter would amount to 529.3 million bond units. Finally, if the total realized expenditure, taken as 3,169.1 million, is broken down into quarterly figures, which are then used to calculate quarterly deficits, the total realized deficit would amount to 748.8 million bond units. Cf. also Hsiao Chi-jung, *Revenue and Disbursement of Communist China* (in English), Hongkong, 1954.

38. See Liu Shan-su, "Introduction to the Standard Budgetary Classifications of 1952," *New Accounting,* Nos. 13 and 14, Peking, January and February, 1952.

39. See, for instance, Shen Ho's article on "China's Fiscal and Economic Reconstruction" in *Economic Yearbook,* p. 11, Hongkong, 1953.

40. The various extraordinary levies and their known receipts are as follows:

	Period	*Amount in billion*	*Note*
"Resist U.S.-Aid Korea Campaign Fund"	November 20, 1950 to January 21, 1952	4,113.9[a]	Actual receipts up to November 29, 1951, were Y 3,911.9 billion
"Arms Fund"	June 1, 1951, to December 31, 1951	5,024.7[b]	
"3-anti" and "5-anti" Drives against Corruption, Tax Evasion, etc.	(a) "3-anti" December 29, 1951 to June, 1952 (b) "5-anti" February to June, 1952	[c]	
Expropriation during Land Reform	1949-1953	[d]	

a. *1951 Economic Yearbook,* p. 31, Hongkong, 1952.

b. *1952 People's Handbook,* p. 15, Shanghai, *Ta-kung pao,* 1953.

c. One unofficial estimate for tax evasion alone was Y43,000 billion. *Economic Weekly,* No. 15, p. 296, Shanghai, April, 1952.

d. No official figures available. See, however, chapter 4 below. Cf. also Hsiao Chi-jung, *op. cit.,* for other estimates.

41. See *People's Daily,* Peking, October 29, 1953.

42. Reports to the second session of the first National Committee of the People's Political Consultative Conference by Po I-p'o and Chen Yün, June 15, 1950, on tax collection and adjustments.

43. Po I-p'o, *ibid.* It should also be noted that the inheritance tax and the income tax on salaries and wages were never enforced.

44. See "Directive on the Differentiation of Government Revenue and Expenditure in 1951," March 29, 1951, and "Directive on the Further Readjustment of Local Finance," *New China Monthly,* pp. 1357-9, Peking, April, 1951.

45. See the following chapter.

46. The original sales tax has now lost its revenue function through the reduction in the number of times these commodities now change hands. See *Economic Weekly, 1953,* No. 2, Shanghai, January, 1953.

47. China News Service report, Peking, April 1, 1954.

48. For the text of the government decree on conversion see, for instance, *Ta-kung pao,* Tientsin, February 21, 1955. The new currency began circulation as of March 1, 1955. The months of March and April were reserved for the conversion.

49. Cf., for instance, Yang P'ei-hsin's article in the Tientsin *Ta-kung pao,* February 21, 1955.

50. Official reports so far have pointed to the continued relative stability of urban controlled prices.

51. Not all this revenue is, however, available for use in current consumption as the government must also assume a larger share of total investment, now that private business is doing less investing on its own and larger amounts will be needed to maintain existing capital intact.

52. The *People's Daily* stated on December 2, 1954: "Compared with 1953, social purchasing power went up by 13.8 per cent in 1954. Such a rate of growth of people's purchasing power has exceeded the rate of increasing production of consumers' goods, thereby causing shortage of certain consumers' goods . . ."

53. The figure given for economic construction includes both the replacement of private investment that would have been made if nationalization and state investment had not been expanded and reinvestment of depreciation reserves. On the other hand, some military spending is probably included under "investments for heavy industries," as well as in administrative expenditure.

54. The new Construction Bonds which are essentially compulsory loans may be regarded as another example of "extraordinary revenue."

55. It seems to follow from our analysis that in the interest of financial stability Communist China would be ill-advised to expand its military expenditure further. The adverse effect of the Korean war on commodity prices may be seen in the price statistics given earlier. However, the upkeep of a Communist Chinese soldier is relatively cheap. At the reported annual cost of 4,000 catties of food (including normal munition supplies), or the equivalent of US$150-200 per soldier, the current budgeted figure is ample for the maintenance of a very large army. See *Economic Weekly*, Vol. X, Nos. 8-9, p. 11, Shanghai, March 1, 1950, and No. 10, p. 4, March 1 1950.

CHAPTER FOUR

Land Redistribution and Its Implications

I

THE NATURE OF CHINA'S LAND PROBLEM

Our discussion of Communist China's fiscal development in recent years has served to point out the vital role of the agricultural tax and, by inference, the importance of agricultural production and its institutional framework in supporting the Communist government's economic activity. A more searching attempt will now be made to unravel the intricacies of this particular phase of Communist China's economic development which has often beclouded the issue of Communism in China and has been the source of endless confusion to the student of Chinese affairs.

The confusion surrounding China's farm problems stems from the fact that a number of different issues are involved and that it has not always been in the interest of organized groups having a particular axe to grind to distinguish publicly between the individual issues. In the first place, it should be borne in mind that there are two interrelated but separate economic aspects regarding agriculture in China; namely, agricultural production and the distribution of farm income and wealth. Since China's teeming millions eke out their meager living principally from tilling the soil, the amount of food and other crops produced and the manner in which the products, as well as the land and other factors used in their production, are shared are matters of serious and general concern. Furthermore, since China's agricultural output, though considerable, has been and still is extremely low relative to the size of the farm population, and since uneven distribution of this small product and the land which brings it forth was regarded by many as a major socio-economic problem long before the Communists' accession to power, the welfare of the peasantry could not be promoted without some change in the status quo. On the one hand, production should be increased; on the other hand, inequities in distribution should be removed. Because conditions favorable to the promotion of the first objective are not necessarily conducive to the attainment of the second, and vice versa, a potential source of confusion is always present.

In the second place, though basically an economic problem, the manner in which agricultural production is organized cannot be divorced from the realities of politics. While the average Chinese peasant, weighed down by the burden of making a living, is probably rather apathetic in the political sense, it remains true that if any organized political force can maintain a firm hold on the peasantry, it will also wield an overwhelming influence over the rest of the country. The existence of genuine economic problems and grievances has afforded militant political groups, of which the Communist Party is the outstanding example, numerous opportunities to make political capital out of them. Since the economic issue is not a simple problem of either distribution or production alone, it is not always easy to determine the precise effect of any set of proposals designed ostensibly to rid the peasantry of all its worries without an objective and thorough analysis. In the circumstances, the demagogue has little difficulty in advocating some high-sounding policy with apparent sincerity on the ground that it would solve some of the genuine problems while pursuing in reality an entirely different objective.

Finally, while the long-term interest of any government in China cannot but be tied to the success of its agricultural policy in both its production and distributive aspects, the short-term interest of a new government bent on consolidating its power need not follow a path that considerations for the welfare of the population alone might recommend. For, as the cynic will agree, once power has been consolidated, a change in policy can always be made.

Bearing the above points in mind, we may now proceed with our analysis. First, the real nature of the problem faced by Chinese agriculture as analyzed in objective studies will be compared with the Communist version. Second, the contents of Communist policy will be examined and tested against the criterion of whether it has been conducive to the solution of the real problems. Third, an attempt will be made to determine other possible motives of the Chinese Communist Party in following the course it has adopted since 1949.

This will require a brief review of the historical development of its agrarian policy in the light of the political fortunes of the Chinese Communist Party. Finally, having determined the raison-d'être of the present institutional framework of Chinese agriculture, we will return in the next chapter to an examination of the course of agricultural production in Communist China and its relation to the development of the Communists' economic policy in general.

OVER-POPULATION AND CAPITAL SCARCITY

As may be seen in Chapter II above, a basic feature of Chinese agriculture is the scarcity of land relative to the size of the population. As a matter of fact, one may even assert without exaggeration that virtually every economic problem concerning Chinese agricultural production and the distribution of land and agricultural income stems in some manner from this single fact—over-population.

The scarcity of land means that the average size of the farm is extremely small. According to a study of the 1929–1933 period which covered 16,786 farms in 22 provinces, the average size of the farm was about 25.4 *shih mow*.[1] This is substantially below the minimum size considered necessary by even the most optimistic for the peasant to make both ends meet.[2] For the small size of the farm, often further divided into scattered parcels, precludes the adoption of mechanized farming even if capital were available for the purpose.

At the same time, capital for the expansion of the farm and for the adoption of improved methods is almost as scarce as land itself. The owner farmer finds it difficult to accumulate capital because the size of his farm is too small to begin with, so that even in a normal year his income can barely keep himself and his family alive, thus ruling out altogether the possibility of savings. The tenant farmer suffers from the additional disadvantage of having to pay rent to the landlord, which, according to a 1934 study, amounted in prewar years to 50 per cent of the crop in most cases when payment was made in kind, or about 11 per cent when it was made in money.[3] Before the Communist regime this was usually a greater deduction to the tenant than the land tax was to the owner farmer. Moreover, at such a low level of income, the danger of getting into debt is always present. Once in debt, interest charges tend to make the financial position of the peasant even worse than ever. Studies of prewar conditions show that most loans to farmers were made for a period of six to twelve months at 20 to 40 per cent interest per annum. While in a small percentage of cases the interest rate might be from 10 to 20 per cent, perhaps not unduly high in view of the state of the Chinese market for rural credit, there were also cases where it exceeded 50 per cent per annum.[4]

As for the few landlords who might be in a position to make improvements, if they were not tempted to invest in non-agricultural activities, the high level of rent and interest rate acted as a strong inducement to have their savings employed merely in the expansion of existing holdings for renting or in usury loans.[5]

Under the above conditions, which were prevalent before the establishment of the new regime and, with certain modifications, are still obtained today, there is no self-generating force working towards larger farms as distinguished from larger holdings. In fact, barring a substantial increase in the amount of cultivated land,[6] larger farms must mean fewer independent farms, and, even without the introduction of machinery, fewer farmers. Unless employment can be found in non-farming occupations, it is difficult to see where the displaced farmers can go.

Thus, the economic problem of Chinese agriculture is, first and foremost, one of over-population. The most important, if not only, long-term solution lies in the opening of alternative employment opportunities which would make possible the enlargement of the farm simultaneously with a reduction of the farm population. Any policy that falls short of reducing the excessive population pressure on farm land cannot claim to be a permanent solution, whereas any policy that fails to increase the size of the farm as an operating unit would be no solution at all. Reduction of land rent and provision of better farm credit to replace usury loans, though necessary to mitigate the lot of the peasantry, cannot by themselves accomplish more than providing temporary relief.

If such is the real nature of the economic problem confronting Chinese agriculture, how does the land program of Communist China fit into the picture? Do the Chinese Communists see the problem in the same light as we have tried to describe, and what is the solution advanced?

THE COMMUNIST VERSION OF CHINA'S LAND PROBLEM

The Chinese Communists are apparently fully aware of the disadvantages of the small farm. This is eloquently proved by their recent emphasis on the need to organize mutual aid teams and cooperative farms, a development which we shall analyze presently. Nor is this realization of the importance of large-scale farming a sudden discovery made after their accession to power. Thus, one of the leading Communist economic experts wrote in early 1948 that after the impending "land reform" only very few new "middle peasants" would be permitted eventually to develop into new "rich peasants," the majority of small farmers being destined to ultimate collectivization.[7] "There is an upper limit," according to the author, "to the continuous increase in the productive efficiency of the small farmer. If we cannot bring about the gradual transformation of individual peasant farming to collectivized farming, we cannot expect an uninterrupted rise of productivity." In view of the emphasis the Communists have always placed upon agricultural developments, it is inconceivable that this same understanding of the nature of Chinese agriculture is not widely shared by others. Since the ultimate collectivization of agriculture has definitely been implied as a part of the Communists' program for China, if not always explicitly stated, there is indeed every reason to believe that the need to expand the size of the farm in order to increase production has always been understood by the Communists.

However, it is extremely significant that between 1950 and 1952 this aspect of the economic problem of Chinese agriculture was given scant public notice. In fact, it may not be an exaggeration to say that until the virtual completion of their land redistribution program in late 1952 the Chinese Communists had purposely presented, at least in public, a version of the problem that possessed an entirely different twist.

Practically all official and semi-official statements on their land program during and before this period were devoted to the issue of land ownership and distribution. The official line of the Party, as, for instance, expounded by Liu Shao-ch'i in his major speech on June 14, 1950,[8] stressed the need for land reform in China on the basis of the mal-distribution of ownership. Thus, according to Liu, some 70 to

80 per cent of China's farm land was supposedly owned by less than 10 per cent of the farm population, consisting of "landlords" and "rich peasants," while over 90 per cent of the farm population owned only 20 to 30 per cent of the land. This mal-distribution was regarded as the underlying cause of all the problems of Chinese agriculture and the fountainhead of the peasants' suffering. Consequently, land should be redistributed. The redistribution of ownership would not only enable the poor peasants to be better off, but would serve to free the productive powers of the peasantry from the "feudalistic fetters" of the oppressive land system. This release of productive energy, according to Liu, would serve to promote the development of Chinese agriculture and prepare for the country's industrialization.

Although, in expounding the Party line, Liu did not deny that land reform in the sense of redistribution could not entirely eradicate the poverty of the peasants, which would have to be accomplished through industrialization, he nevertheless contrived to convey the impression—probably intentionally and especially to the peasants—that considerable relief would be offered the peasants through the new land program. At any rate, he was most emphatic in stressing that the redistribution program was a prerequisite for the "release of productive energy" hitherto held in bound by the mal-distribution of land ownership. Others who echoed the same Party line during the entire "land reform" program also adhered closely to the above argument, though occasionally even going beyond Liu in promising the wonders a redistribution of ownership would perform.

LAND OWNERSHIP AND THE DEGREE OF CONCENTRATION

This Communist thesis on "land reform" was based on two major premises; namely, that there was a high degree of concentration of land ownership in pre-Communist China and that this state of affairs was responsible for under-development in agriculture. While there may be some truth in both of these assertions, serious doubt must be entertained on the degree of their validity, and, in particular, on the quality of the statistical data used to support the argument. First, let us consider the question of land ownership.

From the analytical point of view, it is rather unfortunate that neither Liu Shao-ch'i nor other Chinese Communists before him have ever indicated the original sources of the data that 70 to 80 per cent of China's farm land was owned by less than 10 per cent of the farm population. Our only recourse therefore is to establish whatever circumstantial evidence there is that may point to the origin of these figures.

In the first place, mention should be made of some material compiled by the Land Commission of the Hankow Government in 1928.[9] Since the Commission was dominated by Communists and since the data it provided have been quoted time and again by persons out to prove the high degree of concentration of land ownership, there is every reason to believe that the recent information advanced by Liu and others might bear a close relationship to this source.

Two separate statistical tables were published by the Hankow Land Commission. According to the first table, the total farm population of China was given as 336 million persons. Of these 150 million were land owners, 150 million were tenant farmers, 30 million were farm laborers, and 20 million were "unemployed persons, soldiers, and bandits." A second table then gave a detailed breakdown of the land owners by the size of their holdings. The particulars were:

	Average Land Owned per Household in shih mow	*Per Cent of Farm Households*		*Per Cent of Land Owned*	
"Landlords"	Over 100	5.33		43.00	
	50–100	9.57	14.90	19.40	62.40
"Rich Peasants"	30 to 50		16.21		17.44
"Middle Peasants"	10 to 30		24.73		13.26
"Poor Peasants"	1 to 10		44.45		6.16
			100.00[1]		100.00[1]

1. Totals do not add up to 100, presumably due to rounding.

Since the entire "landlord" group constituted 44.45 per cent of the 105 million land owners in a total farm population of 336 million, it represented only 6.5 per cent of the total farm population. Computed in the same manner, the proportion of "rich peasants" in the total population would be 7.1 per cent; that of "middle peasants," 11 per cent; that of "poor peasants" and the landless, 75.4 per cent. Consequently, one could say that the "landlords" and "rich peasants," while constituting only 13.6 per cent of the farm population, owned 79.84 per cent of the total farm land. On the other hand, the remaining 86.4 per cent of the farm population owned only 20.16 per cent of the farm land. These figures are very close to the more recent version presented by the Communists.

In the second place, reference should be made to the estimates given by two individual Communist authors concerning the distribution of land ownership in China:

Ch'en Han-seng's Estimates

	Per Cent of Farm Households	*Per Cent of Land Owned*
"Landlords"	4	50
"Rich Peasants"	6	15
"Middle Peasants"	20	20
"Poor Peasants"	70	15
	100	100
Total Farm Land	1.4 billion *shih mow*	

Source: Quoted in *Economic Bulletin,* No. 180, p. 11, Hongkong, July, 1950.

T'ao Chih-fu's Estimates

	Average Land Owned per Household in shih mow	*Per Cent of Farm Households*	*Per Cent of Land Owned*
"Landlords"	292	4	50
"Rich Peasants"	70	6	18
"Middle Peasants"	18	20	15
"Poor Peasants"	6	70	17
		100	100
Total Farm land	1.4 billion *shih mow*		

Source: T'ao Chih-fu, *The Present Stage of China's Land Problem,* quoted in Chin I-hung, *Communist China's Land Reform and China's Land Problem,* pp. 5-6, Hongkong, 1950.

According to these later sources, only 10 per cent of the country's farm population as constituted by the "landlords" and "rich peasants" owned 65 to 68 per cent of the total farm land, leaving only 32 to 35 per cent of the land to the remainder of the farm households. These figures, too, are quite compatible with the situation depicted by Liu.

Whether the present Communist officials actually employed the data circulated by the 1928 Land Commission and/or the estimates by T'ao and Ch'en is of little consequence. For they have never published any comprehensive survey of their own while the figures they did use in their arguments, and still do, actually coincide with these earlier estimates. The important issue, therefore, is whether the latter were authentic or representative of actual conditions in pre-Communist China.

The Hankow Land Commission rather characteristically failed to disclose the manner in which the findings were arrived at. As far as the distribution of the farm population by land owners, tenant farmers, and other groups is concerned, it has been suggested by Wu Wen-hui in his *China's Land Problem and Its Solution* that the figures are altogther unreliable and were probably put forward by the Communists for ulterior political purposes at the time their split with the Kuomintang occurred. As for the second table made available by the Land Commission, the data are virtually identical with the information contained in the *Agricultural and Commercial Statistics* published by the former Ministry of Agriculture and Commerce in 1918 which, however, dealt with the distribution of farm households by farm size. In other words, the Land Commission, without disclosing the source of its information, had taken over the data on *farm size* and reproduced them as findings on land *ownership*. Whether this was done inadvertently or with intention cannot now be determined, but the validity of such information is obviously nil.

As for the ownership distribution data furnished by Ch'en and T'ao, which are essentially the same, doubt must also be expressed on their accuracy. As Wu Wen-hui has pointed out, both these authors included in their total number of farm households public and religious bodies and communal organizations.[10] As the latter groups were classified as "landlords," the degree of concentration was consequently overestimated. In an estimate of his own published in 1934, a different set of figures was advanced by Wu as follows:

	Average Land Owned per Household in shih mow	*Per Cent of Farm Households*	*Per Cent of Land Owned*
"Landlords"	173	3	26
"Rich Peasants"	77	7	27
"Middle Peasants"	33	22	25
"Poor Peasants and Farm Laborers"	7	68	22
		100	100

However, even these estimates can hardly be accepted at their face value. For if 68 per cent of total farm households owned only 22 per cent of the land, obviously the peasants in question would have to work as tenants and/or farm laborers. This, however, is not borne out by the statistics on farm tenancy compiled from the *Crop Reports* of the National Agricultural Research Bureau. On the basis of returns from 1,058 counties, for instance, tenant farmers were reported to account for only 30 per cent of total farm households in 1937; part tenants, 24 per cent; owner farmers, 46 per cent.[11] Even lower percentage figures were reported by Professor Buck in his volume on *Land Utilization in China*[12] which was also based on an impressive sampling. In terms of total farm households, the data derived from Buck's study of the 1929-1933 period were: tenant farmers, 17 per cent; part tenants, 29 percent; owner farmers, 54 per cent. If, for the sake of argument, we should use the higher tenancy figures, still only 54 per cent of the total farm households would consist of tenants and part tenants, which is considerably lower than the proportion alloted to "poor peasants and hired laborers," by Wu Wen-hui. Granted that some peasants worked as hired laborers *only* and should not be regarded as tenants or even part tenants, it is equally true that not all tenants and part tenants were "poor peasants."

The same problem may also be looked at from a different angle by comparing the relative importance of owner farmers with that of " landlords" and "rich" and "middle peasants." Clearly, the majority, if not all, of the last three groups would be owner farmers. Yet the latter groups were estimated by Ch'en, T'ao, and Wu as constituting about 30 per cent of total farm households. This compares with 46 per cent for owner farmers. Accepting the latter figure as the more reliable of the two, one could not reconcile them unless one were to assume that some owner farmers were "poor peasants." However, this is hardly plausible inasmuch as if they were "poor peasants," there would be every inducement for them to rent more land and to become part tenants, thus ceasing to be owner farmers.

Lack of complete comparability between studies of tenancy and the various estimates by Ch'en, T'ao, and Wu precludes an absolute refutation of these figures. However, in view of the latter's doubtful quality, the validity of the Communist argument must be seriously questioned. If the degree of concentration of ownership even approximated that alleged by the Communist authorities, there should be a much higher percentage of tenants and part tenants than has been established by objective and extensive studies such as those of Buck and the National Agricultural Research Bureau. Besides, the identification of tenancy with poverty is certainly an over-simplification.

PRODUCTIVITY AND DISTRIBUTION OF OWNERSHIP

As for the second argument of the Chinese Communists, viz., that land redistribution would immediately "release large, latent productive forces," two different interpretations are possible. In the first place, it may mean that tenant farmers and laborers work less or less hard than owner farmers. In the second place, it may mean that investment in various farm improvements tend to be smaller under a land system which has a large number of tenant farmers.

The first point is more than debatable. For tenant farmers in China are often among the more efficient, and it is more than probable that the lower one's income, the harder one will work. The mere fact that tenant farmers have to pay land rent does not mean that they will have less inducement to work hard or will be less efficient. In fact, according to a 1941 study of the former Farmers' Bank of China, tenant farms often showed a higher rate of return than owner farms in cases where the former were larger in size.

As for the second interpretation, obviously capital improvements and similar betterments requiring large outlay cannot be made when income is very low. As we have already pointed out earlier, where land rent and interest rates are unduly high, land owners in a position to make such improvements might be induced to expand their holdings instead of investing further in their existing holdings. However, the basic cause of such developments would appear to lie in the high level of land rent and interest rate which could have been changed independently of any forcible redistribution of land. In fact, abstracting from the factors of high rent and interest rates, an increase in the income of the very poor peasants at the expense of those who are better off may conceivably result in an increase in consumption and a reduction of investment. At any rate, such a redistribution of income and land as envisaged in the Communists' "land reform" program could not automatically increase investments in land and hence agricultural production.

IMPORTANCE ATTACHED TO THE LAND PROGRAM BY COMMUNIST CHINA

Even though the principle of the "land reform" instituted all over China shortly after the inauguration of the Communist regime was on the distributive aspect only and the degree of concentration of land ownership was exaggerated, the program still deserves our close attention, if for no other reason than that great importance was attached by the Communists themselves to its fulfilment.

In his speech on June 23, 1950, at the final meeting of the second session of the National Committee of the People's Consultative Conference in Peking, Mao Tse-tung declared that "the evolution of Communism in China must pass through three critical stages, each of which is the prerequisite of the succeeding stage of development. These three stages are marked by the civil war, the land program, and the realization of socialism." In other words, according to Mao, the realization of the land program would be impossible without the successful conclusion of the civil war, whereas the advent of socialism under the aegis of the Communist Party would be virtually unthinkable without the successful conclusion of the "land reform." In addition to the general pronouncement, further evidence of the vital position occupied by the land problem in the Chinese Communist Party's agenda may be found in the time schedule outlined by Liu Shao-ch'i.[13]

By June, 1950, according to Liu, "land reform" had already been either completely or basically carried out in areas with a farm population of 145 million or a total population of 160 million. On top of this result, some three hundred counties with a total farm population of about 100 million were at the time clamouring for similar "reform" during the winter of 1950. In terms of the size of the farm population to be affected, the regional breakdown of these "requests" was: (1) North China, 3,500,000; (2) Northwest China, 8,000,000; (3) East China, 35,000,000 to 40,000,000; and (5) Central-South China, 47,000,000 to 56,000,000. As for the remaining farm population of about 164 million persons, the program as envisaged in June, 1950, provided for their inclusion partly in the second half of 1951 and partly towards the end of 1952. By the end of 1952 only scattered areas inhabited mostly by the non-Chinese minority races would remain unaffected. However, conditions in certain parts of Manchuria inhabited by Koreans and Mongols would by then be ripe for the same treatment although no time table could as yet be set for the remaining areas inhabited by some 20 million persons of non-Chinese extraction.

Considering the magnitude of the task involved, the schedule announced in June, 1950, was certainly an ambitious one. However, the actual time table was even further shortened. According to official data released in June, 1951,[14] 156.8 million of the farm population, instead of the 145 million mentioned by Liu, had actually been subjected to the "land reform" process before spring, 1950, including the whole of Manchuria and North China, as well as 45 million peasants in East China, 1.8 million in the Northwest, and 17 million in Central-South China. In addition, another 128.3 million peasants underwent the program during the winter of 1950 and in the following spring, as compared with the 100 million originally mentioned by Liu, the latter figure including even parts of North China and Manchuria and the Honan province in the Central-South, which had already completed their work at the time of Liu's speech, but had been left out in his compilation.

The speed-up was brought about through a considerable expansion of the original program in Central-South China, the inclusion of the entire area of East China, and the initiation of the program in the Southwest earlier than it was first contemplated. Apparently, for reasons which will become clear later, Communist China's participation in the Korean War had acted as a spur to the entire process. An indication of the enormous effort exerted by the Communist government in bringing the program to a rapid conclusion may also be found in the number of persons engaged in field teams. According to an official statement by the Deputy Secretary-General of the State Administrative Council,[15] such workers, the majority being Party stalwarts, totalled over 300,000 a year. From the Communists' point of view, as reported later by Chou En-lai, the result was probably well worthwhile. For by August, 1951, the land program had already been completed in an area with a farm population of 310 million, which was 25 million more than the record shown only two months earlier.[16] A year later, in August, 1952, it was again reported that more than 90 per cent of the country's farm population, or some 360 million persons, had undergone "land reform," while the total population involved now reached 428 million.[17] With the exception of Sinkiang, Tibet, and areas inhabited by non-Chinese minority races, only 30 million peasants had not yet experienced "land reform," but they were scheduled for similar treatment not later than the spring of 1953, and reports have since confirmed the completion of the program to all intents and purposes.

PRINCIPLE AND PRACTICE UNDER THE 1950 "LAND REFORM" LAW

The basic law governing "land reform" under the present regime was adopted on June 28, 1950, by the Communist Government Council and was made public at the end of the month.[18] Its 34 main articles, together with six additional articles in a supplement, provide some extremely interesting reading.

A major provision of the law is that land ownership must be transferred from certain persons to others. This process, however, involves several separate steps as described below:

a. *Rent Reduction and Interest Curb*

Restrictions on the level of rent and interest charges are regarded as a preliminary step towards "land reform," or the moderate beginning of a revolution. They were made a prerequisite of "land reform" in a general ruling issued by the Chinese Communist Party in September, 1949, for all newly occupied areas, and the principle was incorporated in the Common Program. Regulations applicable to individual regions were later promulgated by the various regional authorities in the course of 1949 and 1950.[19] The contents of these regulations are generally alike and fall into the same pattern as the wartime rent reduction regulations introduced in Communist-occupied areas.

The provisions on land rent consist of, as a rule: (1) a 25 per cent reduction of existing rent, (2) a rent ceiling equal to 37.5 per cent of the normal annual yield of the principal crop, (3) prohibition of advance rent payment, extra obligations to landlords, and secondary letting, (4) refunding of rental deposits, and (5) cancellation of past unpaid rent. The usual restrictions on loan and interest charges are: (1) an interest rate ceiling of 1.5 per cent per month, (2) cancellation of interest charges if the sum of past payments exceeds the original loan by 100 per cent, and (3) outright cancellation of indebtedness if the sum of past payments exceeds the original loan by 200 per cent. These provisions are, however, directed principally against the so-called "landlords" and "rich peasants" while contractual relations between "middle" and "poor" peasants are exempt. Similarly, exemption from rent reduction may be allowed on small amounts of land belonging to certain groups, including members of the Communist army, Party workers and their families. This preferential treatment accorded to the above special groups suggests a class differentiation which is the next important ingredient in "land reform."

b. *Class Differentiation*

The basic step towards the solution of the problem of identifying the persons who should be deprived of their land holdings either in whole or in part, as well as the beneficiaries, is the artificial division of the rural population into four main social classes. These are:

1. "landlords,"
2. "rich peasants,"
3. "middle peasants," and
4. "poor peasants" and "farm laborers."

Broadly speaking, the losers are the "landlords" and the "rich peasants." On the other hand, the beneficiaries are mostly the "poor peasants" and "farm laborers" and, to a lesser extent, those "middle peasants" who are relatively poor. This being so, a most important factor is obviously presented by the criteria employed in determining the class status of individual peasants and the mechanism through which the class label is affixed.

As early as 1933 two documents were issued by the Communist regime at Jui-Chin in Kiangsi, entitled "How to Differentiate Agricultural Classes" and "Decisions Appertaining to Certain Problems in Land Reform." These documents were reissued by the Central Committee of the Chinese Communist Party on May 25, 1948, and their provisions were applied in practice in the Party's land program subsequent to that date. With only a few modifications, the same documents were reissued by the State Administrative Council following a resolution adopted by the Council at its 44th meeting. The new document contains, therefore, the greater part of the earlier documents together with certain supplementary decisions of the Council. This serves now as the basis of class differentiation. It works as follows:

1. The characteristic which above all relegates a person (and his family) to the "landlord" class is that he does not perform "essential" labor himself in cultivating land. In other words, the "landlord" is a person who leases land to others in return for land rent which constitutes his principal source of income. He does not toil on the land himself.

2. The "rich peasant" is a person who derives his income wholly or in part from "exploitation" by hiring farm laborers and lending money. He may be a land owner himself, or he may be a tenant or a part tenant. He may perform farm labor himself or he may not. But the principal fact that determines his status is his "exploitation" of others as an employer and as a money lender.[20]

3. The "middle peasant" is a person who depends either entirely or largely upon his own labor for his livelihood. He may be a tenant or a part tenant, or he may own his land, but he does not sell his labor to others or lend money or lease land to others to such a degree that his "exploitation" of others would be considered excessive.

4. The "poor peasant" and the "farm laborer" are, of course, those who either own insufficient land or no land at all. They have to rent land from others or be the subject of "exploitation" through loan interest. They are distinguished from the "middle peasants" by the fact that they are forced to sell at least a part of their labor to others.

Several things may be noted in this connection. In the first place, it appears that "exploitation" is a very important determinant. Yet the term has not been clearly defined either in these or in related documents. Second, if we were to assume that exploitation consists of the mere fact of money lending or being an employer of hired labor or a lessor of land, we should immediately have to face the paradoxical situation that it is not really these employer-employee, creditor-debtor, or landlord-tenant relationships as such that determine the class status of a person, but rather whether the income derived from these means constitutes the principal part of the individual's income. The degree of "exploitation" is not measured by the level of the land rent or the rate of interest or the wage rate, but rather by the relative importance to a person of rental and interest receipts and the "exploitation" income squeezed from hired hands. In other words, all these fine distinctions are by no means logically consistent. Nor, indeed, one suspects, are they meant to be. The various distinctions which mark out one class from another serve only as a rough guide to differentiate the rich from the poor within any particular locality.

Since, according to the 1950 law, the redistribution of land is conducted within an individual administrative unit known as a *hsiang* which is composed of a number of villages, and since both the population and the amount of land in a *hsiang* vary from one place to another, so that per capita average holdings differ in size, it is entirely conceivable that a person who may fall into one category in one locality would probably fall into a different category if he were residing elsewhere, although the absolute value of his wealth may be the same. Moreover, as the number of persons performing "essential" labor relative to the size of the family also affects the latter's status as a "landlord family," the determination of class status for an individual often is not separated from the characteristics of the family as a whole. The arbitrariness of the criteria of class differentiation and their extreme flexibility have the effect of vesting tremendous power in the hands of those who actually perform the task of labelling every person in the area of "land reform" with a class tag. Who are these people and how do they operate?

c. *The Peasants' Associations and the Assembly of the Peasants' Representatives*

Supervision and direction of the "land reform" program are provided by special Commissions established at different levels of local government, but the executive function in enforcement is vested in the Assemblies of Peasants' Representatives. The latter consist of delegates from Peasants' Associations and non-Association members whose representative status has been approved by the Associations. The Association itself derives its membership from the "poor" and "middle peasants," "farm laborers," and artisans, as well as members of the poor "revolutionary intelligentsia" of the locality and Party cadres sent to the spot as organizers. The last element constitutes the "charter members" of the Association and is, of course, the leading spirit. The Assembly of Peasants' Representatives is not always in session. Its executive power is therefore vested in a committee of the Peasants' Association elected by the Assembly. Both organizations exist at the level of the *hsiang,* as well as at higher administrative levels; but it is the Peasants' Association, or rather its executive committee, which really exercises supreme power in "land reform" at the grass roots, including the determination of class status and the redistribution of land.

In plain language, what really transpires when an area is to be subjected to the rigors of the land program may be briefly summarized as follows.

First, the local Party authorities would send Party cadres as organizers to the *hsiang*. There they would organize a Peasants' Association by getting together a handful of the poorest and the shiftless. Once officially established, this Association would go through the motion of organizing the election of Peasants' Representatives in order to convene an Assembly. The Assembly would produce in a mass meeting an executive committee for the Association which naturally would consist of Party cadres and a few of their henchmen inasmuch as few of the peasants in general would really know what the entire proceedings were about. Once "legally" constituted, the committee would go about its business of determining the class status of the entire population in an area by following a well-tried technique, the essential elements of which consist of the following:

1. Since "land reform" is supposed to be a spontaneous mass movement, the determination of class status is carried out by means of an initial self-appraisal of his own class status by the individual being processed, followed by so-called democratic and public appraisals by other members of the population at a public meeting called by the Peasants' Association. Arguments that may develop in the course of this discussion would be settled by the Party cadres who keep the meetings under control so that any mistake or deviation from the principles laid down by the Party would be immediately corrected.

2. Since the rural population is neither familiar with the class concepts employed nor necessarily in sympathy with such an artificial differentiation, it is necessary to bring about an emotional frenzy in the mob and to stimulate the natural greed of the poor. Consequently, the Party organizers are invariably instructed to rely upon the "poor" peasants and the farm laborers to provide the initial drive. These are given a more or less free hand to help themselves with the property of the relatively rich members of the local population in order to show how concrete material benefits may be obtained through "land reform." This goes under the name of "participation in enjoying the fruits of the anti-feudal movement."

3. In order to produce a highly hysterical state of mind, individuals are encouraged at these public meetings to relate all past real and imaginary wrongs which they have suffered at the hands of the marked

victims or their forefathers. Planted agents in the mob are always available to keep the meetings at a high emotional pitch just in case no one comes forward to provide a sufficient number of accusations against local "despots."

4. As a result of these accusations, open violence to the accused, resulting in bodily harm and not infrequently violent deaths, will almost always break out.

5. In order to provide a semblance of orderly procedure and due process of "law," some of the accused may be brought in front of local People's Courts, organized especially for the purpose of enforcing the land program. These courts are constituted by a chief judge and his assistant, and a number of "jurors." Both the chief judge and his assistant, as well as one-half of the "jurors," are appointed by the local government, i.e., the Party, while the rest of the "jurors" are elected by local People's Representative Assemblies and People's Associations which in the farming areas are identical with the Peasants' Associations or the Assemblies of Peasants' Representatives. Since the latter are controlled by the Party, this means that the court represents the will of the Party. These People's Courts are empowered to arrest, imprison, and pronounce sentences, including capital punishment. In the case of death sentences, confiscation of property, and imprisonment for a period of more than five years, the principal administrative official at a higher level has the power of review. However, it is further provided in the organizational law of the People's Courts that in the case of "bandit agents and counter-revolutonaries" the death sentence may not be appealed. Moreover, the organizational law of the People's Courts also stipulates that all decisions of the court regarding class determination must be carried out immediately upon pronouncement. Furthermore, it is provided as a sop to the legalistically minded that the accused may have the right to defend himself or to engage a third person for his defense under the condition that the defense counsel in this case must be acceptable to the court and approved by it.

A great deal has been heard about the violence and mob hysteria engendered at these mass "accusation" and "anti-despot" meetings and trials. Communist leaders have every now and then pronounced against such happenings and labelled the excesses as deviations.[21] Yet the practice is of long standing and shows clear signs of being an integral part of a calculated tactical maneuver. Besides, the use of violence appears to have its origin in the Communists' conception of revolution which, in its Chinese version, has been clearly expounded by Mao Tse-tung himself. In his report of March, 1927, on the peasant movement in Hunan, a document which has since become the bible of "land reform" and has been printed in many collections of Communist literature, Mao Tse-tung declared that "those localities where the peasant revolts have been most violent are also localities where the landlords and local despots have been most repressive beforehand.[22] The eyes of the peasants are crystally clear and never perpetrate a mistake." In addition to this explanation that violence is only a reaction to past wrongdoing suffered by the peasants, Mao further points out in the same work that "revolution is violence. . . . It is a violent action in which one class attempts to overthrow the power of another. The agrarian revolution is a revolution by the peasantry aiming at the overthrow of the power of the feudalistic landlord class. . . . Great revolutionary enthusiasm must be generated in the villages in order to arouse the tens of thousands of peasants to forge a tremendous power. . . . These actions (of violence) are extremely necessary during the revolutionary period of the peasant movement. . . . All excessive acts possess their revolutionary significance. In plain language, every village must go through a short period of terror without which counter-revolutionary activities cannot be suppressed." Again according to Mao, the techniques of attack on the political power of the "landlords" during the "land reform" movement are, inter alia, fines, forced contributions, liquidation, "small" accusations, public demonstrations, public insults, imprisonment, and death. From this it would appear that violence is in fact not a deviation, but rather a calculated attempt to stir up artificial class hatred, general distrust, mass hysteria, and social disintegration in order to facilitate the class struggle.

d. *Confiscation and "Requisition"*

Land transferred to the beneficiaries during "land reform" is obtained by confiscation. The exact extent of confiscation has changed from time to time. This is true especially in the case of the property of the "rich peasants" and a historical review of this factor must be made in order to throw light on the real intent of the land program of the Communist Party. For the moment we shall, however, confine ourselves to the propositions of the "land reform" law of June, 1950. According to this enactment, the land, farm animals, tools, and surplus grains and foodstuffs, as well as the surplus houses in the village belonging to a person classified as a "landlord" are to be confiscated.[23] It is noteworthy that just as the word "confiscation" has a clear meaning, the term "surplus" is left deliberately vague. A very significant provision is Article 5 of the law which stipulates that unless the amount of land leased to others is excessive, the lessor may not be considered as a "landlord" if he is a member of the family of a revolutionary soldier or martyr, a worker, an employee of recognized institutions, a member of certain professions, or a small tradesman, who is not able to till his own land for want of physical capacity or time. This is a very significant provision which appears in one form or another in all the various versions of Communist laws and regulations affecting their land policy. It is clearly intended to guarantee to the members of the armed forces and of the Party that their land would not be confiscated by virtue of a legerdemain in class differentiation and to offer similar privileges to the intelligentsia as long as it conforms to the Party line. To this we shall return later.

There are a number of other provisions governing different types of property which may be confiscated, but probably the most interesting part of the law in this respect is the treatment meted out to "rich peasants." According to Article 6 of the same law, land cultivated by "rich peasants" themselves or hired labor and their other assets may not be violated. The same applies to small amounts of land rented out by "rich peasants," with the exception that, in special areas and upon order by higher authorities, a part or even the entirety of land rented out by "rich peasants" may be "requisitioned." Where the amount of land rented out by "rich peasants" of the "landlord" type is large, that part which is not cultivated by themselves and by hired labor should also be "requisitioned."

Very characteristically, the term "requisition" is not defined by the law. It is used in this connection in lieu of "confiscation," suggesting thereby that some compensation will be forthcoming, but as far as one can ascertain, this compensation, which has never been explicitly promised, has also never really been paid. Perhaps one can understand the meaning of the term "requisition" better by referring to an earlier document entitled "Provisional Regulations on the Requisition Purchase of Land Owned by Landlords in the Shensi-Kansu-Ningsia Border Region," published in December, 1946. This regulation stipulates that surplus land in excess of the permissible per capita holding in "landlord" households, which is defined as 150 per cent of the average per capita holding of a "middle peasant's" household, is subject to requisition. Article 6, Chapter 3, of this law stipulates that the price at which the requisitioned land is to be bought must be within the range of value of one to two years' harvest of the land in question. Article 8 further provides that if the compensation thus paid to a "landlord" is under 5 piculs of grain, the entire amount should be paid. If the compensation exceeds 5 piculs but is below 10 piculs, only 80 per cent of the second 5 piculs should be paid. The progressive rates of discount continue in such a way that if the total hypothetical compensation should exceed 30 piculs, any amount over and above this figure would not be included in computing payments. A little computation would demonstrate that no matter how much land is "requisitioned" from an individual "landlord," the maximum amount of compensation he would receive would be 15½ piculs of grain or their equivalent. The same text also refers to payment by land bonds, but no clear provision exists as to how this is to be done. "Requisition" in this particular case is disguised confiscation, and there is reason to believe that the same is true in regard to "requisition" under the 1950 law.

e. *The Method of Land Redistribution*

Once the process of class differentiation has been under way, land for redistribution becomes available. Whatever may be this amount, its redistribution among the eligible section of the population follows several general principles. In the first place, redistribution takes place within individual administrative units known as the *hsiang*. That is, confiscated land within a particular *hsiang* is redistributed to eligible residents of the same *hsiang*. Second, the standard governing the amount of land every eligible person is to receive depends upon the size of the average per capita holding of the *hsiang* in question. In a densely populated area where the average per capita holding is small, redistribution will bring about smaller actual holdings in general than in a more sparsely populated area. It is thus obvious that where the problem of land shortage is most acute, this method of redistribution will bring out its full impact in making practically all farm units well under the economic or optimum size. This factor should, however, be considered in conjunction with the fact that both the amount of land available for redistribution and the number of eligible beneficiaries may be drastically altered by subtle changes in the implementation of the class differentiation process and the treatment accorded separate class categories.

Eligibility to share in the benefit of redistribution is principally determined by class status. The "poor peasants" and "farm laborers" are two main categories, but it is important to note that the occupational criterion of farming is not the only one employed in determining eligibility. Once again, Party workers and members of the armed forces are accorded preferential treatment. Article 13, Chapter 3, of the 1950 Law provides, inter alia, that family members of "revolutionary martyrs" resident in the farming areas, members of the "People's Liberation Army," including officers, privates, honored soldiers, demobilized servicemen, as well as functionaries of the government and workers of "people's organizations" (thus making sure that the Party is included), and family members of persons of the above categories, including those who are camp followers and, therefore, not local residents, are to receive equal shares in land and other means of production in the same way as the peasants, except that in the case of government functionaries and workers of people's organizations, their share may be varied in accordance with their other incomes. In determining the allotment to families within these special groups of persons, not only their family members, but also these persons themselves, who are otherwise employed and usually nonresident, are included in computing the size of land and the amount of other assets they are entitled to as the calculations are based on per capita values within the area in question multiplied by the number of persons within the eligible family. In the case of "martyrs," even the dead are counted, thus transforming the land allotment into a type of post facto life insurance for former Communists. This preferential treatment of Party workers and Communist officials should be considered together with the Communist State Administrative Council's supplementary ruling concerning class differentiation which reinforces the provision of Article 5, Chapter 2, of the 1950 "Land Reform" Law, allowing these special families to lease land to others without being considered as "landlords" and to possess a per capita holding twice the size of the average in the same area without becoming liable to the impediments of being better off than the next man.

A HISTORICAL REVIEW OF THE TREATMENT OF "RICH PEASANTS"

In the carefully engineered class struggle through "land reform," the current slogan employed by the Communists, which may rightly be described as the Party line, consists of the following dicta: "Depend upon the 'poor peasants' and 'hired laborers.' Consolidate the 'middle peasants.' Neutralize the 'rich peasants.'" The different treatments promised these three class categories in the 1950 law correspond closely to this Party line. However, the Party has not always wanted to neutralize the "rich peasants," and the evolution that has led to the present position is well worth explaining.

The early pronouncements of the Communist Party on the fate of the "rich peasant" class were far more outspoken. Article 1 of the provisional Land Law adopted by the First Soviet in Shanghai in May, 1930, stipulated uncompromisingly the confiscation of all holdings owned by "landlords" as well as the land of "rich peasants" not cultivated by the owners.[24] More revealing, however, is a passage from an article by a Communist writer on "How the Chinese Soviet Government Solves the Land Problem" published in the Party's official organ in Shanghai, *The Red Banner*. sometime in 1933–34. "The present stage of the agrarian revolution," according to the author, "naturally also requires the (eventual) liquidation of the 'rich peasant.' His land must, of course, also be confiscated. But . . . the confiscation of the landlord's land aims at the complete liquidation of the landlord class, while the confiscation of land owned by 'rich peasants' does not have the same purpose of liquidating the 'rich peasants,' because the stage of the latter's destruction has not yet been reached at the present time. . . . The imposition of restrictions on the development of 'rich peasants' is meant to enable the 'middle' and 'poor peasants' to reap greater benefit from the agrarian revolution."[25] A little further on in the same article we find the author stating that "the complete elimination of feudal relationship in farm areas can be achieved only through land nationalization which is the inevitable and highest form of rapid development for an agrarian economy." This statement fully anticipated Mao Tse-tung's 1950 speech calling for the eventual socialization of agriculture. Thus the "rich peasants" were scheduled for ultimate liquidation even though the time was not yet ripe in the early thirties. Mao's 1950 pronouncement has the same ring.

The Sino-Japanese War brought about a temporary shift of policy. The civil war was halted for the time being, and increase in agricultural production was a matter of great concern. Even more important was the need to pose as liberal reformers who abhorred violence for the benefit of Western observers and the swelling rank of Chinese sympathizers. Accordingly, the Central Political Bureau adopted a resolution on January 28, 1942, less than two months after Pearl Harbor, calling for the reduction of rent and interest in return for guaranteed payments by tenants and debtors and the suspension of the confiscation and redistribution program. The Party line was to encourage production by "rich peasants" and to join hands with the "rich peasant" class.

The tenancy and interest regulations of the Shansi-Chahar-Hopeh Border Region adopted on January 21, 1943, at the first session of the Political Consultative Council of the Shansi-Chahar-Hopeh Region and proclaimed on February 4, 1943, by the local Communist authorities followed the Party line laid down in 1942.

Among others, the provisions of the regulations include a 25 per cent rent reduction, a rent ceiling fixed at 37.5 per cent of the annual output of the chief crop, safeguards with respect to land tenure, the fixing of interest rates on new loans by free contract, an interest ceiling of 10 per cent per annum for existing debts, the cessation of interest payment if previous payments already total more than the principal of the original loan, and the outright cancellation of indebtedness if previous interest payments amount to more than twice the original principal. These relatively liberal provisions were entirely in line with the wartime Party program which was also at this time cleverly reinforced by Mao through his proposed program for a "new democracy." As we have already noted in an earlier chapter, it was then declared by Mao that during the period of the new democracy, the economy of "rich peasants" would be tolerated.

Once the war was over and the struggle for political power became more acute, the land program took another turn. The liquidation movement in newly "liberated" areas was inaugurated in May, 1946, in order to acquire more land for further redistribution. From May, 1946, to September, 1947, it appears that this aggressive policy was pushed forward with energy. In September, 1947, a National Land Conference was called by the Communist Party which adopted on September 13, 1947, an "Outline of Land Law for China." This last instrument was proclaimed on October 10, 1947, after it had received the wholehearted endorsement of the Party's Central Committee. In proclaiming the abolition of the land system of "feudal and semi-feudal exploitation," the Outline called for the abolition of land ownership of all "landlords" and the confiscation of surplus property of "rich peasants," the redistribution of confiscated property, including land and other assets, on the basis of an equal amount per head, and the abolition of all tenancy and debt contracts dated prior to the inauguration of "land reform."

Since the announcement of the Outline, Party spokesmen repeatedly have pointed to it as a considerable liberalization in the treatment of "rich peasants," inasmuch as not all property of the "rich peasants" would be confiscated, but only their "surplus" property. By "surplus" was meant presumably any excess over the average per capita value in the district. This doubtful betterment was belied by the subsequent official announcements which followed in a public proclamation by the Peasants' Association of the Shansi-Suiyuan Border Region.[26] The local Party authorities stated that all "landlords" were to be liquidated and that although the "rich peasants" should be treated differently, their feudalistic exploitation and oppression had to be eliminated. "Their surplus land, grains, farm animals, implements, and other property must also be surrendered. Those among them who are criminal despots must be punished *in whatever way the people should wish.*" Furthermore, the pronouncement by the Party denounced the redistribution of land according to any principle other than completely equal distribution on a per capita basis as every other way would constitute a deviation in favor of "rich peasants."

As the civil war progressed, new developments in connection with the treatment of "landlords" and "rich peasants" came to light. In his speech on January 12, 1948, at the Northwest Field Army Front Line Committee,[27] the late Jen Pi-shih emphasized the need to placate the "middle peasants" although the latter were admittedly not reliable or enthusiastic in the class struggle. As for the "rich peasants" and "landlords," he saw in them the source of an expanding labor force. "We should require those 'landlords,'" said Jen, "who have surrendered their land and other property to perform labor. We should regard the 'landlords' and 'rich peasants' as the country's labor force, and compel them to seek self-redemption through work." Holding out further the possibility of a reclassification of their class status as an incentive for exemplary conduct, Jen stated in the same speech: "'Landlords' who have performed labor for five years and 'rich peasants' who have ceased to exploit others for three years may be reclassified. . . . The few 'landlords' and 'rich peasants' who have been allowed to join the People's Liberation Army and have served two complete years, as well as members of the intelligentsia born of 'landlord' or 'rich peasant' families or of families of other exploiters who have joined up for a period of 12 months may also attain the status of members of the revolutionary army."

Jen's speech in which he pointed out the manner in which the "rich peasants" and "landlords" should be employed was further supplemented by subsequent announcements and speeches which throw more light on the nature of the land program. While Jen's speech stresses the need to placate the "middle peasants," a directive of the Central Committee of the Communist Party on February 2, 1948, dealing with "land reform" and Party discipline in "old" and "semi-old liberated areas" stated that, if necessary, land of the "middle peasants" could also be redistributed so as to narrow the gap of the average holdings between "middle" and "poor peasants," although it was mentioned in the same directive that the center of support and organization in carrying out the land program should be gradually shifted from the "poor" to the "middle peasants" as the latter became numerically more and more important. This last point regarding the establishment of a firm basis for the land program and for the Party among the "middle peasants" was clearly a policy aimed at reducing the strength of the opposition. This view appears to be confirmed by Mao Tse-tung's speech of April 1, 1948, to the Party cadres of the Shansi-Suiyuan area,[28] while commenting on the systematic destruction of "feudalistic exploitation." Mao declared that it was necessary to practice the policy of neutralizing "rich peasants" and small "landlords" in newly "liberated" areas where firm occupation was still in doubt. This policy, according to Mao, was calculated to be the first stage of the systematic destruction of "feudalism" in the new areas.

As one looks over the gradual evolution of the changing policy of the Communist Party from the early 30's to the late 40's, one cannot help but gain the impression that the twists and turns were entirely calculated to secure political advantages. The Communist Party was probably honest in its assertion in the early days that the destruction of private peasant economy, including the "rich peasants" as well as the "middle peasants," and the nationalization of agriculture constitute the ultimate objective. The wartime policy of rent and interest regulation which approached the then unenforced program of the Kuomintang was a tactical retreat designed, as one now looks at it with the benefit of hindsight, principally to mislead the liberal elements at home and abroad.

The postwar developments mentioned above have shown great flexibility in class differentiation and in the treatment of different class categories. The "rich peasants" and the "landlords" are those subjected to systematic liquidation and are regarded as a potential pool of forced labor. Where Communist power was not firmly established and where strenuous oppression might prove embarrassing, temporary appeasement would be practiced. The "rich peasants" especially should be neutralized whereas the "landlords" as a whole should be subjected to more severe treatment because after all there are more "rich peasants" than "landlords" and it is wise to choose a minority as the first victim. This also explains the repeated emphasis on the corresponding enlargement of the base of support and its shift from "poor peasants" who should be employed as a spearhead in "land reform" because of their natural enthusiasm to the "middle peasants" who are numerically important. Yet even the "middle peasants" may be losers in land redistribution if and when the "poor peasants' " demands cannot be otherwise satiated.

II

SOME ECONOMIC EFFECTS OF "LAND REFORM"

In all probability, most people would readily agree that *other things being equal,* for a segment of the population, namely, some of the small tenant farmers and farm laborers who belong to the "poor peasant" class, rent and interest reduction, cancellation of past debts and deposit refunds, followed by the receipt of small parcels of land and other property, as well as the sharing of spoils, might bring about a certain improvement in material welfare in the short run. For others "land reform" has been little less than a catastrophe. As to whether the different sections of the community taken together have become better or worse off, and whether the advantages enjoyed by those who have benefited in the short run will be permanent and not likely to be outweighed by other new hardships, no final evaluation can be made at this point. In order to arrive at such a conclusion, a number of other factors will still have to be considered. First of all, however, let us point to some of the more obvious economic effects.

In the first place, it would appear that the average size of the farm has decreased as a result of "land reform" while the number of independent operators has increased. As mentioned earlier, certain groups of people formerly not engaged in farming are included in redistribution under the 1950 law, such as village handicraft workers, small traders, professional workers, families of veterans who died during the civil and World wars, servicemen, government and Party workers and their families, families of persons resident in urban areas, unemployed industrial workers, and members of religious bodies. This has had the effect of adding to the farm population without any compensating increase in available farm land. Furthermore, since the amount of land transferred to any person within an area depends upon the per capita size of the land available, the result has been a general gravitation towards uniformity in the size of the farm.

As was reported in August, 1952, some 700 million *shih mow* of land had by then been confiscated and redistributed to some 300 million peasants, after whatever reservation was made for the establishment of state farms.[29] While regional variations exist, it is known that in the Central-South, East, and Southwest, the average holding after the completion of "land reform" is around two *mow* per capita. In the more over-populated areas this downward levelling process has decidedly further aggravated the problem of the small farm. In certain areas in Kwangtung, for instance, "poor peasants" who prior to "land reform" had 0.33 mow each *now* have 0.76 *mow* instead. Hired hands who previously had 0.08 *mow* each, now have 0.77 *mow*. "Middle peasants" who had 0.86 *mow* before now average 1.01 *mow*. On the other hand, "landlords" who formerly had 2 *mow* per capita now average 0.69 *mow,* while "rich peasants" with a previous average of 1.41 *mow* now have 1.09 *mow*. Similar examples may be given for areas in Szechwan, Kweichow, Hunan, Shensi, Anhwei, Chekiang, and many other places.[30]

Although "land reform" has resulted in the consolidation of scattered parcels of land and has thus increased the area available for farm purposes through the elimination of numerous boundaries, this is offset by the fact that the proportion of available area on a farm devoted to non-productive purposes is as a rule larger on small farms than on large farms. Moreover, not only has redistribution eliminated the small number of relatively large farms, it has also brought about the more or less even distribution of farm animals, implements, and other productive resources which are included in the confiscation and redistribution process, thus increasing their scarcity all around.

Finally, it has been tacitly assumed by the Communists that success in farming and the resultant larger size of certain farms in the past had nothing to do with aptitude or efficiency, and that the landless were without exception victims of exploitation pure and simple. Inclusion of the shiftless as beneficiaries of redistribution and the special reliance placed on them for the requisite enthusiasm and mass hysteria has, no doubt, led in a number of cases to penalizing efficiency in favor of the less efficient. Clearly, none of these developments would work to the advantage of production.

MOVEMENT TOWARDS COLLECTIVIZATION

However, if the effect of "land reform" on production tends to be unfavorable, this possibility was well recognized in advance. At any rate, Communist writers had been fully aware of the limitation of "land reform" in enhancing production through the release of productive forces from the trammels of "feudalistic, exploitative" practices, and had consistently pointed to collectivization as the ultimate goal even before the "land reform" program was introduced on an ever-widening scale in China. Once "land reform" has been completed, the urgency of collectivization increases partly because of the need to offset the disadvantage of the small holdings aggravated by "land reform," partly because of the natural tendency for the outcome of equal distribution to be unstable. Though starting out on a more or less equal footing, the more efficient farmers have somehow or other managed to increase their income more than the less able, and, here and there, some holdings have expanded at the expense of others, and usury loans have again reared their head. Apparently, this phenomenon has become quite common in many areas.[31] Since it was considered both necessary and desirable to carry out "land reform" in the first place, reemergence of a large number of "new rich peasants" and "landlords" obviously cannot be tolerated. The movement towards collectivization has now been given an additional impetus.

The appearance of an increasing number of articles in Communist Chinese publications on the need for collectivization in the latter half of 1952[32] when the completion of "land reform" was already in sight suggests that the authorities were convinced either that time was ripe for greater speed in collectivization or that further delay would be unwise. This advanced preparation of the public for a change in emphasis in the Party's agricultural program was followed by the official adoption and public release on December 15, 1953, of a resolution on the promotion of cooperative farms.[33] It was disclosed at the same time that the Central Committee of the Chinese Communist Party had discussed the same program exactly two years earlier and had even then instructed local Party organs to make use of its provisions on an experimental basis. But apparently the decision has now been made to increase the momentum of the program openly.

At the end of 1953 there were only 59 mechanized state farms in Communist China, of which 24 were in Manchuria.[34] These collective farms represent the "highest" form of collectivization. Between the small individual farm and the collectivized state farm, there are three intermediate forms: (1) mutual aid teams organized on a temporary basis and for specific purposes, (2) permanent mutual aid groups in which members may pool some of their draft animals and implements, coordinate some of their individual production plans, and even accumulate communal property, and (3) cooperative farms organized by the amalgamation of individual holdings as well as other resources and managed as single farm units. The present policy is to promote the expansion of cooperative farms wherever this is possible and to organize the more primitive forms of mutual aid where a more gradual evolution is advisable. A relatively cautious procedure is adopted especially in areas where the memory of "land reform" is still vivid and where the peasants are not yet prepared for further innovation. Caution has been recommended because peasants who have only just received land through redistribution would be suspicious of any effort to make them give up their land to common management even if it should nominally remain as their private property. Moreover, it is probably also believed that, given a little time, even those peasants who have come out of the "land reform" with apparently important gains would soon find out for themselves that the small parcels of land to which they hold title nevertheless are too inadequate to help rid all the economic woes for them. However devious the course collectivization may have to take, the trend is quite clear. Individual farmers are to be organized progressively into mutual aid groups and cooperative farms. Then, as a final step, nominal private ownership in the cooperatives could be taken away and the socialization of agriculture would be complete.

The number of farm households engaged in some form of organized farming or other, mostly temporary mutual aid groups, constituted only 10 per cent of total farm households during 1950. The ratio increased to 25 per cent in 1951, 36 per cent in 1952, 43 per cent in 1953, and 60 per cent in 1954.[35] However, up to 1953, only an extremely small percentage of the farm population had actually been integrated into cooperative farms. Even in Manchuria which had progressed farther along this road than other regions there were in 1953 only some 4,817 cooperative farms, representing 1.38 per cent of the area's total farm households. In all other regions in China Proper, except North China, the proportion of farm households engaged in cooperative farming was substantially lower than 1 per cent. For the country as a whole, only 0.25 per cent of the total farm households were organized in cooperative farms as against a little over 10 per cent in perennial mutual aid teams, but the pace of cooperativization has since been stepped up. While, according to official plans, the number of cooperative farms was to have been increased to 35,800 during 1954 from 15,192 in 1953, the actual number was reported to have reached 225,000 in the fall of 1954.[36] According to the original plan, by 1957, upon the conclusion of Communist China's first five-year plan, it was expected that 20 per cent of the farm population would be organized into some 800,000 cooperative farms. The revised schedule announced in September, 1954, now envisages a total of 500,000 cooperative farms composed of 10 million farm households in the spring of 1955 and the expansion of cooperativization by 1957 to include one-half of the country's land and more than one-half of the peasant households.[37] It is, of course, entirely possible that this time-table may be further stepped up in the same way as the redistribution program was unless serious opposition on the part of the peasants is encountered.

THE *raison d'être* OF COLLECTIVIZATION

The determination to promote the establishment of cooperative farms, publicly announced in December, 1953, but privately agreed upon two years earlier, is defended by the Chinese Communists on several different grounds. In the first place, the cooperative farm, being considerably larger in size than the individual farm, as well as the aggregate of individual farms that may be organized into a single mutual aid team, will facilitate the development of specialization with respect to farm labor and land utilization. New techniques and equipment can be more readily adapted to the larger cooperative farms. Second, a smaller number of large farms will facilitate the planning of agricultural production and the consumption and marketing of farm products, as well as the integration of agricultural planning with industrial policy, such as the provision of exportable surpluses for purchase of capital equipment abroad. Third, the cooperative farm will serve as an intermediate form of organized farming between mutual aid groups and final collectivization. It will provide a stage of experimentation and indoctrination for the individualistic peasants and reduce the shock that collectivization might have on the peasantry if it were introduced directly. Finally, the promotion of cooperative farms will prevent the reemergence of "rich peasants" as a class and, in the words of the Communist Party's resolution mentioned before, "will serve to guarantee the solidarity of 'poor' and 'middle' peasants."

Given a country of small land holders, the need for increasing agricultural production points quite clearly to the desirability of larger farm units. Further, given the Communists' policy of socialization and central planning, it is equally obvious that the only compatible form of large-scale farming is the collectivized farm. The present policy of gradual collectivization by passing through the intermediate stages of mutual aid and cooperative farming indicates a prudent approach designed to minimize opposition and the unfavorable effects on production that too violent a change might easily bring about as was the case in Soviet Russia some years ago. In addition, it may be noted that as long as the development of industries is not able to absorb the surplus population on farms, the establishment of cooperative farms would enable the excess population to remain on the farms while pursuing supplementary or new occupations. They would not be able to do this if large-scale farming were developed through the expansion of individual farms.

In view of the Soviet experience in collective farming one may question whether the ultimate goal to collectivize will really furnish all the answers to agricultural production, especially with respect to the problem of incentive. So far, the Chinese Communists appear to believe that collectivization would offer everything. However, Communist China is still very far from this final stage of development. For the time being, we must ask ourselves why the Chinese Communists have chosen to move towards cooperative and collective farming via "land reform." If cooperative farming is desirable, why was it not introduced in the first place? Was "land reform" with all the attending violence and human sacrifice really necessary even if one should concede that the organization of cooperative farms might be easier given the universal existence after "land reform" of equally small farms, none of which can prosper on their own?[38]

III

POLITICAL AND MILITARY ADVANTAGES OF "LAND REFORM" TO THE COMMUNIST PARTY

Few would be so naive as to believe that the Chinese Communists carried out their policy of land redistribution for no other reason but that they had promised to do so. The real reasons for their action, especially for going beyond the initial moderate measures to help tenant farmers, such as the reduction of land rent and rural interest rates, would appear to lie elsewhere.

Since China is predominantly an agricultural economy, the firm establishment of political power, as we have already mentioned before, is predicated upon control of the agricultural population. To a ruthless political party it may appear that this objective calls for the elimination of all potential competitors for control who may act as a focal point in rallying opposition to that party's political policy either at the present time or in the future. As the traditional seat of political influence in rural communities in China was found in the so-called "landlord" and "rich peasant" classes because their members were relatively more educated and more at home in exercising the function of local government, the progressive development of the land program as envisaged by the Communists very naturally, it would appear, necessitates the planned liquidation of these groups.

The past political influence of "landlords" and "rich peasants" was based both on their economic strength and on their social standing and prestige. For this reason attack on the "landlords" was directed during "land reform" both on the political and on the economic fronts. The weakening of their economic power was to be accomplished through the redistribution of their land and other property, while the deliberate destruction of their social standing was to be achieved through the humiliating treatment and physical violence associated with the accusation meetings, the anti-despot movements, and public trials of the People's Courts. The course of events during the recent "land reform" was a complete reenactment of the strategy outlined in Mao Tse-tung's 1927 report on the peasants' uprising in Hunan.

The initiation of such a social revolution could not, of course, be satisfactorily set off without local support. Consequently, at the very beginning of "land reform" the policy was laid down to rely principally upon the disgruntled and malcontent as a spear head of the drive. The latter were mostly found among the ranks of the "poor" peasants and hired hands. Feelings of class enmity were artificially fanned through the arbitrary classification of the population into different classes and the segregation of the people into exploiters and exploited. Rent reduction, interest control, deposit refunds, and the repudiation of contractual obligations, which usually heralded land redistribution, as well as the outright sharing of spoils known as "fruits of land reform," were among the principal material benefits used to incite greed and hence enthusiasm for the Party's cause among the shiftless and the malcontent.

However, the Chinese Communist Party has never ceased to admonish its members that they must never have as their active opponents at any time a sizable proportion of the population with whom they have to deal. Consequently, it is entirely in accordance with this general rule that the liquidation of "landlords" and of "rich peasants" was not carried out simultaneously during "land reform." The initial Party slogan of neutralizing the "rich peasant" class reflected unmistakably the principle that "one should never attack at one time more than 10 per cent of the rural population."[39] The more recent policy to curb the growth of "rich peasants" through the promotion of cooperative farms marks a shift of emphasis that is also in accord with the same obiter dicta for by now the "landlord" class no longer exists. It is for the same reason that Party directives during "land reform" repeatedly emphasized the desirability to shift the base of support from the group of enthusiastic "poor peasants" to the numerically growing group of "middle peasants" although the latter's political consciousness and dependability were not above question.

In order to gain tight control over the "middle peasants," their organization into Communist-controlled Peasants' Associations and the recruitment of Association members into the Party in order to expand the base of the Communist Party itself were among the measures taken concomitantly with "land reform." The implementation of the land program offered an unusual opportunity to test future candidates for Party membership. The creation of a reign of terror and the supply of a vast number of living examples during the public trials also helped to impress upon the public the futility of opposition and the security offered by the Communist Party.

As long as opposition by the potential victims of liquidation might bring about the collapse of the program, that is, as long as the Party did not have sufficient trained personnel and armed might on the spot to suppress opposition, the Communist authorities proved that they were always ready to make some slight and temporary concessions. But as soon as the circumstances changed or the balance between the Party's political strength and the need to crush actual or potential opposition altered, the original policy would be resumed.[40] This explains why in newly conquered territories the initial policy of the Chinese Communists tended almost always to be more moderate than their policy in firmly held territories. The same factor can probably explain the low priority originally assigned to Southwest China in the "land reform" program and the subsequent *tour de face* after the outbreak of the Korean War and the intervention of Communist China.

While the liquidation of potential foes serves to enhance the relative strength of the Communist Party, the latter's power may also be increased more directly. This, as one might expect, can be done by offering Party members some special incentive and by giving material inducement to members of the armed forces. It was obviously for this reason that careful provisions were made during "land reform" to guarantee these privileged groups and their families a favorable class status and an opportunity to benefit from the redistribution of farm land. If the cadres engaged in carrying out the Party's policy should happen to help themselves a little more than it was their due, this would be a "minor" deviation only. For there was very little security the Party could otherwise offer to its members and followers. Land was clearly a suitable reward. Besides, unless these people were given land to grow their own food, they would have to be supported by the treasury. Because land could not be created, the provision of an abundant supply of free land had to be taken care of through the confiscation of land owned by a numerically minority group.

Even as Party recruits were attracted from peasants participating in land redistribution, so did the army obtain its recruits in the same way. In the first place, peasants were impressed directly into the regular army. A second and probably more common practice was to absorb the peasants into the regular armed forces in an indirect manner. The organization of Peasants' Associations was, for instance, invariably associated with the formation of local militia controlled by the Association, i.e., the Party. These militia men were directed to provide the means of enforcement in carrying out the land program and to relieve the regular army for more urgent tasks. As they increased in number and became more experienced, they could be easily absorbed into the regular army. In this way, an almost inexhaustible supply of cannon fodder could be and was found. Thus, as one report tells us, the number of Peasants' Association members had already reached 88 million by the end of 1951 while that of militia men at the same time was 12,800,000.[41] Perhaps the effect of the Korean War on the course of the "land reform" program may be best visualized in this light. The local forces were as a rule first told that their task was to protect their newly acquired land ownership and to prevent the return of the so-called exploiters. Intensive indoctrination would take care of their future attitude later. The military advantage derived from "land reform" was certainly more than a mere incidental effect of the carefully engineered social upheaval.

In the same category as army expansion should be included the creation of a large pool of "voluntary" and forced labor. The use of hard labor as a method of "redemption" for "landlords" and "rich peasants" has already been referred to before. These are the expendable men who have been employed to build dikes, irrigation works, railways, and roads, as well as the numerous construction projects of which we shall have more to say later. Rarely if ever before in history have hunger and terror been more ruthlessly and effectively exploited by a political party on such a scale for the consolidation and perpetuation of its own power.

GRAIN COLLECTION AND GOVERNMENT REVENUE

"Land reform" was of course not only a means to consolidate political power and to destroy the political and economic foundation of potential or active opponents in rural areas. It was also an important measure to provide adequate revenue for the continuation of government activities. Not only did the Communist authorities have special need for large quantities of grain to feed their army and government employees and to maintain control over market prices in urban areas during the initial period of its rule, but increasing need for agricultural exports to foreign countries for the purchase of capital equipment in the government's industrialization program poses a constant problem to the Chinese Communists. If the "landlords" and "rich peasants" had been allowed to collect their usual income from the other peasants and this income had then been taxed away by the government, not only would there have been very strong opposition from the taxpayers themselves, but the effect on the incentive of the peasants in general would have been no less unfavorable. If the peasants had continued to pay land rent, etc., they would have felt very little enthusiasm for the government's policy. In addition, they would have been discouraged by the heavy tax imposed on the "landlords" and "rich peasants," because deep in the heart of every "poor peasant" the fondest dream was to join the ranks of these so-called exploiters, and it would have been very disillusioning indeed if this dream had been prematurely dashed. Consequently, as it appears to us, it was deemed more advisable to liquidate the "landlords"—and now the "rich peasants"—and to divide what was formerly paid in land rent with some of the peasants, the government taking, of course, the lion's share. In this way the "landlords" and "rich peasants" could be eliminated with the help of the rest of the peasantry, instead of against the latter's opposition. Once the core of opposition has disappeared, any further increase in taxes which the peasantry now must bear directly will meet with less effective resistance.

CONCLUSION

In summary, let us repeat that the Chinese Communists did not plunge into the "land reform" program without a thought on the next step they had to take. Nor have they only just discovered the economic disadvantages of small farms. The decision to move towards cooperative farming and eventual collectivization, now that the preliminary "land reform" is largely over, was obviously reached a long time ago. But collectivization was not actively promoted before the completion of "land reform" because it was politically unwise or even unfeasible to do so. On the other hand, the Chinese Communists did not content themselves with the adoption of moderate measures to correct inequality in income and wealth in the farming sector of the economy because such measures per se would not have led to the development of large-scale farming in China. At the same time, they could not allow large-scale farming to develop along individualistic lines because such a development would be ideologically intolerable to them, as well as practically incompatible with their political objective and economic policy. Consequently, for a combination of reasons, they decided upon a policy of redistribution followed by consolidation. That such a policy has entailed unnecessary human suffering and that it had the appearance of a political stratagem on a grandiose scale merely testify to the character of Communism.

NOTES

1. John Lossing Buck, *Land Utilization in China,* pp. 267-269, Chicago, 1937. Both farms of the most usual size and the median are smaller.

2. Estimates of the minimum holding necessary for subsistence in China range from 6.5 to 15 *shih mow* per head. Cf. Chin I-hung, *China's Industrialization, A Communist Fantasy,* pp. 10-11, Hongkong, 1952. Huang T'ung puts the minimum economic size of the farm in China at 10 *shih mow* per person in his article, "The Standard Farm," *Land Reform Monthly,* Taipeh, 1951. The average farm household has a little over five persons.

3. Ch'en Cheng-mo, *Land Rent in Chinese Provinces,* pp. 94-101 and pp. 128-135, quoted in Bureau of Statistics, *A Statistical Analysis of Tenancy in China,* 2nd edition, p. 84, Chungking, 1946. Similar figures are given in other studies such as that of the Legislative Yuan for 1930 and the Crop Reports of the National Agricultural Research

Bureau. Without apologizing for landlords demanding a high rent, one should nevertheless point out that rent was often computed on the basis of the principal crop only. In double-crop areas rent was frequently paid on one crop only, and there was usually no rent on supplementary crops. See John Lossing Buck, "Fact and Theory about China's Land," *Foreign Affairs,* October, 1949, and his summary of the study by the Farmers' Bank of China in Szechwan in 1941.

4. Cf. Tamagna, *Banking and Finance in China,* pp. 205-6. The frequency distribution of rural interest rates in 1934, according to Tamagna, was:

Interest Rate Per Cent per Annum	*Per Cent of Cases*
10–20	9.4
20–30	36.2
30–40	30.3
40–50	11.2
over 50	12.9
	100.0

In his paper presented at the 1947 conference of the Institute of Pacific Relations, Buck mentioned 30 per cent as the rate usually charged on loans from landlords as against 25 to 28 per cent in the case of loans from relatives and friends.

5. See Wu Yuan-Li, *op. cit.*

6. See Chapter II above.

7. See Ti Ch-ao-pai, *China's Postwar Agrarian Problem,* pp. 51-52, Hongkong, 1948. The terms "middle peasants," "rich peasants," etc., are put in quotation marks as their precise implication in Communist usage is at considerable variance with what one might infer from the ordinary meaning of the words. The term "land reform" is also put in quotation marks when reference is made to the land program adopted by the Communists.

8. The Chinese text is contained in many publications. See, for instance, *A Manual for Newspaper Readers,* Hankow, 1950.

9. See Wu Wen-Hui, *China's Land Problem and Its Solution,* p. 119, Shanghai, 1947.

10. Cf. Wu Wen-hui, *Inquiry into Modern China's Land Problem.*

11. *A Statistical Analysis of Tenancy in China,* pp. 6-7.

12. Buck, *op. cit.,* p. 196.

13. Cf. Liu's speech mentioned earlier in this chapter.

14. NCNA, June 29, 1951.

15. See Liao Lu-yen's report in the *People's Daily,* Peking, September 21, 1952.

16. *People's Daily,* Peking, November 3, 1951.

17. *Economic Weekly,* No. 40, p. 802, Shanghai, 1952.

18. English texts of the law and its ancillary documents are available in the Peking Foreign Language Press series.

19. Cf. *Compendium of Important Documents on Land Reform,* pp. 93-105; *Compendium,* Vol. II, Peking, 1951; and Chin I-hung, *Land Rent and Ownership,* Chapter 4, Hongkong, 1951.

20. It should be noted in this connection that the Communists have never bothered to define precisely what constitutes "exploitation" in the context of this law.

21. For instance, a resolution was passed by the Central-South Bureau of the Chinese Communist Party in December, 1949, warning against the continuation of excessive killing and beating during the campaign against rural class enemies on the ground that such acts might alienate the public from the Party.

22. See, for instance, the recently published *Collected Works of Mao Tse-tung,* Peking, 1952.

23. Incidentally, it is provided in this act that his other property may not be confiscated.

24. There are several other versions of early "land reform" laws, which are more or less in the same vein as the above-mentioned document. See Chin I-hung, *Communist China's Land Reform and China's Land Problem,* pp. 22, *et seq.*

25. See the Chinese text reprinted in *The Chinese Communist Party and the Land Revolution,* published by the *Cheng-pao she,* Hongkong.

26. Chinese text reprinted in *The Chinese Communist Party and the Land Revolution,* cited above.

27. Chinese text reprinted in *Some Problems in Land Reform and Three Model Experiences.* A symposium published by the Ch'i-shi Northwestern Bookstore, 1948.

28. Chinese text reprinted in *Land Policy in Newly Liberated Areas,* a symposium published by the New Democracy Publishers, Hongkong, 1949.

29. Cf. *Economic Weekly,* No. 40, p. 802, Shanghai, 1952.

30. See, for instance, reports carried by *Ta-kung pao,* Hongkong, April 18, May 24, and June 21, 1951; *Wen-hui pao,* Hongkong, March 20, 1951; *Kung-sheung yat-pao,* Hongkong, May 27, 1951; and *Sing-tau jih-pao,* Hongkong, January 29, 1951.

There is only approximate equality in the size of the holdings probably due to topographical and other conditions of the land in question.

31. In a report to the Northeastern Bureau of the Chinese Communist Party in 1952, Kao Kang stated that usury loans had again become widespread in Manchuria, with many Communist Party members taking part as lenders. Cf. *People's Daily,* January 24, 1952. Similar reports of a trend towards new "class differentiation" are also available for other areas.

32. See, for example Sun K'ang, "The Resolute and Orderly Transition of Individual Farming to Cooperation," *Economic Weekly,* No. 41, Shanghai, October, 1952, and Tzu Hsuan, "Problems in Collectivizing Agriculture," *Economic Weekly,* No. 40, October, 1952.

33. *People's Daily,* Peking, January 9, 1954.

34. *New China Monthly,* pp. 155-157, Peking, April, 1954.

35. Cf. *People's Daily,* Peking, January 1, 9, 14, and 16, 1954; *Study,* Peking, January 2, 1954; and NCNA, September 24, 1954.

36. These were distributed as follows: Manchuria, 60,340; North China, 79,538; East China, 46,045; Central-South, 18,232; Southwest, 17,745; and Northwest, 3,505. NCNA, December 1, 1954.

37. Report by Teng Tzu-hui to the National People's Congress on September 23, 1954. NCNA, September 23, 1954.

38. Some of the discussion in the following section represents a certain amount of value judgment. It is believed, however, that even critics would probably concede that our interpretation is plausible.

39. Cf. Mao Tse-tung's speech on April 1, 1948, mentioned earlier and the directive of the Communist Party in 1948 on "land reform" in Manchuria.

40. This policy of making temporary concessions whenever necessary was very clearly illustrated in the Directive issued by the Chinese Communist Party Central Committee on May 25, 1948, concerning "land reform" and Party work in that year. "Land reform" in areas bordering on Nationalist-held territories was postponed because of insecure military control.

41. Cf. *People's Daily,* Peking, November 3, 1951.

CHAPTER FIVE

Agricultural Production and Self-Sufficiency

I

INTRODUCTION

In focussing attention on the process of land redistribution and collectivization in our preceding analysis we have so far emphasized two major factors—namely, the overwhelming political bias of the land policy of the Chinese Communists and the rather tenuous relationship between redistribution per se and the ultimate economic objective of increasing agricultural production. Our comments should not, however, detract from the impressive recovery in the production of food crops and cotton that has been achieved since the inception of the new regime even though it cannot be over-emphasized that the completion of "land reform" and the launching of a gradual collectivization process have by no means disposed of the problem of production.

Since agricultural production in a very broad sense may be regarded as including all tangible, non-industrial goods, among which are the products of animal husbandry, fishery, and forestry, we shall obviously have to confine our discussion to a few of these items only. The problem of selection posed cannot be resolved easily. In omitting a number of highly interesting and even important topics, such as the supply of draught animals, meat products, wood oil, other vegetable oils, and bristles, at this point, we do not mean to underestimate their vital role in some important areas of the country's economic life, but lack of space forces us to consider two groups of agricultural products only, namely, the staple food crops and raw cotton.

There is no overriding reason why any country under normal conditions should feel obliged to produce all the food and textile fibers required for the consumption of its population, but, given economic self-sufficiency as a political objective, independence from foreign supply in satisfying these basic needs for survival overshadows self-sufficiency in all other fields in importance. In fact, in a large measure, the degree of freedom of independent action in the international arena that is enjoyed by the Chinese Communist authorities may very well be regarded as a function of self-sufficiency in these two commodity groups. Besides, as we shall see in the following chapters, dependence on imports in the supply of other goods required in the program of economic development necessitates retrenchment in the importation of all consumers' goods, and the ability to be free from foreign supplies of food and cotton may mean a great deal to the success of the country's industrialization plans. Imports of raw cotton and cereals during 1946 and 1947, for instance, accounted for 25.9 and 21.6 per cent respectively of China's total commercial imports in these two postwar years.[1] Excluded from these figures are the sizable imports of cotton, wheat, and flour undertaken by UNRRA in amounts about equal to the above recorded volumes. Although the conditions of these postwar years were not representative of normal circumstances, the significance of self-sufficiency in this respect can hardly be overestimated.

Among the many questions that will be raised even within the scope of our limited discussion the following should perhaps be singled out for particular attention:

1. What is the extent of recovery in production under the Communist regime?

2. How does the present level of cotton and grain output compare with that of former years?

3. Is the present level of production sufficiently adequate to provide for the minimum requirements of the population, assuming that the overall supply is judiciously distributed in accordance with physical needs?

4. Is there any surplus that may be either exported or added to stock if consumption is kept at the minimum level?

5. What measures, if any, have been taken by the Communist government to curtail consumption?

6. In view of the redistribution of land, the growth of total production, the curtailment of consumption, and other developments, is it possible to draw any definite conclusion as to changes in the well-being of the peasantry in comparison with earlier years?

7. What factors accounted for the increase in production after 1949, and, in the light of present conditions, can production be expected to

increase further and to such an extent as to fulfill the requirements of the plan for economic development?

II

INDEX NUMBERS OF GRAIN PRODUCTION[2]

In estimating the extent of recovery in grain production in Communist China since 1949, one logical step to take would be to examine the series of index numbers published by official Communist sources. Without going into the reasons for statistical discrepancies that are found in such official reporting in general, which will be discussed in Chapter VI, it should be noted that among the grain production data published for the successive years since 1949 those of the National Bureau of Statistics and the Ministry of Agriculture, released in 1953 and 1954 respectively, are reasonably close and comparable to each other. If we use 1949 as the base year, the figures contained in these two series, together with an earlier set of official data, are as shown in the following table:

Index Numbers of Grain Production
in Communist China, 1949-1954

	I	*II*	*III*	*IV*
1949	100.0	100.0	100.0	
1950	117.0	117.3	121.2	
1951	128.0	129.3	134.4	
1952	145.0	156.7	156.7	
1953[1]				145.0
1954[2]				150.0

Sources: I. National Bureau of Statistics, *Wen Hui-pao,* Hongkong, September 30, 1953.

II. *New China Monthly,* p. 124, Peking, April, 1953.

III. Ministry of Agriculture, *Science Bulletin,* Peking, May, 1954.

IV. [1]NCNA, February 28, 1954. A preliminary estimate for 1953 given in *Economic Bulletin,* No. 50, Hongkong, December, 1953, was 115 per cent of the 1950-1952 average or 150 with 1949 as the base year.
[2]NCNA, September 24, 1954. Preliminary.

Of the above three, series I and II are virtually the same for the first three years, whereas II and III offer the same figure for 1952. The Ministry of Agriculture data in column III are more recent although the Bureau of Statistics information should not be dismissed lightly. The discrepancies between column III and columns I and II may stem from differences in commodity and/or geographical coverage for the years after 1949 although the 1949 figure in columns II and III is shown in both original sources as 74.6 per cent of the prewar output.[3]

Regardless of the series one chooses to use, there is no denying the fact that impressive gains were scored in grain production during the past few years and that the peak output so far was reached in 1952 when production was frequently referred to in Communist sources as the "highest in history."[4]

ESTIMATES OF GRAIN PRODUCTION

Although absolute figures for grain production in 1950 and 1951 have occasionally been published,[5] it is not quite clear whether information realeased represents final estimates. Accordingly, the most promising way to estimate the absolute quantities of production is to use either the 1949 or the 1952 output in conjunction with the index numbers. The 1949 output is useful for this purpose because it has been consistently given as 110 million metric tons. The 1953 output, given by Po I-p'o in his 1953 budget report as 163.75 million tons, is also reasonably reliable because it can be checked against the acreages of individual crops planted and their respective yields per unit area and because, even if it should err slightly on the high side, the analysis on Communist China's food supply based on it would not run the risk of underestimation as a result.

Grain production in 1949 was said to be 110 million tons during the December, 1949, conference held to plan the expansion of agricultural production in the following year.[6] Moreover, since the 1949 output was also equal to 74.6 per cent of the 1931-1936 average, an estimate could be made on the basis of the latter. According to the official Nationalist Government's 1947 publication on *China's Food Production* and the *Statistical Yearbook* of 1948, the average annual output of the principal food crops in mainland China in 1931-1936 was 147.79 million tons. The principal food crops included are rice, wheat, corn, millet, proso millet, kaoliang, oats, barley, soyabeans, field peas, and sweet potatoes, items that are commonly understood to be components of the collective term "grain." 74.6 per cent of 147.79 million tons happens to be 110 million tons. Finally, the National Bureau of Statistics which has provided us with the index numbers in column I of the preceding table also gives the 1952 output as 160 million tons. If the 1952 output corresponded to 145 per cent of that of 1949, the 1949 output would again be 110 million tons. Thus, the 1949 output as given by the official sources may be used with some confidence in deriving production estimates for the subsequent years.

However, it should be borne in mind that the estimate of 110 million tons for 1949 was made at a time when the Chinese mainland had barely fallen into Communist hands. It is entirely probable that production in certain areas, and especially the southwestern provinces, could not be estimated with any degree of accuracy. Besides, the figure of 110 million tons was in all likelihood a rounded number, as was probably the figure of 160 million tons given later by the National Bureau of Statistics for 1952. Consequently, the actual production date for both 1949 and 1952 may depart somewhat from these rounded estimates.

This consideration leads us to the employment of the figure of 163.75 million tons given by Po I-p'o for 1952. An interesting aspect of this figure is that if yield and acreage data were used to estimate the production of individual crops, the aggregate weight of grain production thus obtained would correspond very closely to this total given by Po. The following table shows this coincidence quite clearly:

Comparative Estimates of the Production of Food Crops in Communist China, 1952

	Acreage Planted (in thousand hectares)	*Yield (in kilograms per hectare)*	*Production (in thousand metric tons)*	
			I	*II*
Rice	27,694	2,445.0	67,710	68,280
Wheat	24,644	735.0	18,110	18,180
Corn	12,566	1,342.5	16,870	16,870
Kaoliang	9,394	1,177.5	11,060	11,140
Millet	9,760	1,140.0	11,130	11,460
Soyabeans	11,346	817.5	9,280	9,380
Tubers	8,540	1,875.0	16,010	16,210
Other	18,056	679.0	12,280	12,280
Total	122,000	Aggregate weight	162,450	163,750

Sources: The data on acreage and yield are taken from Wang Shou's article in *Science Bulletin,* No. 5, Peking, 1954, and *Wen-hui pao,* Hongkong, September 30, 1953. Column I under "Production" is computed from the acreage and yield data. Column II is computed from the percentage distribution by crops given by Wang and the total grain output reported by Po.

In the light of the above discussion, it would appear that one could either employ the 1949 output of 110 million tons or the 1952 output of 163.75 million tons in estimating the total grain outputs of the four years, 1949-1953. In addition, the preliminary output for 1954 may also be obtained. However, since there are three separate series of index numbers, it is theoretically possible to obtain six different figures for each year. In practice, however, it is believed that two of the six series are probably more accurate than the rest.

Estimates of Grain Production in Communist China, 1949-1954
(in million metric tons)

	Estimates Based on 1949 Output			*Estimates Based on 1952 Output*		
Index Number Series	*I*	*II*	*III*	*I*	*II*	*III*
1949	110.00	110.00	110.00	112.93	104.49	104.49
1950	128.70	129.03	133.32	132.01	122.57	126.64
1951	140.80	142.23	147.84	145.57	135.10	140.43
1952	159.50	172.37	172.37	163.75	163.75	163.75
1953	159.50	159.50	159.50	163.75	151.51	151.51
1954 Preliminary[1]	165.00	165.00	165.00	169.39	156.73	156.73

1. The plan was set at 5 million tons above the 1953 output. *People's Daily*, January 1, 1954.

On the basis of the time of information, series I and III are more recent than series II. As far as the period 1949-1952 is concerned, there is no decisive preference for either the first or the last column of the above table. However, from the point of view of the entire period under consideration a decisive consideration is that the 1953 output given in the first column is the same as that of 1952, whereas the 1953 output in the last column is about 8 per cent lower than that of 1952. In spite of the conflicting official pronouncements on grain production in 1953,[7] there are good reasons to believe that production in 1953 was in fact lower than in the preceding year. Consequently, it is the estimates given in the last column that we shall use in our discussion although, as mentioned before, the figures in the first column may also represent a fair approximation.[8]

COMPARISON WITH THE PREWAR PERIOD

Although official Communist sources have consistently claimed that the grain output of 1952 was the highest in Chinese history, this assertion is borne out only if we disregard some of the minor food crops for the prewar years. On the basis of the information given in the 1947 publication on *China's Food Production,* the average annual grain output in 1931-1937 amounted to 19,723,000 tons for Manchuria and 136,103,000 tons for China Proper, or a total of 155,826,000 tons for the entire mainland. This figure, representing the aggregate weight of eleven major crops, is of course almost 8 million tons less than the 1952 output of 163,750,000 tons. However, the National Agricultural Research Bureau which collected the information on the eleven crops also had estimated the production of several other food crops. For the 1931-1937 period the annual outputs of these other items averaged 1,274,000 tons of black beans, 1,449,000 tons of *mung* (green) beans, 1,103,000 tons of buckwheat, and 1,907,000 tons of Irish potatoes.[9] These represented production in China Proper, and, when added to the 136,103,000 tons mentioned above, would raise the aggregate weight of grain output to 141,836,000 tons for China Proper and 161,559,000 tons for all mainland China. Consequently, if the official Communist grain production data include all these items as well, the increase in production in 1952 in comparison with the 1931-1937 average was rather negligible if, indeed, there was an actual gain at all. Given Communist China's predisposition to try to impress the world and its own people with its achievements, one may be justified in assuming that the 1952 output of 163,750,000 tons included all the principal and minor food crops enumerated here.

Be that as it may, in evaluating the 1952 grain output against that of the prewar years, one should also recall the criticism that has been levelled by some authors against the NARB's estimates of crop acreage. According to Ou Pao-san's study on China's prewar national income, for instance, the estimated total weight of food crops in 1933, based on revised acreage and other data, amounted to 229 million tons for China Proper and 14 million tons for Manchuria, or an aggregate of 243 million tons.[10] Granted that Ou's figure may lean towards an overestimate, there is certainly a possibility that production in 1952 might even be smaller than the actual production attained in some of the prewar years.

All this should not be construed as an effort to belittle the degree of recovery in agriculture between 1949 and 1952 especially when one bears in mind that the increase in grain production was accomplished simultaneously with an impressive expansion of raw cotton production which adversely affected the production of some food crops such as wheat.[11] Yet the official claim that the 1952 grain output was the highest in Chinese history, though not without merit in a way, should not be allowed to mislead the student from thinking that all was indeed well.

ACREAGE AND YIELD

If the 1952 grain production was only slightly larger than the adjusted average of the 1931-1937 period, it was obtained from a crop acreage that was appreciably greater. The total food grain acreage in mainland China during 1931–1937, excluding Sinkiang and the acreage of the minor crops as well as that of rice, potatoes, and some coarse grains in Manchuria, averaged 90,600,000 hectares.[12] The actual total, including all the items omitted for lack of information, was, of course, larger. However, it is unlikely that it would be as high as 122 million hectares as reported for 1952 although the latter figure corresponds very closely to Ou's estimate of 107 million hectares for China Proper and over 12 million hectares for Manchuria, or a total of 120 million hectares. The increase in crop acreage occurred mostly in Manchuria where the total grain acreage had reached approximately 18 million hectares by 1951.[13] If the crop acreage in Manchuria in 1952 was no more than that of the preceding year, the corresponding acreage in China Proper would be about 104 million hectares, some 3 million hectares less than Ou's figure for 1933 and possibly somewhat higher than the average for 1931-1937, allowing for the omissions mentioned above.

It was partly this increase in acreage in Manchuria that accounted for the high grain production in 1952. According to one report, the grain output of Manchuria in 1952 was 21 million tons, leaving 142.72 million tons to China Proper and Inner Mongolia, a portion of the latter being originally parts of Manchuria. The grain production of Inner Mongolia was 1.1 million tons in 1949 and, in all probability, greater in 1952.[14] On the assumption that the grain output of Inner Mongolia in 1952 that might be attributed to those parts which formerly belonged to Manchuria was approximately at this level, the grain production in China Proper in 1952 would be 141.65 million tons or almost the same as the corresponding average figure for the 1931-1937 period. By examining the distribution of this total, both by crops and by geographical regions, it could be established quite clearly that there was a general increase in production in Northwest and North China in comparison with the 1931-1937 period, while production in the other regions, with the exception of rice, was actually smaller.[15] On account of the possibility of double cropping the increase in rice output was doubtless partly instrumental to the fact that crop acreage and production in China Proper in 1952 were not smaller than the above estimates indicate.

Thus, two tentative conclusions may be drawn. In the first place, grain production in 1952 was as high as 163.75 million tons principally because of an increase in rice production which more than offset the decline of production of other food crops. Second, grain production was high in 1952 because of the expansion of crop acreage in general which took place principally in Manchuria, as well as in some of the northern and northwestern provinces. But for these developments the large grain production of 1952 would not have been possible.

That it was the large crop acreage that underlay the recovery of grain production finds further support in the relatively low yields attained even in 1952 in comparison with available information from earlier studies. Although information on unit area yields is not available for all the main crops, the following comparison between 1952 and three other earlier periods points unmistakably to the relatively poor showing in the year of "peak" output.

It is noteworthy that the unit area yields of all the major food crops listed below were lower in 1952 than in the 1931-1937 period for China Proper and the 1935-1938 period for Manchuria. Furthermore with the sole exception of corn, the 1952 yields were also lower than the most frequent yields obtained in Buck's study. The exceptionally low yield in the case of tubers in 1952 poses a rather perplexing problem and suggests that as a result of the expansion in crop acreage only land with the worst soil was devoted to this crop. In addition, it should be noted that the prewar most frequent yields were as a rule under 80 per cent of the normal yields and under 70 per cent of the best yields.

Comparative Data on Crop Yields in Communist China
(in kilograms per hectare)

	1952 National Average	*1931-1937 Average China Proper*	*1935-1938 Average Manchuria*	*1929-1933 Most Frequent Yields*
Rice	2,445	2,532	—	3,384–3,273
Wheat	735	1,078	900	1,077–1,213
Corn	1,343	1,379	1,500	1,321
Kaoliang	1,178	1,366	1,400	1,279
Millet	1,140	1,178[1]	1,200	1,178[2]
Soyabeans	818	1,164	1,200	946
Tubers	1,875	7,900	—	5,837[3]

Sources: For 1952, Wang Shou, *op. cit.;* for 1931-1937, Shen, *op. cit.* original data from the National Agricultural Research Bureau; for 1935-1938, Manchuria, *Japan-Manchoukuo Yearbook,* 1941; and for 1929-1933, Buck, *Land Utilization in China,* pp. 224-225, Chicago, 1937, data derived from 20 per cent or more of the farms surveyed in eight agricultural regions.

1. Weighted average of millet and proso millet.

2. Millet only. The most frequent yield for proso millet was 842 kilograms only, but proso millet production was usually about one-fourth of the millet output.

3. Irish potatoes only. The yield of sweet potatoes was higher.

POTENTIAL FOR GROWTH

In the light of the above analysis it is not surprising that the Chinese Communist authorities have devoted increasing attention to raising the average productivity of the farms. The program of production contests was launched ealy in 1951 and has been pursued with great vigor since.[16] Some exceptionally high yields achieved have occasionally been given wide publicity although the national averages do not appear to have advanced greatly. Moreover, according to one official survey, a number of these exceptional achievements were the result of either erroneous reporting or deliberate efforts to falsify records for the purpose of receiving official awards.[17]

However, if favorable conditions for the increase of unit area yields can be obtained, the relatively low yields reported for 1952 do seem to hold out considerable promise for an expansion of grain output well beyond that of 1952. If, for instance, the prewar most frequent yields could be attained for rice, wheat, corn, kaoliang, millet, soyabeans, and tubers, and if their respective acreages remained the same as in 1952, even if the output of all other crops should not register any increase over the 1952 level, total grain production would reach 235,626,000 tons. This would be a 43.8 per cent rise over the

1952 level and would be comparable to Ou Pao-san's estimate of of 243 million tons for 1933.[18]

The initially announced objective of the First Five Year Plan was to increase grain production by the end of 1957 by as much as 30 per cent above the 1952 level and to achieve a 70 per cent expansion at the end of two Five Year Plans.[19] The target set for 1957 has since been lowered to 192.8 million tons or only about 17.6 per cent above the 1952 level.[19a] While the sights set are still fairly high, they do not seem to be completely unrealistic from the purely technical point of view. However, the possibility of further expansion depends upon the existence of certain favorable factors which cannot be guaranteed. Since grain production in 1953 actually declined and the 1954 production did not seem to be much better, one may question whether the long-term plan envisaged can in fact be carried out. In the meantime, the problem of equating demand and supply remains while measures adopted to deal with the issue may in turn affect the expansion of production in an adverse manner.

III

THE MINIMUM LEVEL OF FOOD CONSUMPTION

The extent of recovery in grain production since 1949 and the potential capacity of expansion are meaningful only in relation to the demand for food grains. In view of the reputedly low standard of living in China, the aggregate quantity of food grains demanded in any year may not diverge significantly from the minimum requirement for subsistence. Moreover, in view of Communist China's need to restrict consumption, it may be assumed that the minimum demand for subsistence also constitutes the initial and primary objective the authorities may feel obliged to attain. Consequently, the most important question is whether this minimum goal could be achieved.

According to dietary studies conducted in China prior to the establishment of the Communist regime, the daily consumption of food ranged from 2,300 to 3,200 calories per adult.[20] In a report of the Chinese Medical Council in 1938, however, the figure of 2,400 calories was suggested as the minimum daily requirement for an adult male. The same figure was adopted by the Food and Nutrition Board of the U. S. National Research Council for use by international relief agencies in their postwar operations in China. While it is several hundred calories less than the minimum daily requirement commonly assumed, for instance, in this country, it is meant for a moderately active Chinese male weighing 55 kilograms and takes into account the lower basal metabolism of the Chinese. Consequently, for our present purpose, it may be assumed to be the minimum daily caloric intake for an adult Chinese male.

According to T. H. Shen, probably about 80 per cent of the prewar daily caloric intake of the Chinese population consisted of cereals. Taking into account the legumes and tubers, the share of the three groups of food crops might be as high as 90 per cent. According to the FAO food balance sheet quoted by Shen, the estimated share of the three categories was about 87 per cent of the total caloric intake. Since a more balanced diet would require a far smaller share of the carbohydrates, we might use 85 per cent as a reasonable approximation. On this basis, the caloric intake to be derived from cereals, legumes, and tubers would amount to 2,040 calories per adult male per day.

According to official Communist reports, the present population of the Chinese mainland is 583 million. Only very little is known about the present age and sex distribution of this population, but as an approximation we may assume that from the point of view of food consumption every one hundred persons are equivalent to about 82 adult males.[21] On this basis, a population of 583 million would be equivalent to 478 million adult males. In order to support this population at the minimum subsistence level, the quantity of milled food grains required would amount to 103.8 million tons of milled rice a year, or its equivalent, or 217 tons of rice per 1,000 adult males.[22]

It is interesting to note that when food rationing was officially introduced in Shanghai and Kwangtung at about the end of 1953 the amount promised by the authorities was 182.5 kilograms per person per year[23] although the actual ration was much less. This would be equivalent to the 222.5 tons per 1,000 adult males, which seems to lend further support to our estimate of minimum food requirements. Thus, it remains for us to determine whether the amount of food crops available for human consumption is large enough to provide for this minimum level of consumption.

ADEQUACY OF FOOD SUPPLY

Not all the unprocessed grain produced is available for direct human consumption as food. Provision for seed and animal feed must be made. The remainder is available for direct human consumption as food, manufacturing, export, and addition to stock. However, since manufacturing in this case consists principally of the production of processed foods and distillation, it may be assumed that in the event of a serious food shortage, such activities would and could be curtailed. Consequently, there is no need for our purpose to distinguish between manufacturing and food in the utilization of the grain available. Under normal circumstances, both export and addition to stock may also be regarded as claims upon any surplus that may be available instead of being unavoidable deductions from the total supply. Thus the entire supply of food crops after provisions for seed and fodder may be treated as available for human consumption if necessary.

In addition, two other factors must be considered. In the first place, the unprocessed grain must be milled so that there would be some weight loss. The milling factor, of course, varies by crops and is relatively flexible. Moreover, peasants who grow food crops usually retain a portion for their own consumption although the exact share thus retained varies both with the size and nature of the crop, the market price, and deductions in the form of taxation or compulsory purchase. Consequently, one must distinguish between the overall volume of grain available for consumption and that part which is available for those sections of the population that do not grow their own food, including farmers who raise such cash crops as cotton, tobacco, etc., as well as the urban population. The aggregate amount of food requirements of the population at a minimum subsistence level may not be equal to the sum of the food-growing farmers' own consumption in the absence of external curtailment and the consumption of the rest of the population at the subsistence level. The latter sum would as a rule be greater than the former figure.

The proportion of unprocessed grains available for human consumption after provisions for fodder and seeds varies not only with individual crops, but also with geographical regions due to different farming conditions and dietary habits. Although such information is available in the form of studies by the National Agricultural Research Bureau and other authors, it may be safe to assume that when the supply of food is subjected to central planning on a national scale, such regional differences will to some extent be ignored. Besides, a detailed treatment by individual areas would exceed the scope of the present inquiry. Consequently, as an approximation, we shall adopt the national data used in the FAO Food Balance Sheet for 1931-1937 in determining the maximum amount available for food.

As for the milling factors, we shall also use the FAO figures, where the ratios retained by the peasants for their own consumption in terms of total supply are taken from Buck's prewar work on China's land utilization. By applying these ratios to the individual crops on the basis of their outputs in 1952, and reducing the data into "rice-equivalents," we are able to get a fairly good idea of the food supply situation in Communist China. The relevant data are presented in the following table:

Supply of Food Crops in Communist China in 1952
(quantities in thousand metric tons)
Factors Used in Computing Food Supply

	Per Cent of Total Production Available after Provision for Seeds, Fodder, and Waste	*Per Cent Normally Retained by Food-Growing Farmers for Own Consumption*	*Milling Factor in Per Cent*	*Conversion Factor into "Rice-Equivalents"*
Rice	92.01	56	74	1.00
Wheat	86.47	54	80	1.02
Corn	79.93	63	100	1.03
Kaoliang	78.00	53	88	1.00
Millet	84.20	77	88	1.00
Soyabeans	81.94	47	100	0.99
Tubers	64.00	63	100	0.28
Other[1]	65.00	45	89	1.00

1. Figures for the first four columns under "other" are averages of barley, oats, buckwheat, black beans, broad beans, *mung* beans, and field peas, weighted by their average outputs for the 1931-1937 period.

	Maximum Supply Available for Food	*Quantity Normally Retained by Food-Growing Farmers for Own Consumption (in terms of milled rice)*	*Quantity Available for Other Population Groups*
Rice	46,490	28,295	18,195
Wheat	12,828	8,011	4,817
Corn	13,892	10,947	2,945
Kaoliang	7,646	5,196	2,450
Millet	8,492	7,765	727
Soyabeans	7,019	4,341	2,678
Tubers	2,905	2,859	46
Other	7,104	4,918	2,186
Total	106,376	72,332	34,044

On the assumption that the urban population of China numbers approximately 100 million, the remaining 483 million being mostly farmers,[24] the food balance in Communist China, based on the 1952 production and the level of subsistence assumed, may be summarized below:

	In thousand metric tons of rice	*In million persons*
Maximum supply available for food	106,376	597.6
Consumption requirement at subsistence level		
Rural population	86,032	483.0
Urban population	17,794	100.0
Total	103,826	583.0
Surplus	2,550	14.6
Export	1,550	
Net Surplus[1]	1,000	

1. Annual average for the 1950-1953 period. Cf. Chen Yün's report to the National People's Assembly on the "planned supply and marketing" of commodities on September 23, 1954. NCNA, September 23, 1954.

Thus, a surplus of 2,550,000 tons of rice or its equivalent was at least theoretically available in 1952 if consumption were at the subsistence level assumed. This surplus would be available for manufacturing, export, and addition to stock.

Pursuing the line of thought a little further, we see that the volume retained by farmers for their own consumption amounts to approximately 72,332,000 tons. In practice, the actual quantity might even be somewhat larger as the last figure is derived from Buck's original data which did not include a part of the consumption of landlords who are also members of the peasantry. The difference between 86,032,000 tons and 72,332,000 tons or 13,700,000 tons represents the amount available for that part of the rural population that cannot provide for its own food if total consumption were not to exceed the total estimated consumption requirement. If this residual amount were inadequate, it would be necessary to reduce the quantity retained by the farmers for their own consumption.

Moreover, the surplus available over and above the minimum food consumption requirement was only 2.5 per cent of the total maximum supply available for food. This means that at the same level of production, it would be absorbed by the natural growth of population within a short period of one to two years. Consequently, if a surplus were to be maintained for export and other purposes, it would be necessary for production to increase almost proportionately.[25] On the other hand, if production should decline by more than 2.5 per cent, it would be necessary to curtail consumption below the minimum subsistence level assumed.

INTRODUCTION OF FOOD RATIONING

Since grain production actually declined by an estimated 7.5 per cent in 1953 from the 1952 level, the position of the food balance in Communist China began to worsen in the latter part of 1953 when consumption of the 1953 crop began. If we assume that the distribution of production by crops did not change materially, the maximum supply available for food out of the 1953 production probably declined to 98.4 million tons in terms of milled rice. Compared with the estimated minimum consumption requirement of 103.8 million tons, there would be a shortage of 5.4 million tons. While this amount could perhaps be made up by drawing on stock, such action would be contrary to the policy of building up a grain stockpile for emergency purposes.[26] At any rate, since grain exports based on contractual arrangements with other countries must be maintained, the overall reduction of consumption necessitated by the fall of production would be in excess of 5.4 million tons. Besides, although official policy since 1950 has stressed the need to produce undermilled rice and flour, in practice, the milling factor for rice in many parts of the country towards the end of 1953 was reported to be 60 per cent only as compared with 74 per cent used in our estimate and the official objective of 92 per cent, while that for flour was 70 per cent as compared with our assumption of 80 per cent and the official objective of 81 per cent.[27] Finally, losses in transportation, especially in shipments by water, and spoilage in warehouses due to excessive moisture, fermentation, and improper handling may have contributed to occasionally substantial losses. All these considerations point to the need of a greater reduction of consumption than the 5.4 million tons mentioned above.

According to the official *People's Daily,* at the beginning of 1954, some 10 per cent of the rural population had to obtain all or a part of their grain supply from others.[28] In addition, the famine-stricken peasants following the natural disasters of 1953 constituted another 10 per cent of the rural population. These two groups alone totalled 96.6 million persons. Added to an urban population of about 100 million, about 200 million persons had to be supplied with food. In terms of rice, the grain supply required would total 35 million tons at the minimum subsistence level, or 31.5 million tons if per capita consumption were reduced by, say, 10 per cent. If we assume that the peasants usually retain for their own consumption some 72 per cent of the maximum supply available for food, the residual quantity available for sale and tax payments out of the 1953 grain output would be no more than 27.6 million tons, which was 3.9 million tons less than 31.5 million tons. This situation by itself posed a sufficiently serious problem to the Communist government even if hoarding by consumers and grain merchants in anticipation of further deterioration of the grain supply were completely absent. On the other hand, a rise of grain prices, both through the peasants' increasing reluctance to sell and through competitive bidding on the part of private grain merchants would further threaten the government's control of the price structure and its fiscal program, not to mention that large segments of the population might literally starve.

The conditions described above were, of course, not only typical of 1953-1954, for the supply of grain in the years 1949-1951 was even smaller than in 1953. However, prior to 1952, the land redistribution process had probably yielded substantial stocks which could be freely disposed of by the government while the stepping up of grain exports was not made until the inception of the First Five Year Plan. Besides, the new population census was not completed until late 1953, and the Communist authorities were conceivably not altogether aware of the seriousness of the situation as long as the population's demand for food remained at a low level—*i.e.,* appreciably lower than the minimum subsistence level—prior to the beginning of the large-scale investment program. Nor indeed could rationing have been successfully introduced on a national scale as long as the "land reform" was incomplete and the Communist government was neither in full political control of the rural areas nor in possession of the necessary economic data. These conditions had changed by 1953 when the need to curtail consumption again arose.

Confronted with the threat of grain shortage, the Communist authorities officially introduced grain rationing on November 19, 1953, under the so-called program of planned purchase and supply of grain.[29] The peasants were ordered to sell their entire surplus stock to the government in accordance with predetermined quotas and at prices fixed by the government. All private grain merchants were prohibited to deal in grain on their own account although some were commissioned to act as government agents in selling grain to the public. Private rice, flour, and other mills were also ordered to cease operation for themselves or for private contractors and could only work on govenment processing contracts or for the account of others under official supervision. As for the consumers, the urban residents were to receive their rations against ration cards or, pending the issue of these cards, against residence certificates. In the smaller market towns and rural areas, distribution was to be made on the basis of control figures issued by the government, which would in turn reflect the supply available, and through "democratic consultation" with the persons and groups concerned.

According to official reports, in the months immediately after November, 1953, the Communist authorities were reasonably successful in obtaining the "surplus" grain which the peasants possessed beyond their tax payments, sales to the government prior to the inception of the new program, and what authorities considered to be their requirements.[30] The imbalance between grain purchases and sales by government agencies that was in evidence before was reversed. By the end of January, 1954, grain rationing systems had been set up in 13 municipalities, 156 medium size cities, all the county seats, and many market towns, with a total population of some 60 million.[31]

By June, 1954, rationing was in force in most of the rural areas.[32] A contractual purchase system was further introduced in March, 1954, for forward purchase through the government cooperatives so as to assure the government's grain supply in the future.[33] However, all this was apparently carried out against considerable opposition by the peasants and the grain merchants as may be seen in the large volume of official publications which have appeared in 1954 denouncing the activities of "counter-revolutionary saboteurs" and exhorting the peasantry to cooperation.[34] It appears that there is no absolute certainty that the rationing program will continue to succeed.

IV

CHANGES IN THE AGRICULTURAL TAX BEFORE 1951

As far as the government's grain supply is concerned, the purchase program serves to supplement the agricultural tax which is still levied in kind. Obviously, if the volume of grain collected through tax payments were large enough for the government's purposes, there would be no need to make additional purchases. The institution of government purchases on a very large scale indicates either inability or reluctance on the part of the Communist authorities to raise the agricultural tax even though the substitution of purchases for additional taxation does not necessarily imply a lighter burden on the peasantry at the present time because deferred payments are made by the government by crediting the purchase price to special savings accounts of the peasants who are not free to draw upon the receipts and because the purchase prices set seem to be exceedingly low.

The story of the agricultural tax since 1949 is an extremely complicated one because the tax rates were closely linked to the pattern of land redistribution which underwent constant change during the "land reform," but did not progress at the same speed in individual areas. This factor has led to divergent tax structures for different regions, and the situation has persisted in spite of the completion of the redistribution program.

According to official reports, grain collections in the autumn of 1949 totalled 2.65 million tons in Central-South China, 2 million tons in the Southwest, and 3.45 million tons in East China.[35] No reports were made on collections in Inner Mongolia and Northwest China, but the proceeds from Manchuria were said to be 5 million tons for the year. The share of the tax in Manchuria constituted 38.5 per cent of the area's grain output in 1949. The share in East China was 15.3 per cent of the year's output although tax was collected by the Communists only for the second half of the year. The relative share of the grain tax in the Central-South was said to vary from 15 to 18 per cent of the production of the Central-South provinces. All in all, about 21 per cent of the total grain output of Manchuria, Inner Mongolia, North China, Shantung, Shensi, Kansu, and Ningsia—which together constituted the so-called "old liberated areas"—was taxed away by the new regime in 1949, while in the newly "liberated" areas 18 per cent of the total gross output was appropriated in the same manner.[36] These figures represent official estimates of the total tax burden, and do not reflect the situation with regard to individual areas and persons as apparently no uniform rule prevailed. In the rich rice-growing Central-South provinces, the tax rates employed were based on the class status of the taxpayers, and levies were made at 6 per cent of the entire harvest or less for "poor peasants," 15 per cent or less for "middle peasants," 25 per cent for "rich peasants," and 50 per cent for "landlords." However, it was also officially reported that taxes accounting for 50-100 per cent or even more than 100 per cent of the entire harvest were not unknown in individual cases. It was with reference to this situation that one author went so far as to comment that the grain tax under the new regime was at times even higher than in previous years.[37]

In the summer of 1950, the tax rate on the 1949-1950 winter crop in the newly "liberated" areas was reported to have been reduced to 13 per cent of the gross output while local grain surtaxes were limited to 14.95 per cent of the central government tax instead of the 20 per cent that was theoretically in force previously.[38] But this situation was short-lived, and the tax system was soon to be further altered through the promulgation on September 8, 1950, of another set of provisional regulations on agricultural taxation in the newly "liberated" areas.

According to the new regulations, families with a per capita annual grain output less than 75 kilograms would enjoy complete tax exemption. The initial tax rate began at 3 per cent and rose progressively. The rate was set, for instance, at 13 per cent for families with a per capita annual output of 275.5 to 305 kilograms, rising to 42 per cent in cases where the per capita annual output was over 1,705.5 kilograms, and to 80 per cent when the per capita annual output was 100,000 kilograms or over.

It should be noted, however, that in conjunction with the program to liquidate the "landlord" class, the per capita annual output of a "landlord" was calculated at 120 per cent of the actual output. On the other hand, the crop of "poor peasants," less rent paid to others, was computed for tax purposes at 80 per cent of the actual output. Moreover, the so-called progressive rates were applicable to the *entire* output instead of the excess in total output over that part which fell within a lower tax bracket. Officially, the rather lame excuse advanced for this inequitable method was that it would simplify the mechanics of tax computation. Finally, preferential treatment was accorded to the families of "revolutionary martyrs," members of the armed forces, and government and party officials by allowing these groups to include absentee family members in computing their tax liability even though these persons were otherwise provided for by the government.

According to some Communist writers, the tax rates under the above provisions averaged 13 per cent for "middle peasants," 20 per cent for "rich peasants," and 30-50 per cent for the "landlord" class. These rates did not take into account the local surtaxes or any other "voluntary" contributions and dues imposed by local authorities in order to raise the tax collections above the central government quotas. The local authorities were induced to do so inasmuch as under a March 26, 1950, resolution of the State Administrative Council, 80 per cent of the grain collections in excess of the quotas could be retained by the former for their own use. The fixed quotas and flexible tax rates in force during this period were, by official admission, an important cause of dissatisfaction.[39]

THE STRUCTURE OF THE AGRICULTURAL TAX IN 1951

A partial revision of the agricultural tax was again made in June, 1951, when the State Administrative Council issued its new tax directive.[40] The country was divided into three areas for grain tax collection. First, in the "old liberated areas," tax would continue to be levied at a fixed proportion of the normal yield. The rate varied from 13 per cent in Jehol to 16 per cent in North China, and 20 per cent in the Manchurian provinces of Kirin, Sungkiang, and Lungkiang. Second, in those parts of the newly "liberated" areas where "land reform" had already been completed, tax at progressive rates ranging from 5 to 30 per cent would be levied on the entire output. In the case of tenant farmers, tax payments would be shared between tenants and landlords in the same proportion as the division of output, and additional charges on rental proceeds would no longer be made. Some special allowance was given to "poor peasant" households composed of one to two persons. Otherwise, the June, 1950, provisional regulations would continue to apply. Third, in those parts of the newly "liberated" areas where "land reform" had not yet been completed, the 1950 regulations would remain in force. Finally, the maximum limit of local grain surtaxes was restored to 20 per cent.

In anticipation of further reform in the tax structure and in order to lighten the task of local authorities in collecting the grain tax, the same directive also stipulated that a complete land survey be made and that the normal yields of individual holdings be determined. This program was to be completed in the "old" areas by the end of 1952 and was to be conducted simultaneously with "land reform" in all the other areas with a view to its completion in three to four years' time.

THE AGRICULTURAL TAX DIRECTIVE OF 1952

The process of continual revision was maintained in 1952. According to the directive of June, 1952, the schedule appearing on page 176 was adopted for individual areas.[41]

In addition, the 1952 directive mentioned the government's intention to adopt progressive tax rates for the whole country in 1953. Local surtaxes which had been changed time and again were finally abolished, and a single tax was levied by the central government.

Apparently, following the announcement of the above regulations, the Communist authorities have decided to make no further important changes in the agricultural tax. The 1953 tax directive even went so far as to promise no further increase in the agricultural tax for three years, that the 1952 rates would be continued, and that even the basic program of land survey and determination of normal yields

Schedule of Agricultural Tax in Communist China, 1952

Area	*Tax Rates*	*Exemption*
Manchuria	Proportional rates in per cent of total output	None
Heilungkiang, Sungkiang, and Kirin	23	
Liaotung and Liaohsi	21	
Jehol	15	
Hopeh, Chahar,* Shansi, and Pingyuan*	Proportional rate at 165 kilograms of millet per hectare	Tax exempt on land sufficient to produce 70 kilograms of grain per capita a year
Shantung, Inner Mongolia, and the former Shensi-Kansu, Ningsia Border Region	Proportional rates to be determined	
Newly "liberated" areas where "land reform" had been completed	Progressive rates from 7 to 30 per cent of the entire output	75 kilograms per capita
Newly "liberated" areas where "land reform" had not been completed	Progressive rates in accordance with the provisional regulations of 1950	75 kilograms per capita

* Since abolished.

would be discontinued so as to assure the peasants that "increase in production would not be followed by increase in taxation."[42] The same policy was reiterated in 1954.

TAXATION VERSUS COMPULSORY PURCHASES

The Communist authorities have been extremely reticent on the amount of grain collected through taxation ever since 1950. Although one cannot estimate accurately the tax collections, the proportional rates in force in Manchuria suggest that the share of public grain in gross output is probably not less than 20 per cent of the normal yield. Since normal yields are as a rule higher than actual yields, even allowing for partial tax exemptions for disaster-stricken areas, the tax burden is likely to be somewhat over 20 per cent of the gross production. In fact, if the actual yield were no more than 70 per cent of the normal yield, 20 per cent of the normal yield would amount to 30 per cent of actual output.

At 20 to 30 per cent of gross output, the total grain tax collection in 1952 would amount to 24.9 million to 37.4 million tons in terms of milled rice. Even the lower figure would be more than sufficient to provide for the entire urban population at the minimum subsistence level over and above the government's export and other requirements. But actual demand may exceed the minimum subsistence level assumed, especially through the expansion of government investment and the usual multiplier effect. Moreover, when the output of grain decreased in 1953, the same tax rates could yield only a smaller volume while the emergence of large numbers in the rural population who needed food supply made it impossible for the Communist authorities to provide for the increased demand out of tax collections, even at the minimum level. The only alternatives were an increase in tax rates and compulsory purchases.

Fear of the adverse effect of another tax increase on agricultural production which had already fallen below the 1952 peak was probably the determining factor in the authorities' decision not to increase taxation openly for the time being. As one author has pointed out, in order to produce 2,445 kilograms of rice on one hectare of land, the cost of seeds, fertilizer, animal feed, and labor amounts to a sum equivalent to 1,091 kilograms of rice.[43] Thus the farmer's net income is actually less than 56 per cent of his gross output even though his total receipts may be somewhat higher as not all the cost items represent actual outlays by him. If 20 per cent or more of the gross output is further subtracted by taxation, the net income after tax would be less than 36 per cent of gross output. Under such circumstances, it is quite likely that the point of diminishing return has been reached in agricultural taxation.

However, compulsory purchases of grain by the government do not necessarily leave the peasants better off than an increase in taxation would. For one thing, the Communist authorities have never published the prices at which grain purchases are made, and there is reason to suspect that the prices set are low.[44] Moreover, the peasants are induced to deposit their sales proceeds in special savings accounts for fixed periods.[45] These accounts cannot be drawn upon freely and are subject to frequent charges for various contributions and government loan subscriptions. The reduction of consumption in the end, therefore, may be as severe as if there were an increase in taxation although the government probably enjoys more administrative flexibility in meeting any changes in the situation.

These considerations also lead us to doubt whether the majority of the peasants could be better off now than they were before the "land reform." In the first place, the former owner farmers are in all probability worse off in view of the higher grain tax and stationary or even lower crop yields. The former part owners are unlikely to have fared any better unless their unfortunate experience as land owners could be more than offset by improved circumstances as tenants. But even the majority of the former tenant farmers never had to pay rents as high as the present tax and other deductions, taking into account the fact that as tenants at least a part of their production costs were previously borne by the owners. Only those former tenant farmers and farm laborers whose increase in holdings after "land reform" can more than compensate the decrease in net income per unit area can be considered better off. While one cannot be certain of the number of these persons, reference to our discussion in the preceding chapter should be sufficient to convince us that they can hardly be in the majority. Finally, since all these comparisons refer to farm households, the increase in population must have exerted some further adverse effect on per capita net income after taxes. Given the present scale of taxation and compulsory purchases, the lot of the peasants can scarcely be improved unless the trend of grain production could follow a sharply rising course.[46]

V

COTTON PRODUCTION

Before the establishment of the new regime, the production of cotton in mainland China, influenced by the high cost of domestic transportation, grain prices, and the fluctuating world price of raw cotton and its effect on imports, varied widely from year to year. The location of the large mills in port cities and the small proportion of long staple cotton produced in China tended especially to favor cotton imports. These fluctuations may be seen in the following table:

Raw Cotton (Lint) Production in Mainland China, 1931, 1936, 1941, and 1946
(In thousand metric tons)

1931	374.4
1936	848.7
1941	399.8
1946	371.5

Source: Statistical Yearbook, Nanking, 1948.

According to a preliminary estimate, cotton production in 1949 was 387 thousand tons.[47] Later reports showed a revised figure of 440,000 tons. If the latest figures are used and internal inconsistencies are eliminated, the following output estimates and their corresponding index numbers may be obtained for the 1949-1954 period:

Raw Cotton (Lint) Production in Communist China, 1949–1955

	Index	*Quantity (In thousand metric tons)*
1949	100	440
1950	161	711
1951	229	1,008
1952	293	1,290
1953	266	1,175
1954 (preliminary)	280	1,232[1]
1955 (plan)	338	1,486

Sources: People's Daily, Peking, April 1, 1953, and January 11, 1954; NCNA, November 3, 1953, and September 13 and 24, 1954; and Li Hsien-nien's report on the 1955 budget on July 9, 1955.

1. Actual output reported to be smaller.

The reasonable accuracy of the above estimates may also again be confirmed by the acreage and yield data obtained from various Communist sources as shown in the table appearing on page 180. These represent national averages and may not be as accurate as regional figures and their aggregates would be, but the discrepancies between estimates derived in this manner and those given above are relatively small.

Raw Cotton (Lint) Acreage, Yield and Estimated Production in Communist China, 1949-1953

	Area Planted (in million hectares)	*Yield (in kilograms per hectare)*	*Estimated Production (in thousand metric tons)*
1949	2.6	159.8	418
1950	3.7	190.5	711
1951	5.6	186.7	1,046
1952	5.6	228.6	1,280
1953	5.2	224.8	1,169

Sources: New China Monthly, No. 17, pp. 1070-1072, Peking, March, 1951; *Liberation Daily,* Shanghai, June 20, 1950; *Science Bulletin,* Vol. IV, No. 3, Peking, 1954; *People's China* (in English), Peking, February 16, 1954; and NCNA, September 9, 1954.

ACREAGE EXPANSION AND YIELD

On the basis of the above information, it can be seen that although there was a notable increase in the unit area yield between 1949 and 1952, the increase in total production was to a large extent due to the expansion of acreage. Especially, if comparison is made with the prewar peak output year, 1936, when yield per hectare averaged 242 kilograms of lint on 3.5 million hectares, the larger output in 1952 was entirely the result of larger acreage.

The principal factor in bringing about the greater acreage under cotton during the period under consideration is, by official admission, purely economic. It is the relative price between cotton and grain as fixed by the authorities for tax payment by cotton farmers and grain purchases by the latter from government cooperatives. By offering the cotton farmers increasingly favorable prices in terms of grain, the Communist government succeeded in encouraging the planting of cotton between 1950 and 1952. When the price of cotton was lowered in 1953, following an increase in the tax on cotton land in 1952,[48] cotton acreage promptly declined, and the authorities were forced to raise cotton price again in 1954. The close correlation between cotton acreage and the economic incentive offered presents a very serious problem and further emphasizes the importance of raising unit area yield.

The initial encouragement given to cotton growers was prompted by the desire to achieve self-sufficiency in cotton, an objective which was temporarily attained after the 1952 cotton harvest. The reversal of policy in 1953, on the other hand, was explained by the fact that

Relative Prices of Cotton in Terms of Grain, 1950-1954
(in units of grain in weight to one unit of cotton lint, 7/8″, medium grade)

	1950	*1951*	*1952*	*1953*	*1954*
Wheat region	7.0	8.0	7.5–8.5	6.25–7.5	6.75–8.0
Millet region	8.0	8.5	8.0–9.5	6.75–8.0	7.5 –8.25
Rice region	6.5	8.5	8.0–9.0	6.75–8.0	7.25–8.25

Sources: A Manual for Newspaper Readers, p. 574, Hankow, 1950; *Economic Weekly,* No. 14, p. 3, Shanghai, April, 1953, and No. 21, p. 21, May 28, 1953; and NCNA, March 3, 1954.

---

while cotton acreage had increased rapidly, "the potential of cultivated land had not been fully exploited.[49] The expansion of cotton acreage had encroached upon land formerly devoted to grains, especially wheat.[50] Although it was quite reasonable to aim at the stabilization of cotton acreage and to concentrate on increasing unit area yield, this policy failed to take into sufficient account the reaction of the peasants. According to an official comment,[51] "the trend of unplanned expansion of cotton acreage was overestimated. In fixing the price ratio for cotton and grain, the price for cotton was set too low. In stressing the importance of increasing food output, inadequate attention was paid to cotton production. The target planned for cotton production in 1953 was also less than that of 1952. With additional shortcomings in cotton purchases and the supply of producers' and consumers' goods to the cotton farmers and the sudden suspension of advance purchases of cotton, many party cadres were given the erroneous impression that there was already too much cotton. The government's leadership in increasing cotton production slackened unconsciously, and the population began to doubt the wisdom of increasing cotton output further. As a result, the cotton acreage in 1953 decreased by over 400,000 hectares from the 1952 high, and the total output also fell short of the target . . ."

To remedy the situation, the authorities embarked in early 1954 upon a policy of raising the grain price of cotton, guaranteeing equal tax treatment between cotton and grain farmers, and advance government purchases through the supply and marketing cooperatives. However, all these measures, in so far as they are successful in encouraging cotton planting would only restore the conditions under which cotton acreage was cut back in the first place. Given the same unit area yields, the problem remains to be one of land shortage. Whether it be grain or cotton, shortage will always arise if unit area yields cannot be expanded and/or if the crop area cannot be increased.

ADEQUACY OF COTTON SUPPLY

In order to achieve self-sufficiency in raw cotton, the first and foremost criterion is the availability of sufficient supply for the country's modern cotton mills. In addition, however, there should be enough surplus to meet the demand for home spinning and for padding winter clothing and bedding, a common practice in China. Estimates of these requirements could be made as follows.

First, according to a prewar study on Chinese cotton mills in seven provinces, about 203.6 kilograms of lint cotton was required for each bale of yarn.[52] This rate was achieved during the first years of Communist rule only in some of the government mills which possessed relatively modern equipment taken over from the Japanese by the Nationalists.[53] Considerable gains were subsequently made in increasing efficiency, and the average cotton consumption was said to be 195 kilograms in 1954.[54] On the basis of such a cotton consumption ratio, the 4.6 million bales of yarn produced in 1954 as estimated in Chapter VIII below would require approximately 898,000 tons of raw cotton.

Second, for normal home cotton consumption, an approximate idea may be obtained by using the 1936 cotton production figure, adjusted for incomplete geographical coverage, plus net imports and less mill consumption and addition to stock. The residual amount which may be regarded as the total home consumption, came to about 0.6 kilogram per capita in 1936. Approximately less than one-half of this amount could be attributed to padding, the rest to hand spinning.[55] If the same rate of per capita consumption for padding is assumed for 1954, given a population of 583 million, the total requirement for cotton would amount to approximately 175,000 tons. Allowing the same quantity for hand spinning, a rough balance between the available supply from production in 1953 and our estimated consumption requirements for 1954 would be as follows:[56]

		In thousand metric tons
Production		1,175
Consumption requirements:		
Mill consumption	898	
Padding	175	
Hand spinning	175	1,248
Deficit		73

Thus, under our various assumptions, there would be a deficit of 73,000 tons, which is very small.

As for 1953, since cotton yarn production was smaller than in 1954, while cotton production in 1952 was greater, a surplus of 120,000 tons could probably be assumed. The latter was quite adequate to meet the deficit of the following year. On this basis, Communist China's claim of having achieved self-sufficiency in raw cotton supply could be more or less sustained.

However, in this connection, several other factors should be considered further. First, the above estimates have not taken into account the possible shortage of long staple cotton which is required for spinning fine yarns. Since some of the spindlage available in Communist China may not be adaptable to spinning coarse yarns, and since short staple cotton still predominates in Chinese production, a certain amount of imports of long staple cotton may continue to be necessary. The overall surplus of cotton conceals possible shortages of particular grades. Second, no allowance has been made in the above estimates for waste and other losses which could conceivably more than wipe out the estimated surplus. Third, the per capita cotton consumption assumed for padding represents an extremely low level of consumption and may conceivably be an underestimate of actual consumption in any period. Fourth, in view of the fact that cotton piece goods manufactured in modern mills are still in short supply, the home weaving industry using handspun yarn may actually demand more cotton than has been assumed above although any appreciable expansion of modern machine spinning would tend to reduce the cotton demand of hand spinning. When all these factors are taken into account, it is quite possible that the estimated cotton surplus in 1953 has to be discounted to some extent.

By far the most important factor in evaluating the supply of raw cotton in Communist China is the fact that the cotton yarn output of modern mills in 1954 by no means corresponded to the potential demand for cotton if available spindlage had been fully utilized. The 4.6 million bales of cotton yarn produced in that year corresponded to 0.8 bale or about 320 pounds of yarn per spindle. Assuming that the average productivity of the modern mills was about 1.2 pounds of yarn per 20 spindle-hours,[57] the average yarn production per spindle would entail an annual operation rate of 5,332 hours for each spindle, which was substantially less than what might be expected under the assumption of full-time operation of all available spindles.

If the operation rate at the modern mills were stepped up to, say, three eight-hour shifts a day and a minimum of 300 days a year, the total number of spindle hours could be easily raised to 7,200 a year for each spindle.[58] Given 5.5 million spindles for the country as a whole and an average productivity of 1.2 pounds of yarn per 20 spindle-hours, Communist China's total yarn production could conceivably be increased to 5.94 million bales a year. At 195 kilograms of cotton per bale of yarn, the total mill consumption of cotton would then rise to 1,158 thousand tons. If the demand for home consumption were maintained, while production remained at the 1954 level, the result would be a deficit of 276 thousand tons in 1955. This situation probably underlies Communist China's plan to increase cotton production in 1955 by up to 254,000 tons over the 1954 output.

Estimated Balance of Cotton Supply and Consumption in 1955

		In thousand metric tons
Production		1,232
Consumption requirements:		
Mill consumption	1,158	
Padding	175	
Hand spinning	175	1,508
Deficit		276

Bearing in mind that some of the factors mentioned above, such as waste, etc., might be operative, and that industrial demand for raw cotton other than that of the textile industry might arise, one can easily see the precarious situation in raw cotton supply at the present time.

It was obviously in the light of this development that the Communist authorities decided to extend their compulsory purchase program to cotton as soon as the 1954 crop came in.[59] Under this program, the cotton farmers are required to sell to the government all surplus in excess of tax payments and minimum requirements for the farmers' own use. Use of cotton for padding is also to be curtailed. Thus the situation of cotton supply has taken a parallel course to that of grain.

As we shall see in our discussion on the textile industry later in this book, Communist China probably produced more yarn in the years under consideration than could be made into finished cotton piece goods on account of the small number of machine looms available. Moreover, power shortage may have limited operation in the mills. However, these are situations which the authorities are bent to remedy. If they are successful in this respect and/or if cotton yarn exports could be developed by Communist China, for instance, in some of the Southeast Asia countries, the problem of cotton supply would continue to worsen unless the unit area yield could be boosted. The First Five Year Plan envisages a 25.4 per cent increase in cotton production between 1952 and 1957. Since production in both 1953 and 1954 was actually lower than in 1952, the target appears to have been set too high. Moreover, even if realized, the output in 1957 may still prove to be inadequate in view of the projected expansion of spindlage and population growth.

VI

FACTORS IN THE EXPANSION OF GRAIN AND COTTON PRODUCTION

Both Communist official pronouncements and the apparent conflicting claims between grains and cotton on available crop acreage in certain areas point to the general conclusion that any further increase in overall crop production in Communist China must be sought in greater productivity instead of a larger crop acreage although some further expansion of the latter should not be ruled out.[60] It appears that greater productivity per unit area of land and, incidentally, per man, could be brought about through the following developments.

First, technological changes in the form of improved seeds and methods of cultivation, and other related developments could conceivably raise yields without any other change. Second, without altering the ratio of land to labor appreciably, yield could be increased by the employment of more capital to the form of fertilizers, implements, insecticides, and more irrigation and better water control. All these would, however, require capital investments in certain industries and the carrying out of vast conservation projects. Finally, the size of the farm as an operating unit may be altered with, in all probability, a reduction of the ration of labor to land. It is also true that some of the technological changes and the employment of more capital in the form of farm machinery may not be practicable without an enlargement of the size of the farm, which would result in the emergence of surplus labor on the farm. Given the greater cost of capital on mechanized farms, whether the establishment of large state farms would be economically worthwhile or not depends to a large extent upon what can and has to be done with respect to the displaced farm labor. These are among some of the factors that have obviously engaged the thinking of Communist planners just as they are interesting to us.

SUPPLY OF CHEMICAL FERTILIZER AND INSECTICIDES

Deferring the discussion on water conservancy projects to Chapter IX, we may take a cursory look at some of the other possible developments noted here. First, regarding fertilizer supply, according to a study by the National Agricultural Research Bureau, the annual requirement for rice, cotton, wheat, and rapeseeds amounts to 10 million metric tons on the basis of optimum technical application and a smaller crop acreage than now exists. If the other major crops are also included, the annual requirement would amount to 15 million tons.[61] These figures represent quantities of chemical fertilizers over and above such other substances as oil seed cakes and manure. It is further stated that the optimum application of chemical fertilizers in areas where water is not a limiting factor may increase yields by as much as 25 per cent. However, according to Communist reports, the total supply of commercial fertilizers to farmers through the supply and marketing cooperatives amounted to only 5.7 million tons in 1953 and may reach 7 million tons in 1954.[62] Since the commercial fertilizers supplied obviously did not refer to chemical fertilizers alone, it would seem that a great deal remains to be done in this respect.

The same is true with respect to the employment of insecticides and fungicides. A total of 20,000 tons of such materials was supplied to farmers during 1952 and 1953, and their use on 4 million hectares of cotton land contributed largely to the bumper crop in that year. In 1953, 2 million hectares of land devoted to food grains benefited in the same manner. The planned supply during 1954 was to be twice that of 1953, but even then only 8.8 million hectares were to benefit from this treatment.[63] Compared with the total crop acreage the supply of these chemicals appears to be grossly inadequate, even granted that they may not be needed in all areas simultaneously.

CROP YIELDS AND FARM SIZE

Finally, we have to examine the relation between unit area yields and farm size. Although information on this subject has been rather sketchy and the official sources may be somewhat biased, it is nevertheless interesting to note that of the 59 mechanized state farms reported in operation at the end of 1953,[64] the average size in terms of cultivated area was 2,260 hectares. The latter may be compared with an average farm size of 2,800 hectares for 50 mechanized and semi-mechanized state farms reported earlier in 1953, an average of 2,533 hectares for 15 mechanized state farms and 2 tractor stations in 1950,[65] and an estimated average of only 17 hectares for the 14,000 cooperative farms in 1953.[66] On the basis of available information it appears that the average size of the farm varies directly with the number of hectares per man, as well as the unit area yields. The cooperative farms, for instance, are said to have yields that were 16.4 per cent greater than those of mutual aid teams and 39.2 per cent greater than those of individual farms. On the other hand, yields on the 50 state farms in 1953 were from 50 to 100 per cent greater than those of individual farms in the same areas. These same farms had 5.2 hectares per man as compared with less than 0.7 hectare per man on the state farms and tractor stations reported for 1950, and one-third of a hectare on the cooperative farms. While the cooperative farms in 1953 did not seem to possess tractors, the 50 state farms in 1953 possessed an average of 16 tractors each.

The average number of 15 h.p. tractors on the 59 mechanized state farms at the end of 1953 was 27.4, while the average number of hectares of cultivated area and arable land per man was 2.3 hectares and 8 hectares respectively.

It is, of course, possible that the state farms may have enjoyed preferential treatment in the supply of fertilizers, improved seeds, and credit, but the use of farm machinery made possible by the larger size of the farm and resulting in a lower labor-land ratio can hardly be dismissed as having no relation to the greater yields of the larger farms even if this phenomenon has been highly colored in official reporting.

THE IMPONDERABLE HUMAN FACTOR

The supply of fertilizers, improved seeds, and insecticides may be increased independently of the efforts of the peasants themselves although they have to be effectively used by the peasants. The construction of large irrigation and flood control projects must, however, rely predominantly on labor recruited directly or indirectly from the farms. Aside from forced labor, the importance of the peasants' cooperation becomes even more pronounced when individual farms have to be combined to form cooperative and, later, state farms. Since land ownership is deeply ingrained in the mind of the average peasant, a fact amply substantiated by the Communists' own admission of the emergence of new "rich peasants" after the "land reform," the only compensating factor the authorities could offer would be the higher yields of the larger farms. However, this attraction loses much of its glitter when the agricultural tax and compulsory purchases may take away the bulk of the increased output. If, through collectivization and the resultant larger output, the peasants could receive a higher net income that could be freely disposed of in spite of the high government requisitions, it is conceivable that opposition may eventually melt away.[67] However, collectivization cannot succeed without the initial cooperation of the peasants. Herein lies a dilemma of major proportions which the Communists must resolve.

Perhaps the peasants' opposition to collectivization could be lessened if surplus labor could be removed from the farms in the first place. Yet public works may not be able to absorb all the potential surplus labor available. Such alternatives as labor exports and other means to dispose of surplus labor may have to be considered by the Communist authorities. However, opposition may also be encountered here. The human element remains an imponderable factor in Communist plans for the expansion of agricultural production as an integral part of forced industrialization. It remains to be seen whether the Chinese Communists' political control over the peasantry can deal with this immense problem with a greater degree of success than has apparently been possible elsewhere in the past.

NOTES

1. Cf. T. H. Shen, *Agricultural Resources of China,* Ithaca, 1951. Data compiled from the trade returns of the Maritime Customs of China.

2. The term "grain" includes other items in addition to cereals. For details see below.

3. This is clearly indicated as the 1931-1936 average. Cf. *Popular Agriculture,* Shanghai, February, 1952.

4. Cf., however, Chou En-lai's report to the National People's Congress, September 24, 1954, according to which the 1953 and 1954 outputs were slightly higher.

5. See, for instance, *New China Monthly,* No. 17, pp. 1070-72, Peking, March, 1951.

6. *Ibid.* Cf. also *Chinese Agriculture,* Vol. II, No. 1, Peking.

7. Cf. *Economic Bulletin,* No. 50, p. 15, Hongkong, December, 1953, and NCNA, February 4, 1954.

8. An additional advantage in using 163.75 million tons for 1952 instead of 160 million tons is that this will obviate the danger of underestimating Communist China's food supply in the discussion below.

9. See the Food Balance sheet in T. H. Shen's work.

10. Ou Pao-san, *China's National Income, 1933,* Nanking, 1947.

11. Offsetting the increase in cotton acreage, however, there was probably a decline in acreage under the oil-bearing crops.

12. See Shen, *op. cit.*

13. NCNA, May 7, 1953.

14. See *Northeast Daily,* Shen-yang, May 7, 1950.

15. For preliminary estimates of regional crop distribution see *Economic Bulletin,* No. 309, p. 12, Hongkong, March, 1953.

16. See the various government directives and resolutions in *Compendium,* Vol. III, pp. 779-796, 1952.

17. Cf. *New China Monthly,* No. 42, pp. 132-133, Peking, April, 1953.

18. The breakdown by commodities in thousand metric tons would be as follows:

Commodity	Thousand metric tons
Rice	93,713
Wheat	26,542
Corn	16,600
Kaoliang	12,415
Millet	11,497
Soyabeans	10,732
Tubers	49,847
Other	12,280
Total, all grains	235,626

19. Cf. *People's China* (in English), Peking, March, 1954.

19a. See Li Fu-ch'un's report to the second session of the First National People's Congress on July 6, 1955.

20. Cf. T. H. Shen, *op. cit.,* chapter 18. See also Ou Hui-ch'ing, *Nutrition and Diet,* Shanghai, 1952.

21. This represents the mean between the figure of 76 adult males according to C. M. Ch'iao's study on *China's Food and Population Problem,* Shanghai, 1937, and the figure of 87 adult males according to T. H. Shen's more recent work. Even if the assumption that every 1,000 persons are equivalent to 82 adult males should overestimate food consumption, this would be offset by the low caloric intake assumed.

22. The FAO Food Balance Sheet figure of 3,430 calories per kilogram of rice is assumed here.

23. Based on reports from Hongkong.

24. *People's Daily,* Peking, February 10, 1954.

25. Requirements for animal feed and seeds do not rise proportionately with the population growth.

26. Cf. *Committee for Free Asia Bulletin,* San Francisco, October 29, 1953.

27. Cf. *Ta-kung pao,* Tientsin, November 16, 1953.

28. February 10, 1954.

29. NCNA, February 28, 1954. The rationing of edible vegetable oils was decreed soon afterwards for similar reasons.

30. *People's Daily,* Peking, March 1, 1954.

31. NCNA, February 28, 1954.

32. *Ta-kung pao,* Tientsin, June 3, 1954.

33. NCNA, March 27, 1954.

34. See, for instance, *People's Daily,* Peking, March 7, 1954, and *Reference Sources on the General Line,* Peking, 1954.

35. See *Economic Weekly,* Vol. X, No. 6, p. 15, Shanghai, February, 1950; *Manual for Newspaper Readers,* pp. 408, 633, and 678, Hankow, 1950; *Northeast Agriculture,* No. 35, pp. 1-2, February, 1952; and *New China Monthly,* Vol. IV, No. 5, p. 1101. Cf. also Y. L. Wu, *The Land Program of the Chinese Communist Party, An Interpretation* (in English), San Francisco, February, 1952.

36. *Economic Weekly,* Vol. X, Nos. 8-9, p. 12, Shanghai, March, 1950.

37. *Economic Weekly,* Vol. X, No. 15, p. 8, Shanghai, March, 1950.

38. *Economic Yearbook,* p. 30, Hongkong, 1951.

39. Cf. *People's Daily,* Peking, February 11, 1951.

40. See *New China Monthly,* No. 21, p. 676, Peking, July, 1951.

41. See *People's Daily,* Peking, June 19, 1952.

42. *Wen-hui pao,* Hongkong, August 31, 1953.

43. Cf. *Economic Weekly,* No. 35, p. 691, Shanghai, September, 1952.

44. The present price paid for rice, estimated indirectly, is probably about Y50,000 per picul as compared with a retail price of about Y120,000 per picul. According to official statistics the weighted average grain purchase price index was 117.73 in 1951, 122.72 in 1952, and 131.88 in 1953 (1950=100). The gradual increase since 1950, however, probably reflected a greater amount of rice purchased in line with the expansion of rice production, as rice commands a higher price than coarse grains. Cf. *People's Daily,* Peking, March 1, 1954.

45. NCNA, March 1, 1954.

46. In this connection, however, one should note the benefit of farm crop and livestock insurance which is being gradually introduced. The measure helps to mitigate

the impact of disasters without, of course, raising the net income of the peasants in normal years. Cf. Chen Chu-yuan, *Monetary Affairs of Communist China* (in English), Hongkong, 1954.

47. See Li Jung-shuan's article in *Industrial and Commercial News,* Vol. V, No. 1, pp. 8-9, Shanghai, September, 1951, and the *Far Eastern Economic Review,* p. 726, Hongkong, December, 1950.

48. See Article V of the directive on parity prices between cotton and grain and the land tax in kind on cotton fields in *Liberation Daily,* Shanghai, March 15, 1952.

49. NCNA, March 27, 1954.

50. Cf. *New China Monthly,* No. 42, p. 124, Peking, April, 1953.

51. NCNA, March 27, 1954.

52. Cf. Wang Tzu-chien and Wang Chen-chung, *A Study of Chinese-owned Cotton Mills in Seven Provinces,* Shanghai, 1936.

53. *Economic Weekly,* Vol. II, No. 6, pp. 6-8, Shanghai, August, 1950.

54. *Ta-kung pao,* Hongkong, October 31, 1952, and NCNA, April 14, 1952, and September 9, 1954. According to Li Fu-ch'un, cotton consumption in the Shanghai mills averaged 193.1 kilograms per bale of yarn in the first quarter of 1955. The Shanghai mills, however, are among the relatively more efficient.

55. Cf. *Manchuria's Resources and Chemical Industry,* Vol. I, pp. 40-41, Shanghai, 1934.

56. In the case of cotton, consumption in any year must be met predominantly out of the previous year's output.

57. This figure is derived from Wang, *op. cit.,* and is confirmed by the NCNA report on September 9, 1954.

58. By 1954 some 95 per cent of the total spindlage available was operated on a 3-shift basis, though probably not all the time. NCNA, September 9, 1954.

59. See the decree of the State Administrative Council issued on September 9, 1954. NCNA, September 14, 1954.

60. Th official pronouncement on the further expansion of crop acreage is that future development depends upon the availability of farm machinery. This does not seem to be a satisfactory explanation as land can also be brought under cultivation without the help of machinery. Water is probably the principal limiting factor in some areas. Cf. Chen Yün's report on September 23, 1954. As reported by Li Fu-ch'un, the First Five Year Plan envisages a minimum increase in cultivated land of 2,580,000 hectares over the 1952 level.

61. Cf. T. H. Shen, *op. cit.*

62. NCNA, March 31, 1954.

63. NCNA, April 2, 1954.

64. NCNA, March 17, 1954 and *New China Monthly,* pp. 155-157, Peking, April, 1954.

65. China News Service, February 25, 1954, and *China Agriculture Bulletin,* Peking, Vol. II, No. 12.

66. *Study,* Peking, January, 1954, and NCNA, January 14, 1954.

67. Some doubt may still be expressed even under these hypothetical conditions.

CHAPTER SIX

Industrialization, Planning and Socialization

I

RELATION BETWEEN FORCED INDUSTRIALIZATION, CENTRAL PLANNING, AND SOCIALIZATION

The two cornerstones of the Communists' initial program in China were the restoration of a semblance of economic stability and fiscal viability and the recovery and gradual collectivization of agricultural production through an initial process of land redistribution. At the risk of repetition, let us emphasize again that, from the economic point of view, the Communists' policy of rapid industrialization could not begin without first having suppressed the postwar hyper-inflation and assured the government of an expanding flow of revenue. Nor could the pace of industrialization be stepped up without a large supply of agricultural products under the control of the government. At the same time, the political overtone of the Communists' activities in the fiscal and agricultural spheres is also quite unmistakable inasmuch as without price stability, fiscal order, and tight control over the peasants the new masters of China would not have been able to achieve the degree of consolidation of political power that was necessary for the initiation of any large-scale development program such as was exemplified in the launching of the First Five Year Plan in 1953. Viewed from this particular angle it is perhaps not surprising that the program of industrial development was not initiated earlier. The years between 1949 and 1952 represented in every way a period of consolidation and preparation. Progress in industrial recovery coincided with the realization of the other indispensable conditions of rapid industrialization. By about the end of 1952 the stage was more or less set for a serious attempt to embark upon the path that, supported by the Soviet example, seems to hold the promise of greater national power and, if political conditions permit or require at some future date, also a larger measure of economic welfare.

Needless to say, a socialistic economy has two indispensable elements, central planning and nationalization. When the Common Program delineated the Chinese economy into five sectors, including one for the so-called national capitalists, the policy announced was not a denial of this basic proposition, but rather a concession to expediency. Practical considerations also point to the ultimate need to introduce both planning and socialization even though this may be done only gradually. This is true not only in Communist China, but also in any other underdeveloped country that, motivated by some overriding political purpose, forces itself to industrialize at a pace beyond the rate voluntary domestic savings, supplemented by foreign capital, can support.

In the Chinese case, the consumption of agricultural products must be reduced so that there can be a large enough exportable surplus to pay for imported capital equipment while supplies are made available to support the urban population and laborers who are employed on large public works and paid in food rations and to provide the manufacturing industry with raw materials. At the same time, the consumption of industrial products must be reduced so that domestic resources in general, and specialized equipment in particular, can be allocated in desired quantities to capital accumulation in the form of domestically produced capital equipment. This emphasis on industrialization through domestic accumulation is notable especially in view of the much publicized assistance received from the Soviet Union.

One good illustration of the view that it is impossible to depend upon imports of foreign capital equipment for the country's industrialization, not to mention foreign credit, may be found in an editorial of the official *People's Daily* which stated at the end of the first year of the country's First Five Year Plan:[1] "In order to acquire the source of capital for the development of heavy industry, we can only rely upon the wealth we create through production and through measures such as 'production-increase and austerity.' This will naturally slow down the speed at which the standard of living of the people can be improved. The only way to resolve this conflict is to subordinate the improvement of livelihood to the development of production . . . During the last few years, a part of the country's agricultural produce was used to exchange for a sizable amount of machinery and consumers' goods from the Soviet Union and the People's Democracies. But it must be understood that in the Soviet Union industrial and agricultural goods are produced according to a definite ratio that cannot be altered simply because there is more agricultural produce to be absorbed from China." Besides, even if imported capital equipment is available in substantial quantities, the responsibility of domestic industry is not necessarily lessened. Under the present arrangement with the Soviet Union, some 30 to 50 per cent of the plan and equipment to be installed in the large construction projects undertaken or planned with Soviet assistance for 1950-1959 has to be supplied domestically.[2] Obviously, if capital goods required for a particular enterprise cannot be imported, or imported in entirety, domestic products must fill the gap. The availability of an exportable surplus of agricultural products as such does not automatically provide the solution. The answer lies in domestic production of capital equipment.

While the volume of current consumption cannot be curtailed drastically without government control and planning, it is not enough merely to hold consumption at a low level. For the nature, as well as volume, of investment must be regulated. Investment in the form of an indiscriminate accumulation of inventory, for instance, would not be desirable from the Communist planners' point of view. The selection of industries, production techniques, and geographical location must be determined in accordance with the overall economic policy of the government, which is basically defined by the latter's political objectives. In short, if the government follows a detailed plan at all—as the Chinese Communist regime does in an increasing degree—and if the plan envisages an arrangement of productive forces different from that which would be obtained without government intervention, a program must be devised to determine the allocation of resources (1) temporally, (2) within the current period, and (3) with respect to geographical location, and concrete measures must be taken to implement the program.

The allocation of resources according to a unitary plan implies the subordination of individual plans and decisions to those of the government. Consequently, the effectiveness of central planning cannot but vary in inverse proportion to the scope and importance of that part of economic activity which is determined by individual entrepreneurs and consumers. Perhaps there is no logical necessity why the subordination of individual decision-making to the central plan must lead to the sequestration of private property, but the Communist doctrine abhors private ownership of means of production and the rentier class. Besides, private property, even when deprived of the power of control in production, may well contain the kernel of independent self-assertion, which, conceivably, could be disruptive of the plan at some time or other. This being so, there is a strong case from the Communists' viewpoint for the increasing socialization of the private sector in production and for the regulation of its activities so that they will not hinder the fulfilment of the central plan even though, at the outset, the latter may be of a partial character only. This gradual transformation of private business is clearly reflected in Communist China's policy towards the private sector during the transitional period—a policy of "utilization, restriction, and reform." [3]

Increasing government control is necessary not only to assure the planned allocation of resources in production, but also to make certain that limited quantities of consumers' goods are made available to non-producers. As mentioned in the preceding chapter, this is particularly true in the case of agricultural produce of which, theoretically at any rate, all surpluses above the minimum consumption requirements of the producers themselves must be made available to the government for export and consumption by the non-farm population. Even if total consumption were held at the required low level, any withholding of their crops from the market by the peasants would lead to an accumulation of private inventory which would in all probability yield no direct advantage to future production. Besides, such conduct would offer a strong inducement to private industry to produce certain consumers' goods in order to exchange for farm products, a development which may well be disruptive of the country's industrial plan. As mentioned previously, such a development would also have an adverse effect on the government's ability to control certain key commodity prices that enter into the urban cost of living index and consequently affect the wage level. At the same time, the distribution of industrial products must be government-controlled so that the population will be supplied with what is allowed, no more and no less. This applies not only to the urban industrial population, but also to the farmers from whom the government expects to receive the bulk of their surplus. The most effective way to control distribution rigorously is, of course, to channel the commodity flow between producers and consumers through government trading organs. From this follows the logical necessity of socializing trading activity and of reducing the number of private producers and traders through amalgamation and other forms of concentration in order to facilitate control short of and prior to complete socialization. Furthermore, the reduction of the number of middle men and their gradual replacement by government trading organs would also be useful in effecting the transfer of resources from trade to industry, thereby increasing the physical production of goods.

The foregoing discussion points to several issues with which Communist China has had to contend and which any other underdeveloped country in similar circumstances might also have to resolve even if it were not dedicated to the Communist philosophy. To recapitulate, given a plan of rapid industrialization by domestic means, total consumption must be controlled. The nature and geographical distribution of investment and current production must be regulated. The distribution of products must be supervised. The subordination of individual plans and decisions must be effected in every possible way. From this follows the need for increasing government control which, when coupled with an avowed preference for public ownership, means increasing socialization. The program of socialization and control of private business is therefore an integral part of government planning for industrialization.

Understanding of this process will serve to explain much that has transpired in Communist China since 1949 and what continues to be the country's charted course for the future. The principal implications of the gradual evolution and reshaping of the economic system were contained in the Common Program. Subsequent developments such as the General Line of the Party enunciated in 1953 and the Constitution of 1954 served merely to reaffirm the original plan and to disclose more clearly the time table adopted. Even with the adoption of the First Five Year Plan the scope of government economic planning and regulation is far from being all-embracing. There remains a dwindling area of economic activity in which the private entrepreneur and consumer still to some extent retain the power of individual decision. Outside the agricultural sector, this area now includes a part of internal trade and of the manufacturing industry for consumers' goods. However, the scope is dwindling and may be expected to disappear within the foreseeable future.[4] For a workable system of economic planning and administration has been built up since 1949, and it is now more or less ready to take over.

II

THE FUNCTION OF THE STATE SECTOR

According to the Chinese Communists, the state or socialized sector has the important function of helping to effect the transition to socialism by gradually broadening the sphere of its planning and control. In order to fulfill this function, three conditions must be satisfied. In the first place, the government enterprises[5] must be on a sufficiently broad physical base and must occupy the "commanding heights" of the economy so that their action will be able to exert a decisive influence on the conduct of private business. Second, the state sector must be exemplary in performance in terms of plan formulation and fulfilment. Finally, methods of controlling private business must be devised so that the necessary supervision and guidance can be provided by the state enterprises. Failure to satisfy any one of these conditions would be fatal to the development of an effective planning system with the government enterprises holding the rein.

For any particular country, historical circumstances will necessarily determine the initial size and nature of the state sector from which a socialistic regime can operate. It is probably also true that for any individual country a blueprint of operation can be worked out for the government enterprises only gradually and after a certain amount of trial and error. The same applies to the development of methods to control private enterprise. While similar experience in other countries may be utilized to minimize the extent of avoidable error, even the most extensive program of technical assistance provided by another is unlikely to be able to substitute for the process of learning through practice. This inherent obstacle may be further enhanced if there is no prior experience in large-scale, practical economic planning and in modern business administration. For, over and above the accumulation of capital, the process of economic development is essentially one of investment in man so as to develop the necessary skill in production, administration, and planning. Such a process takes time and is both hazardous and painful.

In the case of China, the Communists were favored by two special circumstances when they took over the government. These were the existence of a large number of government enterprises under the Nationalist regime after World War II and the experience of the Soviet Union in planning and industrial management which could be drawn upon for imitation and inspiration. The first factor obviated the necessity of an immediate and wholesale attempt to socialize existing private production, which might well have wrought political havoc and would certainly have retarded economic recovery. The second factor meant that there were certain broad principles of planning and control that could be followed without the risk of going completely astray. With the physical presence of many Soviet personnel in Manchuria and the ravaged Manchurian industries to restore, it was therefore natural for the Communist authorities to use Manchuria as the proving ground for transplanting and testing Soviet methods on Chinese soil. Once successfully tested, these methods have invariably been adopted for the rest of China as well.

THE INITIAL IMPORTANCE AND NATURE OF GOVERNMENT ENTERPRISES

The growth of the government's role in economic life under the Nationalist regime was largely through the expansion of the National Resources Commission, the principal administrator of government industrial and mining enterprises. In addition to the NRC and other similar establishments the Nationalist government also operated and controlled virtually all the railways, airlines, postal and communications networks, highway transportation establishments, and public works, as well as most of the shipping lines, forest land, and fishery properties. According to one recent estimate, the amount of capital invested in the above government enterprises, as represented by their fixed assets only, including those in Formosa for 1946, increased from CN$1.5 billion in 1933 to CN$4.3 billion in 1946 (both figures at 1933 prices).[6] These figures may be further broken down as in table appearing on page 199.

In terms of the size of the capital stock, the relative share of the state may be gauged by comparing the value of investment in the state sector with the total capital stock of the country. Such a comparison is necessarily of an approximate nature as work on the estimate of China's capital has not progressed too far up to the time of the

Capital Investment in Government Enterprises
(In CN$ thousand at 1933 prices)

	1933	*1946*
Industry and mining	162,830	700,000
Railways	869,488	1,772,000
Highways	291,691	374,000
Shipping	47,250	264,000
Airlines	9,560	72,000
Post and Communications	140,700	284,000
Fishery and Forestry	17,850	100,000
Public Works	713	713,000
Total	1,540,082	4,279,000

Nationalists' evacuation of the mainland. However, there are certain estimates available, of which the one by Wang Foh-shen is probably the most recent and reliable.[7] The following table presents the comparison for 1933:

Capital Stock in China
1933
(In CN$ million at 1933 prices)

	Total[a]	*Government Enterprises*
Manufacturing and Mining[b]	2,632	163
Transport	2,100	1,218
Other Non-agricultural Enterprises	17,739	141
Agriculture	21,450	18
Total	43,921	1,540

a. These data represent the arithmetic mean of Wong's maximum and minimum figures derived from his second method, that is, the use of annual depreciation charges and the average life of the capital stock which is assumed to be from 10 to 50 years. See also Chapter II above. Inventories of finished products and goods in process are not fully covered.

b. Including public utilities.

Insofar as the above data are accurate, it is interesting to observe that, as of 1933, or less than four years before the outbreak of the Sino-Japanese War, government enterprises accounted for less than 4 per cent of the total capital stock available. This is not surprising as about one-half of the total capital was found in agriculture while a substantial part of the non-agricultural capital consisted of residential buildings. The government was not represented to any large extent in these categories. On the other hand, 58 per cent of the capital stock in transportation was accounted for by the government while the government's proportion in industrial capital was 6 per cent.

The situation changed considerably between 1933 and the postwar period. Although lack of a complete estimate for the total capital stock of China after World War II and before 1949 precludes a direct comparison with that of the government enterprises for the postwar period, a reasonably accurate view can be formed by bearing in mind the following circumstances: First, the increase in investment in Free China during the war took place principally in the various enterprises operated by the government, the NRC in particular. Second, elsewhere in China, investment increased mainly in Japanese enterprises or in enterprises supported by the Japanese occupation authorities. All these assets were taken over by the Chinese government at the end of the war, and only a small part was later returned to private operation. Third, imports of capital equipment into China under the various postwar relief and aid programs also contributed primarily to the growth of government capital. All these factors pointed to one conclusion; namely, that the increase in China's total capital stock between 1933 and 1946 took place predominantly in the government sector.

As we have just seen, this increase in government investment was, according to Wang, in the neighborhood of CN$2.8 billion at 1933 prices. It is doubtful that private capital registered any large increase during the same period, if at all. In addition to capital consumption during the war, some of the capital transferred to the government represented what was private capital in 1933. Consequently, the increase in China's total capital stock between 1933 and 1946 was probably not very much greater and might even be less than CN$2.8 billion. The result is a much larger share for government capital, especially in the non-agricultural sectors.

It should be pointed out that Wang's estimate of postwar governmental industrial capital was based on 97 industrial and mining enterprises under the NRC, 85 plants under the China Textiles Corporation, 8 plants under the China Silk Corporation, 18 plants under the China Food Corporation, and the various establishments of the China Vegetable Oil Corporation, together with enterprises operated by local governments.[8] There is a strong possibility that there were certain large omissions in this enumeration, especially with respect to investments in Manchuria. In fact, by aggregating separate estimates of government investments in Free China, Manchuria, North China, and Central and South China, a much larger estimate for governmental industrial capital could be reached. According to this method, it was suggested by Wang that the total for China (including Formosa) should be CN$3.07 billion instead of the 700 million given earlier, which even included investments in Formosa, or at least 1.07 billion if Manchuria were excluded. It is possible that this larger estimate may not have made sufficient allowance for capital consumption during the war years. Yet there is little doubt that the volume of government investment in industry in 1946 was well above CN$700 million and was more likely to be between 1 and 3 billion. If these figures are accepted provisionally, and if we further assume that changes in the stock of private industrial capital after 1933 were negligible, then we might regard the entire increase in industrial capital to have taken place in the government sphere, and the relative share of the government in total industrial capital in mainland China would range from 30 to 55 per cent as a result. If the absolute amount of private capital actually decreased between 1933 and 1946 on account of transfers to the government, then the latter's share would be correspondingly higher.

The order of magnitude envisaged here may be compared with another estimate made by C. M. Wu in 1949.[9] The total industrial capital in 1946, excluding that in Formosa and Manchuria, was, according to Wu, about CN$4.6 billion (at 1936 prices), or 6.7 billion if all confiscated Japanese property were included. Excluding CN$2.2 billion for foreign industrial capital, the shares of governmental and private capital were 67.3 and 32.7 per cent respectively. In terms of total industrial capital, the government's share would be about 46 per cent. While Wu's estimate of industrial capital was probably too high, as he included not only current physical assets but also claims on other enterprises, the proportion of governmental capital in industry derived from his estimate for 1946 is comparable to the range of 30 to 55 per cent suggested above.

The importance of government enterprises at the time of Communist occupation may be further illustrated by some data published in 1951[10] which referred to conditions in a number of industries in 1950. These seem to be in accord with the general order of magnitude developed so far.

	Percentage of Government Enterprises in Terms of Total Available Capacity
Producers' Goods Industries	
Rolled Steel	97
Machinery	45
Cement	54
Petroleum	100
Consumers' Goods Industries	
Textiles—Cotton Spinning and Weaving	44
Wool Spinning	44
Silk Weaving	7
Gunny Bags Manufacturing	75
Paper	49
Rubber Products	17
Matches	30
Flour Milling	37
Cigarettes	26
Oils and Fats	55

Furthermore, it has also been reported that in industrial production as a whole the share of government enterprises accounted for 34 per cent during 1949, which seems to be well in line with the government's relative share in total industrial capital. The fact that government industrial enterprises probably produced a smaller share of the total output than their relative share of industrial capital might lead one to expect was doubtless the result of the poor condition in which many of these enterprises found themselves in 1949, notably in Manchuria.

From the point of view of economic planning and of the gradual transition to a socialistic economy, the initial status of government enterprises in the non-agricultural sectors, especially in transportation and modern industry, therefore provided the Chinese Communist regime with its first advantage. In other words, the physical base was already there in 1949, the important task being the organization and administration of these enterprises and the development of principles and techniques of controlling private business from the bases which these enteprises constituted.

RATIONAL ECONOMIC BUDGETING OR BUSINESS ACCOUNTABILITY

Given the relative importance of government enterprises in general and their preponderance in the capital goods industries in particular, failure to put them on a sound basis would endanger the long-term hope of developing a workable planning system, as well as the immediate objective of the Communist regime to rehabilitate industrial production. From the point of view of the planners, there are apparently two criteria by which "soundness" may be judged; namely, (1) the possibility of appraising the performance of individual enterprises in terms of plan fulfilment, and, (2) the provision of a suitable guide for making adjustments in the allocation of resources on the basis of the individual performance indices thus obtained and in the light of the government's scale of preference for the products and services supplied by the enterprises in question. The basic element of this system is known as *ching-chi he-suan,* an apt translation of the Russian term *khraschet.*

The term *khraschet* has been translated into English in a number of different ways, among which "rational economic budgeting," "economic calculation," "business accountancy," and "business accountability" may be mentioned. Apart from individual preference, these terms do not carry the same connotations because of their emphasis on different aspects. The first two terms stress the aspect of general economic planning with respect to the allocation of resources and reflect the various problems that were frequently summed up under *Wirtschaftsrechnung* in European economic literature on planning and socialism during the twenties and early thirties. "Business accountancy" and "business accountability," on the other hand, stress the management aspect of individual enterprises, perhaps somewhat to the neglect of the broader economic issues involved. The word "accountability" also conveys the notion of a definite and predetermined pattern of job responsibilities and is in fact suggestive of the ideas underlining what the Chinese Communists have since termed the "responsibility system." Since there is no clear-cut advantage in favor of any one of these terms, we shall employ "business accountability" most of the time in the present text, bearing in mind, however, the broader implications of *khraschet.*

As one Communist writer has pointed out,[11] some of the elements of "business accountability" were expressly emphasized by Mao Tse-tung in 1937 in his plan to achieve self-sufficiency in the Shensi-Kansu-Ningsia Border Region. Every individual enterprise was enjoined to have (1) its independent capital, (2) a financial system to account for and control income and outlay, (3) proper computation of costs, adopting complete cost accounting procedures wherever appropriate, (4) monthly and annual production plans supplemented by periodic inspection, and (5) a system for economy in the consumption of raw materials and for safeguarding the equipment used. In the light of later experience, it is doubtful that these postulates were strictly followed or clearly understood at the time, but the need for proper industrial management was apparently felt, although considerable time was to pass before the issue became acute.

After the Communist occupation of all Manchuria towards the end of 1948, the problem of restoring production in this critical area came to the fore. Soviet experience in the theory and practical application of business accountability was held out as an example to be copied first in Sovietized Lü-ta, a new municipality formed out of the Port Arthur-Dairen area. A resolution to enforce the practice of business accountability was adopted by the Northeast Department of Industry in July, 1949, in order to curtail waste of labor, materials, and power, spoilage, industrial accidents, and the adverse effects of improper budgeting. Simultaneously, a great deal of publicity was given to evidences of inefficient management that were reported from coal mines, cotton and paper mills, electric utilities, and virtually every other industry in Manchuria. The campaign to acquaint the managers and workers with the meaning of business accountability began in earnest as government directives and admonitions continued to pour out from the Department of Industry and the Northeast Administrative Council.[12]

Although reports of waste and mismanagement first originated from Manchuria, experience in China Proper followed the same pattern. It was in the spring of 1950, when serious stabilization efforts were being made to curb the runaway inflation, that reports on defective planning and industrial management also began to appear in greater frequency in official Communist publications. One of such adverse reports was, for instance, printed in the party organ, *People's Daily,* in the middle of July, 1950, which also endeavored to explain the matter by pointing to the influence of wartime practice in "crash" programs that stressed the fulfilment of specific assignments while ignoring cost considerations.[13] Such practice was regarded as reflecting the "work style" of the military and was also characteristic of bureaucratic conduct. It was attributed to a complete lack of understanding of the relation between production and cost control on the one hand and internal capital accumulation by government enterprises on the other. The proper solution was, of course, the adoption of business accountability.

In one of the many discussions on business accountability the system was defined as the employment of definite plans and quotas in managing an enterprise.[14] In particular, production plans and quotas should be fixed both by commodities and in monetary terms; computations of labor and motive power requirements should be made; and definite plans should be laid down for the maintenance of fixed capital, the employment and source of funds, and the provision of working capital. Moreover, coordinating contracts should be concluded both among individual segments of the same enterprise, such as different workshops in a plant and among different enterprises. Implicit in this rather cryptic description of the system were the ideas of production according to planned targets, cost control, budget control, and the achievement of equilibrium between supply and demand, both internally within an enterprise and externally in relation to other enterprises.

The above is, of course, an oversimplified version of the business accountability system. According to another Chinese writer,[15] a fuller description of the system in China as taken over from Soviet practice should contain the following elements: (1) the fixing of definite amounts of the total investment and working capital of every enterprise which is to be operated independently, but under an overall economic plan, (2) the establishment of independent accounting and treasury systems with budgetary control and year-end financial statements, (3) the adoption of internal auditing and work supervision independent of the accounting system, (4) the use of periodical plans and authorization procedures, (5) the installation of proper controls for materials, including purchasing, inventory, and requisition, (6) a production inspection system, (7) the adoption of definite technical standards and standard costs, (8) cost accounting, (9) accounting for transportation and marketing, (10) the adoption of definite procedures for settling claims and liabilities, (11) a plan for labor incentive and discipline, and (12) regular statistical reporting. In other words, what is required is (1) the installation of proper financial and cost accounting for every phase of production, marketing, and raw material purchase, together with internal control and supervision, and (2) the operation of the enterprise on the basis of production quotas assigned according to a general economic plan. The first requirement amounts to little more than the usual standards of sound business management, while the second condition places the individual enterprise within the framework of central planning.

CENTRAL PLANNING AND BUSINESS ACCOUNTABILITY

At this point one may very well raise the question as to the manner in which the operation of the business accountability system becomes an integral part of the planning procedure. The answer lies in the method of formulating and transmitting production plans. Here again the technique employed by the Chinese Communists follows closely the Soviet pattern.[16] In the first place, a general plan in broad outlines is formed at the highest political level. This is then transmitted to the various ministries in charge of groups of industries and thence to the many bureaus and administrations supervising the work of individual industries.[17] During this process the very general outlines are developed into detailed figures in terms of commodities. On the basis of its own plan the individual administrative agency then assigns specific quotas to the enterprises under its control. On the basis of its assignment, every enterprise must now produce its own production plan, covering all the aspects previously mentioned, such as labor, motive power, raw materials, working capital, marketing, transportation, etc. These individual plans are then submitted to the successively superior levels of administration for approval. Once approved, authorization is given through the same chain of command and becomes eventually the directive under which the individual enterprises must operate.

In accordance with a resolution of the State Administrative Council on the reconstruction of government industries during 1951[18] and the formulation of their production plans, the overall "control figures" and the production targets assigned to individual enterprises are not quotas in a restrictive sense. A certain degree of flexibility is permitted as the plans submitted by individual enterprises may not coincide entirely with the assigned quantities. The reason for this is that the individual enterprise cannot draw up its plan for the assigned tasks irrespective of the cost involved. It is precisely in this connection that the "supply system" formerly employed in executing crash programs must be discarded in favor of business accountability. The individual enterprise must plan its production with a view to delivering a profit to the government, and the size of the profit must be related to the government's capital investment in the enterprise. As a matter of fact, an integral part of the latter's assigned tasks is to yield a return to the capital employed, calculated according to some standard rate. If an enterprise is not able to produce its assigned quota at a suitable rate of profit, and if the aggregate planned output of the commodity in question falls short of the overall control figure, the superior planning authorities may either revise their control figure or subsidize production. Or, as a third alternative, the planning authorities may try to alter the prices of either the final product or some of the cost items. The last possibility is open only if the government is in a position to regulate the total demand and supply of the commodities involved, which in turn depends in part upon the relative shares of government and private enterprises in their production. On the other hand, if an enterprise is able to produce more than its assigned quota at the standard rate of profit, it may submit a plan for greater production. It may also produce more than the final authorized quota under the provisions of the 1951 SAC resolution provided that it makes adequate arrangements for marketing and the purchase of raw materials, and provided that in doing so, it does not disrupt the government's overall "plan of balances." [19]

From the point of view of the central planning authorities, it is the rate of return on capital investment, supplemented by the political decision that for certain commodities some specified quantities must be produced, regardless of the real and financial cost, that serves as a guide to the allocation of resources, while the actual profit delivered will be available for capital investment or any other use the government may have. Consequently, the individual enterprise must be cost conscious and must plan its production for a profit. In doing so, it must abide by certain technical standards which give rise to standard costs and must plan every phase of its operation on a business basis, both with respect to the technical side of the enterprise and with respect to the financial arrangements. All this is, of course, embodied in the system of business accountability.

THE ROLE OF THE PRICE SYSTEM AND PLAN FOR BALANCES

The application of business accountability in industrial management, however, presupposes several things. In the first place, it presupposes the employment of the price system. In other words, planning is not done on a purely physical basis. The price system is employed in order to facilitate the computation of cost and its comparison with the selling price. In this connection, two different problems are encountered. The first arises as a result of inflation, while the second has to do with the basic issue of balancing demand and supply.

After the introduction of the system of business accountability in Manchuria, its initial operation took place in a period of sustained and rapid rise of the general price level. Plans made on the basis of one set of prices became altogether unrealistic after a short time. In order to deal with this situation, a set of provisional regulations was issued by the Northeast Department of Industry on April 1, 1950, on the method of computing costs. This consisted of the adoption of two different sets of prices known as "plan prices" and "actual prices." The former were the actual prices prevailing at the time of planning in 1950 and were to be used to measure internal efficiency and to exercise price control, while the actual market prices prevailing at the time of sale were used to determine the selling price in order to assure the government enterprises their profit.[20] The plan at the time was to abolish this dual pricing system as soon as the general price level was stabilized, and it was probably for this reason that there was little mention of this method in the case of government enterprises in China Proper as the system of business accountability was not introduced there until the latter part of 1950 when relative price stability was already in sight although this remains a debatable point.[21]

A far more basic problem, however, is the fact that if production is planned on the basis of prevailing market prices, there is no guarantee that the outputs of individual commodities would correspond to the quantities desired by the government when the latter is not prepared to bid up prices for them. And even if production in government enterprises is planned on the basis of assigned quantities, there is still no assurance that the total supply of individual commodities from both government and private enterprises would be equal to the total quantity demanded, apart from the fact that government enterprises may not be able to plan a profit or earn the planned profit. In other words, the prevailing relative prices may not be such as to clear the market. While any disequilibrium between supply and demand reflects a maldistribution of resources, from the short-term point of view of the government, such a maldistribution might be considered to be at its worst only if the total supply of "key" commodities falls short of the government's minimum demand plus the unregulated demand of private individuals and enterprises. In order to forestall such possibilities, the government must be ready to resort to direct controls such as rationing and the allocation of materials in short supply as well as other measures to direct private production into the desired channels. As long as the government does not have complete direct control over both production *and* consumption, complete reliance on the price system in production planning by individual enterprises cannot guarantee the fulfilment of the government's plan in terms of control figures. This appears to be exactly the case in Communist China.[22]

As a concrete example, we may cite the work of the Materials Allocation Bureau of the Northeast People's Economic Planning Commission in 1950 when it undertook to draw up an allocation plan for Manchuria covering ten commodity groups.[23] This was supplemented by the allocation of forty other commodities by individual government enterprises that enjoyed a virtual monopoly in their respective fields. The individual quotas were decided upon on the basis of satisfying the production requirements of what the planners regarded as important enterprises. Actual allocation was made in the course of a series of materials allocation conferences called especially for this purpose during the months of April and May. Following the allocation, contracts were signed between the buyers and suppliers specifying their individual commitments. Thus, direct controls were used to supplement the business accountability system in its application by individual enterprises.

The same methods were followed in the experience of the Ministry of Heavy Industry which undertook to draw up a number of "plans of balances" during 1950, first for the iron and steel and electric machinery industries, then for the other machinery manufacturers. The allocation plan was made by comparing the production plans of individual enterprises with purchase applications and was confirmed by a series of contracts both among the government enterprises and between the latter and private business firms.[24] Needless to say, one such plan of allocation usually leads to another, and the sum total constitutes a national plan of control figures together with a corresponding plan of balances, the latter superseding to a considerable extent the price system in its function as an arbiter in the allocation of resources.

THE "PRODUCTION RESPONSIBILITY" SYSTEM

The adoption of the business accountability system in managing government enterprises also presupposes that the individual enterprise is properly organized in the sense that all the technical requirements and assigned tasks are attended to by persons and departments charged with the respective responsibilities. On the basis of published reports, however, this does not appear to have always been the case in practice even though the matter was given official cognizance from the very beginning. As early as March, 1950, an official resolution was made public by the Northeast Department of Industry on the establishment of a "production responsibility system."[25] This was defined as a system of work specifications and responsibilities for plan fulfilment, safe production, the maintenance of product quality, and the proper accounting of supplies and materials.[26] Yet observance of this rather simple principle in practice has left much to be desired.

Some of the early examples of irresponsible practice resulting in waste and industrial accidents in different undertakings such as the Fu-shun coal mine, the An-shan Iron and Steel Works, timber cutting stations, etc., were given wide publicity in Kao Kang's report on Manchurian economic recovery in the middle of 1950.[27] But these were not isolated instances peculiar to Manchuria, nor were they characteristic of the initial period of economic recovery only. Examples of similar difficulties plaguing many industries in different areas could be found in great abundance in both technical and popular publications in Communist China.[28] In a report published in April, 1953, the increasingly deteriorating quality of certain industrial products and the large percentage of factory rejects were officially deplored.[29] In addition to blaming the poor results on the speed-up in production, the authorities also mentioned inadequate product inspection, laxity in technical supervision, and irresponsibility in general as the major causes of these failures in the application of the business accountability system. The scope and seriousness of such shortcomings were brought out in special relief during the "three-anti" movement in the first part of 1952 when many Party cadres engaged in economic work were purged for crimes of corruption, waste, and bureaucratism, none of which could be countenanced under the banner of business accountability.

CENSUS OF GOVERNMENT INDUSTRY AND ASSET REVALUATION

It would probably be a mistake to regard the many reported instances of errors and poor performance in government enterprises entirely as an official attempt to exhort the industrial and government workers to more strenuous effort. A more likely explanation is that there have actually been an alarming number of failures and that the principal cause has been, and still is, the sheer difficulty in acquainting both Party members and ordinary workers with intricacies of modern business management. In other words, some of the prerequisites of business accountability are not present.

Perhaps an even more glaring deficiency in this respect than the difficulty encountered in making the necessary adjustments in mental attitude and business methods was the apparently profound ignorance on the part of the Communist Chinese planners regarding the physical assets of the government enterprises at the time the new regime was established and for a long time thereafter.It was partly to deal with this problem that the State Administrative Council ordered in March, 1950, a general census in all government industrial enterprises, industrial cooperatives, and joint government and private industrial undertakings, as well as a complete inventory count in all government warehouses.[30] While the inventory-taking was also intended to locate all the surplus materials that could be sold to the public or used by the government to defray expenses at a time when the major economic effort was to stabilize commodity prices, it also served to supplement the industrial census that covered all the important data required for planning, such as the scale and condition of the plants, raw materials required, available equipment, actual production in 1949, and the past history of the plants.

However, even though this first census may have served its immediate purpose, the returns were later said to be defective, incomplete, and not always comparable as a result of different methods and other divergencies in reporting. Besides, the date of reference used in the census was the end of 1949 when considerable confusion prevailed in the enterprises which had just been taken over by the Communist authorities. Violent price changes during 1950 further complicated the issue of determining asset values. Yet, as the official *People's Daily* commented in mid-1951: "The first step in establishing and furthering the system of business accountability is to ascertain the assets (of an enterprise) and to determine its capital. For only then can we get to know the basic condition of government enterprises. . . . Only then can we tell whether the utilization of these assets and working capital has been reasonable, and whether there is any waste."[31] Where assets have not been correctly evaluated, the proper amount of depreciation cannot be determined. This will lead to a misstatement of operating cost, and hence of income. Both profit and capital accumulation are thereby affected.[32] Nor will it be possible to judge managerial performance or make adjustments in allocating resources on the basis of the rate of return to capital. Again, it was stated by the same official source: "A decisive majority of our government enterprises have not had their capital appraised. In consequence, the government does not have full information on the fixed assets of these enterprises or the potential of their available working capital. Management and economic planning are undertaken without accurate knowledge. The present ratio of equipment utilization is extremely low in some government enterprises such as coal mining, power generation, etc. . . . The turnover of working capital has been slow in a number of cases. As an example one may cite the experience of the Shih-ching-shan Iron and Steel Works which had a working capital that was 54 per cent in excess of its requirement until this situation was corrected in April, 1951, when the amount of its capital was adjusted."[33]

A set of general regulations for reappraising the fixed assets of government enterprises in Manchuria was promulgated in December, 1950.[34] This was followed by the adoption of a resolution by the State Administrative Council about six months later to reappraise all assets in government enterprises and to determine for every enterprise the amount of capital required for its operation. The announced purpose for this undertaking, which was scheduled to be completed by the end of 1951, was to eradicate the remnant influence of the "supply system" and to enable the state "to fulfill the planned tasks with the minimum amount of materials and money."[35] Particular emphasis was placed on determining the necessary working capital in an enterprise by fixing standard requirements for (1) raw materials, fuel, and supplies, (2) materials for repair and maintenance, (3) goods in process, (4) inventory of finished products, (5) prepaid expenses, and (6) cash in treasury. The criterion in all these cases is to determine the minimum amounts required on the basis of past experience and the 1951 production assignments. Any surplus working capital and fixed assets were to be adjusted by shifting them from one enterprise to another. It is not difficult to see that the primary purpose in this program was not only to provide the business accountability system with the necessary conditions for operation within a given enterprise, but also to enable the planners to obtain the maximum utilization of available equipment irrespective of the boundaries of nominal ownership, and to increase the turnover of working capital so that within the limits set by the political decision to emphasize production in the capital goods industries at any time, only the minimum amount of resources should be allowed to linger, as if it were, within the pipe line of production in the form of goods in process. With the completion of this particular phase of work in early 1952, the general structure of economic planning and the prerequisites of the business accountability system were more or less in being.

III

PLANNING FOR CAPITAL CONSTRUCTION IN MANCHURIA

The preceding review shows quite clearly that the many problems encountered by the Chinese Communists in establishing efficient business management in government enterprises have stemmed from two principal causes; the usual difficulty in finding a suitable substitute for the normal profit motive, and unfamiliarity with sound business management in large-scale enterprises. However, as long as the work consisted of production along established lines or the restoration of idle plants, the task was still relatively simple. But a far severer test was to present itself in connection with the construction of new plants, the conversion and expansion of existing plants, and the large-scale rehabilitation of devastated factories and mines, of which there were a great many, especially in Manchuria.[36] Since the very basis of a long-term development program depends upon new investment and the construction of new production facilities, the importance of proper planning and management is quite obvious. In this respect, it is particularly instructive to note some of the fumbling attempts that have characterized developments in the last few years.

One of the first general directives on "basic" or "capital construction"[37] was issued by the Northeast Department of Industry in November, 1949. It called for the establishment of separate departments solely responsible for the planning, design, and work supervision of investment projects in all government enterprises and their supervisory bureaus.[38] At the same time, the Department also called for reports on 1949 investment projects and plans for the following year. Several months later, the Department made public a set of provisional regulations governing capital construction in which certain procedural matters, control measures, and management instructions were given in detail.[39] This document was then followed in mid-1950 by a circular summarizing the findings of some inspection reports and listing a large number of unsatisfactory performances, which included poor engineering work, waste of materials, and irresponsibility on the part of leading cadres. Many of these same criticisms were again voiced in a year-end report[40] which noted the following types of deficiencies during 1950: (1) undue haste and improper planning, (2) the dispersion in a large number of enterprises of a very small number of personnel trained in drafting and designing, (3) dispersion of investments, (4) over-emphasis on the construction of auxiliary buildings and installations in comparision with production equipment, (5) lack of business accountability, and (6) the employment in production projects of organizational methods suitable for government administration only.

In the light of its findings, the Northeast Department of Industry offered five major rules to be observed in capital construction projects in 1951. The fact that some of these might appear almost ludicrously elementary is particularly significant. First, individual project planners were reminded that the need and practicability of projects should be carefully examined prior to their submission to higher authorities. Second, actual work should not start without a work plan based on existing blueprints. Third, personnel for detailed planning and designing should be concentrated at the level of industry bureaus under the Department instead of being dispersed among the individual enterprises as heretofore. Fourth, investments should be concentrated on the manufacture and installation of equipment that could be utilized in production quickly and on the development of future potential such as research, technical training and education, and geological prospecting. Finally, the system of business accountability was to be strictly enforced.

The mere issuance of admonitions did not automatically eliminate these errors in planning and administration although some improvement was noted in a mid-year survey in 1952. But in the meantime one noteworthy development was the emergence of lags in detailed planning and the drafting of blueprints as a bottleneck in capital construction, a development that could not but exert a restraining influence on the Communist authorities in their selection of investment projects. The problem was clearly recognized by the Northeast Department of Industry in the middle of 1951 when a standard time table for planning and the preparation of blueprints for a new medium-size mine or factory was given as follows:[41]

	Time Required (Number of Days)
1. Preparation of the preliminary statement of plan objectives and requirements	15
Review and authorization	20
2. Basic planning, including the selection of plant site, geological survey, and assembly of data	90
Review and authorization	30
3. Technical planning and preparation of blueprints	180
Review and authorization	30
4. Preparation of detailed work plans and blueprints	180
Total	545

From the point of view of engineering work, the length of time required in the above schedule may not be at all excessive, especially as the scale and complexity of a "medium-size" plant are rather flexible. However, the fact remains that the length of planning time could act as a serious brake on the rate of capital construction even if the necessary capital equipment were readily available. Morever, planning for current production has to be carried on concurrently. As one author has commented: "For a unit like the An-shan iron and steel combine, more than 1,000 planning personnel usually have to work from September to March in order to compile the annual plan. It was for this reason that the capital construction plan of the Department of Industry for 1952 was not completed until March, 1952, although its preparation had begun in November, 1951. This was the reason why preparatory engineering work in 1952 was delayed."[42] Lag in planning was also largely responsible for the delay in capital construction projects in the first half of 1953 when an estimate number of 150,000 to 200,000 construction workers of the government engineering company were idled for several months in the whole country.[43] By using standard engineering estimates and specifications, the Communist planners are trying to shorten the planning time required, but the net effect still remains to be seen.

A UNIFIED SYSTEM OF CONTROL OVER CAPITAL CONSTRUCTION PROJECTS

Developments in Manchuria in the field of capital construction have been closely paralleled by events in the rest of China, including the types of errors committed.[44] The only difference has been a time lag of about a year due to the later start of large-scale construction in China Proper, the obvious emphasis on developing Manchurian industry, and the desire to use Manchuria as a field of experimentation. The various resolutions and directives adopted by the Northeast Department of Industry were repeated in essence by similar official acts on the part of the Economic and Financial Commission of the central government.[45]

However, attention should be given to one major document issued by the Commission in January, 1952, inasmuch as it constituted a complete restatement of the principles to be followed in all capital construction projects that had been evolved up to that time. This was the "Provisional Regulations Governing Capital Construction."[46] In addition to articles dealing with the various stages required for planning and blueprint preparation, inspection, and work supervision, the most important provisions may be described under two headings.

In the first place, the planning procedure to be followed in capital construction as set forth under the 1952 regulations follows the exact flow outlined earlier in connection with the formulation of production plans in general. In other words, control figures are issued from above while detailed planning is prepared from the individual enterprises up. Authorization is again given from the superior administrative levels downward.[47]

In the second place, all capital construction projects are now divided into two groups, depending upon whether the total investment involved is greater or smaller than certain "quota" figures. Within each group the projects are further divided into two classes according to the absolute amount of the investment in question. In this way, projects are classified according to the amount of total investment into those that are, (1) above quota and over ¥100 billion, (2) above quota but less than ¥100 billion, (3) below quota but over ¥2 billion, and (4) below quota and less than ¥2 billion.[48]

The degree of centralized control to be exercised varies with the classification of the project. Since class (1) projects are obviously the most important, the preliminary statement of plan objectives and requirements has to originate from a ministry of the central government and has to be approved by the State Administrative Council, while the basic plan may be approved by the ministry without consulting the Commission. Approval of the preliminary statement in class (3) projects may be given either by the ministry or by one of its designated agencies. The same applies to recommendations in basic planning. In the case of class (4) projects, both the preliminary statement and the basic plan are dispensed with. Comparable stipulations also exist for the approval of the more detailed technical plans although in no case is the Economic and Financial Commission or the State Administrative Council involved.

It is clear that in devising the above system the intention of the Communist planners was to find some arrangement that would give the central government an opportunity to pass on all important investment projects without being overwhelmed by a vast number of relatively unimportant proposals. The criteria used in judging the importance of a project are (1) the amount of total monetary outlay envisaged in relation to the quota figures, and (2) the nature of the product involved. All projects intended to introduce some new product that has not been produced in China before are automatically regarded as above quota irrespective of the size of the investment. The quota figures vary from one industry to another because investments of the same amount may posses different degrees of importance in different industries. Bearing this in mind, however, one might say that the higher the quota figure in a given type of enterprise, the greater is the possibility for projects to be below quota and hence the greater degree of decentralization in control. A fairly general idea of the scale of importance attached by the planners to different types of capital investments when this system was introduced may be obtained from the following table:

Capital Construction Quotas[1]
(In ¥ billion)

Fuel Industry	
Electric Power	
Generation	50
Transmission	30
Coal Mining (existing mines)	50
New Mines	all above quota
Petroleum Production and Refining	500
Heavy Industry	
Iron and Steel (including coking)	50
Non-ferrous Metals	30
Coal Tar Chemicals	50
Machinery Manufacturing and Repair (including metal products and transport equipment)	30
Electrical Equipment	30
Chemical Fertilizers	50
Other Chemicals	20
Cement	20
Glass	20
Light Industry	
Rubber Products	15
Paper	15
Leather	10
Wood Products	5
Sugar	15
Oils and Fats	10
Brewing and Distilling	5
Edible Salt	5
Flour Milling	5
Textile Industry	
Cotton, Wool, Flax, and Hemp Products	30
Cotton Processing	10
Other Industrial and Mining Projects	10
Railway Transportation	
Construction of New Lines and Double Tracks	all above quota
Bridges	50
Railway Workshops	20

Improvements on Existing Lines	
Subsidiary Enterprises Attached to Railway Stations	10
Automatic Signals	10
Improvements	10
Shipping and Highways	
New River and Sea Ports	all above quota
Navigation Constructions	10
Modification Work on River and Sea Ports	10
Construction of New Highways	all above quota
Rehabilitation of and Modification Work on Existing Highways	20
Highway Bridges	10
Automobile Repair Plants	10
Post and Tele-communications	
Installation of New Dial Telephones	all above quota
Additions to Urban Telephones	30
New Construction and Expansion of Long-Distance Tele-communication Facilities	10
New Radio Stations	10
Agriculture	
New Tractor Stations	all above quota
Marine Products	5
Animal Husbandry	3
Agricultural Implements and Chemicals	8
Forestry	
Timber Felling	10
Afforestation	5
Manufacture of Forest Products	10
Water Conservancy	
Water Reservoirs	50
Flood Control	50
Water Disposal	30
Irrigation	20
Work on Navigation Channels	20
Building	
Warehouses	3
Office Buildings	3
Residential Housing	3
Private Railway Tracks	3
Research and Experiment	3

1. The industry divisions used here are taken from the Provisional Regulations mentioned above and apparently correspond to the divisions of ministries in the central government at the beginning of 1952.

According to Li Fu-ch'un's report on the First Five Year Plan, some of these figures have been revised upward.

IV

CONTROL OVER PRIVATE BUSINESS

Our discussion so far has dealt with Communist efforts in establishing an efficient working system for general planning and for opearting the state enterprises. We must now inquire into some of the methods employed in controlling the remaining but dwindling private sector.

It will be recalled that in addition to the sector of state enterprises the Common Program of 1949 mentioned both a semi-socialistic sector of joint government and private enterprises and a private sector of large and small individualistic enterprises. The distinction between the state and semi-socialistic sectors lies in the degree of public ownership. But this is a legalistic and theoretical distinction, because in practice the influence of the government in a joint enterprise is by no means limited by the proportion of its ownership.[49] At the same time, only a relatively thin line separates the semi-socialistic and the private sectors as few private enterprises can remain completely aloof from the direct influence of the government. As Li Wei-han pointed out in his address to private industrialists and merchants in October, 1953, the intermediate stage of state capitalism is characterized by the award of government orders and processing contracts to private producers and by the government's underwriting of the marketing of private production. However, the relation between the government and private enterprise is designated as a lower form of state socialism if private business acts as the selling agent of government enterprises on a non-exclusive basis and if the government purchases from private producers without any initial intervention in production planning. Obviously the rate of transition from the lower to the intermediate stage may be freely regulated by the government, because private producers cannot take upon themselves to spurn government contracts in favor of production for private orders without infringing upon the overall economic plan of the state and thus automatically relegating themselves to the ranks of "enemies of the people." The same is true with respect to the participation of government capital in existing private establishments to form joint enterprises, for the rate at which this highest form of state capitalism can be multiplied is entirely dependent upon the government's ability to invest and "the number of Party cadres it can spare"[50] for the purpose of exercising control.

Given this pragmatic approach, it is not difficult to see that the opening wedge in fostering government control is the financial power of the government in purchasing and contract-letting.

THE SIGNIFICANCE AND GROWTH OF GOVERNMENT CONTRACTS

In this respect not too much was done during 1949, when the Communist authorities were still groping for some way to curb the inflation and were not prepared to initiate any positive program with respect to the reform of private business. As we have seen in Chapter III above, however, the situation underwent a dramatic change in the spring and early summer of 1950. Heavy tax payments, Victory Loan subscriptions, and the forced liquidation of inventory were induced by the monetary and fiscal measures adopted by the government. In the meantime the decline of the interest rate lagged behind that of commodity prices. Private firms that had engaged in large-scale short-term borrowing for hoarding purposes were caught in a squeeze.[51] The decline in business activity was reflected in high unemployment which, according to the Ministry of Labor, totalled 1,660,000 persons in June, 1950, in twenty-nine cities alone.[52]

It was at about this time that the Communist authorities began to expand their "program of assistance" to private business. Processing and purchasing orders were given, for instance, to private cotton mills, textile finishing plants, flour mills, steel rolling mills, and electric equipment and machinery manufacturing plants in all the major manufacturing centers in China, especially Shanghai and Tientsin, while private firms were also asked to act as sales agents for government enterprises. The volume of government work in 1950 was later reported to have taken up over 50 per cent of the capacity of the country's machinery manufacturing industry, including at one time 87 per cent of the capacity of North China producers and 43 per cent of East China producers. It also accounted for 47.1 per cent of the country's private spindlage in May, 1950, rising to 81.5 per cent in the following month. For private industry in Shanghai as a whole, 32 per cent of its total output was absorbed by the government during the first year of this program.[53]

A sizable amount of the government orders was given to private business through government trading agencies. But many orders were also given during special industry conferences called by the government. Some of these conferences, such as the national heavy industry and machinery industry conferences, were held in the first part of 1950. However, a much longer series of industry conferences took place in the second part of the year, following discussions between the central government and the heads of bureaus of industry and commerce in seven principal cities in May on the problem of "adjusting the relationship between the public and private sectors of the economy." In addition to determining the amount of government orders, these conferences also served the important purpose of acquainting the government with the conditions of private business enterprises and of instructing private businessmen on the government's long-term policy towards them. Among the common topics of discussion were such matters as the establishment of new plants, the training of technical personnel, labor relations, and the allocation among individual producers of production and raw material quotas. In this way, the short-term objective of assisting private production through government orders was artfully combined with the long-term aim of integrating the private sector within the structure of central planning.

As we have already hinted, the purpose of giving government orders to private producers was not merely to offer assistance to private business during a general recession. This purpose predominated only in the beginning of the downswing in economic activity in 1950. While a substantial part of the government's purchases from the machinery manufacturers at the industry's conference in the first part of 1950 was for products that were not immediately useful and while similar purchases were probably made from other producers, it was subsequently decided that government purchases should be planned in accordance with national requirements only. In other words, the government was not to take the passive attitude of encouraging private production whenever necessary but should actively try to regulate it.[54] The extent of regulation was to encompass the reorganization of individual enterprises as well as that of the entire industrial structure. For this purpose two important steps were taken at the end of 1950 when all private firms were called upon to conform to a new set of "Provisional Regulations Governing Private Business" and to reappraise their assets and liabilities for the ostensible purpose of recapitalization and reorganization in the interest of greater efficiency.

It was in this changed atmosphere that the volume of government orders and processing contracts began to grow by leaps and bounds through the subsequent years both in relation to total private production and in comparison with the so-called lower form of state capitalism.

According to a 1953 report,[55] the aggregate value of government contracts rose from 32 per cent of the total output of private industry in Shanghai in 1950 to 44 per cent in 1951 and 58 per cent in 1952. By 1953, the volume of non-government business had declined to less than one-third of total sales. As for individual industries, during 1953, the entire private cotton textile industry, as well as producers of rubber tires, cement, and some commodities of lesser significance, worked exclusively for the government's account. The government also took 80 per cent of the output of 49 industrial products such as electric machines, lathes, electric cables, rolled steel products, electrolytic copper, caustic soda, paper, cigarettes, oils and fats, and dyestuffs.[56] In the case of 66 private industries included in another tabulation for the third quarter of 1953, 67.2 per cent of their total production was taken by the government.[57] Moreover, according to the reports of seven government trading companies in Shanghai, more than 77 per cent of their purchases from private firms was made on direct orders, while less than 23 per cent was done without prior instruction to the manufacturers.[58]

The experience of private industry in Shanghai was paralleled by the Tientsin manufacturers.[59] Similar reports are also available for other lesser industrial centers in China Proper and, of course, Manchuria where the relative importance of private industry was, however, not important.[60] As far as this particular aspect of state capitalism is concerned, the trend is therefore both decisive and unmistakable.

THE BUSINESS CONCENTRATION MOVEMENT AND RECAPITALIZATION OF PRIVATE FIRMS

Once the immediate threat of business recession had been met, the focus of official attention turned to the basic issues. A general statement of official policy came at the end of 1950 when the State Administrative Council adopted the "Provisional Regulations Governing Private Business."[61] According to the Director of the central government's Private Business Bureau, this new law represented a revised and consolidated text of the Bureau's own "Draft Regulations on Investment in Private Enterprises," which had been submitted to the Council in April, 1950, and the "New Draft Company Law" of the Government's Legal Affairs Commission. The two earlier documents were ordered to be combined by Chou En-lai on the ground that business conditions had changed since the spring of the year, when it was thought necessary to encourage private investment, while a company law as such would be too restrictive in its effect. What was required was a set of general regulations for the control of private business preparatory to the implementation of the overall policy of socialization. This was to be the function of the new law.

In the light of Chou's instructions, three specific provisions of the law deserve particular mention. In the first place, it was stated in Article 6 of the law that the government would henceforth be empowered to prepare general production and marketing plans for both public and private enterprises whenever such plans should become necessary in the government's judgment so as to eliminate "chaotic" production, to adjust supply and demand, and to channel efforts towards the establishment of a planned economy. In the second place, it was stipulated that private enterprises should be encouraged to enter into amalgamations and other arrangements for complete or partial joint operation. Finally, it was stated that no private business could be set up or undertake any important change in the manner or scope of its operation without the prior approval of the government agencies concerned. This authorization requirement was superimposed on the ordinary licensing procedure for permission to engage in business.

In advocating the amalgamation and partial consolidation of private firms, the new law only reaffirmed what had been hinted, if not openly proclaimed, at the various industry conferences and what had become an integral part of the policy of "industrial and commercial readjustment" since the summer of 1950, if not earlier. Some of the advantages of such a movement are, of course, quite genuine from the individual firms' point of view, such as greater attraction to new capital and easier credit terms, elimination of competitive price cutting, more efficient purchasing and marketing facilities, including the possibility of lower raw material cost and price maintenance in sales, and greater specialization through the integrated use of existing productive facilities. In fact, these are the usual advantages claimed for rationalization and cartelization schemes in capitalistic economies. In addition to these points, which have been and continue to be used as baits to private businessmen, Party spokesmen have also maintained that it would be easier for the government to award contracts to compact groups of associated private firms instead of a large number of small enterprises. "Besides, the relation between firms with joint operation arrangements tends to be closer and it will be easier (for the government) to engage in their re-education and reform. The concentration movement on the part of small and medium-size private firms will contribute greatly to the effective exercise of the leadership function of state enterprises."[62]

From the point of view of increasing production, it would be clearly desirable for individual private firms to pool their assets and facilities especially if their original size and organization were too small for efficient production. By promoting the concentration movement the Communist authorities doubtless had this advantage of large-scale production in mind, but, in doing so, they were also trying to devise means for more efficient control, and, in the final analysis, determining the best place and time to establish joint government and private enterprises.

In support of our inference, let us consider the highly important announcement of the State Administrative Council on December 22, 1950, to the effect that all private business firms should engage in a complete revaluation of assets and liabilities and that this work was to be completed by the end of June, 1951. Reports should then be submitted to the government authorities giving complete details on the various items of the balance sheet both before and after the appraisal and the methods of evaluation used.[63] The individual firms were further instructed to include in their reappraisal all items hitherto not recorded in their regular books so that the reports as a whole would reflect the actual position of private business.

It may be recalled at this point that in their attempt to introduce the system of business accountability and to establish the foundation of central planning for the state sector the Chinese Communists had conducted a general census of government industrial and mining enterprises in the spring of 1950 and that this census was later supplemented by the wholesale revaluation of the assets of government enterprises which was commenced in the middle of 1951. In the case of private business firms, the series of industry conferences in 1950 may be compared with the 1950 census while the decision to reappraise private business assets was the counterpart of the 1951 decision for government enterprises. The interested observer will not fail to notice that the revaluation program was ordered for private enterprises six months earlier than for government enterprises in China Proper. Even though one may give some credence to the argument that private enterprises in China were not always efficiently operated and that many would benefit from the adoption of sound management methods, one could hardly maintain that their need in this respect was more acute than that of government enterprises. Common sense would suggest that the opposite case might be true. Thus the explanation of the timing of the revaluation program for private business seems to lie in the desire to give an additional impetus to the policy of "industrial and commercial readjustment."[64]

Obviously, it would not be possible for business firms to enter into negotiations for amalgamation or other forms of close association without full knowledge of their own financial condition. It is quite conceivable that such knowledge was frequently lacking in view of the prolonged inflation both under the Nationalist regime and afterwards, the physical destructions suffered, and the prevalent desire on the part of businessmen to conceal assets. However, one should not overlook the fact that even as individual firms might benefit as a result of the revaluation, the government stood equally to gain. As a matter of fact, it would be much easier for the government to take over a properly managed enterprise with complete records and a working system of control and operation than an enterprise that is poorly managed. Even when the government is not yet prepared to assume direct control, the program of business concentration would be facilitated as a result of the revaluation work.[65] The experience of individual industries in different localities during 1951 and later bore ample evidence to this conclusion.

METHODS OF EXTENDING GOVERNMENT OWNERSHIP

Apart from the consideration of rationalizing production, "the industrial and commercial readjustment program" inaugurated in 1950 and continued through the succeeding years has for its ultimate purpose the further development of completely or partially socialized enterprises. In this regard one may safely assert that the Chinese

Communists have never lost sight of their ultimate goal. This conclusion appears to be well warranted as one examines the frequent reports in current Communist publications on the reorganization of hitherto well known private enterprises into joint enterprises between the government and private interests, and that of joint enterprises into government enterprises.

It is noteworthy that there has not been any official account on the exact manner in which private firms have been reorganized to admit government participation in ownership except that, according to the regulations of September 6, 1954, extension of government participation may be brought about through investments in other enterprises by joint enterprises in which the government already holds an interest.[66] Nor has there been any concrete instance of nationalization, partial or complete, that is carried out with due compensation to private owners.[67] However, the procedure involved in nationalization through direct government participation may be surmised by examining the main sources from which government holdings in private enterprises can be derived in the light of published regulations governing the management of such interests the government possesses or may acquire from time to time.[68] These are (1) assets and stock participations of the Nationalist Government and its agencies, including the former government banks, (2) assets and stock participations of the governments and nationals of former enemy countries, and (3) assets and stock participations of war criminals, collaborators, and bureaucratic capitalists confiscated by law, as well as any other assets and stock holdings thus confiscated.[69]

It is not difficult to identify the subjects under the first two categories mentioned above. The question of interpretation arises in connection with the last group of persons; namely, the "war criminals, collaborators, bureaucratic capitalists and others." Although various "black lists" of individuals were published by the Chinese Communists both before and after their victory over the Nationalists, there has never appeared a single list on which all the proscribed persons are enumerated. In the absence of a complete enumeration, how is one to determine whether a person falls under this provision or not?

The answer apparently lies in the phrase "other assets and stockholdings" confiscated by law, the meaning of which was supplied by the State Administrative Council in its "Directive on the Confiscation of Stock Interests and Assets of War Criminals, Collaborators, Bureaucratic Capitalists and Counter-revolutionaries Found in Business Enterprises."[70] According to this ruling, which was issued in February, 1951, the property of "counter-revolutionaries" may be ordered confiscated by a People's Court or Tribunal without much ado. Lest one should have the wrong impression that "counter-revolutionaries" are primarily such persons as spies, saboteurs, and foreign intelligence agents, reference should be made to the "Decree on the Suppression of Counter-revolutionaries,"[71] which was officially announced on February 21, 1951, shortly after the appearance of the "Directive on Confiscation" issued in the same month. In the context of these regulations a "counter-revolutionary" is somewhat obliquely defined as a person who has the intention to overthrow the "people's democratic regime" and to do harm to the "people's democratic undertakings."[72] Within this broad definition, the list of counter-revolutionary activities enumerated encompasses a large enough area so that there should not be any difficulty in bringing private businessmen within the meaning of the law whenever their enterprises are scheduled for partial or complete nationalization.[73]

THE "GLEICHSCHALTUNG" OF PRIVATE BUSINESS

The use of legal devices and sheer political power to achieve the purpose of increasing socialization, for which the officially sponsored program of business concentration, the revaluation of assets, and the decree on confiscation procedures all served to pave the way, was given additional impetus in a nation-wide campaign that swept through all the urban centers of China in the first half of 1952. This was the "five-anti" movement and was launched shortly after the inception of the purge within the ranks of government agencies and enterprises popularly known as the "three-anti" movement.

The signal was given by Chou En-lai who, in an address to the Standing Committee of the National Committee of the PPCC, declared on January 5, 1952: "We cannot speak about the simultaneous preservation of both public and private interests in a vacuum, but should do so only under the condition of obedience to the leadership of the government sector of the economy. . . . Nor can we talk about the benefits that will accrue to both labor and capital in the abstract. To do so we must first accept the leadership of the working class. . . .

Private enterprises that are of little use or harmful to the national economy would not be permitted to develop. The state should centralize the operation of all enterprises that can exert a controlling influence on the economic life of the country. . . . We cannot advocate planless production, but must gradually promote the guiding role of the overall production plan of the state."[74] Rather significantly, Chou's remarks and the subsequent trials and investigations of private businessmen and enterprises were described as a counter-meausure against the attempt of the capitalists as a class to undermine the new economic order.[75] The economic "crimes" against the government, classified into five categories, included bribery of public officials, tax evasion, theft of public assets, fraud in fulfilling government contracts, and theft of official information and were said to have caused serious increases in production costs, low quality of products, price fluctuations, decrease in tax revenue, and general disruption of economic planning. Businessmen were accused of organized attempts to conspire against and defraud the state not as individual offenders, but as members of a class. Consequently, the "five-anti" campaign was not simply an effort of the administration to punish wrong-doers who were exceptions. Instead it was a carefully engineered "class struggle" parallel to the earlier "land reform" but directed against the urban bourgeoisie or what there was left of it.

A combination of circumstances probably accounted for the timing of this attempt to bring private business firms into line. Difficulties encountered in planning both within the government enterprises and in their relation with private business, failures and frustrations, the need for a scapegoat as a result of the stalled military venture in Korea, and the very important function of the program as a means to raise extraordinary revenue were all partly responsible. However, from the point of view of the transformation of the economy to socialism the "five-anti" campaign must be considered primarily as a vital link in the development of Communist China's economic policy.

The analogous position of the "five-anti" campaign to "land reform" was brought out especially distinctly in the classification of private business firms into five categories according to the degree in which they were law-abiding, a technique reminiscent of the differentiation of rural classes.[76] Other resemblances may be found in the organization of special People's Tribunals and the employment of informers and agents provocateurs. The punishment meted out to offenders ranged from fines to confiscation, the last reserved to those persons and firms that had committed the most serious crimes, measured in terms of the amount of money involved.

According to one report, the number of business firms investigated during the campaign totalled 450,000 in the cities of Peking, Tientsin, Shanghai, Hankow, Canton, Chungking, and Shen-yang alone. Of these 340,000 were found guilty in some fashion or other.[77] The scope of the investigations will be better understood by comparing these figures with the total number of registered business firms in China. The latter was reported to be 1,289,253 in 1950, including companies, partnerships, and proprietorships, but excluding the very small handicraft and family workshops.[78] It is only logical to assume that all the larger private enterprises were investigated. The scale of the campaign was most impressive.

There has not been any detailed account of the number of confiscations, although preliminary estimates in Peking and Shanghai put the numbers at 1 per cent of the business firms investigated. This would put the absolute figure at about 4,500 enterprises, which may again be compared to the 10,747 private firms organized as companies in December, 1950. Since confiscation was reserved for those offenders whose "crimes" involved large quantities of money, it is reasonable to assume that these were mostly the larger private enterprises. One could hardly fail to realize the significance of these results in terms of socialization.

A period of consolidation set in upon the close of the "five-anti" campaign which was itself responsible for considerable disruption of production, but as the First Five Year Plan was launched in 1953, the step of socialization was soon stepped up again. The official Party Line for private enterprises for the remainder of the present period of transition continues to be one of "utilization, restrictions, and reform" with the emphasis shifting increasingly to the last objective. The large private textile mills and manufacturers of metal products, many of whom are in Shanghai, are, for instance, apparently among the first scheduled for partial socialization in the immediate future.[79] It will probably take a few more years before complete socialization can be achieved in the non-agricultural sector of the economy, but already the socialized and partially socialized enterprises have grown considerably in importance. Their share in industrial production increased from 34 per cent in 1949 to 58 per cent in 1952.[80] Of the 58 per cent government enterprises accounted for 50; joint government and private enterprises, 5;[81] and government-sponsored cooperatives, 3. If only the large enterprises were included, the share of the socialized and partially socialized sectors would account for 69 per cent of total industrial output. Of the 69 per cent government enterprises were responsible for 60; joint enterprises, 6; and cooperatives, 3. There were 60 large industiral plants under joint government and private operation in Shanghai towards the end of 1953;[82] by mid-1954 the number was 123.[83] For the other industrial and commercial centers the same story of stepped up socialization can also be told.[84] By the time the First Five Year Plan is completed, the share of private industry in total industrial output, excluding that of consumers' co-operatives, is expected to constitute no more than 12.2 per cent.[85]

SUMMARY

In November, 1952, the central government of Communist China formally announced the formation of a State Planning Committee responsible for charting the course of the country's future development. This act gave official recognition to the oft-repeated assertion that the period of preliminary experimentation in building a workable planning system was over. If we look over the various developments of government policy in both the state and the private sectors of the economy which have been reviewed in some detail in the foregoing pages, it would appear that such an interpretation is essentially correct.

Within the sector of government enterprises, the first major landmark in the development of a planning system for current production was represented by the Resolution of the State Administrative Council in April, 1951. This was followed by the equally significant "Provisional Regulations Governing Capital Construction" promulgated in January, 1952. By this time the process of evolution had gone even further in Manchuria where the system of business accountability had already been supplemented by so-called plans of balances. Concurrently, in the sector of private enterprises, the process of socialization has proceeded apace. With the government enterprises now under relatively systematic control, a speed-up was soon to be ordered to integrate the remaining private business more firmly into the general structure of government planning. This explains the decision taken in 1953 to tighten control over private business. Thus the process has almost completed a full circle. As Mao Tse-tung has told us, the period of the "New Democracy" is a period of transition. This period is now nearing its end. The structure of the socialistic economy has grown out of the embryonic stage. The next question is: what will be its capabilities in terms of material development?

NOTES

1. December 16, 1953. For further discussion on this point see Chapter VII below.

2. *People's Daily* editorial, Peking, March 10, 1954.

3. See Li Wei-han's address on October 27, 1953, to the All-China Federation of Industrial and Commercial Circles, and the 1954 Constitution.

4. If one may hazard a guess, the length of the transitional period will probably take not more than a decade and may be concluded in a large measure by the end of the First Five Year Plan, especially in the modern industries.

5. Government enterprises in Communist China are divided into (1) central government or state enterprises and (2) local government enterprises, the latter being limited to the smaller enterprises of local significance only. To all intents and purposes, therefore, the terms, "government" and "state" enterprises, may be used synonymously.

6. Wang Foh-shen, "The Foundation of China's State Economy," *China's Industry,* Vol. I, No. 10, Shanghai, February, 1950.

7. Wang Foh-shen, "Problems in Connection with China's Capital Stock," *Economic Review,* Vol. IV, No. 4, Shanghai, October 23, 1948.

8. Wang, *op. cit., China's Industry,* Shanghai, February, 1950.

9. Wu Ch'eng-ming, "An Estimate and Analysis of China's Industrial Capital," *Economic Weekly,* Vol. IX, Nos. 8 and 9, Shanghai, 1949.

10. *Economic Yearbook,* p. 44, Hongkong, 1951.

11. Huang I-feng, "On Business Accountability," *Business Accountability,* p. 54, Peking, 1950.

12. See the various documents and articles collected in the volume on *Business Accountability* quoted above.

13. *People's Daily,* July 15, 1950. Among the many interesting cases cited were the under-utilization of power plant equipment in North China, the poor quality of the products of the Chi-nan cement plant and the An-shan steel works, the absence of fixed technical standards in industrial plants, damage to a power plant in Kwangtung, and a futile attempt to build trackless vehicles by the Northwest Department of Highways.

14. Ning-chi, "On the Problem of Business Accountability," *People's Daily,* Lü-ta edition, May 21, 1950.

15. Cheng Hung-sui, "Theory and Practice of Business Accountability," *China's Industry,* Vol. I, No. 10, Shanghai, February 15, 1950.

16. See Hsü Ch'ih, "Procedure and Method in Formulating the National Industrial Plan," *People's Daily,* Peking, July 7, 1950.

17. For a list of the ministries see the Appendix.

18. Adopted on April 6, 1951, at the 79th meeting of the State Administrative Council, *Compendium,* Vol. III, pp. 593-599, Peking, 1952.

19. What is meant by "balance" here is simply the equality of demand and supply although the entire market may not be at equilibrium when "balancing" is restricted to the government industries.

20. Cf. Yü Wen-ch'ing, "Cost Computation in Northeast Industrial and Mining Enterprises," *China's Industry,* Shanghai, August 23, 1950. For an actual case see the article on the adoption of the business accountability system at the Ho-kang coal mine in Manchuria in *Business Accountability,* p. 135, 1950.

21. The widespread employment of the commodity-equivalent units during the inflationary period may have, however, obviated the need for explicit dual pricing. See, however, the discussion on the compilation of statistics on gross industrial production in the next chapter.

22. It should be noted that when the price system can be relied upon to produce the planned quantities automatically, it will probably also be no longer a free price system that reflects the consumers' choice.

23. *Northeast Daily,* Shen-yang, July 24, 1950. The ten commodity groups were iron and steel, coal, gasoline, timber, cement, cotton cloth, grain, newsprint, glass, and copper.

24. Cf. Chang Ta-tien, "The Function of the Contract System in Economic Planning for Heavy Industry," *People's Daily,* Peking, September 8, 1950.

25. *Northeast Daily,* Shen-yang, March 4, 1950.

26. *Northeast Daily,* Shen-yang, May 7, 1950.

27. Kao Kang, "On the Forefront of Northeast Economic Reconstruction," *People's Daily,* Peking, June 5, 1950.

28. See, for instance, the discussion at the National Textile Conference, in 1951, *North China Textile Journal,* March 1, 1951.

29. *New China Monthly,* No. 42, p. 143, Peking, April, 1953.

30. See *New China Monthly,* Vol. II, No. 1, pp. 108 and 141-142, Peking, March 15, 1950, and Sung Chen-ch'üan, "Evaluation of Machinery Depreciation and Maintenance," *China's Industry,* Vol. II, No. 6, Shanghai, October, 1950.

31. *People's Daily,* June 4, 1951.

32. It should be noted that under Communist practice depreciation charges are not merely book entries for the purpose of arriving at a correct statement of income, but must be delivered periodically to the government in the same manner as profit.

33. *New China Monthly,* No. 22, pp. 826-827, Peking, August, 1951.

34. See "Provisional Regulations for the Control of Fixed Assets in Government Enterprises in the Northeast," *Compendium,* Vol. II, pp. 195-197, Peking, 1951; and "Resolution on the Census of Assets and Determination of Capital in Government Enterprises," ibid., Vol. III, pp. 88-90, 1952.

35. *New China Monthly,* No. 22, pp. 825-826, Peking, August, 1951.

36. The proportion of new industrial plant constructions (including conversions) in total industrial investment was only 25 per cent in 1949. It increased to 38 per cent in 1950, 80 per cent in 1951, and a planned 90 per cent in 1952. The importance of rehabilitation work decreased accordingly. Cf. *New China Monthly,* No. 34, p. 86, August, 1952.

37. According to one official source, "basic" or "capital construction" includes all outlays on (1) building work, (2) installation work, (3) machinery and equipment, (4) instruments, tools, and laboratory equipment, (5) inspection, surveying, designing, and research, (6) personnel training and miscellaneous organizational expense, (7) purchase and maintenance of animals and perennial plants, and (8) other investment.

In other words, it corresponds to long-term investment in fixed and durable assets. Cf. *New China Monthly,* No. 21, p. 649, Peking, July 15, 1951.

38. "Directive on the Organization and Work of Capital Construction Departments," November 26, 1949. Text in *Capital Construction,* Shen-yang, September, 1950.

39. "Provisional Regulations for the Control of Capital Construction," April 5, 1950, *ibid.*

40. "Report by the Department of Industry on Capital Construction in 1950," dated December 20, 1950, *Northeast Industry,* No. 47, Shen-yang, 1950.

41. "Resolutions on Planning in Capital Construction," adopted June 30, 1951. For text see *Handbook on Capital Construction,* Peking, March, 1953, 2nd edition. It should be noted that work may actually begin without the completion of stage 4.

42. "Use of Standard Estimates in Preparing the Annual Capital Construction Plan," report by the planning section of the Office of Capital Construction, Northeast Department of Industry, *China's Industry,* Vol. IV, No. 8, pp. 56-60, Peking, December 26, 1952.

43. *Economic Weekly,* No. 15, pp. 8-9, Shanghai, April 16, 1953.

44. According to a report of the *People's Daily* on September 9, 1952, capital construction in the first three years of the new regime was not altogether satisfactory. In the field of heavy industry, for instance, 61 projects were under way in China Proper during 1951. Of these 14 should have been completed in the preceding year although only one was actually finished by the end of 1951. The total plan fulfilment for the year was 60 per cent. The highest rate of plan fulfilment in any individual project was only 75 per cent; the lowest, 37 per cent. Haste, incompetent and irresponsible technical planning, or rather the lack of it, poor coordination, absence of overall control, and general failures in the practice of business accountability have dotted the experience of capital construction in China Proper in virtually the same way as in the case of Manchuria discussed earlier. The following instances have been officially reported and provide a rather interesting sample:

(1) Over Y10 billion were spent on construction work at the Ting-hsiang iron mine in a period of two years, at the end of which it was diiscovered that the ore had long been exhausted.

(2) Buildings were constructed for a coal mine at Hsiao-hsi-p'o where it was later established that no coal actually existed.

(3) Factory buildings were erected in 1950 at the T'ai-yuan Iron and Steel Works although there was no machinery available to be installed.

(4) Repair teams were sent to work on a bridge on the Hua-hui Ch'ü in Yunnan, only to discover that the scheduled repair had been done two years earlier.

(5) Construction work in a number of projects was so defective that it had to be done a second time. Among the known examples were the Feng-feng coal mine, road building in Peking, and many projects in Liaotung Province.

(6) Investment funds were allotted equally among the various departments of the Shih-ching-shan Iron and Steel Works with the result that the unused funds of some departments were diverted to the building of a 200-man bath house. Excessive investment was made in workers' dormitories and subsidiary buildings at both Shih-ching-shan and T'ai-yuan.

(7) More than Y6 billion were spent at the Ta-t'ung coal mine on buildings that were not properly designed and served no useful purpose.

(8) During 1950 the Ministry of Heavy Industry reported the completion of 60 to 70 per cent of its planned capital construction for the year, but was not able to tell which projects had been completed or what was the increase in production capacity at individual production enterprises.

Cf. Chang Ta-tien, op. cit., *China's Industry,* Vol. III, No. 7, Shanghai, November, 1951; and *New China Monthly,* No. 22, Peking, pp. 828-829, August, 1951.

45. See in particular "Directive on Capital Construction Planning in 1953," adopted by the Financial and Economic Commission on January 27, 1953. For text see *Compendium,* Vol. III, pp. 651-654, Peking, 1952.

46. Issued on January 9, 1952. Text in *Handbook on Capital Construction,* 1953.

47. Section VII, article 28.

48. Section III, article 15. Prior to the abolition of the Major Administrative Areas, the regional government was given the same degree of authority as a ministry of the central government.

49. As the *People's Daily* has put it: "The leading position of the socialist sector in an enterprise is not determined by the proportion of state investments in individual enterprises, but is determined by the character of state power, by the leading position of the socialistic sector in the national economy, by the coalition of the representative of public shares and the worker masses and the education and reform of capitalists and their agents, and by the capability of this leadership to push the enterprises forward." Peking, September 6, 1954.

50. *People's Daily,* Peking, March 10, 1954.

51. Cf. Ch'ien chia-chü, "No Reason for Pessimism in Private Business," *Kuang-ming jih-pao,* Peking, April 14, 1950.

52. Cf. Ch'en Yün's report on economic and financial work to the third session of the first national committee of the PPCC, dated October 25, 1951. The figure includes "unemployed and semi-unemployed workers and unemployed intelligentsia" but should not be regarded as a measure of total unemployment in the country.

53. See *The Daily News,* Shanghai, May 22, 1950; *Tientsin Daily,* May 23, 1950; Sun Hsiao-ts'un, "The Public-Private Relationship in Processing Orders and Government Purchases," *Forward Look,* Vol. V, No. 21, June, 1950; the Economics Department, Peking University, "The Economic Structure of the New China," *New Construction,* Vol. I, No. 5, Peking, 1949; *People's Daily,* Peking, November 11, 1953; and various issues of *New China Monthly.*

54. *People's Daily,* Peking, June 4 and 8, 1950.

55. *People's Daily,* Peking, November 11, 1953.

56. Report of the Shanghai Bureau of Industry and Commerce quoted in Ai-fang, "Reform of Private Industry in Shanghai in Four Years," *People's Daily,* Peking, March 3, 1954.

57. Ibid.

58. Ibid.

59. Yao Chung-wen, "The Development of State Capitalism in Tientsin in the Past Five Years," *Study,* No. 3, Peking, 1954.

60. *Economic Yearbook,* p. 66, Hongkong, 1954.

61. For the text of the law and Hsueh Mu-ch'iao's report see *Compendium,* Vol. II, pp. 141-185, Peking, 1951.

62. *People's Daily,* Peking, June 17, 1950.

63. The firms were instructed to use current market prices in their appraisals.

64. When the decree to revalue assets was issued, the prevalent attitude of businessmen was that it was an attempt to collect more taxes. In order to allay this fear the Communist Ministry of Finance stated in April, 1951, that additional commodity tax would not be levied on any increase in the value of assets after the reappraisal and that the stamp tax would be levied only on that part of any increase in capital that was due to the inclusion of assets hitherto not on the firm's books, and that no fines would be imposed on delinquent stamp tax payments. This ruling was entirely consistent with the long-term benefit to the government treasury as a result of better accounting records the government would have henceforth. But the immediate fiscal

effect of the revaluation program should probably be regarded as of secondary importance only.

65. See, for instance, Ch'en Wen-ch'uan, "Review of Asset Revaluation Work in Canton," *Economic Yearbook,* Hongkong, 1952.

66. See the "Provisional Regulations Governing Public-Private Jointly Operated Industrial Enterprises," NCNA, September 6, 1954.

67. According to "The Provisional Mining Regulations" of December, 1950, for instance, private mines may be nationalized if they have already been worked for a certain length of time or if the government so decides for reasons of its own. Compensation would be given for private equipment. Not a single instance of compensation has been reported, however. See *New China Monthly,* Vol. IV, No. 1, pp. 141-144, Peking, May 1951.

68. Cf. *Compendium,* Vol. II, Peking, 1951.

69. See "Regulations on the Handling of Public Assets and Stockholdings in Business Enterprises," *Compendium,* Vol. II, Peking, 1951.

70. Ibid., p. 194.

71. Adopted by the Government Council on February 22, 1951. For text see, for instance, *People's Handbook,* pp. 39-40, Shanghai, 1952.

72. Article 2 of the law.

73. That certain large enterprises were confiscated under the law seems to be indirectly proved by the instruction of the SAC in June 1951, that operation in such cases should not be interrupted. Cf. *People's Handbook,* p. 40, Shanghai, 1952.

74. Cf. Nai-hui, "The Broad Prospect of Private Industry and Trade in the New China," *Economic Yearbook,* p. 51 et seq., Hongkong, 1953.

75. See, for instance, Yang Tzu-ho, "Evidences of the Crimes of the Capitalist Class in Their Violent and Crazed Onslaught," *Economic Weekly,* No. 7, Shanghai, February 21, 1952. Reference may also be made to numerous other articles on this subject in the various issues of the same journal in the first half of 1952.

76. Cf. the SAC ruling on the method of differentiating business firms during the campaign in Peking, adopted on March 3, 1952, the report of the mayor of Peking of the same date, the SAC resolution on March 21 to establish special tribunals, and the report of the mayor of Shanghai on March 25 to the Committee for Production Increase and Austerity. Texts in *People's Handbook,* pp. 60-76, Shanghai, 1952.

77. See the reports of the mayors of Peking and Shanghai mentioned earlier.

78. See Hsüeh Mu-ch'iao's report to the SAC on December 29, 1950.

79. *People's Daily,* Peking, March 3, 1954.

80. See *Wen-hui pao,* Hongkong, September 30, 1953. The increase in the relative share of the socialized and partially socialized sectors was, of course, not the result of socialization alone. It also reflected the more rapid increase in the output of the government enterprises which predominated in the capital goods industries. According to Chang Wen-t'ien, the share of government enterprises was 80 per cent in the production of capital goods industries in 1952 but only 50 per cent in that of "light" industries. *People's Daily,* October 1, 1953. See also *People's China* (in English), Peking, January 16, 1954.

81. The share of joint enterprises was reported to have increased to 6 per cent in 1953. Cf. Hsü Ti-hsin's report to the National People's Congress, NCNA, September 24, 1954.

82. Jen-wei, "Private Industry and Commerce in the First Year of the Five Year Plan," *Economic Yearbook,* pp. 64-67, Hongkong, 1954.

83. Reported in *People's Daily,* July 21, 1954.

84. See, for instance, reports in the Tientsin *Ta-kung pao,* June 10, 1954, which emanated from such widely scattered areas as Tsingtao and Chinan in Shantung, Kunming in Yunnan, and Honan, and Kiangsu.

85. See Li Fu-ch'un's report on the First Five Year Plan on July 6, 1955. Li also gave the following percentage figures for the share of the government and partially socialized sectors in total modern industrial production and factory handicraft output: 1949, 36.7 per cent; 1952, 61.0 per cent; and 1954, 75.1 per cent.

CHAPTER SEVEN

An Appraisal of General Industrial Recovery and Development

I

INTRODUCTION

In the preceding chapter we have tried to show how the Communist Chinese authorities have gradually developed a system of economic planning and administration which, though far from being completely adequate, nevertheless constitutes a reasonably workable framework for the pursuit of their industrialization program. The announcement of the Five Year Plan in 1953 signified the determination of the Communist government to embark upon large-scale development on the basis of the accomplishments of the recovery period. The pertinent question at this point is how far the industrial economy has actually recovered from its postwar low and how rapidly industrialization can be carried out in the immediate future. Obviously, there is no simple answer to this question, not only because of the complexity of the issues involved and the many imponderables that will affect the implementation of future policy, but also because of the nature of the statistical data with which the outside observer is compelled to work. However, these are not insuperable difficulties, and, as we shall see presently, a fairly detailed notion of the march of events can be obtained by piecing together the information we have.

In attempting to measure Chinese industrial development quantitatively, a word of warning should be uttered for the benefit of the unwary who may be tempted to draw too precise and sweeping conclusions on the basis of a few "pivotal" quantities, for we are dealing essentially with orders of magnitude instead of accurate measurements. Above all, at the present stage of our knowledge about Communist China, except for illustrative purposes, we should not embark upon the construction of theoretical models that might appear to the layman to present a complete and accurate forecast of economic activity in China for many years to come when they in fact cannot do so. While it is possible to project Chinese economic development for the next two or three years, any attempt to make a quantitative assessment beyond such a short length of time, however interesting as a theoretical speculation on broad trends, must be viewed with a searching skepticism by the man of affairs.[1] Bearing this point in mind, we must therefore regard our present discussion more in the nature of an exploration and an interim report on what must be a continuing study.

NATIONAL INCOME AND INVESTMENT IN THE PREWAR PERIOD

We have already noted before that Communist China must plan to rely largely upon its own resources for the accumulation of capital. So far, the credit provided by the Soviet Union and its other satellites appears to have been on a rather small scale. Of course, this situation may be drastically altered by some political decision of the Communist alliance, but if the inflow of foreign capital could be suddenly augmented through the intervention of external factors, it could also be reduced under the same type of influence. For the student of Communist Chinese development it cannot but be a matter of vital concern to ascertain the extent of potential capital investment on an autarchic basis.

The problem posed may be approached by first examining the volume of potential capital investment in the past and by reviewing then the subsequent changes that have taken place in some of the relevant factors. Unfortunately, as we have seen in Chapter II, national income statistics in China are rather crude, and a long series does not exist. The most recent published data relate to 1946.[2] However, these are derived on the basis of certain bold assumptions and are mostly extrapolated from data dealing with the prewar period. For the prewar period, our previous discussion has shown that thorough analysis is provided in two published sources only—the 1946 exploratory study by Liu Ta-chung and the more extensive study by Ou Pao-san and his associates of the Academia Sinica, which was first published in 1947. To recapitulate, Liu Ta-chung's work attempts to measure the gross national product of the 1931–36 period, while Ou Pao-san's study aims at determining for the same period what is defined as "disposable goods and services" by adding to net income produced international net inpayments in which foreign borrowing and contributions are included. There has been considerable discussion in China on the estimates by Liu and Ou inasmuch as a sizable discrepancy exists between the two series even when they are adjusted to a comparable basis.[3] However, there is no doubt that Ou's results are based on the use of far more extensive material, and may be used as the starting point of our analysis for our present purpose, short of a thorough re-examination of the original data.

If we take the revised "net income produced" figures given by Ou in his 1947 monograph[4] and convert them to 1933 prices by using the same price index employed by Ou in his original work, we obtain an annual average of CN$20,377 million for the 1931–36 period. Subtracting from this figure Ou's estimated consumption of CN$20,441 million, we find a negative average annual net investment of CN$64 million. This figure disregards the net international payments position and may be looked upon as an approximate measure of capital decumulation during the six years immediately preceding the war with Japan if compensatory international factors had been absent.

	Net National Income Produced	*Consumption*	*Net Investment*
	(In CN$ million at 1933 prices)		
1931	20,597	20,441	+ 156
1932	20,296	20,441	— 145
1933	20,319	20,441	— 122
1934	19,457	20,441	— 984
1935	19,824	20,441	— 617
1936	21,767	20,441	+ 1,326
1931-36 average	20,377	20,441	— 64

THE PREWAR POTENTIAL CAPACITY TO INVEST

However, one would not be justified to conclude from these figures that in the absence of compensatory international factors China would not have been able to prevent the disinvestment that would have taken place during this period on the strength of domestic production alone. Two hypothetical circumstances might be considered in this connection.

In the first place, it should be recalled that 1931 was a year of serious floods and that the economic depression in China reached its height in 1934. As may be seen from the above table, there was a small net investment in 1931. Obviously, if agricultural production had not been vastly diminished on account of the flood, the national income produced in 1931 would have been greater and hence the net investment would have been larger. Of course, it could be argued that natural disasters such as the 1931 flood could not have been avoided at the present stage of China's material development, and for this reason we should not disregard 1931 in our evaluation of the potential capacity to invest.[5] However, the depression that took place in the early thirties in China was not due to any unavoidable natural occurrence and could, at any rate, have been mitigated. Consequently, if we should disregard the worst depression year, i.e., 1934, the negative net investment for the prewar period would become a positive annual net investment of CN$99 million instead. If the entire depression period were disregarded and only 1931 and 1936 were taken into account, then the net investment in prewar China would average CN$741 million a year in relation to an average net income of CN$21,182 million. In other words, the annual net investment would have amounted to 3.5 per cent of the net national income produced.

In the second place, it should be noted that the above estimate of a negative net investment for the prewar period is predicated on an annual consumption of CN$20,441 million. If we look closely at the consumption estimate, we find that this figure is the aggregate of the consumption of the agricultural population and that of the non-agricultural population. In both cases the total estimate is again derived from two major geographical sectors, namely, the "lower Yantze region and Southeast China" and the so-called "other regions." In each region the aggregate consumption of each sector represents the sum of consumption by three population groups. For the agricultural population, these are the owner farmers, part owners, and tenant farmers. In the case of the non-agricultural population, they are the upper, middle, and lower income groups. There is a considerable gap between the successive levels of per capita consumption in the three population groups, and if the higher per capita consumptions of certain groups had been reduced, the aggregate consumption would have been smaller. For the sake of argument, we could perhaps take a hypothetical case in which the per capita consumptions of all the highest classes in the two regions are lowered to those of the corresponding middle groups. Under this assumption, the aggregate consumption of the Chinese population in the prewar period would have been reduced by CN$1,278 million which would be made up by 1,032 million from the agricultural population and 246 million from the urban population. This would still leave the per capita consumption of the urban population higher than that of the rural population. In the "lower Yangtze region and Southeast China" the per capita figure of the urban middle group would be CN$177.30 as against CN$41.60 for the rural middle group. For the rest of China the estimated per capita consumption of the middle group would be CN$163.08 for the non-agricultural population and CN$29.93 for the agricultural population. It should also be borne in mind that such a lowering of the consumption levels of the higher groups would still leave their adjusted levels of consumption substantially higher than those of the lowest groups so that there would be some margin of improvement available for the latter through further redistribution. On the assumption of a total reduction in consumption of CN$1,278 million, the net investment in 1931–36 would average CN$1,214 million per annum if the entire period were taken into consideration, or CN$2,019 million if only 1931 and 1936 were taken into account. Such a net investment figure would amount to 5.8 to 9.9 per cent of the national income produced in the correpending prewar years.

There may be some doubt as to whether such a hypothetical reduction of consumption would be at all realistic in view of the bare subsistence level enjoyed by the rural population, but, as Liu Ta-chung has pointed out, actual consumption in real terms by the Chinese population during the prewar years was probably much larger than the above estimates would seem to indicate. Any international comparison of per capita consumption between China and other countries could not be made without a number of adjustments.

II

THE "TOTAL OUTPUT OF INDUSTRY AND AGRICULTURE" AND GROSS INDUSTRIAL PRODUCTION

The question we have to answer now concerns the present potential of investment. As we have pointed out earlier, China's capital stock in the non-agricultural sectors has increased considerably since 1933.

There has also been a sizable increase in the population of the country. On the assumption that agricultural production has not changed substantially, the increase in non-agricultural capital must have brought about an increase in production and hence national income unless the rise of the capital stock and population had been more than counterbalanced by a decrease in productivity. However, while national income may have increased, the question remains as to whether its increase is proportionate to the rise of population and of consumption. Of course, it is quite conceivable for the absolute volume of potential net investment to be greater even if national income has failed to keep pace with the population increase as long as the increment in population brings with it an increment in output greater than that of consumption.

Although official Communist sources have not published any national income statistics so far, estimates of the "total output of industry and agriculture" have been made available for the last few years. These figures represent the sum of industrial and agricultural production and are composed of "output statistics of the major industrial products and estimates for the lesser industrial products, together with estimates for agricultural products, the handicraft industries, and supplementary agricultural products not otherwise included in agricultural production."[6] In the case of industrial production the individual enterprise is the reporting unit. "For every enterprise all its finished and semi-finished products, regardless of the source, i.e., internal or external, of the raw materials used, as well as the value of any industrial construction and service, are included in the gross value output of the enterprise, as long as they represent the final results of the productive activity of the enterprise. For a ministry or bureau, its total value output is the aggregate of the outputs of all its subordinate enterprises. In other words, within the enterprise, its own products that are consumed during the manufacturing process are not included in the total value output to avoid double counting. But within the ministry or bureau, products (obtained from one enterprise) consumed during the manufacturing process (in another) are *also* included in the (latter's) total value output."[7] Consequently, the "total output of industry and agriculture" is a gross concept. It does not correspond to the "value added" concept used in both Liu's and Ou's national income estimates and includes a considerable amount of double counting. The values, however, are expressed in terms of constant prices which are "provisionally those announced by the Economic and Financial Commission in June, 1950, except that in the case of Manchuria the 1943 prices are used."

On the basis of available information, we have been able to construct indices for the "total output of industry and agriculture," as well as for industry in general and modern industry in particular, for the years 1949–1954. As may be seen from the following table, the total output of industry and agriculture rose by 89.4 per cent from 1949 to 1953. In the same period, the increase in industrial output, including both modern industry and handicraft workshop production, rose by 202.6 per cent whereas that of modern industry alone increased by 226.3 per cent.[8] The greater increase in production in the industrial sector and especially in modern industry, of course, reflects the government's emphasis on industrial recovery and the relative ease with which industrial production could be rehabilitated and, at the present stage of Chinese development, expanded with increasing returns in comparison with diminishing returns from agriculture.

GENERAL PRODUCTION INDEX OF INDUSTRY AND AGRICULTURE

	Total Output of Industry and Agriculture	*Industrial Output*	
		Total[1]	*Modern Industry*
1949	100.0	100.0	100.0
1950	—	128.9	—
1951	—	188.1	—
1952	170.0[2]	236.4	260.0[2]
1953	189.4[3]	302.6	326.3[2]
1954 (plan)	213.3[4]	354.0	386.0[5]
(Preliminary)[6]	220.0	402.5	420.0
(Revised)[7]	207.2	354.0	—
1955 (plan)[7]	—	381.3	—

1. Including handicraft industries. For 1949-1952 see *People's Daily*, Peking, December 12, 1953; also quoted in *Economic Yearbook*, p. 25, Hongkong, 1954. For 1953 see Teng Hsiao-p'ing's report on the 1954 budget. For 1954 see *People's Daily*, January 1, 1954; also *Economic Bulletin*, No. 1, p. 5, 1954.
2. See Ts'ai-ching's article in the Tientsin *Ta-kung pao*, June 21, 1954.
3. Estimated at 111.4 per cent of the 1952 output. Cf. Teng Hsiao-p'ing's report. The actual figure may be somewhat higher.
4. Estimated at 112.6 per cent of the 1953 output. Teng Hsiao-p'ing, *ibid.*
5. Estimated at 118.3 per cent of the 1953 figure. Teng Hsiao-p'ing, *ibid.*
6. Cf. Chou En-lai's report to the First Session of the First National People's Congress on September 23, 1954, NCNA, September 24, 1954.
7. Li Hsien-nien's report on the 1955 budget, NCNA, July 9, 1955.

However, there still is the problem of relating industrial production in 1949 to that of the pre-Communist period. According to the Economic and Financial Commission, the index of industrial production, computed on the basis of the output of 33 major industrial products, stood in 1949 at 56 per cent of the pre-1949 peak.[9] However, it is not clear whether production by the handicraft industries was taken into account. Nor can one be certain as to whether the "pre-1949" peak referred to a single calendar year or to some fictitious construction similar to that used in measuring the increase in the production of a number of individual commodities. Consequently, for this purpose, we must resort to some crude arithmetic of our own by adapting Wang Foh-shen's industrial production index for 1931–1946[10] and extending it to the 1949–1953 period. The physical outputs of six key industrial items—namely, pig iron, cement, coal, electric power, cotton yarn, and flour—are used in constructing this adjusted industrial production series which has 1933 as its base. This results in an admittedly very crude index as only six commodities are included although they represent China's principal manufacturing and mining industries. The narrow coverage is forced upon us not only because of our present lack of information on some of the items used by Wang, but also as a concession to the fact that if such commodities as gasoline and rolled steel were included, their phenomenal rise in recent years would seriously distort the series in comparison with 1933. However, for our purpose, such a crude index does afford us some ground for speculative contemplation. As may be seen from the table below, the physical production index thus constructed with 1933 as base is 103.82 for 1949, and is about 56 per cent of that for 1945, Wang's peak year. It rose to 261.63 in 1952 and again to 318.36 in 1953. In addition, it should also be noted that the 1946 index is 92.76 as against 103.82 in 1949, a situation which common sense would suggest to be essentially correct when viewed against the historical background.

We may now take the bold step by using the 1949 index in our physical output series to provide the missing link between prewar industrial production and that of the Communist period as indicated in the official gross industrial production statistics. In this way we may convert the Communist industrial production series for 1949–1954 to the 1933 base. According to the adjusted industrial production series, industrial output in 1953 was 314.16 as against 103.82 in 1949.

INDUSTRIAL PRODUCTION INDEX

	Physical Output Index	*Adjusted Communist Production Index*
1933	100.00	100.00
1945	180.00	180.00
1946	92.76	92.76
1949	103.82	103.82
1950	147.95	133.82
1951	204.29	195.29
1952	261.63	245.43
1953	318.36	314.16
1954	—	367.52

There is no denying the fact that recovery of industrial production was very rapid after 1949 as viewed from the above indices. However, this phenomenon is largely due to the low industrial production in 1949. If one were to compare industrial production in 1953 with that of 1945, instead of 1949, the increase would be about 76 per cent according to our physical output index, or 74 per cent on the basis of the adjusted official industrial production index. This rate of expansion is quite comparable to that obtained from 1933 to 1945, which was also 80 per cent. According to Wang Foh-shen's industrial production index, the 1945 output was the highest ever reached in mainland China. Yet industrial production in Manchuria was disrupted during the latter part of 1945 following the surrender of Japan in World War II, and new industrial establishments installed by the Japanese in the latter part of the war had never been utilized to their full capacity. Following the rehabilitation of Manchuria it is not surprising that the Communist regime has been able to bring industrial output to the above estimated levels during the first year of the Five Year Plan.

THE PROBABLE RANGE OF NATIONAL INCOME IN 1953

According to official Communist statistics,[11] during 1953, the gross value of industrial output, including that of the handicraft workshops, accounted for 39.4 per cent of the total output of industry and agriculture. If we assume as a first approximation that the relative increase in gross industrial output between 1933 and 1953 may also be used to measure that of industry's contribution to "net values added," and that the relative share of industry in the total output of industry and agriculture also measures its share in the aggregate "net values added" by both industry and agriculture, then we may use our industrial production index in conjunction with Ou's revised estimate of net income produced by industry to arrive at some very crude conjecture on net income produced by industry in 1953. From this we may further estimate the aggregate of net income produced from agriculture and industry.

Since we have two industrial production series, there are two possible estimates. On the one hand, given the net income produced by industry in 1933 as CN$2,127 million,[12] if we employ the Communist official industrial production series as adjusted by us, net income produced in 1953 in the industrial sector would amount to CN$6,682 billion at 1933 prices. This would give us a net income produced by industry and agriculture of 16,959 million in 1933 Chinese dollars. On the other hand, if our industrial physical output index is used, the net income produced by industry in 1953 would amount to 6,772 million, and the aggregate by industry and agriculture together would be 17,188 million, both in 1933 Chinese dollars.

According to Ou, the share of industry and agriculture in net income produced in 1946 was 66.1 per cent. With the expansion of government administrative activity and the substantial increase in transportation under the present regime, which probably outweighs any possible decrease in the other remaining sectors, the relative importance of industry and agriculture now is likely to be somewhat different from that of 1946. But, for want of a better estimate, we may provisionally accept this figure. On this basis, our two estimates of Communist China's net national income produced in 1953 would both come to about CN$26,000 million at 1933 prices.

It is possible that the above figure is an underestimate as the relative share of industry in the total output of industry and agriculture may be somewhat exaggerated in the official statistics[13] so that, given the value of industrial production, the national income derived therefrom may also be too low. If, for instance, the share of industrial production in the total output of industry and agriculture were as low as 30 per cent, other things being equal, and using the adjusted official industrial production index, the net income produced in 1953 would be about CN$33,847 million at 1933 prices.[14] This may be treated as a higher estimate. Thus, the probable range of Communist China's national income produced in 1953 was between CN$26,000 amount to 6,772 million, and the aggregate by industry and agriculture together would be 17,188 million, both in 1933 Chinese dollars.

CONSUMPTION AND POTENTIAL NET INVESTMENT IN 1953

Given the possible range of national income produced in 1953 as CN$26,000 million to CN$33,847 million at 1933 prices (US$18.0 to 23.7 billion at 1953 prices), the amount available for investment depends upon the estimate of consumption requirement. Since the population of mainland China is said to have increased from 450 million in 1933 to 583 million in 1953, the total consumption requirement may be assumed to have risen in the same proportion, i.e., 30 per cent. On the basis of Ou's consumption estimate of CN$20,441 million for 1933, the 1953 figure would be CN$26,573 million. Since consumption at this level would not be possible without disinvestment if the actual national income produced were at our lower estimated level of CN$26,000 million, one would be justified in assuming that under such circumstances strenuous measures would be taken by the Communist authorities to curb consumption. Consequently, one should probably use at least the adjusted consumption estimate of CN$19,163 million[15] for 1933 in this case instead of Ou's original estimate so that the estimated consumption requirement for 1953 would be CN$24,912 million. In practice this figure could probably be curtailed further. On the other hand, in the *very unlikely* event that the 1953 national income produced were as high as CN$33,847 million, one would probably be justified in using CN $26,573 million as the consumption estimate. Under these assumptions the possible range of potential net investment in 1953 may be seen as follows:

NATIONAL INCOME PRODUCED, CONSUMPTION, AND POTENTIAL NET INVESTMENT IN 1953
(In CN$ million at 1933 prices)

	Lower Estimate	*Higher Estimate*
National Income	26,000	33,847
Consumption	24,912	26,573
Investment	1,088	7,274

In terms of U.S. currency the potential net investment in 1953 would accordingly be from US$761 million to US$5.1 billion at 1953 prices. A far more detailed study would be necessary in order to determine more precisely the potential capacity to invest. But both the higher and the lower estimates are most improbable and, as we shall see presently, actual performance in 1953 pointed to a range of US$1 to 2 billion as the rate of annual net investment at the beginning of the First Five Year Plan, or closer to the lower and more realistic of the above two estimates. Since the many large industrial projects have a fairly long construction period, it is doubtful that this rate can increase very significantly in the next few years.

It will be noted that even if the higher of our two estimates were correct, the rate of investment would still be relatively low on the basis of western standards. Besides, such a rate of investment would be possible only if consumption were held at not above the prewar per capita standard. There is always the danger that population growth and the popular desire for some investment in the standard of living or at least some relaxation in austerity might play havoc to the program of industrialization unless adequate measures were taken in time.

So far the Communist authorities have not indicated any clear intention to curb the rate of population growth. On the contrary, the various social measures they have taken in regulating family life would seem to point to the opposite effect. They have emphasized a great deal on increasing productivity, but the record so far has been in line with economic rehabilitation, and, except for occasional advances in some fields, there has not been any outstanding improvement in a broad area. The task of technical training is a relatively slow process although an official attitude to experiment with and adopt innovations readily may be helpful.

However, it would probably be a serious mistake if we were to confine our thoughts to the conventional methods of relieving population pressure, for there are at least three other ways in which national income could be increased by putting some of the surplus and underemployed labor into "productive" work. In the first place, such labor could be drafted to work on large construction projects without any adverse effect on the original level of production and could be paid with no more than what it would otherwise have to consume. Second, labor could conceivably be exported as a commodity on a compulsory basis. Finally, the armed forces provide a ready outlet wherever the use of superior manpower could be expected to yield an economic return through military and political conquest.

Moreover, in spite of the extremely low living standard, consumption can still be curtailed. Already the Chinese Communist authorities have introduced the rationing of certain staple foods and cotton cloth, together with the promise of further restrictions. They have also restricted dividend and bonus disbursements in the fast-expanding, semi-socialistic sector of the economy, and have repeatedly stressed the need for capital investments in the cooperative farms. The decisive factor is, in the final analysis, whether popular acquiescence to continued austerity can be enforced indefinitely and whether the political high command has the necessary power and will to do so.

AN ESTIMATE OF ACTUAL INVESTMENT IN THE FIRST PHASE OF THE FIVE YEAR PLAN

Total capital construction expenditure in 1953 was said to account for one-third of total government outlay in Po I-po's 1953 budget.[16] However, as some of the construction projects had a late start and some of the budgeted investments were overestimated, actual outlay on capital construction, based on the 1954 budget report, was considerably less. It was probably about ¥59,130 billion out of a total outlay of ¥86,019 billion on "economic development" or "reconstruction." At the official exchange rate, this would represent an investment of US$2.4 billion at 1953 prices by the government.[17]

However, capital construction expenditure corresponds to gross investment from which depreciation and replacement must be deducted. The annual depreciation charge on China's capital stock has been estimated by Wang Foh-shen at CN$1,464 million for 1933 or about US$1.02 billion at 1953 prices. As an approximation, we might assume that the probably larger depreciation charge required for 1953 was more or less offset by whatever net private investment there was in that year. Accordingly, total net investment in Communist China in 1953 would be around US$1.38 billion. Since Communist government investment in 1953 included that part which was financed with foreign credit, net investment from domestic sources was slightly lower.[18]

NATURE AND TREND OF GOVERNMENT INVESTMENT

On the basis of official reports, total government expenditure on capital construction increased from ¥31,133 billion in 1952 to ¥59,130 billion in 1953—a gain of 90 per cent—as compared with ¥16,827 billion in 1951. It increased further to ¥87,197 billion in 1954 and is planned to reach ¥95,916 billion (in old currency) in 1955, although, as we have argued in the preceding pages, this rate of increase could not be easily maintained.[19] Given the small absolute volume of investment, the importance of husbanding available resources is quite evident. Consequently, the distribution of government investment by types of activity is most revealing.

According to an official report in 1953,[20] capital construction expenditure in 1952 was distributed as follows:

	Per Cent	*Y billion*
Industry	56	17,435
Agriculture, Forestry and Irrigation	16	4,981
Transport and Communications	28	8,717
Total	100	31,133

According to the Bureau of Statistics, the 1952 capital investment by the six ministries of the central government in charge of various industries, which account for the bulk of total industrial investment, was 206 per cent of the corresponding figure in 1951.[21] Since total expenditure on capital construction in 1952 rose by 85 per cent only in comparison with the preceding year, there was a shift of emphasis in 1952 from the other items to industrial investment. The increase in industrial investment in 1953 was again 106 per cent over the 1952 level and more rapid than the corresponding increase in total investment.

This shift of emphasis in official policy will apparently continue through the 1953–1957 period and the present priority given to the manufacturing, mining, and other industries is quite unmistakable. Transportation and communication appear to be second on the list, followed by agriculture, forestry, irrigation, and others. In the absence of detailed breakdowns for capital construction, the following overall expenditure data for 1953–1955 serve to substantiate this conclusion almost equally well:

PERCENTAGE DISTRIBUTION OF GOVERNMENT EXPENDITURE ON ECONOMIC ACTIVITIES 1953–1955

	1953 Budget	*1953* Actual	*1954* Budget	*1955* Budget
Industry	46.01	49.83	47.79	45.02
Transportation and Communications	14.34	14.44	15.59	15.12
Agriculture, Forestry, and Irrigation	11.36	13.16	10.55	9.25
Trade and Banking	4.33	11.61[1]	11.29	20.05
Other	23.96	10.96	14.78	10.56
Total Economic Items	100.00	100.00	100.00	100.00

Sources: 1953 and 1954 budget reports. Economic expenditure, as mentioned before, includes expenditure on defense, especially expenditure by the Second Ministry of Machinery Industry which is believed to be the ministry of armaments.

1. The increase in expenditure under "trade and banking" in 1953 was prompted by the expansion of the government food purchase program for the general implementation of food rationing.

Furthermore, within the industrial field, apart from the armament industries proper, attention seems to have been concentrated on fuels, iron and steel, and machinery. During 1953, while government investment in all industries rose by 106 per cent over the corresponding level in 1952, government investment in the fuel industries was reported to be 245 per cent of that of 1952 and was equal to the total investment made in the entire 1950–1952 period. The increase in government investment in machinery manufacturing in 1953 over that of 1952 was also as high as 141.35 per cent.[22] In 1954 one half of the planned investment in industry, which was 28 per cent higher than the 1953 level, was earmarked for electric power and coal mining.[23] In terms of overall budget provisions, the increase in government expenditure from the 1952 to the 1953 budget was 84.56 per cent in the fuel industries and 47.31 per cent in the machinery industries and industries under the jurisdiction of the Ministry of Heavy Industry, i.e., including chemicals, iron and steel, and nonferrous metals. Finally, according to the 1954 budget, 78.3 per cent of government outlay in the industrial field is earmarked for the "heavy industries" such as coal, electric power, petroleum, chemicals, iron and steel, and machinery manufacturing, while only 21.7 per cent is allotted to the "light industries." In 1955, the corresponding share of "heavy industry" has been raised further to 89.20 per cent.

The increasing importance of investment for further accumulation has been reflected in the composition of industrial output. According to official Communist reports, the share of producers' goods in total industrial output increased from 32.5 per cent in 1949 to 43.8 per cent in 1952 and again to an estimated planned target of 47.5 per cent in 1953.[24] This trend is expected to continue in the remainder of the Five Year Plan period and beyond.

III

THE IMPORTANCE OF INFORMATION ON SPECIFIC INDUSTRIES

So far our discussion on industrial recovery and potential development in Communist China has been in broad terms. We have had occasion to note the relatively small margin available for investment and the predominant emphasis on producers' goods in the composition of investment, but the general discussion has left us without any detailed knowledge of the individual industries, which is most unsatisfactory from several points of view. In the first place, the outwardly astounding rate of industrial recovery since 1949 is rather deceptive inasmuch as the outputs of many key commodities are still very small and, with few exceptions, are barely sufficient to supply the necessary capital equipment required for a modest industrialization program. In the second place, as we examine the contents of the First Five Year Plan, their significance cannot be properly appreciated except in the light of the present state of the various industries. Finally, for those students of Communist Chinese affairs who have to make evaluations for practical purposes, it is especially important to be able to translate the various aggregates into concrete terms. Consequently, we shall try to survey the process of industrial recovery in terms of the outputs of a number of industrial products in this section. We shall then review some of the industries in greater detail in the following chapter. Before we can do this, however, we have to digress for a moment on the development of Communist statistical reporting.

STATUS OF STATISTICAL REPORTING IN COMMUNIST CHINA

Attempts by independent observers to make use of official Communist statistical information have been constantly plagued by the fact that index numbers released at different times and appearing in either the same or different publications, while apparently relating to the same subject matter, are not always identical. Or else, if they refer to different time periods, internal inconsistency is frequently present. This characteristic of Communist Chinese statistics has raised some serious doubt as to their general validity. It has also led some to question whether this situation is not entirely the result of deliberate efforts to conceal information for security reasons. However, upon close examination, it is believed that while the last-mentioned factor is constantly present, much of the confusion and discrepancy stems from somewhat different reasons. These are: (1) the existence of different reporting agencies such as the statistical office of the Economic and Financial Commission and the various subordinate ministries and bureaus under the jurisdiction of the Commission, (2) the employment of different methods and coverages by separate agencies and by the same reporting agency at different times, and (3) the indiscriminate use by Communist writers of planned versus actual figures and of preliminary versus revised and final estimates.[25]

The first attempt to establish some semblance of order in statistical reporting was made in the middle of 1950 when a conference was called in Manchuria to consider the standardization of statistical reports, the training of statistical personnel, and the completion of an industrial census covering private firms.[26] But the existence of divergent practice continued, and it was not until October, 1952, when the National Bureau of Statistics, headed by Hsüeh Mu-ch'iao, was established, that a serious effort was made to reorganize and streamline statistical work. The establishment of the new bureau was in response to the government's policy to inaugurate a more inclusive planned system, and was therefore an important step preparatory to the inception of the First Five Year Plan. Against this background it is perfectly understandable why the Bureau's first assignment was the organization of "national surveys of gross industrial and agricultural production and of employment."

The second national conference on statistical work was convened under the auspices of the new Bureau of Statistics in December, 1952. Following the conference, it was announced that a centralized and unified system of statistical reporting would henceforth be established and that the Bureau would be responsible for the standardization of statistical methods and report forms. At the same time, the conference also decided that the principal statistical work in 1953 was to gather the necessary data for economic planning.

Since the establishment of the Bureau, annual statistical reports have been released for both 1952 and 1953, in addition to regular statistical bulletins at more frequent intervals. According to Hsüeh Mu-ch'iao's report to the third national statistics conference in February, 1954, the Bureau had by then reached the point when it could process, with a time lag of not more than twenty days, national statistical data on the physical and value outputs of the major products under the jurisdiction of the central government ministries in charge of industries, the transport volume on railways, and the sales and purchases of important merchandise.[27] Yet performance in different areas was rather uneven during 1953. In the state sector of the industrial economy, while statistical information on physical and value outputs was fairly complete, the quality of statistical information on wages was very poor. Statistical information on financial and cost data in the government industries was said to be even poorer, while it was virtually non-existent as far as technical data were concerned. In the field of state trading, during 1953, statistical data were available on purchases, sales, and stocks only. Reporting on transportation and the state farms in 1953 was said to be inferior.[28]

From these comments it would appear that reporting on industrial production had apparently become reasonably satisfactory by 1953, but this applied only to the government enterprises from which regular and complete returns were received, and the same situation holds for the present time. For the non-socialized sectors of the economy, sampling remains to be the method used for arriving at estimates.[29] Accordingly, statistical data on the capital goods industries are probably more accurate than those on consumers' goods industries as socialization has gone much further in the former than in the latter.

ESTIMATES OF PHYSICAL PRODUCTION FOR MAJOR INDUSTRIAL PRODUCTS

In the light of the above discussion we may now regard the following index numbers as a reasonable approximation of the physical outputs of certain key commodities. The numbers italicized are selected from among several alternative figures which are all related to the 1949 base. In addition, we also present the 1949 production data for some of these commodities in terms of their respective "peak year" outputs. The so-called "peak year" varies from one industry to another and is not infrequently a purely fictitious concept. In the latter case, the particular "peak year" output is the sum of the peak output in China Proper, which in a number of cases fell in 1936, and that of Manchuria, which as a rule fell in the 1942–45 period. Thus the "peak" outputs for all China that should be used in converting these indices into absolute quantities are not necessarily those of any actual calendar year or years. Finally, for those commodities information on which is more readily available an attempt has been made to convert the official indices into absolute quantities. The estimates are made on the basis of the "peak year" outputs except where information for 1949 is directly available. It is believed that the figures finally arrived at are essentially correct as they can be tested in most cases by aggregating or comparing with estimates for individual regions that may be made independently.

On the basis of the estimated outputs of selected commodities, several tentative observations may be made. In the first place, the outputs of a number of important industrial products during the first year of the Five Year Plan were still extremely small, especially in view of the large population in mainland China. They compared unfavorably not only with the Soviet Union in the late twenties, but also with India at the present time.[30] Moreover, the much vaunted industrial recovery since 1949, while impressive enough, was not as spectacular as the Communist authorities would have us believe. Compared with pre-Communist peak outputs, the production of coal and pig iron might even be lower in 1953, and the increase in rolled steel products was less than 10 per cent. While the increase in the production of steel ingots and cement was notable, this only reflected the small outputs in the pre-Communist period. A most outstanding example of this deceptive development was petroleum production which was doubled between 1943 and 1953, but which was produced in very small quantities in the earlier year. On the other hand, it was in the consumers' goods industries such as the cotton textiles and, to a lesser extent, flour milling, that the advance was really significant in view of the relatively large outputs before the advent of the Communists. These facts are of far-reaching importance in our understanding of the contents of the Five Year Plan, the possibilities of self-sufficiency in individual industries, and the rate at which indus-

INDEX OF PHYSICAL OUTPUT OF MAJOR INDUSTRIAL PRODUCTS IN COMMUNIST YEAR

Commodities	"Peak Year" = 100	1949 = 100												
	1949	1950				1951				1952				
	(1)	(2)	(3)	(4)	(5)	(2)	(3)	(4)	(6) (Plan)	(2)	(7)	(8)	(9)	(10)
Producers' Goods														
I. Pig Iron	10.9	394.0	445.0	–	–	574.0	587.0	–	567.0[a]	764.0	750.0	754.8	963.0	954.1
II. Steel Ingots	15.8	383.0	434.0	–	–	566.0	614.0	–	–	846.0	940.0	798.6	1,076.0	981.1
III. Rolled Steel	17.8	288.0	376.0	–	–	496.0	674.0	–	–	848.0	820.0	–	–	938.0
IV. Cement	30.9	213.0	213.0	–	–	376.0	346.0	–	–	433.0	350.0	417.4	495.0	479.0
V. Metal-cutting Machines	–	200.0	–	–	–	362.0	–	–	–	650.0	–	–	–	–
VI. Soda	62.9	–	154.0	–	–	–	197.0	–	–	–	190.0	263.6	–	–
VII. Caustic Soda	62.2[a]	–	131.9	–	–	–	392.2	–	–	–	520.0	322.3	–	–
VIII. Automobile Tires	35.9	–	184.0	245.0	–	–	546.0	844.0 900.0[a]	796.0	–	–	–	–	–
IX. Coal	44.5	132.0	132.0	–	–	164.0	156.0	–	–	202.0	200.0	193.2	213.0	202.2
X. Crude Oil	38.0	166.0	–	–	158.5	248.0	–	–	–	358.0	310.0	309.8	–	358.0
XI. Gasoline	–	–	–	–	133.3	–	–	–	–	–	–	–	–	–
XII. Fuel Oil	–	–	–	–	364.0	–	–	–	–	–	–	–	–	–
XIII. Electric Power	72.3	106.0	107.0	–	–	134.0	131.0	–	–	164.0	180.0	173.7	158.0	159.1
Consumers' Goods														
I. Cotton Yarn	72.4	134.0	139.0	–	–	149.0	146.0	–	124.0[b]	201.0	200.0	193.6	207.0	198.8
II. Cotton Piece Goods	72.6	154.0	149.0	–	–	197.0	156.0	–	–	287.0	230.0	269.1	226.0	221.7
III. Flour	77.6	93.0	–	63.0	–	143.0	–	106.0 87.6[a]	–	220.0	–	–	–	–
IV. Sugar	39.6	121.0	–	146.0	–	151.0	–	184.0	185.0	199.0	–	193.6	–	–
V. Cigarettes	83.0	116.0	–	116.0	–	116.0	–	133.0	124.0	151.0	–	–	–	–
VI. Matches	85.0	87.0	–	87.0	–	107.0	–	100.0	104.0	129.0	–	–	–	–
VII. Paper	89.5	130.0	128.0	95.0	–	223.0	173.0	163.0 153.1[a]	124.0	331.0	–	336.3	238.0	–

INDEX OF PHYSICAL OUTPUT OF MAJOR INDUSTRIAL PRODUCTS IN COMMUNIST YEAR

(Continued)

Commodities				1953			1954		1957-9	1957
	(11)	(12)	(13)	(14)	(15)	(19)	(16)	(18)	(17)	(20)
				(Plan)	(Plan)		(Plan)	(Prel.)	Planned Goals	Planned Goals
Producers' Goods										
I. Pig Iron	807.0[b]	886.0	879.0	871.0	865.6	909.2	1,151.8[c]	1,240.0	–	–
II. Steel Ingots	–	1,109.0	1,103.0	1,041.6	1,033.0	1,108.3	1,275.4[c]	1,370.0	3,384.0	2,922.0
III. Rolled Steel	–	–	1,064.0	–	1,143.1	1,136.3	1,144.8[c]	–	2,120.0	–
IV. Cement	–	–	–	506.6	561.6	584.6	640.2[c]	720.0	–	930.8
V. Metal-cutting Machines	–	–	786.0[a]	871.0	678.0	968.5	–	850.0	2,275.0	–
VI. Soda	–	–	–	–	–	220.4	–	–	–	–
VII. Caustic Soda	–	–	–	681.2[a]	–	587.6	–	–	–	–
VIII. Automobile Tires	1,554.0 1,510.0[a]	–	–	–	–	a	–	–	–	–
IX. Coal	–	225.4	–	202.0[a]	–	220.0	259.2[d]	260.0	323.0	434.6
X. Crude Oil	–	486.9	509.0[b]	508.4	462.2	515.5	767.0[a]	–	–	–
XI. Gasoline	–	–	b	–	–	b	–	–	–	–
XII. Fuel Oil	–	–	b	–	–	–	–	–	–	–
XIII. Electric Power	–	200.1	203.0[c]	208.3	194.0	206.6	233.0[b]	250.0	328.0	353.3
Consumers' Goods										
I. Cotton Yarn	209.0	–	226.3[d]	219.1	219.9	227.1	253.0[a]	260.0	–	–
II. Cotton Piece Goods	216.0	–	275.9[d]	266.8	254.2	262.2	310.8[a]	–	–	–
III. Flour	136.0[a]	–	–	–	–	253.0	–	–	–	–
IV. Sugar	253.0[a]	–	–	245.0	–	214.9	–	–	–	–
V. Cigarettes	175.0[a]	–	–	–	–	205.4	–	–	–	–
VI. Matches	131.0[a]	–	–	–	–	113.5	–	–	–	–
VII. Paper	249.0 261.0[a]	–	–	351.0	357.1	380.7	–	450.0	–	–

Sources — Index of Physical Output of Major Industrial Products in Communist China.

(1) Report by Li Fu-ch'un to the third session of the First National Committee of the PPCC on October 1, 1951, quoted in *New China Monthly*, p. 27, Peking, November, 1951; also report by Li on September 19, 1952, reprinted in *New China's Economic Achievements in the Last Three Years*, Peking, 1952. Cf. also Shen Ho, "The Glorious Achievements in New China's Financial and Economic Reconstruction in the Past Year," *Economic Yearbook*, p. 13, Hongkong, 1953.
a - Estimated.

(2) Bureau of Statistics Bulletin, quoted in *Wen-hui pao*, Hongkong, September, 1953. Cf. also Li T'ing-hsiu, "The Basic Task of China's First Five Year Development Plan" and Ma Ling-feng, "The Glorious Victory on China's Industrial Front during the Past Year," *Economic Yearbook*, 1954.

(3) Data converted from "peak year" base. Preliminary estimates. Sung Shao-wen, "The Chinese People's Economic Reconstruction Achievements in the Past Two Years," *People's Daily*, Peking, October 6, 1951. Cf. also *New China Monthly*, p. 1301, October, 1951, and Yang P'o, "Industrial and Commercial Recovery and Readjustment in China," *Economic Yearbook*, p. 31, 1952.

(4) Huang Yen-p'ei, "Recovery and Development of the Light Industries in the Last Three Years," *New China Monthly*, p. 146, November, 1952.
a - Huang's report to the State Administrative Council on June 13, 1952, *New China Monthly*, p. 172, October, 1952. Data converted from "peak year" base.

(5) *People's China* (in English), Vol. IV, No. 8, p. 10, Peking, October 16, 1951.

(6) Converted from 1950 base. *Natural Science*, Vol. I, No. 5, p. 365, Peking, report by Ch'en Wei-chi.
a - Actual, converted from 1950 base. *New China Monthly*, April, 1953, p. 139.
b - Actual.

(7) Chia T'o-fu's report to the seventh National Congress of the China Federation of Labor, *Ta-kung pao*, Hongkong, May 9, 1953.

(8) Cf. Po I-p'o's report on the 1953 budget.

(9) Preliminary estimate, NCNA, January 1, 1953. Cf. also Ch'en Ting-wei's article in *Economic Yearbook*, p. 16, 1953. Data converted from "peak year" base.

(10) Estimates given by Li Fu-ch'un in his report on September 19, 1952, in (1). Cf. also *Chinese Youth Journal*, Peking, September 3, 1952, and Ch'en Ting-wei, *op. cit.* Data converted from "peak year" base.

(11) *Wen-hui pao*, October 7, 1953.
a - Huang Yen-p'ei's estimates. Data converted from "peak year" base. See (4) above.
b - See (6)a above.

(12) Teng Hsiao-p'ing's 1954 budget report. Data converted from 1952 base.

(13) New China Monthly, No. 3, pp. 133-4, 1954. Data converted from 1952 base.
a - NCNA, January 31, 1954.
b - Ma Ling-feng, *op. cit.* Data converted from 1952 base, eleven months totals at annual rate. For gasoline and fuel oil, the index numbers are 127.6 and 168.6 respectively (1952 = 100).
c - NCNA, January 11, 1954.
d - Report of the Ministry of Textile Industry, March 6, 1954. Cf. *Ta-kung pao*, Tientsin, June 19, 1954.

(14) Po I-p'o's 1953 budget report. Data converted from 1952 base.
a - Cf. Chou En-lai's report on February 4, 1953, to the fourth session of the PPCC National Committee. Also *Economic Bulletin*, No. 305, Hongkong, February 10, 1953.

(15) Believed to be a revised plan. Cf. Chia T'o-fu's report of May 9, 1953. See (7) above. Data converted from 1952 base.

(16) a - See 13d above.
b - NCNA, February 3, 1954.
c - NCNA, April 19, 1954.
d - *Economic Bulletin*, No. 1, p. 6, January 24, 1954.

(17) *Pravda*, September 28, 1953.

(18) Chou En-Lai's report to the First National People's Congress, September 23, 1954, NCNA, September 24, 1954.

(19) National Bureau of Statistics, NCNA, September 13, 1954.
a - Reported at 117 per cent of the 1952 output.
b - Reported at 140 per cent of the 1952 output.

(20) Li Fu-ch'un's report on the First Five Year Plan, NCNA, July 6, 1955.

ESTIMATED OUTPUT OF SELECTED INDUSTRIAL PRODUCTS IN COMMUNIST CHINA[1]

	1936[7]	Previous Peak[7] (Calendar Year)	1949[7]		1950		1951	
			A	B	A	B	A	B
Pig Iron	795	2,131 (1942)	206	244	812	961	1,182	1,399
Steel Ingots	414	853 (1943)	141	158	540	605	798	894
Rolled Steel	neg.	844 (1943)	87		251		432	
Cement	764[a]	2,220 (1943)	678	657	1,444	1,400	2,549	2,473
Coal	39,646	64,974 (1942)	26,000	31,535	34,320	41,596	42,640	51,680
Crude Oil[2]	neg.	75 (1943)	30		49		74	5,789
Electric Power[3]	1,724	5,654 (1944)	4,500	4,320	4,770	4,579	6,030	
Cotton Yarn[4]	2,039	2,455 (1930)	1,778		2,383		2,206	
Cotton Piece Goods[5]	942	942 (1936)	684		1,053		1,287	
Flour[6]	74,857[a]	–	57,911		53,857		82,813	

	1952		1953		1954		1957
	A	B	A	B	(Preliminary)	Per Capita	(Plan)
Pig Iron	1,574	1,864	1,873.0	2,218.4	3,030	5.19 kg.	
Steel Ingots	1,193	1,336	1,562.7	1,751.1	2,170	3.72	4,120
Rolled Steel	738		988.6		–		
Cement	2,936	2,842	3,963.6	3,840.8	4,730	8.11	6,000
Coal	52,520	63,654	57,200.0	69,377.0	81,990	140.65	113,000
Crude Oil[2]	106		155.0		–		
Electric Power[3]	7,380	7,085	9,054.0	8,925.0	10,800	18.52 kwh.	15,900
Cotton Yarn[4]	3,573		4,038.0		4,600	.008 bale (3.2 kg.)	
Cotton Piece Goods[5]	1,573		2,126.0		–		163,720,000 bolts
Flour[6]	127,404		146,514.0		–		

[a] 1933

[1] In thousand metric tons unless otherwise indicated.

[2] In million gallons.

[3] In million kilowatt-hours.

[4] In thousand bales.

[5] In million meters.

[6] In thousand bags of 22 kgs.

[7] Geological Survey of China, General Statement on the Mining Industry, 7th issue, 1945; Bureau of Information, Iron and Steel, Nanking, 1947; Pauley Reparations Commission Report, 1946; Statistical Yearbook of the Republic of China, 1948; The Chinese Economy in the Last Decade; H. D. Fong, China's Cotton Textile Industry, 1953; Plan for the Industrial Development of China, 1948; and Wang Foh-shen, China's Industrial Production and Li Fu-ch'un's report on the First Five Year Plan, NCNA, July 6, 1955.

Figures in column B in 1949-1953 are derived from preliminary data given in Chou En-lai's report on September 23, 1954, and are more questionable. According to Li Fu-ch'un's report of July 6, 1955, on the First Five Year Plan, the 1952 figures were: steel, 1,350,000 tons; electricity, 7,228 million kilowatt-hours; coal, 63,530,000 tons; cement, 2,860,000 tons; and cotton piece goods, 111,630,000 bolts.

trialization may be carried out apart from the consideration of the overall ability to accumulate capital.

IV

THE FIRST FIVE YEAR PLAN

Although the First Five Year Plan made its official debut in 1953, extremely little information was published on the contents of the plan until July, 1955, when Li Fu-ch'un, head of the planning authority, presented his report to the second session of the First National People's Congress. According to Li, drafting of the Plan began in 1951 and was not completed until February, 1955. However, the decision was made as early as 1950 to undertake 50 construction projects with Soviet assistance. Then, in May, 1953, the construction of another 91 projects with Soviet assistance was decided upon. It is noteworthy that this decision to embark upon large-scale economic expansion was reached only two months before the signing of the Korean armistice, which is probably more than a coincidence.

According to the Plan, the share of industrial output in the total value of agricultural and industrial production should rise to 36 per cent in 1957. Compared with 1952, the increase in industrial production in general and modern industrial production in particular during 1953–1957 is planned to be 98.3 per cent and 104.1 per cent respectively. The latter figures represent an annual increase of 14.7 per cent in total industrial production and 15.3 per cent in the output of modern industry.[31] Of the expanded industrial output only 54.6 per cent will consist of consumers' goods. The overall targets are reasonably conservative and, even if fully realized, will not bring about industrialization in any substantial degree.[32] They also correspond very closely to the estimate of one non-Communist author, who has put Communist China's planned rate of increase in industrial production at 15 to 20 per cent a year up to 1957.[33] The predominant position of industry versus agriculture, however, is quite unmistakable inasmuch as the gross value output of agriculture, including subsidiary agricultural production, is planned to increase by 23.3 per cent only during the five-year period. This special emphasis on industry is clearly reflected in the allocation of development outlay.

According to Li Fu-ch'un, the total outlay for "economic construction and cultural and educational development" during 1953–

1957 will amount to ¥766,400 billion (¥76,640 million in the new currency) of which 55.8 per cent or ¥427,400 billion (¥42,740 million in the new currency) will be allocated to capital investment. At the official rate of exchange, the latter figure would amount to US$17,096 million for the five years or an annual average of US$3.4 billion. In practice, the actual level of investment would be somewhat lower in the first part of the plan period, rising gradually towards the end. However, as mentioned earlier in this chapter, outlay on capital construction as given by the Communist authorities represents gross investment and depreciation charges must be taken into account to arrive at net investment. Since depreciation also increases as the capital stock expands, the net increase in capital stock at the end of the First Five Year Plan will aggregate somewhat lower than US$12 billion, rising from US$1.4 billion in 1953 to over US$2 billion a year in the latter part of the plan period.

For the five-year period the total outlay on capital investment will be distributed as follows:

	Per Cent
Industry	58.2
Transportation, Post, and Telecommunications	19.2
Agriculture, Forestry, and Water Conservancy	7.6
Trade, Banking, and Stockpiling	3.0
Municipal Public Utilities	3.7
Cultural, Educational, and Public Health Institutions	7.2
Miscellaneous	1.1
Total	100.0

The largest share goes to industry which will have 694 major or "above-quota" projects and 2,300 smaller projects, including both the expansion or renovation of existing facilities and new constructions. Of the major projects 156 will be pivotal works undertaken with Soviet supervision and assistance, although eleven of these projects will only have completed the stage of planning and designing during the First Five Year Plan. Some 455 of the major industrial projects are scheduled for completion during the five-year period. In the non-industrial fields, the Plan also envisages 220 major or "above-quota" projects in transportation and communications, 252 in agriculture, forestry, and water conservancy, 180 in public utilities, 156 in the field of culture, education, and public health, and 160 in other fields. All in all, the Plan includes 1,600 major and 6,000 minor construction projects in all fields, and of these 1,271 major projects and most of the minor ones are planned to be completed within the five-year period.

In terms of individual groups of enterprises and commodities, certain production targets were first published in *Pravda* on September 28, 1953, without specific reference to the time period in question. These target figures represented a vast increase in the output of crude and finished steel products, of coal and power, and of machine tools. More details have since been given in Li Fu-ch'un's detailed report on the First Five Year Plan. According to Li, Communist China will build during the five-year period 10,000 kilometers of railways, including 4,000 kilometers of trunk lines, 10,000 kilometers of highways, and an aggregate tonnage of 400,000 tons of steamships. During the same period, it is also planned to set up 91 new mechanized state farms and 194 new tractor stations, to construct 13 large reservoirs, and to begin work on the harnessing of the Yellow River. However, since major effort will be devoted to the installation of new industrial equipment and facilities, the figures presented by Li, appearing on page 264, should be examined with some care.

As may been seen from the table, increase in capacity during the five-year period in the case of a number of industries will amount to only a portion of the total increase in capacity planned on the basis of projects initiated during the period. This is true especially in the manufacture of machinery, motor vehicles, and chemical fertilizer, and, to a lesser extent, in coal mining and the electric power industry. Some doubt may also be cast on the accuracy of the figure for steel in the final column, because the sum total of steel producing capacity in 1952 and the capacity added during the Five Year Plan will in all probability be much smaller than 6.1 million tons.

TYPES OF INDUSTRIAL PROJECTS

Although full details are lacking with respect to individual industrial projects, the list appearing on pages 265, 266, 267, 268 and 269, offers a good sample of the major projects planned, as well as their geographical distribution.

In addition to the plants listed, numbering 144, it should be noted that another 19 coal mining projects and 29–30 textile mills are in-

First Five Year Plan Goals for Selected Industries

	Projected Annual Capacity of All Projects Initiated during the First Five Year Plan upon Their Completion	*Annual Capacity to Be Added during 1953-1957*	*Annual Capacity Added in 1953-1954*	*Projected Total Output in 1957*
	(In thousand metric tons unless otherwise indicated)			
Pig Iron	5,750	2,800	—	—
Steel[1]	6,100	2,530	427	4,120
Metallurgical and Mining Machinery	190,000	70,000	—	—
Power Generating Equipment[2]	800,000	800,000	—	227,000[3]
Trucks[4]	90,000	30,000	—	4,000[5]
Tractors[4]	15,000 (1959)	—	—	—
Cement	3,600	2,360	650	6,000
Electric Motors[2]	—	—	—	1,050,000
Cotton Spindles[4]	1,890,000	1,650,000	700,000	—
Coal	93,100	53,850	13,000	113,000
Electric Power[2]	4,060,000	2,050,000	530,000	15,900[6]
Chemical Fertilizer	910	280	—	—
Machine-processed Sugar	560	428	109	686
Machine-processed Paper	186	95	40	650
Cotton Piece Goods[7]	—	—	—	163,720,000

Source: Li Fu-ch'un's report on the First Five Year Plan, NCNA, July 6, 1955.

1. Probably ingots only.
2. In kilowatts.
3. Generators.
4. Number of units.
5. Trucks only.
6. In million kilowatt-hours.
7. In bolts.

Major Industrial Enterprises under the First Five Year Plan

	Manchuria and Inner Mongolia	*North China*	*Central-South China*	*East China*	*Northwest China*	*Southwest China*
Iron and Steel Industry	*An-shan,* 48 projects, including 3 iron mines, 8 ore concentration and sintering plants, 6 automatic blast furnaces, 3 smelting plants, 16 rolling mills, 10 batteries of coke ovens, and 2 shops for heat-resistant materials *Pen-ch'i* iron and steel plant *Pao-t'ou* iron and steel plant (Inner Mongolia)	*Lung-yen* (Hopeh) iron mine	*Ta-yeh* (Hupeh) iron and steel works	*Ma-an-shan* (Anhwei) iron mine		*Chungking* No. 101 and No. 104 iron and steel plants
Non-ferrous metals and other Metallurgical Industry	*Fu-shun* No. 301 aluminum plant *Shen-yang* smelting and refining plant		*Hsiang-t'an* (Hunan) manganese mine *Hsi-ku'ang-shan* (Hunan) antimony mine		*Pai-yin-ch'ang* (Kansu) copper mine	*Ta-tun* (Yunnan) tin concentration plant *Tung-ch'uan* (Yunnan) copper mine *Ta-pao-shan* (Szechwan) copper mine

Major Industrial Enterprises under the First Five Year Plan

Industry						
Chemical Industry	Chemical plants at *Shen-yang, Ta-lien,* and *Chin-hsi*					
Ordnance	*Ha-erh-pin* plant	*T'ai-yuan* plant	*Han-yang* (Hupeh) plant	*Nanking* plant	*Shui-mo-kou* (Sinkiang) plant	*Chungking* plant
	Ch'ang-ch'un plant	*T'ai-yuan* aeronautical mfg. plant	*Ch'en-ch'i* (Hunan) plant			*Ch'eng-tu* plant
	Shen-yang plant	*Chin-yuan* (Shansi) chemical ordnance plant				
	Lü-ta **plant**					
	Heilungkiang plant					
Machinery Manufacturing Industry	*Shen-yang* No. 1, No. 2, and No. 3 machinery plant	*T'ai-yuan* heavy machinery plant	*Wu-ch'ang* (Hupeh) shipyard	*Shanghai* Chiang-nan shipyard		
	Shen-yang pneumatic machinery plant	Ching-wei *(T'ai-yuan)* textile machinery plant		Hu-tung *(Shanghai)* shipyard		
	Shen-yang electric cable and wire plant			*Shanghai* steam turbine plant		
	Shen-yang heavy machinery plant			*Shanghai* boiler plant		
				Shanghai lathe plant		

Shen-yang transformer plant	*Shanghai* tool plant
Ha-erh-pin electric instrument plant	*Tsingtao* shipyard
Ha-erh-pin measuring and metal cutting equipment plant	
Ha-erh-pin agricultural equipment plant	
Ha-erh-pin boiler plant	
Ha-erh-pin steam turbine plant	
Heilungkiang No. 2 machinery plant	
Fu-shun heavy machinery plant	
Ch'ang-ch'un No. 1 automobile plant	
Shen-yang automobile plant	

	Manchuria and Inner Mongolia	*North China*	*Central-South China*	*East China*	*Northwest China*	*Southwest China*
Oil Industry	*Fu-shun* No. 1 plant				*Yü-men* (Kansu) oil field	
	Fu-shun No. 2 plant				*Lan-chou* (Kansu) refinery	
	No. 5, No. 7 and No. 9 plants				*Yen-ch'ang* (Shensi) oil field	
					Sinkiang oil field	
Electric Power Industry	*Fu-shun* No. 2 plant	*T'ung-chou* (Hopeh) plant	*Cheng-chou* (Honan) plant		*Hsi-an* (Shensi) No. 2 plant	
	Fou-hsin plant	*Tientsin* plant	*Chu-chou* (Hunan) hydro plant		*Ti-hua* (Sinkiang) plant	
	Ta-lien No. 2 plant	*T'ai-yuan* plant	*Ta-yeh* (Hupeh) plant		*Lan-chou* (Kansu) plant	
	Ha-erh-pin plant					
	Feng-man hydro plant					
	Pao-t'ou (Inner Mongolia) plant					

Coal Mining	*Fu-shun* mine	*K'ai-lan* (Hopeh) mine	*Chiao-tso* (Honan) mine	*Huai-nan* (Anhwei) mine	*T'ung-ching* (Shensi) mine
	Ho-kang mine				
	Hsi-an mine	*Ta-t'ung* (Shansi) mine			
	Fou-hsin mine				
	Chi-hsi mine	*Feng-feng* (Hopeh) mine			
	T'ung-hua mine				
Other	*Ha-erh-pin* flax mill				
	Chia-mu-ssu paper mill				

Sources: *The Communist Chinese Problem*, Vol. I, pp. 57-61, Hongkong, 1954, and Li Fu-ch'un's report on the First Five Year Plan, NCNA, July 6, 1955.

cluded in the Five Year Plan. All in all 192–3 projects could be accounted for, covering probably the bulk of the 165 industrial projects to be undertaken with Soviet assistance. Some of these projects, as well as others, were scheduled for the first two years of the Plan.[34] For 1953, the official sources have mentioned the initiation and continuation of construction on 130 projects of which 75 were principal mining and manufacturing enterprises. This was in addition to the program of railway building of which we shall have more to say in a later chapter. Furthermore, among the industrial projects in 1953 21 were large metallurgical and chemical works, 24 were large machinery manufacturing plants, 24 were electric power plants, and several were major coal mines. These, together with some 21 principal textile plants, account for over 90 enterprises out of the 130 projects and give us a very good idea of the nature of the program at this stage.

Although the exact nature of the projects within the several broad categories mentioned above is not known, some of the individual projects either completed or under way during 1953 have been the subjects of official announcements. First, in the iron and steel industry, a seamless pipe plant and a heavy rolling mill were completed at the An-shan Iron and Steel Works in the third quarter of the year. Two large blast furnaces at An-shan were also converted into automatic operation. For the eight-year period between 1953 and 1960, expansion and new construction at the An-shan iron and steel center will include 3 iron mines, 8 ore concentration and sintering plants, 6 automatic blast furnaces, 3 steel smelting plants, 16 rolling mills, 10 batteries of coke ovens, and 2 shops for heat-resistant material. Upon completion of these projects, An-shan will have been restored to the position formerly planned by the Japanese and will have an annual production of 2.5 million tons of pig iron, 3.22 million tons of steel ingots, and 2.48 million tons of rolled steel. Elsewhere, several blast furnaces were repaired at the Ma-an-shan plant in Anhwei province. But, most important of all from the long-term point of view, was the beginning of a development program for a new iron and steel center at Pao-t'ou in the former Suiyuan province which is now a part of Inner Mongolia. Echoing the same type of development was the expansion of the original iron and steel works at Ta-yeh in Hupeh on the strength of new iron ore deposits discovered in the area.

In the machinery manufacturing industry the bulk of the 1953 projects reported consisted of the conversion and expansion of existing plants such as (1) the Northeast No. 1 Machinery Manufacturing Factory at Shen-yang to produce medium-size metal-cutting machinery, (2) the Northeast No. 2 Machinery Manufacturing Factory at Shen-yang specializing in machinery for iron and steel and non-ferrous metals works, (3) a Pneumatic Machine Manufacturing Factory at Shen-yang to produce drilling and riveting machines, (4) the Northeast No. 4 Electrical Engineering Works specializing in turbo- and thermal generators up to 16,000 volts and other power plant equipment,[35] (5) an electric machinery manufacturing plant at Fu-shun producing heavy mining equipment,[36] and (6) the Northeast No. 7 Electrical Engineering Works at Shen-yang producing high voltage cables and insulated wiring. Of these the first four were to be completed in 1954; the last two, in 1955. In addition, construction was started on a number of plants in 1953, including the No. 1 Automobile Factory at Ch'ang-ch'un,[37] the No. 625 Automobile Factory at Shen-yang, the Northeast No. 1 Precision Instrument and Tools Factory at Ha-erh-pin, which will have a capacity ten times that of all similar plants in the country, and the T'ai-yuan Heavy Machine Factory in Shansi province. The precision instrument plant was scheduled for completion in the latter part of 1954, while the T'ai-yuan plant, which will produce large steel cutting equipment, coke ovens, and overhead cranes, would be completed in 1955.

Altogether there were said to be some 70 construction projects for coal mines, power stations, petroleum refineries, and oil wells in 1953. Of these probably the most important were the two open-cast coal mines at Fou-hsin which resumed production in 1953. Among the larger coal shafts under construction were those at Ho-kang, Fou-hsin, Yin-ch'eng, and Chi-hsi in Manchuria, while work to prolong the life of existing shafts was done at the Chiao-tso, Ching-hsing, and Chia-wang mines in China Proper. In addition, one of the principal projects was the attempt to extinguish the underground fire which had been burning for some time at the large Ta-t'ung coal deposit. For the five-year period, 31 projects are scheduled in coal mining. By 1957 the annual capacities of the five largest mines are planned to be 9.3 million tons at Fu-shun, 8.45 million tons at Fou-hsin, 9.68 million tons at K'ai-lan, 6.45 million tons at Ta-t'ung, and 6.85 million tons at Huai-nan.

Work to rehabilitate the No. 2, No. 5, and No. 9 oil refineries in Manchuria was carried on during 1953. As for electric power, a number of new plants were under construction during the year, including one each at T'ai-yuan, Hsi-an, Cheng-chou, Lan-chou, Ti-hua, Pao-t'ou, and Ta-yeh. Both the Hsi-an and the Cheng-chou plants were finished in 1953 and have begun to supply power to the expanding cotton textile, machinery manufacturing, and flour mills of the area. The T'ai-yuan steam and power plant, scheduled for completion in 1957, could probably start partial operation at the end of 1954 or the beginning of 1955 in conjunction with the expanding machinery industry of the area. Moreover, the Hsiao-feng-man hydro-electric plant, as well as the thermal plants at Fu-shun, Fou-hsin, Ha-erh-pin, and Ta-lien, all in Manchuria, was being expanded during 1953. Finally, a number of medium and small hydro-electric plants were also built in Szechwan and Fukien provinces, while the expansion of smaller local plants was carried out in a number of cities. For the five-year period, 15 50,000-kilowatt thermal power plants are planned while the Feng-man hydro plant will have a generating capacity of 560,000 kilowatts upon completion of its rehabilitation program.

In the non-ferrous metals industry, an ore concentration plant at the Yunnan tin works at Ta-tun was rehabilitated in 1953. The Shen-yang electrolytic copper plant was expanded while most of the construction work at another Shen-yang smelting plant was also completed in the same year.

In the consumers' goods industry, the first year of the Five Year Plan saw the principal effort concentrated in the cotton textile industry. A large number of government mills were completed or under construction during the year. In addition, some 20 government and private cotton mills were expanded or renovated. Activities in related fields in the same year consisted of the construction or expansion of 6 printing and dyeing plants, 3 wool weaving mills, 3 gunny bag factories, 1 hemp manufacturing plant and 1 hemp processing plant. For the first five-year period 30 major textile plants are planned.

GEOLOGICAL SURVEY AND EXPLORATION

In addition to the construction and expansion of industrial enterprises, another phase of the First Five Year Plan is the attempt to broaden the material base of the industrialization program through the discovery of mineral deposits. Following the establishment of the Ministry of Geology in 1952, which was in itself an eloquent expression of government policy, government expenditure on geological prospecting in the 1953 budget was increased to 711.5 per cent of the corresponding outlay in 1952.[38] The work volume scheduled in 1953 was more than six times that of the preceding year. The number of persons engaged in geological work in the Ministries of Geology, Heavy Industry, and Fuel Industry was expanded to 45,000, which was twice the number in 1952.[39]

A considerable part of the prospecting has been done in Northwest China both for metals and for petroleum. There were twice as many persons involved in the search for oil in the Northwest in 1953 in comparison with 1952, while the number engaged in active prospecting was two and a half times as large. The number of persons in search for other minerals in the same area in 1953 was four times that of 1952, and there were as many as 240 separate field teams.[40] These and other workers elsewhere are said to have found a number of new deposits of copper, lead, zinc, and other non-ferrous metals, and to have paved the way for the expansion of the Ta-yeh iron and steel center and the establishment of a new metallurgical industry in the Pao-t'ou area.[41]

The announced plan for 1954 has pointed to a further intensification of the search, with the emphasis on coal, refractory clay, ferroalloys, and non-ferrous metals. The trend will doubtless continue throughout the First Five Year Plan.

CONCLUSION

It will be noted that the industrial projects enumerated above were concentrated in a few fields: the iron and steel industry, machinery manufacturing, the textile industry, and the supply of fuel and power. Although the cases mentioned do not in any sense constitute a complete enumeration, the apparent emphasis on these industries can hardly be regarded as accidental. It is not difficult to explain this aspect of Communist policy as it merely confirms the Communists' desire for greater self-sufficiency in the country's industrialization program by providing (1) adequate supplies of fuel and power, (2) capital equipment for the further expansion of the heavy industries, and (3) textile and other basic products to meet the population's most elementary demand for consumers' goods in place of imports and to increase potential and actual export. At the same time, it should be noted that there have been relatively few reports on the development of the non-ferrous metal industries. This again may be interpreted as an admission of China's relative poverty in this sector and the smallness of the known reserves. There are, of course, exceptions to this general statement as we shall see presently, but it is in this area that the greatly intensified search for new ore deposits which has characterized the First Five Year Plan is principally intended to prepare the ground for later development. The same is true with respect to petroleum and iron ore deposits.

Nor can one fail to notice the geographical concentration of the large number of industrial projects in Manchuria, while North China and the Northwest provinces have also been given great emphasis. In contrast, few large industrial projects have been reported in the remaining parts of the country. This seems further to accent the importance of Manchuria and the increasing value of the Northwest, both representing areas of special interest to the Soviet Union. Shanghai, the scene of an industrial exodus following the Nationalist air raids in February, 1950, though still a very important light manufacturing center, has lost much of its pre-eminence. Although considerable industrial development may take place in such areas as Wu-han in Hupeh, Hsiang-tan in Hunan, Chungking in Szechwan, and other localities in the South, the Yangtze basin does not seem to be destined for an important role in Communist China's industrialization program. The economic center of mainland China has apparently shifted northward. While the geographical distribution of natural resources may have dictated this development, the economic facts have manifested a more than accidental coincidence with the shift of the political center of gravity. Closer ties with the Soviet Union are probably acting both as a cause and as an effect.

The nature and geographical distribution of the various projects so far announced further reveal a most vital interdependence among the individual undertakings and, as we shall be able to see more clearly in the next chapter, point to certain pivotal issues on which the success or failure of the Five Year Plan will revolve. The general index of industrial recovery does not disclose the presence of serious weaknesses in the industrial structure of Communist China.

Finally, it should be mentioned that in spite of notable accomplishments, the Five Year Plan has far from been highly successful in terms of planned goals. As the Communist authorities have admitted themselves, actual work on industrial capital construction during 1953 amounted to a little over 12 per cent of the five-year planned total, while the 1954 plan, if accomplished in full, would not account for more than another 15 per cent. Moreover, almost invariably a great deal of work had to be rushed through in the last half or quarter of each year.[42] Taking all fields of activity into consideration, total capital construction during 1953–1954 accounted for less than 35 per cent of the planned goal for the five years. Thus, much of the Five Year Plan remains to be carried out, and there is no assurance of success.

NOTES

1. This is not to belittle the worthiness of such studies, but merely to warn the general reader against oversimplification and the unwarranted employment of broad predictions.

2. See Pao-san Ou, *National Income of China, 1933, 1936, and 1946* (in English), Institute of Social Sciences, Academia Sinica, Nanking, 1947.

3. See especially the interesting discussion by Chang Chi-hung, "Another Estimate of China's National Income," *Central Bank Monthly*, new series, Vol. III, No. 11, Shanghai, November, 1948. For 1933 the net national product was CN$25,030 million according to Liu's estimate, as adjusted by Kuznets from the gross national product. This compares with CN$20,319 million in Ou's estimate of "net income produced," or CN$25,453 million as adjusted by Chang.

4. The revision was made on the basis of information that had become available after the first publication of his two volumes on *China's National Income* and in the light of comments by various critics, including Simon Kuznets.

5. In this connection cf. the discussion on mass labor projects and their effect on national income and investment in chapter IX below.

6. *A Practical Encyclopedia of the National Economy*, p. 1102, Shanghai, 1953.

7. *Ibid.*, pp. 2088-2091.

8. Comparison may be made at this point between the extent of economic recovery in mainland China as a whole and that in Manchuria. The following table, containing our preliminary estimates, shows quite unmistakably a faster rate of progress in Manchuria, especially in industrial production.

Preliminary General Production Index
of
Industry and Agriculture in Manchuria

	Total Output of Industry and Agriculture	*Industrial Output*
1949	100	100
1950	137	209
1951	161	244
1952	172	255

This reflects both the traditional importance of Manchuria as an industrial base and the emphasis on rehabilitating Manchurian industry as the first order of the day. Cf. *Economic Bulletin,* No. 151, p. 10; *New China Monthly,* p. 166, October, 1952; *Economic Yearbook,* p. 55, 1953; and *Ta-kung pao,* Hongkong, October 4, 1952.

9. Quoted in United Nations, *Economic Bulletin for Asia and the Far East,* Vol. IV, No. 3, p. 23, Bangkok, November, 1953.

10. See Wang Foh-shen, *China's Industrial Production,* 1931-1946, Institute of Social Sciences, Academia Sinica, Nanking, 1948.

11. See Teng Hsiao-p'ing's report on the 1954 budget. The share of "modern" industry alone was about 30 per cent.

12. Including manufacturing, mining, and public utilities.

13. Apart from the double counting in the official statistics of industrial production the proportion of agricultural products included in the gross value of industrial production is probably higher than the proportion of industrial products included in the gross agricultural output.

14. Converted into 1933 U. S. dollars and allowing for the latter's depreciation since 1933, these figures would correspond to US$18.0 billion and US$23.7 billion at 1953 prices. Reference may be made here to a Japanese estimate of US$18-20 billion for Communist China's national income in 1952. Cf. Shigeru Ishikawa, "On China's National Income," *Aziya Kenkyu,* Vol. I, No. 1, Tokyo, 1954.

15. CN$20,441 million less a reduction of CN$1,278 million.

16. *Wen-hui pao,* Hongkong, September 20, 1953. The absolute amount budgeted was ¥77,833 billion for capital construction as against a total outlay of ¥103,528 billion on economic development. The latter includes government expenditure in current operations such as grain purchases for resale, imports of consumers' goods, etc.

17. For the official U. S. dollar rate one may use the cross rate of ¥24,620 obtained from the sterling-*jen-min-pi* rate. A higher estimate of ¥75,736 billion or US$3.0 billion of gross investment may be derived from Li Hsien-nien's report on the 1955 budget. NCNA, July 9, 1955. This figure, however, appears to be too high in relation to total expenditure on "economic reconstruction" and may refer to the budgeted instead of actual figure.

18. The net investment for 1953 estimated above is equivalent to CN$1.9 billion at 1933 prices. On the basis of this initial rate of investment we may construct two crude models to illustrate the effect of population growth on potential consumption and investment. In model A, the rate of population growth is assumed to be 1.25 per cent per annum, which corresponds to that in India. In model B, a 2 per cent annual rate of growth, as reported by the Chinese Communists in connection with the 1953 census, is used. Common to both models are the following simplifying assumptions:

(1) New investments (I) made in year O will cause output (Y) to increase only in year 3, the ratio of Y/I being 1/3.

(2) New investments will be maintained at a minimum rate of CN$1.9 billion at 1933 prices.

(3) Aggregate potential consumption (C) and population will increase in the same proportion.

(4) Net investment will not be raised unless actual consumption does not have to fall below potential consumption on the basis of population growth.

Model of National Income, Consumption, and Net Investment for Communist China
(In CN$ billion at 1933 prices)

A. $\Delta C/C = 1.25$ per cent per annum

	Y	C	I	I/Y (%)
1953	26	24.1	1.9	7.4
54	26	24.4 (24.1)[1]	1.9	7.4
55	26	24.7 (24.1)[1]	1.9	7.4
56	26.6	25.0 (24.7)[1]	1.9	7.1
57	27.2	25.3	1.9	7.0
58	27.9	25.6	2.3	8.0
59	28.5	25.9	2.6	9.1
60	29.1	26.2	2.9	10.0
61	29.9	26.5	3.4	11.4
62	30.8	26.8	4.0	13.0
63	31.8	27.1	4.7	14.8
64	32.9	27.4	5.5	17.0
65	34.2	27.7	6.5	19.0
66	35.8	28.0	7.8	21.8

1. Figures in parenthesis indicate the actual level of consumption to which the potential level of consumption on the basis of population growth must be reduced in order to maintain investment at the minimum level.

B. $\Delta C/C = 2$ per cent per annum

	C	I	Y
1953	26	24.1	1.9
54	26	24.6 (24.1)	1.9
55	26	25.1 (24.1)	1.9
56	26.6	25.6 (24.7)	1.9
57	27.2	26.1 (25.3)	1.9
58	27.9	26.6 (26.0)	1.9
59	28.5	27.1 (26.6)	1.9
60	29.1	27.6 (27.2)	1.9
61	29.7	28.1 (27.8)	1.9
62	30.3	28.6 (28.4)	1.9
63	30.9	29.2 (29.0)	1.9
64	31.5	29.8 (29.6)	1.9
65	32.1	30.4 (30.2)	1.9
66	32.7	31.0 (30.8)	1.9
67	33.3	31.6 (31.4)	1.9
68	33.9	32.2 (32.0)	1.9

On the basis of the above assumptions, model B shows that the net investment can never rise above CN$1.9 billion. In fact, by 1969, potential consumption would exceed total output.

The situation would be more favorable if (1) the construction period were shorter, (2) if the output-investment ratio were higher, (3) if the rate of population growth were lower (see model A) or, (4) if output could be increased without new investment by the exploitation of unemployed resources (see Chapter IX). It should also be noted that investment expenditure on the same project is usually spread over several years so that the increase in output at the same ratio of investment to output should be somewhat higher.

19. Some regional difference in the rate of capital investment may be noted here. A later report by the National Bureau of Statistics put the increase in 1953 at only

66 per cent over the 1952 level (see National Bureau of Statistics *Bulletin,* October, 1954), but even this national rate was somewhat higher than the reported rate for Manchuria in 1953, or 52.8 per cent. However, if 1949 is used as the base year, capital construction expenditure in Manchuria rose to 161.84 in 1950, 289.80 in 1951, 650.25 in 1952, and 994.88 in 1953. The largest relative increase so far was scored in 1952, which would seem to be well in line with Communist policy to rehabilitate Manchurian industry before developing other industries in China Proper. It also confirms our general observation that industrial recovery and the development of the planning and administrative apparatus in Manchuria has progressed a year ahead of that in China Proper. A possible exception to this lag in China Proper in comparison with Manchuria, however, is Northwest China where government capital investment increased at an even greater pace in the 1950-1952 period than it did in Manchuria. While this in no way makes Northwest China an industrial center at this time on account of its former economic backwardness, it does seem to point to a distinct trend in industrial location in the not-too-distant future. This observation is amply supported by reports on individual industrial projects and railway constructions in the area discussed elsewhere in this book. Cf. *Wen-hui pao,* Hongkong, August 26, 1953; *Ta-kung pao,* Shanghai, September 24, 1951; NCNA, Shenyang, May 4, 1952, and Hsi-an, December 3, 1953; Cheng Tsu-yüan, *op. cit.,* p. 79; and NCNA, September 13, 1954.

20. NCNA, Peking, May 7, 1953.

21. *People's Daily,* Peking, October 1, 1953, and National Bureau of Statistics *Bulletin,* Peking, October, 1954.

22. NCNA, November 27, 1953, March 24, 1954, and September 24, 1954.

23. NCNA, February 3, 1954.

24. *Economic Weekly,* No. 40, p. 802, Shanghai, 1952, and Lin Po-ch'ü's article in *For a Lasting Peace, for a People's Democracy,* October 2, 1953. In Manchuria the share of producers' goods in the output of all central and local government industries was 67.5 per cent in 1952, and was even higher in the industries under the Department of Industry. Cf. *Economic Yearbook,* p. 55, Hongkong, 1953, and Kao Kang's report on May 13, 1950. According to Chou En-lai's report in September, 1954, the ratio of producers' goods in total industrial production was 42.3 per cent in 1954 as compared with 28.8 per cent in 1949.

25. As a rule, statistical information released on such festive occasions as the first of October of every year, as well as in the New Year reports, if purporting to deal with the current or immediately preceding year, constitutes either preliminary or revised estimates, but not final figures which are not available until the spring of the following year, if not later.

26. See *New China Monthly,* Vol. II, No. 4, p. 834, Peking, August, 1950.

27. *Statistical Work Bulletin,* No. 1, 1954.

28. See *People's Daily,* Peking, March 31, 1954.

29. Cf. Li Fu-ch'un's remarks at the third statistics conference as reported in *People's Daily,* Peking, March 31, 1954.

30. Cf. W. W. Rostow, *The Prospects for Communist China,* Cambridge, 1954, and Y. L. Wu and Robert C. North, "Industrialization in India and China," *Problems of Communism,* Washington, D. C., May-June, 1955.

31. According to Communist spokesmen, the official policy was to increase industrial production by 21-23 per cent in 1953 and by another 17-18 per cent in 1954. The higher rate of increase planned in the first phase of the Plan obviously reflects the possibility of more intensive utilization of existing productive facilities. See *People's Daily,* October 1, 1953, and October 1, 1954. Also *Economic Bulletin,* No. 1, 1954, and Teng Hsiao-p'ing's 1954 budget report.

32. According to Teng Wen-ching, China's industrialization program aims at eventually increasing the share of industrial output to 70 per cent of total industrial and agricultural production. *People's China,* March 1, 1954.

33. Cheng Tsu-yuan, *The New Tendencies of the Chinese Communists' Financial and Economic Policies,* Vol. II, p. 86, Hongkong, 1953. Cf. also Eckstein's estimates in Rostow, *op. cit.,* pp. 284-5.

34. For reference on the remainder of this section see *Wen-hui pao,* June 10, September 20 and 28, and October 1, 6, and 8, 1953; *New China Monthly,* Peking, October, 1953; China News Service release, November 10, 1953; Chuang P'u-ming, *China's Progress in Industrialization,* Peking, 1954; and NCNA, November 4 and 27, 1953, and Li Fu-ch'un's report on the First Five Year Plan, NCNA, July 6, 1955.

35. The present construction work was begun in 1951. Five plant buildings were reportedly completed in 1952. The factory will equip some of the power stations scheduled in the Five Year Plan.

36. When the expansion is completed, the annual capacity of the plant will be boosted to 350 per cent of its previous peak.

37. Work on this factory was started in July, 1953. No completion date has been given.

38. Po I-p'o, report on the 1953 budget.

39. See Chuang P'u-ming, *op. cit.*

40. Tung Cheng, *Geological Work and National Reconstruction,* Peking, 1953.

41. More than 12,000 persons are thus engaged in Manchuria. Cf. NCNA, Shen-yang, March 6, 1954.

42. *People's Daily,* Peking, November 15, 1954.

CHAPTER EIGHT

Survey of Selected Industries

I

INTRODUCTION

Given an estimated annual net investment of US$1–2 billion, the industrialization program of Communist China can theoretically proceed along the path of expansion set by this rate. In practice, however, this does not necessarily follow as the accumulation of capital must be translated into the addition of concrete industrial equipment. If the latter could be obtained entirely from foreign sources, either on credit or through Chinese exports, no serious problem would arise. On the other hand, if foreign supplies were cut off for some reason or other, the question immediately arises as to whether the rate of domestic capital accumulation can find its full counterpart in the production of capital goods at home. In reality, of course, Communist China is able to import some of the capital equipment it needs, partly on credit and partly through current payments, but, since there is no known grant-in-aid arrangement between Communist China and other members of the Soviet bloc, some of the capital equipment required must be produced domestically while imports of consumers' goods must be cut to a minimum in order to permit a larger inflow of capital goods. Thus the success of the industrialization program hinges largely upon the degree of self-sufficiency the country can achieve with respect to a number of key industries.

While it would be impossible to examine the present status of all the important industries in mainland China, a few of the pivotal industries may be reviewed briefly. The industries selected for this purpose may be divided into three categories: (1) sources of fuel and power on which industrial production, as well as transportation, depends, (2) producers' goods industries that must supply the raw materials and finished products for the construction of new plants, railways, and other capital equipment, and (3) consumers' goods industries, the products of which would have to be imported if domestic production is not adequate to maintain either the normal or the minimum level of consumption. The individual industries are:

I. 1. Coal
   2. Electric power
   3. Petroleum

II. 1. Iron and steel
   2. Ferro-alloy and non-ferrous metals
   3. Machinery
   4. Chemicals
   5. Cement

III. 1. Cotton textiles
   2. Food processing

Since we are limited by space, our discussion will have to be extremely brief. However, we shall try to indicate for each industry (1) its present estimated capacity and production, (2) its geographical distribution, (3) the nature and volume of its current demand as far as this can be quantitatively demonstrated within the space available, and (4) official Communist policy towards its future development. In spite of our necessarily superficial treatment of this extensive field, it is believed that such a survey will prove useful in our understanding of the Communist Chinese economic system.

II

THE STRATEGIC POSITION OF COAL

Apart from manpower, coal is the principal source of energy in China because so far all alternative sources have remained undeveloped. The petroleum industry is still in its infancy, while natural gas deposits are believed to be rather limited. Although the potential of water power is very large, the high initial investment required for its effective utilization and lack of a large enough market for the potential volume of electricity that can be generated have precluded its development to the present time. Out of a total potential of 64.7 million kilowatts at low water for all the river systems in mainland China, the capacity of hydroelectric power installations at the end of World War II, including some small plants in China Proper then under construction, was no more than 651,000 kilowatts.[1] Following the destruction in Manchuria wrought by Soviet removals and the civil war and the conversion of the Shanghai Power Company's facilities from fuel oil to coal,[2] nearly 90 per cent of the entire electric generating capacity of Communist China at the end of 1949 was dependent on coal. Thus the entire industrial productive apparatus is powered either directly or indirectly by coal.

The importance of coal is further enhanced if we bear in mind the fact that it is also the most important fuel in the household for heating purposes. In China Proper, for instance, 50 per cent of total coal consumption in 1934 was attributed to household use.[3] In the same year in Manchuria, 26.8 per cent of all the coal consumed was burned in individual households.[4]

One implication of this widespread use for direct consumption is that coal must be made available in all areas with large concentrations of population even where industrial demand itself might be negligible and that it must be shipped from the collieries to meet the demand of both industry and households. In view of this situation, it is not surprising that, excluding Manchuria, about one-half of the total tons carried by Chinese railways in the prewar period consisted of coal and that some 85 per cent of the output of large mines was carried by rail from the pits.[5] Other things being equal, the greater the volume of rail traffic in coal, the greater is the consumption of coal by rail, because, with the exception of the Chinese Changchun Railway, which formerly used both wood and coal, virtually all of China's railway engines burn coal. The same is true with respect to other categories of freight traffic and passenger movement. As railways are the principal means in long distance hauling in China, coal must therefore be regarded as a key factor in commodity movement.

The strategic position of coal in Communist China's industrialization program is paramount. It is perhaps even more important than any of the other basic industries as all the latter's products must be shipped by rail even if they could be produced in the first place. The three important problems posed by coal to Communist planners are: (1) development of alternative sources of power, (2) expansion of coal production, and (3) reduction of long-distance coal movement and, incidentally, coal consumption by the railways. On the first point, apart from an all-out effort to expand the infant oil industry, which, however, cannot be expected to replace coal to any noticeable extent for a long time to come, official policy has shunned the large-scale exploitation of hydroelectric power at the present time beyond some rehabilitation in Manchuria and the continuation of various small, unfinished projects elsewhere.[6] The underlying reasoning remains to be the high cost and long period of construction required for hydroelectric power plants. As for the third point, some attention has been given to the installation of high power transmission lines lately[7] while several of the large thermal power plants under construction in 1954 are located at or near coal production centers.[8] However, in the immediate future, the principal concern is still to increase coal production while the coal produced must continue to be shipped by rail both in bulk and over long distances.

COAL SHORTAGE

Prior to the establishment of the Communist regime coal production in mainland China was at its highest in 1942 when nearly 65 million metric tons were mined. Of this quantity 24.2 million tons came from Manchuria while China Proper contributed 40.8 million tons.[9] By 1947 production in Manchuria had declined to 4.6 million tons[10] or less than one-fifth of the area's peak output of 25.6 million tons (1944). Production in China Proper in the same year was 13.8 million tons or about 33 per cent of the peak 1942 level.[11] From 1947 to 1949 production in Manchuria more than doubled, while a slight gain was also registered in China Proper. The output for the entire mainland in 1949 was 26 million tons, with 10.5 million tons derived from Manchuria and 15.5 million tons from China Proper.[12] On the basis of these figures, the estimated output in 1953, the first year of the First Five Year Plan, was only 57.2 million tons, of which 36.2 million tons were mined in China Proper and 21 million tons in Manchuria. Thus, production in both Manchuria and China Proper was below the peak outputs previously achieved during the war. During 1954, the planned output was 67.4 million tons, of which 23.1 million tons were to be mined in Manchuria and 44.3 million tons in China Proper.[13] It is not difficult to see that recovery in coal mining under the Communist regime has lagged persistently behind industrial production as a whole. In the meantime, railway traffic and its coal consumption has increased. The increase in population must also have brought about a corresponding increase in household demand if the prewar per capita consumption was to be maintained.[14] Although industrial coal consumption need not rise proportionately to industrial output, burning of low-grade coal and the continued operation of obsolete equipment in many of the power plants have tended to increase coal consumption. Without going into a detailed estimate of consumption, it is not difficult to see that until recently coal shortage was a serious problem under the Communist regime and that curtailment of direct consumption of coal and rationing of electricity to the households were the only means to redress the balance.

EXPANSION OF COAL PRODUCTION, 1950–1953

According to our estimates, up to 1953 coal production had lagged particularly in Manchuria while recovery was more rapid in China Proper. This was due to the fact that many of the mines restored to operation consisted of small inclined shafts and that the modern facilities at such mines as Fu-shun and Fou-hsin in Manchuria had been severely crippled. Due to power shortage and loss of mining equipment the Fu-shun coal mine, which produced more than 9.5 million tons a year in 1936 and 1937 and 4.5 million tons in 1944, averaged only 65,500 tons a month in the last quarter of 1948.[15] At Fou-hsin, where production was well over 5 million tons in 1944, a similar decline had taken place. Output at the Pen-ch'i mine, which produced somewhat under 1 million tons annually during 1942–1944, was around 500,000 tons in 1949.[16] Comparable losses in production were also noted at the Pei-p'iao, Hsi-an, T'ung-hua, Ho-kang, and other mines of Manchuria.[17] Outside Manchuria Chinese coal production in the first two years of Communist rule was mainly derived from North and East China with K'ai-lun, Men-t'ou-Kou, and some of the smaller government mines accounting for the bulk of the output.[18]

This gloomy picture was compounded by the official forecast that, of the 322 coal shafts in operable condition in November, 1949, 55 would have to be closed by 1952, and another 120 would have to be given up by 1955. The estimated loss in output would amount to over 13 million tons.[19] The situation was especially critical in Manchuria. The national coal mining conference that made the above estimate in November, 1949, also outlined a program of recovery for the 1950–1952 period, concentrating above all on the Manchurian mines, among which were two open cast mines at Fou-hsin, and giving second priority to the North China mines. For East China the principal purpose was to achieve a greater degree of regional self-sufficiency so as to minimize long-distance hauls.[20]

Apparently the plan was partly successful as may be seen from the rise of the country's coal output from 34.3 million tons in 1950 to 52.5 million tons in 1952. This was attributed to the assistance of Soviet experts in rehabilitating certain mines that were originally scheduled to be abandoned, prolonging their life by 20 to 40 years.[21] As a result it was estimated in 1952 that less than 60 shafts would have to be closed before 1957 instead of the original estimate of 120 shafts up to 1955.[22]

While production contests were responsible for much of the increase in production, some of the improvement was apparently due to increasing mechanization which boosted the output of modern mines from 79.81 per cent of total coal production in 1950 to 81 per cent in 1951. The extent of mechanized extraction, *mostly partial,* was said to have increased from 45 per cent of total coal produced in 1950 to 53 per cent in 1951. By 1953 it had risen to 78 per cent in coal extraction and 70 per cent in coal transport.[23] The national average output per man-day increased from 0.404 ton in 1949 to 0.459 ton in 1950 and 0.62 in 1951.[24] Further increases in 1952–1953 were also reported.[25] However, it is not quite clear whether these figures referred to coal cutters or to all employees at the collieries. If only coal cutters were included in the computation, which might be the case, they were not particularly favorable in comparison with conditions before 1937 when output per man-day ranged from 0.3 ton at the small Fu-hua mine in Hupeh to 1.9 ton at Fu-shun.[26]

However, in spite of the progress made, the expansion of production did not get into full swing until the latter part of 1953. The additional impetus was provided by the beginning of production at the Ping-an mine at Fou-hsin in May, and that of two open-cut mines at Fou-hsin in July and December.[27] Since these additional facilities were not in use in the entire year, their full effect on production was not felt in 1953. Consequently, it was only in 1954 that the Communist authorities could hope to exceed the wartime peak reached in 1942.

PROSPECT OF THE COAL INDUSTRY

According to the Communist authorities, coal consumption in Communist China in 1953 was 27 per cent higher than in 1952 and it will be 80 per cent greater in 1957 than in 1953.[28] The latter estimate might not be very far from the mark in view of the current rate of increase in industrial production and rail traffic. In other words, a substantial rise of coal consumption may be expected unless insufficient supply and resistance to further curtailment of household consumption should limit the rate of expansion of coal consumption and thereby retard the planned rate of industrialization.

An official report towards the end of 1953[29] suggested that the most serious problem in raising production from many coal mines was the lack of "reserve strength." By this was meant that the speed of coal digging lagged behind that of actual cutting and extraction, while geological work lagged further behind the progress in digging. In other words, although production could be stepped up in the short run by labor contests and movements of the Stakhanovist type, the opening of new coal shafts and workings appeared to offer the only long-run solution.

It was in response to this situation that investment in capital construction in coal mines was raised during the First Five Year Plan. We have already noted the increase in government investment in the fuel industries as a whole from 1952 to 1953.[30] Investment in capital construction in coal mining during 1954 was planned to be another 21 per cent higher than the corresponding outlay in 1953.[31] According to one report, work was scheduled at 86 mines in 1954, including continuing projects carried over from the preceding year. Of these projects 10 were to be completed during the latter part of 1954; namely, five pairs of vertical shafts at the Ho-kang, Hsi-an, Pen-ch'i, Shuang-ya-ling, and Chi-hsi mines in Manchuria and five projects involving inclined shafts at the Chi-hsi, T'ung-hua, Ho-kang, and Yin-cheng mines in Manchuria, and Chiao-tso in China Proper.[32] These new constructions were to increase Communist China's coal production by 13 per cent over the 1953 level or an estimated 7.6 million tons.[33] In addition, large-scale construction at the Hai-chou open-cut mine at Fou-hsin would be continued so that production could be increased further by 1955.[34] Construction was also scheduled during 1954 in a number of North China mines, including rehabilitation at Ta-t'ung in Shansi, expansion at K'ai-lun, and the development of Feng-feng in Hopeh into one of China's largest coke-producing centers.[35]

By the time all the 86 projects are completed in about 1957 coal production in Communist China is expected to be 80 per cent greater than in 1953 according to the same authorities who have postulated an 80 per cent rise of consumption. However, this would not result in any large export surplus as equilibrium between demand and supply was barely maintained in 1953.

Several factors, however, should be further considered at this point. First, granted that production might expand according to plan, the maintenance of quality might present a problem. A rather interesting report in mid-1953 mentioned the need to improve the mining method in government mines where too much stone was mixed with coal and to reinstate the process of coal concentration where it had been abandoned previously.[36] Second, as the Communists well know, the capital construction program in coal mining begun in 1953 requires a large number of additional technicians and skilled workers whose training is a program of sizable proportions in itself.[37] Finally, it is only too obvious that the successful execution of the expansion program hinges upon the availability of mining machinery and heavy equipment for excavation and drilling which, as we shall see in the next section, the machinery industry of Communist China could hardly be expected to provide. Thus the prospect of the coal industry is inextricably linked with Soviet technical assistance and machinery imports.

CAPACITY AND PRODUCTION OF THE ELECTRIC POWER INDUSTRY

If there is a constant threat of coal shortage in Communist China, the supply of electric power is apparently in a no less precarious position. The total rated and operating generating capacities in mainland China in 1947, excluding those parts of Manchuria that were then under Communist control, amounted to 1,047,029 and 783,692 kilowatts respectively.[38] Of these 284,500 kw. of rated capacity and 220,000 kw. of operating capacity were in Nationalist-controlled areas in Manchuria. While the capacity in China Proper compared favorably with that before the war, the decline of Manchurian capacity from the wartime high of 1.8 million kw. reflected primarily the result of Soviet removals after the Japanese surrender in World War II.[39]

However, recovery was fairly successful under the present regime. On the basis of various Communist Chinese reports there was some increase in generating capacity between 1949 and 1952 so that the country's total rated capacity at the end of 1952 was probably close to 1.86 million kw. The latter figure was raised to an estimated 2.13 million kw. in the course of 1953 as new plants went into operation.[40] In the meantime a high ratio of operating to rated capacity was said to have been achieved, while the rate of equipment utilization through load adjustments also showed a steady improvement.[41] Under these conditions the volume of electricity generated increased from 4.5 billion kilowatt-hours in 1949 to 9 billion kilowatt-hours in 1953. About 5 of the 9 billion kwh. were generated in Manchuria.

NEW POWER PLANTS AND THE EXPANSION PROGRAM

Using 1950 as the base year, the official index numbers for capital construction in electric power plants were 175 for 1951, 462 for 1952, and 2,495 (estimated) for 1953.[42] During 1954 investment was to increase by another 21.8 per cent over 1953 in the thermo-plants and 42 per cent in the hydro-plants.[43] The phenomenal rise in investment during 1953–1954 in terms of these figures may be explained partly by the fact that imported machinery was installed during these last years on some of the projects although basic construction had begun earlier as the construction period for thermal plants is said to require an average of three years.[44]

Mention has already been made of the principal thermal electric plants under construction in 1953 at Hsi-an (Shensi), Ti-hua (Sinkiang), Cheng-chou (Honan), T'ai-yuan (Shansi), Chungking, Fou-hsin, and elsewhere.[45] In addition, several hydro-electric installations in Manchuria were being expanded. The construction plans of 1954 included the establishment or expansion of more than 160 electric generation and distribution works with eight of the "keypoint" projects being undertaken with Soviet assistance. Besides the projects already enumerated for 1953 work on a large generating plant at Cheng-tu was reported to be under way, while small hydro-plants were being built on the Lung-ch'i in Szechwan and by the Kuan-t'ing Reservoir outside Peking.[46] Together with coal production, these various developments are apparently receiving most of the attention and investment outlay in current Communist plans.

During 1950–1952, in order to provide an adequate supply of power to industry, the Communist authorities attempted in many areas to schedule the time of demand for electricity by individual users to reduce load fluctuations and obtain a higher output. Private households in certain areas, for instance, were not allowed to use electricity during daylight hours while manufacturers were told to stagger their work shifts.[47] It is quite possible that these restrictions are still in force in view of the accelerated industrial activity. The prospect of the electric power industry appears to resemble that of coal mining and to be in a most precarious balance.

THE LIQUID FUELS

In contrast to coal mining, the production of crude oil and refined petroleum products in Communist China is altogether negligible in spite of the reported increase in terms of official index numbers. The two oil-producing areas are Northwest China and Manchuria, production in the latter being from shale and coke distillation plants. In Northwest China the principal center is at Yü-men in Kansu although the Sinkiang wells are being strenuously developed while some output is available at Yen-ch'ang in Shensi.

On the basis of our estimates, crude oil production in Communist China increased from 30 million gallons in 1949 to 155 million gallons in 1953. Of the latter approximately one third was derived from Yü-men. The following table presents the index numbers and the estimated absolute quantities of Yü-men output:

PRODUCTION OF PETROLEUM PRODUCTS AT YU-MEN
(IN MILLION GALLONS)

	Crude Oil		*Gasoline*		*Kerosene**	
	Index	*Quantity*	*Index*	*Quantity*	*Index*	*Quantity*
1949	100	19.6	100	3.7	100	1.7
1950	138	27.1	117	4.3	159	2.7
1951	172	33.7	184	6.8	148	2.5
1952	200	39.2	250	9.3	319	5.4
1953	255	50.0	307	11.5	—	—
1954 (plan)	510	100.0	335	11.5	—	—

Sources: *New China Monthly,* Vol. IV, No. 1, Peking, May, 1952, and No. 37, November, 1952; *Wen-hui pao,* Hongkong, July 19, 1953; *General Statement on the Mining Industry,* 7th issue, pp. 294-5; NCNA, Hsi-an, February 8, 1954; *Chinese Yearbook,* Vol. II, pp. 1572-3, Nanking, 1948; and Fan Ch'ing-p'ing, *op. cit.*
*Kerosene is still used for lighting in towns and villages.

Elsewhere in the Northwest some increase in production has also been reported. At Yen-ch'ang, for instance, where operation was resumed in July, 1948, the index number for crude oil increased from 100 in 1950 to 167 in 1952 and a planned rate of 650 in 1953. In Sinkiang crude production in 1953 was reported to be 19 times that of 1951.[48]

As one compares Yü-men production with that of mainland China as a whole, the increasing importance of crude oil production from sources other than Yü-men from 1952 onward becomes apparent. This phenomenon may be explained by two factors—progress in the rehabilitation of the Manchurian plants and development in Sinkiang. Of the 3 shale oil plants, 7 synthetic oil plants, and 3 refineries in Manchuria, 2 shale plants at Fu-shun, the synthetic oil plants of Chin-hsi and Chin-hsien, and the refineries at Szu-p'ing-chieh, Ta-lien, and Chin-hsi were reportedly being repaired or in partial operation during 1950.[49] Apparently an increase in production capacity was achieved by 1952. Since then new installations and repair at Fu-shun have been reported. In Sinkiang where joint operation with the Soviet Union began in 1950, one refinery was built in 1952; an old plant was repaired in the same year; and a new cracking plant was under construction during 1953.[50]

The future of mainland China's petroleum industry, however, will depend largely upon the success of the prospecting program now under way in Sinkiang and Kansu. As mentioned in Chapter II, according to one recent estimate, petroleum reserves in Northwest China may amount to 1.7 billion tons.[51] However, current production is still so small and refining facilities so inadequate[52] that it will be a long time before Communist China can achieve some measure of self-sufficiency in the face of the increasing needs of its industry, not to mention civilian consumption.

III

THE CHANGING STRUCTURE OF THE IRON AND STEEL INDUSTRY

The structure of mainland China's iron and steel industry has undergone considerable change since the prewar days. Before 1937, China was an exporter of both iron ore and pig iron,[53] but imported finished steel products as well as small quantities of steel ingots. This was due to the greater backwardness of the steel industry relative to the production of pig iron, the greater part of which was smelted in China Proper in native furnaces and the greater backwardness of the pig iron industry relative to iron ore mining. Following the outbreak of the war with Japan, ingot production was stepped up, both in Free China by the Chinese, and in North China and Manchuria by the Japanese. From an annual output of 414,000 metric tons in 1936, production more than doubled in seven years and reached a peak of 853,000 tons in 1943, not including the production of certain North China mills. Of this quantity 844,000 tons were produced in Manchuria. In the same period the production of rolled steel products was also greatly expanded. While only very small quantities were produced in Free China towards the end of the war, Manchurian production, using locally produced crude steel, rose to 486,000 tons in 1943, a part of which was exported to Japan. The total capacities of the Manchurian ingot and rolling mills at the end of World War II were estimated at approximately 1,300,000 and 1,000,000 tons a year respectively. This was accompanied by a greatly expanded pig iron production which reached its peak at 2,131,000 tons in 1942 for all mainland China and an iron ore production of about 10 million tons.[54] Thus, from the point of view of the country as a whole, although iron ore output was still much in excess of that of pig iron and pig iron output was considerably greater than the domestic demand for steel-making, the capacities of steel ingots and finished steel were in much better balance than before, and were estimated to be amply sufficient to meet China's reconstruction needs.

This situation was, however, drastically changed for the worse, first through removals of equipment from Manchuria by Soviet occupation troops, and subsequently through reported destructions by the Chinese Communists and military hostilities between Communist and Nationalist troops. The destruction was apparently greater in rolling than in ingot capacity—especially in the rolling of special shapes such as heavy rails—and greater in ingot than in pig iron capacity.[55] In 1949, the first year of Communist rule in Manchuria, only 100,000 tons of ingots and 72,000 tons of rolled products were produced from the former Japanese mills.[56] This imbalance persisted through 1953 as the capacity for making crude steel was rehabilitated much faster than the reconstruction of the rolling mill that was completed toward the end of the year.[57] Total ingot production in

Manchuria in 1953 was probably about 1,200,000 tons or slightly below the capacity at the end of the war. The production of rolled steel in the same year, not having yet benefited from the reconstructed rolling mill, was probably less than 700,000 tons.[58] On the basis of our estimated outputs for mainland China, the outputs for China Proper were: ingots, 41,000 tons in 1949 and 362,000 tons in 1953; and rolled products, 15,000 tons in 1949 and 289,000 tons in 1953. While still considerably smaller than the corresponding Manchurian outputs, these figures for China Proper which are probably reasonably accurate, suggest both a tremendous advance over previous production and a notable rise of the relative share of China Proper in steel-making, a fact to be attributed largely to developments in Tientsin, T'ang-shan, and T'ai-yuan in North China and Chungking in Szechwan.

Pig iron production, on the other hand, has apparently lagged behind in its recovery. Out of a total output of 206,000 tons in 1949, Manchurian production accounted for 172,000 tons,[59] or about 83.5 per cent. The same ratio was probably maintained in 1953 when total production in mainland China was around 1,873,000 tons. With the addition of the two automatic blast furnaces at An-shan in 1953, pig iron production in Manchuria should increase fairly rapidly. However, in spite of the initial drop of production, pig iron did not become at any time a serious bottleneck in Communist China's iron and steel industry largely because of the small domestic demand by fabricators.[60] Consequently, unless export is stepped up unexpectedly, such as through an expansion of trade with Japan, there does not appear to be any immediate, serious danger of an iron shortage even allowing for a sizable domestic demand for finished iron products.

THE IRON AND STEEL CENTERS

Prior to the Soviet removals, there were 13 large blast furnaces in Manchuria—7 in An-shan and 2 in Pen-ch'i—with a total furnace capacity of over 6,000 tons. In China Proper, blast furnace capacity totalled only just about 3,000 tons, one half of which was located at Shih-ching-shan near Peking. Elsewhere there were approximately 450 tons at Ta-yeh, 310 tons at T'ai-yuan and Yang-ch'üan in Shansi, 375 tons in Szechwan, largely scattered in a number of small plants built during the war; 264 tons in Hunan; and a number of small furnaces in Anhwei, Kiangsi, Kwangsi, Yunnan, and Shanghai.

At the time the Communists took over, there were only five blast furnaces left in Manchuria, of which only four (total capacity 1,400 tons[61]) were in operable condition. Since then, two large automatic furnaces were added in 1953 at An-shan, while work on three others was either continued or started in 1954. By the end of this construction program the number of blast furnaces would be at least eight while actual production might be considerably greater than under the Manchoukuo regime. In China Proper, production has also been expanded at Shih-ching-shan, T'ai-yuan, Ta-yeh, and Chungking.

In the case of steel-making, the original furnace capacity in Manchuria totalled over 4,000 tons with 19 furnaces at An-shan, 6 at Pen-ch'i, and 6 at Fu-shun. The total furnace capacity in China Proper was less than 300 tons. The principal centers, in order of their relative importance were T'ai-yuan, Shanghai, Tientsin, T'ang-shan, and Chungking. In addition, there were several very small furnaces at An-ning in Yunnan, Ta-yeh, and Canton. Rolling capacity was even more concentrated in Manchuria, principally An-shan, although there were some small mills at Chungking, T'ai-yuan, Tientsin, T'ang-shan, Shanghai, and Ta-yeh.

At the time of Communist occupation only one or two furnaces were in operation at An-shan where annual ingot capacity, reduced to an estimated 500,000 tons after Soviet withdrawals, had dropped even further. Apart from certain subsidiary finishing and special plants, only one blooming mill and one small bar mill were left at the An-shan Iron and Steel Works. Since then, however, a number of plants have been rebuilt to replace those dismantled, including one mill each for heavy rolling, steel sheets, and seamless pipes. In addition, the present construction program includes two blooming mills, one sheet mill, and one steel smelting plant. There was no serious loss of equipment in the small steel industry in China Proper before the Communists took over. From 1949 to the beginning of 1954 heaving rolling, such as for rails, was concentrated at Chungking as only light rails could be produced at An-shan and T'ai-yuan. However, ingot capacity at Chungking was inadequate and shipments had to be made from as far as An-shan. The Communist authorities are said to be correcting this by expanding the open-hearth capacity at Chungking.

Thus the present iron and steel centers in Communist China are located at An-shan, Pen-ch'i and Fu-shun in Manchuria; and Chungking, T'ai-yuan, and Ta-yeh in China Proper. In addition, the Tientsin and T'ang-shan steel plants and the Shih-ching-shan pig iron works should be regarded as one complex. While all these plants will no doubt be expanded in the course of the Five Year Plan, and while the immediate goal must be further building at An-shan, the long-range center of interest may well be in North China. Already a small machinery industry is being built up at T'ai-yuan and, as mentioned in the last chapter, the city of Pao-t'ou in the former Suiyuan province has been selected to become a new major iron and steel center. In Central China also new iron ore beds discovered at Ta-yeh are providing the necessary support for further expansion.

SUPPLY AND DEMAND OF FINISHED STEEL PRODUCTS

If our production estimates are at all close to the mark, a much better balance between pig iron and crude steel production was achieved in 1953 than heretofore. With the rolling capacity added in 1953 at An-shan, the ingot and rolling capacities are also in reasonable balance. The predominant question confronting the Communist Chinese authorities, it seems, is no longer whether enough pig iron and ingots could be found for further fabrication or even whether pig iron and ingots currently produced could be further manufactured, but, rather, whether the supply of finished products is sufficient to meet the rising demand, as existing capacity in all branches of the iron and steel industry is being utilized intensively. Should the answer to this question be in the negative, a simultaneous expansion of all the branches of the industry might be necessary, especially in the steel-making stage. It would also follow that in order to raise the output of finished steel products the necessary investment, spread over the successive stages of the production process, would have to be much greater than it is.

Before 1937, Chinese consumption of rolled and steel products was dependent almost solely upon imports. According to the Maritime Customs reports, the annual import of rolled and other steel products of China Proper in 1931–1936 averaged 428,000 tons. Imports into Manchuria during the same period were about 255,000 tons a year. Allowing for some domestic production in Manchuria in 1935 and 1936,[62] the total amount available for consumption in mainland China amounted to 709,000 tons a year.

During the war with Japan, while consumption in China Proper may have decreased, consumption of rolled steel in Manchuria increased to an annual average of 345,000 tons in 1942–1943.[63] Consequently, one might assume that in order to maintain a level of economic activity commensurate to that of Manchuria in 1943 and of China Proper in 1936, the annual requirement for rolled steel and steel products would be around 773,000 tons.

The increase in population since before the war and the higher level of industrial activity that has now been achieved in comparison with both prewar years and wartime would naturally tend to increase the demand for steel products. However, some of the 773,000 tons actually went to new investments before and during the war whereas if no economic expansion had been undertaken in China Proper in 1936 or in Manchuria in 1943, normal demand merely to maintain economic activity at the given level would have been much smaller. It is quite possible that the additional quantity previously devoted to economic expansion would more than offset the greater current demand due to the larger population and higher industrial activity. It would seem, therefore, reasonably safe to assume a present "normal" requirement of not more than 800,000 tons of rolled steel and steel products a year for Communist China.[64] Accordingly, on the basis of our estimated output for 1953, the surplus available for new constructions and, incidentally, armament, would be around 189,000 tons, perhaps substantially more. Such a small supply for new construction purposes would not be sufficient to provide for more than a very modest development program,[65] considering the increasing replacement demand as the industrial base expands, and would preclude altogether any accelerated expenditure of steel products in large-scale warfare. The importance of the new constructions now under way at An-shan and elsewhere can probably be best appreciated in this light. Yet, on the other hand, it is equally significant that the supply of rolled steel is now as large as it is and that complete dependence upon imports has given way to dependence upon Manchuria.

SOME OF THE FERRO-ALLOY AND NON-FERROUS METALS

The backwardness of the iron and steel industry and of industries in general before the war was the underlying reason for the extremely retarded state of the Chinese ferro-alloy and non-ferrous metals industries. Considerable efforts were made by the Japanese during the war in developing such metals as manganese, molybdenum, and copper, both in Manchuria and in China Proper, but the situation was not appreciably altered, and as the development of industries continues and the demand for special steels and other metal products expands, lag in the production of some of these metals may prove to be a very serious bottleneck. The only outstanding exceptions to this general picture are furnished by such metals as tungsten, antimony, and tin—especially the first two—which were important items in China's export of mineral products. Supplies from known deposits of such metals as manganese and molybdenum are also said to be reasonably adequate for China's present and developing needs, but in the case of many other metals, new deposits and the exact extent of known deposits have still to be discovered or ascertained by the intensified geological work mentioned in the preceding chapter.

The principal tungsten-producing mines are found in Kiangsi, Kwangtung, and Hunan, although there is also some ore production in Kwangsi and Yunnan. In the pre-Communist period, the peak output in Kiangsi, in terms of WO_3 concentrates, was about 10,000 tons in 1942. The highest output in Hunan was about 2,700 tons in 1935 while that of Kwangtung was a little over 2,000 tons in 1937.[66] For the country as a whole, the highest output was scored in 1935 when 14,500 tons were produced. Production dropped sharply after World War II, but recovered to a little over 10,000 tons in 1948 according to an NRC Report.[67] The same level of production has probably been maintained up to 1951 although some increase may have taken place since.[68] Since the greater part of the tungsten produced was for export, domestic requirements are more than adequately covered at the present level of production.[69]

Antimony production in mainland China, which is concentrated in Hunan, declined steadily from the twenties onward and through World War II. Production in 1944 was just over 200 tons of regulus. The latest reported figure is 3,280 tons for 1948, but it is not quite clear whether this refers to crude antimony or not.[70] However, like tungsten, this metal has been mined primarily for export, and the problem of a domestic shortage does not arise. Recent reports from Communist China have mentioned plans for new mining developments in Hunan, as well as the discovery of new deposits.

In the case of tin mining, which is concentrated in Yunnan and Kwangsi, constructions in 1953 mentioned in the last chapter suggest the concentration of effort in boosting production at Ko-chiu. Output at this established center of tin mining rose significantly between 1949 and 1953.[71] For the country as a whole, production in 1951 was probably between 7,000 and 8,000 tons as compared with the peak year production of over 17,000 tons.[72] With the new installations at Ko-chiu now completed, production is probably much higher than in 1951. Again, the problem is not one of domestic shortage, but the supply of a large enough export surplus for the country's foreign trade program.

The picture of copper production is less rosy although official reports suggest a considerable increase in production since 1949, especially in Manchuria.[73] Net imports by China Proper throughout the thirties were several times domestic production. Even in Manchuria where production reached 2,239 tons in 1944, large imports were required. Given the present larger output from Manchurian mines, it is nevertheless doubtful that production could keep pace with expanding demand. There are three or more principal mines in Manchuria and some five ore concentration plants.[74] Expansion of the Shen-yang copper works has already been mentioned before and may prove to be a significant development.

Official information on the production of other metals has been notoriously lacking.[75] This may be interpreted either as a sign of no progress or as an attempt to conceal some important achievement. As mentioned earlier, we are inclined to believe that the former interpretation is correct. The establishment of a separate Ministry of Geology in 1952 and the large-scale prospecting work reported so far seem to lend support to such an appraisal.

However, in view of the unpredictability of new geological discoveries, the possibility of some spectacular development in the mining of non-ferrous and other metals cannot be ruled out. In this connection attention should be directed particularly to joint Soviet-Chinese efforts both in exploiting such established Chinese products as tungsten in Kiangsi, Kwangtung, and Hunan and in exploring and developing new metals and deposits in the vast area of Sinkiang. According to a report from Ti-hua on the third anniversary of the Sino-Soviet Non-Ferrous Metals Company,[76] a notable diversification in the production of the company which operates in both northern and southern Sinkiang has been reported. At the same time, overall production in 1953 was said to be about 214 per cent of that of 1951.[77] Mention was also made of new power plants, machine shops, and an ore dressing plant. Geological surveying work by the company in 1953 was 897 per cent of the corresponding 1951 volume while the capital construction work undertaken in 1953 was 550 per cent of the 1952 figure. These are all indications of a sustained effort to expand mining activities in this area. Viewed in this light and in conjunction with the railway development program for this area, one should not be surprised if the present unfavorable prospect of the mining industries were changed in the future.[78]

THE MACHINERY MANUFACTURING INDUSTRY

While the supply of ferro-alloy and non-ferrous metals may pose a serious problem to the effective expansion of the iron and steel industry on an autarchic basis and hence to the industrialization program itself, an even greater bottleneck exists in the machinery manufacturing industry. Not only must the products of the iron and steel industry be further fabricated into machines, but new equipment for the latter, if not obtainable from foreign sources, must also be manufactured by the machinery industry. This important role of machinery manufacturing was given official recognition by the Communist Chinese authorities when the First Ministry of Machinery Industry was organized in October, 1952.[79] Under the jurisdiction of the new ministry are plants producing such diverse items as mining machinery, electric machines, machine tools, ships, and automobiles.

According to official information, the value output of all plants under the First Ministry of Machinery Industry, expressed in terms of index numbers with 1949 as the base year, was 727 in 1952 and 1,200 in 1953. This was accompanied by a 30 per cent increase in labor productivity in 1953 in comparison with 1952 or 190 per cent in comparison with 1949.[80] The production of machine tools and electric motors and generators in 1953 all exceeded their original targets and were greater than the corresponding outputs in 1952 as was the case with mining machinery.[81] In addition, some 600 items were said to be new products for which China had been completely dependent upon imports.

This apparently striking advance in machinery manufacturing is, however, exceedingly deceptive as the production in 1949, the base year used, was virtually negligible. In the first place, according to both Nationalist Chinese reports and the Pauley Reparations Commission, the postwar Soviet removals reduced the capacity of Manchurian industries using machine tools and metal-working machinery by as much as 80 per cent.[82] This estimate does not take into account further losses due to the civil war in 1947–1948. In the second place, outside Manchuria, the machinery manufacturing industry was virtually non-existent. The monthly productive capacity for a number of items in 1947 in 18 principal cities in China Proper[83] was altogether negligible, as most of the firms were nothing but small repair shops. Consequently, with the Manchurian capacity literally eliminated for the time being, the entire machinery industry of China was at a standstill in 1949.

According to a 1951 report[84] the capacity of the Manchurian machinery industry in 1950 was 28 per cent higher than in 1949. Compared with the 1949 outputs the production of machine tools, motors, and lathes in 1950 was 138.1 per cent, 424.8 per cent, and 40 per cent greater respectively,[85] but the entire production of machine tools in 1949 consisted of 439 units, and it can be safely assumed that no heavy machinery was produced.[86] Further increases in machinery manufacturing including such items as machine tools, ball bearings, electric generators, and motors, have been reported for both 1952 and 1953, interspersed with occasional comments on plan failures.[87] While these sources all tend to support the general trend of recovery depicted earlier, they also seriously modify the optimistic note struck by the official index numbers suggesting a twelve-fold expansion in the value output of the machinery industry in the country between 1949 and 1953. On the basis of our present knowledge, dependence upon imports will continue for a long time to come. It is in this light, too, that the role of the various plants under construction in 1953 and 1954 at Shen-yang and Ha-erh-pin must be viewed.

As of 1953 about one-quarter of Communist China's machinery production was derived from Shen-yang where 43 per cent of the city's industrial output consisted of machines.[88] Other centers of the machinery industry in Manchuria are such cities as Ha-erh-pin, An-shan, Fu-shun, An-tung, and Lü-ta. In China Proper, smaller plants are located at Shanghai, Tientsin, Tsingtao, Chungking,

Hankow, Fu-chou, Kun-ming, Kwei-yang, Nan-ch'ang, Chiu-chiang, and the Ch'ang-sha Heng-yang area. Moreover, T'ai-yuan is being gradually built up as a principal center to supply the needs of Northwest China. Of these Shanghai, Tientsin, and T'ai-yuan are probably the most important.[89]

THE BASIC CHEMICAL INDUSTRY

If Communist China's demand for machinery cannot be satisfied by domestic production, how about the basic chemicals? At a conference in June, 1951, called by the Ministry of Heavy Industry, which has jurisdiction over the chemical and metallurgical industries, the belief was expressed that it was possible for Communist China to become self-sufficient in acids, alkalies, and dyestuffs.[90] Moreover, the output of the country's chemical industry in 1950 was reported to be 90 per cent greater than that of 1949,[91] while further increases in the subsequent years have since been told. Is it possible then that self-sufficiency is now in sight if indeed it has not already been reached?

The question, of course, does not refer to the supply of raw materials which are mostly available. Rather it is a problem of productive facilities which are extremely limited. The impressive expansion of production from 1949 to 1950 fails to disclose the fact that in terms of their original capacities the productive capacities in operation of the plants in being in 1950 were, for instance, 62 per cent in pure soda, 13 per cent in ammonium sulphate, and only 10 per cent in sulphuric acid.[92] Subsequent relative increases must therefore be evaluated in the same light. What quantities could be produced at such an operating rate depended largely upon the size of the original capacity which was undoubtedly very small.

Before the war with Japan, Tientsin was the principal center of the chemical industry in China. The largest producer was the Yung-li Company which had an annual capacity of 70,000 tons of soda ash and 10,000 tons of caustic soda. Taken over by the Japanese during World War II, the plants were expanded so that production in 1940 reached 60,000 tons of soda ash, 28,000 tons of caustic soda, 50,000 tons of ammonium sulphate, and 17,500 tons of chlorine gas. The company was returned to private operation after the war, but was brought under joint government ownership in July, 1952. The annual rate of soda ash production in 1952 was said to be equivalent to 400 per cent of the peak output under the Japanese or an estimated 240,000 tons. The output of ammonium sulphate in 1952 was also estimated at 170 per cent of the prewar peak.[93]

In addition to the Yung-li Company, the Japanese also established the Oriental Chemical Industry Company at T'ang-ku and the Po-hai Chemical Company at Han-ku, producing such items as refined salt, potassium fertilizer, and hydrochloric acid. Both of these firms, together with two other Japanese plants at Tientsin, were subsequently taken over by the NRC, and the Tientsin Chemical Industry Company was formed. The latter became the second major chemical manufacturer in Tientsin along with the Yung-li Company.[94] According to Communist sources, its annual productive capacity in 1949 consisted of 1,600 tons of solid caustic soda, 2,400 tons of magnesium hydroxide, 600 tons of magnesium chloride, 5,400 tons of sodium sulphate, 647 tons of cyanogin sulphide, 6,000 tons of sodium sulphate crystals, 2,896 tons of sodium sulphide, 1,000 55-lb. drums of hydrochloric acid, 500 tons of glue, 2,100 tons of bleaching powder, 40,000 cases of soap, 500 tons of gypsum, 45,000 tons of washed salt, 5,100 tons of table salt, and 3,700 tons of bone meal.[95]

Next to Tientsin, Shanghai is probably the principal chemical industry center in China Proper. Although there were 233 plants according to a 1950 report, 30 per cent of these consisted of handicraft workshops only, and most of the remainder were also very small. The largest plant belongs to the Yung-li Chemical Company and had a peak output in 1950 of 140 tons of ammonium sulphate and 180 tons of pure soda a day.[96] Other products of the private firms include sodium sulphide, liquid caustic soda, and bakelite material production of which is said to have increased during 1950–1952.[97] Besides, the government-operated Shanghai Chemical Industry Company has also stepped up its output since 1949, including such products as sulphuric, nitric, and hydrochloric acids, liquid caustic soda, sulphur black, insulating paint, rubber belting, mica sheets, and refractory bricks.[98]

Elsewhere there is the Yung-li Ammonium Sulphate Factory at Liu-ho near Nanking which has an ammonium plant and a sulphuric acid plant. The former had a daily output of 30 tons in 1950, the latter a maximum daily output of 130 tons of concentrated sulphuric acid. A new sulphuric acid plant is said to have since been established by Yung-li in the same area, with operation scheduled to begin in July, 1953.[99] Smaller chemical works are also found at Tsingtao, Lan-chou, Hsi-an, Canton, Kun-ming, and Chungking, producing acids and soda.[100] Little recent information is available on the individual plants except that a potassium chlorate plant in Southwest China is reported to have been expanded with the assistance of Soviet experts.[101]

In spite of incomplete information, it is quite clear that the basic chemical industry of China Proper is altogether inadequate. Thus, there must be continued reliance upon Manchurian production, which was built up by the Japanese during the Manchoukuo period. Of the 80 plants reported upon by the Pauley Commission, 31 were in Communist territory at the time of the Commission's survey. Relatively few plants in Nationalist-controlled areas were said to have suffered complete damage although there was some reduction of capacity in a large number of them.[102] At the end of the war the plants in southern Manchuria were taken over by the NRC and operated by the Shen-yang Chemical Works. Production in 1946–1947 included soda, alcohol, glycerine, and hydrochloric acid. The Hu-lu-tao sulphuric acid plant also resumed production under the NRC's control, producing 1,000 tons of concentrated acid a month.

Following the Communist take-over in 1948, about three-fourths of the chemical industry at Shen-yang, as well as plants at Chin-chou, Chin-hsi, Ssu-p'ing-chieh, Chi-lin, and Hu-lu-tao was being rehabilitated. Surveys in 1949 mentioned 6 plants at Shen-yang, producing caustic soda, hydrochloric and nitric acids, bleaching power, lubricating oil, oils and fats, and cyanogin sulphide; one plant at P'i-tzu-wo in Liaotung province, producing salt, magnesium sulphate, and potassium chloride; 2 plants at Chi-lin, producing phosphorous sulphide and calcium carbide; 2 plants at Ha-erh-pin, producing oils and fats and alcohol; and one plant each at Ssu-p'ing-chieh, Chin-chou, Chin-hsi and Hu-lu-tao.[103]

Compared with the situation at the end of 1949, increases in the productive capacities of Manchuria's chemical industry registered in 1950 ranged from 3.9 per cent in ammonium sulphate to 78.4 per cent in caustic soda. Further impressive gains were recorded for both 1951 and 1952, especially in nitric acid and ammonium nitrate.[104] Thus, as far as southern Manchuria is concerned, it is possible that recovery to the Manchoukuo level in the basic chemicals may have been attained by now. For the aiea as a whole, lack of information on plants under Communist control in 1946–1947 makes a more accurate assessment extremely difficult. However, since Manchurian production was not large enough to permit heavy exports during the period of Japanese rule, it is hardly likely that the supply of chemical products from Manchuria could meet the expanding needs of China Proper at the present time. Like machinery, chemicals as a whole must continue to be imported by Communist China during the current industrialization program and possibly in sizable quantities.

THE CEMENT INDUSTRY

Turing to the basic building activities, we may examine briefly the state of the cement industry, which, in view of the many construction projects scheduled or under way, not only in industry, but also in flood control projects and defense installations, appears to be far from being adequate in spite of recent expansion in China Proper.

Before the outbreak of the war with Japan, there were nine cement plants in China Proper and seven in Manchuria with maximum annual capacities of 1,305,000 tons and 1,355,000 tons respectively.[105] During the war additional plants were built both in China Proper and in Manchuria so that at the end of World War II there were 19 plants in China Proper and 14 in Manchuria. The former had a maximum capacity of 1,887,000 tons; the latter, 2,310,000 tons.[106]

The greater part of the Manchurian plants was, however, either removed or damaged. Of the 9 plants under Nationalist control in 1946–1947 only the Pen-ch'i, Hsiao-tun and Chin-hsi plants were in operation; the one at Liao-yang was being repaired in 1948 when the city fell to Communist hands; the remaining 5 plants, located at Kung-yüan, An-shan, Ch'üan-t'ou, Chi-lin, and Fu-shun, were completely inoperative. Of the last 5, damage was very severe with the exception of the An-shan and the Fu-shun plants. The fate of the 5 plants under Communist Chinese and Soviet control was unknown, but it is unlikely that their original combined annual capacity of 640,000 tons was maintained intact as may be seen from production data for later years.

In China Proper, the principal plants were at T'ang-shan and Liu-li-ho in North China and Lung-t'an, Lung-hua, and Chiang-nan in Shanghai and Nanking. The remaining were smaller plants located at T'ai-yuan (Shansi), Tsing-tai, Chi-nan (Shantung), Canton, Kuei-lin (Kwangsi), Ta-yeh (Hupeh), Ch'en-ch'i (Hunan), Chungking, Lo-shan, Kuang-yüan (Szechwan), Kun-ming (Yunnan), Kweiyang (Kweichow), and Chahar. Although damage to their original capacities was sustained by some of these plants, they were all expected to be in operation in 1948. Since then some new facilities are believed to have been established at Lan-chou (Kansu) and in Sinkiang.

According to our estimates in the preceding chapter, total cement production in Communist China in 1949 was only 678,000 tons, of which less than one-third or 218,000 tons were produced in Manchuria.[107] These figures may be compared with 251,000 tons in 1946, 550,000 tons in 1947, and the planned output of 1,200,000 tons in 1948.[108] Among the Manchurian plants in operation were those at Pen-ch'i, Liao-yang, and Ha-erh-pin.[109] Since then the An-shan, Fu-shun, and Chin-hsi plants have also resumed production,[110] but there has been little information on the other plants. It is perhaps significant that, with the exception of the Ha-erh-pin plant, these were all either in operation or under repair prior to the establishment of Communist rule.

While cement production in Communist China increased to 2.9 million tons in 1952 and 3.9 million tons in 1953, the outputs of Manchuria were probably about 720,000 tons in 1952 and 810,000 tons in 1953.[111] Recovery has apparently lagged behind in Manchuria so that the aggregate output for the country as a whole is still below the maximum capacity available at the end of World War II in spite of the rapid expansion of facilities in China Proper. The small production in Manchuria contrasts rather sharply with the intense building activity in the area. In view of this situation it may not be too far-fetched to trace the defective building on a number of capital construction projects partly to cement shortage.

IV

Given the small domestic machinery industry and the possible shortage of certain metals, basic chemicals, and liquid fuels, success of Communist China's industrialization program hinges upon the rate at which these commodities can be imported. Furthermore, given the total means of foreign payment available, the proportion that can be devoted to the importation of capital equipment and other producers' goods depends upon the amount used for importing consumers' goods. It may be assumed that imports for direct or indirect consumption purposes have been, and will continue to be, kept at a minimum. However, this minimum requirement could still be too high if large deficiencies should exist in the most vital areas of consumption: namely, food and clothing. The supply of food crops and cotton has already been discussed in connection with agricultural production. It now remains for us to examine briefly the manufacturing end of these products.

THE COTTON TEXTILE INDUSTRY

The largest light manufacturing industry in China is represented by the cotton mills. At the time of Communist occupation there were about 247 mills in mainland China with 5.1 million spindles and 68 thousand looms.[112] These were distributed geographically as follows:

	Million Spindles	*Thousand Looms*
East China	3.7	46.5
North China	0.5	11.5
Central-South China	0.3	1.9
Other Areas	0.6	8.0
	5.1	67.9

About one half of the capacities was located at Shanghai.

Production of both yarn and cotton piece goods was extremely low in 1949, the former being 72.4 per cent of the 1930 peak, the latter being 72.6 per cent of the 1936 peak.[113] A great deal of idle capacity existed as a result of the civil war, monetary instability, power shortage, and the precarious supply of raw cotton. With the exception of 1951, when the spinning mills were closed for about two months in the summer because of cotton shortage, yarn production has increased steadily and even greater progress has been made in cotton weaving. As may be seen from our estimates in the preceding chapter, the outputs of yarn and cloth in 1953 were 4,038,000 bales[114] and 2,126 million meters respectively.

This rise of production was achieved through increasing productivity, more intensive utilization of available equipment, and the establishment of new mills. According to official Communist reports, there was a 15.5 per cent increase in spindlage in 1950–1953 and a 21 per cent increase in the number of looms in the same period.[115] Since there was some destruction of spindles during 1949 and 1950, the total spindlage available at the end of 1950 was probably less than 4.8 million. Using the latter figure, the spindlage available at about the end of 1953 would be 5.5 million. Since the officially reported figure may have included mills still under construction, the actual number of spindles available in 1953 was probably smaller although this figure may be regarded as an approximate estimate for 1954. Assuming that the 21 per cent increase in the number of looms is more or less correct, the present number of looms would be about 82,000.

According to official reports, up to the end of 1953, 8 new cotton mills had been established and begun operation. Eleven more were still under construction in 1953, and work on 4 others was started in 1954. All of these are located in cotton-producing areas—especially in Hopeh, Honan, and Shensi—away from the largest established textile center, Shanghai. The tabulation appearing on page 307 illustrates very clearly the official policy to shift production nearer to sources of raw material supply.

Most of the larger mills are planned to be equipped with 50,000 spindles each, as well as one to two thousand looms. The four plants begun in 1954 will have 100,000 spindles.

It can be easily seen from our production and equipment data that the present structure of the textile industry shows a considerable imbalance between spinning and weaving. The yarn production of 1953 was sufficient to produce 5.2 billion meters of average grade cloth.[116] The estimated cloth production of the year from modern mills was only 2.1 billion meters. The potential per capita output was just under 9 meters a year, while the actual per capita output was 3.6 meters. Allowing for handwoven cloth, the supply was too small relative to demand so that rationing was finally introduced in September, 1954. A substantial expansion of the weaving industry would have to be carried out if the consumption level were to be raised although, supplemented by material from other fibers, the population can probably just be clothed.[117] In the meantime there should be a large exportable surplus of cotton yarn.

NEW COTTON MILLS ESTABLISHED IN COMMUNIST CHINA

				Under Construction	
	1951	*1952*	*1953*	*1953*	*1954*
Hopeh	Shih-chia-chuang*		Han-tan No. 1 Plant	Shih-chia-chuang Peking No. 1 Plant	Peking Shih-chia-chuang
Shensi		Hsien-yang (NW. No. 1 Plant)		Hsi-an (NW. No. 2 & No. 3 Plants Hsi-an Weaving Plant	Hsi-an
Sinkiang		Ti-hua (Plant No. 7-1)			
Honan		Hsin-hsiang*	Cheng-chou No. 2 Plant	Cheng-chou No. 1 Plant	Cheng-chou
Hupeh		Wu-han No. 1 Plant			
Kiangsu		Nanking			
Hunan				Hsiang-tan*	
Kiangsi				Nan-ch'ang*	
Szechwan				Chungking (No. 601 Weaving Plant)	
Yünnan				Kun-ming (?)*	
Liaohsi				Location unknown*	

* Smaller mills operated by local authorities.

Sources: Compiled from *People's Daily*, Peking, December 25, 1952, and January 17, 1953; *China News Service*, December 15, 1953; *Wen-hui pao*, Hongkong, October 6, 1953; NCNA, September 30, 1953, December 14, 1953, and February 4, 1954.

According to one official announcement, the First Five Year Plan envisages a 50 per cent increase in the capacity of the textile industry. If distributed equally between spindles and looms, the annual increase in the five-year period would be 500,000 spindles and 7,600 looms. In view of the greater shortage of looms, fewer spindles and more looms would have to be built.

In this connection, it should be noted that during 1950–1953 the textile machinery industry of Communist China produced 18,500 looms and 600,000 spindles or an average annual output of 4,625 looms and 150,000 spindles.[118] This capacity will be doubled upon the completion of the new Ching-wei Textile Machinery Plant at T'ai-yuan which has a planned annual productive capacity of 200,000 spindles and an estimated production of 50,000 spindles in 1954. Thus the goal of achieving self-sufficiency in the manufacture of textile machinery appears to be a reasonably practicable one although, as a result of the lag between the expansion program for cotton mills during the present Five Year Plan and the time full operation will start at the T'ai-yuan plant, imports will continue to be required in the short run.

In addition to the Ching-wei Textile Machinery Plant at T'ai-yuan, there are now six other smaller factories in Communist China, 3 at Shanghai, and 1 each at Tientsin, Tsingtao, and Cheng-chou. The location of the new and largest plant at T'ai-yuan suggests the intention to expand the cotton textile industry in North and Northwest China further and is closely related to the choice of T'ai-yuan as a new machinery manufacturing and metallurgical center.

RICE AND FLOUR MILLING

As industrialization progresses, the urban population will increase and with it the demand for flour and rice by the non-agricultural population. While these staples could be supplied by native mills in the country and small hand mills in the cities, the importance of factory milling will increase on account of the latter's greater efficiency and lower labor cost. Thus the adequacy of the modern mills in meeting the potentially rising demand may pose quite a serious problem in the future even though it is not one of immediate concern.

The production of wheat flour is among the largest modern manufacturing industries for consumers' goods in China, being only next to the cotton textile industry in importance. There are about 970 modern mills in Communist China with a total capacity of 519,725 bags of flour a day or an annual capacity of 137,207,400 bags.[119] The geographical distribution of the productive capacity is: Shanghai, 20 per cent; Wu-hsi (Kiangsu), 8.6 per cent; Tientsin, 7.9 per cent; Hankow, 6.1 per cent; Chi-nan (Shantung), 5.8 per cent; Peking, 5.3 per cent; other, 46.3 per cent.

The great concentration in river and sea ports is due to the lower transport cost by water, the foreign origin of the first modern mills, and importation of foreign wheat. With the disappearance of imported wheat and the greater reliance on land transportation, under the Communist regime, high transportation cost reduced sales between June, 1949, and May, 1950, to 50.2 million bags while 57.9 million bags were produced.[120] Thus more than one half of the capacity of the mills was idle owing to marketing difficulties.

Apparently this problem has since been largely resolved as flour production increased to 127 million bags in 1952 and 147 million bags in 1953 and was fast exceeding the industry's previously estimated capacity. The latter, however, may have expanded somewhat in the meantime as new mills have probably been established in the Cheng-chou (Honan) area to take advantage of the large wheat surplus available. Production has also been stepped up in North, Northwest, and Southwest China.[121] However, as was pointed out by the national food conference in December, 1949, even at the 1949 level of wheat production, the supply available for the modern flour mills exceeded the latter's capacity by 9.6 million bags. As both wheat production and the flour-consuming population of the cities in northern China increase, the problem of insufficient capacity may well arise. However, the problem is not of a pressing nature as long as the farmers can continue to produce their own flour.

Unlike wheat flour milling, factory milling of rice is not highly developed in China as hulls are usually removed from paddy in the villages and further processing is done in the factories that turn out polished rice.[122] According to the 1947 industrial survey, the annual production of polished rice in the 18 principal cities of mainland China was only 0.58 million tons. An earlier survey, dated 1935, which had a wider geographical coverage, listed 1,251 modern rice mills with an annual output of 0.82 million tons.[123] This required approximately 1.26 million tons of paddy or about 2.7 per cent of the country's paddy production. Even though neither of the above surveys is complete, the insignificance of factory milling in rice production is quite unmistakable.

NOTES

1. Ch'en, Hsün-huan, *Development of China's Water Resources,* pp. 11-15, Taipeh, 1952. Of the 651,000 kws. 619,000 were in Manchuria where the potential capacity was estimated at 1.85 per cent of that of mainland China.

2. Cf. *Liberation Daily,* Shanghai, June 6, 1950.

3. The distribution by other uses was: (1) industry, 30.9 per cent, (2) railways, 8.4 per cent, (3) collieries, 5.3 per cent, and (4) shipping, 5.3 per cent. Cf. *General Statement on the Mining Industry,* 5th issue, pp. 113-114, 1932-1934.

4. The distribution by other uses was: (1) industry, 38.8 per cent, (2) railways, 22.6 per cent, and (3) shipping, 11.8 per cent. Cf. *Japan-Manchoukuo Yearbook,* pp. 709-711, Tokyo, 1941.

5. Cf. *Railway Semi-Monthly,* Vol. II, No. 3, p. 41; *Statistics of Chinese National Railways,* 1933-1934; and *General Statement on the Mining Industry,* 5th issue, p. 84.

6. Cf. NCNA, December 2, 1953.

7. A 369.2 km., 220,000-volt transmission line linking An-shan, Shen-yang, Fu-shun, Pen-ch'i and Fou-hsin was completed at about the end of 1953. A 130 km., 110,000-volt transmission line between Peking and Tientsin was to be completed in 1954. Other similar installations that were under construction during 1954 are in Shantung, Shansi, and Anhwei. NCNA, Shen-yang, November 9, 1953, and NCNA, March 18, 1954.

8. The Fu-shun and Fou-hsin power plants in Manchuria and the Tientsin power plant, which has the advantage of coal from nearby K'ai-lun, are cases in point.

9. Cf. *General Statement on the Mining Industry,* 7th issue, and Pauley, *op. cit.*

10. *New Construction,* Vol. I, No. 9, pp. 13-15, Peking.

11. *Loc. cit.*

12. Cf. Ti Ch'ao-pai, "The Chinese Economy during the Past Year," *Economic Weekly,* Vol. X, No. 1, p. 7, Shanghai, January, 1950, and *China's Industry,* Vol. I, No. 11, p. 7, Shanghai, March, 1950.

13. The *preliminary* estimate of actual production given by Chou En-lai in his September 23, 1954, report is 81,990 thousand tons.

14. The prewar per capita annual household consumption was 0.04 ton in North China, 0.02 ton in South China, and 0.08 ton in Manchuria. Cf. L. G. Ting's article in *Nankai Social and Economic Quarterly,* Tientsin, July, 1937, and Wang Kung-ping, *Controlling Factors in the Future Development of the Coal Industry,* New York, 1947 (both in English). In the urban centers the per capita quantities are higher, ranging from 0.11 ton in Canton to 0.47 ton in Peking.

15. Pauley, *op. cit.,* Appendix IV, and *People's Daily,* Peking, February 23, 1949.

16. *Northeast Daily,* Shen-yang, June 19, 1949.

17. *Northeast Daily,* Shen-yang, March 3, 1950, and *People's Daily,* Peking, November 16, 1949.

18. *New China Monthly,* Vol. I, No. 1, Peking, November, 1949, and *China's Industry,* Vol. I, No. 11, p. 80, Shanghai, March, 1950.

19. The geographical distribution of the working and idle shafts was:

	Number of Shafts In Operation	*Idle*	*Total*
Manchuria	169	39	208
North China	22	22	44
East China	43	27	70
	234	88	322

Cf. *People's Handbook,* Vol. II, p. *wei*-10, Shanghai, 1951. The Northwest, Central-South, and Southwest regions were not included in the above survey.

20. For some of the individual projects see *New China Monthly,* Vol. I, No. 2, p. 410, Peking, December, 1949; *New Construction,* Vol. II, No. 11, p. 30, Peking, July, 1950; and *Economic Bulletin,* No. 161, p. 9, Hongkong, March, 1950.

21. Report by the director of the Coal Mining Bureau, Ministry of Fuel Industry, *New China Monthly,* No. 38, p. 117, Peking, December, 1952.

22. *Southern Daily,* Canton, June 4, 1951.

23. *China's Industry,* Vol. IV, No. 2, p. 3, Shanghai, June, 1952, and NCNA, May 5, 1953. The first Donbas-type coal combine was reported to be manufactured at the Chi-hsi Mining Machinery Manufacturing Plant in Manchuria in December, 1953. Cf. NCNA, Ha-erh-pin, January 6, 1954.

24. Figures given by Sung Shao-wen, *op. cit.* Labor productivity in Manchuria was somewhat higher. Cf. *Chinese Workers,* No. 3, p. 11, Peking, April, 1950, and No. 9, p. 1, October, 1950.

25. Cf. Chuang P'u-ming, *op. cit.*

26. Wang Kung-ping, *op. cit.,* pp. 116-117.

27. See NCNA, March 31 and December 15, 1953, and January 7, 1954; *Economic Bulletin,* No. 320, p. 12, Hongkong, May 25, 1953; and *Northeast Daily,* Shen-yang, August 11, 1952.

28. NCNA, February 27, 1954, and *Wen-hui pao,* Hongkong, March 1, 1954.

29. NCNA, November 27, 1953.

30. See the preceding chapter.

31. NCNA, February 17, 1954. Some cost reduction in capital projects in the coal mines in comparison with the plan figures was reported at the fourth conference of coal mining cadres. Cf. NCNA, March 17, 1954.

32. *Wen-hui pao,* Hongkong, March 1, 1954. Other earlier reports mentioned 3 to 5 pairs of vertical shafts and 4 to 9 pairs of inclined shafts as the number to be completed in Manchuria during 1954. Cf. NCNA, Shen-yang, December 15, 1953, and January 5, 1954.

33. NCNA, February 27, 1954. Of the 7.6 million tons the vertical shafts in Manchuria were to contribute 4.3 million tons.

34. NCNA, Fou-hsin, February 25, 1954, and NCNA, Shen-yang, January 9, 1953.

35. The construction work in 1954 included the expansion of four pits and the renovation of two at Feng-feng (completion date, 1957), the sinking of 8 shafts at K'ai-lun (completion date, 1956-1957), which, together with other projects, involved 32 shafts in all. Cf. NCNA, December 28, 1953, February 20, 1954, and March 19, 1954; NCNA, T'ang-shan, February 20, 1954; and NCNA, March 19, 1954.

36. Cf. NCNA, June 12, 1953.

37. Cf. the report on the conference on capital construction in coal mining held in October, 1952. *New China Monthly,* p. 108, Peking, December, 1952.

38. *Chinese Yearbook,* Vol. II, pp. 1537-8, Nanking, 1948.

39. Cf. Pauley, *op. cit.* The available capacity in Manchuria declined steadily after 1945 as a result of civil war destructions so that reported figures vary widely according to the time individual surveys were made and their geographical coverage.

40. Cf. Chuang P'u-ming, *op cit.,* and *Economic Yearbook,* p. 44, Hongkong, 1951. The 1953 figure may be a slight overestimate.

41. Cf. *Southern Daily,* Canton, June 4, 1952; *New China Monthly,* No. 4, p. 123, Peking, April, 1954; and Li Fu-ch'un's report to the PPCC on October 31, 1951.

42. NCNA, May 9, 1953.

43. NCNA, March 18, 1954.

44. NCNA, November 27, 1953.

45. See the preceding chapter. Cf. also *Wen-hui pao,* Hongkong, October 3, 1953.

46. NCNA, Cheng-tu, March 30, 1954; and NCNA, March 18 and 28, 1954.

47. Cf. for instance *Liberation Daily,* Shanghai, June 6, 1950, and November 1, 1951; *People's Daily,* Peking, December 4, 1951; NCNA, Shen-yang, December 21, 1951; *Progress Daily,* April 19, 1952; and *New China Daily,* Chungking, June 9, 1952.

48. See *People's Daily,* Peking, January 27, 1950; *Northeast Daily,* Shen-yang, May 1, 1950; and *Wen hui-pao,* Hongkong, August 24, 1953.

49. *Northeast Daily,* Shen-yang, May 1, 1950.

50. *Wen-hui pao,* Hongkong, August 28, 1953.

51. *Wen-hui pao,* Hongkong, June 15, 1953; figure given by Sun Ching-ch'ih of the People's University of China.

52. About one half of Yü-men's crude oil would have to be refined in Manchuria. Cf. NCNA, Hsi-an, February 7 and 8, 1954.

53. Manchuria was a net exporter of pig iron, while China Proper was a net importer. Both areas also imported scrap and old iron, but, on balance, the country as a whole was a net exporter. Cf. *Trade of China* and *Annual Returns of the Foreign Trade of China.*

54. For pig iron production data in the pre-Communist period see Geological Survey of China, *General Statement on the Mining Industry,* 7th issue; Bureau of Information, *Iron and Steel,* Nanking, 1947; *Statistical Yearbook,* Nanking, 1948; *Chinese Yearbook,* Nanking, 1948; *Chinese Economic Yearbook,* Hongkong, 1947; Pauley, Reparatons Commission Report, 1946; and U. S. Bureau of Mines, *Foreign Minerals Survey,* Washington, D. C., 1948.

55. This conclusion is supported by the report that 71 per cent of the country's existing steel rolling capacity was in operation in 1950 while only 45 per cent of its total ingot capacity was in use. These figures stand in clear contrast to the greater decline in the production of rolled products in comparison with wartime production than that of ingots. Furthermore, the operation ratio for pig iron was 29 per cent of available capacity in 1950, but production was just under 40 per cent of the peak output in 1942. Cf. *New China Monthly,* Vol. II, No. 6, p. 1430, Peking, October, 1950.

56. Kao Kang's report—"On the Forefront of Northeast Economic Reconstruction."

57. Cf. an NCNA report from An-shan, December 27, 1953.

58. NCNA, An-shan, December 26, 1953; *Wen-hui pao,* Hongkong, August 26, 1953, and NCNA, May 7, 1953.

59. Kao Kang *op. cit.*

60. The same is true with respect to iron ore production on which little official information is available.

61. According to another source, blast furnace capacity in 1949 was said to be equal to about 25 per cent of the Manchoukuo peak level, which is in line with the above figure. Cf. *New China Monthly, Peking,* August, 1952.

62. See *Far East Yearbook,* 1941.

63. Pauley, *op. cit.,* p. 120.

64. This figure may be compared to the estimated consumption requirement of 300,000 tons for all iron and steel products made at the 1947 iron and steel conference in 1947. Cf. *Iron and Steel,* p. 39, Nanking.

65. For steel demand for railway building see Chapter X below.

66. *General Statement on the Mining Industry,* 7th issue.

67. *Summary Report of the National Resources Commission Since Demobilization,* Nanking, 1948.

68. See *A Manual for Newspaper Readers,* Hankow, 1950, and *New China Monthly,* p. 1301, Peking, October, 1951.

69. Exports in the 1925-1944 period averaged 7,700 tons a year against an average output of 8,400 tons a year. Thus annual domestic consumption was only 700 tons. Cf. *Foreign Minerals Survey,* p. 63, 1948.

70. *A Manual for Newspaper Readers,* Hankow, 1950.

71. NCNA, Kun-ming, September 29, 1951, and *Wen-hui pao,* Hongkong, June 10, 1953.

72. *Chinese Yearbook,* Vol. II, pp. 1568-9, Nanking, 1948, *New China Monthly,* p. 1301, Peking, October, 1951, and NCNA, September 3, 1954.

73. Cf. *New China Monthly,* Peking, October, 1951. Copper production in Manchuria in 1952 was reported at 110 per cent of the 1951 output, and was to be increased in 1953 to 157.8 per cent of the peak output under the Manchoukuo regime. This would put the 1953 target at just under 3,500 tons. See NCNA, May 7, 1953, and NCNA, Shen-yang, November 15, 1953. Actual production in 1953 was later reported to be 36 per cent higher than in 1952. NCNA, September 13, 1954.

74. Hu Wei-po, *Copper, Lead, and Zinc in China,* Peking, November, 1953.

75. There are, however, some reports of greater production of lead and zinc in Manchuria. See *Northeast Daily,* Shen-yang, January 16, 1951; NCNA, May 7, 1953, and September 13, 1954; and NCNA, Shen-yang, November 15, 1953.

76. *Sinkiang Daily,* Ti-hua, January 3 and 4, 1954.

77. According to another report, total mining production of the company in 1953 was said to be 400 per cent of the 1951 level. Cf. NCNA, January 7, 1954.

78. The planned increase in the production of copper, lead, zinc, and tin in 1954 was said to be from 10 to 27 per cent over their 1953 outputs. See NCNA, April 19, 1954.

79. A Second Ministry of Machinery Industry was organized at the same time. However, no information has ever been released on its activities. It is also rather significant that both the minister and his deputies are military men with field and staff experience. In view of this choice of leading personnel, the veil of secrecy, and the fact that virtually all types of ordinary machinery manufacturing are already under the control of the First Ministry, it is difficult to see what the Second Ministry's function could be if it were not a special department for the manufacture of arms, ammunition, and other related items.

80. See *New China Monthly,* No. 4, p. 137, Peking, 1954. For 1950 the machinery production index, excluding electric equipment, was 341 (1949 = 100). Cf. *Economic Yearbook,* p. 26, 1951.

81. NCNA, January 31, 1954, and Chuang P'u-ming, *op. cit.*

82. Pauley, *op. cit.,* p. 142 and appendix.

83. *An Industrial Survey of China's Principal Cities, Summary of Preliminary Report,* tables in *Chinese Yearbook,* Vol. II, pp. 1499-1537, Nanking, 1948.

84. *Northeast Daily,* Shen-yang, January 16, 1951.

85. *Progress Daily,* Tientsin, September 23 and October 10, 1951.

86. Kao Kang, *op. cit.,* March 13, 1950.

87. See *Economic Yearbook,* pp. 16 and 55, Hongkong, 1953; NCNA, May 7, 1953, and September 13, 1954; *Wen-hui pao,* Hongkong, August 26, 1953; and Kao Kang's report on February 27, 1951, in *New China Monthly,* pp. 1060-61, Peking, March, 1951

88. NCNA, November 2, 1953.

89. On production at some of these centers cf. *Northeast Daily,* Shen-yang, May 29, 1949; *Shanghai Industry and Commerce,* Vol. I, No. 21, August, 1950; *Masses Daily,* Hsi-an, August 11, 1952; *People's Daily,* Peking, January 13, 1953; and *China's Industry,* Vol. IV, No. 3, Shanghai, July 26, 1953.

90. NCNA, July 17, 1951.

91. *Economic Yearbook,* p. 26, Hongkong, 1951.

92. *New China Monthly,* Vol. II, No. 6, p. 1430, Peking, October, 1950.

93. See *Progress Daily,* Tientsin, July 1, 1952.

94. Cf. *Chinese Yearbook,* Vol. II, p. 1555, Nanking, 1948.

95. Cf. *Industry in Liberated Tientsin,* Shanghai, 1950; *China's Industry,* Vol. I, No. 8, December, 1949, and Vol. I, No. 10, February, 1950; and *People's Daily,* Peking, March 2, 1949.

96. *Industry and Commerce in Shanghai,* Vol. I, No. 25, p. 10, Shanghai, July 5, 1950.

97. *Ta-kung pao,* Shanghai, August 6, 1952.

98. *Shanghai Industry and Commerce,* Vol. I, No. 2, Shanghai, August, 1950.

99. Cf. *A Path for the Industrialists and Businessmen of New China,* pp. 163-167, Shanghai, 1950, and *Liberation Daily, Shanghai,* March 3, 1953.

100. *Chinese Yearbook,* Vol. II, Nanking, 1948.

101. *Progress Daily,* Tientsin, December 23, 1952.

102. See Pauley Commission Report, Appendix X.

103. *Northeast Daily,* Shen-yang, May 7 and September 11, 1949.

104. See *Northeast Daily,* Shen-yang, January 16, 1951, and NCNA, May 7, 1953.

105. Bureau of Information, *The Cement Industry,* pp. 8-9 and 19-20, Nanking, 1947.

106. *Ibid.* See also *Foreign Minerals Survey,* pp. 154-5, Washington, D.C., 1948.

107. See Kao Kang, March 13, 1950.

108. Bureau of Information, *op. cit.*

109. *Northeast Daily,* Shen-yang, May 29, 1949.

110. *Northeast Daily,* Shen-yang, April 19, 1950.

111. Estimates based on a 1950 production of 430,000 tons. See Kao Kang, *op. cit.; New China Monthly,* Vol. III, No. 2, Peking, December, 1950, and No. 36, October, 1952; *Northeast Daily,* Shen-yang, May 29, 1949, and January 16, 1951; NCNA, May 7, 1953; and *Wen-hui pao,* Hongkong, August 26, 1953.

112. Cf. Bankers' Association, *Economic History of the Republic of China,* p. 342, Shanghai, 1948; T'an Hsi-hung, *A Preliminary Report on the Industrial Survey of China's Principal Cities,* pp. 36-41, Nanking, 1948; and *Far Eastern Economic Review,* p. 727, Hongkong, December, 1950.

113. See *New China Monthly,* p. 27, Peking, November, 1951.

114. Also reported at 4,090,000 bales. See Chen Yün's report to the National People's Congress on September 23, 1954. NCNA, September 23, 1954.

115. Cf. NCNA, December 14, 1953, and *Wen-hui pao, Hongkong,* October 1, 1953. The increase in the number of spindles and looms between 1950 and the end of 1954 has since been estimated at 22.3 per cent and 26.5 per cent respectively. NCNA, September 9, 1954.

116. The conversion ratio used is 1 bale of yarn for 1,300 meters of cloth. Cf. S. S. Blanchard, *Textile Industries of China and Japan,* New York, 1944, and NCNA, February 12, 1954.

117. There are about 180,000 hand looms in Communist China according to the *Ta-kung pao,* Tientsin, December 24, 1953.

118. See *New China Monthly,* pp. 169-170, Peking, February, 1954.

119. Figures based on a 24-hour day and 22 days a month and given in a survey dated September, 1950. A bag averages 22 kgs. See Huang Chih-ch'iu, China's Flour Industry, Past and Future, *China's Industry,* Vol. II, No. 6, Shanghai, October, 1950.

120. Huang Chih-ch'iu, *loc. cit.*

121. Cf. *Shansi Daily,* T'ai-yuan, January 6, 1954; *Masses Daily,* Hsi-an, January 1 and 9, 1954, and September 26, 1952; and *Ta-kung pao,* Hongkong, January 29–February 11, 1954.

122. See Li Chung-ying, "The Future of China's Food Industry," *China's Industry,* Vol. I, No. 11, Shanghai, March, 1950.

123. Cf. Ku T'ieh-feng, "The Future of China's Staple Food Industry," *China's Industry,* Vol. I, No. 8, Shanghai, December, 1949.

CHAPTER NINE

Forced Labor and Mass Labor Projects

I

THE ECONOMIC BASIS OF MASS LABOR CONSTRUCTION PROJECTS

Notwithstanding the considerable strides made by Communist China in industrial and agricultural recovery, the shortage of both capital and cultivated land remains acute. The only productive factor that exists in super-abundance is unskilled labor. This, of course, is not a new phenomenon as labor has always been used very intensively in all phases of production in China. However, the matter assumes a fresh twist when, in view of the policy of forced industrialization and the desire to expand both agricultural and industrial output, methods have to be devised so that the surplus labor can be used directly in creating new investments.

We speak of surplus labor. What is meant is that, given the productive techniques in use in China, in the absence of active government intervention, it is possible to produce the same output without having as many men ostensibly engaged in the production processes as is normally the case. In other words, there has always been a substantial amount of chronic, disguised, and partial unemployment or under-employment in China. This is true especially, but not exclusively, in the agricultural sector. Peasants and urban workers in small family workshops are not fully employed for want of other necessary productive factors, such as capital and land. As long as small individual farms exist, the personal holdings serve to tie down many of these semi-employed peasants, but, as the farms are consolidated through "cooperativization," the semi-employed become available for other work. The amalgamation movement engendered under the industrial and commercial adjustment programs has brought about the same development in the towns. Occasional reports on the emergence of urban unemployment and the drift of rural population to urban areas point to this general phenomenon in Communist China during the last few years although the situation could have been much worse if outright collectivization had been adopted instead of the comparatively gradual process of "cooperativization."[1]

It may be presumed that this surplus labor in agriculture and other fields is not very productive. Otherwise, disregarding the institutional factors that prevented it from taking up other employment in the past, it would have been possible to absorb it in other branches of production even under a system of free enterprise. However, while a private employer cannot use labor that is incapable of producing as much as it must be paid merely to subsist, for the economy as a whole the situation is somewhat different, for as long as this surplus unemployed labor is not eliminated through sheer starvation, it must continue to account for a certain portion of the national product consumed. In other words, it subsists on the actual or potential savings of those who are employed through provisions by the family, the clan, and other forms of "share work." Consequently, the national output can be increased if available surplus labor is put to productive employment as long as in doing so it does not consume more than it did before and if consumption by the formerly employed population is not allowed to increase now that it does not have to provide for the surplus labor directly. This statement is valid even if the surplus labor in question is extremely inefficient and unproductive. The only arrangement necessary is for the government to curtail consumption in general, principally through the grain tax and compulsory purchases, and to use the food and other consumers' goods thus made available to support the surplus labor now in the government's employ at a subsistence level not above its accustomed or necessary minimum level of consumption.

There is, of course, no need for the government to obtain such labor solely from the gradual release of formerly partially employed persons. Nor does it have to rely upon natural evolution to make surplus labor available. Victims of floods and other natural disasters, soldiers not needed for military operations, and those persons who, for one reason or another, have been permanently severed from their original employment and would have to be resettled, such as former employees of the Nationalist government, all constitute potential sources of labor. The pool of labor is virtually inexhaustible, and it is up to the authorities to regulate its size and to adopt a definite process to select individual persons for work on government projects.

The most obvious fields in which such labor can be used advantageously consist of construction projects which are not bound for technical reasons to require the complement of specific and large quantities of capital equipment and other factors in short supply. "Digging holes in the ground" in its many and varied forms presents itself as the most appropriate type of work. In more technical language, water conservation projects, building of highways and roadbeds for railways, timber felling, construction of defense works, excavation, and other similar projects all belong to this category.

SOME ECONOMIC ADVANTAGES OF RECRUITMENT UNDER COMPULSION

Theoretically, the requisite labor force may be recruited by the government on a voluntary basis. However, the line of demarcation between voluntary and forced labor is a thin one, and the Chinese Communists have expressed a preference for the latter.

There are two types of forced labor. For instance, civilians may be drafted to spend a minimum of ten man-days per person per year on the construction and maintenance of highways, for which they are only partially recompensed through rations.[2] Flood victims may be drafted to repair dykes on a compulsory work-relief basis. In most cases, such relatively short-term labor service represents an additional tax liability to the average person and may best be regarded as such. However, by far the more important type of forced labor in Communist China is on a longer term basis, not infrequently for periods of indefinite duration. This latter category consists of the permanent forced labor contingents recruited from among both ordinary convicts and "counter-revolutionaries."

From the economic point of view, the use of forced labor has several advantages. First, forced labor can be supported more cheaply than free labor. On a strict ration basis, it can be employed at a level of subsistence even below the minimum that must be paid in recruiting free labor.[3] In this way, what would otherwise be submarginal labor can now be employed even in those industrial, mining, and agricultural enterprises which must produce at a profit under the system of business accountability. Second, forced labor, especially by prisoners, can be employed on dangerous work without using some of the costly safeguards against serious accidents. Third, forced labor has the advantage of perfect mobility and can be moved without regard to family and other social ties. Fourth, given perfect mobility, forced labor becomes a readily exportable article and adds to the country's capacity to import capital goods for industrialization.

An offseting factor to the above advantages is that forced labor may be less productive. However, this is by no means certain. Although the lack of positive incentives may dampen the inventiveness of labor, it does not necessarily reduce productivity in purely unskilled work. In the short run, at any rate, fear and compulsion could conceivably be very effective as a means of producing work. Besides, there probably is no greater incentive to a person in a labor camp than the promise that he may one day be set free if the result of his work is satisfactory. Not a few of the labor models extolled in the Communist press have scored their production records in labor camps under such conditions.[4]

EVOLUTION OF THE SYSTEM OF FORCED LABOR

During the civil war the employment of forced labor to build defense works and to transport military supplies was a common practice. But the integration of forced labor to the country's production plans as an important and regular element was not formally recognized in Communist China's organic laws until recently. Apparently, what began primarily as a punitive measure to serve political ends has grown with practice into an accepted economic institution.

It may be recalled that in his exceedingly frank discourse on "Democratic Dictatorship"—a rather paradoxical term with which Mao Tse-tung chooses to describe the new regime—the Chinese Communist leader took pains in distinguishing between those who are the "people" and those who are not. "As for those belonging to reactionary classes or groups, after their political power has been overthrown, we will also give them land and work, permitting them to make a living and to reform themselves through labor into new persons—but only on condition that they do not rebel, commit sabotage, or create disturbances. If they do not want to work, the people's state will force them to do so."[5]

"Feudal landlords, bureaucratic capitalists, and reactionaries in general," again, according to Article 7 of the Common Program, "after they have been disarmed and shorn of their special powers, shall also be deprived of their political rights in accordance with law for a necessary period. But, at the same time, they shall be given some means of livelihood and *shall be compelled to reform themselves through labor so as to become new men.*" Finally, Article 19 of the 1954 Constitution states: "The state shall deprive the feudal landlords and bureaucratic capitalists of their political rights according to law and for specified periods, while granting them the means of livelihood so as *to enable them to reform themselves through labor* and to become self-supporting citizens."

The "land reform," which was the first of the endless array of mass movements we have discussed, probably supplied many of the first recruits of the forced labor contingents. The drive to suppress counter-revolutionaries which began soon after the outbreak of the Korean war and was followed by the three-anti and five-anti campaigns, as well as the commercial and industrial adjustment program, served to broaden the sphere of labor recruitment further. As Chou En-lai reported to the PPCC on October 23, 1951, death sentences passed on those counter-revolutionaries whose crimes were not too grievous could be suspended for two years during which time the prisoners would be put to forced labor. Suspension of the death sentence is not the same as commuting the sentence, for the fate of the doomed prisoner depends upon his conduct during the reprieve. "Only if there is a definite showing of willing acceptance on the part of the prisoner to be reformed will the death sentence be commuted to imprisonment for life or for a number of years during which he will be compelled to perform productive work."[6]

This general line of policy has been pursued through the past few years. Lest we should forget, the *People's Daily* again reminded us with the following revealing passage on September 7, 1954:

"During the past few years, our state has carried out with great fanfare and on a nation-wide scale the movement for the suppression of counter-revolutionaries, and arrested according to law large numbers of bandits, despots, special service agents, backbone elements of reactionary parties and corps, and leaders of reactionary societies and religious sects. . . . Of the many counter-revolutionaries and other criminals, the minority, guilty of arch crimes and persistent in their refusal to repent, had to be given the death penalty in accordance with the law of the state to appease the people's hatred for them.

As for the majority of the criminals, our state organs have generally . . . sentenced them to prison terms, deprived them of political rights, and carried out their reform through forced labor, . . . and during the process of labor, conducted among them political and ideological education."

The above passage appeared at the time when the Communist authorities made public both the Regulations Governing Labor Service for Reform and the report by the Minister of Public Security on the drafting of the regulations.[7] According to the official explanation, the new law summarizes the experience of the last few years and was drawn up with the advice of Soviet experts.

In the first place, labor service is to be rendered in (1) prisons, (2) detention houses, (3) institutes for juvenile delinquents, and (4) labor-service-for-reform corps. Convicts not suited to labor service in the open, including counter-revolutionaries under suspended death sentences or serving life, as well as other important criminals, are to perform compulsory labor service in prison. Criminals serving a two-year or shorter sentence who cannot be conveniently sent to labor reform corps work in the detention houses. Light labor service is reserved for juvenile delinquents between the ages of 13 and 18 in special institutes. All convicted counter-revolutionaries and other criminals suited to labor service in the open are consigned to forced labor corps.

Article 30 of the new regulations provides, "Production in labor service for reform shall serve the interests of national construction, and be *included in the state's production and construction plans.*" The direction of production by this forced labor shall be, according to Article 33, "the concentrated operation of productive activities in provinces and municipalities in all-out efforts for agricultural production; the undertaking of industrial and mining enterprises which have possibilities for development; and the organization of production in water conservation, road building, and other construction projects."

As for the working conditions, the general approach is summarized rather succinctly in the official statement that "such labor is forced, and is carried out without compensation and under strict control. The government organs carrying out this task are thus not ordinary production units, but one of the tools of the people's democratic dictatorship, i.e., organs for the punishment and reform of all counter-revolutionary and other criminals."[8] Consequently, only two days of rest are allowed each month, and the work day is generally from 9 to 10 hours. Furthermore, during periods of peak activity, a 12-hour day may be enforced. Finally, in no case may the period of "study" reserved for the prisoners' "re-education" be less than one hour a day. The long hours are aggravated by the fact that prisoners may be visited by members of their families not more than twice a month, each time for 30 minutes or less, and that they may be shifted from place to place in accordance with "plans for the transfer of criminal manpower" drawn up by the Ministry of Public Security on the basis of "the number of criminals in different areas, conditions relating to production, and the needs of national construction."[9]

THE SIZE AND EFFECT OF FORCED LABOR

The rather elaborate system set up for the management of forced labor[10] and the types of work to which it is usually assigned would seem to indicate that the size of this labor contingent which is available to do the bidding of the state anywhere and at all times, i.e., as long as the government's police control is effectively maintained, is very large indeed. "According to statistical returns from different areas, of the criminals in confinement throughout the country more than 83 per cent have participated in agricultural and industrial production or have been organized into various engineering corps for the felling of timber, construction of buildings, restoration and construction of conservation works, and the building of railways and highways."[11] Thus virtually the entire prisoner population of Communist China has been employed in forced labor at one time or another. No official report has ever been released on the size of the prisoner population. However, it may be safely assumed that the number of persons under detention and sent to forced labor exceeds the number of persons executed. For instance, after the mass arrests in the drive to suppress "counter-revolutionaries" in 1951, the proportion of prisoners sent to forced labor was reported to be 50 per cent in the Central-South, 65 per cent in the Southwest, and as high as 90 per cent in Shansi province in North China.[12] According to Father Tennien's estimate, the number of persons imprisoned in China by mid-1952 totalled 20 million as against 7 million killed.[13] Another estimate has put the total number of killings in 1950–1953 at 15 million.[14] While these figures are all guesses based on incomplete returns, the scale of forced labor is doubtless staggering.

According to a recent report from Nationalist Chinese sources, the number of mainland Chinese doing forced labor is about 23 million.[15] These are distributed in the following manner:

	In million persons
Water conservation projects	10.00
Tele-communication projects	1.00
Government farms	1.00
Labor export	3.00
Transportation projects	0.25
Other	8.00
Total	23.25

Allowing for some exaggeration, it is nevertheless certain that the total number must be exceedingly large. There is no particular reason why the forced labor contingent should not continue to grow as the only important limiting factor is the availability of sufficient party cadres and military force to keep the workers under control. Clearly, without this large labor force, the rate of capital investment in Communist China would be noticeably smaller.

As the Communist Minister of Public Security has reported, income from production by forced labor during 1950–1953, after deducting the living costs of the criminals and the other necessary expenses incurred in the work of reform through labor, "has been accumulated in the forms of fixed capital and working capital to an amount approximately equal to the expenses appropriated by the state for reform through labor."[16] Thus the economic analysis advanced above seems to have been borne out by Communist practice. The same report also mentions that by 1955, as far as the forced labor projects are concerned, "the aggregate income and expenditure in the country as a whole may approach balance." If this means that the forced labor projects can become more or less self-supporting, Communist China's capacity to accumulate capital may rise accordingly. A survey of some of the mass labor projects in which forced labor is an important factor follows.

II

THE SIGNIFICANCE OF WATER CONSERVATION PROJECTS

One of the most important sources of demand for mass labor in Communist China so far, about which considerable information is available, has been the various water conservation projects undertaken in different parts of the country. These constructions promise to constitute a continuing and possibly expanding demand until such time when long-range plans of flood control, irrigation, and the related effort in land reclamation can be executed on a lasting basis so that the task of maintenance can be reduced to normal proportions. This situation is the result of two factors. First, there is an urgent need for flood control and irrigation. Second, mass labor projects, while adequate enough to provide stop-gap relief, do not seem to offer as yet permanent solutions without the constant expenditure of labor for maintenance and repair on a large scale.

During 1949, 6.6 million hectares of the country's farm land were affected by flood while another 1.3 million hectares suffered from drought. In the following year, although the drought area was only 700,000 hectares, some 4 million hectares of farm land were completely inundated. Worst of all was the flooding of the Hwai River and its tributaries in Honan and Anhwei where 2.8 million hectares of farm land were under water and 13 million persons were rendered homeless.[17] It was this situation that prompted the Communist authorities to embark upon a series of large-scale mass labor projects of which the Hwai River control program was one of the most important.

Although water conservation work such as that on the Hwai River serves multiple purposes, improvement of inland water transport and development of hydro-electric power have been of secondary importance thus far. The primary concern of the Communist authorities has been the prevention of serious floods and the extension of irrigation to a larger crop area. The purpose is to minimize loss of farm land thrugh either drought or flood and to raise the unit area yield on irrigated land. In both respects the strenuous efforts have been rewarded with a certain measure of success although favorable weather conditions, especially in 1952, should be given greater credit than the Communist authorities would probably admit.

According to Fu Tso-yi, Communist Minister of Water Conservation, the area of irrigated land in the country was increased by 3.7 million hectares during 1950–1953 as a result of the various projects carried out on the Hwai River, the Yellow River, and the Yangtze, as well as many other smaller undertakings.[18] Compared with the 26 million hectares of irrigated paddy fields estimated for mainland China,[19] this represents a significant step forward and is probably the underlying factor accounting for the increase in rice production during this period. However, only 800,000 hectares were accounted for by the larger irrigation projects while most of the increase was the result of small irrigation schemes and better water utilization on the part of the peasantry. The larger water conservation projects were primarily responsible for the reduction of inundation and the setting of favorable conditions for the expansion of irrigation efforts. Besides, although the flood area declined through 1950–1952,[20] more land was actually affected by drought in 1951 than in the preceding years. Thus for the country as a whole the effect of irrigation was to a large extent liable to be nullified by unfavorable weather conditions.

Even the flood control projects, while eminently successful in the short run, do not appear to have been completely adequate to cope with the vagaries of nature, as may be witnessed by the inundation of some 6 per cent of the country's farm land again in 1954 in spite of the temporary improvement up to that time.[21] According to one official report, the repair of dykes in Hupeh, Kiangsi, Anhwei, Kiangsu, Chekiang, and Hopeh following the 1954 flood damage may require 5 to 6 million civilian laborers working for three months. A great deal of the work has to be done on the Ching-chiang dykes, the site of a major project in 1952.[22] The areas afflicted by flood in Kiangsu and Chekiang in 1954 also happened to be areas of concentrated work in the previous years. While the unusually heavy rains in 1954 may have played an important role in this most recent natural disaster, it is suspected that the basic cause of the recurrence of flood damage so soon after the completion of some of the major conservation works lies in the poor quality of the constructions undertaken.

The stop-gap nature of the water conservation work during recent years is clearly illustrated by the statement of government intention in the *Yangtze Daily* in advance of the Ching-chiang project in 1952. "The aim of the long-range Ching-chiang project is to build dams and reservoirs on the upper course of the river; to dredge the river and to straighten its course on the lower reaches; and to divert flood water into areas north of the Yangtze on the middle course so as to raise the level of the north bank with alluvium. But such a project cannot be carried out completely in the near future because many of the major undertakings cannot yet be started. Consequently, since the water level of the river may exceed that reached during the 1931 and 1949 floods in the next few years, it is necessary to take temporary measures such as reinforcing the main Ching-chiang dyke yearly and building the Ching-chiang reservoir before the high water period begins. The present Ching-chiang project will be useful for 20 to 40 years. Meanwhile, the long-range Yangtze program can be carried out."[23] The obviously short-range objective of the Ching-chiang project in 1952 also characterized most of the other undertakings.

According to the official data of the Communist Ministry of Water Conservation, the volume of work done in 1950–1953 on all water conservation undertakings aggregated 2.7 billion cubic meters of earthwork, 17 million cubic meters of masonwork, and only 600,000 cubic meters of cement and concrete constructions.[24] Although the above figures include the work of individual peasants, as well as the dredging of river channels, and accordingly comprise an unavoidably large amount of earthwork, the preponderance of earthwork relative to other constructions that are more durable is of great significance.[25]

Permanent constructions with materials more capable of withstanding the wear and tear of nature have not been made partly because to carry them out might have taken more time. However, lack of machinery and the necessary construction materials, especially cement and steel, together with the shortage of engineering skill and trained labor, was the really decisive factor. Thus the building of temporary earth construction was an unavoidable but rational choice even though, in adopting such a policy, the authorities also accepted in advance the continuing need for large-scale repair and maintenance during the years to come.

The poor quality of the earth constructions should not detract from the gigantic scale of some of the undertakings. In fact, the employment of mass labor is the only factor that compensates for the lack of construction machinery. As reported by Fu Tso-yi, Communist Minister of Water Conservation, the cumulative total of civilian laborers engaged in water conservation work during 1950 and 1951 amounted to 10,370,000 persons.[26] According to the *New China Monthly,* the 1.7 billion cubic meters of earthwork completed in 1950–1952 represented the effort of 20 million civilian laborers mobilized for this purpose.[27] While these figures are cumulative totals, and the number of laborers at work at any one time was undoubtedly smaller, the gigantic scale of these mass labor projects can be clearly envisaged. During the first period of the Hwai River program, for instance, some 2,200,000 persons were employed in building the dykes. Including the porters for carrying earth and other materials at the work sites, the total number of laborers employed on construction was over 3 million. In addition, in North Anhwei alone, 60,000 persons were employed in transporting the supplies to the work sites by boat while another 900,000 laborers were used in carrying supplies on land. Thus the total number of workers, excluding the troops, technicians, and engineers, was well over 4 million during the first phase of the Hwai River work alone.[28] During the second phase of the Hwai project, 600,000 civilian laborers were at work in the winter of 1951. By the spring of 1952, 2,400,000 laborers were gathered at the work sites. Of these about one million worked on the dykes.[29] Although not all the laborers worked at the same time, the total expenditure of labor in a two-month period in the first phase of the Hwai program during the winter of 1950–1951 amounted to 80 million man-days for dyke work alone.[30] In all East China, including the Hwai project, total expenditure of labor during 1951 amounted to 67.5 million man-days.[31] Other figures for individual smaller projects could be cited almost indefinitely. For instance, during 1950, 320,000 laborers were employed on conservation work on the Yellow River while another 380,000 troops were similarly engaged.[32] On the Ching-chiang project, a much smaller undertaking compared with the Hwai program, 240,000 workers, together with 10,000 troops, were deployed at one time.[33] At one time, during 1954, 60,000 laborers were employed in strengthening the Ching-chiang dykes while one million men were similarly employed along the Yantze in Anhwei province and comparable numbers were mobilized on the lower section of the Hwai.[34]

All these data, though incomplete, point unmistakably to the large numbers of laborers invariably employed on such undertakings. According to the information available, allowing for women and child labor,[35] the amount of excavation done per man-day with the most primitive tools probably averages less than two cubic meters. If we assume that future water conservation work in terms of earthwork should remain at the annual average of the 1950–1953 period or about 670 million cubic meters, about 335 million man-days would be required every year. Assuming further that most of the work has to be done during the winter and early spring in the low water season, on the basis of 100 working days, we could probably estimate the labor force required at 3.4 million persons. This would seem to compare fairly reasonably with the general order of magnitude maintained in recent years. In addition to the above, however, one has to take into account the porters on the work sites, the transport workers for hauling over longer distances, the skilled workers, the technicians and engineers, and, last but not least, the troops and party cadres who oversee the projects. Thus the total labor force required every year might conceivably be 5 million or above. In case of serious floods, repair of damage, together with new constructions and normal maintenance, would, of course, necessitate an even greater expenditure of labor. Until mechanical tools could be adopted widely, it is not difficult to see what a vital role the forced labor contingents are destined to play in carrying out Communist China's capital construction program for the better utilization of its land resources.

In this connection, one might note a most interesting passage in a Communist publication intended to depict the enthusiasm and spirit of self-sacrifice on the part of the laborers working on one particular section of the Ching-chiang project. "The (water conservation) fighters thought of every possible method to cope with the mud. . . . They loaded it into wooden vessels which they pushed on the swamp's miry surface. Sometimes a whole company would stand in a long file, two abreast, using carriers' wooden poles to shove the mud from the center of the swamp outward. Others on the side then filled it in wooden barrels and wash tubs and handed these out (to the shore). When there were not enough containers, many used their own cloth wrappers to carry mud or made sacks out of trousers for the same purpose."[36] One may question whether the laborers' efforts were really spontaneous and voluntary, but there is no better illustration of the virtual absence of construction machinery in this case, which is all the more illuminating as the shortage is in no way unique.

THE HWAI RIVER CONSERVANCY PROJECT

Up to the present time, the most important single project in water conservation undertaken in Communist China is the Hwai River program. As mentioned before, the severe flood in 1950 wrought havoc in the Hwai basin, which runs through the provinces of Honan, Anhwei, and Kiangsu. Upon direct instructions by Mao Tse-tung, a special conference was called by the Ministry of Water Conservation towards the end of August, 1950, to consider the problem. After two weeks' deliberations, the Conference recommended that as a general principle the harnessing of the river should be undertaken with "equal emphasis upon both the conservation and the drainage of floodwater," and that floodwater should be stored in the upper section of the river with a view to developing water resources, while both conservation and drainage should be attempted in the middle section of the river and channels leading to the sea should be opened and dredged.[37] Shortly after the conference, the State Administrative Council decided on October 14, 1950, to establish a Hwai River Conservation Commission with three provincial headquarters and three local project construction bureaus to supervise the prosecution of the program.

The final plan as prepared by the Commission, with Soviet advice, provides for (1) the construction of 13 reservoirs in the mountainous areas on the upper course of the river in Honan province, together with several floodwater storage units on marshy lakes and lowlands, and 3 reservoirs and 9 water storage units in Northern Anhwei; (2) channel improvements and corrections on the main course of the Hwai, as well as its tributaries in Honan and Anhwei; and (3) the opening of a new outlet to the sea at T'ao-tzu-k'ou.[38] In conjunction with the storage of floodwater, the plan envisages the eventual addition of 400,000 to 600,000 hectares of irrigated rice fields in Honan, about 670,000 hectares of rice fields in northern Anhwei, and 1,670,000 hectares of rice fields in northern Kiangsu, or a total of 2,740,000 to 2,940,000 hectares.[39] In addition to the increased yield from the irrigated fields, estimated at 50 per cent[40] of the original output, a potential sizable loss in food crops through the frequent inundation of some 400,000 hectares of farm land in the area can also be avoided. Finally, cheaper transportation will be provided by the Hwai River serving as a more effective link between the Grand Canal and the Yangtze on the one hand, and the Peking-Hankow and the Tientsin-Pukow Railways on the other hand.[41]

The original plan divided the preliminary stage of stop-gap constructions on the Hwai River into two phases. The first phase began in the winter of 1950, although most of the work was done in the spring of 1951. Before the high water season in 1951, work had been completed on one reservoir and four marshy lake and low land floodwater storage areas in Honan, four storage areas and a diversion dam in northern Anhwei, and channel improvements and dyke constructions on a number of the many tributaries of the river.[42] The second phase began in November, 1951. By May, 1952, one reservoir each had been constructed in Honan and Anhwei while construction on the main irrigation channel in northern Kiangsu was also near completion.[43] By October, 1953, total past constructions on the Hwai project included the three reservoirs mentioned above and a total of 16 storage units for receiving flood runoff. Dredging had been done over a total distance of 2,969 kilometers on 77 rivers, and 1,562 kilometers of dykes had been strengthened and repaired. However, the last items are probably cumulative figures and represent to a large extent maintenance work. By 1954, three reservoirs were still under construction, while work apparently had not yet begun on several others.[44] On the basis of these reports it appears that progress has become increasingly slower as the demand for labor and materials by repair and maintenance on previously finished constructions increases. Another contributing factor is that the remaining constructions are probably more difficult from the engineering point of view.[45]

THE CHING-CHIANG PROJECT

Next in importance to the harnessing of the Hwai River is the Ching-chiang project, the preliminary phase of which was carried out in 1952. The section of the Yangtze between Chih-chiang in Hupeh and Ch'eng-ling-chi in Hunan is also known as the Ching-chiang. In case of high water, the Yangtze may burst either its northern or southern dyke at this point. In case of a breach of the northern dyke, some 500,000 hectares of farm land on the fertile Yangtze and Han River plains would be inundated, and more than 3 million persons would be affected. Moreover, flooding of this area would seriously threaten Hankow which is the principal center of trade and transportation connecting the area served by the Yangtze with the Peking-Hankow and Hankow-Canton Railways. On the other hand, if a breach should occur on the southern dyke, water from the Yangtze would surge into the slited Tung-t'ing Lake, which serves as a natural reservoir under normal conditions, and thereby inundate an area of over 700,000 hectares of farm land in the Hunan rice bowl.[46] Accordingly, the Ching-chiang project was designed to avert this threat.

Plans for the Ching-chiang project were drawn up in 1951 by the Yangtze River Water Conservation Commission and were put into operation in the spring of 1952. The first stage of the project consisted of the construction of a large reservoir to retard the river current and to protect the main nothern dyke. In addition, the main dyke was to be reinforced and several lock gates were to be constructed at the reservoir to regulate the flow of floodwater. The entire project, involving some 8 million cubic meters of earthwork, 100,000 cubic meters of cement work, and 10,000 cubic meters of masonwork, took less than three months and was reportedly completed by the end of June, 1952.[47]

However, although no serious flooding was reported in 1952 and 1953, the makeshift work apparently failed to cope with the high water in 1954, when the Hankow area was under water for a considerable length of time during the summer and traffic was halted on the Hankow-Canton Railway. This seems further to confirm the view that water conservation work in Communist China is still of a rather haphazard nature and that the need for technical improvisation, unavoidable as it is under the circumstances, has left much to chance.

THE KUAN-T'ING RESERVOIR PROJECT

Another important construction project undertaken by Communist China, though on a much smaller scale in comparison with the Hwai project, is represented by the Kuan-t'ing reservoir on the Yung-ting river near Peking and Tientsin. The reservoir, which is the largest in mainland China, covers an area of 230 square kilometers and has a total storage capacity of 2,270 million cubic meters. Its construction serves to control flood water on the Yung-ting and is expected to provide irrigation for 100,000 hectares of farm land. However, most important of all, it helps to open up navigation channels in the area, and a hydroelectric plant utilizing the harnessed water will supply power to the new industrial plants in Peking.

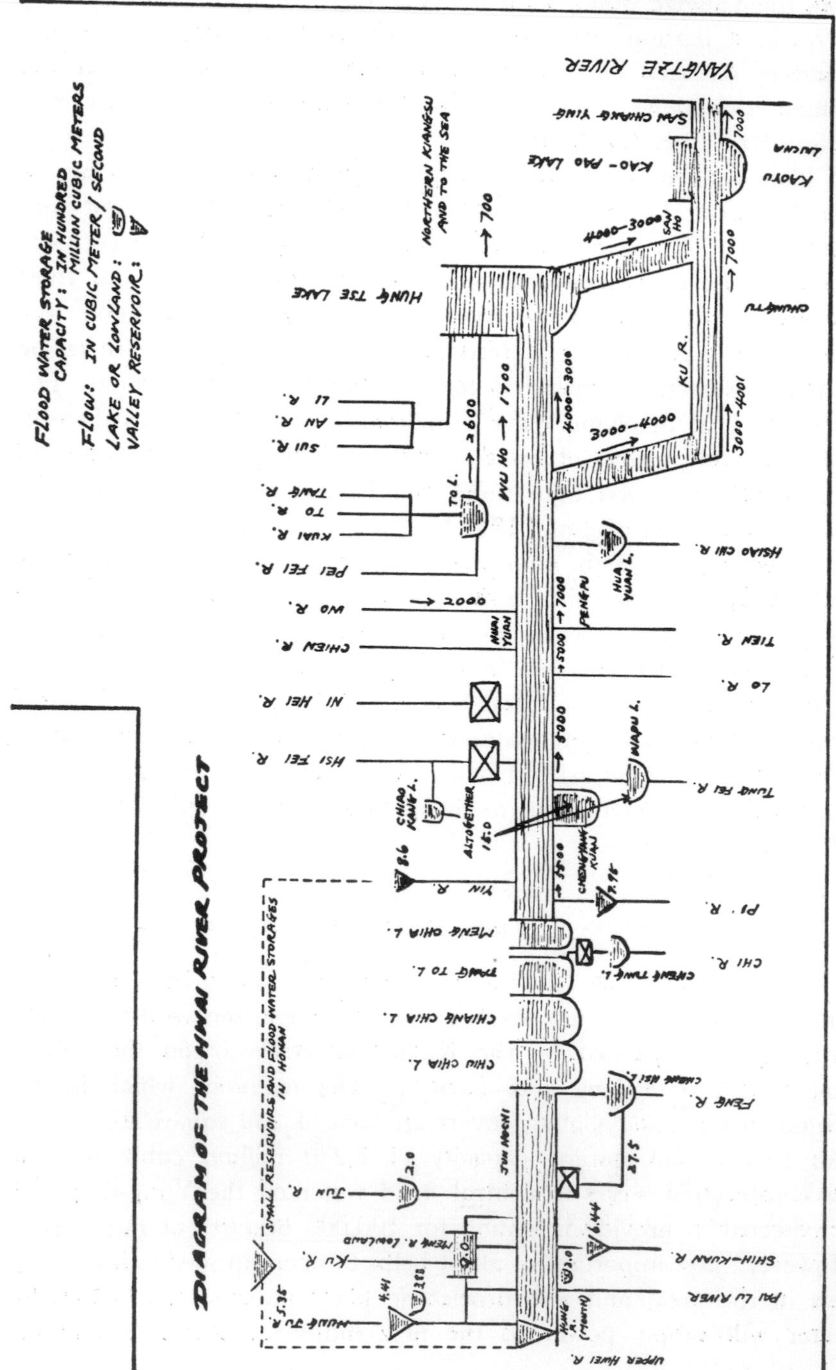
DIAGRAM OF THE HWAI RIVER PROJECT
FLOOD WATER STORAGE
CAPACITY: IN HUNDRED MILLION CUBIC METERS
FLOW: IN CUBIC METER / SECOND
LAKE OR LOWLAND:
VALLEY RESERVOIR:
YANGTZE RIVER
NORTHERN KIANGSU AND TO THE SEA
HUNG TSE LAKE
KAO-PAO LAKE
SAN CHIANG YING
KAOYU
KU R.
WU HO
PEI FEI R.
WO R.
CHIEN R.
NI HEI R.
HSI FEI R.
YIN R.
MENG CHIA L.
CHIANG CHIA L.
CHIU CHIA L.
JUN R.
KU R.
HSIAO CHI R.
TIEN R.
LO R.
TUNG FEI R.
PI R.
CHI R.
FENG R.
SHIH-KUAN R.
PAI LU RIVER
UPPER HWAI R.
SMALL RESERVOIRS AND FLOOD WATER STORAGES IN HONAN
PREPARED BY K. Y. HSU

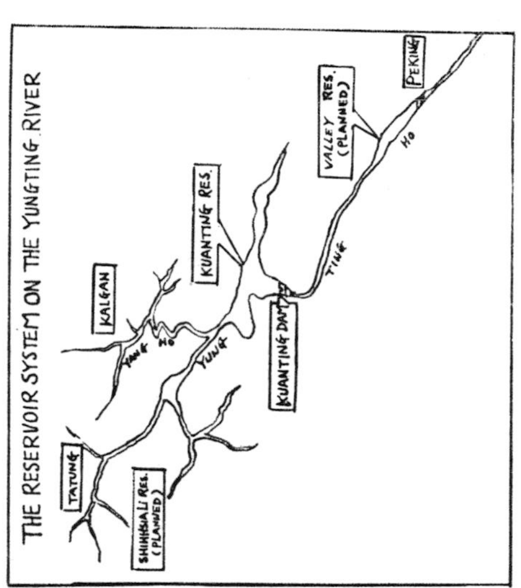
THE RESERVOIR SYSTEM ON THE YUNGTING RIVER
TATUNG
SHIHHSIALI RES. (PLANNED)
KALGAN
YANG HO
YUNG
KUANTING DAM
KUANTING RES.
TING
VALLEY RES. (PLANNED)
HO
PEKING

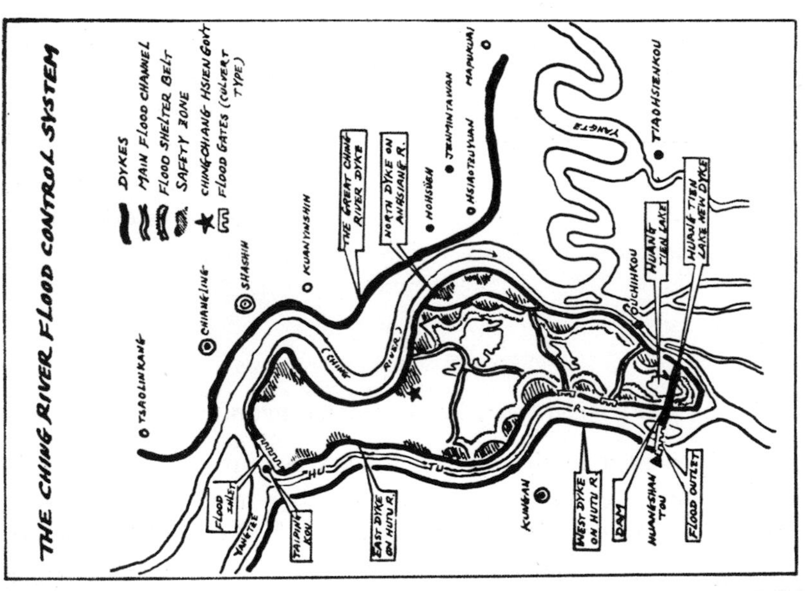
THE CHING RIVER FLOOD CONTROL SYSTEM
DYKES
MAIN FLOOD CHANNEL
FLOOD SHELTER BELT
SAFETY ZONE
CHINGCHIANG-HSIEN GOV'T
FLOOD GATES (CULVERT TYPE)
TSAOLINKANG
CHIANGLING
SHASHIH
KUANYINSHIH
THE GREAT CHING RIVER DYKE
NORTH DYKE ON ANHSIANG R.
HOHSUEH
JENMINTAWAN
HSIAOTSUYUAN
MAPUKUAI
YANGTZE
TIAOHSIENKOU
OUCHIHKOU
HUANG TIEN LAKE
HUANG-TIEN LAKE NEW DYKE
CHING RIVER
HU
TU
R.
FLOOD INLET
YANGTZE
TAIPING KOU
EAST DYKE ON HUTU R.
KUNGAN
WEST DYKE ON HUTU R.
DAM
HUANGSHAN TOU
FLOOD OUTLET

The decision to proceed with the project was made in the winter of 1949. Actual construction began in October, 1951, and was by and large complete by the end of 1953. In the building of the flood water channel alone, 2,500,000 cubic meters of earthwork and 47,500 cubic meters of cement construction were done. Although official reports have not given any detailed account of the number of persons employed on the project, civilian labor was partly drawn from the Kalgan area.[48]

SOME OF THE OTHER FLOOD CONTROL AND IRRIGATION PROJECTS

In addition to the two projects described above, Communist China has also undertaken a number of similar constructions in other areas of the country. Mention should be made especially of the raising of the dyke on the Yellow River and reinforcement on both its lower and upper sections; the dredging of the channels of several rivers in Shantung and Kiangsu; and the construction of new dykes and a water reservoir on the Jao-yang and Hun Rivers in Manchuria. The larger irrigation projects which have been either expanded or repaired under the present regime are located in a large number of provinces, including Honan, Shensi, Ningsia, Sinkiang, Tsinghai, and Szechwan, not to mention the various schemes in Manchuria, Hopeh, Anhwei, Kiangsu, and Fukien.[49] None of these, however, could be regarded as major efforts, and most of the scattered irrigation schemes are essentially little more than the continuation of work initiated by the Nationalists or earlier regimes.[50]

III

AFFORESTATION AND TIMBER PRODUCTION

Closely related to the water conservation projects on the Hwai, Yellow, Yung-ting, and other rivers, a program of afforestation has been actively pursued by Communist China.[51] In addition, the creation of shelter belts and the reafforestation of areas denuded by fire and timber cutting, which has been frequently indiscriminate, have also been given considerable attention. This is quite understandable, both on account of the importance of afforestation as a means of soil conservation and because of the increasing demand for timber for the many construction purposes.

However, it was pointed out by the State Administrative Council in a directive, dated September 30, 1953, that development of the country's forest resources was greatly handicapped by the shortage of machinery and skilled workers, and that mobilization of civilian labor was the only effective remedy.[52] Even in Manchuria, where mechanization has made the most progress, timber cutting is still completely dependent on manual labor.[53] As the area of afforestation increases and as timber production rises, the demand for labor will expand accordingly. Although the mass labor in question can be supplied partly by peasants drafted from nearby places for short periods as the demand is highly seasonal, forced labor contingents have been employed by Communist China all the time. This observation is substantiated not only by such reports as the personal story of an escapee from some of the Manchurian labor camps mentioned earlier, but also by open reference in official publications to the same effect.[54]

According to official reports, the number of persons "mobilized under the leadership of government and party workers" for afforestation in 1950 totalled 100,000 in western Hopeh and 250,000 in Liaohsi province in Manchuria. In the same year, 128,000 civilian workers were employed in cutting timber in the entire country.[55] Although there has not been any detailed information on similar employment in the subsequent years, a rough idea of the size of mass labor in afforestation and timber production may be obtained by referring to the growth of the area afforested and that of timber output since 1950. The relevant data are presented in the following tables:

AREA OF AFFORESTATION IN COMMUNIST CHINA

1950-1953

(In hectares)

Year	Hectares
1950	119,000
1951	404,000
1952	827,000
1953 (plan)	1,498,000

Sources: Economic Bulletin, Nos. 302-303, p. 19, Hongkong, January, 1953; and *New China Monthly,* No. 37, pp. 174-176, Peking, November, 1952, and No. 49, pp. 120-121, October, 1953.

TIMBER PRODUCTION IN COMMUNIST CHINA
1949-1954
(In thousand cubic meters)

1949	4,318
1950	4,750
1951	8,809
1952	9,543
1953 (plan)	13,360
1954 (estimate)	16,690

Sources: New China Monthly, No. 37, pp. 174-178, Peking, November, 1952; *Economic Bulletin*, No. 128, p. 7, Hongkong, July, 1949, and No. 314, p. 12, April, 1953; *Northeast Daily*, Shen-yang, May 7, 1950; and NCNA, April 26, 1954.

Taking into consideration that the 1950 figures for afforestation workers do not include many other areas, the three-fold growth of the annual volume between 1950 and 1953 should be accompanied by at least a corresponding increase in labor requirement. The same is true with respect to timber production, although changes in techniques may have somewhat reduced the average labor input per unit of cut timber. Thus one may put the total annual labor requirement for afforestation and timber cutting in Communist China at between one and two million persons.[56]

IV

OTHER USES FOR FORCED LABOR

While water conservation and afforestation may account for the bulk of forced labor in Communist China, other fields of employment, especially railway construction, are no less important. Without going into details, the variety of activities in which forced labor plays a significant role may be gleaned from several passages in an article entitled "Reform Criminals into New Men" published in the *People's Daily* of October 6, 1954.

"Corrective labor units engaged in agricultural production have now included a number of large farms, some of which are semi-mechanized. In the Ching-ho Farm in Peking, for instance, the average output of rice reaches 741 catties per *mow,* being 54 per cent in excess of the output of local peasants. In the Kwang-han Farm in Szechwan, an average of 851 catties per *mow* has been reported in the wheat fields. In some farms, land tilling has been supplemented by the development of animal husbandry, including the rearing of pigs, sheep, and cattle. The corrective labor farms in different parts of the country have exerted a definite influence over the giving of support to the country's industrial construction.

"Corrective labor production is not confined to agricultural enterprises, but also includes industrial activities, mining, and the operation of kilns. To a certain extent, these undertakings are coordinated with the capital construction of the state and supply in part the consumption needs of the people. The bricks produced by a certain labor unit in a certain locality have met the needs of urban construction in the area. The hosiery works of the Peking prison produced in 1953 32 per cent of all socks manufactured in the whole North China region. A certain corrective labor factory in Shen-yang produced restored rubber and molds of very good quality for casting steel. The various corrective labor engineering corps, such as the Hwai River Engineering Corps, the Tienshui-Lanchou Railways Work Corps,[57] have carried out engineering works in conformity with specifications, and many of them have been repeatedly extolled by the relevant engineering bureaus."

There is no way in which one can arrive at reasonably accurate estimates of the size of forced labor and its relative importance in these various productive activities, especially in industry. However, as the number of state farms increases with the accelerated collectivization program, it may be assumed that the number of corrective labor units engaged directly in agricultural production will expand considerably. The same is probably true in some of the other fields. To quote again the author of the above article, "production from corrective labor, starting from small to large scales, developing from scattered to concentrated units, has now been carried to a definite stage and is producing considerable effects in its coordination with the economic construction of the state." These effects are undoubtedly most significant in two vital areas of general economic development—the conservation and utilization of the country's land resources, and the creation of an effective transportation network, especially railways. We have devoted much of the present chapter to the first of these two items. We shall discuss the second in the next chapter.

NOTES

1. See the government directive on the prevention of the "planless" influx of peasants into cities in *People's Daily,* Peking, March 15, 1954.

2. See *New China Monthly,* No. 21, p. 666, Peking, July, 1951.

3. Cf. *People's Daily,* Peking, February 17, 1951. Even unemployed free labor is not under any pressure to work for less than the subsistence it receives from other sources.

4. Cf. Pei You-ming, *I Came from a Northeast Slave Labor Camp,* Hongkong, 1954, the personal story of an escapee. Also *People's Daily,* Peking, October 6, 1954.

5. Mao Tse-tung, *On People's Democratic Dictatorship,* 1949. All italics are ours.

6. *People's Daily,* Peking, May 1, 1951.

7. NCNA, September 7, 1954. The above regulations were adopted by the State Administrative Council on August 26, 1954.

8. *People's Daily,* September 7, 1954.

9. Articles 52 and 35 of the regulations quoted above.

10. Cf. the descriptive account in Su Wei-ch'üan, *Slave Labor Camps in Northern Shensi,* Hongkong, 1954.

11. *People's Daily,* September 7, 1954.

12. NCNA, October 21, and December 15, 1951, and *Yangtze Daily,* December 13, 1951.

13. Mark Tennien, *No Secret Is Safe Behind the Bamboo Curtain,* New York, 1952.

14. Assistant Secretary of State Walter Robertson's testimony to the House Appropriations Committee, February 23, 1954.

15. Committee for Free Asia report from Taipeh, February 16, 1954. Cf. also Li T'ien-min, *A Factual Account of Communist China's Destruction of Human Rights in the Last Five Years,* pp. 25-27, Taipeh, 1955. The presence of Chinese political prisoners working in the Soviet gold mines at Kolyma has been reported in *Fortune,* p. 159, February, 1954. The export of 1,500,000 laborers to Poland and other parts of eastern Europe in exchange for the import of military supplies was also reported by Li. Finally, Chinese laborers were reported in 1952 to be working on the Trans-Siberian Railway.

16. NCNA, September 7, 1954.

17. *Economic Weekly,* No. 40, p. 802, Shanghai, 1952, and *New China Monthly,* Vol. II, No. 5, Peking, September, 1950.

18. From 1.6 to 1.8 million hectares were brought under irrigation during 1952 while the increase in irrigated acreage was about 1.2 million hectares in 1950-1951 and 0.7 to 0.9 million hectares in 1953. *Ta-kung pao,* Tientsin, June 7, 1954; *New China Monthly,* No. 17, pp. 1083-1084, Peking, March, 1951, No. 35, p. 135, September, 1952, and No. 42, p. 125, April, 1953; and *Economic Weekly,* No. 8, p. 16, Shanghai, February, 1953. The relative importance of small irrigation schemes and water utilization on individual farms may be seen in the following aggregate figures for the 1950-1953 period: wells sunk, 800,000; small irrigation ponds, channels, and ditches, 6 million units; and small dams, 210,000 units. These may be compared with a total of 15,371 irrigation works and only 250 units of larger irrigation ponds, channels, and ditches constructed in the same period. Cf. *Ta-kung pao,* Tientsin, June 7, 1954, and NCNA, January 29, 1954.

19. *Manual for Newspaper Readers,* pp. 562-563, Hankow, 1950.

20. The area of inundated farm land was 1.4 million hectares in 1951 and 1.1 million hectares in 1952 while 4 million hectares were under water in 1950. On the

other hand, the drought area amounted to 2.3 million hectares in 1951 as compared with 700,000 hectares in 1950. Cf. *Economic Weekly,* No. 40, p. 802, Shanghai, 1952, and *New China Monthly,* p. 16, Peking, November, 1951.

21. NCNA, August 22, 1954. This puts the inundated area at well over 6 million hectares and the scale of disaster at above the 1950 level.

22. NCNA, October 11, 1954.

23. Hankow, March 18, 1952.

24. Cf. Fu Tso-yi's report, *Ta-kung pao,* Tientsin, June 7, 1954. For 1952, 1.05 billion cubic meters of earthwork were done in comparison with only 7 million cubic meters of masonwork. *Wen-hui pao,* Hongkong, September 30, 1953.

25. In the Hwai River project, the proportion of masonwork and concrete constructions amounted to 1.5 per cent of the earthwork done in the first period (1950-1951), and less than 0.5 per cent in the second period (1951-1952). Cf. *Control of the Hwai River,* published by the Hwai River Conservation Commission, Shanghai, 1952, and *People's Daily,* Peking, June 23 and August 7, 1952.

26. *People's Daily,* Peking, November 5, 1951.

27. Quoted in Akira Doi, "Facts about 'Unpaid Labor' in People's China," *Aziya Kenkyu,* Vol. I, No. 1, p. 119, Tokyo, 1954.

28. Hwai River Conservation Commission, *op. cit.,* 1952.

29. *Ibid.,* also *Liberation Daily,* Shanghai, March 17, 1952.

30. *People's Daily,* Peking, September 24, 1951.

31. *New China Monthly,* p. 2, Peking, November, 1951.

32. *New China Monthly,* No. 17, pp. 1079-1081, Peking, March, 1951.

33. *Yangtze Daily,* Hankow, April 7, 1952.

34. *People's Daily,* Peking, July 12 and September 8, 1954, and *Ta-kung pao,* Hongkong, August 1, 1954.

35. The presence of women and child labor is shown in a directive of the Ministry of Water Conservation, dated December 30, 1950, warning against the excessive use of women, children, and aged and sick persons in view of the reported incidence of sickness, deaths, and casualties so as to protect the people's health and to safeguard the completion of the projects. Cf. *Compendium,* Vol. II, pp. 1102-1103, Peking, 1951. According to the *New China Monthly* (August, 1952), the average productivity per laborer was said to be two to three cubic meters of earthwork a day for one section of laborers prior to their participation in a labor contest which raised the output considerably. On a long-term basis, however, the estimate in the text is probably more reasonable.

36. Ou-yang An, *The Ching-chiang Flood Diversion Project,* p. 61, Shanghai, 1954.

37. *People's Handbook,* pp. 100-101, Peking, 1951. For the various related government directives, cf. also *Compendium,* Vols. II and III, Peking, 1951 and 1952.

38. *New China Monthly,* Vol. III, No. 1, pp. 94 and 98, Peking, November, 1950, and No. 24, pp. 1317-1320 and 1326-1328, October, 1951.

39. *Ibid.*

40. Cf. Buck, *Land Utilization in China,* pp. 230-233, Shanghai, Oxford, and Chicago, 1937.

41. *Ibid.,* and *People's Pictorial,* Vol. III, No. 5, pp. 17-18, Peking, November, 1951.

42. Report by Tseng Hsi-sheng, Vice-chairman of the Hwai River Conservation Commission, *People's Daily,* Peking, September 24, 1951; and *Daily News,* Shanghai, February 2, 1952.

43. *Liberation Daily,* Shanghai, March 17 and 24, 1952; *People's Daily,* Peking, April 3 and 11 and May 28, 1952; and *Yangtze Daily,* Hankow, November 5, 1951.

44. Report by Fu Tso-yi, *Ta-kung pao,* Tientsin, June 7, 1954.

45. The above view seems to correspond to the gist of the comment in *People's Daily,* Peking, June 23 and August 7, 1952.

46. Cf. *People's Daily,* Peking, April 5, 1952.

47. *Yangtze Daily,* Hankow, April 7, 1952; *People's Daily,* Peking, April 29 and June 11, 13, and 18, 1952; and *Progress Daily,* Tientsin, June 23, 1952.

48. See Ni Ni, *The Kuan-t'ing Reservoir,* Shanghai, 1954, and Wang Shou-jung, *The Kuan-t'ing Reservoir,* Peking, 1954.

49. See Fu Tso-yi's report, *Ta-kung pao,* Tientsin, June 7, 1954.

50. Cf. Bureau of Information, *Farm Irrigation in Recent Years,* Nanking, 1947.

51. Cf. the report on the national forestry conference, in November, 1952. *New China Monthly,* No. 38, p. 138, Peking, December, 1952.

52. Directive on Mobilization of the Masses for Afforestation, Re-afforestation and Care for Forests, *People's Daily,* Peking, November 4, 1953.

53. Liang Hsi, Minister of Forestry, "China's Forestry in the Last Three Years," *China's Forestry,* Peking, October, 1952.

54. *People's Daily,* Peking, September 7, 1954.

55. *Compendium,* Vol. III, pp. 865-884, Peking, 1952.

56. Mention should be made in passing at this point of the shelter belts which account for a considerable part of the annual afforestation. First, there is the West Manchuria Shelter Belt which encloses an area 300 kilometers wide and 1,100 kilometers long. It extends from Fu-yu and Kan-nan in Heilungkiang in the north to Shan-hai-kuan in the south. In the west it reaches as far as Ch'ih-feng in Jehol, and is bound by the Chinese Changchun Railway in the east.

From Shan-hai-kuan the Manchuria Seashore Belt then stretches up to the mouth of the Yalu River. 1,600 kilometers long, it covers an area of 21,850 hectares, and is scheduled for completion in 1955.

In Northwest China, a 1,500 kilometer shelter belt is said to have been planned parallel to the Great Wall. Some stretches have already been planted in northern Shensi, Kansu, and Ningsia.

In North China, a shelter belt is said to have been planted in western Hopeh.

Other shelter belts include one completed in eastern Honan, as well as a long-range plan for three parallel belts from the Gulf of Chili in Shantung to northern Kiangsu.

For reference see *People's Daily,* Peking, November 4, 1953; *New China Monthly,* No. 37, p. 183, Peking, November, 1952, and No. 38, p. 138, December, 1952; NCNA, May 7, 1953, and April 19, 1952; NCNA, Shen-yang, January 23, 1952, and April 4, 1953; and NCNA, Hsi-an, March 31, 1953.

57. The building of the Chengtu-Chungking Railway was apparently another example. During 1951, 100,000 civilian laborers were at work on this line.

CHAPTER TEN

Transportation and Domestic Trade

I

INTRODUCTION

Much of the discussion on agricultural and industrial production in the preceding chapters relates to Communist China as a whole. The implicit assumption is that the Communist Chinese economy may be treated as a single unit and that there are no serious physical and institutional barriers to regional interflow of commodities. While this is generally true today, it was not to be taken for granted in the beginning of the Communist period.

The inflationary rise of prices in the major population centers after World War II which contributed so decisively to the downfall of the Nationalist regime on the Chinese mainland was greatly accentuated by the breakdown of the country's transportation system. The Chinese Communists were, of course, fully aware of the significance of this factor and did their best through guerilla activities and large-scale military operations to cut the rail links both between Manchuria and China Proper and inside the Great Wall. The severance of the principal railway lines connecting North and South China and the lateral line linking the Northwest with the eastern seaboard not only served to hamper the military operations of the Nationalists, but also succeeded in breaking up the economy into separate and semi-isolated areas. Consequently, towards the end of Nationalist rule China no longer constituted an integrated unit from the economic point of view. Deprived of food and raw material supplies which could have been obtained from the interior provinces, the coastal areas fell back upon imports, as indeed they had done so often before. This also further aggravated the country's balance of payments difficulty.

When the Communists took over, the table was turned. It became now incumbent upon them to curb financial instability in the cities by making available large quantities of food, cotton, and coal from the producing areas. This was, of course, predicated upon the restoration of the transportation system which, as we shall see presently, they soon proceeded to carry out.

However, control of commodity prices is not the only consideration. Since Communist China has chosen to achieve self-sufficiency in the shortest time possible, a prerequisite is the effective utilization of regional and local surpluses to offset corresponding deficits elsewhere. In other words, the entire country must be transformed into a single market, and the whole area's imports and exports can then be regulated.

Following Communist China's entry in the Korean war and the imposition of the United Nations' embargo, fear of being completely cut off from foreign supplies gave rise to two related developments. In the first place, it was deemed necessary to concentrate on the development of overland transport routes for imports—i.e., new rail links to Russia—and of internal transport facilities less vulnerable to possible enemy incursions from the coast. As a matter of fact, the Nationalist blockade, which during 1950 was far more effective than it has probably been given credit for, especially in reducing the usefulness of the port of Shanghai, gave warning to the Chinese Communists of what the effect of a full-scale blockade might be. In the second place, additional impetus was given to the drive for self-sufficiency, a movement which not only necessitated the replacement of certain imports by domestic products, but also called for the finding of alternative markets at home for otherwise exportable goods. In both cases, new trade channels had to be found and cultivated, and the resultant changes in commodity movement required corresponding adjustments in transportation services.

Of course, the political and economic considerations underlying the desire for self-sufficiency have only highlighted the basic need for a higher degree of regional division of labor along lines of comparative advantage. Even though the central authorities, instead of the consumers, act as the final arbiter of demand, it is still true that better allocation of resources can be achieved for the country as a whole only when transportation difficulties do not impose insurmountable barriers to domestic trade. Failure to improve transportation facilities would reduce production as a whole and, in the extreme case, might cripple certain enterprises altogether. For example, if it were not possible to ship coal in adequate quantities from the large mines in Manchuria and North China to the industrial centers, the supply of electric power would be immediately curtailed with obviously crippling effects on production in general. Or, if we may take another rather notable instance, up to the end of 1953, the manufacture of standard-weight steel rails in China could be carried out only in Chungking while some of the steel ingots for the Chungking plant had to be shipped from An-shan in Manchuria. For Communist China to carry on its railway building program in Northwest China, it was at one time necessary to transport crude steel from Manchuria to Chungking and then to ship the finished rails to the Northwest, an almost fantastic operation. All this illustrates quite unmistakably the pivotal position of transportation and commodity movement as the lifeline of the Communist Chinese economy.

As a rule, the scale and nature of commodity movements depend upon two factors—the existence of physical facilities for transportation, including such fixed installations as railway tracks and other capital equipment like railway rolling stock, motor vehicles, etc., and the level of freight rates both in absolute terms and with reference to the different means of transportation. However, in the case of Communist China, a third factor has to be considered, because it can no longer be assumed that, given the physical facilities and prevailing freight rates, domestic trade can take its natural course as determined by individual merchants or direct exchange between producers and consumers. The government, partly for the purpose of regulating key commodity prices in urban areas, partly in accordance with the requirements of overall economic planning, must now take a hand in the procurement and distribution of goods at the two ends of the transportation pipe line, in addition to directing the trade flow itself.

Thus, in studying the role of transportation and trade in China, we must first of all examine (1) the rehabilitation and expansion of physical facilities, (2) the structure of freight rates, and (3) the organization of large-scale purchasing and distributive channels. This may then be followed by a review of the pattern of trade in several key commodities, which will serve to shed some additional light on the adequacy of transportation in Chinese economic development.

COMPARATIVE EFFICIENCY AND IMPORTANCE OF THE MAJOR MODES OF SURFACE TRANSPORTATION IN CHINA

One of the first things to bear in mind in studying transportation in China is the fact that traditional methods of transportation are still extremely important and that as a matter of policy the Communist authorities have consciously tried to make the fullest use of such methods. As late as 1952, for instance, the First Northwest Transportation Conference still stressed the need to utilize such means of "mass transportation" as human carriers and animal carts.[1] However, the traditional methods of transport are not highly efficient and are not adaptable to different requirements. This situation may be best illustrated by examining the following table showing the relative efficiency of the different methods:

COMPARATIVE DATA ON SPEED, LOAD CAPACITY, AND PREWAR FREIGHT RATES OF DIFFERENT MODES OF TRANSPORTATION IN CHINA

	Range of Speed (In kilometers per hour)	*Unit Load Capacity (In kilograms)*	*Average Pre-World War II Freight Rates (In CN$ per ton-kilometer)*
Railway Freight Cars	32 –45	15,000– 40,000	0.01327[1]
Junks	2 – 4[2]	1,000– 20,000	0.07000
Steamers	6 –25	5,000–3,000,000	0.08500
Handcarts, 2 men	1.7– 2[2]	300	0.11200
1 man	1.7– 2[2]	180	0.12500
Animal-drawn Carts			
1 animal	1.7– 2[2]	300– 420	0.11700
4 animals	1.7– 2[2]	1,200– 1,500	0.06600
Camels	1.7– 2[2]	120– 200	0.15000
Mules, Donkeys, and Horses	1.7– 2[2]	100– 150	0.19100
Rickshaws	1.7– 2[2]	180– 240	0.27500
Human Carriers	1.7– 2[2]	50– 70	0.32000
Motor Vehicles	40 –60	750– 3,000	0.40000

Source: Chin Chia-fung, *Transportation Development and Trends in China,* pp. 146-7, Shanghai, 1937.

1. Lowest rate on the Tientsin-Pukow Railway.
2. Computed on the basis of 24 hours and the average distance traveled per day.

Although the freight rates given above refer to the prewar period and have doubtless undergone certain changes since, their relative magnitudes indicate quite clearly that for long-distance transportation of commodities in bulk only railways, steamers, junks, and certain large animal-drawn carts are of practical value. However, both junks and the large animal-drawn carts are not suitable for perishable goods on long hauls. Even in the case of non-perishable goods such as coal, timber, and other construction materials, because of their low speed, these methods can be fully utilized only if shipments are planned well in advance. All other surface transportation methods suffer from the extremely small load capacities and low speed which together tend to enhance overhead costs. Consequently, their usefulness is essentially limited to short hauls and in transporting goods to and from points on routes served by railways and ships. Of particular interest was the uneconomic nature of truck transport in prewar China as a result of high costs in operation, maintenance, and depreciation. It is at least questionable whether these costs have been reduced sufficiently in the present time so that trucks can be used extensively in areas served by railways and waterways. Thus, as far as long-distance transportation is concerned, railways and shipping are the only two major factors in China. Of the two inland navigation is further restricted by the geographical fact that most rivers in China flow from the West to the East, while, under present international conditions, coastal shipping is subject to possible external interference. As a result, railways may be regarded as the predominant method of bulk transport.

In this connection we may cite two rather interesting examples. First, during 1951, 84 per cent of the total freight that reached or left the port of Tientsin, not counting highway transport, was accounted for by railways, as against 16 per cent by inland shipping and sea-going vessels.[2] Second, in the case of Shanghai, from June, 1949, to May, 1950, when the Nationalist blockade was in effect, the relative shares of railways and ships, in total freight traffic, including river boats and junks, were in the approximate ratio of 3.2 to 1.[3] Lest one should regard this situation as characteristic of the early period of the present regime only, the same state of affairs could be gleaned from some comparative freight statistics appearing on page 346.

During 1950, the Communist government controlled 41.2 per cent of mainland China's seagoing and river steam shipping tonnage, together with a sizable portion of the available junks and 30 per cent of the motor vehicles. The proportion rose to 45.8 per cent in 1951 in the case of shipping and was also higher in highway motor trans-

FREIGHT TONNAGE, TON-KILOMETERS, AND LENGTH OF AVERAGE HAUL FOR RAILWAYS AND STATE-OPERATED HIGHWAY AND WATERWAY TRANSPORT IN COMMUNIST CHINA 1951–1952

	Million Metric Tons Carried		*Million Ton-Kilometers*		*Average Haul in Kilometers*[1]	
	1951	*1952*	*1951*	*1952*	*1951*	*1952*
Railways	110.50	131.00	51,526	59,461	466.3	453.9
State-operated Inland and Coastal Shipping	3.55	5.31	2,562	3,961	721.6	745.9
State-operated Highway Transport (motor vehicles only)	1.68	4.03	134	255	79.8	63.3

Sources: Po I-p'o's report, *Economic Weekly,* No. 8, p. 16, Shanghai, February, 1953; *Economic Bulletin,* No. 46, p. 13, Hongkong, 1953; and *Far Eastern Economic Review* (in English), Vol. XIV, No. 11, p. 329, Hongkong, March, 1953.

1. The data on average haul are computed from "tons carried" instead of "tons originated" and are therefore only approximate. However, with the exception of railway freight, it is believed that transshipments are quantitatively unimportant.

port.[4] In view of the progressive socialization that has taken place since 1951, these ratios have no doubt increased further.[5] Bearing these facts in mind, we can see quite conclusively (1) that railway transport is quantitatively the most important factor in China, and (2) that truck transport is used predominantly in short hauls. Furthermore, although the average haul in rail transport is less than in shipping, this situation might not hold true if coastal shipping were left out of account.

II

PRIORITY OF RAILWAY DEVELOPMENT AND GOVERNMENT INVESTMENT

The relative importance of rail traffic in comparison with other forms of freight movement in Communist China is not only representative of the original, pre-Communist state of affairs, but is also in part the result of deliberate policy. However, the policy of concentrating all efforts in restoring and expanding the railway system undoubtedly owed its origin to some of the factors mentioned above which tend to limit the present usefulness of other modes of transport.

According to a member of the Planning Bureau of the Economic and Financial Commission, Communist China decided early in 1950 not to stress the recovery of highways and waterways. Instead, emphasis was given to the rehabilitation of railways. Apart from the economic, geographical, and external considerations alluded to earlier, one of the official reasons given was that the country had only 20,000 to 30,000 motor vehicles altogether and that of the 1,200,000 tons of Chinese shipping only a small part was under Communist control.[6] Thus lack of equipment and the apparent inability and undesirability of incurring large initial outlays and, in the case of trucks, also continuing, high operating costs, to expand shipping and truck transport led to the decision to concentrate on railway rehabilitation. Moreover, the time element and shortage of foreign exchange unquestionably also entered into consideration, inasmuch as railway tracks could be rehabilitated with reasonable speed, as distinguished from new construction, whereas ships and motor vehicles would have to be imported.

Given this combination of circumstances, railways were alloted a sizable portion of government investment. According to T'eng Tai-yüan, Communist Minister of Railways, the greater part of government investment in industry and transportation during 1950 and 1951 was devoted to "capital construction" in railways.[7] In terms of total government outlay for economic reconstruction some 20 per cent of the entire amount spent in 1949 and 1950 was said to have been alloted to railway rehabilitation. For 1950 the planned value of total government investment in railways amounted to the equivalent of 1,466 million catties of millet, or roughly about US$70 million, of which 74.4 per cent was earmarked for use in China Proper. As mentioned in Chapter VII above, the relative importance of government investment in railways has probably decreased since the first years of the new regime, especially in comparison with that in the manufacturing and other industries. However, in absolute terms, there was a continuous rise of railway investment through 1952. This development may be seen in the investment index furnished by Ch'i Yü.

INDEX OF GOVERNMENT INVESTMENT IN RAILWAYS IN COMMUNIST CHINA, 1950–1952

Year	Index
1950	100
1951	240
1952	490

Source: Ch'i Yü, *New China's Railway Construction*, p. 21, Peking, 1953.

If we assume that actual investment in 1950 more or less corresponded to the planned figure, investment in 1952 would approximate US$343 million. Since new railway building was stepped up somewhat after 1952, investment in 1953 was conceivably higher. After the 1954 National Conference on Railway Work it was again officially stated that investment for the strengthening of existing railways, engines, and rolling stock during 1954 would be 43 per cent higher than the corresponding level in the preceding year.[8] Thus one may safely conclude that government investment in the rehabilitation and expansion of the railway network in Communist China has been rising steadily even though its importance relative to other types of investment may have declined.

Of course, only a part of the total investment in railways is for the repair and construction of tracks, but a sizable proportion has probably been for this purpose. For instance, of the US$70 million planned to be invested in 1950 about 70 per cent was meant for route construction and repair. Of the latter amount, again, about one-half was devoted to bridge construction, an obvious prerequisite of through train operation. Although some new construction was done in 1950, it was not quantitatively important until 1952 when the period of recovery was virtually over.

REHABILITATION OF THE RAILWAY NETWORK

Among the economic achievements of Communist China that have been given widest publicity the recovery and expansion of the railway network occupy an important place. On this point, the main question that interests us in the first instance is the actual achievement that has been made as distinct from propaganda and its significance, both economic and otherwise.

First, let us take a look at official Communist statistics on the increase in the length of railways in operation. The following data, appearing on page 349, are among those most frequently quoted.

On the basis of these figures, it would appear that tremendous progress has been made since 1949 in comparison with earlier years. However, such a conclusion would be mistaken because of the official practice to exclude railways not under Communist control both during and before 1949 even though they were in operation. For instance, according to the above table, railways in operation in 1947

RAILWAY LINES IN OPERATION IN COMMUNIST CHINA
(IN KILOMETERS)

Year	Kilometers
1947	6,884
1948	12,768
1949	21,715
1950	22,238
1951	23,063
1952	24,232

Source: Ch'i Yü, *op. cit.*

in areas under Communist occupation, including a large part of Manchuria, totalled 6,884 kilometers. On the other hand, 15,812 kilometers of railways were reported to be in operation at the end of 1946 in areas under the control of the Nationalist government. The corresponding figure at the end of 1947 was 13,675 kilometers.[9] One cannot regard the sum of the average of the latter two figures and the 6,884 kilometers in Communist hands as representing the total length of railway lines in operation during 1947 both on account of the inclusion of Formosa in the Nationalist data and overlapping reports from some areas due to military operations. However, it appears quite irrefutable that the total length of railways in operation on the Chinese mainland as a whole was probably close to 20,000 kilometers in 1947, and that, in terms of total length, the expansion of railway lines in operation under Communist rule is not really as spectacular as the official statistics suggest at first glance.

During 1949–1952 Communist China reportedly restored and repaired a total of 9,991 kilometers of railway tracks.[10] This figure presumably included both trunk and branch lines, as well as double-tracking, rerouting, and extensions. It no doubt also included sections which were in operation but needed repair and ordinary maintenance, as well as sections on which repair had to be done more than once. Of this cumulative total, work was done on about 4,925 kilometers in 1949, 2,200 kilometers in 1950, and 743 kilometers in 1952.[11] By inference, work was completed on 2,123 kilometers in 1951.[12] The length of track repair and rehabilitation thus averaged 2,498 kilometers a year, which may be compared with the corresponding figure of 2,560 kilometers a year under the Nationalists during the period between V-J Day and the end of 1947.[13] At their peak Communist efforts in railway rehabilitation undoubtedly surpassed the Nationalists' achievement in the post-World War II period, partly because the new regime was not hampered by deliberate destruction after 1949 and was therefore at a considerable advantage in this respect.

THE PRESENT RAILWAY NETWORK

On the basis of the data on operating length, track repair, and new constructions, it may be safely stated that the period of track rehabilitation had been largely completed by the end of 1951 and that it was over at the end of 1952. However, the close of the rehabilitation period does not mean that the entire pre-Communist trackage is now in being or that new lines built under the present regime represent a net addition in trackage. The entire picture may be seen through a detailed comparison of individual railway lines between a 1948 report by the Vice-Minister of Railways of the Nationalist government and a comprehensive compilation based on various Communist reports up to the end of 1954. (See tables appearing on pages 351 through 358.)

It may be seen from our compilation that the present total length (1954) of Communist China's trunk railway lines amounts to 24,985 kilometers. Since this figure does not include the short branch lines and spurs listed in 1948, totalling 1,318 kilometers,[14] under the assumption that these are now also in operation, the adjusted total network would be 26,303 kilometers.[15]

The pre-Communist network as given in our table totalled 26,448 kilometers. Since some 421 kilometers of lines reported for 1954 were probably also in existence in 1948, the actual total should be 26,869 kilometers. Less an overstatement of 194 kilometers for the Shenyang-Shanhaikuan line, the adjusted total would be 26,675 kilometers or 372 kilometers more than in 1954.

However, the 1954 total includes 2,304 kilometers of new lines not in existence before the Communist period. If the latter were deducted, the present network would be 2,658 kilometers short of the pre-Communist total, and of this deficiency some 2,424 kilometers can be accounted for by dismantling, the rest by discrepancies in the methods of measurement and errors and omissions. In short, disregarding any construction not publicly reported, new constructions under the Communists up to the end of 1954 were not quite enough to offset those railways formerly in existence which the authorities

RAILWAYS IN CHINA
1948–1954
(IN KILOMETERS)

RAILWAYS SOUTH OF THE YANGTZE RIVER:

1948			*1949*		*1954*	
Nanking-Shanghai Line			Nanking-Shanghai	312	Nanking-Shanghai	312
Nanking-Shanghai	311					
Nanking Municipal Br.		15				
Chunghuamen Br.		16				
Sanmin Road Br.		2				
Wusung-Shanghai	16				Wusung Wharf-Shanghai	13
Shanghai-Hangchou-Ningpo Line						
Shanghai-Ningpo	360		Shanghai-Hangchou	196	Shanghai-Hangchou	196
Jihhuikang Br.		4				
Kungchenchiao Br.		6				
Paisha Br.		4				
Suchou-Chiahsing	74[1]					
Nanking-Kiangsi Line						
Sunchiapu-Hsihsien	155		Nanking-Wuhu	91	Nanking-Wuhu	91[1]
Nanking-Sunchiapu	175[1]					
Chekiang-Kiangsi Line						
Hsiaoshan-Chuchou	929		Hsiaoshan-Changshu	668	Hsiaoshan-Chuchou	941
Chinhua-Lanhsi Br.		23				
Kaokang Br.		7				
Anyuan Br.		7				
Hsiangtang-Nanchang	31					
Nanchang-Chiuchiang	128		Nanchang-Chiuchiang	129	Nanchang-Chiuchiang	129
Canton-Hankow Line						
Wuchang-Canton	1,096		Wuchang-Sungting	474	Wuchang-Canton	1,106
Nienyutao Br.		3				
Hsinho Br.		1				
Hsiangchiang Br.		13				
Payang Br.		14				

RAILWAYS SOUTH OF THE YANGTZE RIVER (continued)

1948			*1949*		*1954*	
Yingteh Br.		2				
Huangpu Br.		15				
Canton-Shenchuan	146		Canton-Shenchuan	146	Canton-Kowloon	146
Canton-Sanshui	49[1]				Kwangchou-Sanshui	49
Hunan-Kwangsi Line						
Hengyang-Laipin	605		Hengyang-Liuchiang	533	Hengyang-Munankuan	1,025[2]
Lingleng Br.		13				
Tawan Br.		20				
Ningming-Chennankuan	67[1]					
Kweichow-Kwangsi Line						
Liuchou-Chingtaipo	474		Liuchiang-Nantan	315	Liuchou-Chingtaipo	472
Chengchan Br.		3				
Hunan-Kweichow Line						
Tienhsin-Lantien	175[1]					
Yunnan Railways						
Kunming-Chani	173		Kunming-Chani	174	Kunming-Chani	174
Kunming-Anning	35		Kunming-Shihtsui	12	Kunming-Shihtsui	12
Connecting line		6				
Kunming-Hokou	465				Kunming-Pisechai	287[1]
Chichieh-Kochiuhsien	34				Chichieh-Kochiuhsien	32
Maoerhto-Wucha	66		Chichiang-Wucha	58	Chichiang-Wucha	58
Sungyu-Chiangtungchiao	28					
Shantou-Ichi	42[1]					
Peichieh-Toushan	110[1]					
Ningcheng-Paisha	28[1]					
Pishechai-Shihping	144[1]					
		202				
	5,888					
Total	6,090			3,082		5,043

RAILWAYS NORTH OF THE YANGTZE RIVER:

1948			*1949*		*1954*	
Peiping-Liaoning Line						
Peiping-Shanhaikuan	426		Peking-Shanhaikuan	418	Peking-Shanhaikuan	418
Nanyuan Br.		8				
Hsiku Br.		4				
Tientsin Sta. Br.		2				
Tangku Br.		5				
Peitaiho Br.		10				
Peiping-Suiyuan Line						
Peiping-Paotou	813		Peking-Chihsiaying	618	Peking-Paotou	814
Hsipienmen Br.		3				
West Suburban Br.		5				
Huancheng Br.		12				
Hsipienmen-Ta-tai	56				Peking-Mentoukou	26
Yentungshan Br.		10				
Tatung-Kouchüan	20				Pingwang-Kouchüan	20
Peiping-Kupeikou Line	143		Peking-Miyün	90	Peking-Kupeikou	144
Tunghsien Br.		6				
Fengtai Conn. Br.		4				
Fengchang Conn. Br.		2				
Tientsin-Pukou Line						
Tientsin-Pukou	1,010		Tientsin-Pukou	1,009	Tientsin-Pukou	1,009
Lianchen Br.		26				
Luankou Br.		6				
Tungtaiping-Nanhsintai	66				Tzuyao-Nanhsintai	66
Yenchou Br.		32				
Lincheng Br.		31				
Taochuang Br.		4				
Linchuan Br.		16				
Pangpu-Shuichiahu	61		Pangpu-Shuichiahu	61	Pangpu-Shuichiahu	61
Ferry Line		2				
Techou-Shihchiachuang	181		Tehsien-Shihchiachuang	181	Tehsien-Shihchiachuang	181

RAILWAYS NORTH OF THE YANGTZE RIVER (continued)

1948			*1949*		*1954*	
Huainan Line						
Tienchiaan-Yuhsukou	214		Tienchiaan-Hofei	79	Tienchiaan-Yuchi	214
Tsingtao-Chinan Line						
Tsingtao-Chinan	393		Tsingtao-Chinan	393	Tsingtao-Chinan	392
Ssufang Br.		5				
Poshan Br.		39				
Lochiachuang Br.		7				
Huangshan Br.		7				
Poshan-Patou Br.		9				
Chinlingchen Br.		7				
Huangtaichiao Br.		4				
Peiping-Hankow Line						
Peiping-Hankow	1,213		Peking-Hankow	1,214	Peking-Hankow	1,216
New Main Line Br.		8				
Toli Br.		16				
Choukoutien Br.		15				
Ihsien Br.		33				
Tzushan Br.		44				
Hsitzo Br.		21				
Liuhokou Br.		18				
Chenchuang-Sanliwan	163		Hsienhsiang-Chiaotso	64	Hsienhsiang-(Chiaotso (Chinghua	64
Lunghai Line						
Lienyunkang-Tienshui	1,382		Lienyunkang-Tienshui	1,382	Lienyunkang-Tienshui	1,389
					Tienshui-Lanchow	360[2]
					Lanchow-Huaihsipao	332[2]
Chaotun Br.		31				
Kaifeng Br.		89				
Hsienyang-Tungchuan	135		Hsienyang-Tungchuan	135	Hsienyang-Tungchuan	138

	Main line	Branches				
Chengtai Line						
Shihchiachuang-Taiyuan	234		Shihchiachuang-Taiyuan	235	Shihchiachuang-Taiyuan	236
Yutzu Br.		36				
Huangtankou Br.		16				
Chinghsing Br.		11				
Fengshan Br.		7				
Tungpu Line						
Tatung-Fenglingtu	864		Taiyuan-Lingshih	164	Tatung-Fenglingtu	835
Yuanping-Tayingchen	120				Yuanping-Kuohsien	18[1]
Hsinyao Br.		52				
Hsishan Br.		24				
Hsiming Br.		4				
Tailan Br.		16				
Huancheng Br.		14				
Tungkuan-Luan	175				Tungkuan-Luan	178
Yuanchi Br.		34				
Sanchiatien-Chiafang	64[1]					
Taierhchuang-Tsaochuang	48[1]					
		755				
	7,779					
Total	8,534			6,044		9,071
					Chengtu-Chungking	505[2]
					Chengtu-Hsiaszu	277[2]
					Chining-Erhlien	338[2]
						9,431

HAINAN ISLAND

1948			1949		1954	
Peili-Sanya	180		Peili-Sanya	180	Peili-Sanya	180
Sanya-Yulinkang	20		Sanya-Yulinkang	20	Sanya-Yulinkang	20
Paopan Lumber Mill		20				
Paso Br.		52				
Tienmassu Br.		2				
Tientu Br.		15				
		89				
	200					
Total	289			200		200

RAILWAYS OF THE NORTHEAST (Manchuria)

1948			1949		1954	
Shenyang-Shanhaikuan	620		Shenyang-Shanhaikuan	420	Shenyang-Shanhaikuan	426[3]
Huangkutun Conn. Line		3				
Yuhung Br.		5				
Yukuo Br.		13				
Hulutao Br.		12				
Koupangtze-Yingkou	91					
Hsinlitun-Ihsien	131		Hsinlitun-Ihsien	132	Hsinlitun-Ihsien	131
Kaotaishan-Hsinlitun	61				Kaotaishan-Hsinlitun	61
Tahushan-Chengchiatun	365		Tahushan-Chengchiatun	366	Chengchiatun-Tahushan	366
Chinchou-Kupeikou	542		Chinchou-Ihsien	50	Chinchou-Chengteh	340[1]
Peipiao Br.		18				
Yehpaishou-Chihfeng	147				Yehpaishou-Chihfeng	144
Shenyang-Antung	262		Shenyang-Antung	261	Shenyang-Antung	258
Nanan Br.		13				
Shenan Br.		35				
Shenanpei Br.		24				
Suchiatun-Fushun	53		Suchiatun-Fushun	53	Fushun-Suchiatun	49
Hunho Br.		5				
Funshun Conn. Line		4				

Line	Main	Branch	Line	Km	Line	Km
Penchi-Liaoyang	69		Penchi-Liaoyang	70	Penchi-Liaoyang	71
Penchi-Tienshihfu	86				Penchi-Tienshihfu	85
Fenghuacheng-Kuanshui	82				Fengcheng-Kuantien	112
Chinchou-Chengtzutung	102				Chinchou-Chengtzutung	104
Shenyang-Kirin	444		Shenyang-Kirin	447	Shenyang-Kirin	445
Shennan Br.		11				
Shenpei Br.		4				
Meihokou-Chian	252		Meihokou-Chian	245	Meiho-kou-Chian	246
Hsintung Br.		3				
Ssuping-Meihokou	156		Ssuping-Meihokou	156	Ssuping-Meihokou	155
Yayuan-Talitzu	114		Yayuan-Talitzu	113	Yayuan-Talitzu	113
Changchun-Tumen	530		Changchun-Tuman	528	Changchun-Tumen	527
Tafengman-Lungtoushan	23				Tafengman-Lungtoushan	22
Chinchu Br.		19				
Naitzushan Br.		10				
Hsiaohsin Conn. Line		9				
Lungching-Holung	52		Lungching-Holung	51	Lungching-Holung	50
Chaoyangchuan-Kaishantun	60				Chaoyangchuan-Kaishantun	57
Lafa-Pinchiang	266		Lafa-Harbin	265	Lafa-Harbin	266
Meiyao Br.		30				
Pinchiang-Peian	326		Harbin-Peian	326	Harbin-Peian	333
Harbin Br. Line		9				
Sankoshu Wharf Line		4				
Suihua-Chiamussu	382		Suihua-Chiamussu	382	Suihua-Chiamussu	383
Chiamussu Wharf Line		4				
Lienchiangkou Wharf Line		2				
Hsinpeian-Heiho	303[1]					
Heiho Wharf Line		4				
Ssupingchieh-Lungchiang	571				Ssuping-Chichihaerh	573
Angang Br.		6				
Changchun-Taoan	333		Talai-Paichengtzu	119	Paichengtzu-Changchun	329
Taoan-Tuanlu	377		Paichengtzu-Aerhshan	337	Paichengtzu-Aerhshan	354
Lungchiang-Peian	231		Chichihaerh-Peian	231	Chichihaerh-Peian	231
Ningnien-Holungmen	285		Ningnien-Nunchiang	181	Ningnien-Nunchiang	182

RAILWAYS OF THE NORTHEAST (continued)

1948			*1949*		*1954*	
Tumen-Chiamussu	580		Tumen-Chiamussu	580	Tumen-Chiamussu	577
Wangching Conn. Line		9				
Hsinhsing-Chengtzukou	216[1]					
Linkou-Hutou	336		Linkou-Tungan	172	Linkou-Tungan	171
Chining-Hengshan	12				Chihsi-Hengshan	12
Tungning-Hohsi	91					
Hsichining-Hsiachengtzu	103		Hsiachengtzu-Chihsi	104	Hsiachengtzu-Chihsi	104
Lienchiangkou-Hokang	54		Liho-Hokang	54	Liho-Hokang	54
Nancha-Ichun	105		Nani-Ichun	105	Nani-Ichun	105
Chinese Changchun Line						
Manchouli-Suifenho	1,482		Manchouli-Suifenho	1,484	Manchouli-Suifenho	1,484
Harbin-Dairen	944		Harbin-Dairen	943	Harbin-Dairen	946
Tashihchiao-Yingkou	23		Tashihchiao-Yingkou	23	Tashihchiao-Yingkou	23
Yentai Br. Line		16				
					Tungchiamussu-Chienshan	78[4]
					Kuanshui-Saimachi	46[4]
					Yapoloni-Loushan	70[4]
					Yapoloni-Chihshan	49[4]
					Choushuitzu-Lüshun	50[4]
					Paishan-Huolungkuo	40[4]
		272			Hungchiang-Sanchatzu	18[4]
	11,263				Kutuerh-Tuliho	72[2]
Total	11,535			8,198		10,311

Sources: For 1948, Ling Hung-hsün, *General Survey of Railways in China*, pp. 27-34; for 1949-1950, *People's Handbook*, pp. 5-6, Shanghai, 1951; for 1954, compilation based on *Manual for Newspaper Readers*, Hankow, 1950; *People's Handbook*, pp. 51-53, Shanghai, 1952; *People's Atlas*, Shanghai, 1953; *Current Background*, No. 274, Hongkong, January, 1954; and sources for new constructions given in table later in the text.

1. Figures in 1948 represent dismantled tracks previously in existence. Figures in 1954 which are at variance with the 1948 data are due to dismantling believed not rehabilitated.
2. Increase in kilometrage due to new construction.
3. *General Survey* figure believed to be in error.
4. Spur and branch line trackage not listed on 1948 *General Survey* totals, but believed to have been in existence.

had chosen not to restore. A little more than 1,100 kilometers of these dismantled lines are in the "south of the Yangtze" area. About the same length is in Manchuria.[16]

NEW RAIL CONSTRUCTIONS

According to our compilation, a total of about 2,304 kilometers of new railways were built during 1950–1954. The individual lines and approximate annual constructions are as appearing in table on page 360.

Since the length of new constructions during the period in question was almost equal to that of the lines still not rehabilitated, it is probably fair to say that the Chinese Communists could have completed the restoration of the entire former railway network if they had chosen not to build the new lines instead. That they actually decided upon new construction may be explained by the fact that in the case of practically all the lines not rehabilitated, except those in Yunnan province, alternative routes or other suitable means of transportation are now available. As for the lines in Yunnan, their rehabilitation as such would not have provided any connecting link with the country's railway network. For the same reason, it would also have been difficult to transport construction supplies to Yunnan from other parts of the country.

However, it is interesting to speculate on some of the reasons why Communist China chose to build the particular lines it did. Apart from the short Kutuerh-Tuliho line which serves the timber industry and is being currently extended, several considerations which may have been decisive may be pointed out.

In the first place, political and strategic reasons apparently dictated the early construction of the Laipin-Munankuan section of the Hunan-Kwangsi line in order to establish a direct rail link with Indo-China because the line's economic significance would not have justified the priority it received. The same consideration no doubt also determined the construction of the Chining-Erhlien section of the new China-Outer Mongolia line as an alternative route to the Chinese Changchun Railway, thus not only reducing the transportation cost for imports through Manchuria through a shortening of the line, but also providing a rail link with the Soviet Union, bypassing the militarily exposed coastal stretch between Manchuria and China Proper

New Railway Construction in Communist China 1950–1954 (In kilometers)

Line	Annual Construction 1950	1951	1952	1953	1954	Total Length Completed up to the End of 1954	Remark
Hunan-Kwangsi (section from Laipin to Munankuan, formerly Chennankuan)	240	180				420	Completed January 1, 1952. Trunk line reported at 403 kilometers.
Chengtu-Chungking	65	158	282			505	Completed in May, 1952. Total length also reported to be 530 kilometers.
Tienshui-Lanchou-Tihua		82	278	190	142	692	Total through 1954 up to Huai-hsi-pao.
Chengtu-Paochi				117	160	277	Total to November, 1954, up to Hsia-szu.
Chining-Ulan Bator (Chinese section between Chining and Erhlien)				100	238	338	Completed in December, 1954.
Kutuerh-Tuliho[1]				72		72	Completed in March, 1953.
Total	305	420	560	479	540	2,304	

Sources: *Singtao Daily,* Hongkong, October 30, 1951; NCNA, Lan-chou, October 17, 1953, and April 4, 1954; NCNA, Chungking, December 10, 1951, and June 30, 1952; NCNA, Cheng-tu, November 10, 1954; *Free Asia Bulletin,* San Francisco, December 17, 1954; NCNA, January 5, 1951; *Ta-kung pao,* Hongkong, March 2, 1951; and *People's Atlas,* 1953 edition, Shanghai.

1. There are several other short forest tracks in Manchuria which have not been included. A 314-kilometer line from Li-t'ang in Kwangsi to Kuang-chou-wan and the rerouting of the section between Feng-t'ai and Sha-cheng on the Peking-Paotou line were reported completed in June, 1955.

—namely, the Peking-Shanhaikuan-Shenyang Railway. The same reason, though not the only one, has no doubt prompted the Communists' relentless drive to push the Tienshui-Lanchou Railway westward toward Tihua and thence to Soviet Central Asia, and to complete a north-south rail connection in western China by building the Chengtu-Paochi Railway. The present effort to build bridges across the Yangtze and Han Rivers at Wu-han so as to provide through connection between the Peking-Hankow and Hankow-Canton Railways instead of effecting a crossing at Nanking is at least partly to be explained in the same manner.

At the same time, one may also note the fact that it was not until the summer of 1955 that the first mention was made on railway construction in Fukien, the province opposite Formosa. However, the construction of the railway to Outer Mongolia was not announced until it was nearly completed, and the same veil of security may have been put over construction in Fukien.

In the second place, from the purely economic point of view, construction of the Chengtu-Chungking Railway has opened up the granary of the Cheng-tu plain for shipment down the Yangtze. Once the Chengtu-Paochi line is completed, its connection with the Chengtu-Chungking Railway in the South and the lateral Lunghai Railway in the North would add another loop to the country's railway network and would provide a hitherto non-existent direct transport route between Northwest and Southwest China. The extension of the Tienshui-Lanchou Railway westward will definitely prove to be a decisive factor in spearheading economic development of Northwest China even though there may not be sufficient freight traffic to make the investment a paying proposition at present. However, as the railway stretches westward, one of the immediate effects has already been felt in the shortening of the truck route from the Yü-men oil field to the railway and the consequent increase in crude shipments to Manchurian and East China refineries.

In the third place, since the usefulness of a railway in long distance traffic is predicated upon its being connected with the rest of the rail network or other means of bulk transport, it may be noted that all the new lines built by the Chinese Communists, with the only exception of the Chengtu-Chungking line—which is connected with the Yangtze—are extensions of the present network. Apparently it was for this reason that Communist China chose to extend the Hunan-

Kwangsi line to Indo-China instead of restoring another rail connection that formerly existed in Yunnan.

Finally, it should be noted that the Chengtu-Chungking, Tienshui-Lanchou, and Laipin-Munankuan lines were all built on the basis of previously completed work and that virtually all the lines were included in the initial railway construction plan drawn up by the Nationalists.[17] As far as new rail construction was concerned, the Communist regime was able to fall back on earlier planning and was not forced to start from scratch. While there was some revision of the original plans, such as the rerouting of the Chengtu-Paochi Railway, which was formerly planned to join the Lunghai extension at Tienshui instead of Paochi, as well as some resurveying, most of the engineering plans were already in existence, and much of the earth work had been done.

III

VOLUME OF RAILWAY FREIGHT TRAFFIC

Notwithstanding the fact that actual rail construction by the Chinese Communists has not been as spectacular as it has been frequently made out to be, increase in rail traffic during recent years has been quite impressive. Before the war with Japan, the fourteen national railways of China, excluding the Manchurian rail system, reported for the 1931-1935 period an average freight traffic of a little over five billion ton-kilometers a year only.[18] Of the fourteen railways the Peking-Hankow, Peking-Liaoning, and Tientsin-Pukow lines accounted for the bulk of the traffic. In spite of the nominal reincorporation of Manchuria after World War II, the civil war and Communist occupation of large areas of the country reduced rail freight traffic in all government-controlled territory to 1.7 billion ton-kilometers in 1947. Although the total volume rose to 3.2 billion ton-kilometers in the following year, it was still only about one-half of that of 1935 which did not include Manchuria.[19]

Contrasted with these prewar and post-World War II data which admittedly did not even cover the entire railway system then in existence, the volume of rail traffic under the new regime is substantially greater. It may be expressed in terms of the number of car-loadings per day, tons carried, and ton-kilometers as follows:

ESTIMATES OF RAILWAY FREIGHT TRAFFIC IN COMMUNIST CHINA, 1949–1954

	Number of Carloadings per Day	*Million Metric Tons Carried*	*Billion Ton-Kilometers*
1949	7,240	48.2	18.8
1950	9,698	99.2	38.6
1951	10,794	110.5	51.5
1952	12,780	131.0	59.5
1953	14,786	157.5	64.8
1954	17,077[1]	181.9[1]	74.8[1]

Sources: For car-loadings, reports by T'eng Tai-yüan, *New China Monthly,* Vol. I, No. 2, p. 432, Peking, December, 1949, and Vol. I, No. 5, pp. 1208-1210, March, 1950; *People's Daily,* Peking, June 29, 1952; *New China Monthly,* p. 1258, October, 1951; and NCNA, January 26, 1954.

For tons carried, *New China Monthly,* Vol. I, No. 4, p. 920, February, 1950; Ch'i Yü, *op. cit.,* p. 39; and NCNA, January 26 and April 19, 1954.

For ton-kilometers, NCNA, September 20, 1951; *Economic Weekly,* No. 8, p. 16, February, 1953; and *China News Service, Peking,* November 15, 1953.

1. Preliminary.

According to the above statistics, railway freight traffic registered an increase of over 80 per cent in both tons carried and ton-kilometers between 1950 and 1954, while the number of carloadings increased by just under 80 per cent in the same period. This rising trend was accompanied by a slight increase in the average load per car, and, if comparison is made between 1950 and 1953 or 1954, a slight increase in the length of the average haul. The former reflected the result of a strenuous campaign to load freight cars beyond their rated capacity while the latter indicated the importance of long-distance traffic by rail.

UTILIZATION AND AVAILABILITY OF ROLLING STOCK

By increasing train speed, which rose from a national average of 20.9 kilometers per hour for freight in 1950 to 25.6 kilometers in 1952, and by more efficient use of available engines, the average number of kilometers run per engine per day increased from 336.7 kilometers in 1950 to 436.1 kilometers in 1952.[20] At the same time, speed-up in loading and unloading and reduction of unnecessary stops has lowered the turn-around time,[21] and thus increased the carrying capacity of the existing rolling stock. Through overloading of the cars and increasing the number of cars pulled per freight train, the average train load has in turn been increased. All these indices point to one thing, namely, the better utilization of available equipment, which underlies the supply side of the expanding freight traffic.

A critical issue in this connection is whether the number of freight cars available is adequate enough to sustain a continued rise of freight movement especially in view of the current building program. According to the First Five Year Plan, the projected volume of rail freight traffic will reach 121 billion ton-kilometers in 1957. Even on the existing network a point may be reached beyond which no amount of overloading and economy in equipment utilization can offset the shortage of rolling stock and engines. Moreover, as new rails are built in remote areas, the existing number of engines and cars will be spread progressively thinner over a longer network while the average haul will also increase in distance, thereby accentuating the technical difficulty of rolling stock utilization. How serious this problem is, or is likely to become, will be tentatively examined on the basis of immediately available information.

According to one official report,[22] Communist China possessed at the beginning of 1949 a total of 1,737 railway engines, 3,145 passenger cars, and 29,188 freight cars. Acquisitions during the year through seizure raised the numbers to 3,355 engines, 4,412 passenger cars, and 44,401 freight cars at the end of 1949. However, of these only 2,332 engines, 3,706 passenger cars, and 39,989 freight cars were undamaged. Moreover, only 30,300 undamaged freight cars were then in use.[23] The official plan for 1950 was to put a total of 39,500 freight cars in service and to build 1,500 new cars in Manchuria.[24] In the same year, the number of engines was increased to about 2,900.[25] During 1951 and 1952 probably some 4,000 new freight cars were manufactured.[26] Under the optimistic assumption that all the previously serviceable cars had been kept in use and that all the damaged ones had been repaired, the total number of serviceable freight cars at the end of 1952, excluding additions through import, would be less than 48,500.[27] Since Communist China's domestic production of railway engines was negligible,[28] the total number at the end of 1952 was probably not more than the 3,355 in existence at the end of 1949 if imports were disregarded.

According to the postwar railway construction plans of the Nationalists, the average rolling stock requirements on Chinese railways for every 1,000 kilometers of railway lines are 200 engines and

2,500 freight cars.[29] Given the 24,232 kilometers of railways in operation in 1952, 4,846 engines and 60,580 freight cars would be needed if these standards were used. Our estimated number of engines would be about 30 per cent below this level while that of freight cars would be 20 per cent below.

It is quite possible that, prior to 1952, Communist China was not able to import rolling stock on a scale sufficient to bridge the gap between the standard requirements and supply from domestic manufacture and stock. This is true especially with respect to engines. Since railway trackage in operation increased by about 9 per cent from 1952 to the end of 1954, unless the supply of rolling stock increased more than proportionately, the shortage must have worsened in the meantime. One might even venture to suggest that the availability of rolling stock may actually act as a brake to new railway building.

PLANNING RAILWAY FREIGHT TRAFFIC

Although shortage of rolling stock has not prevented a considerable gain in freight traffic under the new regime, it has necessitated the exercise of exceptional care in scheduling traffic and in determining its priority. Measures have had to be adopted in order to eliminate seasonal peaks—such as the transport of coal in winter and of construction materials in autumn—and cross hauls of the same commodities.

According to a November, 1950, directive of the State Administrative Council,[30] freight traffic by rail was classified into (1) commodity movement under the overall plan of the Ministry of Trade, (2) transportation requirements of other government agencies for machinery, raw materials, and other supplies, (3) military traffic, (4) movement of railway material, (5) intra-regional commodity movement sponsored by local governments, and (6) private trade. The first two categories of demand for railway service were to be coordinated and planned by the Economic and Financial Commission of the central government and the Planning Bureau, while the third category remained under the jurisdiction of the People's Revolutionary Military Committee. The Ministry of Railways was made responsible for carrying out these traffic plans. On the other hand, both intra-regional commodity movement sponsored by local governments and private freight traffic were subject to the availability of rolling stock in accordance with allocations made by the Ministry of Railways to its subordinate railway administrations.[31]

The existence of a priority schedule does not, of course, automatically guarantee either wise planning or proper performance. In fact, it has been said that since the second half of 1950, individual railway administrations have actively engaged in soliciting private business for the sole purpose of inflating traffic statistics so as to attain or over-fulfill assigned quotas. Moreover, some of the plans made have not been in accordance with the actual pattern of commodity movement. All this has, therefore, led to waste and improper distribution of the available rolling stock.[32]

However, notwithstanding the shortcomings in the utilization of available rolling stock and traffic planning, on the whole, Communist China appears to have been reasonably successful in carrying out the transportation work involved in its overall economic plan. Apart from the increasing volume of rail traffic, which points to this conclusion, an examination of the composition of rail freight suggests that under the priorities scheme mentioned above movement of the essential commodities necessary for the government's plans of construction and price control has been kept at a relatively high level.

COMPOSITION OF RAIL FREIGHT TRAFFIC

In terms of tons carried, during the first eight months of 1950, 80 per cent of the entire freight traffic on Chinese railways—not including the Chinese Changchun Railway—consisted of coal, grain, and cotton. Coal alone accounted for 46 per cent of the total.[33] These figures may be compared with the corresponding data for 1935 regarding the railway system in China Proper, when mineral and agricultural products, which included the above three items, represented 64 per cent and 18 per cent of total rail freight respectively.[34]

Although detailed information on the importance of different commodity groups in subsequent years is wanting, official reports have pointed to a large increase in the quantity of iron and steel products, ores, and construction materials transported by rail. Given the quantity of iron and steel transported in 1950 as 100, that in 1952 and 1953 was 162 and 230 respectively. The corresponding index numbers for ores and construction materials, measured against the same base year, was 685 in 1952 and 1230 in 1953.[35] In 1953,

3.8 million tons of grain entered into inter-regional trade, while some 30 million tons were planned to be handled by the state trading companies alone.[36] According to the Communist Ministry of Food, 80 per cent of all grain transport during the 1950–1954 period was by rail.[37] A large increase in the transport of timber has also been noted in the same period.

Since shipments of all the above-mentioned items are under the direct control of the central government, increase in the volume of their transport along with the overall expansion of railway freight traffic is of particular siginficance. In the first place, it suggests that the priority system has been adhered to with some measure of success. In the second place, it is possible that to the extent shortage of rolling stock has exercised a restraining influence on the exchange of goods between regions, the burden has been borne by other "non-essential" goods.

FREIGHT RATES, THROUGH TRAFFIC, AND THE "RESPONSIBILITY SYSTEM"

Within the limits imposed by the capacity of the present railway system, expansion of freight traffic by rail as described above has been facilitated by three other factors which should be mentioned in passing.

First, there are now thirty different classes of freight rates with a ratio of one to seventeen between the highest and the lowest rates.[38] They taper off as the distance traveled increases, beginning with a 10 per cent reduction for shipments over the range of 210 to 500 kilometers and ending with a maximum discount of 70 per cent for the 1,510-2,000 kilometer range. Special seasonal rates for certain farm and marine products, as well as lower rates for less-than-carload shipments are also provided. The special rate applied to coal is said to be below the operating cost. The same is probably true in grain transport. Since even government-owned enterprises have to adhere to the practice of business accountability and must therefore take transport cost into consideration, low freight rates have acted as a subsidy to some industries and users of the railways. At the same time, the larger number of freight classes has given the Communist authorities an added opportunity to regulate production and commodity movement by freight discrimination.

Second, parallel to their role in regulating domestic trade, freight rates have been used to stimulate certain groups of exports. For instance, a discount of 50 per cent from the regular rates is granted on export shipments of tea, silk, casing, etc., while a 30 per cent discount is given to those of wool, camel hair, and wood oil.

Third, the effect of the low freight rates on both domestic and foreign trade is reinforced by the reintroduction of the so-called "responsibility system" on a national scale as of January, 1953, and by through traffic arrangements with foreign railways and other transport facilities. On the one hand, the "responsibility system," which for a long time fell into disuse both before and after the establishment of the Communist regime, now frees the shippers from responsibility during transit. On the other hand, through traffic arrangements have made possible long-distance hauls over routes served by different carriers without the need of making individual arrangements for transshipment.

Based on an agreement reached at the International Railway Through Transport Conference held in July, 1953, in Moscow, Communist China now provides through freight and passenger rail service with such countries as the U.S.S.R., Korea, Outer Mongolia, East Germany, Poland, Czechoslovakia, Rumania, Hungary, Bulgaria, and Albania.[39] A similar arrangement has also been made with Communist-controlled Indo-China. Domestic through traffic has also been made possible by special joint transport agencies in conjunction with different carriers. Thus it may not be an overstatement to say that every attempt has been made by Communist China to develop rail traffic as a means of transforming the Communist Chinese economy into an integrated whole.

IV

NAVIGATION ROUTES

At the end of 1953, 26,000 kilometers of Communist China's inland waterways were reported to be open to navigation by steamers and steam launches.[40] In addition, another 64,000 kilometers were probably also open to native junks. The principal inland waterways may be grouped into (1) the Yangtze and its tributaries which serve a number of the East, Central-South, and Southwest China provinces,

(2) the Hei-lung-chiang, Sungari, and Ussuri system in northern Manchuria, and the Liao-ho in southern Manchuria, (3) the Pearl River system in Kwangtung and Kwangsi, (4) smaller rivers in Chekiang and Fukien, and (5) certain sections of the Hwai River and its tributaries.[41] A detailed list of some of the established routes is given in the following table:

ESTABLISHED PRINCIPAL INLAND WATERWAY ROUTES IN CHINA

River	*Route*	*Length of Established Service (kilometers)*
Ch'ang-chiang (Yangtze)	I-pin, Lu-hsien, Chungking, Wan-hsien, I-ch'ang, Hankow, Chiu-chiang, An-ch'ing, Nanking, Shanghai	2,539
Han-shui	Han-chung, Lao-ho-k'ou, Hsiang-yang, Sha-yang, Han-ch'uan, Hankow	1,171
Chia-ling-chiang	Pai-shui-chiang, Kuang-yuan, Nan-ch'ung, Ho-ch'uan, Chungking	588
Min-chiang	Ch'eng-tu, Lo-shan, I-pin	329
Yuan-shui	Huang-hsien, Tzu-ch'iang, Ch'en-ch'i, Yuan-ling, T'ao-yuan, Ch'ang-te, Han-shou	706
Hsiang-shui	Ling-ling, Ch'i-yang, Heng-yang, Hsiang-t'an, Ch'ang-sha, Ying-t'ien	515
Lishui	Ts'u-li, Chin-shih	112
Tzu-shui	Yuan-chiang, Shao-yang, Wu-kang	481
Kan-chiang	Hu-K'ou, Nan-ch'ang, Feng-ch'eng, Chi-an, Wan-an, Kan-hsien	630
Fu-ho	Kuang-ch'ang, Nan-ch'eng, Lin-ch'uan, Nan-ch'ang	385
Hsin-chiang	Yü-shan, Sang-yao, I-yang, Yu-ch'iang, Nan-ch'ang	375
Chin-chiang	Wan-tsai, Shang-kao, Kao-an, Nan-ch'ang	305
Yuan-shui	I-ch'un, Hsin-yu, Chang-shu, Nan-ch'ang	285
Hsiu-shui	Hsiu-shui, Wu-ning, Yung-hsiu, Nan-ch'ang	280
Chu-chiang (Pearl River)	Chiang-men, Fo-shan, Shih-ch'i, San-fou, Macao, Canton	778
Hsi-chiang	Nan-ning, Kuei-p'ing, Wu-chou, Chao-ch'ing, Canton	992
Pei-chiang	Ying-te, Ch'ing-yuen, San-shui, Chu-chiang	390
Tung-chiang	Lao-lung, Ho-yuan, Hui-yang, Canton	230
Liu-chiang	Ch'ang-an, Jung-hsien, Liu-chiang, Kuei-p'ing	496
Kuei-chiang	Hsing-an, Kuei-lin, P'ing-lo, Ts'ang-wu	459

River	*Route*	*Length of Established Service (kilometers)*
Yu-chiang	Pai-se, P'ing-ma, Nan-ning	468
Tso-chiang	Lung-chou, Nan-ning	334
Han-chiang	Ta-p'u, Ch'ao-an	119
Ch'ien-t'ang-chiang	K'ai-hua, Hua-fou, Ch'ang-shan, Ch'u-hsien, Lan-ch'i, Chien-te, T'ung-lu, Fu-yang, Hang-chou	328
Min-chiang	Nan-p'ing, Fu-chou, Ch'ang-lo, Ch'ang-men	329
Chin-chiang	Nan-an, Chin-chiang, Hsin-p'u	103
Yung-shao-yün-ho (canal)	Yü-yao, Shao-hsing, Hsi-hsing	135
Yü-yao-chiang	T'ung-ming, Yü-yao, Yin-hsien	125
Hei-lung-chiang (Amur)	Mo-ho, Ch'i-ch'ien, Wu-su-li	2,381
Sung-hua-chiang (Sungari)	Ha-erh-pin, Hei-lung-chiang	696
	Ha-erh-pin, Nun-chiang	241
	Nun-chiang-Fu-yu	44
Nun-chiang	Sung-hua-chiang, Ta-lai	47
Wu-su-li-chiang (Ussuri)	Hei-lung-chiang, Hsin-k'ai-ho	619
Liao-ho	Ying-k'ou, T'ai-tzu-ho	53
	Total	18,068

SHIPPING TONNAGE

With the banning of foreign shipping on China's inland rivers,[42] inland waterway transport must now depend entirely upon domestic shipping, the modern part of which is extremely small. According to one estimate, of the 400,000 gross tons of the China Merchant Steamship Company, which was the largest government-owned domestic shipping organization, only 70,000 tons were left to the Communists in 1949. The total volume of domestic-owned shipping available in mainland China after the Nationalists' evacuation was no more than 200,000 tons.[43] Three hundred and sixty-six vessels, totalling 160,000 gross tons, were in the Hankow-Shanghai area. Of these 66 vessels with a total tonnage of 65,000 tons were damaged. Of the remaining 300 vessels fewer than ten were seagoing ones, even including some government-owned small tankers. Two of the three private seagoing vessels that remained in Communist hands were sunk in the mouth of the Yangtze.[44] Next to the China Merchant Steamship Company, the most important domestic shipping line is the Min-sheng Company[45] which had 43,000 gross tons in 1952. Thus, allowing for new shipbuilding since 1949, as well as salvage and destruction through air raids, etc., barring large unreported transfers from the Soviet Union, the total tonnage of steamers, tugboats, etc., now available in Communist China is probably in the order of 300,000 gross tons. It is believed that an equivalent volume of foreign shipping is also available for coastal service.[46]

Even if all the Chinese-owned vessels were concentrated on inland river routes, which is not the case, because of the small tonnage available, plus the fact that some of the vessels cannot be used for freight, Communist China would still have to depend upon the traditional junks for its waterway transport to a great extent. The total tonnage of junks available for river navigation in 1951 was reported to be twenty-three times that of steamers.[47] A later report has put the total tonnage of junks in the country in 1953 at 4 million tons. However, since over a period of time their capacity in transportation is limited by their speed, the aggregate volume of freight carried in relation to that by steamships is considerably less than the ratio in total tonnage would indicate. However, even under such limitations, about one-half of the total freight traffic on inland waterways in 1953 was accounted for by junks. Prior to the opening of the Chengtu-Chungking Railway in 1952, junks were responsible for one-half of all surface freight movement in the entire Southwest Region.[48]

DEVELOPMENT IN WATERWAY TRANSPORT

Unlike railway statistics, information on waterway transport has been relatively poor. However, according to official reports, several developments may be noted.

In the first place, if comparisons are made between 1950 and 1952, the expansion of coastal freight traffic was far greater than that of river traffic. For instance, in terms of tons carried, the increase was 589 per cent in coastal traffic, but only 88 per cent for government-owned shipping on the Yangtze and the Sungari, and 25 per cent for all shipping other than junks on the Yangtze.[49] However, allowing for the fact that the comparison may be distorted as a result of Nationalist blockade activities in 1950, one may use 1951 as the base year. On this basis the increase in coastal traffic between 1951 and 1952 would be 47 per cent as against 36 per cent on the Yangtze and 70 per cent on the Yangtze and the Sungari combined. Since the Sungari is really an international waterway, increase in shipping activity on the river and increase in coastal traffic both may be regarded at least in an appreciable degree as a reflection of the expansion of foreign trade, and possibly also increasing activity by foreign shipping.

Second, the expansion of coastal freight traffic was greater in terms of ton-nautical-miles than in terms of tons carried during the 1950-1952 period. The reverse is true, however, if comparison is made between 1951 and 1952. The considerable increase in the average distance traveled from 1950 to 1952 indicated more effective control by Communist China of its coastal waters and is particularly significant from both the economic and the political points of view.[49a]

Third, waterway transport on the West River in Kwangtung and Kwangsi increased from an index of 100 in 1951 to 190 in 1952 and 800 in 1953.[50] The rate of increase surpasses that for both coastal traffic and freight movement on other rivers. Although different interpretations may be advanced for this phenomenon, one cannot held wondering whether it was not in some way related to Communist activities in the border area between Kwangsi and Indo-China.

OPERATING EFFICIENCY AND FREIGHT RATES

Several factors have contributed to the expansion of water transport during recent years.

Improvement in operating efficiency, for instance, has succeeded in reducing the length of a round trip on the Yangtze between I-ch'ang and Chungking by steamer from 12 days to 4 days in 1952. Similarly, a round trip between Shanghai and Hankow which took up to 10 days before August, 1952, was shortened to 6 days in January, 1954. Round trips between Chia-mu-ssu and Fu-chin on the Sungari have also been reduced from 6 to 3.6 days.[51]

Along with the reduction in time, changes in towing practice through the adoption of "single-file towing," reportedly a Soviet suggestion, has had the effect of increasing transport capacity from

2-3 tons a time in downstream sailings on the Yangtze to an average of 8 tons.[52] The same development has been observed on other rivers.

Because of cost reduction, freight charges have declined. On the Yangtze, for instance, shipping charges have been lowered successively. Compared with the preceding years, freight rate reduction amounted to 39 per cent in 1950, 35 per cent in 1951, and 30 per cent in 1952 respectively.[53] At the same time, freight tonnage carried on the Yangtze increased from 3.1 million tons in 1950 to 3.9 million in 1952, 5.3 million in 1953, and 6.6 million in 1954.[54] The monthly transport capacity by freighters between Shanghai and Hankow now approximates 500,000 tons a month. Together with junks, which probably can carry as much as the freighters, the Yangtze acts as a major channel for east-west traffic of which 70 per cent consists of building materials and industrial products while grain and cotton are also important items.[55]

HIGHWAY MILEAGE AND ROUTES

Highway traffic is the least developed form of surface transportation in China although rapid progress was made in road construction during recent decades. The most serious limitations are quite obvious —namely, lack of domestic manufacturing facilities for motor vehicles, high fuel cost, and the relatively small capacity of trucks, especially the pay load, for long-distance transportation. Shortage of building material for modern highways has also affected the quality of road surfacing so that relatively few roads can sustain heavy traffic even if a large number of motor vehicles were available. Lack of rubber-tired vehicles has also increased the need for road maintenance. As a result of these factors, highway traffic is of little economic significance except for short hauls and as feeder for railways and waterways.

However, there are still a few provinces in which railways either do not exist or are not connected with the national network and in which inland waterways are also unimportant. Fukien on the coast, Kweichow, Yunnan, Sikang, and Tibet in the Southwest, and Sinkiang and the former province of Ningsia in the Northwest belong to this category. Freight movement in these areas is forced to use the existing roads which also assume particular significance from the political and strategic standpoints.

However, a network of highways does exist in China, and it would be a serious mistake to belittle their potential importance in the long run. The exact length of the network cannot be determined without a far more extensive study than it is possible to undertake in this volume. One of the difficulties stems from the fact that Chinese highway statistics are not always comparable because of (1) the existence of national, provincial, and county roads, (2) differences in geographical coverage in individual reports, and (3) lack of uniform treatment concerning roads open and closed to traffic, completed and unfinished constructions, and sections jointly used by different routes.

Bearing the above factors in mind, we may note, in the first place, that the total length of highways in China was first reported by the Chinese Communists at the 1949 conference on waterway and highway transportation as 372,094 kilometers.[56] This figure very obviously included the national and provincial highways of China Proper, as well as Manchuria, because the corresponding figure in all Nationalist-controlled areas in 1946 was no more than 191,198 kilometers.[57] Moreover, the network of national highways, including both class A and class B roads,[58] but excluding roads in Manchuria, totalled 57,102 kilometers (including 6,554 kilometers unfinished[59]) or about 30 per cent of the 1946 total, including provincial highways. Thus one may be justified in assuming that of the 372,094 kilometers of roads reported in 1949 probably 30 per cent, or about 110,000 kilometers, represented class A and class B national highways, and that some 50 per cent of the latter were in China Proper and Manchuria respectively.

The above estimate may be checked against Communist statistics on the length of roads open to traffic which totalled 120,000 kilometers in 1952. Only 1,647 kilometers of new roads were built during 1950–1952. This puts the length of highways in 1949 at 118,353 kilometers, of which 75,000 were open to traffic.[60] The following figures present a complete picture of the progress in highway rehabilitation as officially reported:

Length of National Highways Open to Traffic in Communist China, 1949–1953

(In kilometers)

Year	Kilometers
1949	75,000
1950	102,800
1951	107,400
1952	120,000
1953	130,000

Source: Economic Bulletin, No. 46, p. 13, December, 1953.

One-half of the 1953 total is said to represent all-weather roads. The lengths and routes of the network in existence in China outside Manchuria are given in the tables below.

NATIONAL HIGHWAY NETWORK OF CHINA PROPER
SEPTEMBER, 1947

Line	*Terminals*	*Kms. Completed*	*Kms. To Be Completed*	*Joint Use w/other Lines*	*Kms. Actual Length*
BASIC					
No. 1	Shanghai-Lhassa	4,041	1,180	—	5,221
No. 2	Kowloon-P'angchiang	3,411	—	80	3,331
No. 3	Mawei-Hoerhkuossu	5,386	—	63	5,323
No. 4	Wanting-Ch'engte	4,075	540	208	4,407
LATERAL					
No. 1	Hsiamen-Chennankuan	1,923	—	275	1,648
Br. No. 1	Canton-Hsintu	279	—	19	260
No. 2	Shanghai-T'ienshench'iao	2,782	—	390	2,392
Br. No. 1	T'aiho-Yushuwan	758	—	61	697
Br. No. 2	Yungchia-Yangwan	659	—	34	625
Br. No. 3	Hsiangshan-Hangchou	257	—	—	257
No. 3	Lussukang-Paoch'eng	2,053	—	196	1,857
Br. No. 1	Paoshan-Yunnan-Burma Bdr.	234	—	—	234
Br. No. 2	Ch'ienchiang-Sanchiaop'ing	457	—	—	457
No. 4	Lienyunkang-Mingt'akai	3,345	2,414	487	5,272
Br. No. 1	Anhsi-Huangliukou	759	—	—	759
Br. No. 2	Paiyangho-Shach'e	1,215	217	—	1,432
No. 5	Tsingtao-Ningsia	1,499	450	406	1,543
Br. No. 1	Weihsien-Weihaiwei	480	—	—	480
No. 6	Tolun-Shanpa	1,224	—	70	1,154
LONGITUDINAL					
No. 1	Haian-Shanhaikuan	4,297	—	216	4,081
No. 2	Shant'ou-Chouchiak'ou	2,042	—	76	1,966
Br. No. 1	Hsihsien-Wuhu	242	—	—	242
No. 3	Ch'angte-P'angchiang	2,128	—	198	1,930
Br. No. 1	Jufen-K'aifeng	178	—	—	178
No. 4	K'angchiang-Pailingmiao	3,074	340	1,086	2,328
Br. No. 1	Yulin-Lient'ang	306	78	—	384
Br. No. 2	Kueilin-Hengyang	361	—	—	361
Br. No. 3	Lip'u-Sanhui	584	—	—	584
No. 5	Talo-Shanpao	2,567	1,054	150	3,471
Br. No. 1	Peihai-Shatsuling	1,025	—	29	996
Br. No. 2	Hok'ou-Ch'engkung	279	191	—	470
Br. No. 3	Mienyang-Shuangshihp'u	565	—	—	565

Line	Terminals	Kms. Completed	Kms. To Be Completed	Joint Use w/other Lines	Kms. Actual Length
LONGITUDINAL SECONDARY LINES					
No. 1	Chenan-Hsiaokuanho	278	—	—	278
No. 2	Hsiehwu-Taot'angho	673	—	—	673
No. 3	Chiuch'uan-Ch'atao	360	90	—	450
No. 4	Joch'iang-K'uerhlei	442	—	—	442
No. 5	Wusu-T'ach'eng	354	—	—	354
Total		54,592	6,554	4,044	57,102

Source: Government Information Office of the Executive Yuan, *National Highway Network* [of] *China*, pp. 1-60, Nanking, September, 1947.

Routes of National Highway Network of China Proper

BASIC LINES:

No. 1: Shanghai, Nanking, Wu-hu, An-ch'ing, Chiu-chiang, Hankow, I-ch'ang, Chungking, Ch'eng-tu, Ya-an, K'ang-ting, Yu-shu, Lhassa

No. 2: Chiu-lung, Canton, Ch'u-chiang, Heng-yang, Ch'angsha, Wu-ch'ang, Hankow, K'ai-feng, Tientsin, Peking, Chang-chia-k'ou, P'ang-chiang

No. 3: Ma-wei, Fu-chou (Lin-ch'uan), Nan-ch'ang, Wu-ch'ang, Hankow, Hsi-an, Lan-chou, Ho-erh-kuo-ssu

No. 4: Wan-ting, K'un-ming, Chungking, Hsi-an, T'ai-yuan, Pao-ting, Peking, Chang-chia-k'ou, Ch'eng-te

LATERAL LINES:

No. 1: Hsiamen, Kanhsien, Ch'uchiang, Ta-t'ang, Nan-yang, Chen-nan-kuan

No. 2: Shanghai, Hang-chou, Hsi-hsien, Nan-ch'ang, Ch'ang-sha, Ch'ang-te, Chen-yuan, Kuei-yang

No. 3: Lu-ssu-kang, Nan-t'ung, P'u-k'ou, Ho-fei, Liu-an, Huang-ch'uan, Nan-yang, Lao-ho-ku, Pao-ho, Pao-ch'eng

No. 4: Lien-yun-kang, Su-ch'ien, Hsu-chou, K'ai-feng, Lo-yang, T'ung-kuan, Hsi-an, Hsien-yang, Pao-chi, Lan-chou, Hsi-ning, Jo-chiang, Ch'ien-mo, Yu-tien, Ho-tien, Sha-ch'e, Ming-t'a-kai

No. 5: Tsingtao, Wei-hsien, Chi-nan, Ta-ming, Ch'ang-chih, T'ai-ku, Feng-yang, Sui-te, Ningsia

No. 6: To-lun, Chang-chia-k'ou, Kuei-sui, Pao-t'ou, San-pa

LONGITUDINAL LINES:

No. 1: Hai-an, Canton, Chien-yang, Ch'u-hsien, Hang-chou, Nan-king, Chi-nan, Tientsin

No. 2: Shan-t'ou, Hsin-ning, Kan-hsien, An-ch'ing, Liu-an, Chou-chia-k'ou

No. 3: Ch'ang-te, Hsiang-yang, Lao-ho-k'ou, Nan-yang, Lo-yang, Chin-ch'eng, T'ai-yuan, Ta-tung, P'ang-chiang

No. 4: K'an-chiang, Pin-yang, Kuei-yang, Chungking, Lung-chung, Hsi-an, Sui-te, Yu-ling, Pao-t'ou, Pai-ling-miao

No. 5: Ta-lo, K'un-ming, Hsi-ch'ang, Ya-an, Ch'eng-tu, Mien-yang, Wu-tu, Lan-chou, Ningsia, Shanpao

GOVERNMENT POLICY, TRAFFIC, AND FREIGHT RATES

The preceding survey shows quite clearly that up to 1953 relatively little was done with respect to new highway construction. This is the result of Communist China's policy in the transportation field to which reference has been made several times before.

The decision of the first national conference in 1949 on highway transport and navigation made it quite clear that new roads would be built primarily for military use and that high priority was to be given only to the repair of main national highways and a few provincial roads of economic significance, while only ordinary maintenance was to be undertaken on the other roads by employing mass labor.[61] A second conference on highways was convened in early 1951 when the same policy was reaffirmed. New roads would continue to be built for defense purposes, and government transport companies were to be established especially in developing trade between urban centers and surrounding rural areas and in fostering through traffic.[62]

At the end of 1952 government motor transport companies had a total operating route length of 93,000 kilometers and carried 4.03 million tons of freight for a total of 255 million ton-kilometers. The corresponding figures for 1950 were 960,000 tons and 100 million ton-kilometers.[63] These data may be compared with statistics gathered during the Nationalist period which, while showing a much smaller volume of freight, consistently indicated a much longer average haul.[64] The latter phenomenon was true not only during the war years when Free China was completely dependent on road transport in some of the interior provinces, but also in 1937 and after World War II. The larger volume in tons carried under the Communist regime points to more active freight movement between the countryside and marketing towns while the shorter haul is a logical development in view of the high cost of motor vehicle transport.

As mentioned before, the high operating cost of trucks is due to the costliness of fuel and maintenance. As reported in the official publication, *People's Communications,* in October, 1952, as a result of notable improvements, gasoline consumption by certain types of vehicles had declined from 8 kilometers to 14 kilometers per gallon while the life of tires had risen from 10,000 to 16,000 kilometers. Since the two manufacturing plants for automobiles now under construction are still unfinished, and a plant in Tientsin can only undertake body assembling, practically all motor vehicles in use have been imported, and the consequent depreciation cost is very high.

The level of freight rates may be illustrated by a few examples. For instance, following a general rate reduction in June, 1952, first class freight rates by trucks in Szechwan amounted to ¥3,195 per ton-kilometer for gasoline-driven trucks, ¥3,400 for alcohol-burning vehicles, and ¥2,980 for charcoal-burning vehicles. At about the same time, freight rates in Northwest China, the country's principal petroleum-producing area, ranged from ¥2,640 to ¥3,988 per ton-kilometer. In Fukien province, where oil is not produced locally, while the rate in charcoal-burning vehicles was fixed at ¥3,200 per ton-kilometer in May, 1952, that on gasoline trucks was ¥4,200. The latter rates were already some 20 per cent lower than before the general reduction.[65] It is possible that rates in areas where imported fuels are available may be somewhat lower and that further reductions may have been made since mid-1952. They are, however, a far cry from the basic rate on railways which, even as early as 1951 when coal consumption and other operating costs were still exceedingly high, charged only ¥100 per ton-kilometer.[66] Apparently, highway transport by motor vehicles in Communist China is about thirty times as expensive as rail transport. In certain areas the differential is even larger. This ratio is roughly equal to that of the prewar period pointed out earlier in this chapter and indicates quite conclusively the poor competitive position of highway transport and its limited usefulness. This situation cannot be materially altered even though "mass transportation" methods by primitive means are extensively used.[67]

VI

TRANSPORTATION, TRADE AND ECONOMIC PLANNING

The preceding review has dealt with the physical facilities through which commodities may be moved from one place to another. Since these physical facilities are limited, especially in long-distance movement, their optimum utilization requires that proper reference be made to the pattern of domestic trade. In other words, if large quantities of construction materials produced in North China are required by buyers in South China, sufficient rolling stock must be made available for moving the goods. Since competitive claims for transportation facilities originate from different areas, no transportation plan can be formulated without a corresponding plan for domestic trade.

The function of trade is to bring buyers and sellers together. However, in an economy where both production and consumption are being progressively drawn into the orbit of central planning, it is no longer permissible for trade to look after itself. Certain types of buyers, such as government industrial enterprises and export agencies, must be given preference. Other categories of buyers, such as ordinary consumers, may have to be restricted in their purchases. Similarly, discrimination must be practised with respect to sellers. The freedom with which buyers can obtain supplies and sellers can dispose of their products directly affects freedom in planning of production and consumption. Consequently, given an economic plan that envisages an allocation of resources materially different from the voluntary pattern, one effective method of plan enforcement is to control the link between buyers and sellers, namely, trade. Given adequate trade control, the basis of a transport plan will also be established inasmuch as, outside local exchange, all trade must entail transportation.

In the case of Communist China, there are some additional reasons for government control of trade. One important reason the Communist authorities had immediately after the establishment of the new regime was to control the supply of certain key commodities such as foodstuffs, cotton textiles, and coal for the purpose of maintaining price stability. These and other commodities were sold through government wholesale and retail channels in order to curb speculation and hoarding and to induce inventory liquidation by private businessmen.[68] These same trade channels have since become agencies for rationing of consumers' goods and allocation of other products and raw materials as an integral part of general planning. Another reason for trade control is the policy to reduce the relative, if not absolute, share of resources devoted to trade. This policy is a part of the "industrial and commercial adjustment" program which we have already discussed in an earlier chapter. It owes its origin not only to the Communists' aversion to the middleman, but also to the desire to convert trade capital into industrial capital. By decreasing business inventory less finished products will have to be produced to satisfy a given demand and more resources will be freed for producing other commodities.

STATE TRADING COMPANIES AND COOPERATIVES

Two groups of trading agencies are employed by the Chinese Communists as the apparatus of trade control. These are the state trading companies and the cooperatives. As early as March, 1950, six state domestic trading companies were established as a part of the economic stabilization effort. These deal with the wholesale and retail of grains, cotton textiles (including cotton, yarn, and piece goods), general merchandise, salt, coal and building materials, and "native products."[69] Other state companies since established specialize in metals and machinery, chemicals, communications and electric equipment, petroleum, pharmaceuticals, and silk.[70] The cooperatives are of two kinds—consumers' cooperatives in urban areas and rural marketing and supply cooperatives.[71] The former are supply outlets only, while the latter, together with the state trading companies, engage in both buying and selling. As of 1954, the wholesale of industrial products has been centralized in the hands of the state trading companies, while the wholesale and retail of handicraft products are entirely handled by the cooperatives. Both groups of organizations are required to give each other first priority in supplying commodities. The cooperatives retail industrial products received mostly from the state trading companies to their members, especially the farmers, and act as purchasing agents for the trading companies particularly in such commodities as grain, cotton, and other farm products.[72] Although membership in cooperatives is completely voluntary in theory, it has been officially stated that "in a country like ours there is no possibility for withdrawals."[73] Since the cooperatives are organized in such a way that general direction is given from the top down and since the All-China Federation is under the direct control of the central government, both the cooperatives and the state trading companies must be regarded as government agencies. Both must operate under the system of contracts and business accountability, and both must strive to fulfill government quotas.

DEVELOPMENT OF GOVERNMENT TRADING

According to official statistics, considerable progress has been made by the state trading companies and the cooperatives in expanding their share of domestic trade. Their share in domestic wholesale trade increased from 50 per cent in 1952 to 80 per cent in 1954, while the corresponding share in retail trade in eight principal cities increased from 32 per cent in 1952 to 50 per cent in 1954.[74] During the first half of 1954, the membership of 31,000 rural supply and marketing cooperatives in the country stood at 165 million as compared with 138 million a year earlier.[75]

Under the system of planning adopted, the cooperatives are entrusted with the function of determining the demand for individual commodities, especially in the case of rural demand for industrial goods. They also play a key role in the large-scale purchase of such commodities as grain and cotton for direct distribution to other areas and through government trading companies. Within the limits set by available means of transportation, they have been active in promoting trade fairs at county, provincial, and even regional levels.[76]

TRADE PATTERN OF CERTAIN KEY COMMODITIES

An early example of the large-scale movement of certain key commodities under the sponsorship of the cooperatives may be found in the three-region commodity exchange program undertaken between November, 1950, and June, 1951. During this period 300,000 tons of corn, kaoliang, soybeans, and beancakes supplied by members of Manchurian rural cooperatives were shipped to North and East China in exchange for 600,000 bolts of cloth, 1,000 tons of raw cotton (lint) and varying quantities of handicraft and agricultural products.[77] With the expansion of state and cooperative trading, such organized movement of certain important commodities has vastly increased, as may be seen in the traffic statistics discussed earlier in this chapter.

The significance of commodity movement with respect to transportation needs and regional specialization can be best visualized only through a careful examination of the pattern for individual commodities. Unfortunately, without the benefit of complete traffic statistics, these patterns do not readily reveal themselves. Nor can they be determined a priori short of a clear identification of individual surplus and deficit areas. This would have to be predicated on the determination of regional production and consumption levels for a number of years. While such an attempt could doubtless be made, it would require far more space than can be devoted to it in the present volume. We must therefore content ourselves with a few general remarks.

The pattern of movement for industrial products can be deduced fairly easily since there are only a few centers of industrial production. Heavy industry is still concentrated in Manchuria although the Tientsin, T'ang-shan, and Shih-ching-shan area in Hopeh, T'ai-yuan in Shansi, Shanghai, and, to a lesser extent, Wu-han, and Chungking are also important centers. For the manufacture of consumers' goods, Shanghai, Tientsin, Wu-han, Tsingtao, Cheng-chou, Shih-chia-chuang are among the important centers, while certain areas of Manchuria are also of considerable significance. Accordingly, machinery and other products of heavy industry tend to move from Manchuria and North China to the South while consumers' goods tend to move in the reverse direction. For certain industrial products, such as electrical machinery, there is also some northward movement originating from Shanghai. Moreover, all groups of industrial products flow to the Northwest and the Southwest, especially the former region, where considerable construction activity has been taking place, not the least important of which is railway building.

In the case of construction materials, cement from North China is also shipped to Manchuria. On the other hand, building timber originates mostly from Manchuria and Inner Mongolia, as well as the Central-South province of Hunan.

The main centers of industrial activity are also principal markets for raw materials, food, and fuel. Apart from local and intra-regional movements congregating towards these centers, the following broad pattern may also be noted.

First, in the case of food grains, the exporting areas are roughly Manchuria, Inner Mongolia, Hunan, Hupeh, and Kiangsi in the Central-South, and Szechwan in the Southwest. The principal importing areas are North and East China, especially the Peking-Tientsin-T'ang-shan triangle and the Shanghai-Nanking area, as well as the Northwest. In terms of regions it is possible that future developments may turn East China as a whole into a surplus area and the entire Southwest region as a deficit area although Szechwan would probably continue as an exporter. As long as East China remains a deficit region the pattern of grain movement is roughly as follows:

	Exporting Area	*Importing Area*
1.	Manchuria, Inner Mongolia	North China, Northwest China, East China
2.	Central-South China	North China, East China
3.	Southwest China (certain areas only)	Northwest China, East China

In the group of textile fibers, raw cotton movement is undoubtedly the most important. Exports to East China where the Shanghai mills constitute a major source of demand as a rule originate from North China, Honan in the Central-South, and Northwest China. The same sources also supply Manchuria. Supplies from Hupeh and Hunan in the Central-South are also available to East China via the Yangtze. Cotton production in the Southwest is relatively unimportant. This pattern, however, is being radically altered as new mills are being erected in Hopeh, Shensi, Honan, and other cotton-producing areas. This effort to change the pattern of raw material movement will, of course, also affect that of the finished products.

In the case of coal, which has consistently accounted for one-half of the tonnage carried by rail, the flow is for coal from Manchuria and the northern provinces of Hopeh, Shantung, Shansi, and Honan —which cut across the former administrative regions—to go to Kiangsu, Anhwei, Chekiang, Hupeh, Hunan, and the southern coastal provinces of Fukien and Kwangtung. Northwest China also imports coal from the above exporting areas, and, upon completion of the Chengtu-Paochi Railway, may also derive coal from Szechwan. As coal mining in Northwest China develops, this pattern will be affected accordingly.[78]

PROSPECT AND IMPORTANCE OF RAILWAY CONSTRUCTION

Since much of the commodity movement in China is between the North and the South, and since navigable inland waterways do not provide longitudinal trunk lines over any long distance, railways and, in a more limited sense, coastal shipping are among the principal transportation methods to be developed. So far, Communist China's railway system does not appear to have presented any problem of serious, overall inadequacy to meet the demand of commodity movement. However, as industrial development progresses, the demand on transport facilities will increase. In fact, without new rail transport facilities it would not be possible to develop certain areas. This is particularly true in the case of Northwest China.

There is little doubt that the two railway lines now being built between Ch'eng-tu and Pao-chi and between Lan-chou and Ti-hua are among the most important both economically and politically. However, other constructions are also being actively pushed, notably the lines (1) from Pao-t'ou to Lan-chou and Ningsia, (2) from Ch'eng-tu to K'un-ming, and (3) from Huai-jou to Ch'eng-teh. The length of new lines built between 1950 and 1954 averaged only 460 kilometers a year. At the present rate of rolled steel production it should be possible to increase the pace of rail-laying if engineering plans and technical and construction workers are available, even though the once reported plan to construct some 200,000 kilometers of new lines during the First Five Year Plan is completely unrealistic.[79] The limiting factor is more likely to be the availability of rolling stock, on which Communist China will continue to be dependent on imports for a considerable time to come.[80] Here is another notable example of the effect of serious lags in certain branches of Chinese industry.[81]

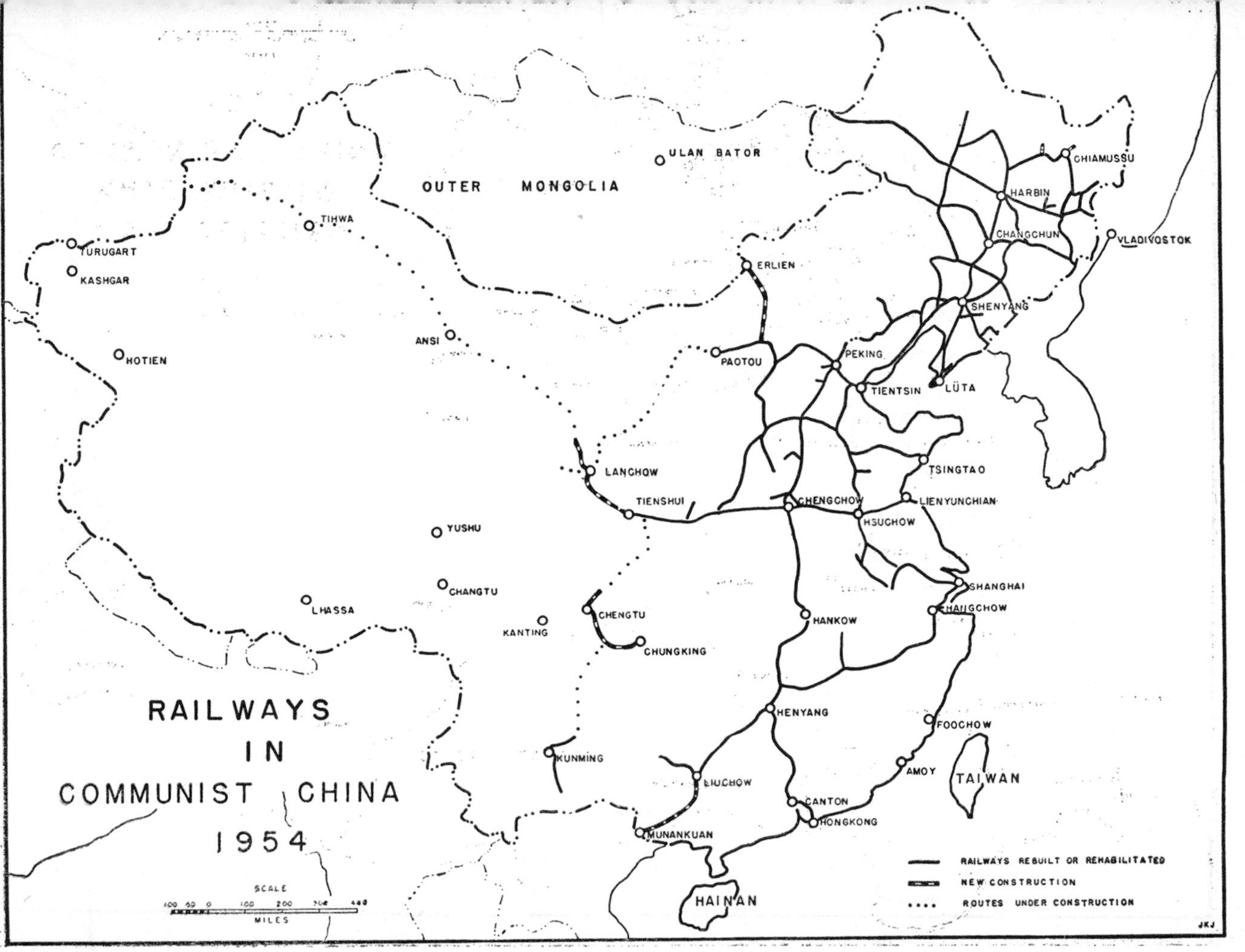
RAILWAYS
IN
COMMUNIST CHINA
1954
SCALE
400 50 0 100 200 300 400
MILES
RAILWAYS REBUILT OR REHABILITATED
NEW CONSTRUCTION
ROUTES UNDER CONSTRUCTION
OUTER MONGOLIA
ULAN BATOR
CHIAMUSSU
HARBIN
CHANGCHUN
VLADIVOSTOK
TURUGART
KASHGAR
TIHWA
ERLIEN
SHENYANG
ANSI
HOTIEN
PAOTOU
PEKING
TIENTSIN
LÜTA
LANCHOW
TIENSHUI
TSINGTAO
CHENGCHOW
LIENYUNCHIAN
HSUCHOW
YUSHU
CHANGTU
LHASSA
KANTING
CHENGTU
CHUNGKING
SHANGHAI
HANGCHOW
HANKOW
HENYANG
FOOCHOW
KUNMING
LIUCHOW
AMOY
TAIWAN
CANTON
HONGKONG
MUNANKUAN
HAINAN
JKJ

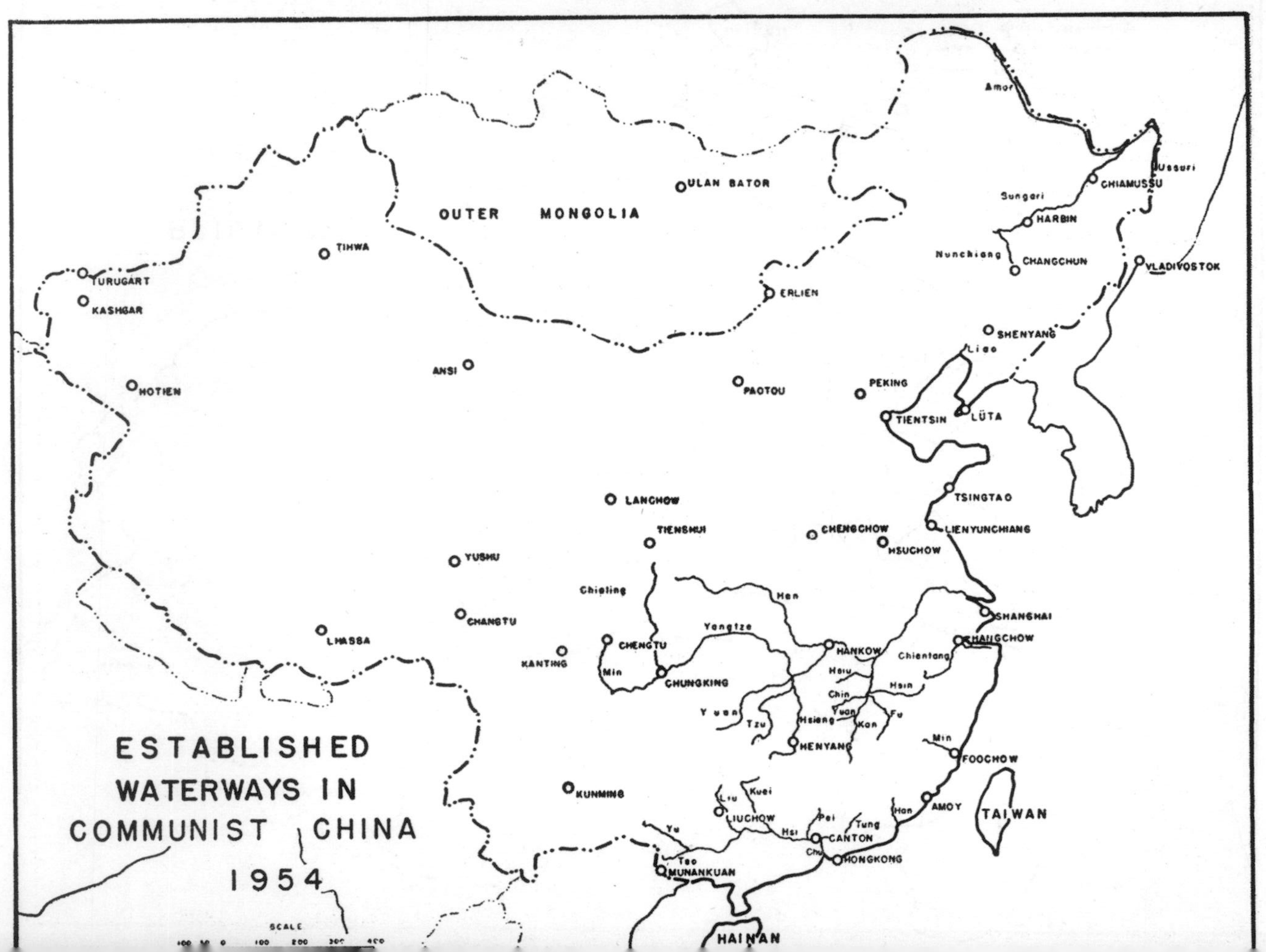
ESTABLISHED
WATERWAYS IN
COMMUNIST CHINA
1954
SCALE
OUTER MONGOLIA
ULAN BATOR
ERLIEN
PAOTOU
PEKING
TIENTSIN
LÜTA
SHENYANG
Liao
CHANGCHUN
Nunchiang
HARBIN
Sungari
CHIAMUSSU
Ussuri
Amur
VLADIVOSTOK
TSINGTAO
LIENYUNCHIANG
CHENGCHOW
HSUCHOW
SHANGHAI
HANGCHOW
Chientang
Hsin
Fu
Min
FOOCHOW
AMOY
Han
TAIWAN
Tung
Pei
Hsi
Chu
CANTON
HONGKONG
HANKOW
Hsiu
Chin
Yuan
Kan
Hsiang
HENYANG
Tzu
Yuan
Yangtze
Han
CHUNGKING
CHENGTU
Min
Chialing
KANTING
LIUCHOW
Liu
Kuei
Yu
Tso
MUNANKUAN
HAINAN
KUNMING
LANCHOW
TIENSHUI
YUSHU
CHANGTU
ANSI
TIHWA
LHASSA
HOTIEN
TURUGART
KASHGAR

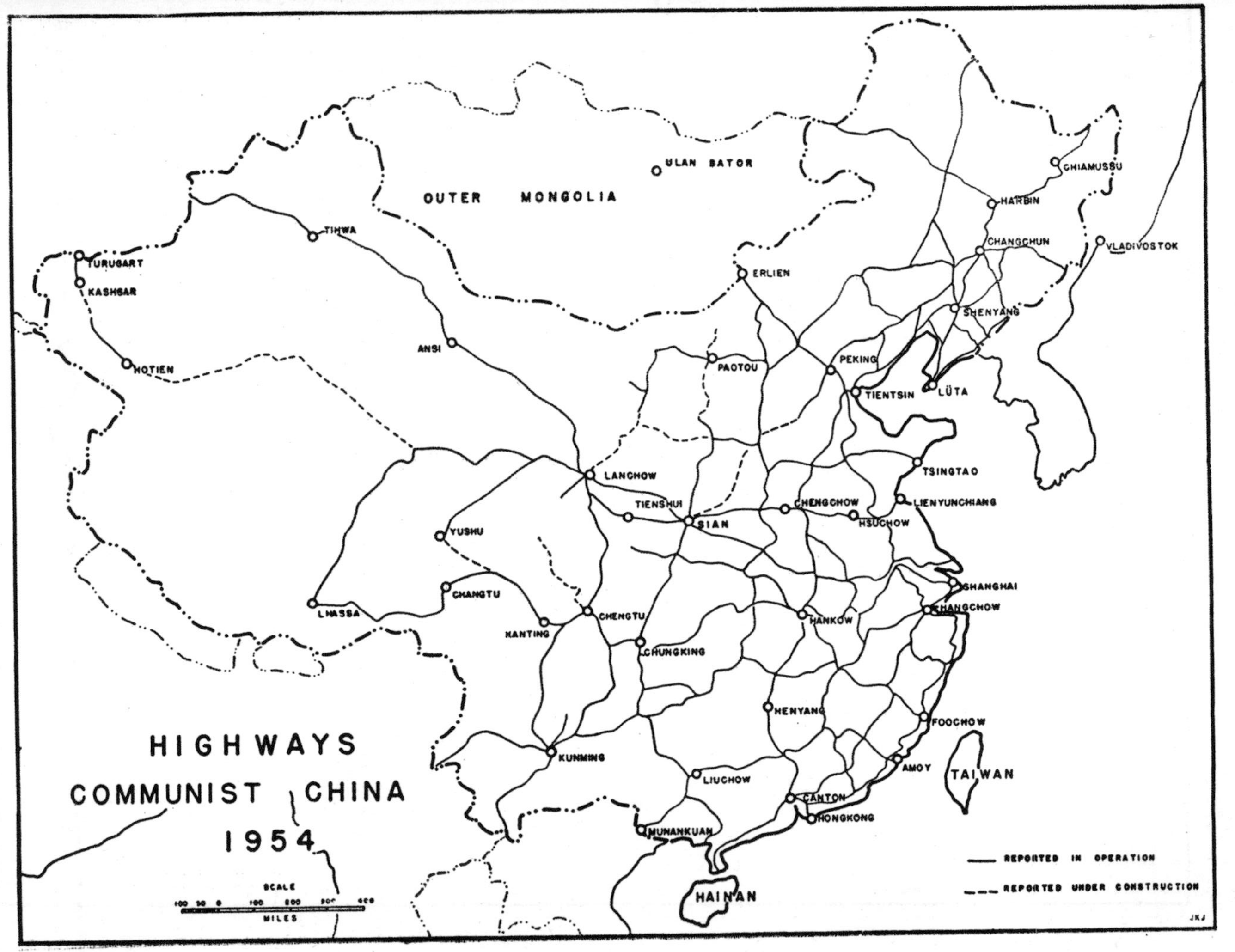
HIGHWAYS
COMMUNIST CHINA
1954
SCALE
MILES
REPORTED IN OPERATION
REPORTED UNDER CONSTRUCTION
OUTER MONGOLIA
ULAN BATOR
TAIWAN
HAINAN
VLADIVOSTOK
CHIAMUSSU
HARBIN
CHANGCHUN
SHENYANG
LÜTA
TIENTSIN
PEKING
TSINGTAO
LIENYUNCHIANG
HSUCHOW
SHANGHAI
HANGCHOW
FOOCHOW
AMOY
HONGKONG
CANTON
HENYANG
HANKOW
CHENGCHOW
ERLIEN
PAOTOU
SIAN
TIENSHUI
LANCHOW
CHUNGKING
CHENGTU
LIUCHOW
MUNANKUAN
KUNMING
KANTING
CHANGTU
YUSHU
ANSI
TIHWA
LHASSA
HOTIEN
KASHGAR
TURUGART
JKJ

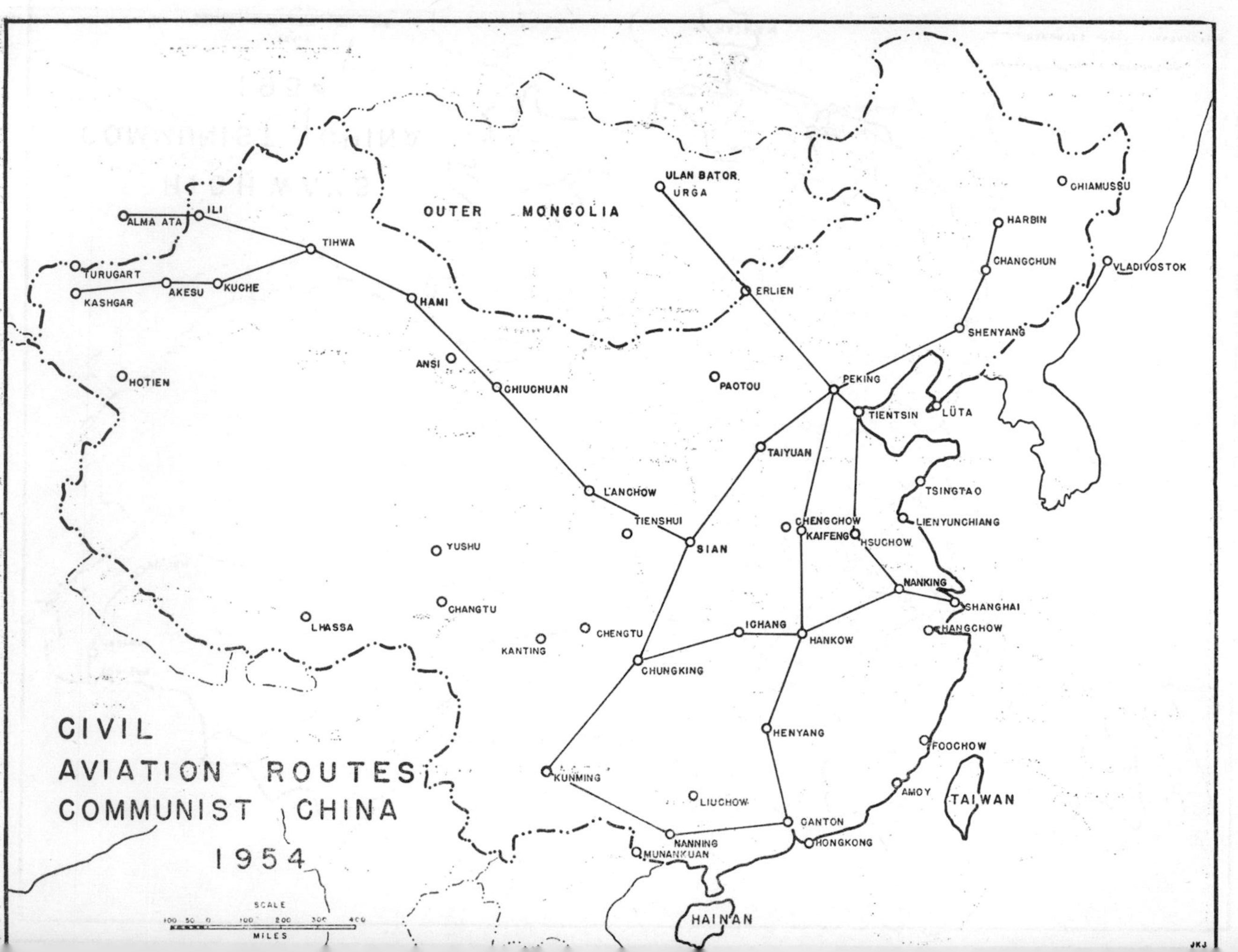
CIVIL
AVIATION ROUTES
COMMUNIST CHINA
1954
OUTER MONGOLIA
ULAN BATOR
URGA
ALMA ATA
ILI
TIHWA
TURUGART
AKESU
KUCHE
KASHGAR
HAMI
ERLIEN
CHIAMUSSU
HARBIN
CHANGCHUN
VLADIVOSTOK
SHENYANG
ANSI
HOTIEN
CHIUCHUAN
PAOTOU
PEKING
TIENTSIN
LÜTA
TAIYUAN
TSINGTAO
LANCHOW
TIENSHUI
CHENGCHOW
KAIFENG
HSUCHOW
LIENYUNCHIANG
YUSHU
SIAN
NANKING
SHANGHAI
CHANGTU
LHASSA
KANTING
CHENGTU
ICHANG
HANKOW
HANGCHOW
CHUNGKING
HENYANG
FOOCHOW
KUNMING
LIUCHOW
AMOY
TAIWAN
CANTON
NANNING
MUNANKUAN
HONGKONG
HAINAN
SCALE
MILES
JKJ

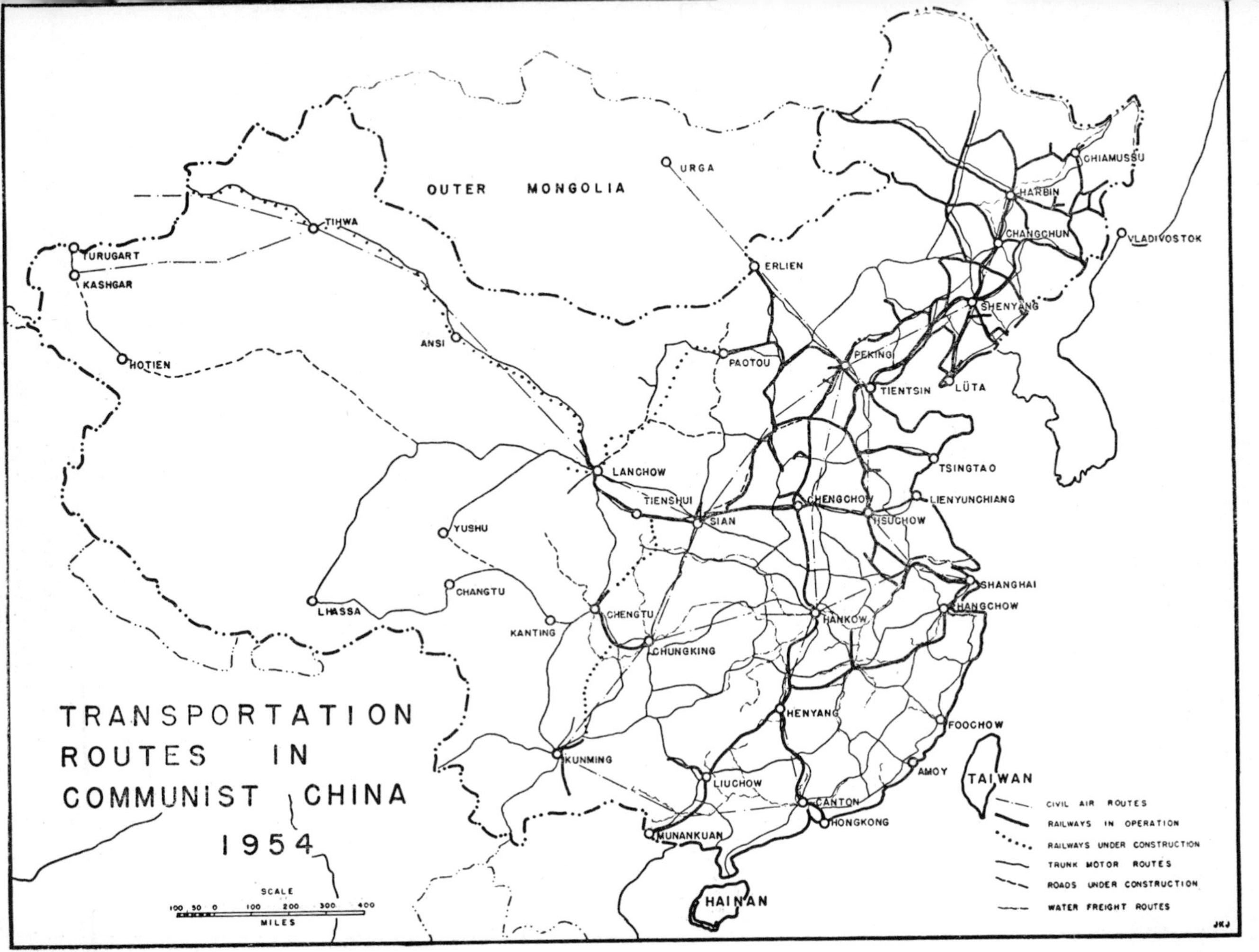
TRANSPORTATION
ROUTES IN
COMMUNIST CHINA
1954
SCALE
100 50 0 100 200 300 400
MILES
CIVIL AIR ROUTES
RAILWAYS IN OPERATION
RAILWAYS UNDER CONSTRUCTION
TRUNK MOTOR ROUTES
ROADS UNDER CONSTRUCTION
WATER FREIGHT ROUTES
OUTER MONGOLIA
URGA
TIHWA
TURUGART
KASHGAR
HOTIEN
ANSI
ERLIEN
PAOTOU
CHIAMUSSU
HARBIN
CHANGCHUN
VLADIVOSTOK
SHENYANG
PEKING
TIENTSIN
LÜTA
TSINGTAO
LIENYUNCHIANG
LANCHOW
TIENSHUI
SIAN
CHENGCHOW
HSUCHOW
YUSHU
CHANGTU
LHASSA
KANTING
CHENGTU
CHUNGKING
SHANGHAI
HANGCHOW
HANKOW
HENYANG
FOOCHOW
AMOY
TAIWAN
KUNMING
LIUCHOW
CANTON
HONGKONG
MUNANKUAN
HAINAN
JKJ

NOTES

1. *Masses Daily,* Hsi-an, February 1, 1952.

2. *Progress Daily,* Tientsin, December 29, 1951.

3. *Liberation Daily,* Shanghai, May 27, 1950

4. *New China Monthly,* Vol. IV, No. 6, p. 1302, October 25, 1951.

5. In 1952 government shipping accounted for 53.8 per cent of total inland waterway freight traffic. The ratio again rose to 57 per cent in 1953. See Ito Tashio, *Chukyo tetsudo no genjo* (The Present Condition of Communist China's Railways) (in Japanese), p. 6, Tokyo, 1954.

6. See Sun Hsiao-ts'un, "Current Financial and Economic Conditions and Economic Plans for 1950," *Economic Weekly,* Vol. X, No. 19, p. 4, Shanghai, May, 1950.

7. Report to the First National Committee of the PPCC in 1951, *New China Monthly,* No. 25, pp. 33-34, Peking, November, 1952.

8. NCNA, Peking, April 19, 1954.

9. *Chinese Yearbook,* pp. 848-849, Nanking, 1948.

10. *People's Daily,* Peking, November 15 ,1953.

11. *A Manual for Newspaper Readers,* pp. 786-788, Hankow, 1950; *Economic Bulletin,* No. 158, pp. 8-9, Hongkong, February, 1950; and *Wen-hui pao,* September 30, 1953.

12. Another report, however, stated that 14,089 kilometers of tracks were repaired during 1951. NCNA, November 4, 1951. This figure is suspect because, according to official reports, the total length in operation did not change by more than 2,000 kilometers between 1950 and 1952.

13. *Chinese Yearbook,* Vol. II, p. 848, Nanking, 1948. According to the same source, during 1947, the Communists destroyed 2,057 kilometers of tracks as well as 1,089 bridges and 236 railway stations.

14. 202 kilometers for south of the Yangtze, 755 for north of the Yangtze, 89 for Hainan, and 272 for Manchuria.

15. If the total of new lines built in 1953 and 1954 (1,019 kilometers) is added to the 24,232 kilometers reported in operation in 1952, the entire length would be 25,251 kilometers. Including the 1,318 kilometers of branches and spurs, the adjusted total would be 26,569 kilometers, which compares quite closely with our figure.

16. For details see the previous table.

17. See, for instance, Bureau of Information, *Postwar Railway Plan of the First Period,* Nanking, 1947. The Chining-Ehrlien Railway may perhaps be regarded as an exception. Though listed as a projected line in their long-term plan, the Nationalists later apparently saw no reason to push forward its construction even if they had been in a position to carry it out. According to the *Chinese Yearbook,* at the end of 1947, 27 per cent of the construction on the Tienshui-Lanchou Railway was finished, while 39 per cent of the Chengtu-Chungking Railway was completed, Vol. II, p. 853, Nanking, 1948.

18. Ministry of Communications and, later, Ministry of Railways, *Statistics of Chinese National Railways,* Nanking, various years.

19. Chin Shih-hsüan, *Railway Transportation,* pp. 219-221, Shanghai, 1948. The 1947-1948 figures given by Chin presumably include returns from Formosa.

20. Ch'i Yü, *op. cit.*

21. That is, the length of time between two successive loadings of the same car.

22. *People's Railways,* Vol. I, No. 2, p. 3, Peking, December 1, 1949.

23. Report by T'eng Tai-yüan, *New China Monthly,* Vol. I, No. 2, p. 432, December, 1949.

24. T'eng, *ibid.*, and *New China Monthly,* Vol. I, No. 5, pp. 1208-1210, Peking, March, 1950.

25. *New China Monthly,* Vol. III, No. 3, p. 632, Peking, December, 1950.

26. Cf. *New China Monthly,* No. 25, p. 33, Peking, November, 1951, and *Ta-kung pao,* Shanghai, December 29, 1952.

27. According to Ito Toshio's estimate, Communist China had 3,224 engines, 22,746 passenger cars, and 72,903 freight cars. However, it is not clear how these figures were arrived at. Cf. Ito Toshio, *op. cit.*, p. 35.

28. The railway workshops and rolling stock manufacturing plants in China are located at Ha-erh-pin (Harbin), Mu-tan-chiang, Huang-ku-t'un, and Dairen in Manchuria, as well as T'ang-shan, Ch'ang-hsin-tien, Nan-k'ou, Kalgan, Tientsin, Ssu-fang, Chi-nan, P'u-chen, Chiu-lung-kang, Shih-chia-chuang, Tai-yuan, Chiang-an, Pao-chi, Hsü-chou, Ch'i-shu-yen, Hsiao-shan, Yü-shan, Wu-tung, Heng-yang, Kuang-chou, Chu-chou, Wu-ch'ang, Kwei-lin, Su-ch'iao, and Ma-wei. *People's Railway,* Vol. I, No. 2, p. 5, Peking, December, 1949. Some of these workshops are very poorly equipped. The first freight locomotive manufactured in China was completed at the Ssu-fang plant in August, 1952. *People's Daily,* Peking, August 9, 1952.

29. Chao Chen-chüeh, *Postwar Reconstruction of Communications,* pp. 68-69, Shanghai, 1947.

30. For the text see *Compendium,* Vol. II, p. 665 et seq., Peking, 1951.

31. The railway system of Communist China is now divided into the following railway administrations: (1) Manchuria: Ha-erh-pin, Ch'i-ch'i-ha-erh, Chi-lin, and Chin-chou; (2) Northern Region: Peking, Tientsin, T'ai-yuan, Chi-nan, and Cheng-chou; (3) Southern Region: Shanghai, Canton, and Liu-chou; (4) the Chengtu-Chungking Railway Bureau; (5) the Kunming Bureau; and (6) the Northwest Trunk Line Engineering Bureau. Cf. Ch'i Yü, *op. cit.*, pp. 6-7.

32. See *New China Monthly,* No. 42, pp. 146-147, April, 1953. For examples of improper handling in the case of coal and lumber transport see *New China Monthly,* Vol. III, No. 1, p. 139, Peking, November, 1950.

33. *New China Monthly,* Vol. II, No. 6, p. 1328, Peking, October, 1950.

34. Chin Shih-hsüan, *op. cit.*, p. 221.

35. NCNA, November 3, 1953, and January 26, 1954.

36. NCNA, June 6, 1953.

37. *Ta-kung pao,* Tientsin, June 6, 1954.

38. Cf. Ch'i Yü, *op. cit.*

39. NCNA, January 14, 1954. The service between China and Russia was started in 1951. Machinery, cotton, and sugar were sent from Russia to Shanghai under this arrangement, while Chinese raw silk and woolen textiles were shipped from Shanghai to Russia. *China News Service,* Shanghai, April 5, 1954.

40. NCNA, Wuhan, December 27, 1953. Also reported at 28,000 kilometers in *Wen-hui pao,* Hongkong, September 30, 1953.

41. Coastal traffic in Communist China is to a large extent dependent on foreign flag ships. Prior to the relaxation of the Nationalist blockade of Shanghai and other southern ports, regular northern routes were at one time limited to (1) Ying-k'ou to Yen-t'ai, (2) Tientsin to Ta-lien, Tsingtao, Ying-k'ou, and Lung-k'ou, (3) Ta-lien to Yen-t'ai and Tsingtao, (4) An-tung to Yen-t'ai and Tsingtao, and (5) Tsing-tao to Lien-yün-kang. Only 14 vessels, totalling 6,830 tons, were in service in early 1950. Cf. *Economic Weekly,* Vol. X, No. 14, p. 2, Shanghai, April, 1950. Since then sailings on some southern routes have been added.

42. See *New China Monthly,* Vol. I, No. 4, p. 924, Peking, February, 1950.

43. Ti Ch'ao-pai, "The Chinese Economy in the Past Year," *Economic Weekly,* Vol. X, No. 1, pp. 7-8, Shanghai, January, 1950.

44. *Economic Weekly,* Vol. X, No. 1, p. 25, Shanghai, January, 1950.

45. This firm is now under joint management with the Communist government.

46. As mentioned earlier, about 46 per cent of the steam and motor boats were owned by the government in 1951. Since modern private Chinese shipping in Communist China could not possibly amount to 100,000 tons even if the Min-Sheng ships were included, most of the private ships would have to be foreign-owned vessels plying in coastal waters.

47. *New China Monthly,* Vol. IV, No. 6, pp. 1301-1302, Peking, October, 1951.

48. *New China Daily,* Chungking, August 22, 1952.

49. Cf. Report by the Bureau of Sea Transport, *People's Communications,* Peking, October, 1952; *Wen-hui pao,* Hongkong, September 30, 1953; and *China News Service,* Peking, November 30, 1953.

49a. The planned objective of coastal freight traffic in 1957 is 5,750 million ton-nautical miles while that of inland water transport is 15,300 million ton-kilometers.

50. Report by the Kwangtung Bureau of River Navigation, *Wen-hui pao,* Hongkong, October 18, 1953.

51. *Economic Yearbook,* p. 25, Hongkong, 1953, and NCNA, Wu-han, January 13, 1954.

52. *Ibid.,* and *New China Monthly,* No. 42, p. 147, Peking, April, 1953.

53. *China News Service,* Peking, November 30, 1953.

54. Excluding junks.

55. *China News Service,* Peking, November 30, 1953.

56. *New China Monthly,* Vol. I, No. 4, p. 924, Peking, February, 1950.

57. Yü Fei-p'eng, *The General Situation of Transportation during the Last Fifteen Years,* pp. 31-34, Nanking, 1946.

58. The maximum loads on class A and class B roads were 20 and 15 tons respectively. Provincial roads are either class C or unspecified. Class C roads had a load capacity of 10-15 tons. Other provincial roads had a load capacity of 5-10 tons. The actual condition of the roads was probably below these standards. Cf. Yü Fei-p'eng, *op. cit.*

59. Bureau of Information, *The National Highway Network of China,* pp. 59-62, Nanking, 1947.

60. *Economic Bulletin,* No. 46, p. 13, Hongkong, December, 1953; *People's Communications,* Peking, October, 1952; and *Ta-kung pao,* Hongkong, December 11, 1952.

61. *People's Daily,* Peking, January 7, 1950.

62. On the basis of a tally of available reports on new road building up to 1954, only the following provinces are represented: Kansu, Ningsia, Sinkiang, Tsinghai, Sikang, Szechwan, Yunnan, Kwangsi, Kweichow, Kwangtung, and Fukien. These are mostly border provinces or areas not served by railways.

63. *People's Handbook,* p. 418, Shanghai, 1952. Cf. also the table in section 1 of this chapter. According to the First Five Year Plan, total motor vehicle freight traffic is expected to reach 3.2 billion ton-kilometers in 1957.

64. The following data on highway traffic in Nationalist-controlled areas have been reported by the Bureau of Statistics in the *Statistical Monthly,* 1948:

	Thousand Ton-Kilometers	*Thousand Metric Tons Carried.*
1937	55	31,464
1938	50	28,572
1939	40	22,718
1940	37	21,937
1941	348	189,205

1942	325	189,167
1943	324	153,636
1944	408	146,692
1945	650	173,622
1946	349	104,937
1947	295	72,784
1948 (10 mos.)	242	49,063

Cf. also report by the Bureau of Highway Transportation, *Chinese Yearbook,* Vol. II, p. 959, Nanking, 1948.

65. *New China Daily,* Chungking, June 20, 1952; *Masses Daily,* Hsi-an, April 3, 1952; and *Fukien Daily,* Fu-chou, May 1, 1952.

66. Ch'i Yü, *op. cit.*

67. According to the Communist Minister of Communications, 200,000 animal-drawn carts had been organized in the country for "mass transportation" by 1953, and another 2,000,000 carts were available.

68. See Chapter III above.

69. Cf. *A Manual for Newspaper Readers,* pp. 422-423, Hankow, 1950. The China National Coal Company which was first established has since expanded its activity to include building materials. "Native products" include mostly dry goods, as well as miscellaneous handicraft products. This list does not include the foreign trade corporations which also engage in domestic buying and selling.

70. Cf. *Taiheiyo Mondai,* Tokyo, September-October, 1954.

71. The term "cooperatives" is used sometimes to include industrial cooperatives which are, however, still relatively unimportant so far. At the end of 1953 there were only about 4,800 such producers' cooperatives, with a total membership of 298,000. There were also other cooperative forms of looser organization. Cf. *Workers' Daily,* Peking, February 2, 1954.

72. Cf. *People's Daily,* Peking, December 21, 1953. As early as 1950, for instance, the government China Grain Company began to purchase grain through rural cooperatives. Since the introduction of grain rationing government purchases on the open market have ceased and are now made through the rural cooperatives only. Cf. *Compendium,* Vol. II, pp. 876-877, Peking, 1951.

73. *People's Daily* editorial on the organization of the All-China Federation of Supply and Marketing Cooperatives, Peking, December 1, 1954.

74. NCNA, December 31, 1953, and September 23, 1954.

75. NCNA, September 23, 1954, and *New China Monthly,* No. 42, p. 153, April, 1953.

76. For a detailed list of numerous such fairs in 1951 and 1952 see *Economic Weekly,* No. 21, p. 7, May, 1953. These large-scale attempts at organized trading in certain appointed places have also facilitated government tax collection.

77. For a full description of the program see *Compendium,* Vol. III, p. 550 ff., Peking, 1952.

78. See Geological Survey of China, *General Statement on the Mining Industry,* No. 5, Chungking, 1935, for a discussion of prewar coal trade in China.

79. According to Chin Shih-hsüan, for every 1,000 kilometers of rail lines to be built in China under the postwar rail construction plan, 150,000 tons of rails and other steels are required. Cf. Chin Shih-hsüan, *Railway Transportation,* p. 475, Shanghai, 1948. See also I-tu Jen Sun, "The Pattern of Railway Development in China," (in English), *Far Eastern Quarterly,* Vol. XIV, No. 2, February, 1955.

80. For every 1,000 kilometers of rail lines in China, according to the postwar rail construction plan, 2,500 freight cars and 200 locomotives are the average require-

ments. Given the present 24,985 kilometers of railway network, the number of cars and engines now available is well below this standard. Cf. Chao Chen-chüeh, *op. cit.*, pp. 68-69.

81. For the principal surface transport and air routes see the maps at the end of this chapter. The maps are drawn by Major John K. Jouett. (The Manchurian section of the road map gives only a few trunk lines.)

CHAPTER ELEVEN

Monetary and Banking Control

I

INTRODUCTION

Since in a money economy by far the greater part of economic activities entails the use of money, the production and distribution of real goods and services are reflected in the monetary flow. When labor and material resources are allocated for the production of certain commodities, and when goods pass from one person to another or are moved from one place to another, money also changes hands accordingly. When money does not actually change hands, credit relationships would arise, which is tantamount to the same thing. At given prices, the disposition of specific quantities of goods and services is reflected in that of specific sums of money.

An implication of this rather commonplace observation with reference to a centrally planned economy is that plans that are drawn up in physical terms must have their corresponding financial counterparts. This is true not only with reference to plans of aggregate consumption and investment, but also with respect to individual commodities and activities. It is conceivable that plan enforcement may be carried out by regulating the monetary flow just as effectively as by direct controls. For instance, if the economic plan aims at restricting the production of certain types of consumer goods, this purpose can be achieved by refusing to allocate resources to their producers. Yet it will be equally effective if ways and means can be found so that producers cannot spend money for the production of these commodities and/or consumers cannot spend money to buy them. By regulating the monetary expenditure of all and sundry, the implementation of the economic plan is greatly facilitated. The execution of the plan in all its ramifications may also be closely supervised by auditing and controlling both the supply and expenditure of funds in individual enterprises.

This line of thinking has apparently motivated Communist China's long-term monetary policy since 1950, which may be described as a painstaking imitation of the Soviet system, with certain modifications in view of China's policy to follow a more gradual path toward complete socialization. An examination of the principal features of this development is essential to our understanding of the operation of the Chinese economy, now that we are familiar with the general structure of Chinese economic planning and the condition of the main branches of its productive apparatus.

THE STRUCTURE OF MONETARY CONTROL

In the Chinese Communist economy monetary expenditure originates from three sources, namely, the government and its subordinate organs, including all government and jointly-operated enterprises and cooperatives, private enterprises, and private persons. For each spending unit, funds from which expenditure is made may come from (1) government appropriations, (2) current earnings, (3) past accumulations, (4) loans, and (5) gifts.[1] Obviously if the government can have control over the funds before they are spent, it will also be in a position to regulate the flow and direction of expenditure. However, the authorities do not possess the same degree of control over the different sources of funds or the different categories of spending units. Government appropriations are made through the budget. Loans may be regulated through control of credit institutions. When it comes to past savings and current earnings, however, especially where private persons and enterprises alone are concerned, the magnitude of the problem multiplies.

The area of control can be extended, however, by channeling the greater part of monetary transactions through banks over which the government has full control. The less currency, i.e., bank notes, is used in making payments, the less is the risk that such payments might result in the employment of resources in contravention to general as well as specific plans. Moreover, if people could be induced to place their past and current savings in accounts with such banks, instead of in currency or other media—gold, for instance—the government would be in an even better position to oversee the disposition of all funds from which expenditure may be made.

Accordingly, in order to integrate monetary control into the system of economic planning as a method of supervising the implementation both of individual production and trading plans and of plans of over-all savings and consumption, the Communist Chinese authorities have developed their monetary policy and financial institutions along precisely the lines indicated above; namely, (1) control of all credit institutions, (2) extension of the use of checks and bank transfers in lieu of currency, (3) supervision by the government banks over the operation of individual enterprises, and (4) expansion of savings deposits to provide for the funds needed for investment and to mitigate the potentially inflationary pressure on prices which have been mounting ever since the inception of the Five Year Plan.

II

CURRENCY UNIFICATION

The establishment of a comprehensive system of monetary control presupposes the existence of an orderly currency, a situation which was far from being true in the early phase of Communist rule. Consequently, the first steps by the Communists in monetary control had as their purpose the abolition of the multifarious currencies which had come into being prior to the establishment of the new regime and the adoption of a single currency for the entire country.

The currencies to be abolished or driven out of circulation were of three kinds: those issued by the Communists themselves, the Nationalist currencies, and foreign currencies.[2] Included in the last two categories were the silver dollars of both old and new coinage which had re-entered circulation during the last years of Nationalist rule on the mainland and were given legal status by the Nationalists in 1949. The abolition of the Nationalist currencies was, relatively speaking, the simplest part of the entire process, but the unification of currencies which the Communists themselves had issued, and the stamping out of foreign currencies, silver dollars, and gold was a much more difficult and time-consuming task.

CONSOLIDATION OF EARLY COMMUNIST NOTE ISSUE

The Chinese Communists had always made a practice of issuing their own currencies to finance activities in areas under their occupation. At least one such currency, for instance, circulated in parts of Kiangsi, Fukien, and Hunan during the Kiangsi Soviet period.[3] During the course of the Sino-Japanese war, many local currencies were issued in various isolated guerilla bases; the highest number reached at one time was over thirty.[4] Toward the end of the civil war, as the Communists' military success began to link together formerly isolated areas held by them, the need to simplify the currency system became more pressing. Preparations for currency unification were made at a Financial and Economic Conference of the North China Liberated Areas in 1947, after which gradual unification took place in the following year. Toward the end of 1948, the People's Bank of China was established through the amalgamation of the North China Bank,[5] the North Sea Bank, and the Northwest Farmers' Bank, and the new *jen-min pi* or "people's currency" was issued to replace some of the local *currencies* on the basis of "100 per cent redemption."

As the table appearing on pages 399 and 400 clearly shows, a most confusing array of bank notes was in circulation on the eve of the Communists' victory in China, even though these diverse issues already represented results of past consolidation efforts. However, by the end of 1948, outside Manchuria, Sinkiang, and Inner Mongolia, the number of Communist currencies in active circulation was reduced to about three. By the end of 1949, of all the Communist currencies in China Proper, only the new *jen-min pi* was left.[6]

ELIMINATION OF NATIONALIST CURRENCIES

Since 1949 was a year of military success over the Nationalists, progress in currency unification consisted primarily of the forcible conversion of the Nationalist currencies into *jen-min pi*. This was carried out at rates that became increasingly favorable to the Communists.

On January 15, 1949, the Communists' Military Control Commission at Tientsin proclaimed the *jen-min pi* as the sole legal tender which was to circulate alongside the Northeast and South Hopeh notes. Circulation of all other Communist currencies in Tientsin was banned, and holders were ordered to convert them into *jen-min pi*. At the same time, the Nationalist GY was declared illegal and the public was free to refuse to accept it in payment, although it could

Sequence of Unification of Principal Local Communist Currencies

	Local Note-issuing Agencies	*Area of Circulation*	*Consolidation Prior to Conversion*	*Conversion Ratio (per jen-min pi[1])*
A.	Shensi-Kansu-Ningsia Border Region Bank	Shensi, Kansu and Ningsia border (Northwest China)	Issue stopped in January, 1948, replaced by D at par.	
B.	Shansi-Chahar-Hopeh Border Region Bank[2]	Shansi, Chahar, and Hopeh border (North China and Inner Mongolia)	Freely exchangeable with C as of April, 1948, at rate of 10 B to 1 C.	1,000
C.	South Hopeh Bank	Shansi, Hopeh, Shantung, and Honan border (North, East, and Central-South China)	Freely exchangeable with D as of October, 1948, at rate of 1 C to 20 D.	100
D.	Northwest Farmers' Bank	Northwestern Shansi and Suiyuan border (North China and Inner Mongolia)	Consolidated with A in January, 1948, and freely exchangeable with C and B as of October, 1948, at the rate of 1 C to 20 D to 10 B.	2,000
E.	North Sea Bank	Shantung (East China)	Freely exchangeable with B and C as of October, 1948, at rate of 1 C to 2 E.	100
F.	Central China Bank	Kiangsu and Anhwei (East China)	Freely exchangeable with E as of November, 1948, at par.	100 (May, 1949)

	Local Note-issuing Agencies	Area of Circulation	Consolidation Prior to Conversion	Conversion Ratio (per jen-min pi[1])
G.	Chung-chou Farmers' Bank	Central China		2 (November, 1949)
H.	Great Wall Bank	Hopeh, Jehol, and Liaoning (North China, Inner Mongolia, and Manchuria)	Conversion to I in February, 1949, at par.	
I.	Northeast Bank	Manchuria		9.50 (April, 1951)
J.	Kwantung Bank	Port Arthur-Dairen area	Conversion to I in June, 1950, at 270 I to 1 J.	
K.	Inner Mongolia People's Bank	Inner Mongolia		9.50 (April, 1951)
L.	Sinkiang People's Bank	Sinkiang (Northwest)		¥350 to 1 Sinkiang silver dollar note. (October, 1951)

Sources: Wang Ching-jan, "A Brief History of the People's Currency," *Economic Weekly,* No. 29, Shanghai, July, 1952, and the same journal, Vol. XIII, No. 15, pp. 283-285, October, 1951.

1. Except as otherwise noted in parenthesis, conversion into *jen-min pi* began in December, 1948.

2. Notes were also issued by this bank bearing markings for circulation in the Hopeh, Jehol, and Liaoning area.

continue to be used up to February 4, 1949. Moreover, the public was told to register its GY holdings at designated places and to have them taken out of the "liberated areas" under seal for the exchange of goods to be imported back to Communist territory. Such imports were restricted to certain categories, while both the routes to be taken and the time of return had to be stated in advance under the personal guarantee of residents in Tientsin. Only in cases of special hardship could holders of small amounts of GY convert their holdings into *jen-min pi* at a rate of CY 6 to ¥1.[7]

This policy of driving out the Nationalist "gold yuan" by denying its holders the right of full conversion to the extent of wholesale repudiation, calculated to enhance the Nationalists' difficulties, was followed subsequently in other areas conquered by the Communists. In the meantime, continued inflation of the GY also led to further depreciation of its own accord. Thus the value of the *jen-min pi* at conversion rose from GY 6 in January 21–February 19, 1949, at Tientsin, to GY 10 in Peking (February 5–22), GY 2,500 in Nanking (April 29–May 8), and GY 100,000 in Shanghai (May 30–June 5). By the time Canton and Chungking were captured, the "gold yuan" had already been displaced by the silver dollar certificates which were also converted into *jen-min pi* in the beginning of 1950. The conversion rates used were ¥100 per silver dollar certificate in Chungking, and ¥1,500 in Canton.

SUPPRESSION OF THE CIRCULATION OF GOLD, SILVER, AND FOREIGN CURRENCIES

Along with the forcible conversion of all Nationalist currencies immediately after the establishment of their rule in new areas, the Communist authorities also undertook to suppress the continued circulation of gold, silver dollars, and foreign currencies. This was achieved by outright prohibition to use them as units of accounts and payment, reinforced by police raids on centers of the clandestine market, especially the goldsmith and silversmiths' shops, wholesale arrests of street corner peddlers of silver dollars and foreign currencies, and control over the movement of gold and silver carried on persons. With the exception of foreign currencies, which for a very brief period had to be surrendered by all holders for conversion into *jen-min pi,* it was, however, most significant that no formal provision was made in all the regulations for the compulsory conversion of these precious hoards into *jen-min pi*. On the contrary, the official prices at which conversion could be made were purposely pegged at such low levels so as to discourage conversion.[8] The obvious explanation for this policy was to avoid a repetition of the Nationalists' experience in 1949 when excessively large quantities of "gold yuan" were issued upon the compulsory conversion of the public's holdings of foreign currencies, silver, and gold bullion. At the same time, the Communist authorities were probably also in part motivated by the consideration that forcible conversion or confiscation at this time would be politically unwise and impracticable. This policy was clearly illustrated by control measures in individual areas.

According to the Financial Control Regulations promulgated in Tientsin on January 16, 1949, all private holders of gold and silver (including silver dollar pieces) were ordered (1) to cease using them in business transactions, including their sales and purchases, (2) to refrain from shipping them out of the city, and (3) to exchange at government-designated places and official rates on a voluntary basis. In the case of foreign currencies, they were to be surrendered prior to the end of the month while the other restrictions would be applicable in the meantime. This treatment of gold and silver was reaffirmed three months later when the Provisional Regulations for the Control of Gold and Silver in North China were promulgated in April, 1949. At about the same time, however, the new Provisional Regulations for the Control of Foreign Exchange in North China[9] stipulated that private foreign currency holdings should henceforth be deposited in the Bank of China in return for foreign exchange deposit receipts which had to be sold within forty days for financing imports. This change in policy not only testified to the failure of the previous order that all foreign currency holdings had to be surrendered prior to the end of January, but also marked a more consistent policy regarding both foreign currencies and gold and silver.[10]

The same development in policy may be observed in the case of Shanghai, where the compulsory exchange of foreign currencies into *jen-min pi* was stopped in June, 1949, and replaced by the system of foreign exchange deposit certificates. A parallel course was also followed in Canton under comparable regulations for South China. However, in the latter case, penalties for violation, especially in speculations involving gold and silver, were further tightened, and the unusually numerous goldsmiths and exchange shops of Canton were told to enter other trades forthwith.

The control measures instituted for gold and silver also restricted the amount of gold ornaments and jewelry that might be freely carried without license to about one ounce per person in North and East China, and as a concession to southern Chinese customs, to about two ounces in South China.[11] Similar restrictions were placed on silverware and personal ornaments made of silver.

As long as mere possession of gold and silver is not illegal, and as long as the stability of the *jen-min pi* is not above question, the black market cannot be entirely eliminated. However, the Chinese Communists have certainly succeeded in limiting the scope formerly enjoyed by these alternative means of payment, although it would be decidedly an overstatement to say that all black market dealings have been stamped out.[12]

CURRENCY UNIFICATION IN 1951

The last stage of currency unification was reached in 1951 after the Communists had successfully halted the rampant inflation in the preceding year.

It will be recalled that when the *jen-min pi* was first issued in December, 1948, it was not freely convertible into the Northeast currency. These two currencies were kept apart and operated as separate monetary systems so as to protect Manchuria against the effects of the inflation of the *jen-min pi*. The much sharper rise of prices in China Proper in relation to commodity prices in Manchuria was partly reflected in the depreciation of the *jen-min pi's* official quotation in terms of the Northeast currency. First quoted at NE¥1,000 on December 1, 1948, the *jen-min pi* dropped to about NE¥180 toward the end of June, 1949. At the end of March, 1950, it was quoted at NE¥11.0 at the People's Bank of China in Shan-hai-kuan, border town between Manchuria and China Proper.[13] Fluctuations after March, 1950, were of a minor order, and on March 20, 1951, the separate Manchurian currency was finally abolished. The bank notes of Manchuria and Inner Mongolia were recalled at the rate of NE¥9.50 and IM¥9.50 to one *jen-min pi* respectively. Lastly, as of October 1, 1951, the silver dollar notes of the Sinkiang People's Bank were also abolished. The unification of Communist China's currencies was now complete.

MOVEMENT TOWARD MULTIPLE CURRENCIES

Since 1951, officially the People's Bank has been the sole bank of issue. However, as the government's program of compulsory purchases from farmers expands, some of the supply and marketing cooperatives have taken upon themselves to issue promissory notes. In some areas the latter have entered into circulation as a subsidiary currency. It is not possible to determine the extent of this practice on a national scale, but it is quantitatively quite significant in some localities. This development is obviously moving in a direction contrary to the unification process described here and may yet prove to be a source of serious embarrassment for the Communists. However, so far, the position of the People's Bank has not been seriously challenged.

III

IMPORTANCE OF PEOPLE'S BANK OF CHINA

Unification of the many local currencies has resulted in a single currency issued by the People's Bank of China. However, the People's Bank is more than a central bank in the usual sense. It virtually represents the entire banking system because all other credit agencies are literally its subsidiary organs. Moreover, it also acts as the cashier and financial watchdog of the expanding apparatus of production and trading within the socialistic and semi-socialistic sectors of the economy. In short, outside the central planning authority, it is probably the most important and powerful organ of economic administration. Why this is so can be best understood by an examination of the various functions the People's Bank exercises.

THE SYSTEM OF "CURRENCY" OR "MONETARY CONTROL"

Apart from being the sole bank of issue, the People's Bank of China has gradually acquired a large number of additional functions since its establishment. Some of its new powers are so wide that they have rendered unnecessary many of the indirect controls previously exercised by the Bank.

First of all, early in 1950 the People's Bank was made the sole depository of government funds, including the funds of all government and cooperative enterprises. Under the control measures introduced in April, 1950, which played a vital role in economic stabilization,[14] all these organizations were required to deposit their entire cash balance on hand,[15] less their minimum currency requirements, enough for three days' normal activity, in the People's Bank.

In the second place, the People's Bank has become the sole source of credit for government and cooperative enterprises, as well as the clearing center and supervisory organ of all transactions involving government, cooperative, and certain joint enterprises. Under a resolution of the State Administrative Council on December 1, 1950, the last group of enterprises were placed under a system of far-reaching "currency" or "monetary control," which, in addition to the cash control features, has the following provisions:[16]

1. All units within the system are directed to conduct their business with other similar units as far as possible. All transactions must be cleared through the Bank; use of currency must be approved and is restricted to transactions with private business and individuals, payroll disbursements, travel expenses, and small sums of petty cash as determined by the Bank.

2. All units within the system have to prepare their respective monthly and quarterly plans of receipts and expenditures, both for currency and for bank transfers. Expenditures and receipts must be in balance, only planned credit, but no overdraft on the Bank, being allowed. The individual plans, when approved by the administrative and planning agencies, are given to the People's Bank for execution. At the same time, the Bank must prepare similar plans for transactions involving private business and persons. The latter are consolidated with the former to constitute a national plan for monetary expenditures and receipts, which is then submitted to the central government for approval. Budgeted transactions may not be made outside the plan period and may not be shifted from one spending unit to another.

3. All units within the system must open accounts with the People's Bank. Two types of accounts are used to distinguish the productive enterprises from organizations operating on government appropriations only. Except those transactions in which currency may be employed, all others are effected through transfers into and from the individual accounts. The Bank credits or debits an account against special transfer checks and clearing certificates which are not negotiable. A copy of all contracts involving any unit within the system must be deposited with the Bank which acts as the government's watchdog in making payments. *The Bank is empowered to hold up any transaction which it considers unwarranted under an existing contract.* Non-cash transactions with private enterprises outside the control system must be effected by special checks which are negotiable only for several days.

4. Units within the system may not enter into any commercial credit relationship with one another. Nor may they establish similar relationships with private firms without the express approval of the People's Bank. Exempt from the general rule are (a) payment of fees in pursuance of a processing contract, (b) purchase orders providing for payment on delivery, (c) advances to purchasing agents, and (d) transfers of sales proceeds by sales agents.

Units within the system that are dependent upon government appropriations, such as certain government agencies and military units, may not borrow from the Bank. Since they may not borrow from any other source either, they are thus prevented from expanding their activities with borrowed funds. Other units, after having fully utilized their own working capital, may borrow from the Bank on short term. Such loans are made by the Bank for less than twelve months and in accordance with previously approved monthly and quarterly plans. Collaterals consisting of current assets only are required, and interest charges are fixed by the Bank. To qualify, the borrower must have made the fullest use of his own working capital, must have an independent accounting system, and must follow the practice of business accountability. In case of default, the Bank may dispose of the collaterals and seize the borrower's outstanding bank balance as long as the payment of wages and taxes is not adversely affected.

5. The bank loans mentioned above are exclusively short-term loans to finance various operating expenses.[17] Special care is taken to distinguish short-term credit from long-term funds which may not be used on everyday operation. The Bank of Communications, one of the specialized agencies under the supervision of the People's Bank, is responsible for overseeing the execution of all approved basic construction projects and for making sure that expenditures correspond to progress in construction as scheduled. Budgeted funds for approved basic construction projects are transferred by the Ministry of Finance to the specialized bank which then prepares the payment plans for submission to the Ministry through the People's Bank. Responsible units having projects in progress are required to submit to the specialized bank regular reports on construction progress and all related information. Payments may be withheld by the bank upon discovering any deviation from the original construction plans, failure to meet the time schedule, or irregularity in the use of funds.

RELATION WITH PRIVATE BUSINESS AND PRIVATE BANKS

As the socialization of private business progresses, the functions of the People's Bank as outlined above will ultimately encompass the entire economic system. During the transitional period, through the reorganization of the private banks under joint operation with the government, all private non-banking firms are forced to look to the government banking system for credit. The principal difference is that as a rule private firms are not subject to the rigorous controls binding the government and semi-socialistic enterprises. Even in this respect, however, the employment of currency in making payments above certain specified amounts has been subjected to special restrictions varying in intensity from time to time.[18]

Prior to the de facto socialization of the entire banking system, the People's Bank also employed some of the relatively orthodox methods of monetary control in dealing with the private banks. At the same time, it competed actively with the latter for private deposits. The general policy followed was decidedly one of "restriction, utilization, and reform," and may be briefly reviewed.[19]

First, the volume of deposits at the People's Bank was greatly increased at the expense of private banks as a result of the financial measures adopted in early 1950. In addition, however, a variety of new savings accounts was instituted by the People's Bank to attract public deposits. Savings deposits in terms of "commodity-equivalent" units were first introduced after the establishment of the new regime. Following the March, 1950, episode, deposits were accepted under different provisions concerning the terms of deposits and withdrawals, as well as lottery features. Especially notable was the type of savings deposits with "double guarantee" features which provided that at the time of withdrawal the principal deposited would be increased in an amount corresponding to any increase in the price index for savings deposits, but that in the event of a price decline the principal amount would not be reduced below the original sum deposited. This type of savings deposits was finally abolished upon the conclusion of the "five-anti" program in 1952 when price stability was, for the time being at any rate, no longer a serious issue and the private banks were well under control.

Second, even before the transformation of private banks into joint operation with the government, private banking credit was controlled by the People's Bank both directly and indirectly. Indirect control was exercised by the introduction of rediscount and remortgage business, acceptance of bankers' deposits at an interest rate 20 per cent higher than that given by the banks on their own deposits, and changes in the legal reserve requirements for bank deposits. Direct control, on the other hand, was exercised by the Bank in two ways. In the case of Shanghai, for instance, a combined board of banks jointly operated with the government was formed on November 20, 1951, under the control of the People's Bank for the special purpose of supervising banking activities involving private business. On a more limited basis, a joint loan agency was formed, for example, by 172 Shanghai banks and trusts as early as September, 1949, for the purpose of extending loans to the cotton textile industry. The agency was subsequently reorganized and its capital expanded a number of times through the last part of 1950 and 1951. Members participating in the joint lending agency were given certain privileges in borrowing from the People's Bank on short term.

REGULATION OF INTEREST RATES

From the very beginning strenuous efforts were made by the People's Bank to regulate private banking credit by adjusting interest rates. The case of Shanghai is most illuminating.

From June 1 to the beginning of September, 1949, the interest rates on collateral loans in Shanghai were determined jointly by the trade associations of commercial banks, native banks, and trust companies, subject to the approval of the People's Bank. In fact, however, the rates were determined during this period by the so-called "black market" or "underground" native banks where loanable funds were concentrated. From September 6 to November 25, 1949, interest rates in Shanghai were determined daily by a 21-member committee of the Association of Financial Institutions, in which two representatives of the People's Bank took part. However, despite increases in the People's Bank's rates, the "black market" rates during this period were consistently from 20 per cent to 100 per cent higher than the open market or official interest rates. Finally, on November 25, 1949, serious measures were taken by the authorities against 26 "black market" native banks, and the People's Bank's control was strengthened over the committee on interest rates. The reduction of interest rates then followed in March, 1950.

From a monthly rate of 27 per cent in March on commercial loans by private banks it fell to 3.9 per cent in June, 1950.[20] Between June, 1950, and April, 1951, the rate of interest remained fairly stable. This was followed by a period of continued reduction through 1951, and a sizable downward adjustment was made in June, 1952, when the "double guarantee" savings deposits were also discontinued. At the latter time interest rates on commercial and savings accounts were also differentiated while private loan rates by the People's Bank and the corresponding loan rates by private banks were standardized and a reduction was effected in the differential between interest rates on bank deposits and on bank loans.

Since June, 1952, the Shanghai interest rates have more or less reverted to the prewar levels. However, the interest rate has also lost much of its significance as a mirror of the state of the money market although it still remains as a determining factor in economic planning by government and other enterprises which operate under the system of business accountability.

PEOPLE'S BANK OF CHINA

INTEREST AT RATES ON SHORT-TERM LOANS TO PRIVATE BORROWERS AND ON CURRENT DEPOSITS IN SHANGHAI, 1949–1952
(Per cent per month)

	LOANS				
DATE OF ADJUSTMENT	*Public Utilities*	*Industrial, Transport and Communications and Cultural and Educational Institutions*	*Commercial Enterprises*	*Agriculture*	*DEPOSITS*
1949					
June 30	15	15–21	24–30	—	7.5
July 18	25	25–35	40–50	—	13
August 11	20	20–30	32–40	—	11
August 22	15	15–21	24–30	—	7.5
November 11	30	30–40	50–60	—	14
November 24	60	60–80	100	—	36
December 7	45	45–55	70–80	—	26
December 16	36	36–48	60	—	21
December 21	27–36	27–36	45	—	16
1950					
January 1	27	27–36	45	—	—
January 9	18–24	18–24	30	—	10
March 16	15–18	15–18	24	—	7
April 5	14.4	14.4	18	14.4	5.4—April 1 4.8—April 3 3.6—April 5
April 6	12	12	15	12	3.3

DATE OF ADJUSTMENT	LOANS Public Utilities	Industrial, Transport and Communications and Cultural and Educational Institutions	Commercial Enterprises	Agriculture	DEPOSITS
April 13	11.2	11.2	14	11.2	3 —April 11 2.7—April 13
April 14	11.04	11.04	13.8	11.04	2.4
April 15	10.8	10.8	13.5	10.8	—
April 17	10.08	10.08	12.6	10.08	2.1
April 18	9.6	9.6	12	9.6	—
April 19	9.12	9.12	11.4	9.12	1.8
April 20	8.64	8.64	10.8	8.64	—
April 21	8.16	8.16	10.2	8.16	1.5
April 22	7.68	7.68	9.6	7.68	—
April 24	7.2	7.2	9	7.2	—
April 25	6.72	6.72	8.4	6.72	1.2
May 2	6.24	6.24	7.8	6.24	—
May 5	5.76	6.5	7.2	5.76	1.1
May 8	5.52	6.2	6.9	5.52	—
May 10	4.56–5.52	5.1–6.2	5.7–6.9	4.56–5.52	1
May 11	3.84–4.8	4.3–5.4	4.8–6	3.84–4.8	0.8—May 12
May 13	3.12–3.84	3.5–4.8	3.9–4.8	3.12–3.84	0.7
May 15	2.4–3.12	2.7–3.5	3–3.9	2.4–3.12	0.5
May 21	2.4	2.7	3	2.4	—
July 1	2.4	2.7	3	1.8	0.7—June 19
July 21	2.4	2.7	3	2.1	—
November 21	2.4	2.7	3	1.6–1.8	—
1951					
January 3	2.4	2.7	3	1.6–1.8	0.7—January
March 1	2.7	2.7	3	1.8	—
July 16	2.7	2.7	3	1.8	0.6
August 1	2.55	2.4	2.55	1.8	—
October 16	2.55	2.4	2.55	1.8	—
1952					
January 1	2.55	2.4	2.55	1.8	0.51
March 1	2.55	2.4	2.55	1.8	—
March 15	2.4	2.25	2.4	1.8	—
March 17	2.3	2.2	2.3	1.8	—
March 21	2.3	2.2	2.3	1.8	0.45
June 25					
1 month	1.05–1.35	1.05–1.35	1.35–1.65	1.05–1.35	0.45
3 months and over	1.50–1.65	1.50–1.65	1.80–1.95	1.50–1.65	

Source: Economic Weekly, No. 26, pp. 512-513, Shanghai, July, 1952.

NATIONALIZATION OF PRIVATE BANKS

The first serious blow to private banking was struck in April, 1950, when government funds deposited in private banks were pulled out and transferred to the People's Bank. According to official reports from Peking, Tientsin, Shanghai, Hankow, Chungking, and Hsi-an, there were 446 private banks in China at the end of 1949, including both modern and native institutions. By June, 1950, the number had decreased to 213. In other words, 233 banks constituting 52 per cent of the total were closed during the six-month period.[21] This initial blow was followed by the government's demand for increase in capitalization by the remaining commercial banks in conformity with the result of a national financial conference held in August, 1950.

Mention has already been made of the formation of banking syndicates for both general and special purposes. These banking syndicates constituted the forerunners of a series of mergers ending in the formation in December, 1952, of an amalgamated bank jointly operated by the government and surviving private interests. The last-mentioned, jointly operated, Amalgamated Bank represented the merger of five groups of consolidated banking institutions. The first group consisted of the combined board of the First Jointly-operated Banks, formed out of a total of 12 separate banks which had 197 branches in 44 cities throughout the country, including such institutions as the Sinhua Trust, Savings and Commercial Bank, the China State Bank, the Young Brothers Banking Corporation, the National Industrial Bank of China, the National Commercial Bank of China, the Bank of Ningpo, the Commercial Bank of China, and the Development Bank of China. The second group of banks incorporated into the Amalgamated Bank in 1952 included the former four northern banks—namely, the Yien Yieh Commercial Bank, the Kincheng Banking Corporation, the China and South Sea Bank, and the Continental Bank—and the United Bank and Trust Company. The third group was represented by the Shanghai Commercial Bank and Trust Company. A fourth group was represented by the combined board of the first and second jointly operated banking syndicates. The first banking syndicate consisted of 14 small, modern, native banks. The second banking syndicate consisted of 14 member banks as of September, 1950. The fifth and last group constituting the Amalgamated Bank was represented by the combined board of the third and fourth banking syndicates. The third banking syndicate, established in July, 1950, consisted of 12 native banks. The fourth banking syndicate, established also in July, 1950, was composed of six native banks. Thus, a total of 64 commercial banks were incorporated into one single unit, and as far as the major banking center, Shanghai, was concerned, the official formation of the joint board of directors and combined head office of the Amalgamated Bank in December, 1952, marked the end of private banking to all intents and purposes.[22] Since the joint board of the Amalgamated Bank also had full control over the branch banks of all the constituent banks in all the major cities, including Peking, Shanghai, Tientsin, Hsi-an, Hankow, Ch'ang-sha, Canton, Chungking, Ch'eng-tu, K'un-ming, Tsingtao, Nanking, Hang-chou, and Amoy, and since similar transformation had taken place in all the important commercial centers, private banking came to an end as of December, 1952. From then on, for the People's Bank, it was no longer a question of how to control private credit by indirect monetary measures, but rather how to direct the policy of the Amalgamated Bank as a part of the government banking system.

THE STRUCTURE OF THE GOVERNMENT BANKING SYSTEM

The People's Bank, which stands at the apex of monetary and credit control, has now under it several groups of institutions:

First, the People's Bank itself and the jointly operated Amalgamated Bank together now provide practically the entire volume of short-term credit. In addition, the People's Bank also exercises the various functions of monetary and currency control discussed earlier. Directly under the People's Bank is a second group of institutions consisting of several specialized banks. Of these three in particular are of importance.

First, there is the Bank of China, which serves as the foreign exchange control organ of the Communist government. Its business consists of all phases of foreign exchange control and the supervision of appointed banks when these existed separately, including all banking operations involving overseas remittances, foreign bonds and stocks, and commercial bills and notes in connection with foreign trade. It conducts international clearing activities and handles all foreign trade barter accounts on behalf of the People's Bank and acts as an agency of the Communist government and the various state trading organs in handling foreign transactions, guaranteeing foreign loans, and conducting related transactions. Originally one of the Nationalists' government banks, it was taken over on June 6, 1949, and was reorganized in April, 1950. Although, since May, 1951, it also undertakes banking business other than foreign exchange transactions, its main function is in the field of foreign trade and related activities. At the present time, overseas offices under its control are found in Hongkong, Singapore, London, Penan, Kualalumpore, Calcutta, Bombay, Karachi, Djakarta, and Rangoon.

Second, there is the Bank of Communications.[22a] Formerly also one of the government banks, it was reorganized under the Communists, and, since June 1, 1951, has become the principal organ under the People's Bank handling basic construction projects as well as all other long-term investment funds. It is also vested with the responsibility of overseeing the government's shares and interests in all jointly-operated enterprises which have been growing in number.

Third, there is the Agricultural Cooperative Bank, which was established in July, 1951, to handle allocations of government investment and long-term credit in the fields of agriculture, forestry, fishery, animal husbandry, land reclamation, and water conservation, as well as in state farms and agricultural cooperatives. In fact, however, the Agricultural Cooperative Bank does not appear to have been very active, while all activities under its control have been provided by the various branches of the People's Bank itself.

Among the remaining financial institutions within the government banking structure are (1) the Investment Bank for Capital Construction in the Northeast, which was established on July 1, 1952, and fulfills the function earmarked for the Bank of Communications elsewhere in China, (2) the People's Insurance Company of China, which is a national organization under the supervision of the People's Bank for the purpose of absorbing private as well as public funds for investment purposes, and (3) investment companies formed in Peking and Canton especially for the purpose of absorbing overseas Chinese capital.

First established in Peking in September, 1950, the investment company aims at the development of industrial, mining, and communications enterprises, as well as public utilities, with subscriptions from overseas Chinese. Since then a similar company was formed in

Kwangtung province in 1953 to handle similar activities in South China. However, neither of these two enterprises has shown any significant accomplishment during the last few years.

Between 1949 and 1950 the personnel of the People's Bank increased by 50 per cent, while the number of new offices established during this period came to 1,300. In May, 1951, the Bank had more than 2,000 branches in the country, as well as a total personnel of 160,000. By March, 1953, the total number employed by the Bank was reported to exceed 300,000. This growth in personnel and branch offices clearly reflects the increasingly powerful role the Bank has come to play.[23]

MONETARY POLICY THROUGH DEFLATION, REFLATION, AND EXPANSION

At this point a few words should be said on the manner in which the People's Bank has exercised its continually augmented powers and has directed Communist China's monetary policy in the light of the country's general economic development.

If 1948 and 1949 were periods of currency unification through which the People's Bank gradually emerged as a central bank of issue, the year 1950 was marked by a concerted effort to achieve price stabilization, to which monetary measures carried out by the Bank contributed a great deal. In fact, the Bank showed a great deal of flexibility in adapting its policy in response to changing economic conditions throughout this period.

From March to May, 1950, following the policy laid down in the March National Financial Conference, the Bank concentrated its effort on inducing deposits from the public, on centralizing the currency holdings of all government agencies and enterprises, and on regulating the inter-regional flow of money. It was during this period that savings in "commodity-equivalent" units were introduced.[24] According to the People's Bank, the volume of notes in circulation contracted by as much as 30 per cent during the three-month period. Simultaneously, the volume of bank deposits rose from being no more than one-third of the amount of notes in circulation in 1949 to three times of the latter in May, 1950. Along with the expansion of government revenue which began at this time, the Bank established no less than 1,657 central government depositories, together with depositories attached to individual government enterprises, including the trading organs, postal and tele-communication units, and railways.[25]

From June to September, 1950, efforts were made by the Bank to correct some of the effects of the severe deflation in the preceding quarter. The decision to expand credit was taken in a general business meeting of the Bank in June, and private banks were called upon to do the same. As a result, the volume of the Bank's outstanding loans increased tenfold during this period. Outstanding loans of the other banks also registered a 60 per cent increase between February and October, 1950, while their deposits increased by 200 per cent in the same period. The apparently receding threat of price instability also gave the Bank a breathing space to consider some of the long-run problems concerning the control of private banks. Accordingly, it was in August, 1950, that the Bank chose to convene a national conference of all financial institutions which led to various arrangements governing bankers' deposits, collateral loans, and domestic remittances with which the activities of the rest of the banking system were to be regulated, as well as the formation of joint investment and loan agencies by private banks, and the reduction of interest rates and interest differentials.

However, the reflation period was rather short-lived. By October, 1950, the international situation had worsened as a result of fighting in Korea, and prices had begun to rise, particularly in textiles and imported goods. The Bank now called for credit contraction all around and threatened all non-conformists with dire consequences. It was at this time that the "double guarantee" savings deposits were introduced and lottery features were added to various types of bank deposits. These measures were accompanied by the temporary freezing of the deposits of all government agencies and enterprises placed under the system of "currency control" which constituted 90 per cent of the Bank's total deposits at the time. Apparently, the need to tighten control over these deposits had become exceedingly urgent.[26] It was the central theme of discussion during the first national conference on "monetary control" convened by the Bank in October, 1950, which preceded the adoption of the various control measures discussed earlier.

The importance of the "monetary control" system instituted in late 1950 in the maintenance of relative price stability during the following year can hardly be exaggerated, especially in the light of the Korean war. In particular, the establishment of banking units attached to the field armies was an innovation of significance. All through 1951 the Bank's principal concern was to set up the system of "monetary control" properly, and it appeared to be fairly successful in this respect. However, as we have shown in Chapter III, the Bank's effort was apparently not sufficient to avoid the reappearance of certain features of inflation during this time, and the "three-anti" and "five-anti" campaigns were started at a most opportune moment from the financial point of view. At the end of June, 1952, the Bank was again in a position to call upon the private banks to expand their lending activities and, at the same time, to bring about a general reduction of interest rates. From then on, a period of steady expansion has set in and, once again, the Bank must concern itself with the problem of encouraging savings.

CREDIT POLICY OF THE PEOPLE'S BANK

Two points of interest may be noted in the credit policy of the People's Bank. The first point relates to differences in interest rates charged on loans, while the second deals with the volume of loans.

For instance, following the general reduction of interest rates in mid-1952, the monthly interest on collateral loans of three months or over for *private* industrial and transportation enterprises, as well as cultural, social, and public health institutions was fixed at 1.5 to 1.65 per cent. The same rate was charged on loans to private handicraft industries, as well as on agricultural, fishery, and animal husbandry loans. Loans for shorter periods were charged lower interest rates. However, interest charges to private trading concerns were fixed at 1.8 to 1.95 per cent on collateral loans of three months or longer. Even self-liquidating loans against trade bills had to bear a uniform monthly rate of 1.35 per cent. Finally, borrowing for large-scale private irrigation projects could be done at only 0.75 per cent a month, and the rate was increased to 0.9 per cent for small-scale irrigation projects.

The preference given to industrial, transportation, and other borrowers—excluding pawnshops—over traders has been a consistent policy maintained by the People's Bank with the exception of the period between August, 1951, and June, 1952, when short-term loans to commercial enterprises enjoyed the same interest rates as public utilities, although they were still higher than rates on other loans. The preference given to agricultural loans began in the second half of 1950, prior to which interest rates on agricultural loans were at a par with those on the most favored industrial loans, the cheapest of which were usually enjoyed by public utilities. The particularly favorable rates given to irrigation loans as of June, 1952, not only further exemplified the emphasis on agricultural credit, but also marked a notable exception to the rule of not extending short-term credit for long-term investment.[27]

The relative levels of interest rates given to different groups of borrowers may be regarded as a fair, though by no means conclusive, indication of the priority attached to their respective fields of activity. During the period immediately after Communist occupation, loans were given primarily to public utilities. Later, the People's Bank began to make general industrial loans, with emphasis on those for wage payments. However, as from 1951, while credit was extended to industrial, mining, and transportation enterprises on a selective basis, loans were concentrated on the promotion of trade between urban and rural areas.[28] In other words, the People's Bank was active in financing the purchase of agricultural products by government trading concerns and cooperatives in a manner which obviated the need of considerable sums of direct loans for increasing agricultural production.

EXPANSION OF RURAL CREDIT

This leads us to some of the problems of rural credit which is provided both by the People's Bank and an increasing number of credit cooperatives, the former accounting for most of the loans extended so far.

The first trial credit cooperative in the Communist period was established by the People's Bank of China in conjunction with the All-China Federation of Cooperatives at Ting-hsien, Hopeh, in 1949. The first trial credit department within a rural supply and marketing cooperative was established in the same year at Ching-wen, also in Hopeh. Since then, as the table appearing on page 418 shows, a very rapid growth has been registered by the credit cooperatives, especially during 1954. According to statistics of June, 1953, the credit cooperatives had an average membership of 618 persons each and an

Expansion of Credit Cooperatives in Communist China, 1950–1954

	Number of Credit Cooperatives	*Number of Credit Teams*	*Number of Credit Departments in Supply and Marketing Cooperatives*
1950 (year end)	103	33	439
1951 (year end)	538	542	953
1952 (year end)	2,271	16,218	1,578
1953 (June)	6,871	14,322	2,137
1954 (June)	42,000	[1]	—

Sources: Study, Peking, January 2, 1954, and NCNA, September 10, 1954.

1. About 42,000.

average capital of ¥12.78 million. The credit teams, which had no separate funds for lending other than the individual members' own ad hoc contributions, numbered 6 to 15 members each.

However, while the number of credit cooperatives had risen substantially since 1950, the number of rural branches of the People's Bank at the *ch'ü*[29] level had also multiplied from 457 in 1950 to 13,290 in 1953.[30] While the *cumulative* total of loans issued by all the credit cooperatives in the country up to June, 1953, i.e., over a period of about four years, reached ¥240 billion.[31] it was very much less than the total of agricultural loans extended by the People's Bank in any single year, even allowing for the fact that a part of the Bank's loans went to government farms and water conservation and forestry projects.[32]

Agricultural Loans Extended by the People's Bank of China, 1950–1953

	¥ billion
1950	2,643.0
1951	4,509.0
1952	13,622.2
1953	15,665.5

Sources: People's Daily, Peking, November 30, 1953, and NCNA, January 25, 1954.

This comparison is all the more striking since a good portion of the loans made by the credit cooperatives represents relending of funds made available to them by the People's Bank.[33] Apparently, the development of credit cooperatives as such has not made available large volumes of savings ready for lending through them.[34]

INCREASE IN RURAL SAVINGS

The rapid increase in the number of rural credit cooperatives in the latter part of 1953 and 1954 clearly reflected the large-scale compulsory purchase of grains after the 1953 harvest and that of raw cotton in 1954. As a result of the purchase program, considerable sums of money have begun to pour into the hands of the peasantry, which in turn has made it necessary for the monetary authorities to absorb this surplus purchasing power that might otherwise create additional demands for industrial products.

Consequently, the expansion in the number of credit cooperatives might be interpreted not so much as an attempt to make available a greater amount of rural credit for the peasantry, but rather as a development in order to induce rural savings. At any rate, the simultaneous expansion of a number of rural credit cooperatives and the initiation of the large-scale compulsory purchase program—as of the latter part of 1954—was no pure accident.

Using 1949 as the base year, the total volume of savings deposits at the People's Bank of China increased by approximately 126 times by the end of 1953. In other words, the total volume of savings deposits at the People's Bank had an outstanding balance of $12,700 billion as against approximately $100 billion at the end of 1949. The greater part of this increase in savings deposits probably took place in urban centers. However, some of this increase no doubt reflected a corresponding development in the rural areas, and it is in the latter respect that further development has to be encouraged from the point of view of increasing the supply of savings for the country's development programs.

Recent reports from Communist China have all stressed the development of various special movements and methods of collecting both urban and rural savings. According to information disclosed during the "three-anti" movement, as well as the later anti-bureaucracy movement in 1953, rural savings have been fostered by means of compulsory allotment in which fixed quotas are assigned by the People's Bank to its lower organs and branch offices down to the village level, and then to individual families. Savings have also been gathered during marathon mass meetings by the ruling that new savings deposits must be made by all individuals participating in the meetings. Similarly, in certain areas minimum quotas of savings have been allotted in the nature of a poll tax. Finally, savings have been made as a part of payment for government purchases of various farm products. These practices have been reported in widespread areas in both North and South China.[35]

It appears that, up to the present time, in spite of the large volume of loans poured into the rural areas by the People's Bank, a certain amount of net savings has probably been made available by the farm population for investment in the non-agricultural sectors of the economy. The moot question is the level to which the volume of rural savings could be stepped up further during the present industrialization program.

V

SOME DEFICIENCIES OF THE COMMUNIST MONETARY AND BANKING CONTROL SYSTEM

The above review has pointed out quite clearly the structure of comprehensive monetary control now existing in the country, as well as the predominant position occupied by the People's Bank. However, one of the disadvantages inherent in the control system that has been established is the rigidity of the system, characterized by over-reliance on the People's Bank as an overall supervisory organ and lack of flexibility with which changes in production plans could be coordinated and adjustments could be made in the corresponding financial transactions. It can be easily imagined that when for any reason production plans fail to be carried out or cannot be carried out exactly the corresponding financial plans would also be affected. Unless adjustments could be made promptly by the Bank which is entrusted with the supervision of the execution of existing production plans, disruptions in production because of inability to make financial adjustments in authorized payments and receipts would inevitably occur. The great amount of paper work involved in monetary control, lack of trained personnel in the branch banks, especially to conduct the monetary control procedures smoothly, and perhaps even the lack of adequate business machines might conceivably create serious bottlenecks in clearly business transactions and consequently in providing the necessary financial arrangements for continued production without violent fluctuations.[36]

The existing monetary control system, however comprehensive, still leaves some room for possible disturbance, especially that of an inflationary character, from the point of view of the authorities. This can be seen quite easily when we consider the various sources from which funds for investment can be derived to fulfill the production and industrialization plans. In the first place, of course, investment funds are obtained from taxation; second, funds may be obtained from profits from state and other semi-public enterprises, depreciation reserves from such enterprises, and insurance payments by both private and public enterprises. As private banking has already been eliminated, and as even private enterprises have been forced to make their deposits in the government-controlled banks, by limiting their practice of cash transactions, the People's Bank is in a position to control in part the use of funds for investment and other purposes by the remaining private business. As nationalization proceeds further and all important private enterprises are brought within the system of monetary control by the People's Bank, even closer supervision by the Bank will be possible. However, all this would still leave a final loophole, namely, the employment and disposition of cash funds in the hands of private individuals. The government still has no sure way to control both the total volume of spending by private persons and the direction of their expenditures. The savings program which has now been stepped up through the expansion of credit cooperatives as well as further development by the People's Bank along the same lines in urban areas is meant in part to close this loophole. Success or failure in this direction may well be decisive not only in terms of overall economic stability but also with respect to certain specific investment plans.

NOTES

1. We shall ignore gifts in the following discussion.
2. For the present purpose gold may be included among the foreign currencies.
3. See *Compendium,* Vol. II, p. 546, Peking, 1951.
4. For Communist wartime and postwar currencies, see Cheng Chu-yüan, *Monetary Affairs of Communist China* (in English), Hongkong, 1954.
5. Established through the amalgamation of the South Hopeh Bank and the Shansi-Chahar-Hopeh Border Region Bank in 1948.
6. For a brief period after the occupation of Canton a separate *nan-fang pi* (southern currency) was issued.

7. Special rates were granted to certain groups of workers, peasants, students, teachers, and other destitute persons for amounts not exceeding GY 500 in each case.

8. Cf. Cheng Chu-yüan, *Monetary Affairs of Communist China,* pp. 39-40, Hongkong, 1954.

9. Promulgated on April 7, 1949.

10. It is still true, however, that while foreign currencies were to be used for financing imports, gold and silver holdings, though equally useful, were not actively sought by the government through conversion.

11. In May, 1951, the maximum amount of gold that could be freely carried was halved, according to the Hongkong *Sing-tao Daily,* May 15, 1951.

12. See Chapter XIII below.

13. See the *Northeast Daily* of this period for day-to-day quotations.

14. See Chapter III above.

15. Current receivables were also included later.

16. For the "monetary control" regulations and other related documents see *New China Monthly,* Vol. III, No. 3, Peking, January, 1951. Cf. also *Compendium,* Vol. II, Peking, 1951.

17. For exceptions see the discussion on agricultural loans below.

18. See Cheng Chu-yüan, *op. cit.,* pp. 9 and 75.

19. On the points discussed below see Liu Kuang-ti, "Financial Developments in Shanghai during the Last Three Years," and Sheng Mu-chieh, "Basic Concepts in Monetary Control," *Economic Weekly,* No. 39, Shanghai, October, 1952.

20. Until June, 1952, the People's Bank consistently charged lower rates than private banks.

21. See *Compendium,* Vol. III, Peking, 1952. For bank closings in Shanghai see Cheng Chu-yüan, *op. cit.,* p. 42.

22. See Hsia Ch'ang-ming, "The Meaning and Function of the Consolidated Bank," *Industrial and Commercial News,* Vol. III, No. 11, pp. 6-7, Shanghai, June, 1951; Hsü Shih-hsün, "Shanghai's Four Banking Syndicates," same journal, Vol. IV, No. 7, p. 16, July, 1951. *Economic Weekly,* No. 50, p. 1004, Shanghai, December, 1952, and *Hsin-wen Daily,* Shanghai, December 25, 1952.

22A. A National Construction Bank was established in the latter part of 1954 to take over some of the functions of the Bank of Communications.

23. Cf. Cheng Chu-yüan, *op. cit.*

24. Credit was also tightened although the money rate of interest had declined following the reversal of the trend of rising prices.

25. See Nan Han-chen, "Report on the Second Anniversary of the People's Bank," Wang Lan, "Consolidating Victory on the Financial Front," and Hu Chin-yün, "Further Implementation of Currency Control," *Chinese Finance,* Vol. I, No. 3, also *New China Monthly,* Vol. I, No. 3, Peking, January, 1951.

26. Whether this development was in anticipation of Communist China's intervention in Korea shortly thereafter remains to be a matter of conjecture.

27. This may be interpreted as another evidence of the failure to develop the Agricultural Cooperative Bank along lines planned for it.

28. Cf. Report of the People's Bank of China, *Compendium,* Vol. III, p. 196, Peking, 1952.

29. Administrative division subordinate to the county or *hsien.*

30. NCNA, March 19, 1954. According to Nan Han-cheu, of the 2,000 offices of the People's Bank in 1951, 80 per cent represented rural branches. These branches accounted for about 60 per cent of the Bank's personnel. Report to the First National Agricultural Credit Conference on May 10, 1951, *Compendium,* Vol. III, Peking, 1952.

31. The cumulative total of deposits for the same period was Y170 billion.

32. This amounted to 10.44 per cent in 1953. NCNA, January 25, 1954.

33. *Study,* Peking, January 2, 1954.

34. A considerable part of the agricultural loans, however, went to waste and could not be repaid. See directive of the State Administrative Council on the settlement of delinquent loans, adopted on December 31, 1953, NCNA, January 6, 1954.

35. *Ta-kung pao, Tientsin,* March 24, 1953.

36. For instance, the Communist press has occasionally reported on serious delays in the remittance and supply of funds by the People's Bank, although such transactions have been approved by the proper authorities.

CHAPTER TWELVE

Labor Organization and Wages

I

INTRODUCTION

Given the theme of increasing production, we have to consider now the manner in which output can be raised through the better utilization of labor, the last major factor of production we have to examine in some detail.[1] In particular, we have to discuss some of the problems related to industrial labor inasmuch as hired labor in agriculture does not appear to have presented any special issue of consequence since the completion of land redistribution.

Focussing our attention on industrial labor, we can readily see that, other things being equal, output can be increased by raising the productivity of labor of given skills, by increasing the skill of labor—which is tantamount to increasing the supply of labor of progressively higher grades of skill—and by working longer hours. First, workers of given skills can produce more within a given period of time under a variety of circumstances. Working conditions may be improved, through, for example, the institution of measures to reduce industrial accidents, rationalization of production procedures, provision of day nurseries in the case of women workers, etc. They may be induced to work harder by such positive incentives as higher wages and bonus payments, as well as the prospect of better working conditions and welfare institutions like labor insurance, or by fear of punishment and group pressure brought about by production contests for the selection of "labor heroes." Second, productivity can be increased as workers acquire more skills. This can be achieved both by learning on the job and by formal training. The latter process is an integral part of the country's educational system, which can only be cursorily examined in the present volume. Third, as for working longer hours, several problems are raised in this connection.

In the first place, a point may be reached beyond which any further extension of working hours would result in a decline of productivity per man-hour and would therefore be self-defeating. In the second place, longer working hours are normally looked upon as a diminution of welfare and must be justified on some plausible ground except where forced labor is involved. The extension of working hours, therefore, has invariably been associated in Communist China with such mass movements as the "Resist-America" campaign and the organization of nationwide production contests.

The last point suggests that in matters involving labor welfare considerations often conflict with the desire to increase production in spite of the beneficial effect of higher wages and greater welfare on productivity. This internal contradiction arises out of the fact that any increase in wages and non-monetary payments to labor almost invariably entails an increase in consumption, whereas Communist China's cardinal economic policy is to augment the volume of current investment in productive facilities devoted to non-consumers' goods. Where to strike the balance not only presents a hard economic problem, but also raises a far-reaching political issue, for the "new democratic" regime supposedly rests upon an alliance of workers and peasants, and somehow the Communist government must show that the workers are actually improving their lot as time passes or otherwise explain away its inability to bring this about. Moreover, since all organized labor movement traditionally aims at the progressive improvement of the material welfare of the groups it represents through collective bargaining and, if necessary, strikes, means must be found to alter this way of thinking and to emphasize instead the need to increase production at the expense of greater welfare at the present time.

Last, but not least, one should not lose sight of the fact that industrial workers and other recipients of salaries and wages, together with their families, constitute a most important segment of the urban population and exert a decisive influence on the operation of the nation's productive and administrative apparatus, and hence the fulfillment of the government's economic policy. To the Communist Party the importance of undisputed control over this segment of the population in the urban centers parallels that of control over the peasantry. The consolidation of the Party's political power in the country must be carried out in both urban and rural areas.

What "land reform" did for the Communists in terms of rural control finds its counterpart in the industrial trade union movement. Moreover, while the completion of "land reform" was followed by "cooperativization," changes in emphasis in the functions of the trade union, reflecting subtle changes in the nature of the labor movement, have also taken place as the nationalization of private enterprises proceeds apace. Nevertheless, a basic difference exists between the techniques of "land reform" and the government-sponsored labor movement. That is, while production could be more or less carried on during land redistribution, industrial production would suffer far more seriously if management were taken over by workers without adequate preparation. Shortage of trained technicians and management personnel loyal to the Party acts as a brake on the employment of organized labor to take the place of capitalists. On the other hand, this does not mean that the importance of the labor movement as an integral part of political and social control should be discounted. As a matter of fact, it can be demonstrated that not only considerations of welfare and of production may result in conflict, but the objective of political control is not necessarily consonant with the objectives of production and welfare. That the Chinese Communists have not succeeded in resolving these problems satisfactorily may be seen in the following discussion.

FUNCTIONS OF THE TRADE UNION

Needless to say, the most vital element in all labor matters in Communist China is the trade union, which is first and foremost an instrument for the implementation of all government policy concerning labor. It does not represent a spontaneous movement and is not an association freely entered into by individual workers for the purpose of improving their material welfare and social status. Nor is it the result of the work of individual labor organizers. The government plays a direct and active role in building both the individual unions and the hierarchy of the entire trade union movement.

According to the constitution applicable to all trade unions, which was adopted in 1953, the latter are charged with the specific responsibility of (1) increasing production, raising labor productivity, and accomplishing and over-fulfilling the production plans of the state, and (2) improving the material welfare of workers insofar as the country's economic development warrants. A distinction is made between trade unions in government enterprises and those in private enterprises. Since Communist China is supposedly a country of workers and peasants, workers in government enterprises are represented as the collective owners of these enterprises. Consequently, the Communist authorities argue, trade unions in these enterprises are primarily responsible for ensuring the fulfilment of production assignments only. On the other hand, trade unions in private enterprises have the additional responsibility of supervising the conduct of the capitalists. In other words, trade unions have the dual function of overseeing production plan fulfilment, including all the ancillary activities connected therewith, and of watching over those capitalists whose enterprises have not yet been taken over by the state. As nationalization advances in scope, emphasis has also shifted increasingly to the former aspect. Moreover, since the accent is on production, members of all trade unions are held responsible for the maintenance of labor discipline and the observance of the government's decrees. Thus, strikes and lockouts, as well as all other methods traditionally employed for the enforcement of labor's demands on management are at one stroke outlawed as far as government enterprises are concerned, because, according to the Communists, labor cannot oppose itself and must not fail to heed its own true interest. The former function of the trade union in organizing and educating workers in order to overthrow the "reactionary regime" of the Nationalists has given way to its present function of enforcing policy on behalf of the government. From a vehicle of labor agitation the trade union has now become an effective instrument of control.[2]

EXPANSION OF TRADE UNIONS

The effectiveness of the trade union as an instrument of the government tends to be enhanced as union membership increases. Accordingly, during a national conference on labor union work in July, 1949, the decision was made to undertake the basic task of organizing the urban workers in one year's time, starting with workers in industrial enterprises.[3] Although unionization did not progress as fast as it was planned in the beginning, substantial expansion was made especially in conjunction with the "five-anti" campaign against the urban capitalists during 1952 and in its aftermath.

According to Li Li-san, total trade union membership in China under the leadership of the All-China Federation of Labor at the time of the sixth National Congress of Labor in August, 1948, was 2,830,000.[4] Following the Communist take-over, the tempo of unionization was stepped up, especially in Shanghai and Tientsin, and official policy stressed the unionization of workers in railways and in maritime, postal, tele-communications, textile, fuel, food, and publications enterprises and educational and cultural institutions, with the purpose of organizing these and others along lines of industrial unions wherever possible. At the end of March, 1950, total union membership stood at 3.8 million and was geographically distributed as follows: (1) East China, 1,829,881; (2) North China, 727,839; (3) Manchuria and Inner Mongolia, 905,353; (4) Central-South, 276,035; (5) Northwest China, 89,311; and (6) Southwest China, 25,538.[5] Of the 3.8 million trade union members, 2.1 million represented the membership of industrial unions, the rest being that of unions organized geographically or on some occupational basis. As may be seen from the following statistics, unionization had progressed most in the metal-working industry, followed by railways, coal mining, the textile industry, and postal and tele-communications establishments.

According to subsequent reports, trade union membership in Communist China had increased to 7.3 million by the first quarter of 1952.[6] At the end of 1952, the number stood at 10.2 million.[7] The figure rose to 10.6 million in 1953.[8] As industrialization proceeds, the organization of more and more workers into trade unions continues, and the basic level unions are charged specifically with this task of expanding the scope of organization.

The movement to expand trade union membership was beset by two types of difficulties. On the one hand, as K'ang Sheng has pointed out,[9] the "close-door" policy of many trade unions had to be abandoned at an early stage and the standards of union membership had to be lowered. On the other hand, indiscriminate expansion has inevitably brought into the trade unions many members who are not active participants in union work. Thus, one should not rely upon the numerical growth of trade unions as an indisputable sign of success. The organizational efficiency and performance of the union's assigned tasks must be examined further.

Membership of Industrial Trade Unions in Communist China, March, 1950

	Number of Employees and Workers	*Trade Union Membership*
Food Industry Workers[1]	1,062,968	138,217
Maritime Workers[2]	700,000	53,580
Shop Clerks[3]	627,300	252,600
Stevedores, porters, etc.	568,548	313,768
Textile Workers	469,085	349,550
Metal Workers	411,340	346,522
Railway Workers	410,519	320,628
Coal Miners[4]	335,268	250,869
Postal and Tele-communications Workers	104,773	67,895
Electric Utilities Workers[5]	31,963	18,727
Total	4,721,764	2,112,356

Source: Statistical Office of the All-China Federation of Labor, *Chinese Workers,* No. 5, p. 69, Peking, June, 1950.

1. Including only the salt industry of Manchuria, North China, Shantung, and Northern Kiangsu; the marine product industry of Manchuria, Shanghai, and Shantung; and government sugar refineries in Manchuria and Canton.
2. The total number of workers is estimated.
3. Including returns from fifteen cities only.
4. Including North China, East China, and Manchuria only.
5. The two figures are *not* comparable. The total number of workers refers to the North China Electric Industry Administration, while union membeship refers to Manchuria.

ORGANIZATION OF THE BASIC UNION

Trade unions in Communist China are organized as a rule without regard to occupational lines and on the basis of individual enterprises or work units such as factories, farms, shops, and schools. In an increasing number of cases, these unions are then grouped into regional and national units by industries. At every level of local government, however, there are also local federations of trade unions which are responsible for overseeing the work of all trade unions in their respective areas and, in the case of unions which have national associations on industrial lines, for supervising their performance with respect to the instructions of their national organizations.[10] This hierarchy of trade unions, criss-crossed by industrial divisions, inevitably enhances the possibility of conflicting policies and increases the usual snarls of bureaucratic organization. However, the quality of trade union work depends ultimately upon the efficiency of the unions at the lowest level. In this respect it appears that there are some serious misgivings.

According to the regulations governing the organization of basic level unions, promulgated by the All-China Federation of Labor in August, 1950, a basic level trade union committee may be organized wherever 25 or more workers and employees are found in a single organization. In organizations of 500 persons or more additional committees may be established for individual workshops or departments. The basic level trade union committee performs its work in accordance with the directives of its superior organizations and the resolutions and suggestions of the meetings of the entire union membership or workers' representatives, and in conjunction with the production plans of the management. The union committee may also establish sub-committees and individual work-groups for the purpose of carrying out the different functions assigned to the trade union.[11]

The extensive scope of trade union work, extending well beyond what may be regarded as the normal sphere of organized labor activity, can be best illustrated by the following list of sub-committees and work-groups which a model trade union at the basic level should theoretically have:[12]

Sub-committees	*Work Groups*	*Functions*
1. Organization	a. Organization	Organization of various ty of major assignments.
	b. Cadres	Promotion and training o activists.
	c. Membership	Supervision over the rig obligations, thought, and activities of the entire union membership.
	d. Statistics	Collection of organization statistics and training of statistical workers.
2. Production	a. Emulation Contests	Promotion of production contests in cooperation w factory management committees, workshop committees, and work-groups.

Sub-committees	*Work Groups*	*Functions*
	b. Quotas	Determination of standard production quotas in conjunction with the administration or the private owners and promotion of production over quota.
	c. Technical Study	Establishment of training courses for adult and young workers and cultivation of labor heroes.
	d. Rationalization Proposals	Study of rationalization proposals and promotion for their adoption.
	e. Wages	Study of the wage system in use in the enterprise and its effect on production.
	f. Statistics	Collection of production statistics and training of statistical workers.
Culture and Education	a. Propaganda	
	I. Newspaper Reading	Organization of collective newspaper reading and tests on current events.
	II. Editing and Publication	Publication of news sheets and wall newspapers.
	III. Broadcasting	Organization of public addresses and news monitoring.
	IV. Artistic and Visual Work	Preparation of slogans, caricatures, and stage setting.
	b. Culture and Education	
	I. Literacy	Basic education in literacy in workshops.
	II. Educational Standards	Stipulation of training courses and teaching methods and judging of labor heroes and work grades.
	III. Organization	Organization of trainees and student-teachers.
	IV. General Affairs	Control of supplies and distribution of public notices.
	V. Evening Schools	Organization of evening classes.
	c. Recreation and Entertainment	
	I. Dancing	
	II. Theatrical Performance	

Sub-committees	*Work Groups*	*Functions*
	III. Music IV. Cinema V. Games VI. Physical Education VII. Circulating Entertainment Instruction VIII. Libraries	
	d. Statistics	Collection of relevant statistics.
4. Labor Insurance	a. Information and Registration	Maintenance of labor insurance card file and public information.
	b. Medical Work	Supervision of hospitals and clinics and medical equipment and supplies.
	c. Visiting	Organization of visits to the sick and injured.
	d. Statistics	Collection of relevant statistics.
5. Labor Safety	a. Safety	Plant safety inspections and prevention of industrial accidents.
	b. Hygiene	Maintenance of sanitary working conditions and hygiene instructions to workers' families.
	c. Inspection	Supervision over the observance of labor insurance regulations by management.
	d. Statistics	Collection of relevant statistics.
6. Living Conditions	a. Service	Provision of miscellaneous services to union members.
	b. Facilities	Organization of barber shops, baths, laundries, etc.
	c. Dormitory	Supervision of dormitories.
	d. Public Kitchens	Organization of public kitchens for workers and their families.
	e. Statistics	Collection of relevant statistics.
7. Mutual Savings	a. Accounting	Collection and deposit of funds.

Sub-committees	*Work Groups*	*Functions*
	b. Cashier	Issue of loan applications and publication of loans granted.
	c. Loan Application	Scrutiny of loan applications.
	d. Organization	Organization of meetings, preparation of reports, and membership drive for savings groups.
	e. Statistics	Collection of relevant statistics.
8. Production Security	a. Protection and Security	Establishment of systems of production safety and responsibility, shop inspection, receiving of visitors, and work shifts.
	b. Security Study	Inquiry into causes of accidents and other incidents and their prevention.
	c. Statistics	Collection of relevant statistics.
9. Statistics		Analysis of departmental statistics.
10. Finance		Handling of all financial matters pertaining to the union.
11. Women Workers	a. Liaison	Supervision of work in all other sub-committees and groups concerning women workers.
	b. Hygiene and Welfare for Women and Children	Organization of medical and public hygiene personnel and welfare institutions.
	c. Family Disputes	Arbitration of family disputes and marriage problems.
	d. Nurseries	Organization of nurseries for women workers.
	e. Statistics	Collection of revelant statistics.
12. Workers' Families	a. Organization and Education	Organization of workers' families in political, cultural, and recreational activities.
	b. Production	Organization of workers' families in supplementary production.

Sub-committees	*Work Groups*	*Functions*
	c. Hygiene	Organization of health cation lectures and p hygiene activities.
	d. Mutual Help	Organization of workers' families for mutual ai distress.
	e. Statistics	Collection of relevant statistics.

Since the above list of twelve sub-committees, forty-five work-groups, and an even larger number of sub-groups is supposed to be representative of the organizational structure of a model basic level union, the average trade union may not have such a stupendous and overlapping organization. However, in the case of a few unions whose activities constituted the object of a sample study in Shanghai,[13] their general structure appears to parallel the one outlined above. The elaborate organization of the basic union not only serves to demonstrate the far-flung activities of trade unions as an instrument of social and political control, but also reveals certain weaknesses inherent in such an organization.

PARTY CONTROL OF TRADE UNIONS

First, as the Communist authorities have openely conceded,[14] there are obviously too many committees and work-groups in the basic level union. The average union in factories and mines now has seven to eight committees. Some unions, in line with the model structure mentioned above, have as many as thirteen committees. In an extreme case cited by the *Workers' Daily,* the union of a 30-man factory at Dairen had 10 working committes; another basic union in Szechwan had a women workers' committee, although the factory in question had only three women workers. As a result, many union workers have to hold several posts concurrently, each of which entails a large number of meetings and paper work, and very little is accomplished for lack of time.

The heavy work load on union organizers and activists results in a particularly demanding role for Communist Party members. Because of the leading role they have to play, they are necessarily separated from the actual production process and become increasingly ill-informed about the workers' real problems. At the same time, their capacity to lead the unions along established Party lines is weakened, and criticisms of union, i.e., Party, leadership have increased. This development is brought out quite clearly in a statement by Lai Jo-yü, Secretary-General of the All-China Federation of Labor: "The majority of responsible trade union workers and basic level union committee chairmen are local Party committee members or branch committee members. Whatever opinion and suggestions they may have may be voiced and properly settled during Party meetings. These are the Party's internal problems. As for the trade unions, their work must be carried out under the leadership of the Party. They may not oppose the Party in any way. It is not permissible to voice dissatisfaction with the Party either openly among the workers or at trade union meetings. Trade unions must accept the Party's leadership. This is heaven's first law. Failure to recognize this is unionism which does not show proper respect to Party leadership and consequently results in serious errors." [15] The same comment was again made early in 1953 when an official notification of the All-China Federation of Labor referred to widespread shortcomings in trade union organizations at all levels. Union officials in the higher echelons were ordered to help local Party committees to launch this struggle at the basic level, and to place trade union work squarely under the supervision of the Party.[16]

As mentioned earlier, there were 10.6 million trade union members in 1953. Of this number 450,000 were Communist Party members, while another 650,000 were members of the Youth Corps. Thus the number of Party members constituted no more than 10 per cent of the entire union membership. There were 180,000 separate trade unions in Communist China at this time. On the average, each union had six Party cadres out of a total membership of 59 workers. Apparently, this ratio of Party men to workers was not sufficient to establish unquestionable Party control over the unions.

In the face of this situation, a directive was issued by the Chinese Communist authorities in November, 1953, to transfer large numbers of Party cadres from government departments to industrial and mining enterprises, and to redistribute cadres among the latter organizations with special emphasis on the newly established factories and mines.[17] At the same time individual enterprises were instructed to train and promote the largest number possible of cadres with experience in production and working ability from among the more skilled workers and Youth Corps members. As the Five Year Plan unfolds and the number of production units multiplies, demands on workers also increase steadily. The shortage of Party stalwarts among trade union workers presents a serious bottleneck which may be of far-reaching consequence.

HOME LIFE AND CONTROL OF LEISURE

Shortage of Party cadres and the consequent threat to Party control of the trade unions stems at least in part from the fact that union work includes so many facets which are not properly the normal sphere of activity of organized labor, but which are essential from the Communists' point of view because of their policy to use the union as an instrument of control of the urban population. This is an aspect of Communist China's labor control program which should not be overlooked.

The extension of government control by means of the trade union to the worker's entire existence outside the factory and work shop is achieved by control of his family and of his non-working hours. On the first point, a resolution adopted by the All-China Federation of Labor to strengthen trade union activities concerning women workers states, inter alia: "Urban workers and their families constitute about one-half of the population of most cities. The organization of workers' families, centering around the trade union, is immensely useful for the purpose of fulfilling production plans; it has a far-reaching political significance with respect to the consolidation of the people's political powers." [18] The responsibility of organizing workers' families falls primarily on the women workers' committee of the basic level union because contact with the wives of workers can be established more easily through women workers and those male union officials whose duty has given them the requisite experience in dealing with women.

According to the Shanghai Federation of Labor, women workers' committee members are directed to "heighten the political consciousness" of workers' families for the purpose of promoting patriotic production contests by such means as public newspaper-reading, story-telling, club meetings, picture-showing, and public addresses dealing with current events and the importance of production. Moreover, workers' families are mobilized in tracking down rumor-mongers and in such work as fire prevention, protection against saboteurs and thieves, and air raid precautions. All these are done in the name of protecting the home. Active members among the workers' families are especially invited to participate in other trade union activities, such as general meetings of workers' representatives, meetings for goving awards to labor heroes, cooperatives, and recreational clubs. Particular attention was given to this aspect of trade union activity during the Korean war and at the height of the "Resist-America" campaign although effort has since been made to sustain the drive to control workers' families.[19] While the same is true in other areas, Shanghai and a few other industrial centers are probably among the more promising places for this type of work because of the large number of women workers in the textile mills concentrated in these cities.

As for control of the workers' leisure hours, a good indication of the method used may be found in the practice of the Wu-san Factory at Shen-yang, which has been set up as an outstanding model to be widely imitated elsewhere. At the Wu-san Factory, after the normal working hours, all workers must take part in "collective study" which takes place every day at 5–6 p.m. Mondays are allotted to the examination of group resolutions. Tuesdays, Wednesdays, and Thursdays are devoted to the pursuit of current drives. Fridays and Saturdays are earmarked for political education. Four times a week, from 6:30 to 8 p.m., there are additional collective cultural study hours for all the workers.[20] In this way, all workers are under the constant supervision of the trade union some twelve hours a day during the greater part of the six-day work week under normal production conditions when no work is done on Sundays. Even then, when they return home, they are still subject to Party control through the union's family organizations. In the case of Party members and other union officials, committee meetings and similar activities would take up even more time. The system of labor control in Communist China thus encompasses practically every waking hour of the individual worker, and the more so if he is also a Party member. The question is whether such control is necessarily conducive to greater production and more efficiency even though it may be useful in consolidating the Party's political power, at any rate in the short run.

II

LABOR-MANAGEMENT RELATIONS

Although maintenance of strict labor discipline under the direction of the Party-controlled union is a primary function of trade unions in Communist China today, the trend towards "unionism," deplored by Lai Jo-yü, was probably more characteristic of the traditional attitude of labor, which was intent on improving its material welfare by every means at its disposal, especially in the initial period of Communist rule. One clear example of this attitude was the large number of industrial disputes reported during this period. It is also probable that some of these disputes were tolerated, if not actively instigated, by the Communists themselves in order to exert pressure on the private industrialists and other businessmen.[21] In Shanghai alone, for instance, a total of 3,324 industrial disputes were reported by the Bureau of Social Affairs during the second half of 1949. Over a third of these disputes originated from workers' demands for re-employment and resumption of operation; about one-third centered around wages, the rest being caused by dismissal of workers, plant close-downs, and other causes.[22] During the same period, a large number of similar disputes were also reported in other cities.

It was at this time that provisional regulations governing labor disputes were issued by the All-China Federation of Labor stipulating definite procedures for conciliation, mediation, and arbitration. As long as disputes were not settled, owners were not permitted to close down their plants or reduce wage payments while workers were told to carry on production and to observe labor discipline.[23] Local regulations governing labor disputes were later published in individual cities, generally following the same principle, especially the maintenance of production and status quo pending settlement.[24]

Obviously the proclamation of these regulations alone could not restore industrial peace once and for all. However, Communist publications after 1950 have rarely mentioned any strikes or other types of serious disputes. Instead, emphasis has shifted to the fulfilment of production plans by workers, especially in the nationalized enterprises. Since activities detrimental to plan fulfilment are regarded as counter-revolutionary, strikes as a weapon to enforce demands on management can no longer exist and become outright sabotage.

COLLECTIVE CONTRACTS AND EMULATION DRIVES

The abolition of strikes does not mean, however, that the role of the trade union is in any way diminished or that the authority of the remaining private employers over the workers is increased. As far as private employers are concerned, the power of the trade union is sustained by the government's decree that collective contracts must be concluded between the employers and workers' representatives, i.e., the union, under the supervision of officials of the local labor departments. Terms of employment, factory regulations, wages, working hours, holidays, special regulations for woman and child labor, and welfare provisions are all covered under such contracts, and both contracting parties must live up to their terms.[25]

At the same time, in the case of government enterprises, the collective contract gives the government-appointed management a formal basis for exacting certain minimum standards of performance from the workers. The most important feature of these collective contracts is the provision that workers must be regularly informed on the production plan and their individual assignments under the plan so that production contests may be organized on the basis of these assignments.[26] Moreover, it is particularly interesting to note that provisions in the contracts concerning wages do not regulate the absolute level of wages, but only determine the relative scale of different grades of workers in terms of index numbers. Thus the so-called collective contracts are not negotiated through collective bargaining in the usual sense, but are merely instruments for binding the workers on a collective basis. Concurrent restrictions imposed by collective contracts on the management of government enterprises are valid only to the extent the government is prepared to bind itself, especially because the workers are represented by officials of the government-controlled union in the first place.

The best example of the status of workers under the collective contract system may be found in the prevalence of the practice of production contests. Started on a large scale after the outbreak of the Korean war, these contests have been kept up without interruption under various patriotic slogans and have become an integral part of economic planning. During 1950, according to Lai Jo-yü, 683,000 workers in the country took part in such emulation drives. The number increased to 2,380,000 in 1951. By the second half of 1952, over 80 per cent of the nation's workers had joined the system as regular participants, which is another way of saying that the majority of the country's workers were working longer hours and under greater pressure than the collective contracts normally require.[27]

PRODUCTIVITY, INCENTIVE, AND LABOR DISCIPLINE

The immediate result of such production contests is usually an increase in total output, but whether this means an actual increase in productivity on a man-hour basis is rather questionable. On the one hand, overall figures on labor productivity such as those given by Lai Jo-yü, who reported a 42 per cent increase in 1951 as compared with the peak postwar level and another 21 per cent increase in the first half of 1952 over the 1951 level,[28] are not particularly meaningful. On the other hand, increases in man-hour or man-day output in individual industries have usually taken place concomitantly with greater mechanization and rehabilitation of the more efficient plants or construction of new facilities. It is not possible to isolate the effect of emulation drives on man-hour productivity even though it is only reasonable to assume that the result may have been favorable in some cases.

However, as a general rule, the effect of emulation drives is an increase in working hours, either in the form of working longer shifts or by working Sundays. This conclusion is warranted by the comment of the *Workers' Daily* to the effect that labor emulation drives must now enter a new stage by paying less attention to extra hours and more to the adoption of technical innovations.[29] The official organ also recommends the encouragement of improvements in technique and management through a proper system of awards and the widespread establishment of committees in government enterprises for the consideration of rationalization proposals. Since the individual trade unions have always had special committees to deal with rationalization proposals originating from the workers, this new emphasis on innovation in preference to sheer hard work is all the more interesting.

Reports on technical innovations and rationalization proposals are frequently reported in Communist Chinese publications, but it is difficult to determine exactly the response of potential innovators to the system of awards currently in use. In this connection, it should also be pointed out that so far Communist Chinese laws have made it a practice to distinguish between "invention rights" and patent rights, the former being limited to single awards in the form of medals, prizes, and money. Moreover, patent rights, which give their holders the right to royalty payments, are not granted to innovations of special importance, including those which should be widely adopted within a short time. It is quite possible that such restrictions have tended to discourage potential innovators.[30]

At any rate, the Communist authorities have apparently decided not to depend upon spontaneous proposals for increasing productivity. On the contrary, great reliance seems to have been placed on negative inducements. In the first place, beginning February, 1954, special workers' courts, directed by local people's courts, have been established under the leadership of the trade unions and are given the responsibility of enforcing labor discipline. Breach of discipline, dereliction of duty, theft, and other offenses are subject to punishments ranging from public rebuke to demotion and dismissal.[31] In addition, an Outline of Labor Regulations in Government Enterprises was promulgated in July, 1954, which further tightened the disciplinary provisions. However, the question whether the problem of suitable incentives can be resolved by disciplinary action alone still remains, not to mention the justifiability of such methods.

Speaking of the 1954 regulations mentioned above, the official *Workers' Daily* stated on January 12, 1955: "First, punishment of workers has become the principal method used to consolidate labor discipline and the 'Outline of Labor Regulations in Government Enterprises' has been made the legal basis for punishing the workers. In carrying out the Outline, some lower level cadres hold the view that 'a wonderful method to ensure the attendance rate is now available; a few dismissals would bring the rest in line.' . . . In some instances, punishment has been meted out illegally (and in excess of the stipulated measures) . . . Second, . . . in drawing up labor regulations, only the systems to be observed by the workers have been fixed in detail while no rigid rules have been laid down for observance by management in discharging its duties. Poor business management, low productivity, and failure to complete the production plans are all blamed on the workers and attributed to breach of labor discipline . . . Third, the management of some enterprises often shift the responsibility for injury and accident to the workers . . . The causes of accident are often described as 'breach of work procedures,' 'carelessness of workers,' and 'clumsiness.' . . . Fourth, in individual enterprises, the management has often abused its administrative power and treated breaches of labor discipline as acts of crime."

III

THE WAGE SYSTEM

It goes without saying that the effectiveness of the wage incentive depends upon the manner in which wages are determined, i.e., whether payments are in any way related to the volume of work done; the possibility of promotion and whether the effort entailed in advancing oneself is adequately compensated by the increase in pay; and, finally, the level of the basic pay at any given grade, excluding bonus payments and other fringe benefits.

As far as the wage system is concerned, Communist Chinese policy has aimed at the abolition of simple time rates and the general adoption of some form of piece rates. The latter system was first put into effect by Soviet-controlled enterprises in the Dairen area and was later extended to the rest of Manchuria, and finally to China Proper. By 1953, 46 per cent of all industrial workers in Manchuria were under piece rates[32] although the practice was probably less widespread in the rest of the country.

While local variations may exist, the general practice in determining wage rates follows the same procedure:[33] on the basis of 7 legal holidays a year and a work week of six days, there are 306 working days a year, and an average of 25.5 days a month. There are 10 working hours per day. Given the basic monthly wage for a particular grade, which is as a rule expressed in terms of wage units, the hourly wage is computed. The latter is then combined with the standard quota, which is determined by the trade union and the management together and is revised usually at six-month intervals as productivity changes. On the basis of the standard quota, i.e., a certain number of pieces per hour, the piece rate for that particular grade of work is then determined, and total payments are made at this rate, modified by penalties or bonuses when actual performance falls short of or exceeds the quota.

When such piece rates were first adopted by Soviet enterprises in the former Kwantung Leased Territory, distinction was made between two groups of enterprises with respect to the basic wage level in corresponding grades. Within each group there were seven grades for factory workers and fifteen grades for salaried employees and other non-production workers. In terms of index numbers within each category the scale was as follows:

Wage Scale in Soviet-Controlled Enterprise
in Lü-ta (Manchuria), 1949

Grade	*Workers*	*Salaried Employees*[1] *and Non-production Workers*
1	100	100
2	120	125
3	145	156
4	175	181
5	215	203
6	260	240
7	320	256
8		281
9		312
10		343
11		375
12		390
13		421
14		453
15		469

Source: People's Daily, Peking, November 14, 1949.

1. The above scale refers to Class B or light industries, but that of Class A industries is virtually the same. All index numbers are comparable only within the same category.

As can be seen from the preceding table, the differences between successive grades of pay within each category of workers were sufficiently wide to offer reasonable inducement to the workers to strive for promotion. At the same time, the gap between the pay of managerial and supervisory personnel, beginning from grade 5 up under the category of salaried and other employees, and that of the workers on the factory floor was also wide enough to offer adequate compensation to the former in accordance with the degree of skill and responsibility involved in their work.[34]

The wage scale introduced in Manchuria, which completely discarded any pretense of egalitarianism, has since been extensively adopted in the entire country. Conditions in China Proper may be illustrated by practice in the Central-South provinces where all government industrial and mining enterprises in the area have been placed under the new system since August, 1952.[35] In the first place, the seven-grade system is maintained for industries such as manufacturing, paper, rubber products, leather goods, oils and fats, tobacco, and matches, while in such industries as coal mining, iron and steel, non-ferrous metals, electric power, machinery manufacturing, heavy chemicals, arms and military supplies, cotton textiles, and printing, an eight-grade system is now substituted. Instead of two groups of industries with two separate pay scales, as was the case in Manchuria in 1949, industries are now divided into a much larger number of groups, and workers of the same grade are paid at different base rates, depending upon the industries in which they work. Arranged in diminishing order of pay scales, the groups are (1) coal mining, the metallurgical industry, and mining of non-ferrous metals; (2) electric utilities, (3) heavy machine manufacturing, manufacture of arms, and the heavy chemical industry, (4) machine repair and the manufacture of machine parts, (5) the cotton textile industry, (6) industries manufacturing paper, rubber products, leather goods, and oils and fats, and the printing industry, (7) food processing and the clothing industry, and (8) match manufacturing and the tobacco industry. Within each industrial group the individual enterprises are again divided into five sub-groups, each with its own pay scale. Within each enterprise differentials similar to those first adopted in Manchuria are maintained between supervisory, technical, and managerial personnel, on the one hand, and the ordinary workers, on the other hand.

Second, in determining the grade of a given type of work within an enterprise, several factors are taken into consideration. These are the requisite technical skill, degree of responsibility, degree of exertion, and working conditions. The weights given to these four factors vary from one industry to another. Once the individual jobs within an enterprise have been properly evaluated, they are classified into seven or eight grades generally maintained in the same industry, with a predetermined pay scale; or, in the alternative case, the "points" allotted to individual jobs are used directly as coefficients for establishing the pay scale. For instance, jobs A, B, and C may have 75, 89, and 105 "points" respectively. In the first case, A and

B may both fall within Grade 1 while C may be in Grade 2. If the base pay for Grade 1 is 100 wage units, then the base pay for jobs A and B in terms of wage units is both 100. In the second case, the "points" themselves are used as index numbers which are then applied to a starting base pay in terms of wage units.

On the basis of the experience of the Central-South government enterprises, it is said that productivity per man-hour has increased since the adoption of piece rates based on the new system. Furthermore, the reclassification of jobs has had the effect of retaining for individual enterprises those workers who are most essential to their uninterrupted and efficient operation. The higher pay scale for certain enterprises in comparison with that in force in other enterprises has also had a similar effect in guaranteeing labor supply to the former, which presumably conforms to the scale of priority given by the Communist authorities to different industries. Finally, the higher differentials between successive pay grades is said to have reduced labor turnover in individual enterprises as workers can now increase their income appreciably by moving up the grades within the same enterprise instead of changing their employment.[36]

MONEY AND REAL WAGES

The new wage system in Communist China may have given the workers more incentive in working harder because of the increasing use of piece rates and the prospect of promotion which, at any rate, appears better on paper than before. However, there remains the question of the level of wages itself.

As mentioned above, the base pay of an individual worker depends, in the first place, upon the number of wage units his grade commands. The monetary value of the base pay depends in turn upon the value of the wage unit. The latter varies geographically from one area to another in more or less the same manner as that of "commodity-equivalent" units formerly in use in many cities for savings deposits. Fluctuations over time are also comparable to those of the "commodity-equivalent"units. The composition of the wage unit consists of a few basic commodities. During 1950 in Manchuria, for instance, the value of a wage unit was the sum of the retail values *in government stores* of 1.63 *shih* catties of coarse grain, 5.5 *shih* catties of coal, 0.035 *shih* catty of bean oil, 0.045 *shih* catty of salt, and 0.2 square *ch'ih* of rough cloth.[37] In some areas, such as Shanghai and Wu-han, no separate wage units were quoted for long periods and the "commodity-equivalent" units were also used in computing wages.[38] In April, 1952, a new wage unit was adopted by the Communist authorities, its commodity composition being 0.8 *shih* catty of food grain, 0.2 *shih ch'ih* of cloth, 0.05 *shih* catty of vegetable oil, 0.02 *shih* catty of salt, and 2 *shih* catties of coal.[39] Some regional variations may still exist, but the general principle remains the same.

The average level of wages in Communist China varies from one region to another. On the whole, it is highest in Manchuria and East China, especially the Shanghai area, and somewhat lower in North China and the Central-South. The wage level of Southwest and Northwest China is said to be the lowest. Lack of detailed wage statistics makes it very difficult to arrive at accurate estimates of the current wage levels in different regions. However, if we may take the Central-South as an illustrative case, it is still possible to arrive at a general picture of the situation.

In the case of the Central-South, official reports have stated, for instance, that the base pay of the lowest grade of industrial workers ranged between 85 and 126 wage units a month in mid-1951. At the time, one wage unit was quoted at ¥2,278.[40] Thus the money wage in different industries amounted to ¥193,630 to ¥284,750 a month for the lowest paid workers. At the same time, the base pay of workers of the highest grade was 378 wage units or ¥861,084. Following the enforcement of the new wage system and the reclassification of jobs, the range of the lowest base pay was increased to 100–137 wage units in mid-1952, while the highest base pay was also raised to 381 wage units. In the meantime, prices had declined in the course of the "five-anti" drive from their post-Korean war high, and the wage unit was approximately equivalent to ¥2,200 each. Thus, in monetary terms, the corresponding figures were ¥220,000-¥301,400[41] a month for the worst paid workers and ¥838,200 a month for the best paid.

It must be borne in mind that the above figures refer to gross pay, which is subject to various deductions in taxes, union dues, and other compulsory contributions.[42] At the same time, the family's total income may be larger if more than one person works. Furthermore, additional pay may be earned through participation in the numerous production contests. Consequently, the money income of the average working family may depart appreciably from the base pay level. It is doubtful that these conflicting considerations could offset one another completely. However, it is interesting to note that during 1952 the base pay in the Central-South provinces for the lowest paid workers, who constituted the majority of industrial labor, was equivalent to no more than U.S. $9.85-13.49 a month at the then prevailing official exchange rate and that under the favorable assumption of two adult workers in the family, a family of five persons would have a per capita money income equivalent to U.S. $3.94-5.36. Even in the case of the highest paid worker, the per capita monthly income would be no more than U.S. $15.01 under the same set of assumptions. Bearing in mind that wages in the Central-South are comparable to those of North China and are even higher than those of the Southwest and the Northwest, though lower than wages in Manchuria and East China, we can readily envisage the extremely small compensation the Chinese worker receives in exchange for the long hours and strict regimentation under the union.

According to official statistics, which offer no clear explanation of the terms used, the average wage level of both workers and salaried employees in government industries rose from an index of 100 in 1949 to 116.3 in 1950, 121.3 in 1951, 134.7 in 1952, and 141.4 in 1953.[43] However, it is hard to say how meaningful these figures really are, not only because workers and salaried employees of many grades have been thrown together, but also because changes in commodity prices since 1949 are not taken into full account even if these index numbers refer to increases in wages units instead of monetary payments.[44] Moreover, since the first introduction of the wage unit, its composition of commodities has been reduced at least once. That is to say, the present wage unit represents a smaller "basket" of goods than before. Finally, granted that wages have actually increased in real terms, the extension of rationing has had the effect of thwarting any attempt to increase consumption.

PRODUCTION AND WAGES

The official reports on wage increases since 1949 may also be compared with increase in industrial production in the same period. While industrial production probably increased by 136.4 per cent between 1949 and 1952, average wages increased by 34.7 per cent only, assuming that the latter actually depicted a rise of real wages. Furthermore, increase in wages has fallen short of the reported rise of labor productivity. In the Wu-san factory at Shen-yang, for instance, labor productivity increased by 347 per cent between 1949 and 1952, while wages increased by only 17 per cent in the same period,[45] even though the factory is said to represent a case of model achievement in labor relations. In the Central-South, according to reports from thirteen government mines and manufacturing plants, labor productivity increased by 88 per cent in 1951 over the preceding year while the increase in wages was just above 13 per cent.[46] Again, in the country as a whole, increase in wages in all government enterprises in 1952 averaged 11 per cent in comparison with 1951, but increase in labor productivity, with the exception of the non-ferrous metals industry, was much higher, ranging from 12 per cent in the electric power industry to 42 per cent in heavy chemicals.[47] The corresponding figures in 1953 compared with 1952 were 5 per cent for wages and 13 per cent for labor productivity.[48] Although one may question the precise meaning of labor productivity as employed by the Communist authorities, there seems to be little doubt that whatever improvement labor may have received in the wage rate since 1949, it has been purposely kept below the increase in productivity. This is achieved by the periodic upward revision of the production quotas assigned to individual workers and reflects unmistakably the Communists' policy to curb consumption and to advance the workers' welfare only insofar as the planned pace of capital accumulation warrants.

IV

LABOR INSURANCE

At this point mention should be made of a countervailing factor, viz., the development of labor insurance, which the Chinese Communists have boasted as a major advance in labor welfare, although the matter must be considered against such adverse factors as (1) the relatively small number of persons covered so far, (2) the exclusion of persons under forced labor, (3) the insignificance of those cash benefits that are tied to the extremely low wages, and (4) the apparently great hazards to which workers are now exposed as evidenced by official reports on industrial accidents.

According to Li Li-san, the general principle of labor insurance was discussed during the sixth All-China Labor Congress, and the first labor insurance regulations of Communist China were promulgated in Manchuria in December, 1948.[49] Under the Manchurian law, a labor insurance fund was set up to which monthly contributions were made by all public enterprises at 3 per cent of the payroll. However, since medical payments and wage benefits in case of accidents and illnesses had to be paid separately by the individual enterprises and not out of the general fund, and since the financial position of most enterprises at this time was rather chaotic, the net effect of the regulations was somewhat nebulous.

A national labor insurance law was promulgated by the State Administrative Council only at the end of February, 1951.[50] It has since been revised in regard to certain coverages.[51] According to these regulations, all government and private industrial and mining enterprises employing more than 100 persons, as well as all railway, shipping, and communications agencies, including the capital construction units, have to adopt labor insurance, and have to make regular payments for this purpose at 3 per cent of their respective payrolls. During the first two months following the introduction of labor insurance in any organization the entire contributions are paid into a general insurance fund under the control of the All-China Federation of Labor. Subsequent to this initial period, only 30 per cent of the contributions are paid into the general fund while the rest is retained by the basic level trade unions for the payment of benefits under the insurance. The general fund may be used for various undertakings and activities aiming at the improvement of industrial safety and the general welfare of the workers. At the end of November, 1952, some 3,861 enterprises and other units were under this system. The number increased to 4,802 during 1953, and the total number of workers and other employees covered amounted to 4,830,000 persons. The latter figure may be compared to the 13,738,000 persons reportedly employed by government enterprises engaged in economic activities and private industrial and commercial firms in the country at the end of 1953[52] and the total trade union membership of 10.6 million. In other words, only about 35 per cent of the persons employed in economic construction, most of whom should probably be included under the law, has been covered so far.

Among the features of the revised coverage the following benefits may be noted:

Benefits for sickness and accident related to work	
1. Payment of wages	100 per cent of regular wages during period of treatment.
2. Relief payments	75 per cent of regular wages in case of total disability, payable to death. 60 per cent of regular wages in case of temporary total disability not requiring care by others, payable to recovery of ability to work. 10–30 per cent of regular wages in case of partial disability and currently working.
3. Hospitalization, medical care, and drugs	All paid by the employer.
Benefits for sickness and accident unrelated to work	
1. Payment of wages	60–100 per cent of regular wages during the first six months.
2. Relief payments	40–60 per cent of regular wages after the initial six months for an unspecified period.
3. Hospitalization, medical care, and drugs	Payment of surgery cost, doctor's fees, and "ordinary" drugs by the employer, other cost not covered, with possibility of a subsidy.
Death benefits	
1. Death related to work	3 months' wages.
2. Death unrelated to work	2 months' wages.
Retirement pension	50–70 per cent of regular wages. Retirement age: men, 60; women, 50. Length of time worked: total, 25 years (women, 20 years); same job, 5 years.
Maternity benefits	
1. Leave and wages	56–70 days, regular wages.
2. Medical examination and obstetrician	Paid by employer.
3. Special benefit	¥40,000.

As the *People's Daily* admitted on January 10, 1953, even the revised coverage as listed above was still rather limited, because, from the Communists' point of view, welfare considerations should not be allowed to interfere with the country's economic development. Thus, although the various benefits may appear liberal under the circumstances and on paper, in reality much depends upon interpretation and administrative discretion, which, as we have shown in our discussion on labor discipline, has tended to render some of the provisions a mere farce.

INDUSTRIAL ACCIDENTS

Finally, the effect of labor insurance, especially against sickness, death, and accidents, must be evaluated against the incidence of their causes. If workers are driven to accidents by overwork and other contributory factors under a program of sustained production contests, and if the health of workers is impaired for similar reasons, the availability of certain benefits cannot fully compensate for the additional hazard to which the workers are exposed as a result of the policy which has brought about more accidents, deaths, disabilities, and illnesses. Nor can one dispute the fact that the all-out drive for greater production has led to a phenomenal rise of accidents in spite of the Communists' effort to keep them under control. Apparently, overwork and mass recruitment of untrained workers, together with inadequate safety measures, have been the principal causes.

According to the *People's Daily,* the beginning of the First Five Year Plan brought with it a serious upsurge in the number of accidents compared with 1952, which was not a particularly good year, especially in Manchuria and North China.[53] The number of accidents in the country's coal mines in the first half of 1953 more than doubled that of the corresponding period in 1952.[54] Developments in 1954 have confirmed the trend.[55] Information on individual areas is somewhat spotty, but it again shows the same general situation. In Shanghai, for instance, some 3,000 persons were killed or suffered injuries in industrial plants during the first 8 months of 1951 as compared with 1,691 persons in the entire year of 1950.[56] In the Central-South an official report mentioned a 22.7 per cent rise in the number of industrial injuries and deaths in government enterprises during the first half of 1952 in comparison with the second half of 1951.[57] In the Southwest accidents in the government coal mines followed a continuously rising trend since the first quarter of 1952.[58] In Manchuria, industrial accidents in 1952 were considerably more numerous than in the preceding year in the electric, non-ferrous metals, coal mining, and chemical industries.[59] These instances could be enumerated almost indefinitely. While one cannot make any unequivocal statement regarding industrial accidents and the beneficial effect of labor insurance, one cannot help feeling that the extent to which existing labor insurance has helped to ameliorate the effect of accidents has been rather limited, and that working in Chinese factories appears to be highly hazardous.

V

TRAINING AND THE SUPPLY OF SKILLED LABOR

Other things being equal, obviously, industrial accidents could be reduced and productivity increased if the supply of skilled labor were greater. A greater supply of skilled workers, including planning and supervisory personnel, would not only have a salutary effect on the factory floor, but also on the flow of production and the elimination of high work peaks which have often occurred in the latter part of each month and year. However, the shortage of skilled labor is especially acute in Communist China.[60]

In the face of this situation, a far-reaching program of training has been launched by Communist China through the revamping of the entire educational system, the initiation of large-scale training classes for workers, and the expansion of apprenticeships. According to the lastest official statistics,[61] there were 3.6 million students in middle schools in the whole country in 1953 as compared with 3.1 million in the previous year, and only about 1.5 million in 1950. Of the 3.6 million some 748,000 persons were enrolled in special occupational schools. Again, there were 194,000 persons enrolled in institutions of higher learning in 1952. The number increased to about 216,000 in 1953. Of the 216,000 only 4,200 students were in graduate schools, while the rest consisted of undergraduates or students in special programs. Excluding the graduate students, engineering students constituted 37.7 per cent; medical students, 13.7 per cent; natural science students, 5.8 per cent; education students, 18.8 per cent; agriculture students, 6 per cent; students in the humanities, 6.5 per cent; and others, 11.5 per cent. Compared with 1952, there was a slight increase in the number of engineering and education students. Finally, 2.3 million workers and 27 million farmers were enrolled in adult education and training courses. These represented a 16 per cent and 207 per cent increase over the corresponding levels in 1951 and 1950 respectively in the case of workers. In the case of farmers the 1952 figure represented a 75 per cent increase over the corresponding 1951 level and a 677 per cent increase over the 1950 level.[62]

ALLOCATION OF LABOR

Although the quality of training cannot be gauged on the basis of the numerical growth of students and trainees alone, the seriousness with which the program of skilled labor shortage is being attacked needs to be closely scrutinized. Unfortunately, further discussion of this issue would lead us to an entirely different field, and we must be satisfied with the simple observation that the problem cannot be satisfactorily solved in a short time.

In the meantime, allocation of labor, especially skilled workers, has been instituted to prevent raiding and distribution contrary to official plans. Official cognizance of this problem was given, for instance, in the promulgation of labor registration and allocation regulations in Kwangtung in January, 1954.[63] The local labor department has been put in charge of clearing recruitments, together with the placement of unemployed workers with precisely the above-mentioned purpose in mind. Similar reports from other areas, though by no means complete, have indicated that this is a general trend.

NOTES

1. Forced labor is excluded from consideration in this chapter.

2. *Constitution of the Trade Union in the People's Republic of China,* pp. 4-5, 8-9, and 24, Peking, 1953. See also Hsü Chih-chen's report on the revision of the constitution of the trade union, pp. 34 and 38, *ibid.*

3. *Liberation Daily,* Shanghai, September 13, 1949.

4. Report on the experience and development of China's labor movement by Li Li-san in *Labor Movement in Shanghai after the Liberation,* p. 235, Shanghai, 1950.

5. *Chinese Worker,* No. 5, p. 68, Peking, June, 1950.

6. *Economic Weekly,* No. 40, p. 802, Shanghai, 1952.

7. NCNA, May 2, 1954.

8. *China Weekly,* Hongkong, January 4, 1954.

9. See *Liberation Daily,* Shanghai, September 18, 1949, and *Yangtze Daily,* Hankow, September 13, 1949.

10. *Documents Concerning Trade Union Organization,* pp. 89-90, Shanghai, 1952.

11. *Ibid.,* pp. 4-7.

12. Speech by Chou Ping-ku'en, chief of the Organization Department of the Shanghai Federation of Trade Unions, *Labor Daily,* Shanghai, September 26, 1951.

13. See *Experience in Basic Level Union Work,* p. 110, Shanghai, 1951.

14. *Workers' Daily,* Peking, February 9, 1954.

15. Report by Lai Jo-yü at the national conference on basic level union work on December 2, 1952, *Trade Union Work Experience at the Wu-san Factory,* p. 21, Peking, 1953.

16. *Far Eastern Economic Review,* Hongkong, April 16, 1953.

17. NCNA, November 22, 1953.

18. *Women Workers in the Trade Union,* p. 3, Shanghai, 1951.

19. *Ibid.,* pp. 16-18.

20. *Trade Union Work Experience at the Wu-san Factory,* p. 52, Peking, 1953.

21. The employment of labor disputes to harass foreign businessmen during this period was a common practice.

22. *Labor Movement in Shanghai after the Liberation,* p. 149, Shanghai, 1950.

23. *Ibid.,* p. 186.

24. *Liberation Daily,* Shanghai, September 18, 1949.

25. *Labor Movement in Shanghai after the Liberation,* pp. 190-191, Peking, 1950.

26. *Collective Contracts,* pp. 28-36, Peking, 1950, and various issues of the *Chinese Worker.*

27. See *Far Eastern Economic Review,* Hongkong, April 16, 1953.

28. *Ibid.*

29. April 16, 1954. See also *Documents Concerning Rationalization Proposals,* pp. 5-6, Shanghai, 1951, and *Documents Concerning Trade Union Organization,* pp. 21-22, Shanghai, 1952.

30. *Documents Concerning Rationalization Proposals,* pp. 8-12, Shanghai, 1951.

31. NCNA, February 18, 1954.

32. NCNA, Dairen, December 24, 1953.

33. Central-South Wage Reform Committee (ed.), *Lectures on Wages,* pp. 28-29, Shanghai, 1952.

34. The lowest grade of supervisory personnel in Class B. industries had a monthly base pay of Kwantung *yuan* 6,500 (Grade 5) while the highest base pay for workers was Kwantung *yuan* 7,040 (Grade 7).

35. Introduction of the new regulations in the Central-South followed the adoption by the State Administrative Council in March, 1951, of the resolution on the composition of wages in the drafting of plans for individual enterprises and the implementation of the business accountability system. *New China Monthly,* No. 17, pp. 1017-1018, Peking, March, 1951. For details on the Central-South wage system, see *Lectures on Wages* cited above.

36. This last point is somewhat questionable, because, in some cases, this effect may be more than offset by the different pay scales in use both in different industrial groups and in different enterprises in the same industrial group.

37. *People's Railways,* Peking, June, 1950.

38. See *Labor Movement in Shanghai after the Liberation,* pp. 157-158, Shanghai, 1950, and various issues of the *Daily News,* Shanghai, the *Yangtze Daily,* Hankow, and the *New China Daily News,* Chungking.

39. Li T'ien-min, *op. cit.,* p. 44.

40. Quoted in the *Yangtze Daily,* Hankow.

41. This sum was enough to buy 110-151 kgs. of rice at the time. In terms of gross receipts it compared slightly more favorably than the wages of the worst paid workers in the thirties, especially some of the women workers. See *Chinese Economic Yearbook,* 1933-1934.

42. Workers in certain Manchurian plants were said to be subject to numerous kinds of exactions at one time which, in the case of the Pen-ch'i power plant, numbered 17. See Li T'ien-min, *op. cit.,* p. 45.

43. *New China Monthly,* No. 49, p. 116, Peking, October, 1953, and *Enlightenment Daily,* Peking, September 29 and October 1, 1954.

44. Like the "commodity-equivalent" unit for savings deposits, the wage unit includes only a few basic commodities. It does not include many industrial products which the workers may buy or such items as light and rent which constitute a part of the worker's budget.

45. *People's Daily,* Peking, December 28, 1952.

46. *Lectures on Wages,* p. 48, Shanghai, 1952.

47. *Enlightenment Daily,* Peking, September 29, 1954.

48. *Bureau of Statistics Bulletin,* Peking, December, 1954.

49. *Labor Movement in Shanghai after the Liberation,* pp. 237-238, Shanghai, 1950.

50. For text see, e.g., *New China Monthly,* No. 17, pp. 1010-1013, Peking, March, 1951.

51. *Labor Insurance Regulations of the People's Republic of China,* Peking, 1953.

52. *National Bureau of Statistics Bulletin,* Peking, December, 1954.

53. Peking, September 1, 1953.

54. *Ibid.*

55. *People's Daily,* Peking, September 13, 1954.

56. *Liberation Daily,* Shanghai, September 9, 1951.

57. *Yangtze Daily,* Hankow, November 24, 1952.

58. *New China Daily,* Chungking, April 21, 1953.

59. *New China Monthly,* No. 42, p. 143, Peking, April, 1953.

60. In 1950, for instance, the ratio of "technical" personnel to ordinary workers in Manchurian industry was said to be 1 to 600. *China's Industry,* Vol. I, No. 10, p. 14, Shanghai, February, 1950. This situation has no doubt improved considerably since, but the general shortage of technical and skilled workers remains undiminished.

61. *National Bureau of Statistics Bulletin,* Peking, October, 1954.

62. In 1946-1947 there were 1.8 million middle school students, as well as 129,336 university students. See *Chinese Yearbook,* Vol. II, pp. 1585, 1626, and 1657, Nanking, 1948.

63. *Southern Daily,* Canton, February 22, 1954.

CHAPTER THIRTEEN

Foreign Economic Relations

I

INTRODUCTION[1]

The predominance of political considerations in Communist China's economic development and government policy, such as we have noted in the course of "land reform," the perversion of the trade union movement, and the forced pace of industrialization, to mention just a few examples, is even more pronounced in the field of foreign economic relations. Problems of the balance of international payments, both in the wake of the hyper-inflation and as a result of the long-term program of industrialization, are intertwined with such developments as the United Nations' embargo against Communist China and the latter's reaction to it. Superimposed on these issues are the logical inclination and, possibly, political necessity for Communist China, as a member of the Soviet Bloc, to reorient its trade towards other members of the Bloc and to recast its traditional pattern of economic ties. In this area, also, the working of the market's economic forces and the profit motive have continued to assert themselves in the face of stringent controls. The British free port of Hongkong, which is used as a principal transit point for western trade with Communist China, also provides a convenient point at which the strictly controlled *jen-min pi* may be bought and sold. In view of Communist China's industrial backwardness and the government's overwhelming desire to industrialize rapidly, dependence on imports may be regarded as one chink in the armor, which gives us an additional vantage point from which foreign economic relations may be viewed.

FOREIGN TRADE POLICY IN 1949–1950

As mentioned in Chapter II, China's postwar balance of international payments was in a precarious position. The deficit on current account stood at US$1.07 billion in 1946, $0.58 billion in 1947, and $0.20 billion in 1948. These figures may be compared with deficits of $0.96 billion on merchandise trade account in 1946, $0.55 billion in 1947, and $0.21 billion in 1948. Although at least a part of the deficits of this period might not have arisen if the means of payment had not been known to be available in advance, the new Communist regime was nevertheless seriously handicapped by the cessation of American economic aid, compounded by the fact that a considerable part of the country's official gold and dollar resources was still controlled by the Nationalist Government even after the latter's evacuation of the mainland.

The Communist authorities approached the problem of foreign trade in 1949 and early 1950 with two broad principles in mind, the reduction and eventual elimination of the persistent trade deficit and the inauguration of a system of protection and trade regulation geared to the country's economic stabilization and development.[2] These general principles were clearly discernible in all the foreign trade regulations promulgated by the regional authorities[3] throughout 1949, as well as the statement of the State Administrative Council on tariff policy on January 27, 1950. Local variations apart, the practice at the time was to divide all merchandise trade into "permissible," "special," "limited," and "prohibited" imports and exports. Since all trade was subject to licensing, these commodity classifications only served to determine the degree of administrative control applicable according to the characteristics of the goods in question. In the case of imports, sufficiency of domestic supply and availability of foreign exchange were the criteria used, while in the case of exports, the criterion of adequate domestic supply was supplemented by special "strategic" considerations in connection with the export of such non-ferrous metals as tungsten, antimony, and tin. At the same time, exporters were required to surrender their foreign exchange proceeds in return for exchange deposit certificates issued by certain designated banks. Importers, on the other hand, had to purchase these certificates through the designated banks for foreign exchange settlement with foreign exporters. As it is the case in similar exchange restrictions practiced in other countries, the entire system of exchange control was designed to conserve foreign exchange and to channel all foreign transactions through the control authority, which, in this case, was the Bank of China, acting as the foreign exchange bank of the People's Bank. Aided by tax concessions, government subsidy, preferential freight rates, a realistic exchange rate, and, above all, a severely deflationary policy, exports increased more than imports, and the Communist authorities were able to trumpet to the world the closing of the trade gap and the realization of an "unprecedented" export surplus in 1950.

THE NEW "WARTIME" POLICY

However, this policy was soon to be completely reversed. Already in July, 1950, shortly after the outbreak of the Korean War, possible changes in policy were discussed during a national foreign trade conference. By November of the same year, at about the time Communist China actively intervened in the Korean fighting, the barter or compensation system which had been discontinued earlier in the year was reinstated at several ports in order to tighten the selective control of imports, as well as to give the authorities more leeway in building up exchange reserves from exports. After a period of experimentation which lasted two months and which paralleled, if not actually antedated, the United States' freezing and shipping control orders, the Ministry of Trade summoned the chiefs of the foreign trade control bureaus of eight major ports, together with representatives of the Maritime Customs, the Bank of China, and the government import and export companies in a two-week conference to revamp the foreign trade policy of the country.[4] The result was summarized in the Barter Trade Control Regulations of March 14, 1951.[5]

The new trade policy, which Communist China has pursued with occasionally slight modifications since the end of 1950 when the threat of stoppage of foreign supplies became serious for the first time, consists of the following points:[6]

1. Regulated trade with the non-Communist countries will be continued at the highest level the loopholes in the latter's embargo system will permit, making certain, however, (a) that, if at all possible, virtually all imports will precede exports, (b) that no favorable trade balance will be built up unintentionally, (c) that strategic exports, if allowed to be sold to the "capitalistic" countries at all, will be exported only in exchange for the most essential imports, and (d) that the monopolistic position of the country as a buyer or seller, as well as any temporary market advantage it may enjoy, will be exploited to the full in order to assure the country of the best terms of trade possible.

2. The above policy is to be supplemented by a sustained propaganda effort against the "pernicious" effect on the expansion of world trade of the United Nations' embargo and by dangling the supposedly unlimited prospect of expanded trade with Communist China in front of the eyes of would-be traders in some of the Western countries.
3. Trade with the Soviet Bloc countries and "neutrals" is to be expanded to provide replacement for the lost markets and sources of supply.

The spirit of the new policy was unmistakably expressed by the Deputy Director of the Department of Trade for East China when he stated on January 12, 1951, "For over a year we have been engaged in the energetic promotion of the export of domestic products and the re-export of imports after processing. Some of the exports have been made possible only as a result of domestic austerity and the reduction of consumption. All this has been done so that we may earn enough foreign exchange to import. If importing on a large scale is no longer possible, there is no apparent reason why we should concern ourselves with the cultivation of foreign markets." The new policy was, first, to import as much as possible while exporting only enough to pay for the assured imports, and, secondly, to regulate the composition of trade in a fashion favorable to Communist China. Should the practical result of this outlook be a temporary drop of the official exchange reserve of the country, that was not to be averted or even regretted as the paramount consideration was to obtain foreign supplies to beat the "blockade" which for a time threatened to broaden itself.[7] At any rate, should the American freezing order be emulated elsewhere, the possession of large blocked funds in foreign countries would be of a little consolation and a poor reward to a country which had been assiduously building up its official reserve.

Under the new barter regulations, imports and exports are divided into three schedules, A, B, and C, according to their general "strategic" importance, the degree in which they are needed by Communist China in its economic and defense program in the light of its domestic supply, and the bargaining position the country is believed to enjoy under some form of state trading on such foreign markets as are still accessible. This division is superimposed on the earlier classification so that each schedule of imports and exports contains "permissible," "special," and "state-monopolized" items.[8] The original classification deals with the economic significance of the individual commodities and aims at giving them the appropriate degree of control. The new division, as represented by the three schedules, A, B, and C, is to serve the purpose of matching or pairing certain types of exports with certain types of imports. Thus an item belonging to Export Schedule A may be exported only against an item on Import Schedule A, a "B" export may exchanged for either an "A" or a "B" import, and a "C" export may be exchanged for an "A," "B," or "C" import. The reasoning is simply that in trading with the "capitalistic" countries, Communist China would not stand to gain if, say, its wolfram ore were exported without obtaining in return a sorely needed item such as electric motors or burlap bags, whereas it would not matter too much what imports were received against the export of Chinese beche de mer or medicinal herbs.[8a]

In addition to the above provisions, four different procedures of trading with the "capitalistic" countries have been set up. These are:

1. *Direct barter,* under which the commodities involved, together with their quantities and values, are determined at the time of license application, with importation preceding exportation, though both may be conducted by installment under a consolidated license. This was the common practice in Shanghai during the trial period from late 1950 to early 1951.

2. *Clearing,* under which, following importation, the importer undertakes to export within a stipulated period of time either by himself or by another person.

3. *Compensation,* or the export-import link system, under which the exporter, *following* exportation, undertakes to import within a stipulated period of time. This was the common practice in both North and South China prior to the proclamation of the standard regulations. Since this procedure does not offer the same degree of assurance as the other two that importation would not be delayed or hindered after the exports have left the country, the official attitude is to be especially watchful in licensing such applications. In practice, the authorities have generally attempted to limit the use of this method to trading with adjacent territories such as Hongkong whence imports could be rushed at a moment's notice. Furthermore, this form of trading is restricted to exports on Schedule C.

4. Trade financed by related letters of credit opened simultaneously in both directions, under which importers and exporters determine simultaneously the commodities traded and their quantities and values, and arrange with their foreign agents or correspondents for simultaneous financing. This is really a variation of the clearing system under which the foreign importer pays the foreign exporter, with commercial banks filling the gap and serving to bring the two together.

It is a concession to the traditional practice of financing foreign trade by commercial letters of credit, but as there is no guarantee that imports thus financed will actually enter the country before the corresponding act of exportation, although the regulations stipulate that they must be shipped from the foreign ports not later than the corresponding exports, it is again frowned upon.

To facilitate the conduct of the above procedures "barter exchanges" have been set up at the major ports to enable an importer to transfer the evidence of importation to an exporter. The transfer is usually accompanied by payment from one party to the other, the direction of payment being governed by the relative profitability of the export and import trades at the time and the particular Schedules involved. As one would expect under the policy of import promotion, it was the importer who had to pay the exporter most of the time.[9]

Moreover, a government agency known as the China National Import-Export Corporation has been set up through the consolidation of several scattered government monopolies formerly in existence. The corporation conducts trade according to the new procedure for the account of the government and is responsible for assisting private exporters and importers, whose numbers have been fast diminishing, to engage in organized bargaining with their foreign counterparts. This development has brought about a further expansion of the share of state trading in foreign trade, rising from 70 per cent of imports and 53.5 per cent of exports in 1950 to 92 per cent of total imports and exports in 1953.[10]

Although the above procedures do not rule out the possibility of importing by the usual method of applying for foreign exchange from the official control and the repatriation of assets from abroad in the form of imports, they have come to dominate Communist China's foreign trade with the non-Communist countries. Moreover, due to the excessive spending of foreign exchange in the first half of 1951, the granting of exchange outside the barter system was often restricted or partially suspended as in the last quarter of 1951 and the first quarter of 1952.

CHANGES IN THE VOLUME AND DIRECTION OF TRADE

The effect of the adaptation and reorientation of external trade policy as described above, modified by balance of payments considerations, has, of course, been reflected in the volume of Communist China's foreign trade, the relation between imports and exports, the distribution of trade by countries, and the composition of trade.

Full publication of foreign trade statistics by Communist China was discontinued in 1951. However, on the basis of incomplete official statistics and other sources, it is nevertheless possible to arrive at some reasonable estimates as given below:

Communist China's Foreign Trade
1949–1954[1]
(In US$ million)

	Total Trade	*Import*	*Export*	*Balance*
1949	343.50	178.72	164.78	— 13.94
1950	902.90	436.40	466.50	+ 30.10
1951	1,705.70	1,033.30	672.40	— 360.90
1952	1,195.01	717.01	478.00	— 239.01
1953	1,625.21	989.47	635.74	— 353.73
1954	1,852.74 (preliminary)	—	—	—

Sources: The above estimates are based on Wu Sho, *op. cit., Economic Bulletin,* No. 231, pp. 2-3, Hongkong, July, 1951; Yang P'o, *op. cit., Selected Economic Essays,* pp. 285-288, Peking, 1951; *Economic Bulletin,* No. 242, p. 30, Hongkong, October, 1951, and No. 25, p. 3, June, 1952; *People's China* (in English), Vol. IV, No. 8, p. 35, Peking, October, 1951; *Economic Weekly,* No. 39, Shanghai, 1952; *Daily News,* Shanghai, October 1, 1952; *New China Monthly,* Vol. III, No. 6, p. 1345, Peking, April, 1951; NCNA, April 27, 1954; National Bureau of Statistics *Bulletin,* Peking, October, 1954; and *Hongkong Economic Yearbook,* Hongkong, 1955.

1. These figures differ from those estimated on the basis of trade returns published by some of the non-Communist countries. Cf. W. W. Rostow, *op. cit.,* p. 251.

It may be readily seen from the above figures that an overall favorable trade balance was obtained by Communist China in 1950 following the Communists' stringent deflationary policy at home and the policy of export promotion and import restriction in the foreign field. The small favorable balance of 1950 then became a large unfavorable balance in 1951 as a result of the deliberate policy to encourage imports in anticipation of a further tightening of economic sanctions and a possible naval blockade by the allied powers fighting in Korea. Apparently an attempt was made to correct the severe drain on the government's foreign exchange resources during 1952. This effort, coupled with the "five-anti" movement of the year which played havoc with private business, including the foreign traders, brought about a substantial drop of both imports and exports, resulting in a smaller net deficit for the year. Finally, in 1953, the inception of the first Five Year Plan led to a large rise of imports. Although exports also increased, their rise fell short of the expansion of imports, and the trade deficit again began to mount.

In this connection, an interesting question is how the total trade of this period was distributed among different country groups, and what the trade balance was with respect to these different groups. If we can supply even partial answers to these questions, we shall be in a better position to tell the manner in which the successive trade deficits have been met, as well as the effects of the United Nations' embargo.

According to official Communist reports, the share of the Soviet Union and other members of the Soviet Bloc in Communist China's total foreign trade, i.e., the sum of imports and exports, rose from 26 per cent in 1950 to 61 per cent in 1951, 70 per cent in 1952, and 75 per cent in 1953.[11] However, these figures cannot be taken at their face value, because even if they accurately measure the volume of imports and exports classified by country of shipment, they do not indicate the actual values by country of origin. Discrepancies arise not only because, for instance, goods of West German or British origin may be re-exported to Communist China by one of the eastern European countries in accordance with the latter's trade agreements with China, but also because such trade may be conducted between Communist China and one of the western European countries at the outset of negotiations by using an eastern European port as a staging point in transit.[12] Conversely, Chinese exports to the "capitalistic" countries may be made via the Soviet Bloc either as a part of the latter's own foreign trade program or with the latter acting on behalf of Communist China. In other words, trade with the non-Communist countries may be much larger than the totals shown above.[13]

That re-exports and transit trade are possible, the United Nations' embargo notwithstanding, has been amply borne out by available Chinese reports on the subject. One good example is given in an article extolling the success of the new trade policy. "We are able," according to the author, "to obtain contrabands from the imperialist countries by virtue of our trade relations with the Soviet Union and the People's Democracies. For instance, tinned plates are sold by the United Kingdom to the Soviet Union in exchange for grain and may be imported by China via this channel. Similarly, many parts of the Hsiao-feng-man hydro-electric power plant have been obtained from West Germany through the intermediary of East Germany."[14]

Bearing the above point in mind, we may now examine a little further Communist China's balance of trade with the two principal country groups. On the basis of available Communist sources, the following estimates for 1950–1952 may be used:

Distribution of Communist China's Foreign Trade by Countries, 1950–1952 (In US$ million)

	U.S.S.R. and the "People's Democracies"			*Non-Communist Countries*		
	Import	*Export*	*Balance*	*Import*	*Export*	*Balance*
1950	92.56	141.05	+ 48.49	343.84	325.45	− 18.39
1951	759.20	520.00	− 239.20	274.10	152.40	− 121.70
1952	479.19	345.92	− 133.27	237.82	132.08	− 105.74

Source: Same as in the previous table.

Since the possibility that the non-Communist countries might serve as a middleman for the re-export of goods produced in the Soviet Bloc to Communist China, and vice versa, can be disregarded,[15] it may be assumed that the above figures under-estimate the importance of trade with the non-Communist countries, and one might even hazard the guess that Communist China's trade deficit with the non-Communist countries was in fact larger during 1951 and 1952. Although detailed information on the division between imports and exports by countries is still wanting, there is reason to believe that the same situation prevailed in 1953 and 1954 as in the two preceding years.[16] However, the deficit balance with the non-Communist countries might conceivably be less in 1953 than in 1952, and the corresponding deficit with the Soviet Bloc might be somewhat larger. This is because of the start of the Five Year Plan in 1953 and the undoubtedly higher imports from the Soviet Union and its European satellites.

Trade between Communist China and members of the Soviet Bloc is conducted on a barter basis. Consequently, any trade deficit with the Soviet Bloc that is not financed under a loan would have to be paid for by cash. This general statement, however, has to be modified on two counts. In the first place, imports have undoubtedly been received from the Soviet Union under the several agreements to establish Sino-Soviet joint enterprises. These were outside the loan agreements between the Soviet Union and China. If included in the merchandise trade statistics, these imports would certainly account for a part of the deficit. In the second place, some of the trade agreements with Soviet Bloc countries are known to be "barter and payment agreements" as distinct from simple barter agreements. It is conceivable that over short periods Communist China could import on credit either under terms agreed to or by simply delaying export shipments.

The total volume of Soviet aid to Communist China has never been fully disclosed. Under a long-term credit granted by the Soviet Union, Communist China was to receive US$300 million worth of aid over a period of five years, i.e., at an annual rate of $60 million. A *New York Times* report[17] in 1953 mentioned a new credit arrangement totalling US$1 billion, including the $300 million granted in 1950, for a ten-year period. Assuming that the first loan was used up to the tune of $180 million in 1950–1952, available credit would average $117 million a year for seven years beginning with 1953. Finally, in October, 1954, a joint Sino-Soviet communique announced the conclusion of a new long-term loan of $130 million, together with the increase in capital goods shipment by another $100 million, the latter presumably to be paid for by current Chinese exports.[18]

Disregarding imports made under the joint enterprise agreements, possible short-term credits from the European satellites, and the very remote possibility of unpublicized economic aid[19] by the Soviet Union, probably not more than $117 million of imports could be accounted for during 1953 by long-term credit. Although the amount might be somewhat larger in 1954 this would leave a net overall deficit of $236.73 million in 1953, and the actual amount might be somewhat smaller for the various reasons indicated above. The situation was even worse in 1952 and 1951 when the regular line of credit was limited to an average of $60 million a year. That something like a serious drop in the official reserve actually took place during 1951 seems to be beyond doubt. Not only did imports begin to taper off in the third quarter of 1951, but the granting of foreign exchange for imports without corresponding exports was virtually suspended during the last quarter of the year and the first quarter of 1952. The official reserve was somewhat replenished during the first half of 1952 as a result of the "five-anti" drive against the bankers, industrialists, and other businessmen. The decline of imports and the smaller drop of exports served to narrow the trade gap, but the retrenchment was probably insufficient. Following a long period of time during which the official exchange rate was pegged at the same level, the *jen-min pi* was openly devalued. Even though the exchange rate had lost much of its significance in view of the increasing share of state trading, the measure was clearly designed to stimulate inward remittances by overseas Chinese and possibly also exports by the remaining private traders. However, since the trade deficit continued through 1953 and may be expected to persist, the problem is a serious one. It would seem that Communist China erred in 1951 in believing that the United Nations' embargo would be expanded and tightened at a more rapid pace than it actually did and that, for a time, the Communists, virtually panicked, went too far in pursuing their "counter-blockade" policy. Since then the problem confronting the country in the face of the embargo is not whether imports could be obtained, but how they could be paid for, although further analysis will show that the trade deficit would have been smaller if the embargo, full of loopholes as it is, had been completely lifted.

SOME OF THE INVISIBLE ITEMS ON CURRENT ACCOUNT

Of course, merchandise trade, however important, is not the only item on the current account of Communist China's balance of international payments. Some of the other factors must be considered in arriving at the balance on the current account as a whole.

First, while imports are probably reported on a c.i.f. basis in accordance with traditional practice, the export values are usually not recorded net of transport charges. In the same category, we should include banking and insurance charges requiring payments in foreign exchange. The greater the volume of trade, the heavier these charges tend to be.

Second, expenses by Communist Chinese government agencies abroad constitute another debit item on current account. These, however, are perhaps more than offset by similar expenditure by foreign missions in Communist China.

Third, it is not clear how the large number of Soviet technicians and other advisers in Communist China are compensated. If paid in foreign exchange, the amount involved would be considerable.

Fourth, export of labor service by Communist China is probably sizable and may constitute an important offsetting item vis-à-vis the trade deficit.

Finally, interest payments on existing loan and credit arrangements with the Soviet Bloc have not been important so far and may be disregarded for the present.

All in all, one may be justified in assuming that of the many "invisible" factors export of forced labor may offer a net credit balance applicable to the trade deficit. At any rate, it is one of the most promising methods with which Communist China can increase its current earnings of foreign exchange.

REMITTANCES BY OVERSEAS CHINESE

However, there is little doubt that the total supply of goods and services in Communist China's balance of international payments has consistently yielded a net debit balance.[20] Traditionally, this debit balance is met in part by inward remittances from Chinese emigrants in foreign countries who send money home both to help defray the living expenses of their families in the home country and to build up personal estates, mostly in land holdings. Prior to World War II, the annual total on this account was usually estimated at US$100 million. After World War II, as a result of war devastation in Malaya, the Philippines, and Indonesia, remittances were greatly reduced. The unrealistic official exchange rate set by the Nationalists during the inflationary period further reduced the amount that went to the exchange control. The problem confronting the Communist authorities is therefore a twofold one—an enlargement of the inward flow and extension of government control over the channels of remittance.

Several developments have occurred in favor of the Chinese Communists. First, economic recovery in certain areas has made it possible for the overseas Chinese to make larger remittances home. Second, suppression of galloping inflation and more rigorous control over the foreign exchange market, including the prohibition of the possession and circulation of foreign currencies and the virtual elimination of private banking, have helped to channel inward remittances through the government banks. At the same time, Communist policy to permit recipients of remittances to keep their money in special foreign currency deposits without having to convert the entire amount into *jen-min pi* at one time was also an effective factor during the period when the official exchange rate was allowed to fluctuate frequently.

However, these developments are apparently more than offset by unfavorable factors of a different nature. Financial control imposed by the United States in December, 1950, prohibiting direct remittances to Communist China while regulating remittances to Hongkong, has helped to cut off perhaps up to 40 per cent of the normal flow of inward remittances. Even more important is the treatment accorded by the Communist Chinese to "overseas Chinese landlords" during the land "reform" and drives to suppress "counter-revolutionaries." This has tended to discourage inward remittances by making it impossible for the overseas Chinese to accumulate home estates as heretofore. In the face of this situation Communist China has even resorted to blackmailing and other techniques forcing Chinese emigrants to send money home.

Official Communist sources have been extraordinarily reticent on the volume of overseas remittances received in recent years. Although a Japanese estimate has put the total in the first half of 1954 at as high as US$170 million, it is more than doubtful that this could be the case.[21] A Hongkong report, on the other hand, stated that remittances made through Hongkong in 1953 were no more than 5 per cent of the corresponding level in 1952.[22] Without attempting to speculate unnecessarily, it would appear more than likely that the present flow of remittances has fallen below the prewar level, even allowing for the greater ability of overseas Chinese to remit money home in depreciated currencies. The deficit on Communist China's trade balance can hardly be met from this source except in a small part.

COMMODITY COMPOSITION OF IMPORTS AND EXPORTS

One thing which the foreign trade estimates given above do not show is the radical change in the nature of Communist China's external trade as compared with previous periods, especially with regard to imports. The policy of austerity and autarchy had already reduced the import of "luxuries" or "non-essentials" and of consumers' goods in general soon after the Communists' occupation of China's major ports during 1949, but the trend became even more unmistakable in 1950 when the import of consumers' goods fell to about 8.6 per cent of total imports. The corresponding figure in 1947, when total commercial imports were $451 million or only slightly higher than our 1950 estimate, was 19.37 per cent.

Composition of Imports in 1950
(In per cent of total imports)

	Capital Goods		*Raw Materials and Fuel*		*Consumers' Goods*	
1950	Iron and steel products	11.34	Cotton	18.04	Sugar	1.99
	Machinery	8.25	Rubber	11.52	Rice	1.03
	Ships, vehicles, tires and tubes	4.39	Petroleum Products	8.48	Drugs	4.03
			Copper	1.76	Other	1.55
	Cables and wires	1.47	Ammonium Sulphate	1.96		
	Other	5.27	Other	18.92		
	Total	30.72		60.68		8.60
1947	Total	18.55		62.08		19.37

Sources: The percentage figures for 1950 are given by the Maritime Customs of Communist China. The 1947 figures are from the *Central Bank Monthly,* Vol. III, No. 4, p. 112, Shanghai, April, 1948. See also *New China Monthly,* Vol. III, No. 6, p. 1345, Peking, April, 1951.

A more detailed comparison between the data of these two years would show that the decline in the importance of consumers' goods in Communist China's imports is matched by a corresponding increase in the relative share of capital goods.[23] Furthermore, it is said that in 1951, 78 per cent of all imports were composed of industrial machinery, transportation and communications equipment, and a few major raw materials, and that 97 per cent of the goods imported under the Sino-Soviet trade agreements belonged to similar categories.[24]

The same picture may also be gleaned from changes in the composition of imports at the port of Shanghai. Between 1949 and 1951 imports in Shanghai consisted chiefly of machinery, metals, chemical raw materials, scientific instruments, drugs, and textile fibers, with raw cotton heading the list. Import of manufactured consumers' goods was at a minimum. In addition, import of raw materials for processing and re-export or for making luxuries for domestic consumption as was formerly characteristic of the cotton textile, flour milling, tobacco, and paper manufacturing industries was also discouraged although for a short period after the Communist occupation cotton was imported and yarn exported.[25]

The emphasis on capital goods is a natural outcome of the policy to bring about forced industrialization. This policy has apparently not been hampered by the United Nations' embargo as the volume of capital goods import has actually increased. The smaller volume of imports from the non-Communist world, from which non-essential consumers' goods have been eliminated, are now largely, though not exclusively, concentrated in a few raw materials and "essential" consumers' goods such as rubber, drugs, and fertilizer.

Increase in the production of food grains, better distribution, and, since 1953, an increasingly stringent rationing system have eliminated the demand for food imports. Similarly, the demand for imported raw cotton has been reduced, and it looked in 1953 as if domestic production would be completely adequate although the 1953 crop was somewhat disappointing and some import was probably required in 1954. However, in the case of such basic consumers' goods as food grains and raw cotton, any shortage that might develop in the immediate future with reference to an extremely low level of consumption could probably be met by rationing instead of expanding imports to any appreciable extent.

Contrary to the radical change in the composition of imports, Communist China has continued to export the same broad groups of commodities as before although there has been a relative increase in the export of food and other agricultural products and a decrease in that of coal and iron ore.[26] During 1950 the composition of Communist China's merchandise exports, which may be compared with that of 1936, was as shown in table appearing on page 471.

According to a 1954 report, well over 3 million tons of soyabeans were exported during the year, accounting for a sizable portion of total exports. In the same year, frozen pork export constituted 2.15 per cent of the year's output while 7 per cent of the year's egg production and 18.7 per cent of the output of cured tobacco were exported.[27] However, as the Communist authorities have admitted themselves, the volume of such traditional exports as raw silk and

Composition of Communist China's Exports in 1950
Compared with Exports in 1936

Per cent of Total Exports

	1950		1936	
Agricultural Products				
Soyabeans	14.4		16.7	
Peanuts	4.7		1.7	
Edible vegetable oils	7.4	26.5	3.7	22.1
Wood oil		7.0		6.4
Eggs and egg products	4.7		3.8	
Hogs	2.2	6.9	0.4	4.2
Bristles		6.7		2.5
Wool	4.1		1.4	
Raw silk	1.9	6.0	2.7	4.1
Tea		3.3		2.6
		56.4		41.9
Non-ferrous metals		3.0		3.2
Coal		1.2		3.2
Other		39.4		51.7
Total		100.0		100.0

Sources: New China Monthly, Vol. III, No. 6, p. 1345, Peking, April, 1951. See also *Economic Weekly,* No. 25, p. 4, Hongkong, 1952, and *Trade of China,* 1936.

silk products, tea, peanuts, egg products, and coal has continued to lag behind, and, in some cases, quite seriously.[28]

Reasons for the failure for certain exports to rise are not far to seek. Higher domestic demand due to increasing economic activity and population growth relative to production have resulted in a smaller exportable surplus, as in the case of coal. The traditional market for such products as raw silk and bristles has been narrowed considerably through the widespread use of synthetic products. Failure to meet the necessary standards may also have affected the export of certain commodities adversely.[29] Finally, foreign demand for Chinese exports, consisting mostly of agricultural products also obtainable elsewhere, is probably quite easily saturated. For the Chinese Communists this means that even greater reliance must be placed on just a few exports like soyabeans and food grains in spite of the clamor of domestic consumers. Ironically, failures in Soviet agricultural production may be rather helpful from the point of view of Communist China, although higher demand for certain agricultural products exported by Communist China does not necessarily mean greater demand for some of the other agricultural exports. Nor does it necessarily prevent the Soviet Union from exacting terms of trade deterimental to Communist China. Lack of export capacity on the part of Communist China is a far more serious and real obstacle to the expansion of its foreign trade than the United Nations' embargo has been.[30] This is true especially in relation to the non-Communist countries where there is no market for Communist China's largest potential export, namely, conscript labor.

II

BILATERAL TRADE AGREEMENTS

While the barter trade regulations adopted in March, 1951, strive to regulate direct trade with the Western countries and most of the other non-Communist countries, unrelenting effort has also been exerted by Communist China to conclude trade agreements with foreign governments. So far governmental trade agreements have been concluded only with the Soviet Union, some of its satellites, and a few "neutrals" in South and Southeast Asia. At the same time, semi-official agreements with private interests in Japan and other non-Communist countries, mostly in western Europe, have also been concluded and even more loudly trumpeted ever since the International Economic Conference held in April, 1952, at Moscow. Although information on the individual agreements remains scanty, a careful search of available sources has yielded sufficient data to show an unmistakable trend of the increasing use of bilateral trade agreements in a manifest desire to reorient the country's trade towards the Soviet Bloc. Some of these data may be presented in tabular form as follows:

Government bilateral trade and credit agreements:

Country	Year in which Agreement Became Operative	Date Concluded	Length of Agreement	Communist China's Imports	Communist China's Exports	Value	Nature of Agreement and Other Data
A. Soviet Bloc							
1. U.S.S.R.	1949	July, 1949	1 Year	Industrial equipment; motor vehicles; kerosene; medical supplies and equipment	Corn, rice, soya-beans, and vegetable oils	1/	Concluded with the Northeast (Manchuria) Regional Government
		October 12, 1949	Single transaction	Newsprint and paper pulp, 8,000 metric tons	Raw silk, 800 bales; bristles, 614 metric tons	1/	Concluded with the East China Regional Government
		October, 1949	Single transaction	Diesel oil, gasoline and kerosene	Tea, 4,500 metric tons	1/	Concluded with the East China Regional Government
	1950	February 14, 1950	5 years	Mostly capital equipment	Loan to be repaid in raw materials, gold, and U.S. dollars	Average $60 million a year, total $300 million	Long-term credit, 1st installment of repayment in 1954, interest at 1 per cent per annum
		April 19, 1950	1 year	Industrial material and equipment, 63.7 per cent; railway and communications equipment, farm machinery, livestock for breeding, seeds, newsprint, medical supplies and equipment, 33.2 per cent; kerosene, etc., 3.1 per cent	Tungsten, antimony, coal, soyabeans, peanuts and peanut oil, wood oil, silk, tea, bristles, furs, hides, etc.	1/	First barter agreement with all Communist China
	1951	June 15, 1951	1 year	1/	1/	1/	Barter agreement of 1951
	1951	June 15, 1951	1 year	Industrial machinery, including equipment for power plants, metal and machine works, and mining machinery, rails, rolling stock, and other transportation equipment		1/	Protocol under long-term credit agreement of 1950

Country	Year in which Agreement Became Operative	Date Concluded	Length of Agreement	Communist China's Imports	Communist China's Exports	Value	Nature of Agreement and Other Data
	1952	April 12, 1952	1 year	1/	1/	1/	Barter agreement of 1952
		April 12, 1952	1 year	1/			Protocol under long-term credit agreement of 1950
		September 21, 1952	To end of 1952	From Finland	To U.S.S.R.	34 million rubles	Sino-Finnish-Soviet tripartite agreement on supply of commodities in 1952, and the Sino-Soviet and Sino-Finnish protocols attached
	1953	March 24, 1953	1 year	Equipment and supplies for the metallurgical, mining, machinery manufacturing, electric power, and other industries; transportation equipment and supplies; modern farm implements; livestock for breeding purposes; plant seeds; etc.	Non-ferrous metals; rice, vegetable oils; oil seeds; meat; tobacco; tea; fruit; animal hair; raw silk and silk products, skin and hides; hemp; etc.	1/	Protocol under long-term credit agreement of 1950 and barter agreement of 1953
	1954	May 29, 1954	1 year	Equipment for the metallurgical, mining, and power industries; tractors and agricultural machinery; construction machinery; rolled steel, non-ferrous metal and petroleum products, chemicals, etc.	Non-ferrous metals, soyabeans, rice, peanuts, vegetable oils, meat, tea, tobacco, fruit, wool, silk and silk fabrics, skin and hides, etc.	1/	Protocol under long-term credit agreement and barter agreement of 1954
2. Eastern Europe a. Czechoslovakia	1950	June 14, 1950	1 year	Heavy industrial machinery and cast iron products; locomotives, trucks, and cars; rubber products; cosmetics, shoes, etc.	Tungsten, mercury, lead, mica, and asbestos; silk, hemp, skin and hides, bristles, and tea	1/	Barter and payment agreement
	1951	June 21, 1951	1 year	Industrial equipment	Raw materials	4 times greater than the volume under agreement, June, 1950	Barter and payment agreement
	1952	1/	1 year	1/	1/	1/	1/

Country	Year in which Agreement Became Operative	Date Concluded	Length of Agreement	Communist China's Imports	Communist China's Exports	Value	Nature of Agreement and Other Data
Czechoslovakia (Continued)	1953	May 7, 1953	1 year	Machinery, rolled metal products, tele-communications equipment and supplies, and consumers' goods	Mineral products, soyabeans, other grains and agricultural products, animal products, and other consumers' goods	Volume increased by one-third over the 1952 level	Barter and payment agreement
	1954	August 18, 1954	1 year	Power plants, sugar refining equipment, metal-working machines, cranes, excavators, diesel engines, heavy trucks, chemicals, and paper products	Raw materials for the metallurgical, textile, leather, and chemical industries, egg products, tea, essence oils, canned food, fruit, etc.	1/	Barter and payment agreement
b. Poland	1950	March 1, 1950	1 year	Rails, steel plates and metal products; industrial equipment; chemicals; and textiles	Soyabeans, peanuts, tobacco, fats, etc.	1/	Barter and payment agreement
	1951	January 29, 1951	1 year	Iron and steel, industrial and mining equipment, machine tools, farm machinery and implements	Tungsten, soyabeans, vegetable oils, tea, casing, and silk	1/	Barter and payment agreement
	1952	July 11, 1952	1 year	Hardware, metals, machinery and tools, chemicals, and paper	Minerals, graphite, cotton and other textile fibers, skins and hides, foodstuffs, tobacco, tea, peanuts	1/	Barter and payment agreement
	1953	May 25, 1953	1 year	Machinery, rolled metal products, and consumers' goods	Mineral products, soyabeans, grains, and other consumers' goods	1/	Barter and payment agreement
	1954	February 19, 1954	1 year	Complete sets of factory equipment, lathes, rolled metal products, laboratory equipment, medical supplies, fabrics, sugar, paper, and other industrial products	Non-ferrous metals, and other minerals; vegetable oils and oil seeds; silk products; cotton and other fibers, rice, tea, tobacco, etc.	1/	Barter and payment agreement of 1954

Country	Year in which Agreement Became Operative	Date Concluded	Length of Agreement	Communist China's Imports	Communist China's Exports	Value	Nature of Agreement and Other Data
c. East Germany	1950	October 10, 1950	1 year	Iron and steel products, electric generators, motors, chemicals, dye-stuffs, tele-communications equipment, precision instruments, etc.	Non-ferrous metals, wood oil, bristles, tea, soyabeans, peanuts, egg products, casing, etc.		Barter and payment agreement
	1952	May 28, 1952	1 year	1/	1/	1/	Barter and payment agreement
	1953	April 30, 1953	1 year	Machinery, surveying equipment, testing machinery, electric equipment and supplies, and chemicals	Soyabeans, other grains, mineral products, oils and fats, other consumers' goods	34 per cent greater than 1952	Barter and payment agreement
		August 8, 1953	To end of 1953	1/	Additional supplies of skin and hides, egg products, oils and fats, meat and canned food	50 million rubles	Supplementary protocol to 1953 agreement
	1954	March 30, 1954	1 year	Lathes, cranes, excavators, trucks, bicycles, ball bearings, testing apparatus, X-ray equipment, optical equipment, chemicals, fertilizer, photo equipment, and miscellaneous instruments	Mineral products, wool, silk fabrics, casing, fur, fruit, etc.	Increase over 1953 level reported	Barter and payment agreement
d. Hungary	1951	January 22, 1951	1 year	Industrial and building materials	Raw materials and agricultural products	1/	Barter and payment agreement
	1952	July 21, 1952	1 year	1/	1/	1/	Barter and payment agreement
	1953	March 30, 1953	1 year	Tele-communications equipment, machinery, and other consumers' goods	Minerals, soyabeans, other grains and agricultural products, and consumers' goods	51.7 per cent greater than in 1952	Trade and payment agreement
	1954	April 30, 1954	1 year	Trucks, busses, refrigerators, power plants, rugs, medical apparatus	Non-ferrous metals and other mineral products, hides and skins, wool, feathers, casing, textile fibers, cured tobacco, etc.	Volume reported to exceed the 1953 level	Trade and payment agreement of 1954
e. Bulgaria	1952	July 21, 1952	short-term	1/	1/	1/	Barter agreement

Country	Year in which Agreement Became Operative	Date Concluded	Length of Agreement	Communist China's Imports	Communist China's Exports	Value	Nature of Agreement and Other Data
Bulgaria (Continued)	1953	December 3, 1952	1 year	Machinery, electrical equipment, and chemicals	Non-ferrous metals, cotton, grains, etc.	70 per cent greater than the 1952 volume	Barter and payment agreement
	1954	March 25, 1954	1 year	1/	1/	1/	Barter and payment agreement
f. Rumania	1952	July 30, 1952	1 year	Petroleum	Soyabeans and other grains	1/	Barter agreement
	1953	January 19, 1953	1 year	1/	1/	Increase of 200 per cent over the 1952 level	Barter agreement
	1954	April 19, 1954	1 year	Petroleum products, chemicals, cotton piece goods, and other industrial products	Cotton, jute, non-ferrous metals, silk fabrics, and raw materials for the food processing industry	1/	Barter and payment agreement
g. Finland	1953	June 5, 1953	short-term to February 28, 1954	Paper boards, $5,070,000; machinery, $5,000,000; copper, $475,000; crude pulp, $4,000; etc.	Soyabeans, $2,050,000; flaxseed, $1,377,000; wood oil, $2,170,000; bristles, $750,000; raw silk, $400,000; green tea, $564,000; black tea, $256,000; etc.	$11,750,000	Barter and payment agreement
	1954	June 21, 1954	1 year, May 1, 1954, to April 30, 1955	Paper, paper boards, machinery, and metal products	Oil seeds, wood oil, tea, silk fabrics, etc.	$12.5 million	Barter and payment agreement, part payment in foreign exchange by Communist China
h. Albania	1954	April 7, 1954	1/	1/	1/	1/	Barter
		December 3, 1954	1/	1/	1/	1/	Trade and payment agreement
3. Asia							
a. Outer Mongolia	1953	August 20, 1953	1/	Livestock, raw materials, and metals	1/	1/	Trade and payment agreement

Country	Year in which Agreement Became Operative	Date Concluded	Length of Agreement	Communist China's Imports	Communist China's Exports	Value	Nature of Agreement and Other Data
b. North Korea	1954	September 4, 1954	1 year	Electricity, minerals, marine products, and medical supplies	Coal, fishing boats construction material, machinery, and industrial products	1/	Barter
		November, 1954	1954-1957	1/	Coal, cotton, grains, railway rolling stock, etc.	Total ¥ 8,000 billion	Economic aid to Korea
c. Northern Indo-China	1954	July 7, 1954	1 year	Non-ferrous metals, tea, coffee, pepper, livestock, and hides	Cotton yarn and piece goods, machinery, tele-communications equipment and supplies, transportation equipment, paper, medical equipment and supplies	1/	Barter agreement and agreement on border trade
B. South and Southeast Asia							
1. India	1951	January 3, 1951	short-term	Burlap bags, 16,500 bales	Rice, 50,000 tons	1/	First rice barter. Five shipments of rice made between February and April, 1951
		April 25, 1951	short-term	1/	Rice, 50,000 tons	1/	Second rice barter. Shipments began in April
		May 22, 1951	short-term	1/	Rice, 400,000 tons	1/	Third rice barter
	1952	December 13, 1952	short-term	1/	Rice, 50,000 tons	1/	Fifth rice barter
	1954	April 29, 1954	1/	1/	1/		Sino-Indian transportation and trade agreement concerning Tibet and India
		July 2, 1954	1/	Tobacco	1/	1/	
		October 14, 1954	1/	Rice, uncured tobacco, beans, ores and metals, vegetable oils, chemicals, pharmaceuticals, electrical supplies, scientific machinery, machine tools, iron and other metal products, cotton piece goods, jute products, bicycles, autos, cement, tires, water pumps, storm lanterns, sewing machines, agricultural implements, mica, films, etc.	Rice, soyabeans, machine tools, machinery, pneumatic machinery, transformers, cotton spindles, medical equipment, antimony, silk fabrics, wool, leather, paper, stationery, chemicals, wood oil, cassia bark, mint extract, resin, porcelin, glassware, knitting needles, vegetables and vegetable products, canned food, films, etc.		Sino-Indian trade agreement and over-all agreement on categories, pending individual contracts

Country	Year in which Agreement Became Operative	Date Concluded	Length of Agreement	Communist China's Imports	Communist China's Exports	Value	Nature of Agreement and Other Data
India (Continued)		October 19, 1954	1/	Tobacco, 9 million pounds	Raw silk, 90 tons	1/	Individual contracts still to be concluded
		December 15, 1954	1/	1/	Silk	1/	Contract signed under October 19, 1954, agreement
2. Ceylon	1952	October 4, 1952	1 year	Rubber, cocoanut oil; cocoa, skin and hides	Rice, 80,000 tons; coal, wheat flour, and newsprint	1/	Trade agreement; rice and rubber to form the subject of separate protocol
	1953	December 18, 1952	5 years	Rubber, 50,000 metric tons, each year	Rice, 270,000 tons; soyabeans, 5,000 tons; newsprint, 10,000 tons; sulphur, 2,000 tons, each year	250 million rupees each way	Sino-Ceylon five-year agreement on exchange of rubber and rice
		September 21, 1953	1 year	Rubber, 50,000 tons	Rice, 270,000 tons	1/	Two contracts signed under overall agreement of December, 1952
	1954	September 21, 1953	2 years	1/	1/	1/	Trade agreement of October, 1952, extended by two more years beginning January 1, 1954
		October 8, 1954	1 year	Rubber, 50,000 metric tons	Rice, 270,000 tons	1/	Two contracts for export of rubber and rice signed under December, 1952, agreement
3. Indonesia	1953	November 30, 1953	To end of 1954	Many categories	Many categories	1/	General trade agreement
	1954	September 1, 1954	1 year	Cocoanuts and cocoanut oil, sugar, quinine, and timber	Textile machinery, motors, machine tools, cotton yarn and piece goods, silk fabrics, and knitted products	£6 million each way	Protocol signed under the 1953 agreement; latter extended to the end of July, 1955, renewable for another year if not canceled beforehand

4. Pakistan	1953	March 14, 1953	short-term	Cotton	Coal, 200,000 tons	1/	Barter
5. Burma	1954	April 22, 1954	3 years	Rice and rice products, beans, oil seed cakes, minerals, timber, rubber, and cotton	Coal, silk and silk fabrics, cotton textiles, paper, agricultural implements, handicraft and light industrial products, enamelware porcelain, tea, cigarettes, canned food, native medicines	1/	Trade agreement
		November 3, 1954	short-term	Rice, 150,000 long tons	1/	1/	First protocol under the April, 1954, trade agreement

TRADE AGREEMENTS CONCLUDED DURING AND AFTER THE MOSCOW INTERNATIONAL ECONOMIC CONFERENCE WITH NON-GOVERNMENTAL REPRESENTATIVES OF NON-COMMUNIST COUNTRIES:

C. Western Europe							
1. United Kingdom	1952	June 12, 1952	To December 31, 1952	Textiles, 35 per cent; chemicals, 30 per cent; metals, 35 per cent	Coal, bristles, and casing, 25 per cent; egg and egg products, 20 per cent; soyabeans, vegetable oils, etc., 55 per cent	US $28 million (£10 million) each way	Detailed protocols based on this overall agreement will be negotiated by private concerns separately
	1953	July 6, 1953	1/	Metals and metal products, machinery, electric equipment and supplies, chemicals, tools, medical supplies and equipment, communications and transportation equipment	Vegetable oils and oil seeds, animal products, egg products, minerals, tea, raw silk, and handicraft products	£30 million each way	Same as above, payment in sterling
2. France	1952	June 11, 1952	1/	Metals, machinery, chemicals, and medical supplies	Silk and silk piece goods, tea, livestock, tung oil, oil seeds, handicraft products, manganese ores	US $11.2 million (£4 million) each way	Same as above
	1953	June 5, 1953	1/	Steel, machinery, medical supplies, scientific instruments, and industrial chemicals	Tea, silk, casing, vegetable oils, bristles, and feathers	£10 million each way	Same as above
3. Belgium	1952	June 12, 1952	1/	1/	1/	1/	Same as above

Country	Year in which Agreement Became Operative	Date Concluded	Length of Agreement	Communist China's Imports	Communist China's Exports	Value	Nature of Agreement and Other Data
4. Holland	1952	June 14, 1952	1/	Sugar, paper, chemicals, fertilizer, drugs, and metal products	Soyabeans, minerals, peanuts, peanut meal, silk, sheep skin, handicraft products, wood oil, egg products, tobacco, ceramics, rugs, etc.	US $6.44 million (£2.3 million) each way	Detailed protocols based on this overall agreement will be negotiated by private concerns separately
5. Italy	1953	June, 1953	1 year	Chemical fertilizer, cameras, etc.	Raw silk, etc.	$11.5 million	Same as above
D. Japan	1952	June 1, 1952	To December 31, 1952	Metals and metal products, machinery, small ships, vehicles, office machines, textiles, fertilizer, chemicals, etc.	Coal, tung oil, manganese and iron ores, soyabeans, bristles, oil seeds, etc.	US $84 million (£30 million) each way	Barter agreement extended to June, 1953, and again to December, 1953
	1953	October 29, 1953	To December 31, 1954	**Group A:** Copper and aluminum ingots, steel plates, pipes and tubes, tin plates, black steel sheets, galvanized iron sheets, steel drum sheets, structural steel, railway equipment, heavy machinery, cargo vessels equipped with refrigeration, other sea-going vessels, 35 per cent of total value	**Group A:** 35 per cent of total value Iron ore, manganese ore, soyabeans, and coal	£30 million each way	Same as above, payment in sterling
				Group B: Textile machinery, cranes, ball bearings, miscellaneous machinery, radio and other electrical equipment and supplies, motor vehicles, optical equipment, medical supplies, insecticides, fertilizer, synthetic fibers, dyestuffs, etc. 40 per cent of total value	**Group B:** 40 per cent of total value Salt, magnesite, China clay, kaolin, fluospar, apatite, asbestos, antimony, bristles, wool, cassia, wood oil, beans, oil seeds and vegetable oils, ramie, wild silk, etc.		

Country	Year in which Agreement Became Operative	Date Concluded	Length of Agreement	Communist China's Imports	Communist China's Exports	Value	Nature of Agreement and Other Data
Japan (Continued)				Group C: Agricultural machinery, scientific and office equipment, bicycles, clocks and watches, household electrical appliances, radio and television sets, photographic material, marine products, cotton yarn and piece goods, etc., 25 per cent of total value	Group C: 25 per cent of total value Talc, graphite, gypsum, pig skin, rugs, lacquer, cotton and silk waste, straw braids, bran meal, oil seed, cakes, resin, medicinal herbs, etc.		
E. Others 2/							
1. Chile	1952	October 23, 1952	1/	1/	1/	1/	Signed in Peking between the representatives of China National Import-Export Corp. and Christian Casanova, representative of the Sino-Chilean Trade Corp.

Sources: Among the sources from which these data are taken are *New Construction*, Vol. I, No. 9, p. 11, Peking, January, 1950; *Handbook for Newspaper Readers*, p. 735, Hankow, 1950; *Industrial and Commercial News*, Vol. II, No. 10, pp. 11-13, Shanghai, March 5, 1951, Vol. IV, No. 3, pp. 9-10, July 2, 1951; *People's Handbook*, p. 194, Shanghai, 1952; *Economic Yearbook*, p. 313, Hongkong, 1952; *Wen-hui pao*, Hongkong, July 17, 24, and 28, and December 1 and 31, 1952; *Far Eastern Economic Review*, Vol. VIII, No. 18, p. 578, Hongkong, October, 1952, and Vol. VIII, No. 26, p. 840, December, 1952; *Ceylon News Letter*, Colombo, November 15, 1952; *Liberation Daily*, Shanghai, June 3, 1952; NCNA *Bulletin*, London, October 24, 1952, and Hongkong, September 27, 1952; *People's China*, Peking, July, 1952; *Hongkong Economic Yearbook*, pp. 182-186, Hongkong, 1955; Asia Bureau, Foreign Ministry, Government of Japan, 1954.

1/ Particulars not available.

2/ Trade with Switzerland has also been reported.

SOME FURTHER OBSERVATIONS ON COMMUNIST CHINA'S FOREIGN TRADE

As one examines the above table, several points of interest may be noted.

First, the number of Soviet Bloc countries trading with Communist China increased from 4 in 1950 to 11 in 1954, plus Finland. As far as information is available, this was accompanied by a continual expansion of trading volume.

Second, through its bilateral arrangements with individual countries, Communist China has apparently sought to enhance its own role as an intermediary in multilateral trading. For instance, Communist China imported rice from Burma in 1954 while exporting rice to Ceylon at the same time. Similarly, the same group of nonferrous metals is apparently imported from Indo-China and exported to other countries. Political instead of purely economic considerations are probably paramount in these arrangements.

Third, employment of the technique of state trading and bilateral agreements has not always succeeded in securing for Communist China favorable terms of exchange. In fact, there are some interesting examples pointing to the contrary. For instance, in the rubber-rice exchange with Ceylon concluded in September, 1953, Communist China agreed to buy rubber from Ceylon at a price that was 75 per cent above the then Singapore market. At the same time, Chinese rice was sold to Ceylon at a price that was substantially below that of other exporting countries.[31] Similarly, some doubt must be entertained on the prices at which imports from, and exports to, the Soviet Bloc, especially the Soviet Union, are bought and sold. Communist China has not published any meaningful statistics comparing the prices of identical imports originating from the Soviet Bloc and non-Communist countries respectively. Whenever generalizations are made on the low prices of Soviet products there is no mention of the prices of corresponding Chinese exports to the Soviet Bloc.[32]

Fourth, in the case of the various non-governmental agreements with private traders from non-Communist countries, the overall trade figures are altogether meaningless, because actual trade is governed by individual contracts negotiated with individual foreign firms. In the case of Japan, for instance, according to reports from the Bank of Japan, actual trade during 1953 between Japan and Communist

China amounted to £3,975,000 of Chinese exports and £5,071,000 of Japanese exports while the planned volume was £30 million in each case. As the Japanese report quoted above[33] stated, the difficulty was that Japanese goods demanded by Communist China could not be exported under the United Nations' embargo, while supplies of Chinese exports demanded by Japan were too small. One should probably add that even if the embargo were completely lifted, while Japanese exports might undergo some change in their composition, there would still be no assurance that they would increase substantially in volume unless means of payment could be found by Communist China.

ECONOMIC SANCTIONS AND SEA TRAFFIC

On the basis of the preceding discussion, it would appear that Communist China's foreign trade has not been seriously affected by the United Nations' embargo in terms of the volume and composition of imports. Apparently, to the extent its trade with the non-Communist countries has to be adjusted, Communist China has been fairly successful in finding replacement in the Soviet Bloc and "neutral" countries and in evading the economic sanctions by transit trade and re-export arrangements. However, these developments are not sufficient to warrant the conclusion that such trade restrictions as still remain in view of the many loopholes have been completely useless in adversely affecting the country's economic development.

First of all, one may point out the fact that the need to accommodate itself to those who are willing to trade has weakened Communist China's bargaining position. This is evidenced in the terms of trade in the exchange of rice and rubber with Ceylon. The same situation may exist in Chinese trade with the Soviet Union and other satellite countries.[34]

Second, the Nationalists' blockade of certain sections of the China coast and economic sanctions, such as they are, have compelled Communist China to rely more on overland routes for its external trade, which is an extremely costly development. The high rail transportation cost to Europe from Communist China means that a larger share of its export earnings has to be allotted to freight charges, thus reducing its ability to pay for imports which have also become correspondingly more expensive for the same reason. Undoubtedly, this consideration, together with military reasons, weighed heavily in the

Communists' decision to build the new rail link between Chi-ning and Outer Mongolia. While this development has served to shorten the rail route between the Soviet Union and China Proper by bypassing Manchuria, it has not completely disposed of the transport problem. Nor has freight cost to Manchuria itself been affected. Moreover, every restriction of the sea lanes, including coastal traffic, serves to increase the traffic load on the railways.

The relative importance of overland and sea traffic in Communist China's external trade may be further gleaned from a comparison between the total volume of trade and that part which uses the Hongkong entrepot.

	Total Imports (In US$ million)	*Imports[1] from Hongkong*	*Imports from Hongkong as % of total*	*Total Exports (In US$ million)*	*Exports[1] to Hongkong*	*Exports to Hongkong as % of total*
1950	436.4	292.0	66.9	466.5	164.9	35.3
1951	1,033.3	320.6	31.0	672.4	169.1	25.1
1952	717.01	106.6	14.8	478.00	156.1	32.6
1953	989.47	110.1	11.1	635.74	161.7	25.4

1. The Hongkong figures here include trade via Macao. Both are taken from the *Hongkong Government Gazette.*

Although Hongkong trade with China is partly conducted by land, all traffic between Hongkong and the rest of the world is by sea. Since Hongkong accounts for only a diminishing part of the seaborne trade as a result of the existing United Nations' embargo and the expansion of the northern ports, particularly Tientsin—where a new harbor has been completed—Ying-k'ou, Ch'ing-huang-tao, and the Russian-controlled ports of Dairen and Port Arthur, the relative importance of Hongkong in Communist China's external trade could be regarded as reflecting the *minimum* importance of seaborne traffic in China's total foreign trade. As can be seen from the above table, 88.9 per cent of Communist China's imports and 67.4 per cent of its exports in 1953 were carried on either by land or through ports other than Hongkong.[35] The proportion of overland to total trade was consequently somewhat less than the above figures indicate, perhaps substantially less. Obviously, any forcible diversion of the remaining sea traffic via Hongkong and the other sea ports would cause a further increase in rail traffic and total freight cost, even though such a development would be far less damaging to the Communist Chinese economy now than it might have been before the completion of the rail link through Outer Mongolia and the changes brought about in the country distribution of Communist China's external trade since 1951.

III

FOREIGN EXCHANGE RATES

The evolution of Communist China's foreign trade policy is closely paralled by its policy with respect to control over the exchange rate. As mentioned in Chapter XI above, private persons were required under the various regional regulations to deposit all their foreign exchange assets and earnings with the government banking system in return for special deposit certificates which may or may not have to be sold to the government within a short period of time.[36] Depending upon their origin, these deposits may or may not be used to finance imports. Generally speaking, the policy was to prohibit the use of foreign exchange deposits obtained from foreign currencies surrendered by the public to finance private imports so as to discourage illicit dealings in such currencies.[37] Demand for foreign exchange was placed under control by the import licensing system and by subjecting all other would-be foreign exchange purchases to licensing.

Uniform exchange rates were not introduced prior to July, 1950. For instance, in the middle of January, 1950, U.S. dollar currencies were quoted at ¥20,700 in Shanghai and ¥14,000 in Canton, while telegraphic transfers in New York were quoted at ¥23,000 in Shanghai and ¥16,500 in Canton. At the same time, special rates were quoted for inward remittances by overseas Chinese. The latter rate was usually at or about the highest of the various regional rates. Finally, by September, 1950, the official control began to quote separate buying and selling rates, which was another step toward the sytematization of foreign exchange regulation.

However, the most interesting aspect of foreign exchange policy concerns the level of the exchange rate.

Up to the beginning of 1951, the official rate of the *jen-min pi* in terms of foreign currencies exhibited a great deal of flexibility. Between March, 1950, when the *jen-min pi* began to be quoted regularly on the free exchange market in Hongkong, and February, 1951, the highest premium at which the Hongkong dollar was quoted in terms of *jen-min pi* on the Hongkong market over the official rate was only 12.4 per cent.[38] There was a continual appreciation of the Communist currency during this period. Occasionally, as during May and June, 1950, the market quotation of the *jen-min pi* in Hongkong was even higher than the official rate. This unusual phenomenon coincided with the severest deflationary period following the March, 1950, financial reform measures. The gradual appreciation of the *jen-min pi* from March, 1950, to the end of the year also coincided with the emergence of an export surplus for the year. Nor was the appreciation interrupted by the renewed rise of commodity prices following the outbreak of the Korean war in the summer of 1950. All this may be explained by the official policy to fix the exchange rate at a level reasonably close to the market rate, by the severe deflationary movement initiated in March, which removed speculation as a determining factor in the exchange market and probably brought about some repatriation of flight capital, and by a general feeling of confidence in the stability of the Communist currency.[39]

The situation changed radically after February, 1951. From then on the official exchange rate was kept constant and was depreciated only once in December, 1952. In the meantime the free market rate fluctuated widely, often in response to military developments in Korea and the international situation in general. In terms of *jen-min pi,* the Hongkong dollar was quoted at a premium of 39.3 per cent above the official rate in the fourth week of November, 1951. Almost exactly a year later, in the first week of November, 1952, the premium reached a high of 43.6 per cent. The official devaluation in December, 1952, helped to bring the premium down from 41.3 per cent at the end of November to 27.4 per cent at the year end. Finally, the premium reached an all-time high of 50 per cent in the second week of February, 1954, when the *jen-min pi* was quoted at HK$117 per million against the official rate of HK$234.

During 1951, the official rate was not adjusted in response to fluctuations in the free market rate, because official trade policy had shifted from export promotion to import encouragement. Although this policy has since been modified, the official rate was altered only once in December, 1952, not only because the Korean war made it all the more imperative for the Communist authorities to avoid any severe or frequent revaluation which might engender speculation on the future stability of the *jen-min pi,* but also because the progressive expansion of state trading has succeeded in minimizing the effect of the exchange rate on the volume of exports and imports. Overvaluation of the Communist currency has little effect on the conduct of the state trading agencies which are able to withstand any loss in domestic currency by falling upon the treasury. The level of the official rate no longer has any important effect on the country's external balance except in two respects. First, overseas remittances may be discouraged. Second, an ever-increasing divergence between the official and market rates may by itself encourage transactions on the Hongkong free market, thus threatening the entire system of foreign exchange control.

BLACK MARKET OPERATIONS IN FOREIGN EXCHANGE

What we have described as the Hongkong free market for the *jen-min pi* is the black market from the Chinese Communists' point of view. Obviously, the *jen-min pi* could not be sold at other than the official rate if supply of the Communist currency could not be obtained from non-official sources. Although free market quotations in Hongkong are not published locally day by day, allowing for the clandestine nature of the transactions involved, reports on both the market rate and the volume of transactions have been reasonably regular, suggesting the existence of a lively black market in Communist China from time to time.

In fact, on the basis of reports published by the *Far Eastern Economic Review,* it is possible to conduct transactions not only in *jen-min pi* notes in Hongkong, but also in drafts on such cities as Shanghai, Canton, Hsia-men (Amoy) and San-t'ou (Swatow) although the market is not always active in the latter cases. Moreover, remittances can often be made between Hongkong and the other cities in terms of gold and United States dollars. That is to say, one may remit, for instance, specific amounts expressed in gold or United States dollars between Hongkong and Shanghai by paying a fairly high remittance charge. The level of the charges apparently varies with the severity of police control in Communist China, while the direction of the remittances seems to change in accordance with such factors as the activity of the black market in Communist China, the need for capital repatriation to meet tax payments and other Communist exactions by private businessmen, and the intensity of capital flight.

So far operations on the black market do not appear to have reached serious proportions, and activity is probably predominantly influenced by the international political scene, instead of purely economic factors such as a resumption of open inflation. However, the very existence of the black market is an interesting comment on Communist China's exchange control. It may also be regarded as a price Communist China has to pay in tolerating the existence of a free economy in Hongkong.

Official Exchange Rate of the *Jen-min pi*[1]
In thousand JMP per one U.S. dollar T/T (Shanghai)

	1949	*1950*	*1951*	*1952*
January		22.30	24.13	22.47
February		25.40	22.51	22.47
March		37.70	22.51	22.47
April		39.50	22.51	22.47
May		37.00	22.47	22.47
June		37.00	22.47	22.47
July		35.00	22.47	22.47
August		33.80	22.47	22.47
September	3.72	31.00	22.47	22.47
October	4.42	31.16	22.47	22.47
November	7.65	31.16	22.47	22.47
December	17.90	30.2	22.47	24.20

Source: Compiled from newspaper daily quotations.

1. No quotations on the U.S. dollar have been published since January, 1952. The above rates for 1952 are computed from the sterling rate at $2.80 per pound. The official rate remained at ¥24,620 per dollar through 1953 and 1954.

Comparison between the Official and Free Market Exchange Rates of the *Jen-min pi*
1950–1954

	I	*II*	*III*	*IV*	*V*
	Period Ending	*Free Market Rate in Hongkong Dollars per ¥ Million*	*Official Rate in Hongkong Dollars per ¥ Million*	*III — II*	*(III — II) / III* %
1950	March 30 (from 3/15)	140	154	14	9.09
	April 20	158	158	0	0
	April 27	159	166	7	4.22
	May 4	167	166	— 1	— 0.60
	May 11	166	160	— 6	— 3.61
	May 18	170	166	— 4	— 2.41

	I	II	III	IV	V
	Period Ending	Free Market Rate in Hongkong Dollars per ¥ Million	Official Rate in Hongkong Official Rate Dollars per ¥ Million	III — II	(III — II) / III %
	May 25	168	163	— 5	— 3.00
	June 15	164	163	— 1	— 0.61
	July 6	166	170	4	2.35
	July 13	170	173	3	1.73
	July 20	169	173	4	2.31
	August 3	175	175	0	0
	August 10	177	202	25	12.38
	August 31	200	202	2	0.99
	September 7	197	210	13	6.19
	September 14	200	210	10	4.76
	September 21	196	210	14	6.67
	September 28	198	210	12	5.71
	October 5	200	210	10	4.76
	October 12	195	210	15	7.14
	October 19	198	210	12	5.71
	October 26	201	210	9	4.29
	November 2	202	210	8	3.81
	November 9	202	210	8	3.81
	November 16	196	210	14	6.67
	November 30	189	210	21	1.00
	December 7	187	210	23	10.96
	December 14	190	210	17	8.10
	December 21	200	210	10	6.67
	December 28	205	210	5	2.78
1951	January 6	237	237	0	0
	February 18	250	257	7	2.72
	February 24	233	257	24	9.34
	March 3	228	257	29	11.28
	March 31	223	257	34	13.23
	April 14	226	257	31	12.06
	April 20	226	257	31	12.06
	April 28	222	257	35	13.62
	May 5	221	257	36	14.01
	May 12	224	257	33	12.84
	May 19	255	257	2	0.78
	May 26	245	257	12	4.67
	June 2	255	257	2	0.98
	June 9	243	257	14	5.45
	June 16	252	257	5	1.95
	June 30	250	257	7	2.72
	July 7	241	257	16	6.23
	July 14	235	257	22	8.56
	July 28	224	257	33	12.84
	August 4	216	257	41	15.95
	August 11	213	257	44	17.12

	I Period Ending	II Free Market Rate in Hongkong Dollars per ¥ Million	III Official Rate in Hongkong Dollars per ¥ Million	IV III — II	V (III — II)/III %
	August 18	217	257	40	15.56
	August 25	215	257	42	16.34
	September 1	211	257	46	17.90
	September 8	201	257	46	21.79
	September 15	189	257	68	26.46
	September 29	212	257	45	17.51
	October 6	228	257	29	11.28
	October 13	205	257	52	20.23
	October 20	201	257	54	21.01
	October 27	194	257	63	24.51
	November 10	164	257	93	36.19
	November 17	160	257	97	37.74
	November 24	156	257	101	39.30
	December 15	181	257	76	29.57
	December 22	187	257	70	27.24
	December 29	200	257	57	22.18
1952	January 5	197	257	60	22.35
	January 19	213	257	44	17.12
	January 26	219	257	38	14.79
	February 11	229	257	28	10.89
	March 1	216	257	41	15.95
	March 15	204	257	53	20.62
	April 5	201	257	56	21.79
	April 19	199	257	58	22.57
	April 26	198	257	59	22.96
	May 3	193	257	64	24.90
	May 17	193	257	64	24.90
	May 24	199	257	58	22.57
	May 31	199	257	58	22.57
	June 7	226	257	31	12.06
	June 14	222	257	35	13.62
	June 21	235	257	22	8.56
	June 28	229	257	28	10.90
	July 5	206	257	51	19.84
	July 12	195	257	62	24.13
	July 19	190	257	67	26.07
	August 2	186	257	71	27.63
	August 9	190	257	67	26.07
	August 16	187	257	70	27.24
	August 23	188	257	69	26.85
	August 30	187	257	70	27.24
	September20	191	257	66	25.68
	September 27	205	257	52	20.33
	October 4	189	257	68	26.46

	I	*II*	*III*	*IV*	*V*
	Period Ending	*Free Market Rate in Hongkong Dollars per ¥ Million*	*Official Rate in Hongkong Dollars per ¥ Million*	*III — II*	*III — II / III* %
	October 11	189	257	68	26.46
	October 18	184	257	73	28.40
	October 25	165	257	92	35.80
	November 1	161	257	96	37.35
	November 8	145	257	112	43.58
	November 15	147	257	110	42.80
	November 22	147	257	110	42.80
	November 29	151	257	106	41.25
	December 6	145	234	89	34.63
	December 27	170	234	64	27.35
1953	January 1	187	234	47	20.09
	January 17	199	234	35	14.96
	January 24	202	234	32	13.68
	January 31	182	234	52	22.22
	February 7	179	234	55	23.50
	February 21	182	234	52	22.22
	March 7	210	234	24	10.26
	March 14	202	234	32	13.68
	March 21	201	234	33	14.10
	April 18	157	234	77	32.91
	April 27	160	234	74	31.62
	May 9	166	234	68	29.06
	May 23	162	234	72	30.77
	May 30	170	234	64	27.35
	June 13	182	234	52	22.22
	June 21	182	234	52	22.22
	June 27	177	234	57	24.36
	July 4	167	234	67	28.63
	July 11	169	234	65	27.78
	July 18	177	234	57	24.36
	July 25	187	234	47	20.09
	August 1	181	234	53	22.65
	August 8	182	234	52	22.22
	August 15	180	234	54	23.08
	August 25	180	234	54	23.08
	September 12	180	234	54	23.08
	October 3	160	234	74	31.62
	October 24	160	234	74	31.62
	November 2–7	158	234	76	32.48
	November 17	160	234	74	31.62
	November 31	159	234	75	32.05
	December 12	160	234	74	31.62
	December 19	160	234	74	31.62
	December 26	160	234	74	31.62

	I	II	III	IV	V
	Period Ending	*Free Market Rate in Hongkong Dollars per ¥ Million*	*Official Rate in Hongkong Dollars per ¥ Million*	*III — II*	*(III — II) / III* %
1954	January 21	170	234	64	27.35
	February 11	117	234	117	50.00
	February 18	135	234	99	42.31
	February 25	135	234	99	42.31
	March 25	142	234	92	39.32
	April 15	140	234	94	40.17
	April 29	145	234	83	35.47
	May 6	151	234	83	35.47
	May 13	150	234	84	35.90
	June 10	159	234	75	32.05
	July 8	171	234	63	26.92
	July 29	176	234	58	24.79
	August 12	144	234	90	38.46
	September 2	146	234	88	37.61
	September 9	150	234	84	35.90
	September 16	140	234	94	40.17
	September 30	150	234	84	35.90
	October 28	135	234	99	42.31
	November	123	234	111	47.44
	December 2	130	234	104	44.44
	December 16	129	234	105	44.87

Source: Compiled from the ***Far Eastern Economic Review,*** Hongkong.

These figures are for ***jen-min pi*** notes and are averages computed from the high's and low's reported for the individual periods. Notes as a rule command a small premium over drafts.

IV

SOVIET AID AND SINO-SOVIET JOINT COMPANIES

A word must now be said on the last principal source of additional foreign exchange in-payments; namely, direct capital investments from abroad. Again, in this case, the only instances reported so far have been a few Sino-Soviet joint enterprises established under special agreements, dealing respectively with civil aviation, the Chinese Changchun Railway, the exploitation of petroleum and non-ferrous metals in Sinkiang, and ship-building at Dairen.

It is not at all clear whether the Chinese Changchun Railway represented much more than a management agreement giving the Soviet Union full control of the railway until 1952, though placing the road nominally under joint supervision. The joint shipbuilding enterprise at Dairen was also established by transferring to the Soviet Union part ownership of an existing firm taken over from the Japanese. Only in the case of the civil aviation company and the two Sinkiang enterprises for the development of petroleum and non-ferrous and rare metals did the Soviet Union undertake to supply Communist China with machinery and equipment as a part of its investment. This is reflected in the rise of imports from the Soviet Union to Sinkiang and the high ratio of industrial equipment and supplies in total Sinkiang imports.[40] However, since 1955, all these joint enterprises have been or are being reorganized so as to give Communist China sole ownership. The transfer involves every one of the above-mentioned firms with the exception of the Chinese Changchun Railway which had been returned earlier. While this development does not necessarily entail relinquishment of control by the Soviet Union, which can continue to exercise supervision by the well-tried technique of employing Soviet advisers, it nevertheless poses a problem to Communist China's balance of payments in the form of capital repatriation.[41] Moreover, according to the original terms of the 1950 agreement, repayment of the $300 million loan should also begin in 1954, although the date may have been postponed under the program of expanded aid from the Soviet Union.

Thus it is entirely possible that the volume of net capital inflow from the Soviet Union is extremely limited. This means not only that Soviet material assistance since the establishment of the new regime in China has been largely on a current basis, but also that, even allowing for imports currently paid for by Communist China, the total supply of goods and services from the Soviet Union to Communist China has not yet equalled the volume of damage suffered by the Manchurian economy alone as a result of Soviet removals in the post-World War II period. This situation may eventually pose a serious dilemma to Communist Chinese planners, and the choice between reducing the rate of industrialization and curtailing domestic consumption to make more exportable goods available is not a pleasant one. As a stop-gap measure, there is always the possibility of dipping into official foreign exchange reserves, which is probably a very good reason for diplomatic moves which, the Communists hope, might result in the freeing of frozen Communist Chinese dollar assets. However, none of these methods can really offer a satisfactory solution to the underlying problems in the balance of payments as determined by low productivity, a limited range of exportable commodities, rising consumption and population growth, and an investment program largely dependent upon imported capital goods.

SOVIET TECHNICAL ASSISTANCE

The small volume of Soviet material aid should not, however, detract from the important role played by the Soviet Union in Communist China's present industrialization program, especially in technical assistance. In the case of large industrial plants recently established in Communist China, such as the An-shan rolling mills, complete sets of bluprints are supplied by the Soviet Union. Allowance is openly made for this factor in the planning schedule for construction and installation. A Soviet adviser, Bukhov, has played a key role in all the principal water conservation projects. Soviet technicians have also helped in railway building and in bridge construction. Similar examples may also be given in the case of coal mining and the electric power industry. In addition to the provision of technical plans and other data, Soviet assistance has also taken the form of on-the-spot supervision of production, as well as the training of skilled workers and technicians, not only in production techniques, but also in management methods and organization. The widespread adoption of the business accountability system and the various related methods is a case in point. The Chinese Changchun Railway, for instance, has served as a training ground for Chinese railway workers. Finally, the adoption of Soviet control methods in such fields as monetary and budgetary control and overall planning procedure owes a great deal to Soviet assistance. The 1954 regulations governing the employment of forced labor have also been officially attributed to Soviet advice.

Information on the exact number of Soviet advisers in Communist China and their assignment to individual industries and activities as well as geographical areas has been rarely published. An inherent difficulty lies in the definition of the term "adviser," which is further complicated by the fact that military, administrative, and technical personnel cannot always be distinguished. According to one estimate,[42] some 15,000 Russian military, engineering, and administrative advisers have been sent to Communist China by the Soviet Union since 1950. Other unconfirmed reports from private sources have mentioned much higher figures, ranging from 20,000 to 90,000 persons or more. There is little doubt that the number is exceedingly large and that, from the point of view of foreign exchange payment, the salary account is bound to be an important factor. A new agreement on scientific and cultural cooperation was signed between the Soviet Union and Communist China in 1954 and was mentioned at the time of the Sino-Soviet joint communique on October 12, 1954. Exchange of technical personnel and special programs for Chinese trainees in Soviet enterprises may well be set up under this arrangement although the method of payment and other details have again not been revealed.

Dependence on Soviet technique in general, together with the small but important contribution of Soviet industrial equipment in key construction projects, may have a much larger influence on Sino-Soviet economic and, incidentally, political relations, in the long run than their absolute scale may suggest. As long as Communist China cannot be self-sufficient in both technicians and capital goods, reliance on Soviet assistance at the present time may lead to dependence for a much longer period due to the need for replacement, designing specifications, and a general technical orientation towards the Soviet Union. In the meantime, Soviet technicians in management and supervisory positions will have a stranglehold on Communist China's industrialization program, if not directly on the country's economic life as a whole.

NOTES

1. A preliminary draft of certain parts of this chapter has appeared in an article by the author in the *Pacific Spectator,* Stanford, Fall, 1953.

2. For the use of flexible tariffs and export taxes to exercise selective control over imports and the manner in which the licensing status of a commodity is subject to continual reclassification in the light of conditions prevailing on the domestic market, see Yang P'o, "Foreign Trade and the Customs Policy of the New China," in *Selected Economic Essays,* pp. 285-288, Peking, 1951. A complete tariff schedule and the Provisional Maritime Customs Law were both published in May, 1951. These are fully discussed in Wei Cheng-huan, "On the Provisional Maritime Customs Laws," *Industrial and Commercial News,* Vol. III, No. 8, pp. 14-16, Shanghai, May, 1951.

3. As regional Communist authorities were established in 1949, foreign trade control regulations were issued separately. In particular, the major instruments were the Foreign Trade Control Regulations for North China and the corresponding regulations for East and South China, issued on March 15, June 9, and December 7, 1949, respectively. For the original texts see *The Urban Policy of the New Democracy,* pp.

128-132 and 138-149, Hongkong, 1949, and *Handbook on Trade with South China*, edited by the *Southern Daily*, pp. 19-63, Canton, January, 1950. These regional regulations were later consolidated in a set of nationwide regulations on December 8, 1950, which were themselves soon to be supplemented by the Barter Trade Control Regulations. For the text of the December, 1950, Order, see *Foreign Trade Handbook*, pp. 1-3.

4. See Li Jung-hsüan, "Barter Trade, Beginning of a New Page," *Industrial and Commercial News*, Vol. II, No. 10, pp. 7-8, Shanghai, March, 1951.

5. See *Foreign Trade Handbook*, edited by the Canton Foreign Trade Control Bureau, Canton, March, 1951.

6. Retaliatory measures which were taken in late December, 1950, such as the control and blocking of American assets in China, the diversion of export shipments away from American, Canadian, Japanese, and Philippine ports and the prohibition of export of bristles, tung oil, and certain ores to the above countries are of secondary importance from our point of view. Cf. Wu Sho, "On the Result of the U.S. Trade Embargo in China," *Economic Bulletin*, No. 214, Hongkong, March, 1951.

7. At least the Communist authorities behaved as if they thought this was the case.

8. The category of state monopolies was added in the December, 1950, regulations. A fourth category consists of prohibited imports and exports.

8a. The construction of the three schedules and its significance may be best illustrated by the following examples:

	Exports	*Imports*
Schedule A	Hog bristles, soyabeans, antimony, wolfram, tin, tung oil, coal and coke, etc.	Burlap bags, cotton, electric generators, machine tools, arms and ammunition, wood pulp, industrial explosives, petroleum products, chemicals, precision instruments, etc.
Schedule B	Feather, various coarse grains, vegetable oils, beans, etc.	Hardware, bicycles, motor boats, newsprint, cement, photographic material, etc.
Schedule C	Tobacco, china, grocery items, handicraft products, etc.	industrial soap, paper products, Processed food stuffs, leather, etc.

9. In June, 1951, the gross profit on imports and exports was reported to be 16 per cent and 9 per cent respectively. By July, 1951, following the expansion of trade under the new system, the gross profit on imports rose to 24 per cent, while that on exports fell to 5.9 per cent. A situation of import surplus developed at all the principal ports of entry. In Shanghai imports exceeded exports by 100 per cent or more and payments equal to 6-7 per cent of the value of the import certificate had to be made by importers to the corresponding exporters who undertook to export under the import certificate. See *Industrial and Commercial News*, Shanghai, October 5, 1951.

10. See *Economic Bulletin*, No. 231, Hongkong, July, 1951, and National Bureau of Statistics *Bulletin, Peking*, October, 1954.

11. NCNA, April 27, 1954. Cf. also Lei Jen-min's report in *People's China* (in English), Peking, January, 1954.

12. The manner in which re-exports and different standards of determining country origin or destination between the trade statistics of two trading countries gives rise to discrepancies may be clearly seen from the following data which compare Communist China's external trade figures in 1950 as derived from official statistics with those given in the 1950 *Foreign Commerce Yearbook*. Only countries for which both sets of data are available are given on page 498.

Communist China's Foreign Trade
with Selected Countries
(In US$ million)

Countries of Origin or Destination	*Import* I *Foreign Commerce Yearbook*	*Import* II *Derived from Communist Chinese Sources*	*Export* I *Foreign Commerce Yearbook*	*Export* II *Derived from Communist Chinese Sources*
Western Europe and Dependencies				
United Kingdom	10.1	36.1	29.0	28.1
West Germany	11.4*	9.4	14.7*	7.5
Holland	0.3	—	11.3	17.3
Belgium	7.4**	6.3	7.5**	4.6
French Morocco	—	—	10.7	6.8
Asia				
Malaya	40.5	50.6	31.3	—
India	7.3†	25.3	1.3†	—
Japan	19.6	23.0	39.5	18.1
Pakistan	26.2*†	13.8	22.2*†	—
Hongkong and Macao	292.0	6.4	164.9	123.6
U.S.A.	46.5	125.7	146.4	82.3

* Including Formosa.

** Including Luxembourg.

† Fiscal year ending March 31 in the following year.

13. Cf., for instance, statistics on Western trade with Communist China published in the U.S. *Foreign Commerce Yearbook* and various reports by the Administrator of the Battle Act. See also Rostow, *op. cit.*, p. 251.

14. Cf. Wang Ya-hsien, "Tremendous Success in New China's Foreign Trade," *Economic Bulletin*, No. 254, p. 7, Hongkong, January, 1952.

15. Hongkong may be an exception in this case.

16. According to the statistics of Western countries, the trade balance in both 1950 and 1952 was in Communist China's favor. This may be explained by the practice of crediting to Communist China imports of Chinese origin obtained from eastern Europe and the Soviet Union and failure to account for all exports that went to Communist China through re-export and transshipment. At the same time some imports that went to Hongkong may have been recorded as exports to China which, added to Hongkong's reported exports to Communist China, result in double counting. Moreover, exports to Hongkong may be re-exported to areas other than China.

17. October 5, 1953.

18. *People's Handbook*, pp. 296-300, Tientsin, 1955.

19. Excluding military aid.

20. It is believed that 1950 was no exception to this rule in spite of the small favorable trade balance.

21. Asia Bureau, Ministry of Foreign Affairs (Japan), *Chukyo no 1954 nen kokka yosan*, pp. 20-21, Tokyo, July, 1954.

22. *Hua-ch'iao jih-pao*, Hongkong, January 7, 1954.

23. If our estimate of total imports in 1950 is correct, the import of capital goods, raw materials, and fuel would amount to $426 million. Of this amount it seems that

$160 million, or more than a third, was earmarked for the rehabilitation of Manchuria. Cf. the economic report of the chief of the Manchurian regional government in *New China Monthly,* Vol. II, No. 2, p. 339, Peking, June, 1950.

24. Cf. *Economic Bulletin,* No. 276, p. 1, Hongkong, June, 1952, and Nos. 290-291, p. 34, September, 1952, and *Economic Yearbook,* p. 48, Hongkong, 1952.

25. Li Shou-ts'u, "Shanghai's Foreign Trade in the Last Three Years," *Economic Weekly,* No. 39, Shanghai, October, 1952.

26. Roughly the same situation existed in 1947 as in 1936, but exports were rather distorted in that year because of the inflation and disruption of production. Communist China will probably try to increase its exports of manufactured products to such countries as Indo-China and Indonesia.

27. *Ta-kung pao,* Tientsin, June 21, 1954.

28. *Ibid.* See also *Economic Bulletin,* No. 25, p. 4, Hongkong, 1952.

29. This point was stressed in a special directive of the Ministry of Foreign Trade in October, 1953.

30. For the indirect effect of the embargo on Communist China's foreign trade see below.

31. One report has put the price of rubber at 80 per cent of the world market price. According to another report, the price of rice was 34 per cent lower. See *Wen-hui pao,* Hongkong, August 29 and September 27, 1953.

32. In the 1950 Sino-Soviet agreement, valuation of imports under the Soviet loan, as well as that of Chinese exports in repayment, was to be made on the basis of world prices. How this has worked out in practice has not been reported so far.

33. Report of the Asia Bureau, Ministry of Foreign Affairs, April 1, 1954.

34. There have been some reports that Chinese products can sometimes be obtained by Western importers more cheaply from eastern Europe than from Communist China direct, which seems to suggest low export prices to eastern Europe.

35. The diminishing importance of Hongkong in Communist China's foreign trade does not really reduce Hongkong's economic usefulness to Communist China seriously. Consequently, one might be justified in deducing from this the conclusion, which is probably comforting to many diverse interests, that the existence of Hongkong as a British colony would continue to be unaffected in the immediate future. First, trade with Hongkong has since 1952 yielded an export surplus in favor of Communist China. Since Hongkong has a free foreign exchange market, this export surplus can be used to help pay for Chinese imports from all other countries in all currency areas. Second, a preponderant part of Communist China's exports to Hongkong consists of foodstuffs and other commodities for consumption in Hongkong by the local population. This source of foreign exchange supply, which cannot be replaced by any other visible source, would disappear if Hongkong became a part of Communist China.

36. Where such time limit was set as in North China and, in the case of foreign exchange deposits derived from other than foreign currencies surrendered and remittances from overseas Chinese residents, also in South China, 40 days were the usual rule.

37. From the very beginning foreign currencies have been quoted by the official exchange control at a discount of about 10 per cent below telegraphic transfers.

38. This took place in the week ending August 10, 1950, when the weekly average market rate stood at HK$177 per ¥1 million against an official rate of HK$202.

39. During the period of hyperinflation, exchange depreciation generally went further than the rise of commodity prices, which was at least partly responsible for the continuation of exchange appreciation beyond the period of falling prices when hyperinflation came to an end.

40. According to the Tientsin *Ta-kung pao,* May 24, 1953, the proportion of industrial equipment and supplies in total imports from the Soviet Union to Sinkiang rose from 30 per cent in 1950 to 70 per cent in 1952.

41. At the time the 1950 Sino-Soviet Pact of Friendship, Alliance, and Mutual Assistance was signed (February 14, 1950), the Soviet Union agreed to return to Communist China 18 barracks, warehouses, and other establishments in Peking, as well as a large number of factories and other installations in Dairen and elsewhere in Manchuria. If these do not represent all the assets that might later be returned, the volume of capital "repatriation" may increase further. See *New China Monthly,* No. 17, p. 1063, Peking, March, 1951.

42. W. W. Rostow, *The Prospects for Communist China,* p. 192, Cambridge, 1954.

CHAPTER FOURTEEN

Conclusion

There is no denying the fact that, economically, a great deal has been accomplished by Communist China in a short span of six years. Moreover, what has been done economically has been carried out for a relentless political purpose. Revolutionary changes have already taken place in the form and spirit of economic organization, the distribution of wealth, the division of the national product between consumption and investment, the geographical distribution of industry, and the reorientation of the country's economic relations with the rest of the world. All this has been done in order to make China into an industrialized and socialistic society *and* to bolster the Communist Party's control over the country. Given the dual purpose of economic transformation for the society and greater political power for the Communist Party, not the least remarkable are the logic and purposefulness with which the various economic measures have been adopted, revised, and pursued. Equally notable, however, are the frequent conflicts between the two objectives and the difficulties and failures encountered, because the increasingly ruthless control has tended to generate resistance, stifle initiative, breed inefficiency, and create a ponderous, overdeveloped administrative machinery which at times threatens to break down altogether.

The experience of Communist Chinese economic development means many things to many people. To the student of economic development in underveloped countries Communist China's economic recovery since 1949 and its present program of industrialization contain some lessons which are so obvious that one is only too prone to forget their basic validity and import. The rapid recovery between 1949 and 1952 once more testifies to the resilience of most economic systems once war and galloping inflation are removed from the scene. The fluctuation in agricultural production in response to price changes is another convincing demonstration of the power of the economic incentive. The evolution of the system and method of economic planning and business management reconfirms the conviction among most economists today that the allocation of resources among different productive activities cannot be meaningful without the assistance of the price system even though prices as such may be tampered with by the government, and that the rate of return to investment is a sensitive barometer for enterpreneurship. Communist Chinese planners have clearly demonstrated that like all practicing planners they have come to appreciate the fact that there must be "plans of balances" as well as plans for individual enterprises, and that the most disturbing influence in overall planning is the unpredictability of the individual. In its attempt to force the pace of industrialization, Communist China has also shown that for an under-developed country capital accumulation without foreign investment is a painful process and that the country's ability to pull itself up by its own boot straps is largely a function of totalitarian control. To some of the Communists it may have come as a rude shock to learn that the way to translate an exportable agricultural surplus into capital goods import is by no means to be found simply in bilateral trading schemes, even when these are fortified by state monopolies, on the one hand, and the political "solidarity" of the working class and of the oppressed peoples of former colonial territories on the other. Foreign technical assistance is indispensable, but it is also not enough. Moreover, technical dependence on a foreign power can be equally detrimental to the maintenance of national control.

The experience of Communist China has also thrown some interesting light on the techniques of control. For one thing, it clearly shows that redistribution of land ownership in the name of social justice may only be the opening wedge for extending organized party supervision over the peasantry. Similarly, use of the trade union movement as an instrument of all-pervasive control over industrial workers and other organized groups is another example to be noted. The extension of overall economic control, especially in the regulation of investment and consumption, points to the key role played by bankers in the economy, and hence the priority accorded to them in socialization. Businessmen whose principal activity is trading may also ponder over the fact that in under-developed countries like Communist China conversion of trading capital to industrial capital is considered more than desirable. In short, wherever transition to socialism is advocated as a gradual process, so gradual as to be painless, in the light of developments in Communist China, it would henceforth behoove many people to be less gullible and to indulge in less wishful thinking than it has been their wont.

One of the less obvious lessons which Communist China has taught us is that, given a large population, the employment of forced labor on labor-intensive projects can be a means to increase the social overhead capital and hence future production. Moreover, stripped of human and moral considerations, an authoritarian state can look upon labor as an exportable article not in the ordinary sense of voluntary or even planned emigration, but as an item of current export. This possibility, however, is predicated upon the existence of a foreign demand for such labor, which tends inevitably to narrow down the range of countries open to this trade.

The national product can be augmented only through increases in the employment and supply of factors of production and/or in their productivity. Communist China has attempted to bring this about in many ways. However, in simultaneously attempting to channel the production and disposition of the national product along certain lines which the population would not have chosen voluntarily and in trying to do too much too soon, Communist China has also had to introduce progressively more and stricter controls. In certain aspects, at any rate, government intervention and the control system as such have now become an obstacle to development. The system of banking and monetary control over the productive apparatus, the intense regimentation of workers, and the cooperativization of agriculture are cases in point. This dilemma would not be a serious one but for the fact that while controls could theoretically be modified, the possibility is ruled out in practice because the enforcement of economic controls is inextricably involved in the consolidation of the fundamental position of the Communist Party. Even though overregimentation may affect the worker's efficiency, the Party demands that his loyalty be closely checked. While resistance to cooperativization may sap the peasant's initiative, the Party demands that every possible re-emergence of a "rich peasant" class must be nipped in the bud. Although meticulous financial control by the government banks tends to slow down production, the Party's interest is best served only when the reins of control can be centralized in every phase of economic activity. The Communist Party may well realize that in the long run it will suffer from this overextension of control. However, since the Party must also maintain itself in power in the short run, short-term considerations tend always to appear more urgent and the inevitable trend is towards more control, instead of less.

Notwithstanding the impressive forward strides Communist China has made so far in increasing production and in shaping the economic life of the people according to the dictates of government policy, there are some serious and even glaring deficiencies on the economic scene. In the field of heavy industry, machinery manufacturing, cement and construction materials, chemicals, and the non-ferrous metals are little more than infant industries by any modern standard. The supply of coal and electric power is barely able to meet the country's current demand, while domestic production of petroleum products is altogether negligible. Although the iron and steel industry has virtually fully recovered from the effects of Soviet devastation in Manchuria, it is in no position to meet any extraordinary increase in demand such as might be expected in a modern war. Besides, in spite of attempts to develop new industrial areas, modern industry in Communist China is still concentrated in a few centers, and the development of industry elsewhere necessitates the maintenance of an efficient transportation system. Similarly, control of consumption through rationing cannot be effective unless unimpeded commodity movement can be maintained. Yet to meet this demand Communist China has only a railway system which, except in Manchuria, has some notable bottlenecks both with respect to the network itself and with respect to available rolling stock. At the same time, highway transportation offers only limited possibilities because of the shortage of both fuel and vehicles, while inland river transportation is subject to the limitations of geography. The Communist monetary system, though exhibiting outward stability, depends for the suppression of inflation upon the government's continued success in mopping up excess income and in controlling the expenditure of the public. The government budget, while showing a nominal surplus from year to year, is by no means in balance and has to rely on extraordinary means to supplement normal revenue. The foreign exchange black market, of limited proportions so far, may well erupt into uncontrollable fury if open inflation is resumed or if the international political climate becomes less favorable. Thus, like a tight-rope walker, suspended in mid-air and with a long way to go, Communist China has been barely successful in maintaining a precarious balance. It is in no position to engage in any foolhardy adventure that might provoke an external adversary into retaliatory action which could easily throw the economy into chaos.

There is no doubt that the Communist Chinese economy cannot support the demand on its resources that an all-out war would make. In view of the extremely realistic and rational conduct of the Communists in their economic affairs, one might venture the guess that Communist China would not run the risk of open war except with Soviet support[1] and perhaps only at the bidding of the Soviet Union. Although the Korean adventure did not cripple the country's economic life, it did not do so only because fighting was limited to relatively short periods, and the domestic economy was not subjected to any physical destruction. Even then the budget difficulties of 1951 and 1952 were admittedly phenomenal, and the Five Year Plan might not have been launched had the war continued. While it is true that the war threat and the call to patriotic duty may be used as a spur to greater production, it is nevertheless important to realize that such an incentive is most effective only when the threat does not become a reality. Accordingly, from the economic point of view, while Communist Chinese propaganda may blow hot and cold, the Communist Chinese government is most unlikely to embark upon a real trial of strength with the West.

All this is not to say that the challenge of Communist China can be discounted, or that the material base of its military capability may not expand at an increasing rate. While the West has little cause to fear Communist China, it also has no cause for complacency. Technological changes may radically alter our present assessment of the status of different industries, while the accelerated pace of industrialization, given adequate assistance from the Soviet Union, may change the Chinese economic structure in an unrecognizable manner within a measurable span of time. Left to itself, unmolested, if not actively helped by those countries which it regards as its implacable, ideological enemy, the regime will not collapse of its own accord. However inefficient and ultimately corruptible, the system of control Communist China has built up cannot be lightly dismissed. It may not stand the test of time when we think in terms of centuries, but it will probably endure when we think in terms of decades. Unless the weaknesses are exploited by its opponents relentlessly, there is little hope for an immediate, nationwide, and spontaneous collapse, at any rate not on purely economic grounds. On the other hand, if the weaknesses are effectively exploited, serious disruptions of the economy can conceivably be brought about, and even a ruthless regime may fall.

To repeat, the present greatest challenge of Communist China is not a military one, paradoxical as this may sound. The military threat becomes serious only in those areas adjacent to China where there is no will to resist and where political infiltration is possible. However, even then this is true only if Communist China is allowed a respite from external pressure in other areas. A far greater challenge posed by Communist China is the fact that the economic system and pattern of development it offers may appear to point to an effective way for industrialization and for the enhancement of national prestige under an all-powerful government. If not understood in its true light, the example of Communist China may appear all too glittering. If an effective alternative is not presented by the non-Communist countries, the remaining underdeveloped countries of Asia and elsewhere may be led to believe, albeit erroneously, that there is no other alternative. We have tried in this book to bring to light some of the circumstances which have enabled the Chinese Communists to attain a limited measure of success. It remains for the statesmen and the citizens of non-Communist countries to show that an equally effective and far more palatable pattern of economic development can become a reality, especially in areas close to Communist China.

Finally, it should be noted that, economically speaking, the dependence of Communist China on the Soviet Union, in spite of the small material aid the latter has so far proffered, is complete. Under such conditions, independent political action on the part of Communist China, even if ideologically possible, is practically unthinkable. Chinese Titoism, a fond hope of wishful thinkers, can hardly develop when the very life of the country's industrialization program and economic activity could be seriously crippled before any such deviationist movement can take shape.

There is no logical reason why one should oppose a program of rapid industrialization necessitating the reduction of consumption if such is the voluntary choice of the population, and if the population retains the unchallenged right to change its mind. But where there is no such guarantee, it would appear eminently prudent not to indulge in an experiment that imposes sacrifice on the population without its consent. As these remarks show, in the ultimate analysis, our criticism of Communist China cannot stop at the methods it uses to achieve the ends chosen by its self-appointed rulers. Our basic objection aims at the ends themselves, especially the manner in which self-perpetuation of the Party in power has taken precedence over the people's welfare as defined and understood by the people themselves as well as the subordination of the individual to the state in every phase of human activity. However, the economist must abdicate to the political philosopher at this point because, in the scale of values and matters of philosophical conviction, there is no such thing as an infallible logic.

It is perfectly possible that others who study the development of Communist China may arrive at conclusions different from ours. We submit, however, that these conclusions, tentative as they are, will at least give us cause to ponder.

NOTES

1. Dependence on the Soviet Union for supplies of heavy arms and liquid fuels makes this inevitable.

Appendix

A SELECTED BIBLIOGRAPHY

A number of bibliographies on China in general, and Communist China in particular, have been published in the last few years. The following selected bibliography is not meant to duplicate or supercede these. Instead we have concentrated primarily on publications dealing with the economy and other immediately related areas. Part one of the bibliography contains books, periodicals, pamphlets, newspapers and various *ad hoc* publications which should be consulted by serious students of the Communist Chinese economy. In the case of Chinese language sources, both the English translations and the original Chinese titles, which are romanized according to the Wade-Giles system, are given. Since many of the Chinese sources have been referred to in the text where only the corresponding English translations are used, we have departed from the usual practice by listing the English translations first so as to facilitate identification by the reader. Moreover, since many Communist publications are actually compilations of government documents and/or articles by individual authors and are issued by different branches of the same official press, the official issuing agency has been omitted in many cases so as to simplify the listing. Pre-1949 government publications issued in Nanking or Chungking are of Nationalist Chinese origin while those published in Peking or elsewhere during or after 1949 are issued by the Communist authorities. No date is given in the case of periodicals and newspapers which it is believed are still being published. Part two of the bibliography consists of articles primarily in English and other western languages which frequently, though not exclusively, offer information bearing on individual localities and/or problems. They have been selected to aid those students of the Chinese economy who do not read the Chinese language, but who nevertheless wish to obtain some detailed information on individual regions and problems often not available in books. Both parts of the bibliography should be consulted by the serious reader although it should be clearly understood that some useful items may have been left out quite unintentionally.

PART 1

All-China Federation of Labor, Finance Department, *Financial Work in Trade Unions (Kung-hui ts'ai-wu kung-tso wen-ta),* Peking 1953

Allen, G. C., *Western Enterprise in Far Eastern Economic Development — China and Japan,* New York 1954

Annals of the American Academy, Philadelphia

Asia Bureau, Foreign Ministry, Government of Japan, *"Chiyo no 1954 nen kokka yosan (The 1954 Budget of Communist China),* Tokyo 1954

——————, *1953 nendo Chugoku keizai gaikan (1953 Economic Report on China),* Tokyo 1954

Association of Chinese Workers, *The Wage Struggle in Shanghai (Shanghai ti kung-tzu tou-cheng),* Hongkong 1947

Atlas of the People's Republic of China (Chung-hua jen-min kung-ho kuo fen-sheng ti-t'u), revised edition, Shanghai 1953

Aziya kenkyu (Research on Asia), Vol. 1, No. 1, Tokyo 1954

Barnett, Robert W., *Economic Shanghai: Hostage to Politics, 1937–1941,* New York 1941

Blanchard, S. S., *Textile Industries of China and Japan,* New York 1944

Buck, John Lossing, *An Agricultural Survey of Szechwan,* New York 1943

——————, *Chinese Farm Economy,* Shanghai and Chicago 1930

——————, *Land Utilization in China,* Chicago 1937

——————, *Some Basic Agricultural Problems of China,* New York 1947

Bureau of Information, *The Cement Industry (Shui-ni kung-yeh),* Nanking 1947

——————, *Coal (Mei),* Nanking 1947

——————, *The Customs Administration (Kuan cheng),* Nanking 1947

——————, *The Distribution and Reserves of Tungsten, Antimony and Tin (Wu, t'i, hsi ti fen-pu chi ch'u-liang),* Nanking 1947

——————, *The Electric Industry (Tien-ch'i shih-yeh),* Nanking 1947

——————, *Engineering Plan of the Yangtze Gorges (Ch'ang-chiang san-hsia shui-li kung-ch'eng chi-hua),* Nanking 1947

——————, *Farm Irrigation in Recent Years (Chin-nien lai ti nung-t'ien shui-li),* Nanking 1947

——————, *Iron and Steel (Kang t'ieh),* Nanking 1947

——————, *The National Highway Network of China (Kuo-tao wang),* Nanking 1947

——————, *Petroleum (Shih yu),* Nanking 1947

——————, *Postwar Railway Plan of the First Period (Chan-hou ti-i-ch'i t'ieh-tao chi-hua),* Nanking 1947

——————, *The Textile Industry (Fang-chih kung-yeh),* Nanking 1947

Bureau of Statistics, *A Statistical Analysis of Tenancy in China (Chung-kuo t'u-ti wen-t'i chih t'ung-chi fen-hsi)*, 2nd edition, Chungking 1946

Bureau of Statistics Bulletin (Kuo-chia t'ung-chi chü kung-pao), Peking 1954

Bureau of Statistics, *Statistical Yearbook of the Republic of China (Chung-hua min-kuo t'ung-chi nien-chien)*, Nanking 1948

Business Accountability (Ching-chi ho-suan chih), Peking 1950

Capital Construction (Chi-pen chien-she), Shen-yang 1950

Carr-Saunders, Sir Alexander M., *World Population; Past Growth and Present Trends*, Oxford 1936

Central Bank of China Bulletin (Weekly), Nanking, up to 1949

Central Bank of China Monthly (Chung-yang ying-hang yüeh-pao), Shanghai, up to 1949

Central Health Research Institute, Department of Nutrition, *Food Composition Tables (Shih-wu ch'eng-fen piao)*, Shanghai 1952

Ceylon News Letter, Colombo

Chang, Kia-ngau (Chang Chia-ao), *China's Struggle for Railway Development*, New York 1943

Ch'ang-chiang jih-pao she, *Handbook for Newspaper Readers (Tu pao shou-ts'e)*, Hankow 1950

Chao, Kuo-chün, *Current Agrarian Reform Policies in Communist China*, Philadelphia 1951

————, *Northeast China (Manchuria) Today*, Cambridge, Massachusetts 1953

Chao, Tseng-chüeh, *Postwar Reconstruction of Communications (Chan-hou chiao-t'ung chien-she kai-lun)*, Shanghai 1947

Chao, Yung-seen, *Railways in Communist China*, Hongkong 1955

Ch'en, Han-seng, *Gung Ho*, New York 1947

————, *Industrial Capital and the Chinese Peasant*, Shanghai 1939

Ch'en, Hsün-huan, *Development of China's Water Resources (Chung-kuo shui-li tzu-yüan k'ai-fa t'u-ching)*, Taipeh, 1952

Ch'en, Po-ta, *Land Rent in Modern China (Chin-tai Chung-kuo ti-tsu kai-k'uang)*, Shantung 1948

————, *On Industrial and Commercial Policy (Kuan-yü kung-shang-yeh ti cheng-ts'e)*, Hongkong 1948

Ch'en, Ta, *Population in Modern China*, Chicago 1946

Cheng Pao She, *The Chinese Communist Party and the Land Revolution (Chung-kuo kung-ch'an-tang yü t'u-ti ko-ming)*, Hongkong (no date)

Cheng, Tsu-yüan, *An Analysis of Communist China's Financial and Economic Policy (Chung-kung ts'ai-ching cheng-ts'e t'ou-shih)*, Hongkong 1952

———, *Anshan Steel Factory in Communist China,* Hongkong 1955

———, *Monetary Affairs of Communist China,* Hongkong 1954

———, *The New Tendencies of the Chinese Communists' Financial and Economic Policies (Chung-kung ts'ai-ching cheng-ts'e hsin tung-hsiang),* Hongkong 1953

Chi, Ch'ao-ting, *Key Economic Areas in Chinese History,* London 1936

Ch'i, Yü, *New China's Railway Construction (Hsin Chung-kuo ti t'ieh-tao chien-she),* Peking 1953

Ch'iao, C. M., *China's Food and Population Problem (Chung-kuo jen-k'ou yü shih-liang wen-t'i),* Shanghai 1937

Chin, Chia-feng, *Transportation Development and Trends in China (Chung-kuo chiao-t'ung chih fa-chan chi ch'i ch'ü-hsiang),* Shanghai 1937

Chin, I-hung, *China's Industrialization, A Communist Fantasy (Chung-kung kung-yeh hua Chung-kuo ti mi-meng),* Hongkong 1952

———, *Communist China's Land Reform and China's Land Problem (Chung-kung t'u-kai yü Chung-kuo t'u-ti wen-t'i),* Hongkong 1950

———, *Land Rent and Ownership (Ti-tsu yü ti-ch'üan),* Hongkong 1951

Chin, Shih-hsüan, *Railway Transportation (T'ieh-tao yün-shu hsüeh),* Shanghai 1948

China Agriculture Bulletin (Chung-kuo nung-yeh) (Monthly), Peking

China Committee for the Promotion of International Trade, *China and the Moscow International Economic Conference (Mo-ssu-k'o kuo-chi ching-chi hui-i yü Chung-kuo)* (no place, no date)

China Handbook Editorial Board (comp.), *China Handbook 1953–1954,* Taipeh 1953

———, *China Handbook 1952–1953,* New York 1952

China Monthly Review, Shanghai, up to 1953

China News Service News Releases (Chung-kuo hsin-wen she tien-hsün), Peking

China Quarterly, Shanghai, up to 1941

China Reconstructs (Bimonthly), Peking

China Weekly (Tsu-kuo chou-k'an), Hongkong

China Weekly Review, Shanghai, up to 1939

China Wins Economic Battles, Peking 1950

China's Forestry (Chung-kuo lin-yeh) (Monthly), Peking

China's Industry (Chung-kuo kung-yeh) (Monthly), Shanghai

Chinese Economic Journal (Monthly), Nanking, up to 1937

Chinese Finance (Chung-kuo chin-yung) (Monthly), Peking

Chinese Workers (Chung-kuo kung-jen) (Monthly), Peking

Chinese-Yearbook (Chung-hua nien-chien), Nanking 1948

Chinese Youth Journal (Chung-kuo ch'ing-nien) (Monthly), Peking

Ching-chi tao-pao she, *New Accomplishments of China's Economic Construction in 1954 (I-chiu-wu-ssu nien tsu-kuo chien-she ti hsin ch'eng-chiu),* Hongkong 1954

——————, *The New Achievement of Economic Reconstruction in China (Tsu-kuo ching-chi chien-she ti hsin ch'eng-chiu),* Hongkong 1953

——————, *Economic Yearbook (Ching-chi nien-pao),* Hongkong 1949, 1950, 1951, 1952, 1953, 1954, 1955

Chou, En-lai, *Report to the National People's Congress (Cheng-fu kung-tso pao-kao),* Peking 1954

Chu, Shih-huang, *Economic History of the Republic of China (Min-kuo ching-chi shih),* Shanghai 1948

Chuang, P'u-ming, *China's Progress in Industrialization (Tsu-kuo tsai kung-yeh hua ti tao-lu shang ch'ien-chin),* Peking 1954

Chugoko keizai nenpo—chugoku soran (Chinese-Economic Yearbook—An Overall View of China), Tokyo 1954

Clark, Colin, *Conditions of Economic Progress,* second edition, London 1951

Collective Contracts (Chi-t'i ho-t'ung), Peking 1950

Committee for Free Asia (Asia Foundation), *Bulletin,* San Francisco

The Communist Chinese Problem (Chung-kung wen-t'i), Hongkong 1954

Compendium of Central Government Financial and Economic Regulations (Chung-yang ts'ai-ching cheng-ts'e fa-ling hui-pien), Peking 1951, 1952

Compendium of Financial and Economic Regulations in East China (Hua-tung ch'ü ts'ai-cheng ching-chi fa-ling hui-pien), Shanghai 1951

Compendium of Important Documents on Land Reform (T'u-ti kai-ko chung-yao wen-hsien hui-chi), Peking 1951

Constitution of the Trade Union in the People's Republic of China (Chung-hua jen-min kung-ho-kuo kung-hui chang-ch'eng), Peking 1953

Control of the Hwai River (Chih huai), Shanghai 1952

Cressey, George B., *China's Geographic Foundation,* New York 1934

Daily News (Hsin-wen jih-pao), Shanghai

The Development of Upland Areas in the Far East, New York 1949

Documents Concerning Rationalization Proposals (Ho-li hua chien-i yu-kuan wen-chien), Shanghai 1951

Documents Concerning Trade Union Organizatiion (Kung-hui tsu-chih kung-tso yu-kuan wen-chien), Shanghai 1951

Draft Constitution of the People's Republic of China (Chung-hua jen-min kung-ho-kuo hsien-fa ts'ao-an), Peking 1954

Economic and Financial Commission, *Compendium of Central Government Financial and Economic Policy Directives and Regulations*
Economic Bulletin (Ching-chi tao-pao) (Weekly), Hongkong
Economic Review (Ching-chi p'ing-lun) (Weekly), Shanghai, up to 1949
Economic Weekly (Ching-chi chou-pao), Shanghai
The Economist (Weekly), London
Enlightment Daily (Kuang-ming jih-pao), Peking
Experience in Basic Level Union Work (Chi-ts'eng kung-hui kung-tso ching-nien tien-ti chieh-shao), Shanghai 1951
Fan, Ch'ing-p'ing, *The Industrial Economy of Communist China (Chung-kung kung-yeh ching-chi yao-lun),* Hongkong 1953
Fang, Fang, *Several Problems of the Present Agrarian Movement (Tang-ch'ien nung-min yün-tung ti chi ko wen-t'i),* Canton 1951
The Far East Yearbook, Tokyo 1941
Far Eastern Economic Review (Weekly), Hongkong
Far Eastern Quarterly, New York
Far Eastern Survey (Fortnightly), New York
Fei, Hsiao-t'ung, *Peasant Life in China,* London 1939
Fitzgerald, Charles Patrick, *Revolution in China,* London 1952
Fong, H. D., *China's Cotton Textile Industry (Chung-kuo chih mien-fang-chih yeh),* Shanghai 1934
————, *The Postwar Industrialization of China,* Washington, D. C., 1942
————, *The Tientsin Carpet Industry,* Tientsin 1929
For a Lasting Peace, for a People's Democracy (Cheng-ch'ü ch'ih-chiu ho-p'ing, cheng-ch'ü jen-min min-chu) (Weekly), Peking
Foreign Trade Handbook (Tui-wai mou-i shou-ts'e), Canton 1951
Forward Look (Chan wang) (Monthly), Peking
Fu, Jun-hua and Yüeh-sheng T'ang, *China's Industry and Commerce (Chung-kuo kung-shang yao-lan),* Nanking 1948
Fukien Daily (Fu-chien jih-pao), Fu-chou
Geological Survey of China, *General Statement on the Mining Industry* (7th issue, 1935–1942), Chungking 1945
Government of Hongkong, *Hongkong Government Gazette,* Hongkong
A Guide to New China (second revised edition), Peking 1952
A Guide to New China (third revised edition), Peking 1953
Handbook on Capital Construction (Chi-pen chien-she shou-ts'e) (second edition), Peking 1953
Ho, Yü-wen, *An Analysis of Communist China's Finance (Chung-kung ts'ai-cheng chieh-p'o),* Hongkong 1953
Hongkong Industrial and Commercial Annual Review (Hsiang-kang kung-shang nien-pao), Hongkong 1952

Hsia, Ronald, *The Role of Labor-Intensive Investment Projects in China's Capital Formation,* Cambridge, Massachusetts 1954

Hsiao, Chi-jung, *Revenue and Disbursement of Communist China,* Hongkong 1954

Hsin min-chu ch'u-pan-she, *Land Policy in Newly Liberated Areas (Lun hsin chieh-fang-ch'ü t'u-ti cheng-ts'e),* Hongkong 1949

Hsin, Ying, *The Foreign Trade of Communist China,* Hongkong 1954

———, *The Price Problems of Communist China,* Hongkong 1954

Hsü, Ti-hsin, *The Economy of the New Democracy (Hsin min-chu chu-i ti ching-chi),* Hongkong 1949

Hu, Wei-po, *Copper, Lead, and Zinc in China (Chung-kuo ti t'ung, ch'ien, hsin),* Peking 1953

Important Documents of the Chinese Communist Party since 1947 (I-chiu-ssu-ch'i nien i lai Chung-kuo kung-ch'an-tang chung-yao wen-chien chi), Hongkong 1949

The Important Documents of the First Plenary Session of the Chinese People's Political Consultative Conference, Peking 1949

Industrial and Commercial News (Kung-shang hsin-wen) (Daily and Weekly), Shanghai

Industrial Labor Heroes in the Central South (Chung-nan kung-yeh lao-tung mu-fan), Hankow 1950

Industry and Commerce Daily (Kung-sheung yat-pao; Kung-shang jih-pao), Hongkong

Industry and Commerce in Shanghai (Shang-hai kung shang) (Daily), up to 1953

Industry in Liberated Tientsin (Chieh-fang hou ti T'ien-chin kung-yeh), Shanghai 1950

International Monetary Fund, *Balance of Payments Yearbook,* Washington, D. C.

Ito Tashio, *Chukyo Tetsudo no genjo (The Present Condition of Communist China's Railways),* Tokyo 1954

Japan-Manchoukuo Yearbook, Tokyo 1941

Kann, E., *The History and Financing of China's Railways,* Shanghai 1937

Ko, Lin, *Agricultural Credit (Nung-ts'un chin-yung kung-tso),* Shanghai 1953

Kunming Highway Research Laboratory, *Highway Journal* (Kung-lu *ts'ung-k'an),* Kunming 1942

Labor Daily (Lao-tung pao), Shanghai

Labor Insurance, Questions and Answers (Lao-tung pao-hsien kung-tso wen-ta), Peking 1953

Labor Insurance Regulations of the People's Republic of China (Chung-hua jen-min kung-ho kuo lao-tung pao-hsien t'iao-li), Peking 1953

Labor Movement in Shanghai after the Liberation (Chieh-fang hou Shang-hai kung-yün tzu-liao), Shanghai 1950

Land Reform Monthly (T'u-kai yüeh-k'an), Taipeh

Lectures on Wages (Kung-tzu ch'ang-shih chiang-hua), Shanghai 1952

Li, Chi and others, *New China's Progress towards Industrialization (Hsin Chung-kuo hsiang kung-yeh-hua mai-chin),* Hongkong 1954

Li, K. C. and C. Y. Wang, *Tungsten, Its History, Geology, Ore-dressing, Metallurgy, Chemistry, Analysis, Applications and Economics,* New York 1947

Liberation Daily (Chieh-fang jih-pao), Shanghai

Li T'ien-min, *A Factual Account of Communist China's Destruction of Human Rights in the Last Five Years (Chung-kung p'o-hai jen-ch'üan chi-shih),* Taipeh 1955

Lin, W. Y., *China and Foreign Capital,* Chungking 1945

————, *The New Monetary System of China,* Shanghai 1936

Ling, Chu-ke, *China's Railway Rolling Stock; a Study of Postwar Purchase,* Seattle 1946

Ling, Hung-hsün, *General Survey of Railways in China (Chung-kuo t'ieh-lu kai-lun),* Taipeh (?) 1950

Liu, Ta-chün (D. K. Lieu), *China's Economic Stabilization and Reconstruction,* New Brunswick 1948

————, *Growth and Industrialization of Shanghai,* Shanghai 1936

Liu Ta-chung, *The National Income of China,* Washington, D. C. 1946

Ma, Chi, *China's Forests (Chung-kuo ti sen-lin),* Shanghai 1952

Manchuria's Resources and Chemical Industry (Tung-san-sheng wu-chan tzu-yüan yü hua-hsüeh kung-yeh), Shanghai 1936

Mao, Shou-chin, *Common Sense on Highways (Kung-lu ch'ang-shih),* Shanghai 1951

Mao, Tse-tung, *Collected Works (Mao Tse-tung hsüan chi),* Peking 1952

————, *The Current Situation and Our Task (Mu-ch'ien hsing-shih ho wo-men ti jen-wu)* (no place), 1949

————, *The New Democracy (Hsin min-chu chu-i lun),* Yenan 1940

————, *The People's Democratic Dictatorship (Lun jen-min min-chu chuan-cheng),* Peking 1949

Maritime Customs of China, *Annual Returns of the Foreign Trade of China,* Shanghai 1931–1936

Masses Daily (Ch'ün-chung jih-pao), Hsi-an

Ming, I, and others, *A Symposium on the Chinese Communist Regime (Ssu nien lai ti chung-kung cheng-ch'üan),* Hongkong 1953

Ministry of Agriculture, Planning Department, *Survey of Chinese Farm Economy in the Last Two Years (Liang nien lai ti Chung-kuo nung-ts'un ching-chi tiao-ch'a hui-pien),* Shanghai 1952

Ministry of Agriculture, *Reference Sources on Agricultural Co-operatives (Nung-yeh sheng-ch'an ho-tso-she ts'an-k'ao tzu-liao),* Peking 1952

Ministry of Economic Affairs, *Gold Mining Journal, Yunnan and Kweichow (Chin-k'uang ts'ung-k'an, tien-ch'ien chuan hao),* Chungking (no date)

Ministry of Industry, *China's Industry (Chung-kuo shih-yeh chih),* Shanghai 1935

————, *Chinese Economic Yearbook (Chung-kuo ching-chi nien-chien),* Nanking 1933–1934

Ministry of Railways, *Statistics of Chinese National Railways,* Nanking, up to 1937

Ministry of Textile Industry, *Innovation and Improvement in the Textile Industry (Fang-chih kung-yeh ti ch'uang-tsao yü kai-chin),* Peking 1951

Moraes, Frank, *Report on Mao's China,* New York 1953

Mordecai, Ezekiel (ed.), *Towards World Prosperity, through Industrial and Agricultural Development and Expansion,* New York and London 1947

Motor Vehicles and Highways (Ch'i-ch'e ho kung-lu) (Monthly), Shanghai

Nan-fang jih-pao she, *Handbook on Trade With South China (Hua-han mou-i shou-ts'e),* Canton 1950

Nankai Social and Economic Quarterly, Tientsin, up to 1937

National Agricultural Research Bureau, *Crop Reports (Nung-ch'ing pao-kao),* Nanking, up to 1949

National Resources Commission Quarterly (Tzu-yüan wei-yuan-hui chi-k'an), Chungking, Nanking, up to 1949

National Resources Commission, *Summary Report of the Work of the National Resources Commission since Demobilization (Fu-yüan i lai tzu-yüan wei-yüan-hui kung-tso shu-yao),* Nanking 1948

Natural Science (Tzu-jan k'o-hsüeh) (Monthly), Peking

New Accounting (Hsin K'uai-chi) (Monthly), Peking

New China Daily (Hsin-hua jih-pao), Chungking

New China Monthly (Hsin-hua yüeh-pao), Peking

New China News Agency, *Bulletin,* London; Hongkong

————, *News Releases (Hsin-hua she tien-hsün)*

New China's Economic Achievements in the Last Three Years (San nien lai hsin chung-kuo ching-chi ti ch'eng-chiu), Peking 1952

New Construction (Hsin chien-she) (Monthly), Peking

New York Times

New Times (Weekly), Moscow

Ni, Ni, *The Kuan-t'ing Reservoir (Kuan-t'ing shui-k'u),* Shanghai 1954

1950 Report on Government Administration (I-chiu-wu-ling cheng-fu kung-tso pao-kao hui-pien), Peking 1951

North China Textile Journal (Hua-pei fang-chih) (Monthly), Peking

Northeast Agriculture (Tung-pei nung-yeh) (Monthly), Shen-yang

Northeast Daily (Tung-pei jih-pao), Shen-yang

Northeast Industry (Tung-pei kung-yeh) (Monthly), Shen-yang

Northeast Industry Editorial Board, *Handbook for Shop Stewards (Ch'e-chien chu-jen shou-ts'e)* (no place, no date)

Ou, Hui-ch'ing, *Nutrition and Diet (Ying-yang yü shan-shih chi-hua)*, Shanghai 1952

Ou, Pao-san, *China's National Income, 1933 (1933 Chung-kuo kuo-min so-te)*, Shanghai 1947

——————, *National Income of China, 1933, 1936 and 1946*, Nanking 1947

Ouyang, An, *The Ching-chiang Flood Diversion Project (Ching-chiang fen-hung)*, Shanghai 1954

Overseas Chinese Daily (Wah-kiu yat-pao; Hua-ch'iao jih-pao), Hongkong

Paauw, Douglas S., *Chinese Public Finance During the Nanking Government Period* (thesis), Harvard University 1950

The Pacific Economic Research Institute, *Chinese Economic Yearbook (Chung-kuo ching-chi nien-chien)*, Hongkong 1947, 1948

Pacific Spectator (Quarterly), Stanford

A Path for the Industrialists and Businessmen of New China (Hsin Chung-kuo kung-shang yeh chia ti tao-lu), Shanghai 1950

Pauley, Edwin W., *Report on Japanese Assets in Manchuria to the President of the United States*, Washington, D.C. 1946

The Peasant Movement During the First Period of the Revolutionary War (Ti-i-tz'u kuo-nei ko-ming chan-cheng ti nung-min yün-tung), Peking 1953

P'ei, You-ming, *I Came From a Northeast Slave Labor Camp (Wo lai tzu tung-pei nu-kung ying)*, Hongkong 1954

People's China (Monthly), Peking

People's Communications (Jen-min chiao-t'ung) (Monthly), Peking

People's Daily (Jen-min jih-pao), Peking

People's Handbook (Jen-min shou-ts'e), Shanghai 1950, 1951, 1952; Tientsin 1955

People's Pictorial (Jen-min hua-pao) (Monthly), Peking

People's Railways (Jen-min t'ieh-tao) (Monthly), Peking

A Practical Encyclopedia of the National Economy (Kuo-min ching-chi shih-yung tz'u-tien), Shanghai 1953

Pravda

Problems of Communism (Bimonthly), Washington, D.C.

The Productive Construction Bonds (Sheng-ch'an chien-she kung-chai), Shen-yang 1950

Progress Daily (Chin-pu jih-pao), Tientsin

Railway Semi-Monthly (T'ieh-tao pan-yüeh k'an), Nanking, up to 1937

Reference for Study on the "General Line" During the Transition Period (Kuo-tu shih-ch'i tsung-lu-hsien hsüeh-hsi ts'an-kao tzu-liao), Peking 1954

Report of the Third World Power Conference 1936, Washington, D. C. 1938

Robertson, Walter (Assistant Secretary of State), *Testimony Before the House Appropriations Committee, 83rd Congress, on February 23, 1954*

Rostow, W. W., *The Prospects for Communist China,* Cambridge 1954

Science Bulletin (K'o-hsüeh t'ung-pao) (Monthly), Peking

Selected Economic Essays (Ching-chi chuan-k'an lun-wen hsüan), Peking 1951

Selected Press Reports on Economic Construction (Ching-chi chien-she t'ung-hsün pao-kao hsüan), Peking 1954

Shanghai Industry and Commerce (Shang-hai kung-shang) (Monthly), Shanghai

Shansi Daily (Shan-hsi jih-pao), T'ai-yüan

Shen, T. H., *Agricultural Resources of China,* Ithaca 1951

Shih, Kuo-heng, *China Enters the Machine Age,* Cambridge 1944

Singtao Daily (Hsing-tao jih-pao), Hongkong

Sinkiang Daily (Hsin-chiang jih-pao), Ti-hua

Some Problems in Land Reform and Three Model Experiences (T'u-ti kai-ko chung ti chi-ko wen-t'i ho san-ko tien-hsing ching-nien), Tsitsihar 1948

South Manchuria Railway Company, *A Brief Survey of the Manchoukuo State Railways* (second edition), Shen-yang 1936

———, *South Manchuria Railway,* Dairen 1939

Southern Daily (Nan-fang jih-pao), Canton

Statistical Monthly (T'ung-chi yüeh-pao), Nanking 1948

Statistical Work Bulletin (T'ung-chi kung-tso t'ung-hsün) (Monthly), Peking

Strickland, C. F., *Rural Finance and Cooperation,* Shanghai 1937

Study (Hsüeh-hsi) (Monthly), Peking

Su, Wei-ch'üan, *Slave Labor Camps in Northern Shensi (Shan-pei nu-hung ying),* Hongkong 1954

Ta kung pao (Daily), Shanghai (discontinued); Hongkong; Tientsin

Taiheiyo mondai (Problems of the Pacific) (Monthly), Tokyo

Tamagna, F. M., *Banking and Finance in China,* New York 1942

———, *Financial Problems in Postwar China,* New York 1946

T'an, Hsi-hung, *A Preliminary Report on the Industrial Survey of China's Principal Cities (Ch'üan-kuo chu-yao tu-shih kung-yeh tiao-ch'a ch'u-pu pao-kao t'i-yao)*, Nanking 1948

T'ao, Ta-yung, *On the New Economy (Hsin ching-chi lun-ts'ung)*, Peking 1951

————, *On the People's Economy (Jen-min ching-chi lun kang)*, Peking 1951

Tawny, R. H., *Land and Labor in China*, London 1937

Tennien, Mark, *No Secret Is Safe Behind the Bamboo Curtain*, New York 1952

Thirty Years of Chinese Engineering (San-shih nien lai chih Chung-kuo kung-ch'eng) (second edition), Nanking 1948

Ti, Ch'ao-pai, *China's Postwar Agrarian Problem (Chan-hou Chung-kuo nung-min wen-t'i)*, Hongkong 1948

————, *New China's Cooperatives (Hsin Chung-kuo ti ho-tso-she)*, Hongkong 1949

Tientsin Daily (T'ien-chin jih-pao), Tientsin

Tientsin Federation of Trade Unions, Preparatory Commission, *The Labor Movement (Kung yün hui chi)*, Tientsin 1949

Trade Union Work Experience at the Wu-san Factory (Wu-san kung-ch'ang kung-hui kung-tso ching-nien), Peking 1953

T'ung, Ch'eng, *Geological Work and National Reconstruction (Ti-chih kung-tso yü tsu-kuo chien-she)*, Peking 1954

United Nations, *Economic Bulletin for Asia and the Far East*, Bangkok 1953

————, *Economic Survey of Asia and the Far East* (Annual), New York

————, *Statistical Yearbook*, New York

United Nations, Food and Agricultural Organization, *World Food Survey, Washington*, D. C. 1946

United States Bureau of Mines, *Foreign Minerals Survey*, Washington, D. C. 1948

United States Consulate-General in Hongkong, *Current Background*, Hongkong

————, *Review of Hongkong Chinese Press*, Hongkong

————, *Survey of China Mainland Press*, Hongkong

United States Department of Commerce, *Foreign Commerce Yearbook*, Washington, D. C.

United States Department of Commerce, Bureau of Foreign and Domestic Commerce, Far Eastern Unit, *A Brief Survey of Important Industrial and Power Plans in Manchuria*, Washington, D. C. 1942

Urban Policy of the New Democracy (Hsin min-chu chu-i ch'eng-shih cheng-ts'e), Hongkong 1949

Wagner, Augusta, *Labor Legislation in China,* Peking 1938

Wales, Nym, *The Chinese Labor Movement,* New York 1945

Wang, Foh-shen, *China's Industrial Production, 1931–1946, Nanking* 1948

Wang, Hai-ch'i, *The Economy of the New Democracy (Hsin min-chu chu-i ti ching-chi),* Peking 1950

Wang, K. P., *The Mineral Situation in the Far East,* Washington, D. C. 1951

Wang, Kung-ping, *Controlling Factors in the Future Development of the Coal Industry,* New York 1947

Wang, Shou-yung, *The Kuan-t'ing Reservoir (Kuan-t'ing shui-k'u),* Peking 1954

Wang, Tzu-chien and Chen-chung Wang, *A Study of Chinese-owned Cotton Mills in Seven Provinces (Ch'i sheng hua-shang sha-ch'ang tiao-ch'a pao-kao),* Shanghai 1936

Wen-hui Daily (Wen-hui pao), Hongkong

Women Workers in the Trade Union (Kung-hui nü-kung kung-tso), Shanghai 1951

Worker's Daily (Kung-jen jih-pao), Peking

Wu, Wen-hui, *China's Land Problem and Its Solution (Chung-kuo t'u-ti wen-t'i chi ch'i tui-ts'e),* Shanghai 1947

Wu, Yüan-li (Y. L. Wu), *The Land Program of the Chinese Communist Party, an Interpretation,* San Francisco, 1952

————, *China's Postwar Economic Policy—Planning or Free Enterprise,* New York, 1946

Yangtze Daily (Ch'ang-chiang jih-pao), Hankow

Yao, Kung-chen, *Problems of Economic Reconstruction in Chinese Villages (Chung-kuo nung-ts'un ching-chi chien-she wen-t'i), Shanghai* 1953

Yeh, Liang, *Production and Marketing of Textile Products in China (Chung-kuo fang-chih p'in ch'an-hsiao chih),* Shanghai 1935

Young, Arthur N., *China's Economic and Financial Reconstruction,* New York 1947

Yü, Fei-p'eng, *The General Situation of Transportation During the Last Fifteen Years (Shih-wu nien lai chih chiao-t'ung kai-k'uang),* Nanking 1946

PART II

"Achievements of the Chinese People on the Economic Front," *New Times,* 307 (February 7, 14, 1951) 10–13

"Acid and Soda Manufacture," *Chinese Economic Journal,* 12 (1933) 386–393

Alley, Rewi, "An Anhwei Motor Tour," *China Journal,* 25:3 (September 1936) 144–149

———, "Outlook for Small Industry in China," *China Weekly Review,* 117 (May 13, 1950) 181–182

"Alum Deposits at Lukiang, Anhuei," *Chinese Economic Bulletin,* 26 (1935) 214–215

"Alum Industry in Pingyung, Chekiang," *Chinese Economic Bulletin,* 24 (1934) 229–232

"Aluminum Industry Extends Operations in China," *Far Eastern Review,* 29:2 (February 1933) 81–82

"Antimony Mining in Kwangsi Province," *Chinese Economic Bulletin,* 21 (1932) 31–32

"Antimony Production in China," *Chinese Economic Journal,* 12 (1933) 57–64; *Far Eastern Review,* 29:8 (August 1933) 377–378

Avarin, V., "Gosudarstvennoe i khoziaistvennoe stroitel'stvo kitaiskoi Narodnoi Respubliki," *Voprosy ekonomiki* (February 1950) 44–64

Barclay, G. W., "China's Population Problems: A Closer View," *Pacific Affairs,* 23 (June 1950) 184–192

Belden, W. and M. Salter, "Coal Resources of China," *Economic Geography,* 11 (July 1935) 304–306

Beloff, Max, "Manchuria as a Prize," *The Orient* (Hongkong) (June 1951) 36–37

"Bibliography of Antimony, 1917–1924," *Journal of the Association of Chinese-American Engineers,* 6:3 (March 1925) 14–34

"Bibliography of Antimony, 1924–1932," *Journal of the Association of Chinese-American Engineers,* 14:5 (September 1933) 18–50

"Blunders of State-run Industry in China," *Far Eastern Economic Review,* 14:12 (March 19, 1953) 359

Bodde, Derk, "Price Fluctuations in Tientsin, Aug. 1948–Aug. 1949," *Far Eastern Survey,* 19 (April 19, 1950) 78–80

Boldyrev, B., "Finansy, den'gi i kredit na sluzhbe ekonomicheskogo stroitel'stva kitaiskoi Narodnoi Respubliki," *Voprosy economiki* (September 1951), 33–48

Booth, Lionel E., "A Wartime Effort to Boost China's Metal Output: Project for Increasing Production of Copper from Mines in Yunnan Ends with Japan's Surrender," *Engineering and Mining Journal* (Booth Engineers, Salt Lake City), 147 (1946) 84–89

"Brick and Tile Industry," *Chinese Economic Journal and Bulletin,* 18 (1936) 63–75

Brown, H. D. and Li Min Liang, "A Survey of Fifty Farms on the Chengtu Plain, Szechwan," *Chinese Economic Journal,* 2:1 (January 1928) 44–74

Brown, J. C., "The Mines and Minerals of Yunnan," *Far Eastern Review,* 17:4, 6–7 (April, June–July 1921) 248–254, 391–395, 465 467

Buck, John Lossing and C. M. Ch'iao, "Composition and Growth of Rural Population Groups," *Chinese Economic Journal,* 2 (March 1928) 219–236

————, "Fact and Theory about China's Land," *Foreign Affairs* (October 1949)

"Budget of China," *Far Eastern Economic Review,* 14:10 (March 5, 1953)

"Campaign Against Middle Peasant in China," *Far Eastern Economic Review,* 16:1 (January 7, 1954) 4

"Camphor, Its Oil and By-Products in China and Formosa," *Far Eastern Economic Review,* 6 (March 23, 1949) 351–352

Canning, Charles J., "The Future of Shanghai," *China Weekly Review,* 114 (August 13, 1949) 204–205

Cardew, J., "The Oil Industry of China," *Petroleum Times,* 56 (March 21, 1952) 222–223, 226

"Centralization of Imports and Exports in China," *Far Eastern Economic Review,* 8 (March 30, 1950) 413–414

Chang, Betty C., "One Year of Progress in Tientsin," *China Monthly Review* (October, 1950) 58–59

Chang, B. T., "Modern Highways in Chekiang," *Chinese Economic Journal,* 12 (March 1933) 231–240

Chang, C. C., "Geology of the Tin Deposits of Nantanhsien, Kwangsi," *Bulletin, Geologic Survey, China,* 34 (January 1941) 31–34

————, "On Native Copper Deposits in Chao-chuo, Sikang," *Bulletin, Geologic Survey, China,* 24:3–4 (1946) 259–261

Chang, C. C. and P. H. Tan, "Public Works in Peiping," *Journal of the Association of Chinese-American Engineers,* 16:4 (July–August 1935) 193–204

Chang, C. D., "Agrarian Reform in Communist China, the New Agrarian Reform Law," *Far Eastern Economic Review,* 9 (September 7, 1950) 271–274

Chang, C. D., "Rents, Rural Depots and Grain Levies in China," *Far Eastern Economic Review,* 9 (September 7, 1950) 332–334

Chang, Chih-yi, "China's Population Problem: A Chinese View," *Pacific Affairs,* 22 (December 1949) 339–356

————, "Land Utilization and Settlement Possibilities in Sinkiang," *Geographic Review,* 39 (1949) 57–75

Chang, C. M., "Local Government Expenditure in China," *Monthly Bulletin on Economic China,* 7:6 (June 1934) 233–247

————, "Mao's Strategem of Land Reform," *Foreign Affairs* (July 1951) 551–563

———, "Tax Farming in North China," *Nankai Social and Economic Quarterly,* 8:4 (January 1936) 824–852

Chang, D. C. and N. L. Liu, "Antimony Deposits of Chuchianghsien, Kwangtung," *Bulletin, Geologic Survey, Kwangtung and Kwangsi,* 1 (July 1943) 63–81

Chang, George H., "A Brief Survey of Chinese Native Banks," *Central Bank of China Bulletin,* 4:1 (March 1938) 25–32

———, "Economic Conditions in Kansu," *Central Bank of China Bulletin,* 5:1 (March 1939) 33–38

———, "Economic Conditions in Kwangsi," *Central Bank of China Bulletin,* 4:3 (September 1938) 226–240

———, "The Practice of Shanghai Native Banks," *Central Bank of China Bulletin,* 4:4 (December 1938) 310–319

Chang, K., "Native Antimony of Lamo, Nantan, Kwangsi," *Bulletin, Geologic Survey, China,* 21:1 (April 1941) 59–66

Chang, Ke-chung and Hung Y. Chang, "Gasoline from Waste Cotton Seed Oil," *Journal of Chinese Chemical Society,* 2 (1934) 211–215

Chang, Pei-kang, "Role of Agriculture in China's Industrialization," *National Reconstruction Journal,* 6:2 (October 1945) 50–59

Chang, Shan-pao, "The Trust Business in China," *Central Bank of China Bulletin,* 4:4 (December 1938) 300–309

Chang, Shu-chi, "Farm Nursery in Honan," *China Monthly Review* (October 1951) 207–208

Chao, Ching-hsueh, "The Chengtu-Chungking Railway Completed," *People's China,* 14 (July 1952) 26–28

Chao, Ti-sheng and Tung Sheng, "Soviet Experts and China's Economic Construction," *People's China,* 4 (February 16, 1952) 5–7, 31

"Chekiang Power Plants," *Chinese Economic Bulletin,* 22 (February 25, 1933) 108–111

Chen, Chien-ke, "China's Outstanding Financial and Economic Achievements," *People's China,* 4:8 (October 16, 1951) 9–11

Ch'en, Han-seng, "The Agrarian Problem of China," *Problems of the Pacific* (1933) 271–299

Chen, Jack, "New Peking," *People's China,* 4:3 (August 1, 1951) 21–23

Chen, Lawrence M., "Highways in China," *Information Bulletin* (Nanking), 2:8 (1936) 133–154

Chen, P. T., "Foundations of China's Wartime Finance and Economy," *Central Bank of China Bulletin,* 5:3 (September 1939) 209–221

Chen, Ping-tsang, "Public Finance," *Chinese Yearbook 1935–1936* (Shanghai) (1935) 1163–1422

Chen, Po-tah, "How Industry Is Run in Liberated China," *China Digest,* 6:3 (May 17, 1949) 3–4

Ch'en, Ta, "The Labour Policy of the Chinese Government and Its Reactions on Industry and Labour," *International Labour Review,* 4:9 (January 1949) 34–62

Chen, Yun, "Economic Situation and the Readjustment of Industry, Commerce and Taxation, A Report Submitted to the National Committee of P. P. C. C.," *China Weekly Review,* 118 (July 1, 1950) 88–90

————, "Report on China's Financial and Food Situation," *China Weekly Review,* 113 (April 22, 1950) 138–140

————, "Report on Financial and Economic Conditions at the End of the First Year," *China Weekly Review* (November 1950) 107–108

Chesneaux, J., "Reconstruction et réorientation dans la vie économique de la Chine nouvelle," *Annales de géographie,* 60 (March–April 1951) 88–109

Chi, Ch'ao-ting, "China's Foreign Trade," *People's China,* 20 (October 16, 1952) 16–17

Chi, Y. S., "Additional Fossil Corals from the Weiningian Limestones of Hunan, Yunnan and Kwangsi Provinces," *Palaeontology Sinica,* B12:6 (1935) 1–38

————, "Geology of the Chang-hsing Coal Fields, Chekiang Province," *Bulletin, Geologic Survey of China,* 24 (September 1934) 37–45

Ch'iao, C. M., "Rural Population and Vital Statistics," *Chinese Economic Journal,* 14:3 (March–April 1934) 391–425

Chien, Feng, "Northwest Survey," *People's China,* 3 (February 1, 1954) 15–19

"China, Agricultural Tax," *Far Eastern Economic Review,* 15:4 (July 23, 1953) 109

"China—Analysis of Population Census," *Keesing's Contemporary Archives* (January 15–22, 1955. Population. D. China) X (1955–1956) 13999.

"China Is Awake to Its Petroleum Possibilities," *Oil Weekly,* 116:2 (December 11, 1944) 130

"China Is Rich in Oil," *China Reconstructs,* 2 (March–April 1952) 18–19

"China, 1950 Production of Oil," *World Oil,* 133 (July 15, 1951) 242

"China, 1951 Activities," *World Oil,* 135 (July 15, 1952) 216

"China Taxes," *Far Eastern Economic Review,* 14:26 (June 25, 1953) 828

"China's Agriculture Program in 1950," *Far Eastern Economic Review,* 8 (March 2, 1950) 287

"China's Coal Production and Trade," *Chinese Economic Journal,* 20 (1937) 379–397

"China's Finances: Surplus or Deficit," *Far Eastern Economic Review,* 14:17 (April 23, 1953) 536

"China's Grain Problems," *Far Eastern Economic Review,* 14:18 (April 30, 1953) 565

"China's National Budget for 1953," *Far Eastern Economic Review,* 14:11 (March 12, 1953) 329

"China's National Economy," *Far Eastern Economic Review,* 14:21 (May 21, 1953) 661

"China's Public Finance in 1950," *Far Eastern Economic Review,* 8 (March 30, 1950) 412–413

"China's Railroad Network," *Geographic Review,* 41 (July 1951) 470–474

"China's Star, Aniseed Oil," *Far Eastern Economic Review,* 6 (May 4, 1949) 567–568

"China's Tin Production and Export," *Chinese Economic Journal,* 10:4 (1932) 333–340

"China's Tung Oil," *Far East Economic Review,* 7 (December 22, 1949) 813–816

"China's Wool Industry," *Far Eastern Economic Review,* 12:9 (1952) 277

"Chinese Antimony Exports," *Far Eastern Review,* 30:5 (May 1934) 239

"Chinese Engineers and Soviet Experience," *Far Eastern Economic Review,* 14:6 (February 5, 1953) 162

"Chinese Government Loans Outstanding on July 1, 1938," *The Central Bank of China Bulletin,* 4:2 (June 1938)

"Chinese Metals and Minerals," *Far Eastern Economic Review,* 6 (February 2, 1949) 141–142

"Chinese Reserves Still a Mystery," *Petroleum Engineering,* 17:2 (November 1945) 184

"Chinese Tin," *Far Eastern Economic Review,* 7 (July 7, 1949) 15–16

Chong, T. Y., "China on Oil Map," *Mining Journal* (London), 225:5733 (July 7, 1945) 435

————, "Modernization of China's Tin Industry," *Mining Journal* (London), 222:5669 (April 15, 1944) 218

————, "Reviving Copper Mining in China," *Mining Journal* (London), 224:5732 (June 30, 1945) 413

————, "World's Largest Wolfram Mine," *Mining Journal* (London), 222:5672 (May 6, 1944) 262

Chow, C. P., "Pawnshops in Shanghai," *Central Bank of China Bulletin,* 4:3 (September 1938) 185–203

————, "Szechwan, An Economic Survey," *Central Bank of China Bulletin,* 5:4 (December 1939) 323–349

Chow, Hsueh-sheng, "A Private Cotton Mill," *People's China,* 3:3 (December 1, 1950) 19–21

Chu, H. C., "A Review of the Coal Reserve in Hopeh Province," *Mining and Metallurgy,* 24 (1934) 107–110

Chu, Hsueh-fan, "Labour Insurance in New China," *People's China,* 3:9 (May 1, 1951) 6–8

Chu, H. J., "The Copper Deposits of China," *Copper Resources of the World,* 2 (1935) 663–680

———, "The Genesis of Some Copper Deposits in Western Szechwan," *Bulletin, Geologic Survey of China,* 14 (1935) 255–278

Chu, Johnson, "Antimony Production in Hunan," *Chinese Economic Journal,* 17 (1935) 291–305

"Civil Aviation in China," *Far Eastern Economic Review,* 8 (April 13, 1950) 499–500

"Coal and Iron Mines of Szechwan," *Chinese Economic Journal,* 18 (1936) 54–62

"Coal Deposit of Hunan," *Chinese Economic Bulletin,* 27 (1935) 109–117

"Coal Industry of Shansi," *Chinese Economic Bulletin,* 24 (1934) 115–119

"Coal Liquefaction and the South Manchuria Railway Company," *Contemporary Manchuria,* 4:1 (January 1940) 17–27

"Coal Mines in Shantung," *Chinese Economic Bulletin,* 23 (1933) 74–75; 25 (1934) 243–249

"Communications in the Northwest," *Far Eastern Economic Review,* 18:2 (January 13, 1955) 49

"The Communists in Kwangtung," *Far Eastern Economic Review,* 15:25 (December 17, 1953) 782

"Complete Description of the Shanghai Municipal Electricity Plant," *Far Eastern Review,* 25:7 (July 1927) 305–315

"Conditions in China Internal Markets," *Far Eastern Economic Review,* 14:16 (April 23, 1953) 533

"Conditions in Kwangtung," *Far Eastern Economic Review,* 15:24 (December 10, 1953) 147

"Conditions in Shanghai Today," *Orient* (Hongkong) (December 1950) 18–19, 36–38

"Construction Bonds of China," *Far Eastern Economic Review,* 15:26 (December 24, 1953) 818

"Consumption of Gasoline and Kerosene in China," *Chinese Economic Bulletin,* 18 (1931) 131–132

"The Copper Works of Fukien," *Journal of the Association of Chinese-American Engineers,* 6:3 (March 1925) 9–11

"Cost of Living Index Numbers for Shanghai Workers During 1936," *Chinese Economic Journal,* 20:3 (March 1937) 315–318

Cotton, J. S., "Concrete Making in China," *Journal of American Concrete Institute,* 19 (January 1948) 381–398

Cressey, George B., "Changing the Map of China," *Economic Geography,* 31 (January 1955) 1–16

"Crisis on the Land in Kwangtung," *Far Eastern Economic Review,* 14:13 (March 26, 1953) 389

"Current Development in Peking," *Far Eastern Economic Review,* 18:3 (January 20, 1955) 75–76

Dawson, Owen, "Agricultural Policies in Unoccupied China Since 1937," *Foreign Agriculture,* 5:10 (October 1941) 407–422

———, "Agricultural Reconstruction in China," *Foreign Agriculture* (June 1943) 123–134

———, "China's Food Problem," *Foreign Agriculture* (May 1944)

"Defects of State Commercial Bodies in China," *Far Eastern Economic Review,* 15:25 (December 17, 1953) 780

"Difficulties in Peking's Land Policy," *Far Eastern Economic Review,* 14:15 (April 9, 1953) 457

Djang, T. K., "Factory Inspection in China," *International Labour Review,* 50:3 (September 1944) 284–299

———, "Social Policy in China," *International Labour Review,* 52:5 (November 1945) 465–478

———, "Some Problems of Labour Law Enforcement in China," *International Labour Review,* 53:1, 2 (January, February 1946) 39–48

"Domestic Trade of China," *Far Eastern Economic Review,* 14:20 (May 14, 1953) 646

"Economic Changes in China and Taiwan Since 1949," *Far Eastern Economic Review,* 11 (August 30, 1951) 268–270

"Economic Development in China During 1949–1953," *Far Eastern Economic Review,* 17 (August 5, 1954) 11–14

"Economic Development in Manchuria," *Far Eastern Economic Review,* 9 (July 20, 1950) 71–72

"Economic History of China: the Manchus and the Moderns," *Far Eastern Economic Review,* 14:6 (February 5, 1953) 164

"Economic Planning in Peking," *Far Eastern Economic Review,* 8 (April 27, 1950) 546

"Economic Reports from China," *Far Eastern Economic Review,* 16:14 (April 8, 1954) 437

"Economic Reports from North China," *Far Eastern Economic Review,* 8 (January 26, 1950) 109–112

"Economic Situation in Manchuria," *Far Eastern Economic Review,* 9 (August 10, 1950) 158–160

"Economic Situation in Shanghai," *Far Eastern Economic Review,* 9 (October 19, 1950) 475–476

"Economic Transformation of Shanghai," *Far Eastern Economic Review,* 9 (August 17, 1950) 187–188

Egloff, G., "China's Potential Oil Resources Large," *Oil and Gas Journal,* 45:34 (December 28, 1946) 245–246, 248

"Electric Enterprises in China," *Chinese Economic Journal and Bulletin,* 20 (May 1937) 530–542; *Far Eastern Review,* 33:8 (August 1937) 309–312; *Journal of the Association of Chinese-American Engineers,* 18:6 (November–December 1937) 391–405

"Electric Progress in Shantung," *Chinese Economic Bulletin,* 25 (September 22, 1934) 199

Electric Utility Regulation Board, National Construction Commission, Nanking, "Electric Power Development in China," *Transactions, Third World Power Conference,* 2 (1936) 105–130

"Electrical Communications in Manchuria," *Contemporary Manchuria,* 2:4 (July 1938) 25–43

"Electricity in Manchuria," *Contemporary Manchuria,* 1:1 (1937) 97–108; *Far Eastern Review,* 33:9 (July 1937) 274–276, 288

"Electrification of the Lower Yangtze Area," *Far Eastern Review,* 27:5 (May 1931) 282–284

"The End of Monetary Inflation in China," *Far Eastern Economic Review,* 9 (August 10, 1950) 160–162

"Engineering Development in Szechwan," *Far Eastern Engineer,* 3:1 (January 1940) 23, 57

Erickson, John, "Railway Development in the New China," *Eastern World,* 4:2 (February 1950) 14–15

"Failure of State Farm in China," *Far Eastern Economic Review,* 15:12 (September 17, 1953) 858

Fan, Moh, "Agricultural Producer's Cooperative," *People's China,* 13 (July 1, 1952) 16–22

Fang, Fu-an, "Shanghai Labor," *Chinese Economic Journal,* 7:2 (August 1930) 553–585

————, "Ten Years of Road Building in China — a Statistical Study," *Chinese Economic Journal,* 6 (May 1930) 542–557

Faulder, H. C., "The Chinese Aluminum Rolling Mills," *Far Eastern Engineer,* 2:11 (October 1939) 652–654, 678

Fei, Hsiao-t'ung, "New Peking — the People's Capital," *People's China,* 1:3 (February 1, 1950)

Feng, Cheng-hai, "Labour Conditions in China During 1934," *Chinese Economic Journal,* 15:2 (February 1935) 185–199

Feng, H. T., "Notes on Peasants' Tax Burden in a Hopei Village," *Monthly Bulletin on Economic China,* 7:3 (March 1934) 105–109

Fetter, Frank W., "China and the Flow of Silver," *Geographical Review*, 26:1 (January 1936) 32–47

"Financial and Commercial Reports from Tientsin," *Far Eastern Economic Review*, 7 (July 7, 1949) 14–15

Fleming, R. C. and C. Li, "Modern Marco Polo Examines a Coal Field; Men-tou-kou Anthracite Field," *Explosives Engineer*, 19 (February 1941) 48–53

"Floods and Kwangtung's Main Task for 1953," *Far Eastern Economic Review*, 14:26 (June 25, 1953) 818

"Fluor-spar Deposits in Chekiang," *Chinese Economic Bulletin*, 25 (1934) 115–119

Fong, H. D., "Bibliography of Silver and China," *Monthly Bulletin on Economic China*, 7:12 (December 1934) 513–524

————, "China's Factory Act and the Cotton Industry," *Monthly Bulletin on Economic China*, 7:3 (March 1934) 93–104

————, "China's Silk Reeling Industry," *Monthly Bulletin on Economic China*, 7:12 (December 1934) 483–506

————, "The Cooperative Marketing of Cotton in Hopei," *Nankai Social and Economic Quarterly*, 8:3 (October 1935) 551–577

————, "The Growth and Decline of Rural Industrial Enterprise in North China: a Case Study of the Cotton Handloom Weaving Industry in Paoti," *Nankai Social and Economic Quarterly*, 8:4 (January 1936) 691–772

————, "Industrial Capital in China," *Nankai Social and Economic Quarterly*, 9:1 (April 1936) 27–94

————, "Industrialization and Labor in Hopei," *Chinese Social and Political Review*, 15:1 (April 1931) 1–28

————, "Industrialization and Rural Industries," *China Quarterly*, 2:2 (Spring 1935) 259–279

————, "Local Government Expenditure in Hopei," *Monthly Bulletin on Economic China*, 7:12 (December 1934) 507–512

————, "Review of C. P. Wang's Indigenous Cooperative Associations in China," *Nankai Social and Economic Quarterly*, 8:4 (January 1936) 920–923

————, "Rural Manufacturing Industries in Chekiang," *Monthly Bulletin on Economic China*, 7:2 (February 1934) 60–71

————, "Rural Weaving and the Merchant-Employers in a North China District," *Nankai Social and Economic Quarterly*, 8:1 (April 1935) 75–120

————, "Terminal Marketing of Tientsin Cotton," *Monthly Bulletin on Economic China*, 7:7 (July 1934) 275-321

————, "Industrial Organization in China," *Nankai Social and Economic Quarterly*, 9:4 (January 1937) 919–1000

Fong, S. L. and B. C. Chang, "The Tungsten Deposits of Talingshan, Chungshan, Kwangtung," *Geological Bulletin, Geologic Survey, Kwangtung and Kwangsi,* 2 (1928) 95–108

"45,000,000 Gallons of Petroleum To Be Produced in China This Year," *Far Eastern Engineer,* 5:10 (October 1947) 431

Gavin, M. J., "Petroleum in Kansu Province, China," *Petroleum Engineering,* 17:1 (October 1945) 181–182, 184

"Geology of Hsiu-Wu Coal Field, Honan," *Bulletin, Geologic Survey, China,* 24 (September 1934) 1–3

"Geology of Tzu-yao Coal Field, Tsing-yuan, Kansu," *Bulletin, Geologic Survey, China,* 37 (July 1948) 7–10

Gew, Lewis, "Land Reform in Communist China," *Eastern World,* 5:1 (January 1951) 19–20

Gilman, W. F., "Electricity Supply for the Province of Kwangtung, Macao, and Hongkong," *Far Eastern Review,* 27:5 (May 1931) 285–286, 306

Ginsburg, N. S., "Manchurian Railway Development," *Far Eastern Quarterly,* 8 (August 1949) 398–411

"Gold in Amur Valley," *Manchurian Economic Review,* 18 (September 15, 1937) 14–15

"Gold Mining Industry in Manchoukuo," *Contemporary Manchuria,* 2:6 (November 1938) 21–42; *Far Eastern Review,* 35:1 (January 1939) 34–37

"Gold Mining Operation," *Manchurian Economic Review,* 9 (May 1, 1937) 5–7

"Grain Miracle in Flood Years," *Far Eastern Economic Review,* 18:10 (March 3, 1955) 266–267

Gull, E. M., "Agrarian Reform in China," *Contemporary Review,* 179 (January 1951) 16–20

Han, Ting, "First Steps in Mechanized Farming," *People's China,* 4:8 (October 16, 1951) 28–30

"The Hankow Light and Power Company," *Far Eastern Review,* 27:5 (May 1931) 300–301, 314

"Harnessing of the Hwai River," *China Monthly Review* (November 1951) 244–247

"Highway Construction in Shensi," *Chinese Economic Bulletin,* 27 (October 26, 1935) 256–260

"Highway in Kweichow," *Chinese Economic Bulletin,* 23 (October 7, 1933) 230–232

"Hitches in China's Capital Construction," *Far Eastern Economic Review,* 14:23 (June 4, 1953) 721

Ho, Chieh, "Alexandrite and Its Popularity as Gem-stone in North China," *Bulletin, Geologic Survey, China,* 3 (1924) 183–190

Ho, Chih-hsiang, "Southwest China, a Political Social and Economic Survey," *China Quarterly,* 3:4 (Autumn 1938) 415–430

Ho, C. S., "The Phosphate Deposits of Tungshan, Chengchiang, Yunnan," *Bulletin, Geologic Survey, China,* 35 (April 1942) 41–43

Ho, C. S. and E. T Chang, "Geology of Tsiao-chia-ping Coal Field, I-chün, Shensi," *Bulletin, Geologic Survey, China,* 37 (July 1948) 39–43

Ho, C. S., T. C. Liu and E. T. Chang, "Geology of the Coal Fields of Eastern Kansu," *Bulletin, Geologic Survey, China,* 37 (July 1948) 11–22

Ho, Franklin L., "Land Problem of China," *Annals of the American Academy,* 276 (July 1951) 6–11

————, "Land Tax in Chekiang," *Monthly Bulletin on Economic China,* 7:1 (January 1934) 1–14

————, "Rural Economic Reconstruction in China," *Nankai Social and Economic Quarterly,* 9:2 (July 1936) 469–535

Ho, Pei-yang, "The Production of Tungsten in China," *Economic Studies,* 16 (1941)

Hok, C. S. and H. L. Tu, "Mineral Resources of Lienhsien, Kwangtung," *Bulletin, Geologic Survey, Kwangtung and Kwangsi,* 1 (1943)

Hou, T. F., "Notes on the Asbestos Deposit of Laiyuan District, Hopei," *Bulletin, Geological Survey, China,* 25 (March 1935) 39–43

Hou, T. F. and K. C. Yang, "Geology of the Sodium Sulphate Deposit of Pengshanhsien, Szechwan," *Bulletin, Geologic Survey, Szechwan,* 1 (1938) 85–92, 93–96

Hsieh, C. Y., "China's Future Producing Possibilities More Promising Than Developments Indicate," *Oil Weekly* 80:3 (December 30, 1935) 20–22

————, "How the New Hwainan Coal Field Was Discovered," *Science and Technology in China,* 1 (1948) 49–54

————, "A Microscopical Study of the Bauxite Deposit in the Tsechuan-Poshan District, Central Shantung," *Bulletin, Geologic Survey, China,* 25 (March 1935) 55–62

————, "The Petroleum Resources of China," *Bulletin, Geologic Survey, China,* 30 (September 1937) 53–67

————, "Tin Placer Deposits in Fuhochung-kiang Area, Northern Kwangsi and Southern Hunan and With a Note on the Distribution of Tin Belt in China," *Bulletin, Geologic Survey, China,* 23:1–2 (June 1943) 79–93

Hsieh, C. Y. and C. H. Chao, "Note on the Phosphate Deposits in China," *Bulletin, Geologic Survey, China,* 28:1–2 (1948) 71–74

Hsieh, C. Y. and Y. C. Cheng, "Lead-Zinc Deposits of Central Hunan," *Bulletin, Geologic Survey, China,* 29 (March 1937) 1–47

Hsin, Jen, "Land Reform and China's Industrialization," *People's China,* 2:6 (September 16, 1950) 4–6

Hsin, Wen, "Victories on the Financial Front," *People's China,* 2:7 (October 1, 1950) 7–8

Hsiung, K. H., "Analysis of the Ores and Minerals in Kiangsi," *Bulletin, Geologic Survey, Kiangsi,* 4 (January 1940) 153–174

Hsiung, Y. H. and Y. C. Cheng, "The Geology of Liulingcho Gold Deposits, Yuanling District, Western Hunan," *Bulletin, Geologic Survey, China,* 27 (March 1936) 47–54

Hsu, Chih, "The First Seamless Steel Tube Made in China," *People's China,* 1 (January 1, 1954) 27–28

————, "A Survey of Central South," *People's China,* 6 (March 16, 1954) 25–31

Hsu, K. C., "Tungsten Deposits of Southern Kiangsi," *Economic Geology,* 38:6 (October 1943) 431–473

Hsu, K. C. and C. J. Peng, "Geology of the Copper Deposits of Yungching and Tientsuan, Sikang," *Bulletin, Geologic Survey, China,* 34 (January 1941) 21–30

Hsu, Ti-hsin, "Remaking Shanghai's Economy," *People's China,* 1:12 (June 15, 1950) 10–11, 30

Hsu, Ying, "New Tientsin," *People's China,* 4:10 (1951) 24–26

————, "The Transformation of a City," *People's China,* 1:3 (February 1, 1950) 11–12

Hu, Chiao-yue, "Agricultural Land Use of Szechwan Basin," *National Reconstruction Journal,* 5 (July 1944) 43–89

Hu, Tao-chieh, "Helping Private Enterprise in Shanghai," *China Monthly Review* (November 1951) 261–263

Huang, Chin-t'ao, "The Coal Industry in China," *Chinese Economic Journal,* 17:5 (1935) 425–438

Huang, Euchinic, "Organizing a New Labor Union in Chuanchow," *China Monthly Review* (January 1951) 11–13

Huang, Hsin-sheng, "Prospects for the Banking Industry," *China Weekly Review,* 114 (July 2, 1949) 104–105

Huang, S. H. and H. C. Tu, "Geology of the Coal Field Between Shihtan-ching and Ta-we-kou, Ninghsia," *Bulletin, Geologic Survey, China,* 37 (July 1948) 49–51

Huang, T. K. and others, "Report on Geological Investigation of Some Oil Fields in Sinkiang," *Memoirs, Geologic Survey, China,* Series A: 21 (1947)

Huang, Yen-p'ei, "Progress in China's Light Industry," *People's China,* 24 (December 16, 1952) 4–7

Huzimoto, H., "On the Geology of the Yang-ch'üan Coal Field in Shansi," *Journal of the Geological Society of Japan,* 52 (January 1946) 41–47

Hwa, Sen, "Industrialization of Manchuria," *China Digest,* 6:5 (June 14, 1949) 8–9

"Imports and Exports of North China," *Far Eastern Economic Review,* 6 (May 25, 1949) 662–665

"Industrial Position of Shanghai," *Far Eastern Economic Review,* 6 (May 18, 1949) 631–633

"Industries of Kwangtung," *Far Eastern Economic Review,* 6 (May 18, 1949) 634

"Inter-Movement of Goods in Red China," *Far Eastern Economic Review,* 14:8 (February 19, 1953) 230

Jao, Shu-shih, "Report on Land Reform in East China," *China Monthly Review* (Supplement) (September 1950) 2–5

"Japan's New Mainland Trade: Revival of Sino-Japanese Trade," *Economist,* 161 (October 13, 1951) 868

Kann, E., "The Big Problem of Small Money in China," *Central Bank of China Bulletin,* 1:2 (September 1935) 36–48

————, "A Brief History of China's Loan Policies," *Central Bank of China Bulletin,* 1 (March 1935) 10–31

————, "Modern Banknotes in China," *Central Bank of China Bulletin,* 3:2 (June 1937) 126–153

————, "Wood-oil, an Important Chinese Export Commodity," *Central Bank of China Bulletin,* 4:3 (September 1938) 204–216

Kao, Fan, "Reconstruction in New China," *China Monthly Review* (October 1951) 194–197

Kao, Kang, "A Year of Achievement in Manchuria," *People's China,* 2:9 (November 1, 1950) 7–8, 31

————, "Economic and National Defense Construction in the Northeast," *People's China,* 3:8 (April 16, 1951) 8–9, 31

Kao, P., "Notes on the Geology of Eastern Chekiang," *Bulletin, Geologic Survey, China,* 25 (March 1935) 45–54

Kao, P. and K. C. Hsu, "Geology of Western Kiangsi," *Memoirs, Geologic Survey, China,* Series A, 16 (December 1940) 61–72

Ke Chia-lung, "The Korean War and the Price Situation in China and the United States," *People's China,* 3:3 (February 1, 1951) 22–23

————, "Manchuria's Economic Victories," *People's China,* 1:11 (May 16, 1950) 7–9

"Kiangsi's Output of Tungsten Ore," *Chinese Economic Bulletin,* 16 (1930) 196–199

King, T. P., "The People's Railways," *China Weekly Review,* 115 (November 26, 1949) 203–204

———, "The Work of the People's Bank," *China Weekly Review,* 117 (March 25, 1950) 57–60

"Kitai" ("China"), *Bolshaia Sovetskaia Entsiklopediia* (2nd ed.) (1950) 167–312

Knowlton, A. B., "Power Supply for Chinese Industrialization Program," *Electric World,* 123 (May 12, 1945) 92–94

Koppel, H., "Chinese Tungsten and American Market," *Engineering and Mining Journal,* 111 (February 12, 1921) 308–309

Krejci-Graf, Karl, "Kohle und Eisen in China," *Natur and Volk* (Senckenb. Naturf. Ges), 69:4–5 (April–May 1939) 163–169, 249–258

Ku, S. L., "Present Trading with Manchuria," *Far Eastern Economic Review,* 6 (April, 27, 1949) 533–535

Kung, H. H., "China's Financial Problems," *Foreign Affairs,* 23:2 (January 1945) 222–232

Kwan, S. C., "Geology of the Chi-chang-hu Coal Field of Turfan, Sinkiang," *Bulletin, Coal Survey, China,* 37 (July 1948) 47–48

Kyi, Zuh-tsing, "How the Business Tax Is Applied in Chekiang," *Chinese Economic Journal,* 9:3 (September 1931) 939–956

"Labor Conditions in China," *Monthly Labor Review,* 60:1 (January 1945) 18–40

"Labour Conditions in China," *International Labour Review,* 27:5 (May 1933) 664–667

Lane, E. W., "Hydraulic Lime for Masonry Construction in China," *Journal of the Association of Chinese-American Engineers,* 10:1 (September 1929) 19–34

Lee, H. C., "Geology of Sungpan Gold Deposits, Yuanling, Hunan," *Bulletin, Geologic Survey, Hunan,* 17 (1934) 8–9

Lee, J. S., "Coal Resources of China," *Asiatic Review,* 31 (July 1935) 571–585

Lee, Shu-ching, "The Heart of China's Problem, the Land Tenure System," *Journal of Farm Economics,* 30 (1948) 259–270

Lee, Tien-chen and Cheng-luen Ho, "Gold Deposits of Huangmatang, Maofungshan, Tsengcheng, Kwangtung," *Annual Report, Geologic Survey, Kwangtung and Kwangsi,* 4:2 (1933) 51–65

Lee, Y. Y. and S. Chu, "Geology of Kenkou on the Hunan-Kwangtung Border and its Bearing to the Geology of the Nanling Ranges," *Bulletin, Geologic Survey, China,* 13:2 (1934) 183–196

Lei, Jen-min, "Trade with Capitalist Countries," *People's China,* 2 (January 1954) 8–11

Leibbrand, R., "Pastoral Products of China," *Chinese Economic Journal,* 7:3 (September 1930) 984–988

Leo, Shoo-tze and Wei-cheng Wei, "Po-shan Bauxite as a Possible Raw Material for the Production of Aluminum in China," *Journal of Chemical Engineering, China,* 3:2 (June 1936) 113–123

Li, C., "Report on the Geology and Mineral Resources of I, Tang and Yu Districts of Western Chihli," *Bulletin, Geologic Survey, China,* 4 (1922) 137–140

Li, Chingyuan Y. and C. Y. Hsieh, "Potential Sources of Aluminium in Southwestern China," *Mining Technology,* 10:1 (January 1946) 1–6

Li, Choh-ming, "Wartime Inflation in China," *Review of Economic Statistics,* 27:1 (February 1945) 23–33

Li, Li-san, "Trade Union Work and Movement in China," *China Digest,* 7:6 (December 14, 1949)

Ling, C. D., "The End of Wall Street in Shanghai," *China Monthly Review* (July 1951) 48–50

Liu, Chen-an, "East China's Agricultural Research Institute," *People's China,* 9 (May 1, 1954) 23–25

Liu, C. B., "General Statement on the Antimony Industry of Hunan," *Bulletin, Geologic Survey, Hunan,* 3 (Special Report I) (1928)

Liu, Shao-chi, "On the Agrarian Reform Law," *People's China,* 2:2 (July 16, 1950) 5–9, 28–31

Liu, Shin-hwa, "The Record Restoration of China's Railways," *People's China,* 1:4 (February 16, 1950) 10–11

Lo, Chen-chun and Ping-shu Kao, "China Wood Oil (Tung Oil)," *Far Eastern Economic Review,* 6 (April 27, 1949) 521–527

Lochow, H. J. van, "Sechzig Jahre Eisenbahn in der Mandschurei," *Internationales Archiv. für Verkehrswesen,* 3 (erstes Augustheft 1951) 347–352

Logan, L. J., "Oil and China's Future," *Oil Weekly,* 120:1 (December 3, 1945) 37, 39–40, 43

Lowe, Chuan-hua, "Labor Conditions in China," *Information Bulletin,* Council of International Affairs, Nanking, 4:5 (July 7, 1937) 93–116

Lu, C. H. and C. C. Pai, "The Gold Deposits of Chingchingchieh, Yungsheng, Yunnan," *Bulletin, Geologic Survey, China,* 36 (April 1936) 25–26

Lu, C. H. and M. H. Chen, "Geology of Siao-lu-tang Coal Field, Chingtai, Kansu," *Bulletin, Geologic Survey, China,* 37 (July 1948) 27–29

Lu, K. C., "China's Oil Policy," *Oil Weekly,* 121:10 (May 6, 1946) 27

———, "War's End Brings Accelerated Activity in Yunnan, China's Only Oil Field," *Oil and Gas Journal,* 44:34 (December 29, 1945) 253–257

Lu, Mark, M., "Honan's Flood Control Project," *China Weekly Review,* 117 (April 15, 1950) 110–111

Lung, Men, "Sino-Japanese Trade Agreement," *People's China,* 12 (June 10, 1952) 9–10

Makarova, M., "Ob economicheskikh uspekhakh Kitaiskoi Narodnoi Respubliki," *Bolshevik* 27 (1950) 38–51

Malabard, J., "L'inconnu chinois," *Actualité économique,* 25 (January–March 1950) 642–666

"Manchuria's Electric Communications," *Far Eastern Review,* 34 (September 1938) 339–343

"Manchuria — Key to the Five Year Plan," *Economist,* 160 (March 10, 1951) 547–548

"Manganese Production in Hunan," *Chinese Economic Bulletin,* 27 (1935) 335–338

Mao, Y. J. and Y. T. Hsu, "Report on the Shangwu-pao Field, Kianghua, Hunan," *Bulletin, Geologic Survey, Hunan,* 17 (1934) 1–5

Marker, A. E., "A Survey of Economic Problems in China," *International Affairs,* 25 (January 1949) 23–36

Maslennikov, V., "Narodnoia respublika kitaia," *Vestnik Statistiki* (May–June 1950) 45–58

Masuda, H. M., "Fushun: Mining Metropolis," *Far Eastern Review,* 36 (October 1940) 363–385

Meng, C. Y. W., "China's Agricultural Development and Planning," *Far Eastern Economic Review,* 10 (April 5, 1951) 417–420

————, "China's First Labor Insurance Law," *China Monthly Review* (January 1951) 19–20

————, "China's Industrial Development and Industrial Capital," *Far Eastern Economic Review,* 10 (1951) 178–183

————, "China's New Foreign Trade Policy," *Far Eastern Economic Review,* 10 (April 19, 1951) 481–485

————, "Chinese Cotton Textile Industry," *Far Eastern Economic Review,* 9 (December 14, 1950) 723–739

————, "New China's Economy Shapes up," *China Monthly Review,* 120 (April 1951) 209–212

————, "New Direction for Shanghai Business," *China Weekly Review,* 117 (May 27, 1950) 223–226

————, "The Remodelling of Shanghai's Economy," *Far Eastern Economic Review,* 9 (November 9, 1951) 557–562

Meng, H. M. and others, "Geology and Tungchuang District, Northern Yunnan," *Memoir, Natural Resources Institute,* 17 (1948)

"Metallic Coinage of Modern China," *Far Eastern Economic Review,* 15:26 (December 24, 1953) 882

"Mineral Resources of Kwangsi," *Far Eastern Review,* 28 (March 1932) 130–133

"Minimum Wage Law, Labour Contract Law and Provisional Regulations Governing Labourers' Savings," *Chinese Economic Journal,* 20:2 (February 1937) 184–199

"Modern Highways for Northwestern Provinces," *Chinese Economic Bulletin,* 24 (April 21, 1934) 245–250

"Modern Highways in Central Provinces," *Chinese Economic Bulletin,* 24 (April 28, 1934) 268–269

Moh, Ju-chien, "New China's Customs Administration," *People's China,* 4:2 (July 16, 1951) 13–14, 35

Morrison, H., "China: the Dragon Aches for Capital," *Canadian Business,* 23 (May 1950) 29–30, 114

Moyer, Raymond, T., "Agricultural Practices in Semi-arid North China," *Scientific Monthly* (October 1942) 301–317

————, "Agricultural Soils in the Loess Region of North China," *Geographic Review* (1936) 414–425

Moyer, Raymond T. and others, "Farm Tenancy in China," *National Reconstruction Journal,* 8:1 (July 1947) 13–24

"The Mui Tsai System in China, Hongkong and Malaya," *International Labour Review,* 34:5 (November 1936) 663–676

Nan, Y. T., "Ore Deposits of Chinchuangtang, Chenhsien, Hunan," *Bulletin, Geologic Survey, China,* 15 (1936) 391–410

"New Taxation in China," *Far Eastern Economic Review,* 14:5 (January 29, 1953) 134

Nieh, Jung-chen, "Municipal Construction in Peking," *People's China,* 3:3 (February 1, 1951) 8–9, 31

"1950 Plan for Increasing Production of Food and Cotton," *People's China,* 1:3 (February 1, 1950) 26

Nolde, John J., "The United States and the Chinese 'Blockade,'" *Far Eastern Survey,* 19 (March 22, 1950) 57–61

"North China's Agricultural Taxation Policy," *Foreign Agriculture,* 14 (February 1950) 34–36

Odinetz, V., "Gold Mining in Manchuria," *Manchurian Economic Review,* 18 (September 15, 1936) 10–14

O'Donnell, J. P., "China's Production of 3,000 Barrels Daily Starts Nation Toward Self-Sufficiency," *Oil and Gas Journal,* 43 (March 9, 1944) 34–35

"Oil Reserves in China," *Far Eastern Review,* 31:1 (1935) 37–38

"Oils and Oilseed Exports," *Foreign Commerce Weekly,* 5 (October 18, 1941) 29

"Oils and Oilseeds; 1946 Supplies in China," *Foreign Commerce Weekly,* 25 (December 21, 1946) 39

"On Chinese Coinage," *Far Eastern Economic Review*, 16:3 (January 21, 1954) 70

Orchard, D. J., "Manpower in China," *Political Science Quarterly*, 50:4 (December 1935) 561–583

"Organization of Investment Companies in Communist China," *Far Eastern Economic Review*, 9 (November 20, 1950) 656–657

Ou, Pao-san, "A New Estimate of China's National Income," *Journal of Political Economy*, 54:6 (December 1946) 547–554

———, "Notes on the Food Problem and Price Control," *Pacific Affairs*, 15:3 (September 1942) 345–361

Ou, Pao-san and Fo-shen Wang, "Industrial Production and Employment in Pre-war China," *Economic Journal*, 56 (September 1946) 426–434

Paauw, Douglas S., "Chinese National Expenditures During the Nanking Period," *Far Eastern Quarterly*, 12:1 (November 1952) 3–26

"Pai-kung-shan Coal Field, a New Discovery in the Huai-nan Basin, Northern Anhui," *Economic Geology*, 44 (March 1949) 128–142

P'an, C. H., "Non-Marine Origin of Petroleum in North Shensi, and Cretaceous of Szechuan, China," *Bulletin, American Association of Petroleum Geologists*, 25 (November 1941) 2058–2068

———, "The Oil Shale Deposit of Northern Shensi," *Bulletin, Geologic Survey, China*, 24 (September 1934) 9–14

"Peiping's Handicraft Industries," *Far Eastern Economic Review*, 6 (June 1, 1949) 688–690

"Peking and the Grain Merchants," *Far Eastern Economic Review*, 16:4 (January 28, 1954) 98

"Peking and Trade Union Problems," *Far Eastern Economic Review*, 14:16 (April 16, 1953) 496

"The Political and Economic Construction of the Chinese People's Republic," *(Voprosy ekonomiki) Soviet Press Translations*, C 5 (July 1, 1950) 387–402

Pon, Alexander C., "Agricultural Construction in the Northeast 1949–1950," *Regional Studies*, 202 (May 1951)

"Power Development in North China," *Oriental Economist*, 4:9 (September 1937) 517–519

"Production and Marketing of Shantung Coal," *Chinese Economic Bulletin*, 25 (1934) 305–310

Pu, Shou-chang, "The New Industrial Labor," *National Reconstruction Journal*, 6:2 (October 1945) 60–75

"Railways in China," *Far Eastern Economic Review*, 9 (September 21, 1950) 341–342

Rankin, B. I., "Chinese Communists Amalgamate Currencies in Controlled Areas," *Foreign Trade* (Canada), 5 (April 9, 1949) 754–757

———, "Foreign Trade in North China Now Transacted Through Tientsin," *Foreign Trade* (Canada), 6 (December 3, 1949) 1050–1051

Read, Thomas T., "Economic-Geographic Aspects of China's Iron Industry," *Geographical Review,* 33:1 (January 1943) 42–45

"Red China Joint Operation for Russia's Benefit Only," *World Oil* (November 1951) 334

"Report from Canton," *Far Eastern Economic Review,* 9 (September 7, 1950) 274–276

"Report from Manchuria and North China," *Far Eastern Economic Review,* 7 (July 28, 1949) 111–112

"Resources of Sinkiang Province," *The Orient* (Hongkong) (February 1951) 15

"Review of Economic Conditions in Shanghai and Tientsin," *Far Eastern Economic Review,* 8 (January 26, 1950) 114–115

Riggs, Fred W., "Can Economic Sanctions Check Communist China?" *Foreign Policy Bulletin* (May 18, 1951)

———, "The Economics of Red China," *Foreign Policy Report* (New York), 27:6 (1951)

"The Rise of Communism in China," *Far Eastern Economic Review,* 10:23 (June 7, 1951) 716

"Road Building Progress in Kiangsi," *Chinese Economic Bulletin,* 26 (April 27, 1935) 260

"Road Construction in Shansi," *Chinese Economic Bulletin,* 23 (December 20, 1933) 417–420

"The Role of the National Corporation in China's New Democratic Economy," *Far Eastern Economic Review,* 9 (November 9, 1950) 562–564

Roth, Andrew, "Communist China's Slow-Motion Industrial Revolution," *China Weekly Review,* 113 (April 30, 1949) 196–197

"Russian and American Pressures on China," *Far Eastern Economic Review,* 14:11 (March 12, 1953) 321

"Salt Production in China," *Foreign Commerce Weekly,* 13 (October 2, 1943) 20

Scott, D., "New Pattern of Chinese Trade," *Wirtschaftsdienst* (English Edition), 31 (March 1951) 21–22

Shan, H. K., "World's Richest Antimony Mines," *Far Eastern Review,* 36 (December 1940) 447

Shan, J., "Tin Industry in Yunnan," *Mining Journal* (London), 230:5878 (April 17, 1948) 270–272

"Shanghai, North China and Manchuria Reports," *Far Eastern Economic Review,* 7 (July 14, 1949) 46–48

"Shanghai Exports in 1950," *Far Eastern Economic Review,* 10:16 (April 19, 1951) 486

Shen, Jenshine, "Bristles of Yunnan," *Far Eastern Economic Review,* 6 (March 23, 1949) 353–354

Shen, L. Y., "A Brief History of Savings Institutions in China," *Central Bank of China Bulletin,* 1:2 (September 1935) 56–70

——————, "Chinese Currencies; Old and New," *Central Bank of China Bulletin,* 4:1 (March 1938) 10–17; 4:2 (June 1938) 111–122; 4:3 (September 1938) 217–225

Shu, C. A., "Geology of the Pingtoushan Tin Deposits, Chungshan, Kwangsi," *Science Report* (National Tsing Hua University), Series C, 1:4 (1948) 243–262

Shurcliff, Alice W., "The Control of Industrial Labor in Communist China," *Monthly Labor Review,* 76:8 (August 1953) 821–825

"Sino-Soviet Economic Agreements Widely Acclaimed," *People's China,* 1:8 (April 16, 1950) 25

"La situation économique en Chine: Etudes et conjoncture," *Economie mondiale,* 4 (March–April 1949) 85–100

"The Situation in Kwangtung," *Far Eastern Economic Review,* 8 (March 9, 1950) 302–304

"Situation in Recent Months; Condition in Principal Cities," *Foreign Commerce Weekly,* 35 (June 27, 1949) 18–19; 37 (October 10, 1949) 15–16; 37 (December 5, 1949) 18–20

"The Situation in Shanghai," *Far Eastern Economic Review,* 8 (February 16, 1950) 204–206

"The Situation in Shanghai," *Far Eastern Economic Review,* 8 (April 13, 1950) 483–484

Small, A. D., "China — Its Future in Petroleum," *Petroleum Engineering,* 18:1 (October 1946) 98, 100, 102, 104, 106, 108

Smith, C. A. Middleton, "Hydroelectric Power in Kwangtung, Harnessing the Yung River to Supply Canton with Electricity," *Far Eastern Review,* 30:5 (May 1934) 216–218, 235

"Some Recent Family Budget Enquiries in Shanghai," *International Labour Review,* 23:4 (April 1931) 550–557

"Soya Beans of Manchuria," *Far Eastern Economic Review,* 6 (June 1, 1949) 690–691

Spencer, J. E., "On Regionalism in China," *Journal of Geography* (April 1947) 123–136

"State-Ownership in China," *Far Eastern Economic Review,* 14:19 (February 26, 1953) 256

"Statistical Survey of Working Conditions of Railway Employees," *Chinese Economic Journal,* 14:2 (February 1934) 201–221

Su, Tuan, "Victory on the Cotton Front," *People's China,* 2:11 (December 1, 1950) 12–13

Sullivan, Walter, "Land Reform Plans in China," *Far Eastern Survey,* 19 (February 22, 1950) 33–38

Steiner, H. Arthur, "Chinese Communist Urban Policy," *American Political Science Review,* 44 (March 1950) 47–63

Stepanek, J. E. and C. H. Prien, "Small Chemical Industries for China," *Chemical and Engineering News,* 28 (September 4, 1950) 3032–3035

Stewart, John R., "Search for Oil in Manchoukuo," *Far Eastern Engineer,* 3:12 (December 1940) 805–815

"Story of Soybean Milk," *Far Eastern Economic Review,* 15:18 (October 29, 1953) 568

"A Study of 65 Labor Families in Nanking," *Chinese Economic Journal,* 9:3 (September 1931) 1002–1007

"Sulphur Mines in Shansi," *Far Eastern Review,* 22:7 (July 1926) 326

Sun, H. T., "L'évolution économique et financière de la Chine en 1950," *Problèms économiques* (June 12, 1951) 14–17

Tam, Wah Ding, "Present Status and Future Outlook of the Chinese Tungsten Industry," *Far Eastern Review,* 25:11 (November 1929) 519, 521

Tamagna, Frank M., "China's Post-war Finances," *Pacific Affairs,* 18:2 (June 1945) 117–136

T'an, H. C. and C. Y. Li, "Mineral Deposits and Eastern Sikang," *Bulletin, Geologic Survey, China,* 17 (October 1931) 1–4

Tang, Chen-hsu, "Water Resources Development of Post-war China," *National Reconstruction Journal,* 6:2 (October 1935) 83–97

Tao, Wei-lien, "Rural Production Is Key to Reconstruction," *China Weekly Review,* 118 (July 15, 1950) 113–115

Taylor, C. S., "The Shanghai Power Houses," *Far Eastern Review,* 27 (May 1931) 287–298

Taylor, J. B., "The Hopei Pottery Industry and the Problem of Modernization," *Chinese Social and Political Science Review,* 14 (April 1930) 184–211

————, "The Possibilities of Rural Industries in China," *Monthly Bulletin on Economic China,* 7:2 (February 1934) 45–59

Thorp, James, "Soil Conditions and Land Use in China," *Proceedings of the Sixth Pacific Science Congress,* 4 (1939) 921–931

Thorp, James, and Daniel S. Dye, "The Chengtu Clays — Deposits of Possible Loessial Origin in Western and Northwestern Szechuan Basin," *Bulletn, Geologic Survey, China,* 15 (1936) 225–246

Tien, C. C. and others, "The Manganese Ores of Hunan," *Memoir, Geologic Survey, Hunan,* Series A:2 (1935) 1–43

Tien, C. C. and H. C. Wang, "Report on the Wuhsi Antimony Deposit, Yuanling, Hunan," *Bulletin, Geologic Survey, Hunan,* 17 (1934) 6–7

Tien, Huo-nung, "Chinese Agriculture in Speedy Rehabilitation," *People's China,* 1:3 (February 1, 1950) 7–9

Tien, Liu, "China's First Collective Farm," *People's China,* 14 (July 1954) 17–25

"Tientsin Industrial Survey," *Far Eastern Economic Review,* 9 (July 20, 1950) 69–70

"Tin Mining in Kwangsi," *Chinese Economic Bulletin,* 25 (1934) 193–194

"Tin Production in Hunan," *Chinese Economic Bulletin,* 26 (1935) 317–320

Ting, Leonard, "China's Cotton Industry," *Nankai Social and Economic Quarterly,* 9:2 (July 1936) 398–445

———, "Chinese Modern Banks and the Finance of Government and Industry," *Nankai Social and Economic Quarterly,* 8:3 (October 1935) 578–616

———, "The Coal Industry in China," *Nankai Social and Economic Quarterly,* 10:1 (April 1937) 33–74

"Tin Mining Industry of China," *Tin* (London) (December 1942) 1–2

Ting, V. K., "The Manganese Deposits at Hsi Hu Tsun, Chang Ping Hsien, Chihli," *Bulletin, Geologic Survey of China,* 4 (1922) 91–95

"Tobacco Production and Trade," *Chinese Economic Journal,* 20:2 (February 1937) 121–139

Todd, O. J., "The Road to Langchow from Sian," *Journal of the Association of Chinese-American Engineers,* 14:3 (May 1934) 6–11

———, "Shansi Water and Power Problems: A Progress Report," *Journal of the Association of Chinese-American Engineers,* 16:4 (July–August 1935) 205–225

Todd, O. J. and S. Eliaseen, "The Yellow River Problem," *Proceedings of the American Society of Civil Engineers* (December 1938) 1921–1991

Torgasheff, P., "Mining Labor in China," *Chinese Economic Journal,* 4:4 (April 1930) 392–417; 4:5 (May 1930) 510–541; 4:6 (June 1930) 653–676; 4:7 (July 1930) 770–795; 4:8 (August 1930) 909–927

"Trade with China," *Far Eastern Economic Review,* 18:8 (February 24, 1955) 250

"Trade with China and the Hongkong Export Prohibition Order," *Far Eastern Economic Review,* 9 (August 31, 1950) 243–245

"Trade with China Controlled," *Economist,* 160 (June 23, 1951) 1521–1522

"Trade with Communist China," *Economist,* 157 (November 19, 1949) 1138

"Transportation and Communications of China," *Far Eastern Economic Review,* 6 (April 27, 1949) 532–533

Trewartha, Glenn T., "Ratio Maps of China's Farms and Crops," *Geographical Review* (January 1938) 102–111

Tsao, S. L., "Gypsum Deposit of P'ing Lu District, South Shensi," *Bulletin, Geologic Survey, China,* 8 (1929) 327–341

Tseng, F. J., "Geology and Mineral Deposits of Lantsang District, Yunnan," *Bulletin, Geologic Survey, China,* 36 (April 1945) 31–34

————, "The Gold Deposits of Kunyung, Mechiang, Yunnan," *Bulletin, Geologic Survey, China,* 36 (April 1945) 35

————, "The Rock-Salt Deposits of Mohei, Ningerh, Yunnan," *Bulletin, Geologic Survey, China,* 36 (April 1945) 37

Tseng, Shan, "Report on East China District Financial and Economic Work," *China Monthly Review* (Supplement) (September 1950) 5–8

Tsha, Kingwell J., "Developing Highways in the Northwest," *Far Eastern Review,* 27:10 (October 1931) 622, 650

Tsha, T. Y., "A Study of the Wage Rates in Shanghai 1930–1934," *Nankai Social and Economic Quarterly,* 8:3 (October 1935) 459–510

"Tungsten Deposits in Hunan," *Chinese Economic Bulletin,* 26 (1935) 267–271

"Tungsten Ore, Antimony, and Tin Exports of China," *Far Eastern Economic Review,* 6 (May 11, 1949) 594–595

"Tungsten Production in China," *Chinese Economic Journal,* 16 (1935) 200–205

"Two Years' Construction Achievements of the People's Railroads," *Soviet Press Translation,* 6 (November 15, 1951) 626–628

"Wages and Hours of Labor in Greater Shanghai, 1929," *Monthly Labor Review,* 33:3 675–677

Wang, C. C., "The Phosphate Deposits of Talungtan, Kunming, Yunnan," *Bulletin, Geologic Survey, China,* 35 (April 1942) 39–40

Wang, C. C. and C. S. Huo, "Geology of Hou-so Coal Field, P'ing-yi, Yunnan," *Bulletin, Geologic Survey, China,* 36 (April 1945) 9–10

————, "The Phosphate Deposits of Chichiaoshan, Cheng-kung, Yunnan," *Bulletin, Geologic Survey, China,* 36 (April 1945) 7–8

Wang, H. C., Y. T. Hsu and H. C. Hsiu, "Report on Ch'ang-chen-ling Antimony Mine, Ichang Hsien, Hunan," *Bulletin, Geologic Survey, Hunan,* 10 (1930) 12–13

Wang, K. P. and T. T. Read, "Controlling Factors in China's Coal Development," *Pacific Affairs,* 19 (June 1946) 165–181

Wang, Tao, "China's Cement Goes to War," *Rock Production,* 47 (August 1944) 110

Wang, Tsung-yen, "Canton Workers Forge Ahead," *China Monthly Review* (July 1951) 13–14

Wang, Y. L., "Geology of the Lomachang Lead-Silver Deposit, Lutien, Yunnan," *Bulletin, Geologic Survey, China,* 36 (April 1945) 1–3

————, "Phosphate Rocks of Chungyitsun, Kunyang, Yunnan," *Bulletin, Geologic Survey, China,* 35 (April 1942) 35–38

Wang, Y. L. and C. S. Pien, "Geology of the K'o-pao-ts'un Lignite Deposits, I-liang, Yunnan," *Bulletin, Geologic Survey, China* 36 (April 1945) 15–18

Wang, Y. L. and others, "Geology and Mining Industry of A-kan-chen Coal Fields, Kao-lan, Kansu," *Bulletin, Geologic Survey, China,* 37 (July 1948) 1–5

Wang, Y. Tsenshan, "Gold Ore Deposits of the Linglungshan Region, Tsaoyuen, Shantung," *Far Eastern Review,* 19:6 (June–July 1923) 383–389, 462–467

Wen, Chao, "Jenchienhu Conquers Flood and Famine," *People's China,* 1:11 (June 1, 1950) 19–20

White, J. R., "Yenchang Oil Field," *Petroleum Engineering,* 21:6 (June 1949) B38, B40, B42, B45–6, B48

"Why China Preserves the Rich Peasant Economy," *People's China,* 2:8 (October 16, 1950) 12–14

Wolff, P. R., "Manganese Ore Production in China," *Chinese Economic Bulletin,* 184 (August 30, 1924)

"Wolfram Ore Mining and Trade in China," *Far Eastern Economic Review,* 6 (May 11, 1949) 595–596

Wong, C. C., "Waterworks and Power Plants in Central China," *Far Eastern Review,* 36:1 (January 1940) 26, 37

Wong, Wing-wah, "Road Construction in Kwangsi," *Far Eastern Review,* 31:3 (March 1935) 111–112

Woo, Wm. H. F., "Some Notes on Highway Construction in the Provinces of Kiangsu, Chekiang, and Anhwei," *Journal of the Association of Chinese-American Engineers,* 16:5–6 (September–December 1935) 253–260, 327–334

"Working Conditions and Output of Coal Mines in China," *Monthly Labor Review,* 42 (February 1936) 236–238

"Working Conditions in Shanghai Factories," *International Labour Review,* 25:4 (April 1932) 535–540

"Workers' Insurance System in China," *Far Eastern Economic Review,* 14:24 (June 11, 1953) 768

Wu, Chih, "Handloom Weaving in Kaoyang," *Monthly Bulletin on Economic China,* 7:6 (June 1934) 248–257

Wu, Francis, "The Banking Industry in China Today," *Far Eastern Economic Review,* 9 (October 5, 1950) 400–402

———, "Canton After One Year under the New Regime," *Far Eastern Economic Review,* 9 (October 26, 1950) 498–499

———, "Shanghai's Economic Recovery," *Far Eastern Economic Review,* 9 (October 12, 1950) 433–435

———, "Shanghai's Economic Recovery," *Far Eastern Economic Review,* 9 (October 12, 1950) 524–526

———, "Unemployment Relief in Shanghai," *Far Eastern Economic Review,* 9 (November 2, 1950) 524–526

Wu, Wen-hui, "Inquiry into Modern China's Land Problem (Hsien-tai Chung-kuo t'u-ti wen-t'i chih t'an-chiu)," *New Social Science Quarterly (Hsin she-hui k'o-hsüeh chi-k'an)* 1:4 (no date)

Wu, Y. L. and Robert C. North, "China and India: Two Paths to Industrialization," *Problems of Communism* (May–June 1955)

Yang, H. C., "Economic Conditions in Kweichow," *Central Bank of China Bulletin,* 3:4 (December 1937) 295–300

Yang, H. K., "The Cooperative Movement in China," *Central Bank of China Bulletin,* 3:2 (June 1937) 111–125

———, "Economic Conditions of Ninghsia," *Central Bank of China Bulletin,* 4:4 (December 1936) 320–326

———, "The Rise and Decline of the Shansi Native Banks," *Central Bank of China Bulletin,* 3:4 (December 1937) 301–316

Yang, Hsien-tung, "China Grows More Cotton," *People's China,* 4 (February 16, 1954) 15–23

Yang, J. Y., "Tungsten Ore: China's Supply and Hongkong Mining," *Far Eastern Economic Review,* 12:22 (May 29, 1952) 693–696

Yang, Pei-hsin, "China Tackles Her Financial Problems," *China Digest,* 7:8 (February 1, 1950) 4–6, 21; *People's China,* 1:3 (February 1, 1950) 5–6, 27–28

———, "How China Conquered Inflation," *People's China,* 1:12 (June 16, 1950) 7–9

Yao, H. H. and T. H. Mi, "Geology of Kangsu Coal Field of Urukchat, South Sinkiang," *Bulletin, Geologic Survey, China,* 37 (July 1948) 45–46

Yao, Shan-yu, "The Chronological and Seasonal Distribution of Floods and Droughts in Chinese History, 206 B. C. — 1911 A. D.," *Far Eastern Quarterly,* 2:4 (August 1943) 357–378

Yarham, E. R., "China's Northwestern Province," *Eastern World,* 4:7 (July 1950) 21

Yeh, Chow, "Hsingang — China's New Northern Port," *People's China,* 4:11 (December 1, 1951) 26–28

Yeh, L. T. and S. C. Kwan, "Geology of the Liang-chih-szu Coal Field, Liang-tang, Kansu," *Bulletin, Geologic Survey, China,* 37 (July 1948) 23

Yeh, Tseng-ke, "The Huai River Battle," *People's China,* 4:4 (August 16, 1951) 21–23

Ying, C. Y., "The P. L. A. Makes the Desert Bloom," *People's China,* 15 (August 1952) 29–31

Yu, Chang-chin, "New Farm Implements," *People's China,* 3:3 (February 1, 1951) 23–24

Yu, Li-ting, "Textiles for the People," *People's China,* 3:5 (March 1, 1951) 9–11

Yu, Wah, "Land Reform in North China," *China Weekly Review,* 114 (June 18, 1949) 53–55

Yuan, H. T., F. C. Kou, and Y. C. Huang, "A Brief Description of Shantung Bauxite and Extraction of Alumina by the Wet Process," *Science and Technology in China,* 2 (April 1949) 21–24

Yuan, P. L., "Hengkeh-Henglu Zinc of Yunnan," *Science Report* (National Tsing Hua University), Series C:1 (1948) 238–242

Yuan, P. L. and Ting-chiang Ju, "The Gold Field of Wali, Yenyuanhsia, Sikang," *Science Report* (National Tsing Hua University), Series C:1 (1948) 308–320

Yui, H. C., "Economic Conditions in Hunan," *Central Bank of China Bulletin,* 4:2 (June 1938) 123–132

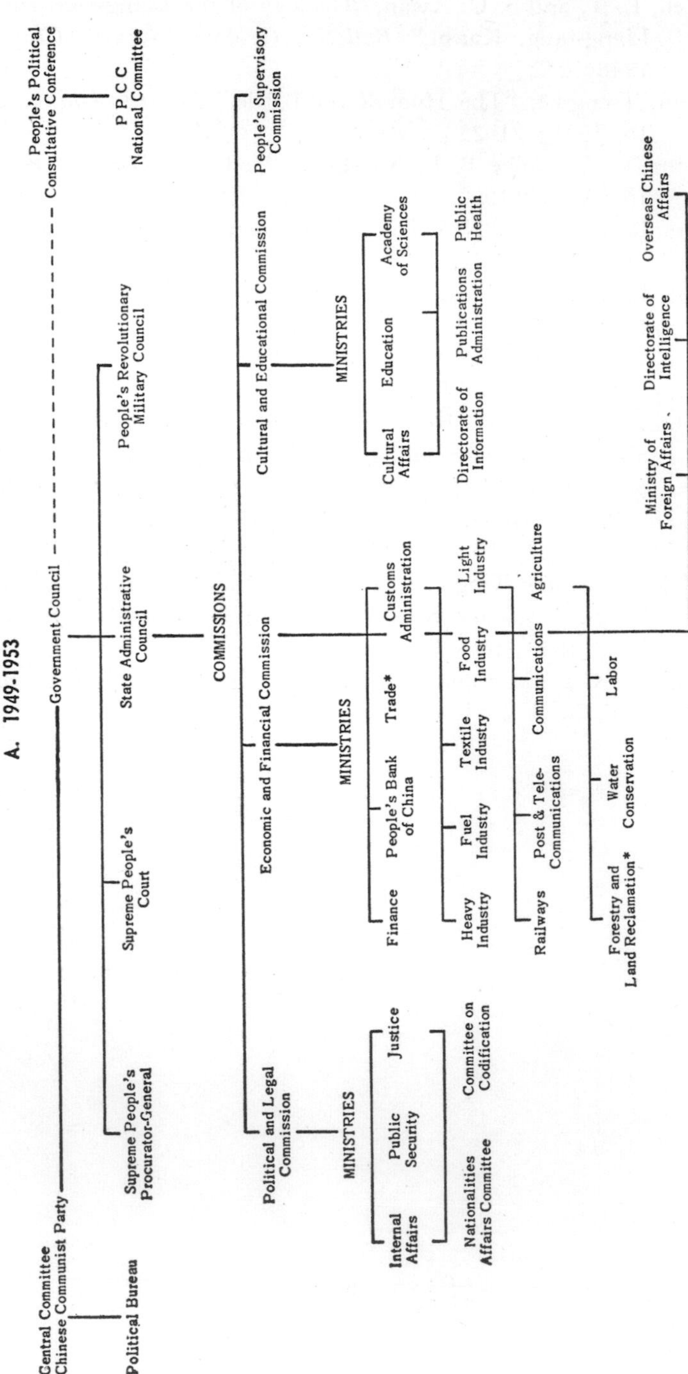

APPENDIX
ORGANIZATIONAL CHART OF THE CENTRAL GOVERNMENT OF COMMUNIST CHINA
A. 1949-1953
Central Committee Chinese Communist Party
Political Bureau
Government Council
People's Political Consultative Conference
P P C C National Committee
Supreme People's Procurator-General
Supreme People's Court
State Administrative Council
People's Revolutionary Military Council
COMMISSIONS
Political and Legal Commission
Economic and Financial Commission
Cultural and Educational Commission
People's Supervisory Commission
MINISTRIES
Internal Affairs
Public Security
Justice
Nationalities Affairs Committee
Committee on Codification
MINISTRIES
Finance
People's Bank of China
Trade*
Customs Administration
Heavy Industry
Fuel Industry
Textile Industry
Food Industry
Light Industry
Railways
Post & Tele-Communications
Communications
Agriculture
Forestry and Land Reclamation*
Water Conservation
Labor
MINISTRIES
Cultural Affairs
Education
Academy of Sciences
Directorate of Information
Publications Administration
Public Health
Ministry of Foreign Affairs
Directorate of Intelligence
Overseas Chinese Affairs

Changes In:	Under the Political and Legal Commission		Under the Economic and Financial Commission	
1950-1951	Ministry of Personnel (est. Sept., '50)	Bureau of North China Affairs* (est. Sept., '50)	Ministry of Food Industry (abolished Dec., '50)	Ministry of Forestry and Land Reclamation (changed into Ministry of Forestry (Nov., '51)
1952-1953	State Planning Committee (est. under Government Council, Nov., '52)	Bureau of N. China Affairs changed into N. China Administrative Committee (April, '52)	Economic and Financial Commission Five Ministries established: The First and the Second Ministries of Machine Manufacturing; Ministry of Building and Civil Engineering; Ministry of Geology; and Ministry of Food. Ministry of Trade abolished and changed into Ministry of Foreign Trade and Ministry of Commerce (Aug., '52)	Under the Cultural and Educational Affairs Committee Established: Commissions on Physical Education, on Elimination of Illiteracy, and Ministry of Higher Education, (Nov., '52). Abolished: Directorate of Information, Directorate of Intelligence, (Nov., '51).

- - - - - indicates organizational relationship
———— indicates line of control

Sources: *Manual for Newspaper Readers*, pp. 75-104, Hankow, 1950; *People's Handbook*, pp. 164-177, Shanghai, 1952; *Ta-kung pao*, Hongkong, December 1, 1952; *Current Background*, American Consulate General, Hongkong, October 1, 1953.

B. 1955*

CHAIRMAN OF THE PEOPLE'S REPUBLIC OF CHINA: MAO TSE-TUNG
VICE-CHAIRMAN: CHU TEH

CENTRAL COMMITTEE (CCP)

POLITICAL BUREAU

CHAIRMAN: Mao Tse-Tung

Deputy Chairman: Liu Shao-Ch'i

MEMBERS:
Chou En-lai, Tung Pi-wu
Chu Teh, Lin Po-ch'u
Ch'en Yun, Chang Wen-t'ien
K'ang Sheng, P'eng Teh-huai
P'eng Chen

(Since April, 1955)
Lin Piao
Teng Hsiao-p'ing

PARTY SECRETARIAT:
Mao Tse-tung, Chou En-lai
Liu Shao-ch'i, Ch'en Yun
Chu Teh

NATIONAL PEOPLE'S CONGRESS (N P C)

Standing Committee of the NPC
Chairman: LIU SHAO CH'I

Vice-Chairmen: Sung (Soong) Ch'ing-ling, Lin Po-ch'u
Li Chi-shen, Chang Lan
Lo Jung-huan, Shen Chun-ju
Kuo Mo-jo, Huang Yen-p'ei
P'eng Chen, Li Wei-han
Ch'en Shu-t'ung, Dalai Lama Dantgenj'atso
Saifudin

Secretary General: P'eng Chen
65 members

SUPREME STATE CONFERENCE

Mao Tse-tung
Liu Shao-ch'i
Chou En-lai
(and others)

SUPREME PEOPLE'S PROCURATOR GENERAL
Chang Ting-ch'eng

SUPREME PEOPLE'S COURT
President Tung Pi-wu

CENTRAL PEOPLE'S GOVERNMENT
(State Council)

NATIONAL DEFENSE COUNCIL

Chairman: Mao Tse-tung

Premier: Chou En-lai

Vice-Premiers: Ch'en Yun, Lin Piao, P'eng Teh-huai, Teng Tzu-hui, Ho Lung, Teng Hsiao-p'ing, Ch'en Yi, Ulanfu, Li Fu-ch'un, Li Hsien-nien

Secretary General: Hsi Chung-hsun

Vice-Chairmen: Chu Teh, Lin Piao, Ho Lung, Teng Hsiao-p'ing, Hsu Hsiang-ch'ien, Yeh Chien-ying, Chang Chih-chung, Ch'en Yi, Lung Yun, P'eng Teh-huai, Liu Po-ch'eng, Lo Jung-huan, Nieh Jung-chen, Ch'eng Ch'ien, Fu Tso-yi

Ministry of the Interior	Ministry of Foreign Affairs	Ministry of Defense	Ministry of Public Security	Ministry of Justice	Ministry of Supervision				
Ministry of Finance	Ministry of Food	Ministry of Commerce	Ministry of Foreign Trade	Ministry of Heavy Industry	The First Ministry of Machinery Manufacturing	The Second Ministry of Machinery Manufacturing	The Third Ministry of Machinery Manufacturing	Ministry of Geology	Ministry of Building and Civil Engineering
Ministry of Textile Industry	Ministry of Light Industry	Ministry of Local Industry	Ministry of Railways	Ministry of Communications	Ministry of Posts and Tele-Communications	Ministry of Agriculture	Ministry of Forestry	Ministry of Water Conservation	
Ministry of Labor	Ministry of Culture	Ministry of Higher Education	Ministry of Education	Ministry of Public Health					
State Planning Commission	National Constructions Commission	Nationalities Affairs Commission	Overseas Chinese Affairs Commission	Physical Culture and Sports Commission					

*A Third Ministry of Machinery Manufacturing in charge of certain industrial enterprises of local significance was established in April, 1955. The Ministry of Fuel Industry was abolished in June, 1955, and in its place a Ministry of Coal Industry, a Ministry of Electric Power Industry, and a Ministry of Petroleum Industry were established. A separate Ministry of Agricultural Products Procurement was set up at the same time.

Sources: *People's Daily*, Peking, September 28 and 30, 1954; *Current Background*, No. 298, October 12, 1954; and *Wen-hui pao*, April 10, 1955.

Index